Handbook of Research on Sustainable Development and Economics

Ken D. Thomas
Auburn University, USA

A volume in the Advances in Finance, Accounting, and Economics (AFAE) Book Series

BUSINESS SCIENCE Reference
An Imprint of IGI Global

Managing Director: Lindsay Johnston
Managing Editor: Austin DeMarco
Director of Intellectual Property & Contracts: Jan Travers
Acquisitions Editor: Kayla Wolfe
Production Editor: Christina Henning
Typesetter: Amanda Smith
Cover Design: Jason Mull

Published in the United States of America by
Business Science Reference (an imprint of IGI Global)
701 E. Chocolate Avenue
Hershey PA, USA 17033
Tel: 717-533-8845
Fax: 717-533-8661
E-mail: cust@igi-global.com
Web site: http://www.igi-global.com

Library of Congress Cataloging-in-Publication Data

Handbook of research on sustainable development and economics / Ken D. Thomas, editor.
pages cm
Includes bibliographical references and index.
Summary: "This book explores topics such as poverty, gender equality, health, security, and the environment through global empirical studies and fundamental frameworks, with the goal of promoting sustainable techniques for the global future"-- Provided by publisher.
ISBN 978-1-4666-8433-1 (hardcover : alk. paper) -- ISBN 978-1-4666-8434-8 (ebook : alk. paper) 1. Sustainable development. 2. Economic development. I. Thomas, Ken D., 1982-

HC79.E5H31854 2015
338.9'27--dc23

2015009472

This book is published in the IGI Global book series Advances in Finance, Accounting, and Economics (AFAE) (ISSN: 2327-5677; eISSN: 2327-5685)

British Cataloguing in Publication Data
A Cataloguing in Publication record for this book is available from the British Library.

Advances in Finance, Accounting, and Economics (AFAE) Book Series

Ahmed Driouchi
Al Akhawayn University, Morocco

ISSN: 2327-5677
EISSN: 2327-5685

Mission

In our changing economic and business environment, it is important to consider the financial changes occurring internationally as well as within individual organizations and business environments. Understanding these changes as well as the factors that influence them is crucial in preparing for our financial future and ensuring economic sustainability and growth.

The **Advances in Finance, Accounting, and Economics (AFAE)** book series aims to publish comprehensive and informative titles in all areas of economics and economic theory, finance, and accounting to assist in advancing the available knowledge and providing for further research development in these dynamic fields.

Coverage

- Accounting information systems
- Economics of Agriculture and Biotechnology
- Applied economics
- Taxes
- Risk Analysis and Management
- Economics of Migration and Spatial Mobility
- Accounting Standards
- Ethics in Accounting and Finance
- Economics of Innovation and Knowledge
- Corporate Finance

IGI Global is currently accepting manuscripts for publication within this series. To submit a proposal for a volume in this series, please contact our Acquisition Editors at Acquisitions@igi-global.com or visit: http://www.igi-global.com/publish/.

The Advances in Finance, Accounting, and Economics (AFAE) Book Series (ISSN 2327-5677) is published by IGI Global, 701 E. Chocolate Avenue, Hershey, PA 17033-1240, USA, www.igi-global.com. This series is composed of titles available for purchase individually; each title is edited to be contextually exclusive from any other title within the series. For pricing and ordering information please visit http://www.igi-global.com/book-series/advances-finance-accounting-economics/73685. Postmaster: Send all address changes to above address.

Titles in this Series

For a list of additional titles in this series, please visit: www.igi-global.com

Promoting Socio-Economic Development through Business Integration
Shalini Kalia (IMT Ghaziabad, India) Bhavna Bhalla (IMT Ghaziabad, India) Lipi Das (IMT Ghaziabad, India) and Neeraj Awasthy (IMT Ghaziabad, India)
Business Science Reference • copyright 2015 • 337pp • H/C (ISBN: 9781466682597) • US $210.00 (our price)

Handbook of Research on Globalization, Investment, and Growth-Implications of Confidence and Governance
Ramesh Chandra Das (Katwa College, University of Burdwan, India)
Information Science Reference • copyright 2015 • 572pp • H/C (ISBN: 9781466682740) • US $345.00 (our price)

Green Economic Structures in Modern Business and Society
Andrei Jean-Vasile (Petroleum-Gas University of Ploiesti, Romania) Ion Raluca Andreea (Bucharest Academy of Economic Studies, Romania) and Turek Rahoveanu Adrian (University of Agronomic Sciences and Veterinary Medicine, Bucharest, Romania)
Business Science Reference • copyright 2015 • 325pp • H/C (ISBN: 9781466682191) • US $195.00 (our price)

Handbook of Research on Behavioral Finance and Investment Strategies Decision Making in the Financial Industry
Zeynep Copur (Hacettepe University, Turkey)
Business Science Reference • copyright 2015 • 525pp • H/C (ISBN: 9781466674844) • US $245.00 (our price)

Agricultural Management Strategies in a Changing Economy
Gabriel Popescu (Bucharest Academy of Economic Studies, Romania) and Andrei Jean-Vasile (Petroleum - Gas University of Ploiesti, Romania)
Business Science Reference • copyright 2015 • 439pp • H/C (ISBN: 9781466675216) • US $225.00 (our price)

Handbook of Research on In-Country Determinants and Implications of Foreign Land Acquisitions
Evans Osabuohien (Covenant University, Nigeria & German Development Institute, Germany)
Business Science Reference • copyright 2015 • 430pp • H/C (ISBN: 9781466674059) • US $265.00 (our price)

Handbook of Research on Strategic Developments and Regulatory Practice in Global Finance
Özlem Olgu (Koç University, Turkey) Hasan Dinçer (Istanbul Medipol University, Turkey) and Ümit Hacıoğlu (Istanbul Medipol University, Turkey)
Business Science Reference • copyright 2015 • 433pp • H/C (ISBN: 9781466672888) • US $235.00 (our price)

Regional Economic Integration and the Global Financial System
Engin Sorhun (Istanbul 29 Mayis University, Turkey) Ümit Hacıoğlu (Istanbul Medipol University, Turkey) and Hasan Dinçer (Istanbul Medipol University, Turkey)
Business Science Reference • copyright 2015 • 355pp • H/C (ISBN: 9781466673083) • US $200.00 (our price)

To Darrion, Jayden, Kristen, and Zai. Cannot wait to see what the future holds for you all.

Editorial Advisory Board

List of Contributors

Table of Contents

Detailed Table of Contents

Diarrhea is the second leading cause of death and is the major cause of malnutrition in children under age 5 worldwide. More than 50 percent of the cases occur in developing countries, particularly in sub-Saharan Africa and Southeast Asia. Open defecation, substandard fecal disposal systems, and contaminated water supplies are the typical causes of diarrheal diseases. This public health crisis in low income countries mirrors the experiences of today's industrialized nations two centuries ago. The lessons learned from their sanitary evolution can be instructive in charting a sustainable path towards saving the lives of almost 2 million children annually. In this chapter a case study of Cuba's sanitary reformation is also presented to showcase successes, similar to those of developed countries, within a developing country and economically challenging context.

This chapter analyses the dynamic of the development of cycling in Italy situating it also in the European context from an economic and strategic perspective. With this aim, first there was a study of the challenge of rapidly growing urban populations in spatially very limited areas affects not only residential housing construction. It also relates to urban infrastructure and services. This led to identification of new mobility needs, met mainly by private means, with implications in terms of congestion and air pollution. Results are analysed in terms of total trips of non-motorized urban mobility and help at understanding how promoting cycling is important for individual health, environmental sustainability and transport demand management. The chapter brings the debate on sustainable transport policy into direct confrontation with the embodied practice of cycling in an urbanized environment.

This chapter examines the challenges and opportunities associated with planning for competitive, smart and healthy cities. The chapter is based on the assumptions that a healthy city is an important prerequisite for a competitive city and a fundamental outcome of smart cities. One of the major decision support systems to support healthy cities is e-health. This chapter focuses on the role of e-health planning, by utilising web-based geographic decision support systems. The chapter proposes the implementation of a novel decision system which would provide a powerful and effective platform for stakeholders to support access online information. This would also provide for better decision-making as well as empower community participation. The chapter highlights the need for a comprehensive conceptual framework to guide the decision process of planning for cities in association with opportunities and limitations. This chapter provides critical insights into using information science-based frameworks.

Municipalities have variety of tools for improving environmental sustainability. The effects of climate change increase the renewable projects developed by municipalities and public private sectors. Turkish municipalities practiced the early steps of sustainability projects, some of which were small-scale projects. In addition, Turkish municipalities have gained experience in LA 21 Process since the late 1990s. Some of the city models for sustainability, such as CittaSlow and healthy city projects developed by Turkish Municipalities. The work in this chapter represents research about variety of issues for environment and sustainability in Turkish Municipalities. Visions, strategies and projects of these municipalities have been analysed to attain this goal. A literature review and SWOT analysis were used for the methodology to determine the Turkish municipalities' potential for sustainability.

As urban development has become an increasing problem, urban planning is required to integrate social and economical needs with the sustainable use of natural resources. Since the urban development is favoured by the amount and diversity of the natural resources (land, mineral resources, green areas, aquatic surfaces) available in the area of influence of the cities and its negative externalities aren't limited inside the urban limits the conservation of those resources became an important issue in the scientific circles. Lately planners have been using GIS techniques and remote sensing, based on international and local databases, in finding the most probable scenarios and the best available solutions in order to promote a sustainable development of urban areas. Four models of natural resources conservation have proved effective in the influence areas of cities: protected areas, yellow-green belts, regional parks and oxygen generating surfaces. The establishment and management of these can be better realised by GIS techniques, because of their efficiency and ease of use, the suitability and general availability of data.

Section 2
Energy Options for a Sustainable Future

The provision of adequate, reliable, and affordable energy, in conformity with social and environmental requirements is a vital part of sustainable development. Currently, countries are facing a two-fold energy challenge: on the one hand they should assure the provision of environmentally sustainable energy, while, on the other, energy services should be reliable, affordable, and socially acceptable. To evaluate such aspects of energy services one needs energy sustainability barometers, which provide the means to monitor the impacts of energy policies and assist policymakers in relevant decision making. Although sustainability is an ambiguous, complex, and polymorphous concept, all energy sustainability barometers incorporate the three major sustainability dimensions: social, economic, and environmental. In this chapter, we review three models for assessing the sustainability of energy development of countries: ESI, SAFE, and EAPI. We also present a brief discussion of the results, the applied methodologies, and the underlying assumptions of these sustainability barometers.

This chapter examines European energy security in the EU-Russian context. Europe is extremely dependent on Russian energy imports. This dependency requires sustainable energy solutions. Russian economy is characterized by high energy consumption and intensity. Russian energy sector needs massive investments, technological and management improvements. They become problematic due to the nation's poor investment climate, stagnating economy, and isolationist foreign policy. These, along with Russia's emerging reorientation of its energy exports toward Asia tend to worsen European energy security. The chapter explores trends in the global energy and analyses the dynamics and outlook for sustainable energy security in Europe in the context of import dependency in energy. It looks at the drivers, constrains and trends in the Russian energy sector in the Eurasian regional context. Despite technological advances, policies toward sustainable development and renewable energy, in the next two decades Europe will predominantly depend on fossil fuels and Russian energy imports.

The move towards a low-carbon world, driven partly by climate science and partly by the business opportunities it offers, will need the promotion of environmentally friendly alternatives, if an acceptable stabilisation level of atmospheric carbon dioxide is to be achieved. This chapter presents a comprehensive review of energy sources, and the development of sustainable technologies to explore these energy sources. It also includes potential renewable energy technologies, efficient energy systems, energy savings techniques and other mitigation measures necessary to reduce climate changes. The chapter concludes with the technical status of the ground source heat pumps (GSHP) technologies. The purpose of this study, however, is to examine the means of reduction of energy consumption in buildings, identify GSHPs as an environmental friendly technology able to provide efficient utilisation of energy in the buildings sector.

Augmenting recent coverage of the topic of regional energy planning, this chapter introduces an Integrated Regional Energy Policy and Planning Framework (IREPP), which is conceptually comprehensive and also enhances feasibility of implementation. This framework contains important concepts of sustainable energy planning, including integrated resource planning, soft energy path, distributed generation using decentralized energy technologies, and energy-environment-economy-equity balance (E4). The IREPP also includes implementation feasibility analysis and highlights the importance of monitoring and evaluation. In the second part of this chapter, the IREPP is applied to the case of Jeju. Jeju's "Mid- and Long-Term Roadmap of Renewable Energy Planning" intends to promote renewable energy applications in order to build a carbon free energy system. This chapter evaluates Jeju's overall Roadmap via the lens of IREPP, assesses the rationale and feasibility of achieving its individual renewable target set for 2050, and, additionally, reviews progress made in some individual targets as of 2014.

This chapter presents the foundations of a holistic model for connecting the key elements necessary for corporations to adopt sustainability and sustainable development in the context of the global economy and strategic innovation. The complexities of doing business on a global scale have increased dramatically over the last two decades. While sustainability involves many perspectives, strategies, actions, and management constructs, the chapter focuses on how global corporations employ strategic innovations in

This chapter revisits the author's earlier findings that scrutinized online marketing strategies employed by the world heritage sites (WHS) based on a predetermined set of sustainability indicators. Recent data shows that, for the most part, the WHS continue to lack behind in sustainable initiatives to promote their sites in a responsible manner. Only slight improvement is noted in terms of efforts to seek host community views on how the local heritage should be showcased and the manner on which culturally appropriate representations can be promoted. In the light of unexpected decreased visitation levels at most of the WHS, as reported by literature, a retro brand marketing strategy is suggested which strives to marry the rich historical past of the sites with the present need. A smart sustainable marketing agenda is proposed to improve brand equity and facilitate coordination between different stakeholders of the heritage sites and to attract increased visitations.

Sustainability is one of the most important challenges of our time. How can prosperity be developed without compromising the life of future generations? Companies are integrating sustainability in their marketing, corporate communication, annual reports and in their actions. The concept of sustainability has more recently also been linked to project management. Sustainability needs change of business models, products, services, resources, processes, etc. and projects are a frequently used practice of realizing change. Several studies explored how the concept of sustainability impacts project management. This chapter elaborates on the impact of sustainability found in literature and analyses the most influential standards of project management processes for their coverage of this impact. The study concludes that the most important standards of project management processes still fail to refer convincingly to sustainability considerations. Based on the author's analysis, this chapter also provides guidance for the further development of the process standards towards a 'sustainable project management' process.

Managing project sustainability is becoming important in the last two decades since the Earth Summit in 1992. An increasing number of projects have built in sustainability considerations into project design and implementation. Recent research findings show that lack of sustainability knowledge for project managers is a key barrier to drive projects and programs contributing towards a sustainable society. Definitions and approaches (pillar-based and principles-based) to sustainability in project management together with project manager competence requirements are discussed. The purpose of this chapter is to devise an assessment tool for project managers incorporating the concept of pillar-based and

Foreword

Increased population growth, environmental emissions, water use, energy use, and consumption of various natural resources are some of the drivers that contribute to current global challenges such rising sea-level, increased frequency and intensity of disasters, increased poverty, and increased health issues. Increasing levels of these drivers are unsustainable with an urgent need for development and implementation of mechanisms to decrease them while still maintaining societal health and wealth.

Development of new and sustainable technologies, processes, and activities provide a way to address these drivers while at the same time improving human lives (social progress) through better, smarter ways of conducting activities. This also has the potential to spur economic development provided that the new sustainable mechanisms and strategies are cost-effective. Sustainable development is defined as "development that meets the needs of the present without compromising the ability of future generations to meet their own needs" (World Commission on Environment and Development, 1987). While there is no consensus on the definition of sustainability, what is clear is that it strives for the maintenance of economic, environmental, and societal well-being of all individuals, communities, and the environment (Muga & Mihelcic, 2008). Further, it recognizes the need to design human and industrial systems that ensure the proper use of natural resources to support current and future generations without adverse impacts on social conditions, human health and the environment (Mihelcic et al., 2003).

Since the advent of the concept of sustainability/sustainable development, a plethora of innovative sustainable practices such as improved products, processes, services, policies, and organizational and management strategies have since been implemented and integrated into the various facets of society. For example, at the global level, organizations such as the United Nations and the World Bank strive for the improvement of the lives of individuals in struggling economies in the Global South. At the country or national-level, practitioners and policy-makers strive for the use of alternative energy use, alternative building materials, access to clean water, and the use of technologies that reduce or capture carbon dioxide emissions. At the community or household level, especially in the Global South, there is repurposing of items to extend usefulness, teaching of community members to conserve resources and be thrifty while diffusing vital survival skills of sustainable practices to the youth. At the educational institutional-level, educators strive to incorporate the theories, concepts and application of sustainability into their curriculum.

Sustainable development has been playing a role in our daily lives since the 1960s and will continue to play a larger and larger role well into the 21st century. Professionals, decision-makers, scientists, engineers, and other stakeholders, have been turning to sustainable practices as a way of doing business. Environmentally-consciousness businesses have been and continue to look for ways to reduce cost, make their products more efficiently, reduce their environmental footprint, and comply with increasingly stringent environmental regulations. In the construction industry, engineers continue to look for alternative, environmentally safe, construction materials. This endeavor has been more pronounced in developing nations, where there has been a push to build infrastructure, e.g. houses, from locally available, indigenous materials such as bamboo. In the energy sector, relevant stakeholders strive for the diffusion and use of alternative energy such as solar panels, wind-turbines, and geothermal as a way of reducing carbon dioxide and reliance on fossil fuel. In academic institutions, educators have been and continue to strive to incorporate sustainability concepts, theories, and case studies into their curriculum. In essence, sustainable practices are becoming the norm in today's society. What remains to be explored and captured is how much of the innovative sustainable practices have enhanced and contributed to economic growth in society. A common objective of this work is to shed some light into sustainable development and economic development.

This book provides a valuable window into:

1. The development of sustainable healthy communities and cities,
2. The different types of energy options available for a sustainable future,
3. How sustainable development contributes to business, and
4. The different information and communication technologies available for sustaining livelihoods.

The development and implementation of sustainable healthy communities and cities is directly and indirectly linked to economic development and growth. For example, access to basic health services such as water and sanitation services is linked to improved health of a person and ultimately a functioning, contributing member of society. Lack of access to these services renders a person a burden to society. Energy options are also linked to economic development and growth. Sustainable energy options such as solar and wind turbines emit less carbon dioxide into the atmosphere. While these options may incur high start-up costs and a longer time to break-even, they save the user significant money over its lifetime. A win-win scenario for manufacturers of solar and wind turbines and users would be a low start-up cost and therefore shorter time to break-even. Incorporating sustainable practices in industrial processes (e.g. in mining, manufacturing) is also important to the triple bottom line. Process improvement, e.g. improvement in energy efficiency or material efficiency, can lead to reduction in carbon emissions and possibly enable a business to participate in carbon trading.

The challenges in developing and implementing sustainable practices that make economic sense are both difficult and interesting. Professionals, businesses, decision-makes, scientists, engineers, and other stakeholders have been working on developing new sustainable technologies, processes, activities and policies, to address current global challenges. Because of the interconnectedness of sustainable development and economics, it is necessary to provide practitioners, both professionals and students, with state-of-the art knowledge on the frontiers on these two topics. This book is a good step in that direction.

Helen E. Muga
University of Mount Union, USA

REFERENCES

Mihelcic, J. R., Crtittenden, J. C., Small, M. J., Sonnard, D. R., Hokanson, D. R., Zhang, Q., & Schooner, J. L. et al. (2003). Sustainability Science and Engineering: Emergence of a New Metadiscipline. *Environmental Science & Technology*, *37*(23), 5314–5324. doi:10.1021/es034605h PMID:14700315

Muga, H., & Mihelcic, J. R. (2008). Sustainability of Wastewater Treatment Technologies. *Journal of Environmental Management*, *88*(3), 437–447. doi:10.1016/j.jenvman.2007.03.008 PMID:17467148

World Commission on Environment and Development. (1987). *Our Common Future*. Oxford, UK: Oxford University Press.

Preface

It is well known, and widely accepted, that sustainability and sustainable development have at the core society, economics and the environment. According to Mihelcic et al. (2003), sustainable development is the design and use of human and industrial systems to ensure that humankind's use of natural resources and cycles do not lead to diminished quality of life due either to losses in future economic opportunities or to adverse impacts on social conditions, human health and the environment. Sustainable development therefore is a vision of development that encompasses populations, animal and plant species, ecosystems, natural resources and that integrates concerns such as the fight against poverty, gender equality, human rights, education for all, health, human security, intercultural dialogue, etc. This is a complex system.

Even now, decades after the Brundtland Report was released, sustainability and sustainable development remain, to very many, as ideals that are utopian and unattainable. The research presented in the chapters of this book provides mechanisms, ideas and techniques to continue to edge towards sustainability and sustainable development.

This handbook aims to provide global empirical studies as well as relevant and current frameworks in the sphere of sustainable development that has widespread and crossover application appeal. The enhanced nature of the chapters of this book allows users to use both the original chapter and the enhanced chapter in tandem to garner improvements, breakthroughs, innovations that could be applied to similar situations. This is indeed a benefit as strides are being made to make sustainable development less utopian and more realistic. The trajectory of improvement in the sustainability/sustainable development body of knowledge that is represented by the span of the original and new enhanced chapter pair most definitely assists in making sustainable development less conceptual and more practical.

In this book the views and expertise of thirty seven authors, from fifteen countries, are presented. Their contributions span studies in the Caribbean, North America, South America, and Asia.

ORGANIZATION OF THE BOOK

Scholarly Value and Impact of Book

The chapters in this book expand on the fields of the public health, engineering, education, and business. Some of the main themes that the chapters in this book attempt to expand upon include:

- Human rights,
- Sustainability and sustainable development metrics,
- Green technologies,

- Project management for sustainability,
- Marketing for sustainability,
- Sustainability in a global economy,
- Strategic innovation for sustainable development,
- International/political arrangements for sustainability,
- Local and regional spatial planning,
- Education for Sustainable Development (ESD).

Target Audience

This book is relevant to a diverse audience inclusive of business research and development professionals, educators/teachers/trainers at all levels of education, sustainable development practitioners, the public at large, and environmental/sustainability policy makers. The book is timely as professionals, researchers, educators, and leaders pursue innovative solutions to numerous challenges with economics at the core of every solution. The content of this book is useful to practitioners, researchers, and educators in the various disciplines of the social sciences, public health, business, and engineering. This book serves as an excellent reference guide for persons working in the fields of economic development as well as sustainability/sustainable development.

The Content

There are eighteen chapters in this book that were developed from the perspectives of academics, researchers, practitioners, and program administrators. Of these eighteen chapters, Chapter 1is an original chapter and the others are enhanced versions of chapters that were previously published by IGI Global. This allows for further research and chapter development as well as greater addition to the sustainability body of knowledge by inclusion of findings from the original time of publication to present.

The eighteen chapters are divided among four sections. These sections were developed in consideration of the true root of sustainability and sustainable development: protecting human lives today and in the future. The sections are:

Section 1: Developing Sustainable Healthy Communities and Cities (five chapters);
Section 2: Energy Options for a Sustainable Future (four chapters);
Section 3: The Business of Sustainable Development (six chapters);
Section 4: Information and Communication Technologies for Sustaining Livelihoods (three chapters).

The foreword is written by Helen E. Muga. She has already contributed widely to the field of sustainability and sustainable development through research and university teaching. In her foreword she explores how sustainable development is achieved through sustainable practices and its reliance on economics. She also gives her thoughts on why she thinks that this book helps with the understanding of this interdependence.

Section 1: Developing Sustainable Healthy Communities and Cities

In Chapter 1, Monica Gray, presents her study entitled "A Systems Approach for Sustainably Reducing Childhood Diarrheal Deaths in Developing Countries". This chapter delves into the public health crises that exist in many low income and developing economies as they attempt to keep their populations alive. The financial burdens of these counties are amplified through a case study on Cuba with focus on the impacts of diarrhea and sanitary reformation in an economically challenging context. This chapter calls for decision makers in developing countries to come to the realization that ensuring environmental justice for all cohorts of their populations benefits everyone and moves the country forward as a whole.

Donatella Privitera of University of Catania, Italy explores the idea of the use of cycling as a mechanism for creating a healthier city from economic, strategic, and environmental perspectives in Chapter 2. Her study "Towards a Competitive Sustainable City: Cycling as an Opportunity" focused on Italy where most cycling is recreational. Culture, habit and custom are important but if cycling is to be a viable mode of transportation with extreme variation in the experience of its users, it must have appropriate facilities. In this chapter she elaborates on the lack of space in Italian cities and that any solution to this complex problem to ensure a sustainable urban mobility requires a strong commitment with respect to innovation as well as methods and content of urban policies inclusive of educational plans.

Ori Gudes, Sarah Jane Edwards, Tan Yigitcanlar, and Virendra Pathak authored Chapter 3: "Competitive Smart Cities through Healthy Decision-Making". In their chapter they focus on the role or e-health planning in consideration of localized health, economic, and social factors. E-health could be an effective solution to address the issues of equitable health services allocation and enhance a level of the competitiveness, sustainability and smart urban systems of a city, particularly given that it acts as a 'disseminator' of local information and knowledge. These authors propose a novel platform to access information about a city's health while highlighting the need for a robust and comprehensive conceptual framework to guide the decision making process. They report that this guidance is imperative to use an e-health approach to create any healthy, competitive, and smart city.

In Chapter 4, Seda H. Bostancı explores her study entitled "Sustainable Strategies and Project of Turkish Municipalities". Here she uses a literature review of Turkish eco-projects and SWOT analysis methodology to determine the Turkish municipalities' sustainability potential. This is with the aim of devising sustainable development model(s) for Turkish municipalities that consider and incorporate costs. The author believes that this is attainable through application of LA 21 processes, cittaslow, and healthy city models by Turkish municipalities to eventually lead to a holistic sustainable municipality model.

Mihai Răzvan Niţă, Mihăiţă Iulian Niculae, Diana Andreea Onose, Maria Pătroescu, Gabriel Ovidiu Vânău, and Cristiana Maria Ciocănea of the University of Bucharest, Romania are the authors of Chapter 5. Their study is called "Recommendations for Natural Resources Conservation in the Influence Areas of Cities: A Case Study of Bucharest, Romania" and presents four models for the environmental protection of the influence areas of cities. These are

1. Protected areas;
2. Yellow-green belts;
3. Regional parks; and
4. Oxygen generating surfaces.

The establishment and management of these influence areas can be better realised by GIS techniques, because of their efficiency and ease of use, the suitability and general availability of data. These authors conclude that in order to preserve the natural resources in the influence areas of cities the local, regional and national authorities should encourage the implementation of the optimum approaches and better regulate the aspects related with territorial planning.

Section 2: Energy Options for a Sustainable Future

In Chapter 6, Evangelos Grigoroudis, Vassillis S. Kouikoglou, and Yannis A. Phillis review various models of sustainability assessment of national energy systems in their work entitled "Energy Sustainability of Countries". These models serve as mechanisms to attain an overall energy sustainability index. These authors also present a discussion of the sustainability indicators, aggregation tools, and data imputation techniques used in each approach. The concepts of sustainability and sustainable development have received much attention among policy-makers and scientists as a result of the existence of limits to growth and the dramatic environmental changes of the last decades but there is still a major lack of accepted assessment techniques for sustainability. This chapter delves into measurement approaches that can be utilized but, according to the authors, there is still a lot to be done in this sphere of research.

"Energy and Sustainability in the European Region: The Russian Factor" is the title of Chapter 7 which was co-written by Anatoly Zhuplev and Dmitry A. Shykhno. It is well known that Europe's wellbeing and sustainable economic growth are highly dependent on Russian imports of oil and gas. In this chapter the authors examine European energy security, its strategic constraints, choices, and implications with the view of sustainability and the EU-Russian energy dialog. Globalization and increasing geo-regional interdependence have serious political-economic impacts and implications for the energy sector and its stakeholders worldwide. In this study the authors dissect the nature and implications of this asymmetric mutual political-economic relationship with respect to Europe's energy dependency. They also get into discourse on competition and sustainability of energy solutions that encompasses investments, management, emergence of green technologies, and investments in green resources.

Abdeen Mustafa Omer of Energy Research Institute, UK authored Chapter 8: "Renewable Energy Technologies, Sustainable Development and Environment". In this chapter the author argues that by adopting coherent strategy for alternative clean sustainable energy sources, the world as a whole would benefit from savings in foreign exchange, improved energy security, and socio-economic improvements. This study presents a comprehensive review of energy sources, and the development of sustainable technologies to explore these energy sources. It also includes potential renewable energy technologies, efficient energy systems, energy savings techniques and other mitigation measures necessary to reduce climate changes. The study concludes with the technical status of the ground source heat pumps technologies.

In Chapter 9, Wei-Ming Chen, Young-Doo Wang, Jong Chul Huh, and Youn Cheol Park elaborated on regional energy planning in their study entitled "A Regional Energy Planning Approach: An Integrated Framework and Its Application to Jeju Island's Renewable Roadmap". This chapter introduces an integrated regional energy planning framework (IREPP) and then evaluates the mid- and long-term renewable energy roadmap for Jeju Island on the basis of the IREPP. Embedded in the IREPP is the concept of energy-environment-economy-equity balance (E^4). In this work, renewable technology options identified in the Roadmap are also evaluated for their technical feasibility, along with policy suggestions, based on experiences with renewable developments from the EU countries, Japan, and the US states.

Section 3: The Business of Sustainable Development

David L. Rainey of Renssealer Polytechnic Institute, USA presents his study entitled "A Holistic Model for Linking Sustainability, Sustainable Development, and Strategic Innovation" as Chapter 10. In this chapter he presents the building blocks of a truly holistic model which factors in globalization from a multi-dimensional perspective. The holistic model discussed in the chapter provides a framework for creating win-win outcomes that are balanced in terms of the social, political, ethical, economic, technological, and environmental forces. The author suggests that balanced solutions require an integrated approach with strategic leaders and contributors working together using strategic innovations. He further prompts that the decision making methodology for strategic innovations has to become more comprehensive and farsighted.

"Developing Sustainable Governance Systems at the Regional Level: The Case of Emissions Trading" by Tim Cadman, Margee Hume, Tek Maraseni, and Federico Lopez-Casero is presented in Chapter 11. With a business-oriented approach, the authors provide a critical analysis of the implementation of governmental systems in relation to regional sustainability programmes and environmentally friendly firms' activities. This chapter looks at market-based sustainability initiatives and investigates the strengths and weaknesses of two emissions trading schemes from a quality of governance perspective. The study concludes with reflections on market-based approaches to environmental problem solving.

In Chapter 12, Michelle Edith Jarvie-Eggart explored the "Development and Progress of The Mining Association of Canada's Towards Sustainable Mining Program". In this study, the author evaluates the Towards Sustainable Mining (TSM) protocols developed by the Mining Association of Canada (MAC). TSM protocols were developed to address public concerns in the area of environmental and social responsibility of mining actions. The TSM protocols incorporate sustainability indicators that evaluate the social, environmental, and economic impacts of mining. The author's findings indicate that (1) great progress has been made by mining companies across Canada in adopting the TSM protocols and the development of new standards; (2) there has been an improved public image of the industry due largely in part to addressing public concerns; and (3) further progress is still needed in the industry for sustainable mining to occur.

Deepak Chhabra's study entitled "Smart Sustainable Marketing of World Heritage Sites: Teaching New Tricks to Revive Old Brands", as presented in Chapter 13, critically analyzes online marketing strategies employed by world heritage sites (WHS) and suggests a more contemporary approach to smart marketing of WHS. In this new approach – smart sustainable marketing – the focus is on improving brand equity through a retrobranding strategy. This study details the steps in developing such a strategy and the benefits of retrobranding for brand sustainability.

Chapter 14 makes the case for the emergence of the Sustainable Project Management field in the study entitled "Considering Sustainability in Project Management Processes". Author Gilbert Silvus remarks that "Projects can make a contribution to the sustainable development of organizations. It should therefore be expected that the concepts and principles of sustainability are reflected in projects and project management and their standards." The author concluded that typical project management processes like PMBOK® Guide, PRINCE2® and ISO 21500 do not adequately address sustainability in project management and so he calls for further research in the development of criteria and concepts to practically implement sustainability into the management of projects.

In Chapter 15 ("Managing Project Sustainability: A Tool for Project Managers") by Gilman C. K. Tam there was a main aim to move the body of knowledge forward to be able to devise a practical assessment tool for project managers in managing project sustainability. As part of this study pillar-based, principles-based, EIA-driven, and objectives-led assessment approaches to sustainability in project management are discussed along with relevant project manager competencies. In this work, selection criteria are developed to help project managers in choosing appropriate sustainability impacts assessment methodology.

Section 4: Information and Communication Technologies for Sustaining Livelihoods

"The Influence of Information and Communication Technologies on Societies and their Cultures: A Historical Perspective" is presented in Chapter 16 and authored by Lee E. Allen. Contemporary sustainable development does, and will continue to, involve Information and Communication Technologies (ICTs). In this work the author reminds us that "it will be up to us, as the human beings responsible for the development and use of new technologies, to see that our new-found tools and resources provide positive outcomes for our future, as well as the future of our children." This discourse allows us to think about ICTs in terms of their revenge effects as well as their potential positives on route to sustainable development.

Flavio Leandro Caldas and Leandro Norberto Giglioli of Provincial College of Technical Education (EPET) No. 12, Argentina explored "ICTs in Schools and Their Relationship with Indigenous Communities in Patagonia" in Chapter 17. In this chapter the authors engage in dialogue that hinges on intercultural education being the key to the sustainable development of indigenous cultures. In this study the authors evaluate the diffusion and adoption of ICTs in schools in the Patagonian province of Neuquén through opinion surveys of students from both aboriginal and urban backgrounds. They also analyze the performance of the students with respect to the use of technology.

The book's last chapter, Chapter 18, by Albena Antonova is fittingly titled "How can ICTs Contribute Towards a More Sustainable Future?" According to this study, ICTs have hastened globalized business activity and has therefore transformed every aspect of human life. This has led to both positives (e.g. wealth accumulation) and negatives (e.g. scarcity of natural resources). Thus this chapter outlines some of the challenges of new technologies and ICT practices. This work also proposed a practice-oriented framework for adoption of sustainable ICT strategies by corporations.

REFERENCES

Mihelcic, J. R., Crtittenden, J. C., Small, M. J., Sonnard, D. R., Hokanson, D. R., Zhang, Q., & Schooner, J. L. et al. (2003). Sustainability Science and Engineering: Emergence of a New Metadiscipline. *Environmental Science & Technology*, *37*(23), 5314–5324.

Acknowledgment

First and foremost, the editor would like to thank each one of the authors for their contributions. His sincere gratitude goes to the authors who contributed their time and expertise to this book.

The editor also wishes to acknowledge the valuable contributions of the reviewers regarding the improvement of quality, coherence, and content presentation of chapters. Without their support, this book would not have become a reality.

To Dr. Helen E. Muga, the editor's esteemed colleague and friend; he wishes to express a multitude of thanks for writing the foreword to this volume.

The editor would like to give a heartfelt thank you to his IGI Global Editorial Assistant, Mr. Austin Demarco, for his unwavering patience and support through an arduous process.

Finally, the editor would like to express gratitude for the support of his affiliate institution: The Honors College & Biosystems Engineering Department, Auburn University, Auburn, Alabama, USA.

Ken D. Thomas
Auburn University, USA

Section 1

Developing Sustainable Healthy Communities and Cities

Chapter 1
A Systems Approach for Sustainably Reducing Childhood Diarrheal Deaths in Developing Countries

Monica Gray
The Lincoln University, USA

ABSTRACT

Diarrhea is the second leading cause of death and is the major cause of malnutrition in children under age 5 worldwide. More than 50 percent of the cases occur in developing countries, particularly in sub-Saharan Africa and Southeast Asia. Open defecation, substandard fecal disposal systems, and contaminated water supplies are the typical causes of diarrheal diseases. This public health crisis in low income countries mirrors the experiences of today's industrialized nations two centuries ago. The lessons learned from their sanitary evolution can be instructive in charting a sustainable path towards saving the lives of almost 2 million children annually. In this chapter a case study of Cuba's sanitary reformation is also presented to showcase successes, similar to those of developed countries, within a developing country and economically challenging context.

INTRODUCTION

Diarrhea is the second leading cause of death and the major cause of malnutrition in children under age 5 (World Health Organization (WHO), 2013b). Of the more than 1.5 million childhood deaths due to diarrhea each year, over 50 percent of all cases occur in developing countries, particularly in sub-Saharan Africa and Southeast Asia (Walker et al., 2013). Diarrhea is usually a symptom of an infection of the intestinal tract and presents as the passage of three or more loose or watery stool at least three times per day or more frequently than normal for an individual (WHO, 2013b). The most common etiologic agents, namely bacteria, viruses and protozoa, are primarily transmitted via the fecal-oral route (Tinuade et al., 2006). This means that most diarrheal pathogens are transmitted from the feces of an individual to his/her and/or the mouth of another. The underlying

DOI: 10.4018/978-1-4666-8433-1.ch001

assumption is: an individual must be exposed to or come in contact with the causative agent(s) to become infected and thus acquire the disease. This also implies that if the disease agents are removed or prevented from the environment of the at risk population, members will not become exposed and consequently develop the disease. Open defecation, substandard sanitation systems and subsequent pollution of nearby drinking water sources are usually implicated in disease causation (United Nations (UN), 2014). This is because fecal matter and its environmental repositories contain most common diarrheal etiologic agents. Thus, sanitation interventions such as latrines and, providing clean water and washing hands facilities, interrupt the fecal-oral transmission pathways. They are therefore effective in preventing and reducing diarrheal incidence, associated morbidity and mortality as wells as subsequent sequelae such as malnutrition. For example, research has shown that access to improved system of feces disposal may reduce the rate of childhood diarrhea by up to 43 percent (Cumming, 2009; WHO, 2013a).

In general diarrhea is, a very common, easily preventable and treatable disease, considered to be no more than a nuisance in most cases. In fact, there are about 1.7 billion incidence of diarrhea each year in both developed and developing countries (WHO, 2013b). However, developing countries are characterized by more adverse morbidity (persistent and reoccurring episodes) and higher mortality (death) health outcomes. For example, in developed countries the average disease incidence range from 1-3 episodes per person per year compared to 5-18 per person per year in developing countries (Guerrant, Hughes, Lima, & Crane, 1991). Rotavirus, which is a common cause of diarrhea in children under age 5 in the United States (US) causes about 300 deaths annually compared to over 220,000 actual hospitalizations (Pont, Grijalva, Griffin, Scott, & Cooper, 2009). In contrast, Rotavirus-induced diarrhea can be a death sentence for children in poor countries. For example, in 2008, the number of Rotavirus associated diarrheal deaths in some sub-Saharan African countries included, Angola (8,788), Uganda (10,637), Ethiopia (28,218), DR Congo (32, 653) and Nigeria (41,057) (Tate et al., 2012). The implication of this is, sadly, every 20 second a child, particularly in a low income country, dies of this relatively innocuous disease for which vaccine exits, is therefore preventable and for which treatment exists (Onda, Crocker, Kayser, & Bartram, 2014; UN, 2014). The World Health Organization (WHO) reports that children in sub-Saharan Africa are thus 16 times more likely to die before age 5 than children in developed regions and over half of these deaths could have been prevented by simple and affordable water and sanitation interventions (WHO, 2013a).

When one considers these somber numbers, it begs the question, is every life on this planet of equal value? In addition, should a child be condemned to unnecessary morbidity, misery and inevitable death, simply on the basis of a lottery of birth? This flies in the face of environmental justice, which demands that no one group should disproportionately bear the burden of adverse health outcomes from environmental hazards while not being able to enjoy the benefits available to other groups simply on the basis of geography and income. The solutions for sustainably providing and implementing clean water and improved sanitation and, reducing childhood diarrheal deaths exist, they are affordable and history has provided precedence that they work. What is left is the focused economic, social and political will of the international community and the affected countries to employ them. In other words, these large scale community health challenges are best tackled by employing a systems approach.

BACKGROUND

Why Children under 5?

Child Mortality, also known as Under-5 Mortality, is a population measure that estimates the number of infants and children that will die before reaching age 5 in a particular geographic location. It is measured as a rate per 1,000 live births. For example, the Under-5 Mortality for Cuba is 7 while for Sierra Leone it is 182 (WHO, UN, United Nation Children's Fund (UNICEF), & The World Bank (WB), 2013). Based on these figures, the probability exists that for every 1,000 children born alive, 7 and 182 will die before their fifth birthday in Cuba and Sierra Leone respectively. Similar to Life Expectancy, which measures how long an individual may live if born in a particular country, Under-5 Mortality, highlights the overall health and wellbeing of a society and measures the long-term health trajectory of a country. Children, age 5 years and under represent the segment of the population most sensitive to environmental threats and are thus perceived, as it were, the "canaries-in-the-coalmine" for the entire populace (Meckel, 1998).

Not all persons exposed to fecal infectious organisms get sick and how adverse the episode is depends on the susceptibility of the individual. Children, in general, are particularly susceptible to diarrheal infections for a number of reasons. They have underdeveloped immune systems and are more likely to become sick or have more severe symptoms once exposed to pathogenic organisms. Malnutrition, concurrent infections and co-morbidities (e.g., HIV, malaria), which are often indigenous to developing areas, further overtax already fledgling immune systems, leading to more adverse and fatal outcomes (Avery, Anchang, Tumsweige, Strachan, & Goude, 2014; Checkley et al., 2008). Children tend to play in the dirt more and often put things in their mouths. Therefore, if their environments are unhygienic and contaminated with fecal matter, they are more likely to come in contact with infectious agents than their adult counterparts. Finally, small children commonly do not use latrines because they are typically not designed with them in mind and child-sized potties may not be available in poorer settings (Valerie Curtis et al., 1995; Yeager, Huttly, Bartolini, Rojas, & Lanata, 1999). As a result, they may defecate in areas that they play and/or frequent. This practice may be compounded by cultural ignorance about the infectious nature of stools from children (Brown, Cairncross, & Ensink, 2013). In fact, by virtue of their behaviors, children's stools tend to have higher concentrations of pathogenic organisms than their adult counterparts (WHO & UNICEF, 2009). These conditions operate individually and concomitantly to predispose children to reoccurring infections.

Repeated episodes of severe and/or persistent diarrhea in the early years of life can lead to serious, lifelong health problems and have been estimated to be responsible for about half of diarrheal related deaths (Brown et al., 2013). Diseases from enteric infections can lead to malnutrition, stunted growth, and impaired cognitive development (Checkley et al., 2008). Developing countries like Africa are home to the world's youngest population (Fatusi & Hindin, 2010). The youth cohort, typically ages 10-24 years, is the driver of population growth because they are in the potential and projected childbearing age range. With almost 70 percent of this population group living in developing countries, one can expect population explosions in these regions in the upcoming decades (Fatusi & Hindin, 2010). From a population dynamics perspective, this means diminished opportunities and productivity over a lifetime for potentially large proportions of the world's populations. Therefore, the long-term sustainable health and economic trajectory of our planet could potentially be short-circuited by high incidence of an otherwise preventable and curable disease. For example, the UN reports that sub-Saharan Africa loses 5 percent of Gross Domestic Product (GDP) annually due to health problems caused by lack of water and sanitation (Moszynski, 2006).

Traditional Approach to Solving Community Health Challenges

The traditional or reductionist approach to solving community health challenges has been; isolation of each health outcome, determination of the dominant cause and suggestion of vertical intervention programs to address each cause (Buchholz, Volk, & Luzadis, 2007; Novick, Morrow, & Mays, 2008). For example, if a rural community in a developing country is found to have a high incidence of diarrheal deaths, a Non-Governmental Organization (NGO) may determine that the major cause is the lack of proper excreta disposal or poor quality water or personal and domestic hygiene. The affected community then receives discipline-specific programs such as Oral Rehydration Therapy (ORT) (Pignatelli & Musumeci, 2003), or excreta disposal (Corrales, Izurieta, & Moe, 2006; Pruss & Mariotti, 2000), or wells (Caslake et al., 2004; McGuigan, Joyce, Conroy, Gillespie, & Elmore, 1998), or hygiene education (Val Curtis & Cairncross, 2003). This outlook has persisted despite emerging evidence that problems solved in this manner often fail or worse, create new problems (Corrales et al., 2006; Espinosa, Harnden, & Walker, 2008; Stepek, Buttle, Duce, & Behnke, 2006; Sterman, 2006).

Research show several instances of counterintuitive results from vertical interventions. Areas with high diarrheal deaths incidence tend to have high rates of open defecation (Schmidlin et al., 2013). As a result, latrine interventions have been aggressively promoted to interrupt the fecal-oral transmission of diarrheal disease. These relatively low cost infrastructures serve to remove feces from the living environment and in some cases protect the contents from flies which are indeed vectors of diarrhea-causing organisms. However, while well intentioned, latrines can actually increase disease incidence and prevalence in affected communities and may create new problems. Most latrines are simple pits in the ground with a superstructure as shelter. These pits are not typically lined and therefore the liquid content seeps out into the ground water taking along infectious organisms and nutrients (Dzwairo, Hoko, Love, & Guzha, 2006; Knappett et al., 2011; Mkandawire, 2008; Nyenje, Foppen, Kulabako, Muwanga, & Uhlenbrook, 2013; Suthar et al., 2009). Consider also if a water well had been dug within the flow path of the microbial and nutrient rich contaminant plume radiating from the latrine. Consequently, the water supply becomes a continual vector for not only diarrheal infectious organisms but also nutrient-related illnesses such as methemoglobinemia (blue-baby syndrome) (Suthar et al., 2009). Another unexpected finding is, over time, latrines may become transmission loci for increase disease incidence if there is no concurrent change in hygiene behavioral practices. For example, if an earth floor in a latrine is poorly maintained, it can become the focal point for disease transmission (Grimason, Davison, Tembo, Jabu, & Jackson, 2000). In fact, dirty latrines may result in higher disease incidence than would occur if people were practicing widely scattered open defecation (Cairncross, 1983). Finally, without adequate security infrastructure, latrines can become rape target areas where women and girls run the risk of being ambushed and brutally attacked (Amesty International (AI), 2010; WaterAid, 2014).

The preceding discourse is not intended to completely castigate current efforts and deny that they have shown some measure of success. For example, the proportion of the population in sub-Saharan Africa with improved sanitation, increased from 20 to 30 percent between 1990 and 2011, while those practicing open defecation decreased from 36 to 26 percent over the same period (WHO & UNICEF, 2013). Campaigns such as the UN's Millennium Development Goal (MGD) and the WHO's, "International Year of Sanitation 2008" have brought international attention to this very important cause. However, any optimism must be tempered with the reality that 115 people in Africa die every hour from diseases linked to poor sanitation, poor hygiene and contaminated water and that MGD for sanitation will not be met by 2015 (Onda et al., 2014). Further, only about 37 percent of the population in sub-Saharan Africa use improved sanitation, while globally about 2.5 billion people still do not have access (Letema, van Vliet, & van Lier, 2014; Zawahri, Sowers, & Weinthal, 2011).

Interventions to correct these public health challenges at this scale and magnitude require a systems approach. This framework acknowledges that the current health emergency arose out of centuries of ignorance, inertia and indifference. The systems approach also recognizes the inherent nonlinearity of the synergistic interactions among geo-political, socio-economic and environmental factors that have caucused to hinder solutions or exacerbate diarrheal disease establishment. Therefore, political advocacy by both national and international stakeholders, as well as the simultaneous or scaffolded application of multiple public health interventions, is needed to create solutions that are economically viable, culturally sensitive and ecologically sustainable.

Lessons from the Last Two Centuries

About two hundred years ago, the current public health crisis in developing countries, epitomized the experiences of today's developed countries such as the Great Britain (Chadwick, 1843). During that period, consequently, they too experienced similar morbidity and mortality rates (Burstrom, Macassa, Oberg, Bernhardt, & Smedman, 2005). In retrospect, it was the confluence of geo-political, social-economic and ecological factors which aided and/or hindered the sustainable transfer of solutions to these challenges for developed nations (Konteh, 2009). Today, advances in supplying clean water and safe sanitation systems, adequate nutrition, widespread use of vaccines in conjunction with enforced and progressive legislature, have contributed to a dramatic drop in deaths due to diarrheal diseases, which were at one time entrenched national problems. For example, in 1897, 54 percent of the infants' deaths in in the US city of Chicago were due to diarrheal infection (Wolf, 2001). European countries such as the UK consistently had infant mortality rates above 100 per 1000 live births (Chadwick, 1843; Regidor et al., 2011). Canadian babies fared no better with 145 infants dying per 1000 live births in the 1890s (Mercier & Boone, 2002). As it is today, social and political inertia played a significant role in hindering or aiding technology transfer and adaption. Thus, change did not always happen quickly after scientific discoveries elucidate and confirm disease causation. For instance, while the city of Philadelphia understood the connection between clean water and disease outbreak from as early as 1799 and the germ theory was widely accepted by the 1890s, up to 85 percent of its untreated wastewater continued to be dumped in the Delaware River as late as the 1940s (Philadelphia Water Department (PWD), 2002). Philadelphia was not unique in this practice, but was among many large cities with combined sewers who continued to subscribe to the theory that running water purify itself even after being disproved in both the US and Europe (Tarr, 1979). In the summer of 1832, disease broke out in Baltimore claiming 853 victims, yet the city's leadership delayed building comprehensive sewer systems until 1905, only acting after experiencing two more and similarly devastating epidemics (Rosenberg, 1987; Schultz & McShane, 1978). Contemporary high-income societies also faced unintended consequences during their sanitary reformation. For example, in the 1800s, mothers in the US were encouraged to feed their babies milk to help reduce childhood mortality rates, but the milk was contaminated with feces laced water thus increasing infant mortality rates (Ward & Warren, 2007).

Similarly, for developing countries, poor sanitation and high disease burden arise out of and are driven by concomitants of socio-economic underdevelopment and an environment that facilitates the proliferation of pathogens (Santiso, 1997;

WHO & UNICEF, 2013). While being cautious not to assume that the sanitary and health dynamics of developed and contemporary developing nations are uniform in their trajectory, it is beneficial to observed commonalities in progression and adaptation of lifesaving public health interventions. This is with the hope of finding evidence of successes that worked over the years and that can be modified and made applicable within contemporary low income contexts.

PUBLIC HEALTH TRAJECTORY IN THE DEVELOPED WORLD

Reoccurring cycles of industrialization, chaotic urbanization and sanitation-related disease outbreaks in 19th century's developed countries served to socialize the connection between public health and the environment among the general populace. As industries grew, great swarms of people flock to urban areas in search of work and a better life (Ausubel, Meyer, & Wernick, 2001). Rawlinson (1853), in the minutes of proceedings of the Institution of Civil Engineers (Great Britain) highlighted these dilemmas. Rawlinson mentioned great population increases, some of over a million people in just a decade; the inability of the infrastructure to support such influx; and the subsequent increases in disease incidence with highest mortality, as much as ten to one, in the "unhealthy parts of town". The disparity in the death rates between rich and poor was so pronounced that the lower class in Paris surmised that the disease outbreaks were a conspiracy by the nobility to wipe them out (Rosenberg, 1987). In the US, the prognosis was no better. In the summer of 1832, disease broke out in Baltimore claiming 853 victims, most of whom were poor (Schultz & McShane, 1978).

These empirical observations helped to establish the connection between disease epidemics, poor sanitation and personal hygiene, and unhealthy environments (Tarr et al., 1984). As acceptance to the germ theory grew, in the 1890s, public health advocates in concert with public outcry, lobbied municipalities to implement many public works projects including comprehensive sewer systems, and water and wastewater treatments systems (Wolf, 2007). At first, gross mortality rates were used to measure the efficacy of these interventions. However, this rate was easily confounded by so many other variables that causality was not easily ascertained. The age-adjusted mortality, more specifically child mortality rate was a more proximate measure and had the added advantage of eliciting empathy from decision makers and the public in general (Rosenberg, 1987; Wolf, 2007). Concurrent to these activities was the promulgation and enforcement of a series of legislatures and policies designed to streamline the decision making processes for activities that affect the health of citizens (Perdue, Stone, & Gostin, 2003). One benefits of these laws was to authorize local and state government to tax and spend, and in turn gave them control over the direction of their development, which up until then was a mélange of private interests and public pressure (Jon, 1979).

Accompanying these large scale public works projects and, changes in legislature and community governance were ubiquitous educational campaigns aimed at socializing scientific discoveries in popular culture and help the ordinary citizen make the connection between their hygiene behaviors and the spread of disease (Ogle, 1993; Tomes, 1998). Communities thus armed with socially instrumental knowledge were able to forcefully lobby their local, state and national governments to make public health investments such as water purification and sewerage systems, garbage removal and children immunization.

As the mortality rates decreased as a result of these efforts the discussion moved on from how to achieve universal coverage to how best to engineer the system. For example, there were vigorous arguments on whether to use separate vs combined sewer (Tarr, 1979) or small-pipe vs large culvert (Jon, 1979). Notwithstanding, successful sanitary revolutions in developed countries all seemed to follow similar trajectories. Once the gravity of the public health crisis has been acknowledged by authorized stakeholders, a process was typically implemented to reduce the mortality and morbidity outcomes of those already affected such hydration therapy or increasing the availability of training medical professionals. Once disease outcome rates start to respond to interventions a series of disease disruption and prevention strategies are then employed whether in tandem or as next steps. These typically involve, public health legislature (e.g., Public Health Act of 1875, 1936 & 1984 in the UK), hygiene education campaigns, creating environments that protect whole community such as sewerage system and piped water while providing universal access and, employing prevention efforts such as immunization and chlorination (Ausubel et al., 2001; Center for Disease Control and Prevention (CDC), 1999; Coker & Martin, 2006). The final stage in this evolutionary process is that of protecting the health of the environment in an effort to protect the health of the community. For example, starting around the early 1970s, the US enacted a series of environmental legislature authorizing the US Environmental Protection Agency (EPA), Clean Water Act, the Safe Drinking Water Act and the National Pollutant Discharge Elimination System (NPDES) (Kapp Jr, 2014). The UK also enacted comparable legislature dating back to 1860s but more recently the Environmental Protection Act of 1990 (Holland & Boon Foo, 2003).

Sustainable Access in the Context of a Developing Country: The Case of Cuba

"Lack of resources" is typically invoked by policy and decision makers in developing economies to justify the lack of progress towards realizing sustainable access to water and sanitation for their constituents. This excuse is by no means unique to developing countries and has been historically used to hinder the progress of previous sanitary reforms (Hanley, 2007). Therefore, providing an environmental that supports the health of each citizen is not simply about wealthy and poor countries, though that plays a role, but it is more importantly about societal and political will and focus. For example, Cuba has a lower Under-5 Mortality rate than the US, coming in at 5.5 per 1,000 live births (Cooper, Kennelly, & Orduñez-Garcia, 2006). In the 1960s, Cuba's Under-5 Mortality rate was almost thrice that of the US (29 per 1000), topping out at 91 per 1,000 live births (Kuntz, 1994). Even more remarkable is that the country made these health gains in spite of tremendous economic struggles cause by trade embargos that impacted food and medicine supplies.

Cuba's health status indicators, such as Under-1 or -5 Mortality rates, transitioned from those typical of a contemporary developing country to those synonymous with the developed world. Similar to today's lower income nations' health profile, the main causes of Cuba's historically high childhood mortality were infectious diseases. In the early 1950s to mid-1960s communicable diseases such as diarrhea accounted for 80 percent of the Under-1 infant mortality rate (Valdés, 1971). In response to this colossal human tragedy, hospital administered rehydration therapy programs were instituted and the rate fell to 16 percent in about four years (Drain & Barry, 2010). While mortality rates declined, diarrheal disease incidence, however, continued to be high in the general population with almost a million cases in 1984 (Terris, 1989). As it is today among developing countries, this was primarily due to low water and sanitation coverage (McLeod, 2010).

Currently in developing countries, open defecation rates and low access to medical services in rural areas and consequent diarrheal disease incidence are significantly higher than urban regions. A similar urban – rural divide existed in 1960s Cuba. For example, there was only one rural hospital and rural infant mortality was about

100/1000 live birth. Most physicians practiced in urban areas where patients could more likely pay for services. In a 1959 comprehensive health study, the health authorities found that about 70 percent of all Cubans had parasites while the rural incidence was closer to 90 percent (Valdés, 1971). Thus, the areas that needed the most help had the least service. To overcome this socio-economic and subsequent health disparity and inequity, both rural and urban medical services were provided to all for free at the neighborhood level. As disease incidence declined, the strategy changed from providing medical services to as many people as needed to one of prevention and health promotion. This included the implementation of a series of nutrition, vaccination, housing and environment improvement, sewage disposal and improved water supply programs (Kuntz, 1994).

As mortality (less people dying) and morbidity (less people getting sick) rates decline, Cuba undertook a public health path similar to that of developed countries by enacting legislature and made steps to provide sanitation and health access to all Cubans. As part of their 1976 Constitution and 1983 Public Health Law, Cuba created national public health system with the aims of universality and accessibility, vertical integration, and inter-sectoral planning, as seen in the following fundamental principles (Iatridis, 1990; De Vos et al., 2009):

- Health care is a right, available to all equally and free of charge.
- Health care is the responsibility of the state.
- Preventive and curative services are integrated.
- The public participates in the health system's development and functioning.
- Health care activities are integrated with economic and social development.
- Global health cooperation is a fundamental obligation of the health system and its professionals.

The process was not without its own fits and starts. While high level rights were being enshrined in the constitution to provide comprehensive coverage, patients were complaining of long waiting times to see doctors and that the visits were too short to address their needs (Márquez, 2009). In response to these complaints the government created community-based polyclinic system with the mandate to providing comprehensive care in residents' local community (Wong & Wylie, 2010). Policymakers understood that health and illness emerged out of a confluence of people interacting with their environment, therefore all community members from health workers to school students are taught not only the health status of their community, but also the environmental, social, cultural and economic factors that affect it (Spiegel & Yassi, 2004). By the early 1980s Cuba spent about US$ 49 per person on health while providing about 6 beds per 1,000 persons and about 55 health professionals per 10,000 persons. By 2009 Cuba provided physician and nurses at a rate of 63 and 84 per 10, 000 population. To put this in context, the US's rates are 23 and 79 respectively (Márquez, 2009).

Cuba is known for its many skilled doctors and trained health professionals, a comprehensive network of regional and national hospitals and, community clinics, universal literacy, and seamless integration of public health and clinical medicine that emphasize prevention and health promotion. Prevention strategies include neighborhood environmental cleanup and in home hygiene (Dresang, Brebrick, Murray, Shallue, & Sullivan-Vedder, 2005). The Cuban experience models sustainable solutions to community health challenges, in a developing world context, when decision makers choose to prioritize human capital development in the face of limited resources. For example, in 2006 Cuba spend $355 per capita on health while the US spent $6714 per capita while achieving similar population health outcomes (Drain & Barry, 2010; Márquez, 2009).

WHERE ON THE SANITARY REFORM TRAJECTORY ARE DEVELOPING COUNTRIES?

Based on the preceding case studies, sustainable reduction in childhood diarrheal deaths followed a health trajectory that includes mortality and morbidity control, systemic and universal access to clean water and improved sanitation as well as supporting legislature along the way. Where along this progressive process are contemporary developing countries? Based on the discussion in the "Traditional Approach" section above, developing countries have experienced a hodgepodge of targeted health interventions in each of these phases without any long term plan and coordination.

For example, starting in the mid-1980s, ORT was dubbed "the most efficacious strategy for reducing mortality" (Taylor, Ha, Frank & Whiter, 1990). Studies later found that while ORT was effective against acute diarrheal episodes, it was helpless against persistent and reoccurring cases, which are more likely to have mortality outcomes (Guerrant et al., 1991). That is, while ORT may save a child from one particular bout of diarrheal infection, he/she may later die due to reoccurrence of this disease and/or its sequelae. In addition, programs were implemented over definite periods and then stopped before gains could be institutionalized or reached less well-off members of the communities (Gwatkin, 2003; Miller & Hirschhorn, 1995; Taylor et al., 1990).

Water and sanitation efforts have led to fragmentation and disproportion in coverage. After research in 7 developing countries by WHO between 1960 -1965 found that children under age 6 had a 40 percent monthly diarrheal prevalence rate, the international financial community donated a total of US $9 billion for water supply and $3.4 billion for sanitation improvements between 1970 – 1975 (Yongsi & Dovie, 2007). Today, the world is off track to meet the 2015 Target 10 of Millennium Development Goal 7 for improved sanitation while the goal for water was met 5 years ahead of schedule (UNICEF & WHO, 2012).

LAWS AND LATRINES: HUMAN RIGHT TO WATER AND SANITATION

With regards to legislature, there has also been an assortment of legal instruments and policies that have cropped up over the years. On July 28, 2010, the UN General Assembly, for the first time, explicitly recognized the right to both water and sanitation as a singular human right and acknowledged that access to clean drinking water and adequate sanitation is essential to the realization of all human rights (Luh, Baum, & Bartram, 2013). Resolution 64/292, though non-binding, calls for member States and international organizations to provide financial resources, help capacity-building and technology transfer to help countries, particularly developing countries, to provide safe, clean, accessible and affordable drinking water and sanitation for all. A few months later, the UN Human Rights Council affirms that the right to water and sanitation is indeed part of existing international law and confirms that the right is legally binding upon States Parties (Council, 2010). This breakthrough came after decades of arduous and exasperating debates and is welcomed news for the over 700 million and 2.5 billion people without access to safe drinking water and improved sanitation respectively (UNICEF & WHO, 2013).

It would not be good form to understate the gravity of such monumental achievements, however, the undeniable fact remains; too many children are unnecessarily sentenced to this colossal daily tragedy. Indeed, in the years leading up to 2010 several conventions, initiatives, goals and resolutions, alluding to varying degrees of human right to water and sanitation, were proposed with mixed success. For example, in November 2002, the UN General Assembly confirmed the right to water in international law (UN, 2002). Though not legally binding, General Comment No. 15 interpreted the International Convention on Economic, Social and Cultural Rights (ICESCR), explicitly outlined States Parties' obligations to the right and defined what actions would constitute a violation. The majority of States in the world are parties to the Convention with a few exceptions (UN, 1966). Yet during the period 2002 to 2010 these signatories fell short of realizing and protecting the right to safe drinking water for their citizens.

South Africa showed exceptional foresight by including these rights in its constitution. Article 27 of the Constitution of South Africa (1996),

1. Everyone has the right to have access to ... (b) sufficient food and water; and ... 2. The state must take reasonable legislative and other measures, within its available resources, to achieve the progressive realization of each of these rights.

South Africa's Water Services Act and National Water Act further elaborated on this constitutional right in 2001 when it recognized the right to water in its Reconstruction and Development Plan in its Free Basic Water policy. This policy has the aim to ensure adequate access by mandating 25 liters of water per day per person (Curry, 2010). Unfortunately, large discrepancies in coverage exist around the country where on average "wealthy, mostly white South Africans...use 600 liters per person per day...poor and largely black residents... 10" (Bakker, 2003).

A large scale example of poor implementation is the African Charter on the Rights and Welfare of the Child (AfCRC) 1990, which most African States were party to (Khalfan et al., 2007). This regional legal instrument mandated States to "ensure the provision of adequate nutrition and safe drinking water". Yet from 1990 to 2000, Africa is the only region in the world to show a decline in the proportion of the population that has access to water and sanitation (Boschi-Pinto, Lanata, Mendoza, & Habte, 2006). What if anything is now different? Will an explicit, legally binding international instrument change what happens on the ground in rural villages in Southeast Asia or Africa?

Every country in the world is now party to at least one health-related human rights treaty which typically includes provisions of related conditions to facilitate the privileges promulgated by the legal instrument. However, being signatories of international human rights instruments and/or inclusion of access to water and sanitation in countries' constitution do not inevitably lead to implementation and subsequent realization in the lives of the average household. As the international community explicitly acknowledges that access to safe water and improved sanitation is indeed a single human right, what prerogatives does this right afford the average citizen? Member States must in turn adopt legislation identifying the legal duties of national and municipal authorities, and prescribe normative course of action in response to violations to the explicitly stated entitlements of each citizen. As history has shown, this is an important phase in the progressive journey of sustainable sanitary reform.

CONCLUSION AND RECOMMENDATIONS

Diarrhea is in general, an easily preventable and treatable disease. Yet, it kills so many each year, especially children in developing nations. Diarrheal disease incidences in developing countries are typically as a result of fecal-oral transmission. History has provided case studies indicating the strategies needed in order to sustainably reduce diarrheal morbidity and mortality. A systems approach has been shown to be most effective. This include public health investment, laws, political advocacy as well as the simultaneous or scaffolded application of multiple universal public health interventions such as hygiene education, and water and sanitation systems. Each of these interventions has been deployed in developing countries at one time or the other. However, their implementation has been ad hoc without long term and sustained efforts.

Disease transmission is a complex process and no single intervention is foolproof. In fact, single intervention strategies tend to be unsustainable and in worse cases can create new problems. Contemporary developed countries faced similar challenges in the past and it was only through a series of sustained implementation of several public health programs that they were able to break the cycle of death and disease. While lack of resources is certainly a barrier for developing economies, the case of Cuba points to the need for social and political will to want to increase the human capital of the constituents.

The health and sanitation trajectories of Cuba and developed countries have many things in common. One important factor is that of sovereignty. That is, the countries involved, had the freedom to create long term goals and implement them without the constant pressure of external reporting and auditing. Governments of many developing countries do not have this freedom and tend to align their public health policies and priorities to the interests of advanced nations who provide funding (Konteh, 2009). For example, up until the mid-1970s, the World Bank seemed to only support sanitation projects where industrial demand indicated that it would produce a good economic return on the investment. Much of the capital aid provided was therefore earmarked for industrial output rather than human capacity building under the assumptions of 'trickle down' economics and that wealth creation was a fundamental precondition for improving health to rural areas and the urban poor (Pickford, 1980). Cuba provides a natural experiment – it was able to develop and implement policies without the financial backing and therefore mandates of the international community. Indeed it got support from the Soviet Union, but it saw fit to develop it human, medical and environmental resources to meet health needs of its populace.

As the international community acknowledges the once implicitly mentioned, right to access safe water and adequate sanitation, it is important that developing countries seize this opportunity to exert sovereignty in creating and implementing policies that promote sustainable access to water, sanitation and good health within the context of their own socio-economic, geo-political and ecological reality. With regards to the lack of structural, social and political infrastructure that is typically cited as being a barrier in developing countries for technology transfer and institutionalization of gains, one only has to look back in history to see that such were also the conditions that existed in currently successful developed nations.

Therefore, sustainable and permanent change can only occur when affected countries, governments and citizens treat and expect the provision of improved sanitation systems and the subsequent health benefits, as fundamental rights commensurate with any other fundamental human right, such as the right to life, liberty and security of person. This right to good health and freedom from disease can only be realized when local and national governments acknowledge that providing equitable access to water and sanitation is a crucial component of social and economic development and support intensive efforts to educate and raise awareness of all segments of society. Decision makers in developing countries must come to the realization that ensuring environmental justice for all cohorts of their populations benefits everyone and moves the country forward as a whole. President Franklin Delano Roosevelt echoed this sentiment in his second Inaugural Address, "The test of our progress is not whether we add more to the abundance of those who have much; it is whether we provide enough for those who have little" – Second Inaugural Address (Jan. 20, 1937), in Great Speeches 61 (John Grafton ed., 1999).

REFERENCES

Amnesty International. (2010). *Kenya: Risking Rape to Reach a Toilet: Women's Experiences in the Slums of Nairobi, Kenya*. (AFR 32/006/2010).

Ausubel, J. H., Meyer, P. S., & Wernick, I. K. (2001). Death and the human environment: The United States in the 20th century. *Technology in Society*, *23*(2), 131–146. doi:10.1016/S0160-791X(01)00005-7

Avery, L. M., Anchang, K. Y., Tumsweige, V., Strachan, N., & Goude, P. J. (2014, November). Potential for Pathogen reduction in anaerobic digestion and biogas generation in Sub-Saharan Africa. *Biomass and Bioenergy*, *70*, 112–124. doi:10.1016/j.biombioe.2014.01.053

Bakker, K. (2003). Archipelagos and networks: Urbanization and water privatization in the south. *The Geographical Journal*, *169*(4), 328–341. doi:10.1111/j.0016-7398.2003.00097.x

Boschi-Pinto, C., Lanata, C. F., Mendoza, W., & Habte, D. (2006). Diarrheal Diseases. In D. T. Jamison, R. G. Feachem, M. W. Makgoba, E. R. Bos, F. K. Baingana, K. J. Hofman, & K. O. Rogo (Eds.), *Disease and mortality in Sub-Saharan Africa*. Washington, DC: World Bank.

Brown, J., Cairncross, S., & Ensink, J. H. J. (2013). Water, sanitation, hygiene and enteric infections in children. *Archives of Disease in Childhood*, *98*(8), 629–634. doi:10.1136/archdischild-2011-301528 PMID:23761692

Buchholz, T. S., Volk, T. A., & Luzadis, V. A. (2007). A participatory systems approach to modeling social, economic, and ecological components of bioenergy. *Energy Policy*, *35*(12), 6084–6094. doi:10.1016/j.enpol.2007.08.020

Burstrom, B., Macassa, G., Oberg, L., Bernhardt, E., & Smedman, L. (2005). Equitable child health interventions: The impact of improved water and sanitation on inequalities in child mortality in Stockholm, 1878 to 1925. *American Journal of Public Health*, *95*(2), 208–216. doi:10.2105/AJPH.2003.034900 PMID:15671452

Cairncross, S., & Feachem, R. G. (1983). *Environmental health engineering in the tropics: an introductory text*. West Sussex, England: Wiley.

Caslake, L. F., Connolly, D. J., Menon, V., Duncanson, C. M., Rojas, R., & Tavakoli, J. (2004). Disinfection of Contaminated Water by Using Solar Irradiation. *Applied and Environmental Microbiology*, *70*(2), 1145–1151. doi:10.1128/AEM.70.2.1145-1150.2004 PMID:14766599

Centers for Disease Control and Prevention. (1999). Achievements in Public Health, 1990-1999: Changes in the Public Health System. [MMWR]. *Morbidity and Mortality Weekly Report*, *48*(50), 849–859. PMID:10563522

Chadwick, E. (1843). *Report on the sanitary condition of the labouring population of Great Britain. A supplementary report on the results of a spiecal inquiry into the practice of interment in towns*. London, UK: H. M. Stationery.

Checkley, W., Buckley, G., Gilman, R. H., Assis, A. M. O., Guerrant, R. L., Morris, S. S., & Black, R. E. et al.The Childhood Malnitrition and Infection Network. (2008). Multi-country analysis of the effects of diarrhoea on childhood stunting. *International Journal of Epidemiology*, *37*(4), 816–830. doi:10.1093/ije/dyn099 PMID:18567626

Coker, R., & Martin, R. (2006). Introduction: The importance of law for public health policy and practice. *Public Health, 120. Supplement*, *1*(0), 2–7.

Cooper, R. S., Kennelly, J. F., & Orduñez-Garcia, P. (2006). Health in Cuba. *International Journal of Epidemiology*, *35*(4), 817–824. doi:10.1093/ije/dyl175 PMID:16931525

Corrales, L. F., Izurieta, R., & Moe, C. L. (2006). Association between intestinal parasitic infections and type of sanitation system in rural El Salvador. *Tropical Medicine & International Health*, *11*(12), 1821–1831. doi:10.1111/j.1365-3156.2006.01737.x PMID:17176347

Cumming, O. (2009). The sanitation imperative: A strategic response to a development crisis. *Desalination*, *248*(1-3), 8–13. doi:10.1016/j.desal.2008.05.031

Curry, E. (2010). Water Scarcity and the Recognition of the Human Right to Safe Freshwater. *Northwestern Journal of International Human Rights*, *9*(1), 103–121.

Curtis, V., & Cairncross, S. (2003). Effect of washing hands with soap on diarrhoea risk in the community: A systematic review. *The Lancet Infectious Diseases*, *3*(5), 275–281. doi:10.1016/S1473-3099(03)00606-6 PMID:12726975

Curtis, V., Kanki, B., Mertens, T., Traore, E., Diallo, I., Tall, F., & Cousens, S. (1995). Potties, pits and pipes: Explaining hygiene behaviour in Burkina Faso. *Social Science & Medicine*, *41*(3), 383–393. doi:10.1016/0277-9536(94)00341-P PMID:7481932

De Vos, P., De Ceukelaire, W., Malaise, G., Pérez, D., Lefèvre, P., & Van Der Stuyft, P. (2009). Health through People's Empowerment: A Rights-Based Approach to Participation. *Health and Human Rights*, *11*(1), 23–35. doi:10.2307/40285215 PMID:20845848

Drain, P. K., & Barry, M. (2010). Fifty Years of U.S. Embargo: Cuba's Health Outcomes and Lessons. *Science*, *328*(5978), 572–573. doi:10.1126/science.1189680 PMID:20430999

Dresang, L. T., Brebrick, L., Murray, D., Shallue, A., & Sullivan-Vedder, L. (2005). Family Medicine in Cuba: Community-Oriented Primary Care and Complementary and Alternative Medicine. *The Journal of the American Board of Family Practice*, *18*(4), 297–303. doi:10.3122/jabfm.18.4.297 PMID:15994475

Dzwairo, B., Hoko, Z., Love, D., & Guzha, E. (2006). Assessment of the impacts of pit latrines on groundwater quality in rural areas: A case study from Marondera district, Zimbabwe. *Physics and Chemistry of the Earth Parts A/B/C*, *31*(15–16), 779–788. doi:10.1016/j.pce.2006.08.031

Espinosa, A., Harnden, R., & Walker, J. (2008). A complexity approach to sustainability - Stafford Beer revisited. *European Journal of Operational Research*, *187*(2), 636–651. doi:10.1016/j.ejor.2007.03.023

Fatusi, A. O., & Hindin, M. J. (2010). Adolescents and youth in developing countries: Health and development issues in context. *Journal of Adolescence*, *33*(4), 499–508. doi:10.1016/j.adolescence.2010.05.019 PMID:20598362

Grimason, A. M., Davison, K., Tembo, K. C., Jabu, G. C., & Jackson, M. H. (2000). Problems associated with the use of pit latrines in Blantyre, Republic of Malawi. *The Journal of the Royal Society for the Promotion of Health*, *120*(3), 175–182. doi:10.1177/146642400012000307 PMID:11077806

Guerrant, R. L., Hughes, J. M., Lima, N. L., & Crane, J. (1991). Diarrhea in Developed and Developing Countries: Magnitude, Special Settings, and Etiologies. *Reviews of Infectious Diseases*, *12*(Supplement 1), S41–S50. doi:10.1093/clinids/12.Supplement_1.S41 PMID:2406855

Gwatkin, D. R. (2003). How well do health programmes reach the poor? *Lancet*, *361*(9357), 540–541. doi:10.1016/S0140-6736(03)12558-5 PMID:12598134

Hanley, J. G. (2007). Public Health, London's Levels and the Politics of Taxation, 1840-1860. *Social History of Medicine*, *20*(1), 21–38. doi:10.1093/shm/hkl084

Holland, L., & Boon Foo, Y. (2003). Differences in environmental reporting practices in the UK and the US: The legal and regulatory context. *The British Accounting Review*, *35*(1), 1–18. doi:10.1016/S0890-8389(02)00127-0

Iatridis, D. S. (1990). Cuba's Health Care Policy: Prevention and Active Community Participation. *Social Work*, *35*(1), 29–35. PMID:2315760

Jon, A. P. (1979). The Impact of Sanitary Reform upon American Urban Planning, 1840-1890. *Journal of Social History*, *13*(1), 83–103. doi:10.1353/jsh/13.1.83 PMID:11632375

Kapp, R. W. Jr. (2014). Clean Water Act (CWA), US. In P. Wexler (Ed.), *Encyclopedia of Toxicology* (3rd ed., pp. 979–981). Oxford: Academic Press. doi:10.1016/B978-0-12-386454-3.00830-7

Khalfan, A., Roaf, V., Grimes, H., Langford, M., Fairstein, C., Russell, A., & Kiefer, T. (2007). *Manual on the Right to Water and Sanitation*. OHRE, AAAS, SDC and UN-HABITAT.

Knappett, P. S. K., Escamilla, V., Layton, A., Mckay, L. D., Emch, M., Williams, D. E., & Van Geen, A. et al. (2011). Impact of population and latrines on fecal contamination of ponds in rural Bangladesh. *The Science of the Total Environment*, *409*(17), 3174–3182. doi:10.1016/j.scitotenv.2011.04.043 PMID:21632095

Konteh, F. H. (2009). Urban sanitation and health in the developing world: Reminiscing the nineteenth century industrial nations. *Health & Place*, *15*(1), 69–78. doi:10.1016/j.healthplace.2008.02.003 PMID:18359263

Kuntz, D. (1994). The Politics of Suffering: The Impact of the U.S. Embargo on the Health of the Cuban People. Report to the American Public Health Association of a Fact-Finding Trip to Cuba, June 6-11, 1993. *Journal of Public Health Policy*, *15*(1), 86–107. doi:10.2307/3342609 PMID:8027364

Letema, S., Van Vliet, B., & Van Lier, J. B. (2014). Sanitation policy and spatial planning in urban East Africa: Diverging sanitation spaces and actor arrangements in Kampala and Kisumu. *Cities (London, England)*, *36*, 1–9. doi:10.1016/j.cities.2013.08.003

Luh, J., Baum, R., & Bartram, J. (2013). Equity in water and sanitation: Developing an index to measure progressive realization of the human right. *International Journal of Hygiene and Environmental Health*, *216*(6), 662–671. doi:10.1016/j.ijheh.2012.12.007 PMID:23333082

Márquez, M. (2009). Health-workforce development in the Cuban health system. *Lancet*, *374*(9701), 1574–1575. doi:10.1016/S0140-6736(09)61919-X PMID:19897113

McGuigan, J., Conroy, G., & Elmore, M. (1998). Solar disinfection of drinking water contained in transparent plastic bottles: Characterizing the bacterial inactivation process. *Journal of Applied Microbiology*, *84*(6), 1138–1148. doi:10.1046/j.1365-2672.1998.00455.x PMID:9717300

McLeod, M. (2010). "We Cubans Are Obligated Like Cats to Have a Clean Face": Malaria, Quarantine, and Race in Neocolonial Cuba, 1898-1940. *The Americas*, *67*(1), 57–81. doi:10.1353/tam.0.0272

Meckel, R. A. (1998). *Save the babies: American public health reform and the prevention of infant mortality, 1850-1929*. University of Michigan Press.

Mercier, M. E., & Boone, C. G. (2002). Infant mortality in Ottawa, Canada, 1901: Assessing cultural, economic and environmental factors. *Journal of Historical Geography*, *28*(4), 486–507. doi:10.1006/jhge.2002.0442

Miller, P., & Hirschhorn, N. (1995). The Effect of a National Control of Diarrheal Diseases Program on Mortality: The Case of Egypt. *Social Science & Medicine*, *40*(10), S1–S30. doi:10.1016/0277-9536(95)00001-N PMID:7638641

Mkandawire, T. (2008). Quality of groundwater from shallow wells of selected villages in Blantyre District, Malawi. *Physics and Chemistry of the Earth Parts A/B/C*, *33*(8–13), 807–811. doi:10.1016/j.pce.2008.06.023

Moszynski, P. (2006). Worldwide water crisis is a "silent emergency," UN agency says. *BMJ (Clinical Research Ed.)*, *333*(7576), 986–986. doi:10.1136/bmj.333.7576.986-a PMID:17095767

Novick, L. F., Morrow, C. B., & Mays, G. P. (2008). *Public health administration: Principles for population-based management* (2nd ed.). Burlington, MA: Jones and Bartlett Pub.

Nyenje, P. M., Foppen, J. W., Kulabako, R., Muwanga, A., & Uhlenbrook, S. (2013). Nutrient pollution in shallow aquifers underlying pit latrines and domestic solid waste dumps in urban slums. *Journal of Environmental Management*, *122*(0), 15–24. doi:10.1016/j.jenvman.2013.02.040 PMID:23542227

Ogle, M. (1993). Domestic Reform and American Household Plumbing, 1840-1870. *Winterthur Portfolio*, *28*(1), 33–58. doi:10.1086/496603

Onda, K., Crocker, J., Kayser, G. L., & Bartram, J. (2014). Country clustering applied to the water and sanitation sector: A new tool with potential applications in research and policy. *International Journal of Hygiene and Environmental Health*, *217*(2-3), 379–385. doi:10.1016/j.ijheh.2013.07.017 PMID:24054545

Perdue, W. C., Stone, L. A., & Gostin, L. O. (2003). The built environment and its relationship to the public's health: The legal framework. *American Journal of Public Health*, *93*(9), 1390–1394. doi:10.2105/AJPH.93.9.1390 PMID:12948949

Philadelphia Water Department. (2002). *Philadelphia Water Department Baxter Water Treatment Plant*. Source Water Assessment Report. (ME350056), 221.

Pickford, J. (1980). UN Water and Sanitation Decade. *Habitat International*, *5*(3/4), 459–467. doi:10.1016/0197-3975(80)90032-6

Pignatelli, S., & Musumeci, S. (2003). Comparison of Three Oral Rehydration Strategies in the Treatment of Acute Diarrhea in a Tropical Country. *Current Therapeutic Research*, *64*(3), 189–202. doi:10.1016/S0011-393X(03)00021-3 PMID:24944365

Pont, S. J., Grijalva, C. G., Griffin, M. R., Scott, T. A., & Cooper, W. O. (2009). National Rates of Diarrhea-Associated Ambulatory Visits in Children. *The Journal of Pediatrics*, *155*(1), 55–61. doi:10.1016/j.jpeds.2009.01.075 PMID:19394047

Pruss, A., & Mariotti, S. P. (2000). Preventing trachoma through environmental sanitation: A review of the evidence base. *Bulletin of the World Health Organization*, *78*(2), 258–266. PMID:10743299

Rawlinson, R. (1853). *On the drainage of towns.* Paper presented at the Minutes of the Proceedings Ambulatory VisiOn the Drainage of Towns.

Regidor, E., Pascual, C., Martínez, D., Calle, M. E., Ortega, P., & Astasio, P. (2011). The role of political and welfare state characteristics in infant mortality: A comparative study in wealthy countries since the late 19th century. *International Journal of Epidemiology*, *40*(5), 1187–1195. doi:10.1093/ije/dyr092 PMID:21737401

Rosenberg, C. E. (1987). *The cholera years, the United States in 1832, 1849, and 1866*. Chicago, USA: University of Chicago Press. doi:10.7208/chicago/9780226726762.001.0001

Santiso, R. (1997). Effects of chronic parasitosis on women's health. *International Journal of Gynaecology and Obstetrics: the Official Organ of the International Federation of Gynaecology and Obstetrics*, *58*(1), 129–136. doi:10.1016/S0020-7292(97)02865-8 PMID:9253675

Schmidlin, T., Huerlimann, E., Silue, K. D., Yapi, R. B., Houngbedji, C., Kouadio, B. A., & Raso, G. et al. (2013). Effects of Hygiene and Defecation Behavior on Helminths and Intestinal Protozoa Infections in Taabo, Cote d'Ivoire. *PLoS ONE*, *8*(6). PMID:23840358

Schultz, S. K., & Mcshane, C. (1978). To engineer the metropolis: Sewers, sanitation, and city planning in late-nineteenth-century America. *The Journal of American History*, *65*(2), 389–411. doi:10.2307/1894086 PMID:11614685

Spiegel, J. M., & Yassi, A. (2004). Lessons from the Margins of Globalization: Appreciating the Cuban Health Paradox. *Journal of Public Health Policy*, *25*(1), 85–110. doi:10.1057/palgrave.jphp.3190007 PMID:15134135

Stepek, G., Buttle, D. J., Duce, I. R., & Behnke, J. M. (2006). Human gastrointestinal nematode infections: Are new control methods required? *International Journal of Experimental Pathology*, *87*(5), 325–341. doi:10.1111/j.1365-2613.2006.00495.x PMID:16965561

Sterman, J. D. (2006). Learning from evidence in a complex world. *American Journal of Public Health*, *96*(3), 505–514. doi:10.2105/AJPH.2005.066043 PMID:16449579

Suthar, S., Bishnoi, P., Singh, S., Mutiyar, P. K., Nema, A. K., & Patil, N. S. (2009). Nitrate contamination in groundwater of some rural areas of Rajasthan, India. *Journal of Hazardous Materials*, *171*(1–3), 189–199. doi:10.1016/j.jhazmat.2009.05.111 PMID:19545944

Tarr, J. A. (1979). The Separate vs. Combined Sewer Problem: A Case Study in Urban Technology Design Choice. *Journal of Urban History*, *5*(3), 308–339. PMID:11614824

Tarr, J. A., McCurley, J. III, McMichael, F. C., & Yosie, T. (1984). Water and Wastes: A Retrospective Assessment of Wastewater Technology in the United States, 1800-1932. *Technology and Culture*, *25*(2), 226–263. doi:10.2307/3104713 PMID:11611516

Tate, J. E., Burton, A. H., Boschi-Pinto, C., Steele, A. D., Duque, J., & Parashar, U. D. (2012). 2008 estimate of worldwide rotavirus-associated mortality in children younger than 5 years before the introduction of universal rotavirus vaccination programmes: A systematic review and meta-analysis. *The Lancet Infectious Diseases*, *12*(2), 136–141. doi:10.1016/S1473-3099(11)70253-5 PMID:22030330

Taylor, M. S., Ha, M., Frank, J., & Whiter, N. (1990). The Risk Approach in Diarrheal Disease Intervention in Grenada. *Social Science & Medicine*, *30*(10), 1089–1095. doi:10.1016/0277-9536(90)90295-4 PMID:2363059

Terris, M. (1989). The Health Status of Cuba: Recommendations for Epidemiologic Investigation and Public Health Policy. *Journal of Public Health Policy*, *10*(1), 78–87. doi:10.2307/3342945 PMID:2715341

Tinuade, O., John, O., Saheed, O., Oyeku, O., Fidelis, N., & Olabisi, D. (2006). Parasitic etiology of childhood diarrhea. *Indian Journal of Pediatrics*, *73*(12), 1081–1084. doi:10.1007/BF02763049 PMID:17202634

Tomes, N. (1998). *The gospel of germs: men, women, and the microbe in American life*. Cambridge, MA: Harvard University Press.

UN Committee on Economic, Social and Cultural Rights (CESCR). (2003). *General Comment No. 15: The Right to Water* (Arts. 11 and 12 of the Covenant). 20 January 2003, E/C.12/2002/11, Retrieved from http://www.refworld.org/docid/4538838d11.html

UN General Assembly. (1966). *International Covenant on Economic, Social and Cultural Rights*. 16 December 1966, United Nations, Treaty Series, vol. 993, p. 3, Retrieved from http://www.refworld.org/docid/3ae6b36c0.html

UN General Assembly. (2010). *Resolution 15/9, Human rights and access to safe drinking water and sanitation*. A/HRC/RES/15/9 (6 October 2010), Retrieved from http://daccess-dds-ny.un.org/doc/UNDOC/GEN/G10/166/33/PDF/G1016633.pdf?OpenElement

United Nation. (2014). *International Decade for Action 'Water for Life' 2005-2015*. Retrieved March 20, 2014, from http://www.un.org/waterforlifedecade/sanitation.shtml

United Nation Children's Fund & World Health Organization. (2012). *Progress on Drinking Water and Sanitation 2012 Update*. Retrieved March 20, 2014 from http://www.unicef.org/media/files/JMPreport2012.pdf

United Nation Children's Fund & World Health Organization. (2013). *Progress on Drinking Water and Sanitation 2013 Update*. Retrieved March 20, 2014 from http://apps.who.int/iris/bitstream/10665/81245/1/9789241505390_eng.pdf

Valdés, N. P. (1971). Health and Revolution in Cuba. *Science and Society*, *35*(3), 311–335.

Walker, C. L. F., Rudan, I., Liu, L., Nair, H., Theodoratou, E., Bhutta, Z. A., & Black, R. E. et al. (2013). Global burden of childhood pneumonia and diarrhoea. *Lancet*, *381*(9875), 1405–1416. doi:10.1016/S0140-6736(13)60222-6 PMID:23582727

Ward, J. W., & Warren, C. (2007). *Silent victories: the history and practice of public health in twentieth-century America*. Oxford, UK: Oxford University Press.

Wateraid. (2014). *Risking rape to reach a toilet in India's slums*. Retrieved December 12, 2014, from http://www.wateraid.org/news/news/risking-rape-to-reach-a-toilet-in-india-slums

Wolf, J. H. (2001). *Don't Kill Your Baby: Public Health and the Decline of Breastfeeding in the 19th and 20th Centuries*. Columbus, Ohio: Ohio State University Press.

Wolf, J. H. (2007). Saving Babies and Mothers: Pioneering Efforts to Decrease Infant and Maternal Mortality. In J. W. Ward & C. Warren (Eds.), *Silent victories: the history and practice of public health in twentieth-century America* (p. 484). Oxford, UK: Oxford University Press.

Wong, J. K. F., & Wylie, A. (2010). Community- and Hospital-based Teaching in the Medical Currirulum: Examples from Cuba and the UK. *International Journal of Canadian Studies*, *2*(3/4), 343–350.

World Health Organization. (2013a). *Children: Reducing Mortality. WHO Factsheet* (Fact Sheet Number 178), 4.

World Health Organization. (2013b). *Diarrhoeal Disease. WHO Factsheet* (330). 4.

World Health Organization, & Unicef, United Nation Children's Fund. (2013). *Progress on Sanitation and Drinking Water*. 2013 Update. 40.

World Health Organization, & Unicef, United Nations Children's Fund. (2009). *Diarrhoea: Why children are still dying and what can be done*. 68.

World Health Organization, United Nations, United Nations Children's Fund, & The World Bank. (2013). Levels and Trends in Child Mortality. *Report, 2013*, 34.

Yeager, B. A. C., Huttly, S. R. A., Bartolini, R., Rojas, M., & Lanata, C. F. (1999). Defecation practices of young children in a Peruvian shanty town. *Social Science & Medicine*, *49*(4), 531–541. doi:10.1016/S0277-9536(99)00119-7 PMID:10414812

Yongsi, H. B. (2007). Diarrheal diseases in the history of public health. *Archives of Medical Research*, *38*(2), 159–163. doi:10.1016/j.arcmed.2006.11.001 PMID:17227723

Zawahri, N., Sowers, J., & Weinthal, E. (2011). The Politics of Assessment: Water and Sanitation MDGs in the Middle East. *Development and Change*, *42*(5), 1153–1177. doi:10.1111/j.1467-7660.2011.01730.x PMID:22175085

KEY TERMS AND DEFINITIONS

Diarrhea: Usually a symptom of an infection of the intestinal tract and presents as the passage of three or more loose or watery stool at least three times per day or more frequently than normal for an individual. It is a very common disease and affect individuals in every country and from every socio-economic background. In healthy individuals there is usually little cause for concern as episodes tend to be self-limiting. However, for undernourished and disease weakened patients, especially children, persistently reoccurring episodes are typically life-threatening. The interaction between diarrhea and malnutrition is bidirectional and synergistic. During a diarrheal episode, the increased rate of the passage of food through the intestines reduces the digestion and absorption of macro and micro nutrients. In addition, patients with persistent diarrhea may have poor appetite and thus have a reduction in food intake. With limited nutrients, the immune system becomes impaired and is unable to respond to attacks from enteric pathogens. Therefore both diarrhea and malnutrition work in synergy to predispose affected individuals to reoccurring episodes, more severe symptoms and higher rates of mortality. Children are particularly susceptible because their immune systems are underdeveloped.

Disease Incidence: Incidence is the rate of new (or newly diagnosed) cases of the disease in a defined population (e.g., children under 5 years old) during a specific time period (e.g., a calendar year). It is generally reported as the number of new cases occurring within a period of time (e.g., 20 new cases of HIV infection occurred in village A during 2013. The defined population refers to the population at risk. This means that for the defined population, children under 5 years old, they are all at risk of getting diarrhea but do not have the disease at the beginning of 2013.

Disease Prevalence: Prevalence is the actual number of cases alive, with the disease in a defined population either during a period of time (period prevalence) or at a particular date in time (point prevalence). While incidence deals with entirely new cases, prevalence counts what exists. It is typically reported as a prevalence rate which is the proportion of ad defined population that has specific disease or attribute at a specific time.

Enteric Infections: Infectious disease of the intestines. Typical bacterial enteric infections include E. coli and cholera. These infections are accompanied by diarrhea, nausea and sometimes vomiting.

Environmental Justice: Requires that no one group should disproportionately bear the burden of adverse health outcomes from environmental hazards simply on the basis of ethnic and racial background, geography and income. Each cohort and/or people group must be fairly represented in all environmental related decision-making processes – so as to prevent environmental discrimination. Environmental discrimination occurs when certain communities, because of their minority or disadvantage status, bear a higher burden of risk from environmental hazards without enjoying the benefits that are easily accessible to other groups.

Health Outcomes: Simply put, are symptoms or result of health-related activities. They are measured on a continuum from morbidity (illness) to mortality (death).

Infant and Child Mortality Rates: Infant mortality rate is the number of children that die before their first birthday per 1000 live births in a country or geographical location. While child mortality is the number of children that dies under age five per 1000 live births in a country or geographical location.

Life Expectancy: The mean number of years an individual is expected to live if born and/or exposed to specific environmental conditions in a country or geographical location.

Open Defecation: The practice of depositing human stool outside particularly in areas where there is no access to improved feces disposal systems. It is typically a rural activity and about 1 billion persons practice it around the world. It is one of the main cause of diarrhea in developing countries.

Oral Rehydration Therapy (ORT): A mixture of clean water and electrolyte solution typically given in response to a diarrheal episode.

Sanitation: Generally speaking, sanitation encompasses fecal disposal systems, water treatment and delivery systems, personal and environmental hygiene education and practices as well as solid waste (garbage) disposal systems. In this work, sanitation typically refer to fecal disposal systems such as latrines in order to differentiate from water treatment interventions.

Sustainable Development: The conceptual framework for organizing plans and activities to achieve sustainability. Where a community's developmental activities is considered sustainable if it produces resources faster than they used, those resources are mostly renewable and/or infinite and, works in harmony with ecological systems to eliminate its wastes.

Systems Approach: A problem solving approach that views the problem (s) as part of an overall system. The component parts of the overall system are view in context to each other rather than in isolation. Therefore, rather than reducing a problem into the properties of its parts or causative components (as in the case of reductionist approach), this approach focuses on the arrangement of and the relations between the parts which connect them into a whole – based on the principle that the whole is greater than the sum of its parts. Instead of simply looking at problems through a linear cause and effects model, the systems framework recognizes the inherent nonlinearity of the synergistic interactions among systems components that can produce unintended consequences through emergence.

Chapter 2
Towards a Competitive Sustainable City:
Cycling as an Opportunity

Donatella Privitera
University of Catania, Italy

ABSTRACT

This chapter analyses the dynamic of the development of cycling in Italy situating it also in the European context from an economic and strategic perspective. With this aim, first there was a study of the challenge of rapidly growing urban populations in spatially very limited areas affects not only residential housing construction. It also relates to urban infrastructure and services. This led to identification of new mobility needs, met mainly by private means, with implications in terms of congestion and air pollution. Results are analysed in terms of total trips of non-motorized urban mobility and help at understanding how promoting cycling is important for individual health, environmental sustainability and transport demand management. The chapter brings the debate on sustainable transport policy into direct confrontation with the embodied practice of cycling in an urbanized environment.

INTRODUCTION

The global population is increasingly concentrating in cities. Globally, more people live in urban areas than in rural areas, with 54 per cent of the world's population residing in urban areas in 2014. In 1950, 30% of the world's population was urban, and by 2050, 66% of the world's population is projected to be urban. Levels of urbanization vary greatly across regions. In 2014, high levels of urbanization, at or above 80 per cent, characterized Latin America and the Caribbean and Northern America. In Europe, around 73% of the population lives in urban areas (United Nation, 2015). Cities and urban areas face many challenges — economic, social, health and environmental and their shape is changing dramatically. They present the typical features of the current process of urban transformation "characterized by growth and the differentiation of urban activities which are resulting in new metropolitan spaces that are enlarged and distantiated in terms of scale and scope" (Salet, 2007, p. 6). As the major function of cities is to provide places for people to trade,

DOI: 10.4018/978-1-4666-8433-1.ch002

produce, communicate and live, the urban environment needs to be assessed from a very specific human perspective: to provide an agreeable place to live while minimising or balancing negative side effects. Quality of life in cities relies on a range of components such as social equity, income and welfare, housing, a healthy environment, social relations and transport (EEA, 2010). Transport is associated with positive connotations, but the impacts and the benefits have a high price (Geerlings et al., 2012). However, the negative effects resulting from mobility cannot be ignored when sustainability is considered.

It's important to identify new mobility needs in the cities. Sustainable mobility is a priority for action for the EU, although the issue is limited resources (CEC, 2001) the cities could use plus investments fund for sustainable urban development. There are opportunities and benefits associated with urban living in terms of sustainability and resource use.

The role reserved for the urban quality of life and livability of the cities is significant and is reflected in numerous studies in national and foreign literature. High human activity, population density, the excesses of motor traffic and traffic congestion, and not least the many spatial elements and the air quality are all factors contaminating the quality of urban life. The power of the automobile has reduced the alternatives offered by other transport modes since, besides the psychological attachment to the private comfort of speed and seamlessness offered by the car (Sheller & Urry, 2000; Urry, 2006), it has inevitably shaped the physical form of urban mobility so that other modes of mobility do not fit in: cyclists and pedestrians have to fight against the symbol of cars, and space for bicycle paths or pavements has to be "stolen" from the "natural". The importance of urban policies and their effectiveness is closely linked to the ability to exploit the land in all its components by focusing on quality of life and meeting the needs of residents. A quality of life, and more specifically quality of urban life, is defined as "the state of social wellbeing of an individual or group, either perceived or as identified by observable indicators" (Pacione, 2005, p. 673) oriented also to the principles of sustainability. Urban quality, based on strong elements of identity and specificity, has thus become the determining factor in a process of continuous economic development in an integrated way that involves public and private resources (Travisi & Camagni, 2005).

In this context, strong planning policies that favour non-auto modes of transport assume increasing importance (Kenworthy & Laube, 1997). The efficiency and effectiveness of the transport system help to qualify the supply of city services; also it cannot ignore the important role in shaping the image on tourism (Page, 2009). In this perspective, addressing the issues concerning sustainable mobility would make a positive contribution to the environmental, social and economic sustainability of the communities they serve, where the aim is also to contribute in an integrated network of actors involved to the development of eco-friendly cities.

Cycling is a sustainable mode of transport (CEC, 2001; 2007) and it has a role in building a better, healthier and ecological society while at the same time offering a tourist attraction role as a possible niche to exploit and promote among the different ways of enjoying the city (Gatersleben & Haddad, 2010; Lumsdon, 2000). Increased cycling should contribute to reducing noise and air pollution and it has important implications for both personal health, having been linked to lower rates of overweight and obesity (Wen & Rissel, 2008), as well as livability and environmental resources.

The aim of this chapter is describes the importance of sustainability in urban areas and to promote the bicycle as a means of transport fitting with wider social and environmental agendas. It shows also an analysis of Italian cities in terms of development, sustainability and infrastructures to promote cycling as an opportunity to reduce environmental degradation.

BACKGROUND TO CYCLING LIKE SUSTAINABLE MOBILITY

Mobility is a multifaceted term when used in different contexts and meanings (Adey, 2010; Kellerman, 2012). In social sciences, mobility refers to two main areas of research, social mobility and spatial mobility, but they are interrelated (Urry, 2007). On one side, social mobility (or intergenerational mobility) corresponds to those studies connected with social stratification and measures the degree to which people's social status changes between generations (Breen, 2004). On the other side, spatial mobility (or motility) is the objective of those researchers who analyze movements, the activity of people within space, thus considering a spatial or a territorial perspective (Kaufmann et al., 2004). Spatial mobility is also the ability to move between activity sites (Hanson, 1995), a meaningful condition, implying modernity, freedom, speed and extensibility (Cresswell, 2006). Mobility is a complex term, since it involves aspects connected to transportation, travel, journey and movement, depending on the focus of attention. Mobility ranges from the analysis of the tools and modes of transport utilized by people, such as cars, bicycles and buses, to the "direction" of and the reasons for movement, thus where people move to and why, as in tourism or home-work commuting.

Transport is one of the sectors of the economy with the most challenging tasks facing decision makers (UNECE, 2008). Transportation refers to the study of how the need for mobility is connected with the size and the organization of the city. By assuming a rational-choice approach, transportation analysis has been addressed in particular by urban economists, who try to determine how cities are dependent upon transportation needs and costs (O'Sullivan, 2003).

Sustainable mobility is an evolving concept and there is no universally accepted definition (Zito & Salvo, 2011). The first appearance of the term (CEC, 1992) refers to strict environmental standards for all modes of transport in connection with the reduction of transport volume. Then attention was paid to the development needs of individuals, businesses and society in a manner consistent with human and ecosystem health (OECD, 2004), and then to the reduction of traffic, particularly in urban areas. A modern transport system must be sustainable from an economic and social as well as an environmental viewpoint, and able to adapt to the requirements of sustainable development (CEC, 2001).

In recent times, the policies for sustainable mobility and transport planning have attracted increasing interest from the European Union (CEC, 2007; 2011) and therefore the priority of policies being expressed as binding rules of law. Only France and England seem to have made strict choices with regard to strategic planning of transport in terms of sustainability. Among other countries, such as Italy, Germany and Spain, there are regulations that are binding on the realities of sustainable urban planning, but only as not mandatory instruments: the urban mobility plane, introduced by the Italian legislation in 2000 (decree of 27/3/98 on the integration of "sustainable mobility in urban areas") for cities with over 100,000 inhabitants, has no binding force and is a prerequisite for access to national funds in case of investments (Socco, 2010). In particular, according to White Paper (CEC, 2011), with a broad strategy and the long-time horizon until 2050, transport will also help sustainable competitive policies of urban and regional planning. The European Commission adopted a road map of 40 concrete initiatives for the next decade to build a competitive transport system that will increase mobility and remove major barriers in key areas including increasing fuel prices and unemployment. At the same time, the proposals will dramatically reduce Europe's dependence on imported oil and cut carbon emissions from transport by 60% by 2050. The central point is that the transport system should meet society's economic, social and environmental needs.

Mobility is a central problem for the city. Cities need efficient transport systems to support their economy and the welfare of their inhabitants. In many EU countries, especially in Italy, the emergence of a mobility model focused mainly on the car, and the lack of proper planning resulted in excessive land consumption and processing functions in the city with new residential, tertiary and trade shapes. Moreover, the predominance of speculation and lack of recovery of the existing buildings have certainly not helped a mobility model centred on urban sustainability. In urban areas, the mobility model is relevant from the point of view of the quality of life of those directly involved (time devoted to the movement, chronic congestion, costs, etc.), in terms of environmental pressure exerted by automobile mobility. The statement is explained by car use in situations characterized by poor quality of public transport. In fact, the car is the best means to manage a mobility that has taken on a space-time profile that is increasingly fragmented (Hochschild, 1997) due to the progressive changes that have occurred in the styles of mobility of the actors who, in turn, refer to most common changes of urban societies. Steg (2005) examines various motives for car use and suggests that policy makers should not focus exclusively on instrumental reasons, but they should, likewise, take into consideration the various social and affective causes. The centrality of the automobile and its increased use is only one aspect of the general mobility, although the dependence on the use of private transport is the principal factor that helps to characterize the profile in the sense of its lack of sustainability, not only environmental and economic but also social.

Many studies have investigated how the externalities of the transport system (non-renewable fuel use and greenhouse gas emissions, traffic congestion, low and unequal mobility, pollution, accidents and fatalities, degradation of ecosystems) may be minimized, while the benefits of mobility are maximized and shared equally through sustainable urban and transport development means (Banister et al., 2000; Kenworthy et al., 1996; Shore, 2006). Unfortunately, global emissions of carbon dioxide (CO_2) – the main cause of global warming – increased by 3% in 2011, reaching an all-time high of 34 billion tonnes and continue to increase with time (primarily due to electricity generation and road transportation). It is worth considering that in many OECD countries CO_2 emissions decreased – in the European Union by 3%, in the United States by 2% and in Japan by 2% – mainly due to weak economic conditions in many countries, mild winter weather in several countries and high oil prices. However, it is significant that CO_2 emissions from OECD countries now account for only one-third of global emissions – the same share as that of China and India, where emissions increased by 9% and 6%, respectively, in 2011 (United Nations, 2012).

Movement and risk are linked with high probability of collisions but behaviour and interactions between road users depend on the attitudes of individuals, the road space available, infrastructure and traffic and environmental conditions (Parkin & Koorey, 2012). Road fatalities in Italy have also been showing downward trend as shown in Table 1.

Clean and energy-efficient vehicles aim to reduce vehicle-and fuel-related greenhouse gas and exhaust gas emissions, fuel consumption and fossil fuel dependency, through the use of measures including exhaust gas treatment systems, alternative drive trains and the use of alternative fuels and energy storage systems (Maragkogianni et al., 2013). All these facts points to the necessity of reducing the dependence on motorized vehicles and promoting an alternate mode in the urban centers.

In 2010, 7.4% of European citizens used the bicycle as their preferred mode of transportation but also walking was mentioned (13%) (Eurobarometer, 2011): alternative modes which can reduce the unwanted impacts of motorization but at the same time are user friendly. The wider benefits (economic, social, environment, etc..) of cycling to communities (increase in quality of life

Table 1. Total of car and two wheeler accidents in Italy

Year	Total Accidents				Two Motorized Wheeler			
	Accidents	Killed	Injured	Killed Index	Accidents	Killed	Injured	Killed Index
2006	238,124	5,669	332,955	2.4	87,303	1,615	102,401	1.8
2007	230,871	5,131	325,850	2.2	87,258	1,701	103,152	1.9
2008	218,963	218,963	4,725	2.2	80,012	1,458	87,241	1.8
2009	215,405	4,237	307,258	2.0	77,877	1,321	85,214	1.7
2010	211,404	4,090	302,735	1.9	71,108	1,214	78,449	1.7
2011	205,638	3,860	292,019	1.8	n.a.	1,142	78,461	1.7
2012	188,228	3,753	266,864	1.9	n.a.	1,028	68,416	1.6
2013	181,227	3,385	257,421	1.8	n.a.	907	61,158	1.7

(Source: Istat, 2014).

due to higher accessibility, improved quality of the public realm, increased interaction between residents, a boost to the vitality of town centers, etc.) are numerous.

The largest single benefit of cycling is on the health side but others categories combined as congestion-easing, fuel savings, reduced CO_2 emissions, reduced air pollution, reduced noise pollution accumulate to an economic benefit of € 143.2 – 155.3 bn (ECF, 2013). In addition, a number of industry sectors benefit from cycling, in particular the tourism industry due to recreational and tourism cycling, as well as the bicycle industry (retail and employment effects in manufacturing industry).

MOTORIZATION IN ITALY

Italian Trends in Mobility Levels and Trip Purpose

The city is defined by the forms and structures of its network of mobility and hence in accordance with user requirements and management of the car (Thrift, 2004). Indeed, cities have been shaped by the needs of cars: parking places, garages, huge mobility infrastructures etc. have been created to serve automobile use. One major impact the motor car has had is on the geography of road space. In fact, motor roads have shaped our experience of space and place, and their design, inhabitation and regulation, but they have also facilitated social and cultural relations with individual freedom of movement (Merriman, 2009). However road transport is by far the most emitting transport subsector, in terms of greenhouse gas emissions.

Automobile dependence has been studied with many different motivations – social, cultural, economic, climatic and political – but without doubt it is interconnected with planning and the contemporary urban landscape (Gatersleben & Uzzel, 2002; Gorham, 2002; Newman & Kenworthy, 1999, 2000; Urry, 2004).

In Italy, the global economic crisis, in recent years, has affected the lifestyles of the population and, consequently, the mobility of people and goods (Figure 1).

From Isfort's survey, some elements emphasize the peculiarities of urban areas and mobility: some people are abandoning cars for bikes (at least for some trips), others bikes for cars (often for all trips). But even within a specific town, at any particular time, there are, of course, major mobility inequalities. Both levels of mobility and attitudes tend to vary, often quite dramatically,

Figure 1. Modal share in cities of Italy (%)
(Source: Isfort, Osservatorio "Audimob" on Italian mobility).

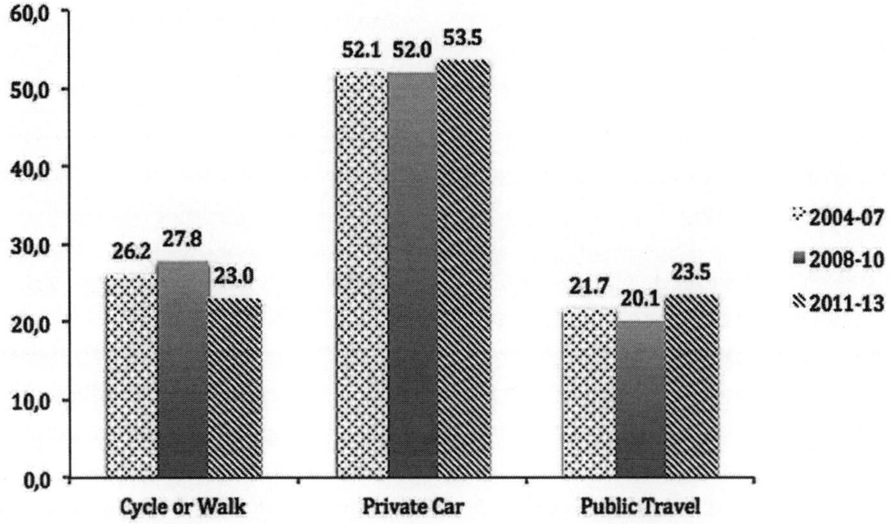

according to gender, class, ethnicity and age. In 2013, public transport gained space and increasingly assumed a role for popularity, a perspective of sustainable urban mobility, especially in the face of the structural decline of non-motorized transport. In the previous two years a decrease in trips had been recorded that was more compatible with environmental needs (pedestrians), but clearly the dependence on the car continued to prevail (53.5%), although there was some variation in user behavior.

Travelling for reasons of work and study was the main reason for mobility; also, between 2007 and 2012, the distribution of displacements recorded significant changes: the sharing of trips for study and family, along with a decrease in the number of journeys to work and, especially, leisure (-11% and 25.2%). In 2012 this reason for travelling lost the leadership in favour of the family (Isfort, 2013). Walking together cycling use continue to be used primarily for leisure and car modal share for work trips has risen as well (Table 2).

Table 2. Modal split of travel in urban area Italian (%)

	Work		Study		Family		Leisure	
	2007	2012	2007	2012	2007	2012	2007	2012
Walk/Cycle	17.3	16.4	25.1	17.2	35.5	31.7	38.9	34.0
Motorcycle	8.8	5.9	12.2	11.3	2.3	1.4	5.0	4.8
Car	63.3	63.8	35.9	32.1	56.6	59.3	50.2	52.8
Public Travel	10.6	13.9	26.8	39.4	5.6	7.6	5.9	8.4
Total	100	100	100	100	100	100	100	100

(Source: Isfort, Osservatorio "Audimob" on Italian mobility).

Developments and Determinants of Cycling in Italy

In Italy, the development of cycling as a sustainable mode of transport is still far from that of other northern European countries. There are 0.44 bicycles per capita in the Netherlands, more than one for every Dutch inhabitant, and they cover on average 1,019 km a year. Furthermore, the cycle paths in countries such as Denmark, Germany and the Netherlands are convenient, safe and attractive. In these countries, cycling is not only recognized as an important means of daily transport but it remains a symbol of national identity and the strong bicycle culture contributes to sustainable urban behaviours (Carstensen & Ebert, 2012).

We note that sustainable mobility fails to adopted n in urban areas (the same is happening in the extra-urban), disregarding the expectations vested in the middle of the last decade. One reason is the lack of space in Italy and bike lanes where the cycling index (m_eq/100 inhabitants) is equal to 34.86 (metres per 100 inhabitants) in Reggio Emilia, a city that boasts 155.5 km the longest network in absolute terms and of 0.0 for l'Aquila and Nuoro (Urban Ecosystem, 2011), although it must be said that some cities lend themselves more easily to cycling, even for morphological and configuration issues and the quality of services offered. In big cities (with over 250,000 inhabitants), pedestrian mobility numbers in 2011 were slightly below the overall average (22.9% vs. 23.2%), with a decided downturn compared to 2010. The bicycle has a traditional lack of penetration, with just 2.3% of trips served (a slight increase from 2010). In the complex sustainable mobility is in the big cities of unsatisfactory levels. In the midsize towns (100,000-250,000 inhabitants) confirm an important role. Conversely, the increased use of "two wheels" to replace a portion of the pedestrian mobility in urban areas reaches 20% of intermediate demand; the smaller towns favour cycling and walking instead (5.1%, a share slightly above the overall average).

In fact, the land of some cities in some cases is 10-15 times smaller than others, implying a different density of population (Table 3). It's worthy of note that specific studies demonstrate that moderate and high-density populations both correlate well with less motor traffic and create more attractive conditions for cycling (Dumbaugh & Li, 2010). But high density city populations may also intensify exposure to pollution, less safe travel, etc., so generally smaller cities more cycle friendly than large ones (Krizek, 2011). Furthermore, the urban structure of some cities, particularly in southern Italy (e.g. Reggio Calabria, Siracusa, Palermo, Catania), is founded on their relationship with the sea and the use of the seafront. They alternate high-density to low-density areas, with a high level of urbanization, in particular by the seaside. That widely increases the distance between different points inside the cities with a consequent increase in the average travel distance.

Isfort's survey (2013) shows how cycling has a typological relief in part similar to that of walking as the choice is derived from motivations which tend to be diversified by social references.

Table 3. Total trips of non-motorized urban mobility with amplitude of the cities

	Towns with > 250,000 Inhabitants			Towns with 100,000-250,000 Inhabitants			Towns with < 250,000 Inhabitants		
	2010	2011	2012	2010	2011	2012	2010	2011	2012
Cycle	2.1	2.3	n.a.	7.9	8.4	n.a.	6.0	5.1	n.a
Walk	27.5	22.9	n.a.	19.5	18.2	n.a.	27.0	24.5	n.a
Total	29.6	25.2	26.0	27.4	26.6	25.3	33.0	29.6	30.3

(Source: Isfort, Osservatorio "Audimob" on Italian mobility, 2013).

Figure 2. Urban non-motorized mobility of Italian population (% trips)
(Source: Isfort, Osservatorio "Audimob" on Italian mobility).

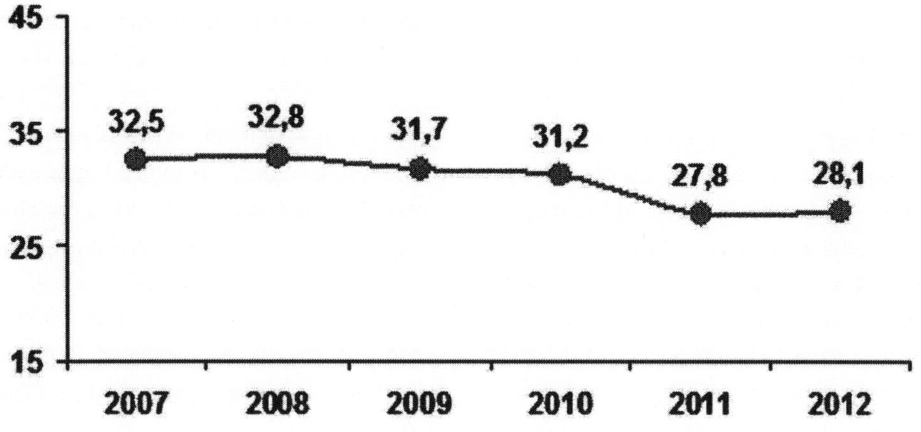

The reasons are to be found in the economic and ecological characteristics but in sum the cycling is not preferable to a quick and more comfortable car.

All over the country in 2012 the share of non-motorized travel (walking or cycling) is equal to 28.1% of the total (Isfort, 2013). Focusing on urban centres, the percentage increases: in the city, one-third of journeys are made on foot, but despite the numbers, the attention given to pedestrians (and cyclists) by national and local administrators is relatively low (Figure 2).

The systematic displacement cycle have a minority of those generated by the need for family and leisure, with a marked characteristic of regularity – 53.7% of the mileage is repeated every day, or almost – confirming that choice is always less determined by contingent causes more and more, but rather, connected to a structured model of a search for modal and sustainable solutions in response to daily transport needs.

Wide, however, the difference in cycling in a part of North-European cities: the mobility bike, properly protected and encouraged, has become a significant part of the management of urban mobility (Pucher & Buehler, 2008). The available data show that the spread of cycle paths is a primarily cultural factor, independent of climatic conditions: they are all in small and medium-sized cities like Helsinki and Aarhus – those in which the network appear than a metre per inhabitant. Medium to large areas such as Stockholm and Copenhagen also have a good supply per capita (Ambiente Italia, 2007). Dutch, Danish and German cities have reinforced the safety, convenience and attractiveness of their excellent cycling rights of way with extensive bike parking, integration with public transport, making their cities people-friendly rather than car-friendly and thus more livable and more sustainable than American and British cities (Pucher & Buehler, 2008).

In many parts of Italy the emergence of modern lifestyles and a new mobility model, which recognizes the important role of cycling, faces difficulties, but in some places (and times) the practice of cycling is easier than in other places. As the contributions which follow also demonstrate, different cycling practices are either encouraged or discouraged by variously favourable and unfavourable conditions. Within any city, cyclists tend to favour some routes over others. Within a region, some cities are considered more cycle-friendly than others, which may nonetheless still be identified with cycles and cycling, through an association with long-established cycle races, for example (Krizek, 2012).

After World War II, also a political choice, Italian cities have grown around a mobility essentially based around the private car and not responded to the application of the principles of sustainability instead of less polluting modes of transport. Especially in urban areas, "car regime" vision (Holtz et al., 2008), which still continues, has changed the landscape. In fact "(...) it is important to recognise the car as part of a system (…) which we have called the 'automobility paradigm'. It is often not appreciated to what extent our modern culture is integrated with the car and its systems: we have literally built our world around the car in its current form (…)." (Nieuwenhuis et al., 2004, p. 10) and has gradually transformed the urban environment (Marletto, 2011). The environment is occupied with increased traffic congestion, air pollution and noise, a lack of safety, accidents as well as difficulty with lifetime management and excessive individual and social costs (Urry, 2007).

The analysis of indicators of sustainable urban mobility (Ispra, 2013) reveals a growing trend on average (2000-2012), but it is not yet sufficient to guarantee adequate levels of sustainability in transport and in the movement of Italian citizens. One cause is related to public transport since the possibility of easy access to quality public transport contributes to the spread of forms of sustainable mobility. There is little evidence of growth in the number of trams, trolley buses and subways other than for buses and railways. In Europe the main approach to increasing cycling and making it safer has been the provision of more bike paths and lanes (Pucher et al., 2010). In Italy there is a spatial inhomogeneity. In general, the use of these lanes, as well as those used for recreation and sports for systematic trips of a short distance, is more common in the cities of North Italy. The recent focus has been on expanding bike lanes, off-street bike paths are often the most heavily used and highest profile cycling facilities but tend to serve mainly recreational purposes. From 2002 to 2013 the km of cycle paths for the municipal area of 100 km^2 are more than doubled, from 6.9 to 18.9 km on principal cities (Isfort, 2013).

There are 17 cities in Italy who have not made their paths (e.g. Napoli, Taranto, Sassari). Among others, Padova (164.8 km), Brescia (132.3), Bolzano (97.3) and Torino (134.4) have the highest density and Imperia (0.9 km per 100 km^2 land), Reggio Calabria (0.6) and Ragusa (0.2) are characterized by the lowest. On average, in large cities such as Milano - still dominated by the car (covering 42.4% of trips) rather than the bike (which accounts for 3.8% of the total) – the network of cycle tracks has been redesigned to more precisely defined links, with "direct" paths from the centre connecting with the periphery in order to improve mobility between home and work and home and school. This is in line with the objectives of the municipality to reinvent Milan, and make it a more green and sustainable city. Separate facilities are not sufficient but they are certainly necessary to ensure that cycling is possible for a broad spectrum of the population (Garrard et al., 2008). It therefore seems essential to regulate mobility in urban centres by encouraging cycling as well as the use of public transport. Looking, for example, at data related to the space for pedestrians, in 2011 (2% from 2010), the different urban realities had, on average, for every 100 inhabitants, 32.6 m^2 of area closed to motorized traffic (Istat, 2013). The municipalities of Verbania, Cremona and Terni exceed 100 square metres for every 100 inhabitants, but the big cities present more surface area for pedestrians: Venezia (which has 486.9 m^2), Roma (396.195) and Milano (362.410). Eight cities say they do not have traffic islands within their territory (e.g. Ascoli Piceno and Agrigento).

The actions taken in Italian cities friendly bike are in order to continue to increase the share of cycling. In fact, they were not limited to the development of infrastructure, but would include a wide set of promotion, education and social measures focusing on the ecological, health, economic benefits of cycling.

The Status of Cycling

In Italy, and also in other and low-cycling countries, very few people use a bike on a regular basis infact for many people driving a car, not cycling, is perceived as normal and habitual option for short urban journeys (Horton & Parkin, 2012). Within a mass motorized context like Italy, cycling as a mode of transport exists by comparison with, and not in competition with, motorized modes. The motorized street is an arena of identity formation, where transport modes have complex, differentiated implications for social identities. Aldred (2012) has shown that for cyclists in the UK, stigmas attached to the 'cyclist' identity are complex: people who cycle are caught between two threats appearing too competent as a cyclist (a proper cyclist), and appearing not competent enough (a bad cyclist).

Urbanczyk (2010) has identified different types of cyclists, which coincide or differ depending on the routine, the frequency and the purpose of their cycling. It should be noted that studies of this kind are numerous and similar (Davies et al., 2001; Jensen, 1999), and identify distinctions mostly related to the motivations for and frequency of use (commuting, health, shopping, leisure), or at least the attitude towards individual sustainability and lifestyle. Social identities are important to the promotion of cycling because in marketing they are often used to promote products (Gatersleben & Haddad, 2010). The goal, in fact, is to encourage people to use bicycles on holiday, at leisure, but transferring this "good practice" to everyday use becomes a tool for disseminating sustainable behaviour within an urban mobility mainly characterized by the use of the automobile (Sener et al., 2009).

It therefore appears to be a social phenomenon – a different leisure culture – and particularly in urban areas related to the deployment of bike sharing, which is playing an important role in urban mobility services in many cities worldwide. These are interesting recent developments in cycling for recreation, but at present in Italy it appears to be a niche business. The cyclists using the bicycle as their main mode of transport in the activity, although not exclusively recreational (Ritchie, 1998) depending on whether the cyclists "excited" or "occasional", in reference to the parameters of time and purpose of the holiday (Simonsen & Jorgenson, 1998). The bicycle is used by a wide variety of individuals and offers potential market segments in terms of sustainable development in tourism (Lumsdon, 2000); it may refer to either a circuit to a journey of at least one day as an integral part of a trip or vacation, for both short and long recreational sports but not (Sustrans, 1999), although it also includes participation in cycling events (Faulks et al., 2008; Lamont, 2009). It is still experience an activity that involves both recreation and transportation as the relationship between tourism and transport is inseparable (Chang & Chang, 2003).

In 2009, the Italian government, like many other international governments, actively examined methods to promote cycling and other sustainable modes of transport. These policies were driven by the desire to contribute to sustainable transport goals reducing greenhouse gas emissions and decreasing congestion, particularly the policies introduced to promote cycling by reducing the cost of purchasing a bicycle and not alone. In many cities the success was significant, but no data demonstrate that citizens have changed their perceptions of cycling and improved accessibility to the bicycles and cycling after using this scheme.

It's worthy of note that specific studies demonstrate that moderate and high-density populations both correlate well with less motor traffic and create more attractive conditions for cycling (Dumbaugh & Li, 2010). But high density city populations may also intensify exposure to pollution, less safe travel, etc., so generally smaller cities are more cycle friendly than large ones (Krizek, 2011). Furthermore, the urban structure of some cities is founded on their relationship with the sea and the use of the seafront (in the south Italy).

They alternate high-density to low-density areas, with a high level of urbanization, in particular by the seaside. That widely increases the distance between different points inside the cities, with a consequent increase in the average travel distance.

DISCUSSION, CONCLUSION, AND PROSPECTS

Cycling continues to increase in popularity and garner attention for its ability to achieve various environmental, health and congestion-mitigating benefits for local communities. However, in Italy very few people use a bicycle on a regular basis and most cycling is for recreation. Culture, habit and custom are important but if cycling is to be a viable mode of transportation with extreme variation in the experience of its users, it must have appropriate facilities.

The diffusion of cycling currently has limited added value for the study area but if properly supported could meet the requirements of sustainability by many operators, public authorities and users in particular in urban areas. From synthetic and fragmented a small fraction but potentially growing.

The image is one of a city still characterized by the proliferation of cars, public transport and little-used eco-friendly mobility. The use of the bicycle is limited; big cities with more than 10% of the local population using sustainable mobility include Milan and Bologna. Residents of the south cities are car-dependent with costs for the quality of life and health that are likely to remain high. While implementation of innovative facilities such as bicycle boulevards and coloured bike lanes is low, surveys have indicated that there are projects currently being implemented or in the process of approval. The number of cities that report having implemented innovative facilities has increased significantly in recent years but there is no image of cycling in Italy. Indeed, actually, cycling has a positive environmental image but in the cities cyclists suffer and combat with disobedience of traffic laws.

To implement a system of bicycle paths (from different regions) means promoting and implementing soft mobility which is the first step towards a sustainable development perspective. One likely development to be maintained and enhanced over time is the awareness of communities and local governments. The sustainable vision of urban mobility is present, at least in its potential, and the idea of cycle paths should be communicated and disseminated with its territorial, economic and social implications. Informal programmes and policies (e.g. marketing programmes) and several independent bicycle organizations and events may also help create a "bicycle culture" that will likely influence cycling behaviour. Cycling may be combined with other modes of transportation and be used by adults to meet the recommendations for daily physical activity, but a network of different types of infrastructure is necessary to attract new people to cycling (Dill, 2009). Cycling is a clean and efficient mode of transportation especially suited for short to moderate distances. Cycling provides numerous benefits compared to motorized vehicles, including healthy exercise, does not use fossil fuels or create air or noise pollution, and helps reduce traffic congestion.

The solution to a complex problem to ensure a sustainable urban mobility requires a strong commitment on innovation as well as methods and content of urban policies. Sustainable urban mobility, like cycling, requires good use of transport infrastructures, coordination between different transport modes and the promotion of strategies of less polluting modes.

Today, space, especially in Italian cities, is unfortunately a limited resource and its distribution appears consequential to government policy. On the other hand, the development prospects for encouraging more cycling for urban travel are strongly affected by the policy choices of mobility, urban and environmental planning, protection of landscape and local governance. With increasing pressure for cities to reduce their carbon footprint and to enhance their part in providing for healthy living, there is a greater need for more research focusing on the economic, social and environmental benefits of cycling for quality of life in urban areas, including leisure and cycling tourism specifically. The results presented also demonstrate the potential success of government policies to encourage cycling and how these types of intervention can achieve a modal shift. Information and advertising could take the shape of an "educational plan", addressed to mobility, which we consider the key issue to induce the change, starting from the young generations (Pronello & Camusso, 2011).

REFERENCES

Adey, P. (2010). *Mobility*. Abingdon, UK: Routledge.

Aldred, R. (2012). Incompetent or too competent? Negotiating everyday cycling identities in a motor dominated society. *Mobilities*, *8*(2), 252–271. doi:10.1080/17450101.2012.696342

Banister, D., Watson, S., & Wood, C. (1997). Sustainable cities: Transport, energy, and urban form. *Environment and Planning. B, Planning & Design*, *24*(1), 125–143. doi:10.1068/b240125

Breen, R. (2004). The Comparative Study of Social Mobility. In R. Breen (Ed.), *Social Mobility in Europe* (pp. 37–75). Oxford, UK: Oxford University Press. doi:10.1093/0199258457.003.0003

Carstensen, T. A., & Ebert, A. (2012). Cycling cultures in Northern Europe: from "golden age" to "renaissance". In J. Parkin (Ed.), *Cycling and sustainability* (pp. 23–58). UK: Emerald Group Publishing Limited. doi:10.1108/S2044-9941(2012)0000001004

Chang, H. W., & Chang, H. L. (2003). A strategic study of bicycle tourism in Taiwan. *Journal of the Eastern Asia Society for Transportation Studies*, *5*, 1675–1685.

Commission of the European Communities (CEC). (1997). *Towards a Urban Agenda in the European Union. COM (1997) 197*. Bruxell.

Commission of the European Communities (CEC). (1998). *Sustainable Urban Development in the European Union: a Framework for Action. COM (1998)*. Bruxell.

Commission of the European Communities (CEC). (1999). *Green Paper on the Urban Environment. COM (1999) 218*. Bruxell.

Commission of the European Communities (CEC). (2001). *A Sustainable Strategy for a Better World: a European Strategy for Sustainable Development. COM (2001) 264*. Bruxell.

Commission of the European Communities (CEC). (2001). *European transport policy for 2010: Time to decide. COM (2001) 370*. Bruxell.

Commission of the European Communities (CEC). (2004). *Towards a Thematic Strategy on the Urban Environment. COM (2004) 60 final*. Bruxell.

Commission of the European Communities (CEC). (2007). *Towards a new culture for urban mobility*. Green Paper. Retrieved from http://www.eur-lex.europa.ue

Commission of the European Communities (CEC). (2011). *Roadmap to a Single European Transport Area: Towards a competitive and resource efficient transport system*. White Paper. COM/2011/0144 final, Bruxell.

Cresswell, T. (2006). The Right to Mobility: The Production of Mobility in the Courtroom. *Antipode*, *38*(4), 735–754. doi:10.1111/j.1467-8330.2006.00474.x

Davies, D., Gray, S., Gardner, G., & Harland, G. (2001). *A quantitative study of the attitudes of individuals towards cycling*. TRL Report 481, Crowthorne. Retrieved December 13, 2013, from http://www.trl.co.uk/online_store/reports_publications/trl_reports/cat_traffic_and_transport_planning/report_a_quantitative_study_of_the_attitudes_of_individuals_to_cycling.htm

Dill, J. (2009). Bicycling for Transportation and Health: The Role of Infrastructure. *Journal of Public Health Policy*, *30*(S1), 95–110. doi:10.1057/jphp.2008.56 PMID:19190585

Dumbaugh, E., & Li, W. (2010). Designing for the Safety of Pedestrians, Cyclists, and Motorists in Urban Environments. *Journal of the American Planning Association*, *77*(1), 69–88. doi:10.1080/01944363.2011.536101

European Cyclists' Federation (ECF). (2013). *Calculating the economic benefits of cycling in EU-27*. Retrieved February 10, 2014, from www.ecf.com

Ecosystem, U. Legambiente. (2011). *XV Report about environmental quality of Italian provinces*. Retrieved from http:/www.legambiente.eu

Eurobarometer. (2011). *Future of transport. Analytical report. Flash EB Series #312*. Retrieved December 12, 2013, from http://ec.europa.eu/public_opinion/flash/fl_312_en.pdf

European Environment Agency (EEA). (2006). *Urban sprawl in Europe. "The ignored challenge" Report*. Copenhagen. Retrieved June 12, 2012, from www.eea.europa.eu/publications/eea_report_2006_10

European Environment Agency (EEA). (2010). *The European environment state and outlook 2010. Urban environment*. Copenhagen, Denmark: Publications Office of the European Union. Retrieved March 10, 2011, from www.europa.eu

Garrard, J., Rose, G., & Lo, S. (2008). Promoting transportation cycling for women: The role of bicycle Infrastructure. *Preventive Medicine*, *46*(1), 55–59. doi:10.1016/j.ypmed.2007.07.010 PMID:17698185

Gatersleben, B., & Haddad, H. (2010). Who is the typical bicyclist? *Transportation Research Part F: Traffic Psychology and Behaviour*, *13*(1), 41–48. doi:10.1016/j.trf.2009.10.003

Gatersleben, B., & Uzzell, D. (2002). Sustainable transport and quality of life. In W. R. Black & P. Nijkamp (Eds.), *Social Change and Sustainable Transport* (pp. 135–140). Bloomington, IN: Indiana University Press.

Geerlings, H., Shiftan, Y., & Stead, D. (2012). The Complex Challenge of Transitions Towards sustainable Mobility: An introduction. In Geerlings, Shiftan, & Stead (Eds.), Transition towards Sustainable Mobility, (pp.1-9). Ashgate.

Gorham, R. (2002). Car dependence as a social problem: A critical essay on the existing literature and future needs. In W. R. Black & P. Nijkam (Eds.), *Social Change and Sustainable Transport* (pp. 107–116). Bloomington, IN: Indiana University Press.

Hanson, S. (Ed.). (1995). *The Geography of Urban Transportation*. New York: Guilford Press.

Hochschild, A. R. (1997). *The Time Bind. When Works Becomes Home and Home Becomes Work*. New York: Metropolitan Books.

Holtz, G., Brugnach, M., & Pahl-Wostl, C. (2008). Specifying 'regime': A framework for defining and describing regimes in transition research. *Technological Forecasting and Social Change*, *75*(5), 623–643. doi:10.1016/j.techfore.2007.02.010

Isfort. (2014). *La domanda di mobilità degli italiani*. Retrieved from www.isfort.it

Isfort, ANAV-ASSTRA. (2013). *10° Rapporto sulla mobilità in Italia*. Retrieved from www.isfort.it

Ispra, Istituto Superiore per la Protezione e la Ricerca Ambientale. (2013). *Qualità dell'ambiente urbano. VII rapporto*. Retrieved from www.isprambiente.it

Istat, Istituto Nazionale di Statistica. (2014). *Focus Mobilità urbana*. Retrieved from www.istat.it

Italia, A. (2007). *Urban ecosystem Europe. An integrated assessment on the sustainability of 32 European cities*. Retrieved March 10, 2012, from www.ambienteitalia.it

Kaufmann, V., Bergman, M. M., & Joice, D. (2004). Motility: Mobility as capital. *International Journal of Urban and Regional Research*, *28*(4), 745–756. doi:10.1111/j.0309-1317.2004.00549.x

Kellerman, A. (2012). *Daily Spatial Mobilities. Physical and virtual*. Surrey, UK: Ashgate Publishing Group.

Kenworthy, J., & Laube, F. (1996). Automobile dependence in cities. An international comparison of urban transport and land use patterns with implication for sustainability. *Environmental Impact Assessment Review*, *16*(4-6), 279–308. doi:10.1016/S0195-9255(96)00023-6

Krizek, K. J. (2012). Cycling, urban form and cities: what do we know and how should we respond? In J. Parkin (Ed.), *Cycling and sustainability* (pp. 23–58). UK: Emerald Group Publishing Limited. doi:10.1108/S2044-9941(2012)0000001007

Krizek, K. J., & Stonebraker, E. W. (2011). Assessing options to enhance bicycle and transit integration. *Journal of Transportation Research Board*, *2217*(-1), 162–167. doi:10.3141/2217-20

Lamont, M. J. (2009). Reinventing the wheel: A definitional discussion of bicycle tourism. *Journal of Sport & Tourism*, *14*(1), 5–23. doi:10.1080/14775080902847363

Lumsdon, L. (2000). Transport and tourism: Cycle tourism - a model for sustainable development? *Journal of Sustainable Tourism*, *8*(5), 361–377. doi:10.1080/09669580008667373

Maragkogianni, M., Papaefthimiou, S., & Zopounidis, C. (2013). Emissions Trading Schemes in the Transportation sector. In Vasile, Turek, & Subic (Eds.), Sustainable Technologies, Policies, and Constraints in the Green Economy (pp. 269-289). Hershey, PA: IGI Global. doi:10.4018/978-1-4666-4098-6.ch015

Marletto, G. (2011). Structure, Agency and change in the car regime. A review of literature. *European Transport*, *47*, 71–88.

Merriman, P. (2009). Auto mobility and the Geographies of the Car. *Geography Compass*, *3*(5), 586–599. doi:10.1111/j.1749-8198.2009.00219.x

Newman, P. W. G., & Kenworthy, J. R. (1999). *Sustainability and Cities. Overcoming Automobile Dependence*. Washington, DC: Island Press.

Nieuwenhuis, P., Wells, P., & Vergragt, P. J. (2004). Introduction to the Special Issue on Technological Change and Regulation in the Car Industry. *Greener Management International*, *47*, 5–11. doi:10.9774/GLEAF.3062.2004.au.00003

O'Sullivan, M., & Watling, D. (2011). Visions for a walking and cycling focused urban transport system. *Journal of Transport Geography*, *19*(6), 1580–1589. doi:10.1016/j.jtrangeo.2011.03.011

OECD. (2004). *Implementing sustainable urban travel policies: moving ahead. National policies to promote cycling*. Paris, France: OECD.

Olivier, J. G. J., Janssens-Maenhout, G., & Peters, J. A. H. W. (2012). *Trends in global CO_2 emissions. 2012 Report. The Hague: PBL Netherlands Environmental Assessment Agency*. Ispra: Joint Research Centre.

Pacione, M. (2005). *Urban Geography. A global perspective*. Abingdon, UK: Routledge.

Page, S. J. (2009). *Transport and Tourism: Global perspectives*. Harlow, UK: Prentice Hall.

Parkin, J., & Koorey, G. (2012). Nework planning and infrastructure design. In J. Parkin (Ed.), *Cycling and sustainability* (pp. 131–160). UK: Emerald Group Publishing Limited. doi:10.1108/S2044-9941(2012)0000001008

Pronello, C., & Camusso, C. (2011). Travellers' profiles definition using statistical multivariate analysis of attitudinal variables. *Journal of Transport Geography*, *19*(6), 1294–1308. doi:10.1016/j.jtrangeo.2011.06.009

Pucher, J., & Buehler, R. (2008). Making cycling irresistible: Lessons from the Netherlands, Denmark and Germany. *Transport Reviews*, *28*(4), 495–528. doi:10.1080/01441640701806612

Pucher, J., & Buehler, R. (2009). Integrating Bicycle and Public Transport in North America. *Journal of Public Transportation*, *12*(3), 79–104. doi:10.5038/2375-0901.12.3.5

Salet, W. (2007). New metropolitan spaces and metropolitan strategies in the face of modernisation, *Metropoles, 2*, 1-26. Retrieved August, 2012, from http://metropoles.revues.org/262

Sener, I., Eluru, N., & Bhat, C. R. (2009). Who Are Bicyclists? Why and How Much Are They Bicycling? *Transportation Research Record*, *2134*(1), 63–72. doi:10.3141/2134-08

Sheller, M., & Urry, J. (2000). The City and the Car. *International Journal of Urban and Regional Research*, *24*(4), 737–757. doi:10.1111/1468-2427.00276

Shore, W. B. (2006). Land-use, transportation and sustainability. *Technology in Society*, *28*(1-2), 27–43. doi:10.1016/j.techsoc.2005.10.014

Simonsen, P. S., & Jørgensen, B. (1998). Cycle tourism. An economic and environmental sustainable form of tourism? In C. Simonsen, S. Jørgensen, L. Robbins (Eds.), *Cycling tourism*. Unit of Tourism Research at Research Centre of Bornholm. Retrieved from www.crt.dk/media/Cycling_tourism.pdf

Socco, C. (2010). *Il Piano Urbano di Mobilità Sostenibile. Annessi*. Osservatorio Città Sostenibili, Department Territorio Politecnico and University of Turin.

Steg, L., & Gifford, R. (2005). Sustainable transportation and quality of life. *Journal of Transport Geography*, *13*(1), 59–69. doi:10.1016/j.jtrangeo.2004.11.003

Thrift, N. (2004). Driving in the city. *Theory, Culture & Society*, *21*(4-5), 41–59. doi:10.1177/0263276404046060

Tight, M., Timms, P., Banister, D., Bowmaker, J., Copas, J., Day, A., & Watling, D. et al. (2011). Visions for a walking and cycling focused urban transport system. *Journal of Transport Geography*, *19*(6), 1580–1589. doi:10.1016/j.jtrangeo.2011.03.011

Travisi, C., & Camagni, R. (2005). *Sustainability of Urban Sprawl: Environmental-Economic. Indicators for the Analysis of Mobility Impact in Italy*. The Fondazione Eni Enrico Mattei. Retrieved from http://www.feem.it/Feem/Pub/Publications/WPapers/default.htm

United Nations, Department of Economic and Social Affairs, Population Division. (2014). *World Urbanization Prospects: The 2014 Revision, Highlights* (ST/ESA/SER.A/352). Retrieved January 30, 2015, from www.esa.un.org

United Nations, Economic Commission for Europe. (2008). *Working Together for Sustainable and Healthy Transport: Guidance on Supportive Institutional Conditions for Policy Integration of Transport, Health and Environment.* Retrieved June 10, 2012, from www.unece.org

Urbanczyk, R. (2010). *PRESTO Cycling Policy Guide. Promotion of Cycling.* Retrieved June 22, 2012, from www.presto-cycling.eu

Urry, J. (2004). The "System" of Auto mobility. *Theory, Culture & Society, 21*(4-5), 25–29. doi:10.1177/0263276404046059

Urry, J. (2006). Inhabiting the car. *The Sociological Review, 54*(S1), 7–31. doi:10.1111/j.1467-954X.2006.00635.x

Urry, J. (Ed.). (2007). *Mobilites.* Cambridge, UK: Polity Press.

Van der Helm, R. (2009). The vision phenomenon: Towards a theoretical underpinning of visions of the future and the process of envisioning. *Futures, 41*(2), 96–104. doi:10.1016/j.futures.2008.07.036

Wen, L. M., & Rissel, C. (2008). Inverse associations between cycling to work, public transport, and overweight and obesity: Findings from a population based study in Australia. *Preventive Medicine, 46*(1), 29–32. doi:10.1016/j.ypmed.2007.08.009 PMID:17904210

Zito, P., & Salvo, G. (2011). Toward an urban transport sustainability index: An European comparison. *European Transport Research Review, 3*(4), 179–195. doi:10.1007/s12544-011-0059-0

ADDITIONAL READING

Carse, A., Goodman, A., Mackett, R. L., Panter, J., & Ogilvie, R. (2013). The factors influencing car use in a cycle-friendly city: The case of Cambridge. *Journal of Transport Geography, 28*, 67–74. doi:10.1016/j.jtrangeo.2012.10.013 PMID:24954981

European Commission. (2013). *Building a Green Infrastructure for Europe.* Luxembourg: Publications Office of the European Union.

Grabow, M. L., Spak, S. N., Holloway, T., Stone, B., Mednick, A. C., & Patz, J. A. (2012). Air quality and exercise-related health benefits from reduced car travel in midwestern United States. *Environmental Health Perspectives, 120*, 66–76. PMID:22049372

Heinen, E., Maat, K., & Wee, B. V. (2010). The role of attitudes toward characteristics of bicycle commuting on the choice to cycle to work over various distances. *Transportation Research Part D, Transport and Environment, 38*, 1–8.

Rashid, K., Yigitcanlar, T., & Bunker, J. (2011). Sustainable Transportation Development. In Green Technologies: Concepts, Methodologies, Tools and Applications (Vols. 1–3). pp. 1044–1058). Hershey, PA: IGI Global. doi:10.4018/978-1-60960-472-1.ch426

Reiter, K., & Wrighton, S. (2013). *Moving Europe forward. Potential to shift goods transport from cars to bicycles in European cities.* Retrieved March 20, 2014, from www.cyclelogistics.eu

Yigitcanlar, T. (Ed.). (2010). *Rethinking Sustainable Development: Urban Management, Engineering, and Design.* Hershey, PA: IGI Global. doi:10.4018/978-1-61692-022-7

KEY TERMS AND DEFINITIONS

Cycling: one of the more sustainable modes of transport for people and goods; for individual is a healthy and cheap mode of transport because is a physical activity and physical activity is beneficial for health.

Quality of Life in Cities: It relies on a range of elements such as income, social equity, housing, a healthy environment, culture, good infrastructure.

Sustainable Development: The development that meets the needs of the present generations without compromising the ability of future generations to meet their own needs. The definition is the integration of economic efficiency, ecological stability and social equity.

Travel Behaviour: It can generally be referred to as the study of what people do over space and how people use transportation.

Chapter 3
Competitive Smart Cities through Healthy Decision-Making

Ori Gudes
Curtin University, Australia

Tan Yigitcanlar
Queensland University of Technology, Australia

Sarah Jane Edwards
The University of Western Australia, Australia

Virendra Pathak
Uttar Pradesh Technical University, India

ABSTRACT

This chapter examines the challenges and opportunities associated with planning for competitive, smart and healthy cities. The chapter is based on the assumptions that a healthy city is an important prerequisite for a competitive city and a fundamental outcome of smart cities. One of the major decision support systems to support healthy cities is e-health. This chapter focuses on the role of e-health planning, by utilising web-based geographic decision support systems. The chapter proposes the implementation of a novel decision system which would provide a powerful and effective platform for stakeholders to support access online information. This would also provide for better decision-making as well as empower community participation. The chapter highlights the need for a comprehensive conceptual framework to guide the decision process of planning for cities in association with opportunities and limitations. This chapter provides critical insights into using information science-based frameworks.

INTRODUCTION

This chapter looks at a new method of how to achieve competitive and healthy smart cities. There are a number of future city visions that contain different focuses on health such as competitive cities, smart cities, healthy cities, resilient cities, knowledge cities, creative cities, green cities and ubiquitous cities. For example, excellent health service delivery, healthy built environments and a high level of health in the population are integral to achieving competitive cities. This is because the qualities that reflect health can make a 'location' more attractive and, therefore, competitive in comparison to global standards. Smart cities, on the other hand, focus on developing urban systems integrated through technology, which leads to the achievement of healthier cities by enabling

DOI: 10.4018/978-1-4666-8433-1.ch003

improved health qualities. Therefore health is an outcome of creating a smart city. For the past few decades, there has been emerging evidence of a close relationship between health and place. This is displayed in the Healthy Cities movement (WHO, 1999) which reflects the amount of work going into creating environments that promote both health and wellbeing. Healthy Cities was officially introduced in 1986 by Ilona Kickbusch at a conference of the World Health Organisation (WHO) in Copenhagen, Denmark. This movement has been very popular with over 3000 cities, towns and villages joining the movement from 1985 to 2010 (Healthy Cities Illawarra, 2010). *Johnson argues that* a healthy community is a critical component of a competitive city (Johnson, 2002). Smart cities include "important ingredients for a healthier environment and for improved quality of life and well-being of city dwellers" (Boulos & Al-Shorbaji, 2014, p.5).

There is evidence that planners require a new approach to enable them to respond to this agenda. Specifically, they need timely access to local information, collaborative planning processes and mechanisms for engaging the public in decision-making. The WHO has concluded that e-Health systems hold great promise for both low- and high-income countries. The benefits of an online approach to health planning apply not only to effective and efficient health-care delivery, but also to public health governance, finance, education, research, and health-related economic activities (WHO, 2008). The purpose of this chapter is to examine an online approach to planning that can respond to the call for healthy, smart and competitive cities. In this chapter, we will first review competitive cities in the context of health. Then we will review smart cities in the context of health. Next, the chapter will explore e-health decision support systems in the context of collaborative health planning practice. This will be followed by the conceptual framework for planning healthy, smart and competitive cities. Lastly, we will introduce a participatory model for implementing collaborative health planning and apply the conceptual framework in practice. In summary, we conclude that e-health Geographical Information System (GIS) based Decision Support System (DSS) can contribute to the development of healthy, smart and competitive cities, particularly if the challenges presented by an online environment can be addressed.

BACKGROUND

The term 'competitiveness' has been well defined by Webster and Muller (2000, p. 1): "The ability of an urban region to produce and market a set of products (goods and services) that represent good value (not necessarily lowest price) in relation to comparable products of other urban regions. Non-tradeables, e.g., local services, are part of the competitiveness equation. An urban economy that produces goods and services for local people of high value relative to price, supports the export economy of the city, making it more competitive, as well as directly raising the quality of life and standard of living for people living in the urban region". Thus, like the healthy cities movement, the call for competitive cities is based on the notion of better city lifestyles. The economic competitiveness of a city is defined by the prosperity of its citizens. A competitive city is known as a city of opportunities for families, lifestyle and business. Similarly, a healthy city is "one that is continually creating and improving [its] physical and social environments and strengthening the community resources which enable people to mutually support each other in performing all the functions of life and achieving their maximum potential" (Flynn, 1996, p. 300). It is not surprising, that the task of applying knowledge to the process of building a healthy and competitive city has become an important focus for urban planners. One of the recent, approaches that encourage this is the Smart City approach.

The concept of a smart city encompasses aspects of both competitive cities and healthy cities. A smart city is a broad concept which can be roughly defined as a city with an Information and Communication Technology (ICT) infrastructure that facilitates an inter-connected urban system that is sustainable while also supporting the knowledge economy (Giffinger, Haindlmaier, & Kramar, 2010; Giffinger et al., 2007; Lazaroiu & Roscia, 2012; Lee, Phaal, & Lee, 2013; Neirotti, 2014, Boulos & Al-Shorbaji, 2014). The literature covers two main perspectives of the role of ICT infrastructure for the city. The first perspective is to facilitate top down decision making for example by collecting data to inform policy decisions information on parking spaces, security cameras or traffic lights. The second perspective is to facilitate bottom up decision making, for example, providing access to information for citizens on the fastest transportation route option, encouraging innovation or providing education (Neirotti, 2014). The following literature on smart cities focus on the health aspects of smart cities for example the role of ICT in delivering healthcare services or providing access to an efficient healthcare system (Accenture, 2011; Atzori et al., 2010; Correia & Wunstel, 2011; Dirks et al., 2009; Nam & Pardo, 2011; The Climate Group et al., 2011; Washburn et al., 2010; Neirotti, 2014).

COMPETITIVE CITIES IN THE CONTEXT OF HEALTH

The importance of public health and community well-being for the development of a competitive city is highlighted in recent literature. According to Kipfer and Keil (2002), public health policies are amongst the most important components of a competitive city agenda. This reflects how integral the public health agenda is to the future city visions.

Jonhnson (2002) argued that there is a direct link between enhancing community health and promoting the competitiveness of a city. As he stated: "the model for enhancing community health and competitiveness is predicated on the ability of the leadership of city government to leverage its polity capital assets to forge win-win and/or reciprocal relationships with for-profit (business) and nonprofit institutions" (Jonhnson, 2002, p. 764). Improving the local health and socioeconomic state of the community may improve the overall cities' competitiveness in the global marketplace. A number of the case studies explored in *Making Competitive Cities* focus on health both in terms of services and industries. Health services are cited as a key aspect that impacts on the perceived attractiveness of a city for creative knowledge workers. Health industries are cited as playing an important role in local economic development such as biotechnology and pharmaceutical companies' knowledge circulation contributing towards competitiveness (Musterd, 2010).

The important role of place in attracting and retaining knowledge and creative workers in order to achieve competitive cities is explored in *Place-making and Policies for Competitive Cities*. Important elements to attracting and retaining workers were found to include health services, schools, and greater amounts of open space and community integration workers (Lawton et al., 2013). The importance of the medical related industries for city competitiveness is highlighted in the Budapest Innopolis Development Pole Programme which focuses on three themes, Information society technology pole, MediPole and the EcoPole. The MediPole concentrates medical industry clusters for medical device manufacturing and medical biotechnological innovation (Musterd, 2013). For example, the city of Charlotte, North Carolina – United States, has worked jointly with some of its private sector companies (i.e., banks) over the years to improve the community health and well-being of the city. As a result of these collaborative efforts, the city of Charlotte has experienced population economic growth and greater prosperity (Perlmutt, 2001; Jonhnson 2002). The 'Livable city' Toronto hinged on the high degree of environmental-health enjoyed by its residents (Porter, 1995). In his seminal work, Porter (1995) focused on the world class health facilities in the inner city of Boston as the most important contributor to the city's competitiveness. By harnessing the private sector and improving their commitment to the local community health, a significant positive impact on cities' competitiveness was generated in the global market arena. Thus, well-being, health and lifestyle have become essential promotional tools in the quest to make a location more competitive.

However, in discussing the creation of competitive and healthy cities, Moutinho (2006) emphasised the need for more attention to be given to the digital infrastructure including local E-government, E-health, E-business and entertainment. In defining successful 'Smart Cities', Moutinho concluded that they require consistent public policies, evaluation frameworks, innovative systems, openness to the society and large investments if they are to create the conditions for enhanced competitiveness and most importantly, competitive cities need to foster a 'culture of knowledge'. Drawing on all these arguments, it is clear that a healthy city depends on the creation of wellbeing through excellent health services, a healthy built environment and health promotion. These qualities are also precursors to, and features of, a competitive city and are interrelated with smart cities. Both healthy and competitive cities depend on the efficient use of digital infrastructure, which in turn depends on a culture of knowledge, collaborative planning and timely access to local place-based knowledge. The efficient use of digital infrastructure in itself links to the smart cities concept and highlights to strategic importance of web-based geographic decision support systems to assist planners with healthy planning decisions.

To plan effectively for healthy, smart and competitive cities, it is necessary to revive the historic collaboration between urban planning and public health professionals, who together can conduct informed evidence-based decision-making (Northridge et al., 2003). Further, planning efforts must focus on the creation of structures and processes that actively work to dismantle existing health inequalities and create economic, political, and social equality (Schulz & Northridge, 2004). To date, urban planning has not focused on the creation of cities that can promote health and prevent disease. Although health is a consequence of the activity planners undertake (i.e., developing effective transport systems, planning community facilities), it has not yet been their direct focus. One of the reasons why planning has not yet been able to effectively contribute to the healthy cities movement is that there are no models to define the type of information that must be considered by planners and there is no method for sharing this information in a meaningful form (Gudes et al., 2010). As Flynn (1996) concluded, every community is unique, with different physical, social, political and cultural contexts that must be understood in the planning process. As these contexts are likely to impact heavily on health, it is necessary for planners to develop a thorough understanding of each individual community health profile and the features that influence health.

To promote health and, therefore, competitiveness, two critical features must be present in a city, namely the ability to organise, access and share local information and the ability to plan collaboratively across multiple sectors and systems. One of the ways to increase accessibility to health information and promote collaborative use of that information is to adopt an e-health approach to decision-making. This in turn links into the concept of smart cities as an e-health system needs to be supported by an inter-connected web of ICT.

Smart Cities in the Context of Health

A wide range of literature focus on the health aspects of smart cities for example the role of ICT in delivering healthcare services or providing access to an efficient healthcare system (Accenture, 2011; Atzori et al., 2010; Correia & Wunstel,

2011; Dirks et al., 2009; Nam & Pardo, 2011, The Climate Group et al., 2011; Washburn et al., 2010; Boulos & Al-Shorbaji, 2014). Reports released by Accenture and Forrester highlight the potential of an intelligent healthcare system built on scalable storage systems which could facilitate storage and sharing of patient records as well as an open communications platform that can facilitate faster emergency response services (Accenture, 2011; Washburn et al., 2010) One of the examples given is the Taiwanese Telehealth Pilot Project which facilitates senior citizens to have health data transmitted from the comfort of their private homes (Acenture, 2011). An IBM report on smarter cities states that a smart city transforms its core systems to be digitalized, interconnected and intelligent. This will boost economic competitiveness and assist in meeting the goals of providing a "healthy, pleasant and safe living environment for their residents" (Dirks et al., 2009). Smart cities can be seen as one of the goals along the way to developing competitive cities.

Boulos and Al-Shorbaji's article focuses on the method of achieving smart eco-friendly, sustainable environment cities through an interconnected web of people and things such as geo-tagged electronic sensors or devices; this concept is termed as the Internet of Things (IoT). The article highlights the link between smart cities, healthy cities and the application of geographical information systems. A few of the outcomes that are possible through IoT are health surveillance and crisis management (Atzori et al., 2010; Boulos & Al-Shorbajo, 2014). Through applying IoT to collect geospatial health related data it is possible to identify spatial trends which can be monitored and problem areas can be targeted for improvement with the result of improving the health of all citizens. In other words, "IoT-powered smart cities stand better chances of becoming healthier cities" (Boulos & Al-Shorbaji, 2014, p. 1).

Smart, healthy and competitive cities need the ability plan collaboratively across multiple sectors and systems. A method to increase accessibility to health information and promote collaborative use of that information is to adopt an e-health approach to decision-making.

E-Health Decision Support Systems and Collaborative Health Planning Practice

Online Geographical Information System (GIS) based decision support systems (DSS) are likely to provide a 'place' in which collaborative planning can occur. GIS is a way of analysing and or displaying complex spatial information. DSS are information and communication technology (ICT) tools that provide the mechanism to help decision-makers and related stakeholders assess complex problems and solve these in a meaningful way (Shim et al., 2002).

The overall aim of DSS, without substituting decision-makers, is to improve the efficiency of the decisions made by stakeholders, optimising their overall performance and minimising judgmental biases (Turban, 1993). Technologies such DSS are reported in the literature as being the best means of "circulating" information and improving its 'interoperability'. DSS incorporates two main domains; the first domain is policy-making, which is the process of making decisions to solve problems. The second domain is technology, which uses computational problem solving tools to support those decisions. Given that cities represent distinct geographical locations, one of the most relevant methods for this type of planning is the spatially-based GIS technology. GIS has become a central spatial component of DSS because it embraces computational, analytical, problem solving and visualisation capabilities (Gudes et al., 2009). As Conway et al. (2008) indicated, spatial maps are likely to be particularly helpful to stakeholders, improving decision-making by visualising and simulating spatial phenomena.

It is essential to expand the use of DSS through online ICT platforms to capitalise on broader e-health initiatives. A collaborative online platform can improve accessibility to information, conceivably to a point that even the public could engage in the process of decision-making and health policy-making. The capacity to share information in a variety of forms, improves stakeholders' involvement in decision-making, creates horizontal knowledge sharing and simplicity of the decision process (Dur et al., 2009). For example, the ACT Government has recently run a web based community consultation process in order to select the location of twenty new drinking fountains in public places. The page hosted by their time to talk community consultation website has a link to an ESRI supported GIS interactive map showing the pre-selected thirty potential locations of the drinking fountains and a survey for the community to select which locations are most desirable (ACT Government, 2014).

A project that is linking researchers with public health data access is the Australian National University's National Centre for Geographic & Resource Analysis in Primary Health Care project that aims to support primary health care researcher's access and analysis of spatially based primary health care data by providing an online data portal. The projects goal is to promote spatial analyses on this publically available data. This aims to overcome one of the core issues with health data, which is privacy and confidentiality (Australian National University, 2014). This will in the long term assist identification of health issues that are geographically correlated and eventuate in improved health planning for the locations analysed.

The West Australia Department of Health has developed an online GIS-based DSS application named "Healthtracks" which improves their health planning capacity (Spatial Vision, 2010). Another example is the Social Health Atlas online (www.publichealth.gov.au) that allows user to map specific health outcomes and associated socio-economic status for administratively defined boundaries (Baum et al., 2010). Although there are several good examples of GIS-based DSS models in Australia (mostly facilitated by Victoria, West Australia and South Australia health government initiatives), the majority of the applications are focused on specific health issues (e.g. National Diabetes Service Scheme and the Social Health Atlas of Adelaide Health Service website) (Central Northern Adelaide Health Service, 2008) rather than the promotion of health in the community in its broad sense. Baum et al. (2010, p.30) concluded that: "In Australia there appears to be a lack of examples illustrating the use of these online tools".

These examples demonstrate the potential utility of GIS-based DSS models, yet all these models lack the communication channels and the collaboration mechanism which are so imperative for developing healthy cities. Thus, online GIS-based DSS are likely to provide a 'place' in which collaborative planning can occur, it is also necessary to adopt a systematic way of organising local information to increase its usability. Specifically, if planners aim to develop healthy, smart and competitive cities, then the information and ICT infrastructure they need to access should address the determinants of these outcomes.

A Conceptual Framework for Planning Competitive, Smart, and Healthy Cities

Mooney and Fohtung (2008) pointed out that understanding the complex relationships between the determinants of health and actual health outcomes may lead to better informed decisions about policies that could influence the healthy city. Therefore, the DSS based on a broad information framework will allow planners to develop effective spatial analyses of complex urban issues. In this section, we propose a conceptual framework for the structural organisation of local information to support collaborative health planning. Given that the factors of this framework have been identified to determine health outcomes, they are also closely related to the competitiveness of a city. Indeed, some elements of the framework have been directly linked to competitive cities by having the potential to improve health and wellbeing (Johnson, 2002).

Schulz and Northridge (2004) developed an analytical framework for public health impact assessments (Figure 1). This framework shows the four levels of factors that have a fundamental impact upon health and wellbeing. . According to Northridge et al. (2003), these factors that contribute to health and wellbeing can be divided into four levels: Macro, Meso, Micro and Individual, which all combine to a health profile of a particular community. In this model, each factor interacts to contribute to health in the community. For instance, the natural environment, macro social factors, and inequalities (i.e., fundamental factors) influence health outcomes and well-being (i.e. individual level factors) via multiple pathways through differential access to power, information, and resources. These fundamental factors, in turn, affect intermediate factors (i.e. the built environment and the social context). Intermediate factors include the development of land use policies and built environment. Consequently, it is here that the impact of the built environment is especially subject to policy management by planners (Gudes et al., 2012).

Figure 1. Public health framework for health impact assessment and health profiling
(Derived from Schulz & Northridge, 2004)[1].

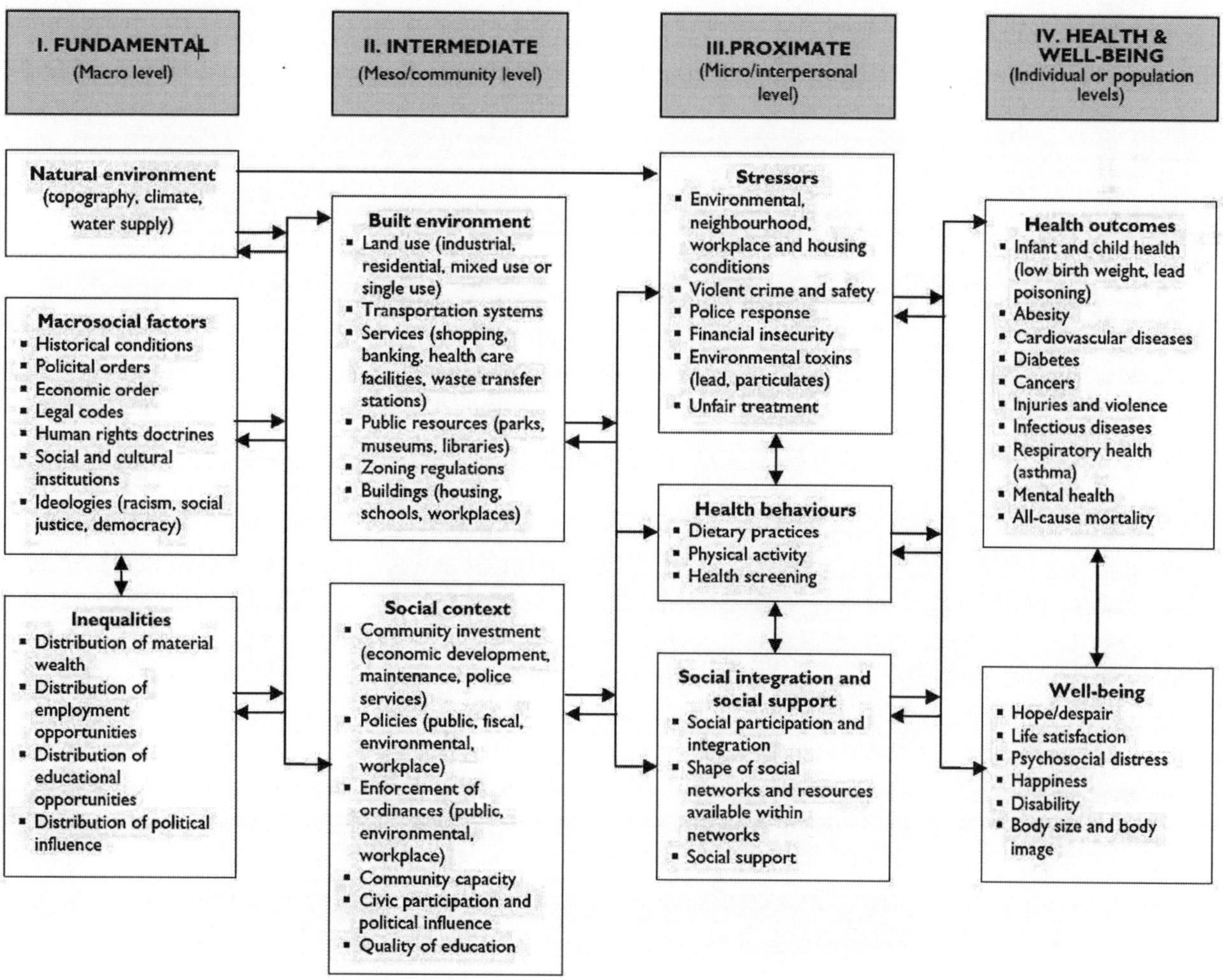

Regarding the proximate factors (public health practitioner territory), it consists of three domains: stressors, social integration and social support, and health behaviours. The literature argues that proximate factors have been given greater scientific attention in recent years (Northridge et al., 2003). The last column in Figure 2 contains two key domains: health outcomes and well-being, as these in turn influence the individual habits. This figure also shows the interactive and dynamic relationships among the various domains, between the fundamental and intermediate factors as well as between the intermediate and proximate factors, and their impacts on health outcomes over an individual's life course. Thus, it is suggested that by adopting such a framework, we can improve our

Figure 2. A conceptual framework for planning a healthy city
(Derived from WHO 1997b; Schulz & Northridge, 2004)[2].

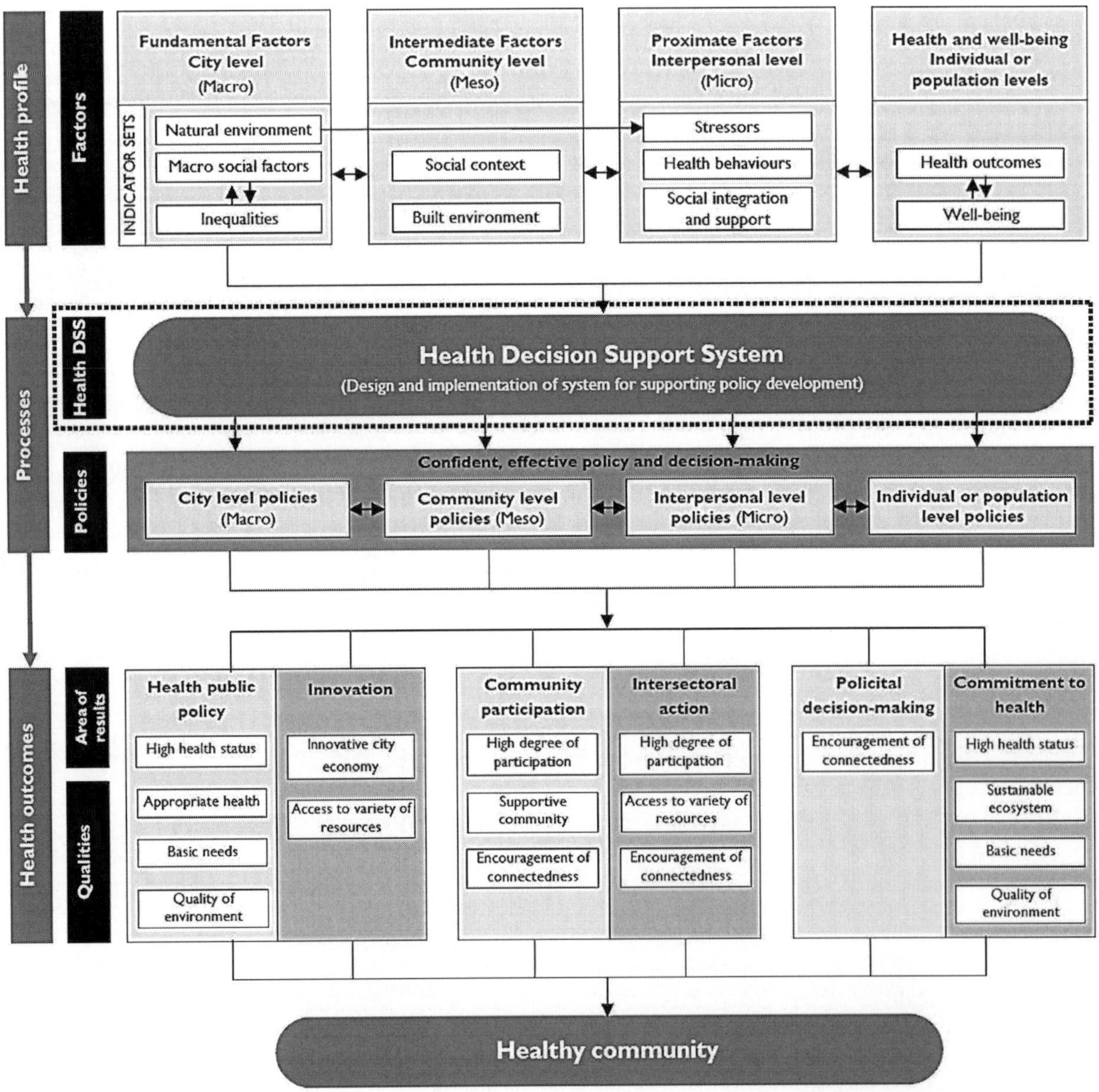

understanding of health in place, increase accessibility to health information and build knowledge about the role of the social determinants of health (Gudes et al., 2012).

A collaborative health-planning framework that has been developed for this study illustrates the overall place of DSS within a healthy cities' planning initiative (See Figure 2). However, the literature emphasises the importance of grounding a DSS in a broad information framework. In particular the Information Management Framework described by Schulz and Northridge's (2004) needs to further guide the development of a community health profile, with information derived from multiple sources. In this regard, Duhl and Sanchez (1999) defined a list of six fundamental characteristics: health public policy, innovation, community participation, intersectional action, policy decision making and commitment to health, which creates a healthy city. If these characteristics are well coordinated, it is likely that a healthy city will emerge. Thus, this framework suggests that by utilising a DSS as part of a broader city health- planning process, it is more likely that a healthy community will form, and this in turn can improve the city's competitiveness and smart urban systems (Gudes et al., 2012).

However, increasing accessibility to effectively organised information through e-health DSS initiatives is not sufficient to ensure effective planning for a healthy, smart and competitive city. Unless health planning is being practiced in an integrated manner, the solutions may only meet the needs of a small minority of the residents. Although the online environment such as e-health enhances the likelihood of ubiquity by multiple stakeholders and knowledge sharing to underpin decisions, it does not imply a collaborative and participatory planning process. Thus, a participatory planning is a critical method of collaborative health planning.

Participatory Planning Process: A Method of Collaborative Health Planning

Direct involvement of a wide range of stakeholders and the affected communities in planning decision-making can improve the overall capacity of cities to address the issue of health inequalities (Beyer & Rushton, 2009). Indeed, collaborative health planning procedures are essential to the policy-making process. Ridley and Jones (2001) argued that most significant forms of collaboration are those that become part of the day-to-day practice of health care and planning. In collaborative health planning, it is necessary to have a clear understanding and recognition of the stakeholder relationships, behaviour patterns and potential outcomes. This level of clarity, in turn, may empower users and enable them to influence the collaborative policy-making dialogue. The broad involvement of different segments of the community remains a promising approach for dealing with urban problems and promoting positive conditions within cities (Flynn, 1996).

Participatory Action Research (PAR) is regarded as an appropriate method in collaborative health planning. Recently PAR has increasingly been used as an overarching name for an orientation to practice that places all stakeholders in equal positions of co-learners. PAR puts a heavy accent on community participation and the translation of knowledge into action (Minkler, 2000). Recently, the method is gaining increased attention in health, particularly in the public health context (Minkler & Wallerstein, 2003). One of the most important characteristics of PAR is the fact that participants whose lives are affected by the knowledge or decisions take an active role of its design. Israel et al. (2001) defined PAR by the following principles:

- Participation of community members in planning;
- Engaging all stakeholders in a joint process where they contribute equally;

Figure 3. A practical PAR model for designing and evaluating an e-health-based DSS

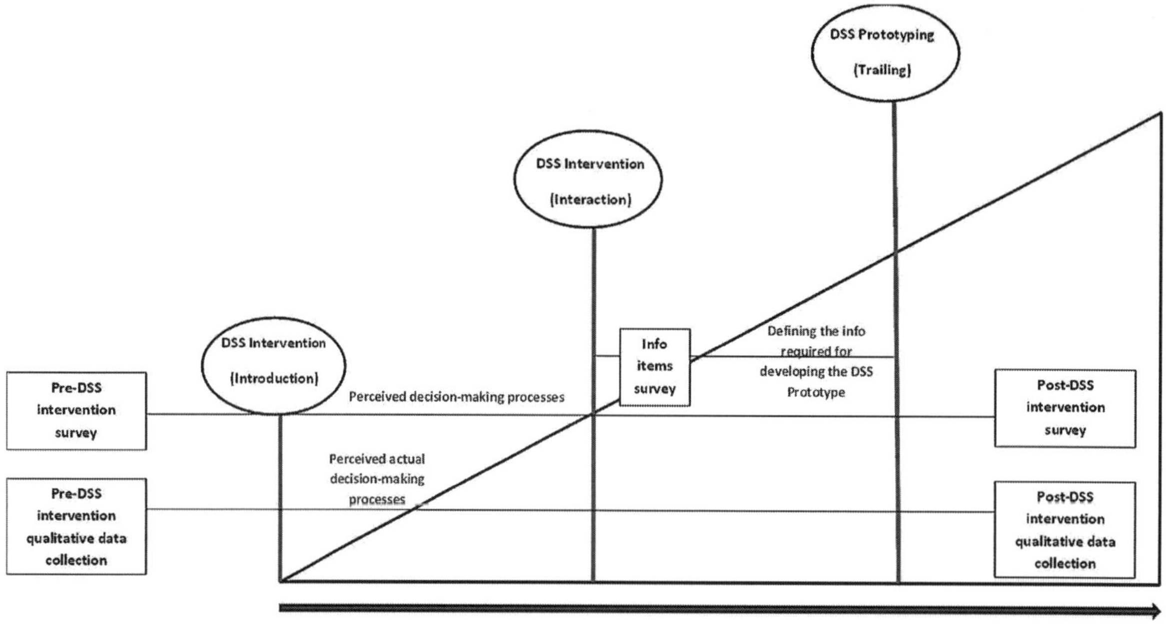

- A co-learning process for all stakeholders;
- A method for systems development and local community capacity building;
- An empowering process through which participants can increase control over their lives nurturing community strengths and problem-solving abilities; and
- A way to balance knowledge and action.

Some key advantages which inherently co-exist in PAR approach, which include: a ground-up approach rather than top-down by experts, empowering the degree of community input into decision-making, a democratic participatory process, driven by community priorities based on community input to create a health community. Duhl (1996) argued that PAR is a community-driven approach oriented toward social change. Stakeholders involved in a PAR initiative come together as co-learners rather than teachers or students (Minkler, 2000). Vajjhala's study outlines the potential application of GIS interfaces for participatory mapping (Vajjhala, 2005). Other applications of GIS and public participation include the use of internet-based public participation geographic information system to identify ecosystem services in Grand County, Colorado (Brown et al., 2012).

PAR has been applied to the process of planning using an e-health GIS-based DSS. For instance, spatial information contained in the DSS can be shared and discussed through iterative focus groups, consultation meetings and surveys, as suggested by Rowe and Frewer (2009). All stakeholders (e.g. health planners, professionals, researchers, community representatives etc.) could be consulted in iterative cycles, with each consultation feeding into the further refinement and development of both the DSS itself and the decisions or policies that are made. To exemplify these statements, and to address the collaborative challenge of developing and evaluating e-health based DSS, this study suggests a practical PAR model (illustrated in Figure 3 to collect quantitative and qualitative data for evaluating the application of such a system. Further, the model also embraces the practical procedures required for designing such systems (e.g., information items, etc.).

Overall, two phases of study data collection are required: Once before the implementation of DSS (pre-DSS intervention) and then after the implementation of DSS (post-DSS intervention). The rationale for this method is to enable to identify the ways in which decisions (i.e. health planning) were being made before and after DSS intervention occurred, and draw the differences accordingly. The post-DSS study data collection should be conducted after trialling the DSS interface for several months. Consequently, it may give decision-makers sufficient time to familiarise themselves with the DSS interface and to incorporate it into their daily routine (Gudes et al., 2012). This is represented in Figure 3 by the rubrics placed subsequent to the DSS intervention (i.e., post-DSS). In line with the recommendation of Meang and Nedovic-Budic (2010), it is suggested that qualitative data should also be collected in order to support the quantitative data collection.

The DSS design also needs a series of consultation meetings with the aim of obtaining input from end-users about the prospective GIS information items, workflows and functionality. This feedback would be included in the DSS interface. For instance, the DSS intervention phase may commence with an introductory presentation about GIS, followed by a series of DSS consultation meetings (i.e., Interaction Phase), whereas additional data obtained from prospective participants and end-users (e.g., information items) should be used for developing the DSS interface. This process may conclude with trialling the DSS prototype (i.e., Trialling Phase) for several months. Thus, the PAR approach could be utilised to develop a practical and efficient model to design an e-health DSS for health planning.

However, a few important limitations of PAR need to be noted. Implementing PAR within a health planning initiative is a time consuming task, and requires significant attention to issues of power, trust, rigor of information and conflicting interests or agendas among the stakeholders (i.e., scientists, policy-makers, providers and citizens). The literature reveals that through effective community consultation processes, many healthy cities have effectively incorporated a high level of participation from all stakeholders (Minkler, 2000; Stern et al., 2009). As Minkler (2000) emphasised, PAR offers a promising approach for realising community participation in planning, thus articulating the vision of the healthy cities movement. In particular, the use of a PAR approach to planning raises a few key barriers to the implementation of an online e-health sharing platform, including accessibility to secure and private data, infrastructures, regulations and procedures. The following section provides more details about these challenges in practice.

CHALLENGES FOR AN E-HEALTH APPROACH TO DECISION-MAKING

Despite a rise of the DSS approach to e-health, there is little discussion as to how the e-health service can contribute to more equitable, sustainable and context specific DSS. Han and Lee (2013) pointed out the three areas of challenges in e-Health provision with DSS:

1. E-health technology stabilisation;
2. E-health service redistribution;
3. Equitable accessibility to e-health allocation.

Firstly, a rapid technology convergence and adaptation ever demand new DSS and e-health services over time. E-health policy should consider the future changes in the needs of the speed and adaptation to the e-health technology shift. The rapid pace of technology development needs to interact with existing health information management and remain aware of the practical impacts by which health related decisions are developed incrementally through corrective actions over time (Han and Lee, 2013). Secondly, the e-health strategy should address the issue of digital disparity in terms of the distributions of health information and

ICTs with a spatial reconfiguration of activities at different scales – homes, suburbs, cities and states. In particular it should minimise inequalities in access to the internet, the extent of the internet's use, knowledge of search strategies, quality of technical connections and social support, ability to evaluate the quality of information, and diversity of uses (DiMaggio et al., 2001). Finally, the e-health should be able to provide an equitable e-health service allocation to alleviate digital inequality in provision of e-health service. Recently the challenge in e-health has shifted from the digital divide to digital inequality (Han et al., 2010). While the digital divide considers the variations in actual access to the internet, digital inequality refers to the quality of the e-health service. This is generally conceptualised as encompassing five main variables: technical means (inequality of bandwidth); autonomy (whether users log on from home or at work, monitored or unmonitored, during limited times or at will); skill (knowledge of how to search for or download information); social support (access to advice from more experienced users); and purpose (whether they use the internet for increased economic productivity, improvement of social capital, or consumption and entertainment) (Warschauer, 2003).

There is a vast amount of literature focusing on e-health. The literature can be divided into two main areas, firstly, those focused on clinical informatics, such as electronic patient or health records. Secondly, it is also divided into those interested in health informatics, including the provision of information through the web to support decision-making and policy development. Although there are some examples where research focuses on both clinical and policy domains (Bernard et al., 2007), generally scholars tend to focus on one or the other. In both areas, however, e-health solutions introduce a range of emerging challenges such as the digital divide, information security, privacy, regulation and policy design, information technology infrastructure and regulatory compliance, all of which need to be considered from the perspective of each stakeholder. In this regard, Kluge (2007) argued that ethical considerations should play a fundamental role in the structuring and implementation of e-health. Wickramasinghe et al. (2005) provided a framework for increasing the potential of e-health through four critical pre-requisites:

- Information communication technology infrastructure;
- Standardised policies, protocols and procedures;
- User access and accessibility; and
- Government regulation.

Each element is considered critical as they combine to create an overall favourable environment. For example, irrespective of accessible internet, a poor physical infrastructure or a high level of bureaucracy will lead to significant impediments to formation of a successful e-health initiative. However, the Annual Survey of Health Information Exchange (2009) published recently in the United States, concluded that addressing privacy and confidentiality issues were among the main challenges of successful implementation. There is some evidence to suggest that a large number of individuals are not willing to engage in e-health because they do not trust the underlying information and communication technologies (Baur, 2008; Croll & Croll, 2007). This effect was also observed by Katsikas et al. (2008), who argued that the lack of appropriate security measures is one of the most severe restraining factors for the proliferation of e-health initiatives in Australia. The literature has also identified a growing digital divide in terms of access to digital technologies depending on ethnicity and income (Ahern, 2007).

In order to deliver practical, secure and comprehensive solutions that protect privacy but improve accessibility it is necessary to apply different approaches For instance, Baur (2008) suggested a user-centred approach that places the needs, preferences, capacities, values, and goals of e-health users at the core of e-health initiatives. Baur also identified the following components of a successful e-health implementation:

- Consumers with diverse perspectives, circumstances, capacities, and experiences are included in the design of and have meaningful access to evidence based e-health tools with strong privacy and security protections;
- Diverse consumers have the skills and support to evaluate, choose, and use e-health tools to derive benefits for themselves and those they care for;
- Healthcare organizations and practitioners use the full range of e-health tools to engage and support diverse consumers in their own health management as a routine element of care;
- Local, state, and national policies and programs support the sustainable development and dissemination of evidence-based consumer e-health tools to diverse individuals and communities, including those served by safety-net providers;
- Alliances and partnerships facilitate sustained consumer access to and use of e-health tools, consistent with the value propositions and perspectives of each participating stakeholder; and
- Appropriate funding and incentives exist in public policy and the market to enable sustainable business models for tools with demonstrated effectiveness.

If e-health is to represent a successful solution to the process of developing healthy, competitive and smart cities, these challenges need to be thoroughly considered and addressed. The result would be e-health implementations that have the potential to contribute to a country's economy and future growth, thus creating healthy and competitive cities. E-health may be an efficient tool for increasing the competitiveness of a country, city or a region, particularly if it becomes part of an evidence-based and informed dissemination and a participatory decision-making process (Gudes et al., 2012).

CONCLUSION AND FUTURE RESEARCH DIRECTIONS

This chapter has identified some challenges and constraints associated with using an e-health GIS-based DSS to contribute to planning for healthy, smart and competitive cities. By proposing the use of spatial information organised in a meaningful framework, we have bridged an existing gap in the knowledge about how to make evidence-based decisions that can increase a city's competitiveness. We introduced an overarching framework for conceptualising the e-health-based DSS and described how a shared framework could become an integral component of the healthy cities planning process. This chapter also discussed how access to effective health information could be enhanced by e-health approaches, particularly if issues of digital disparity, equality and privacy are addressed. E-health could be an effective solution to address the issues of equitable health services allocation and enhance a level of the competitiveness, sustainability and smart urban systems of a city, particularly given that it acts as a 'disseminator' of local information and knowledge. However, increasing accessibility to effective health information through e-health initiatives may not be sufficient, unless health planning is also being practiced in a collaborative manner over the planning decision process. Thus, we suggested a practical model to guide the planning process (i.e., PAR) to ensure participation and collaboration of all stakeholders in designing an e-health-based DSS. It has been noted that to overcome health inequities and create cities that are liveable for all citizens, "we should direct our attention towards the development of adequate tools and strategies" (Beyer & Rushton, 2009).

The tools and strategies we have outlined in this chapter will contribute to planning competitive and smart cites by promoting in general public health, and more specifically increasing the access to effective health systems.

ACKNOWLEDGMENT

This study is part of a broader Australian Research Council (ARC) project: Coalitions for Community Health: A Community-based Response to Chronic Disease. The authors would like to acknowledge the work of Professor Scott Baum and Dr. Heidi Muenchberger as chief investigators in this project.

REFERENCES

Ahern, D. K. (2007). Challenges and Opportunities of eHealth Research. *American Journal of Preventive Medicine*, *32*(5), 75–82. doi:10.1016/j.amepre.2007.01.016 PMID:17466822

Annual Survey of Health Information Exchange. (2009). eHealth initiative, Migrating Toward Meaningful Use: *The State of Health Information Exchange.* A Report based on the Results of the eHealth Initiative's 2009.

Australian National University. (2014) National Centre for Geographic & Resource Analysis in Primary Health Care (GRAPHC) on-line mapping and related geo-spatial analysis systems: A GRAPHC Project. Retrieved May, 2014, from http://aphcri.anu.edu.au/projects/anu/national-centre-geographic-resource-analysis-primary-health-care-graphc-line-mapping

Baum, S., Kendall, E., Muenchberger, H., Gudes, O., & Yigitcanlar, T. (2010). Geographical information systems: An effective planning and decision-making platform for community health coalitions in Australia. *Health Information Management Journal*, *39*(3), 28–33. PMID:21905331

Baur, C. (2008). An analysis of factors underlying e-health disparities. *Cambridge Quarterly of Healthcare Ethics*, *17*(4), 417–428. doi:10.1017/S0963180108080547 PMID:18724881

Bernard, P., Charafeddine, R., Frohlich, K. L., Daniel, M., Kestens, Y., & Potvin, L. (2007). Health inequalities and place: A theoretical conception of neighbourhood. *Social Science & Medicine*, *65*(9), 1839–1852. doi:10.1016/j.socscimed.2007.05.037 PMID:17614174

Beyer, K. M. M., & Rushton, G. (2009). Mapping cancer for community engagement. *Preventing Chronic Disease*, *6*(1), 1–8. PMID:19080009

Boulos, M. N. K., & Al-S horbaji, N. M. (2014). On the Internet of Things, smart cities and the WHO Healthy Cities. *International Journal of Health Geographics*, *12*(10), 1–6.

Brown, G., Montag, J., & Lyon, K. (2012). Public Participation GIS: A Method for Identifying Ecosystem Services. *Society & Natural Resources: An International Journal*, *25*(7), 633–651. doi:10.1080/08941920.2011.621511

Central Northern Adelaide Health Service. (2008). *Central Northern Adelaide Health Service Social Health Atlas 2008*. Retrieved November 24, 2008, from http://www.publichealth.gov.au/interactive_mapping/sa_sha_cnahs_2005/atlas.html

Conway, M. D., Rizzuto, C. D., & Weiss, L. M. (2008). *A better way to speed the adoption of vaccines*. Retrieved November 20, 2008, from http://www.mckinseyquarterly.com/home.aspx

Croll, P. R., & Croll, J. (2007). Investigating risk exposure in e-health systems. *International Journal of Medical Informatics*, *76*(5-6), 460–465. doi:10.1016/j.ijmedinf.2006.09.013 PMID:17126069

DiMaggio, P. J., Hargittai, E., Neuman, R., & Robinson, J. (2001). Social implications of the Internet. *Annual Review of Sociology*, *27*(1), 307–336. doi:10.1146/annurev.soc.27.1.307

Duhl, L. J. (1996). An ecohistory of health: The role of 'healthy cities'. *American Journal of Health Promotion*, *10*(4), 258–261. doi:10.4278/0890-1171-10.4.258 PMID:10159706

Duhl, L. J., & Sanchez, A. K. (1999). *Healthy cities and the city planning process. A Background Documentation on Links Between Health And Urban Planning*. Copenhagen, Denmark: WHO, Regional Office for Europe.

Dur, F., Yigitcanlar, T., & Bunker, J. (2009, March). *A decision support system for sustainable urban development: the integrated land use and transportation indexing model.* Paper presented at the Postgraduate Infrastructure Conference. Brisbane, Australia: Queensland University of Technology.

Flynn, B. C. (1996). Healthy cities: Toward worldwide health promotion. *Annual Review of Public Health*, *17*(1), 299–309. doi:10.1146/annurev.pu.17.050196.001503 PMID:8724229

Government, A. C. T. (2014). Drinking fountains with refill stations locations. Retrieved May 7, 2014, from http://www.timetotalk.act.gov.au/consultations/?engagement=drinking-fountains-with-refill-stations-locations

Gudes, O., Kendall, E., Yigitcanlar, T., Han, J., & Pathak, V. (2012). Developing a competitive city through healthy decision-making City Competitiveness and Improving Urban Subsystems: Technologies and Applications. In M. Bulu (Ed.), *City Competitiveness and Improving Urban Subsystems: Technologies and Applications* (pp. 107–121). Hershey, PA: IGI Global. doi:10.4018/978-1-61350-174-0.ch006

Gudes, O., Kendall, E., Yigitcanlar, T., Pathak, V., & Baum, S. (2010). Rethinking health planning: A framework for organising information to underpin collaborative health planning. *Health Information Management Journal*, *39*(2), 18–29. PMID:20577020

Gudes, O., Yigitcanlar, T., & Pathak, V. (2009, March). *A community health support system for the planning of healthy cities.* Paper presented at the Postgraduate Infrastructure Conference. Brisbane, Australia: Queensland University of Technology.

Han, J. H., & Lee, S. H. (2013). Planning ubiquitous cities for social inclusion. *International Journal of Knowledge-Based Development*, *4*(2), 157–172. doi:10.1504/IJKBD.2013.054092

Han, J. H., Sunderland, N., Kendall, E., Gudes, O., & Henniker, G. (2010). The need for an equitable approach to e-health: Spatial variation in internet accessibility, chronic disease and disadvantage. *Health Information Management Journal*, *39*(2), 30–36. PMID:20577021

Healthy Cities Illawarra. (2010). *Working with the community for a healthier, safer, greener and more caring Illawarra. Wollongong: Illawarra city council.* Retrieved October 10, 2010, from http://www.healthycitiesill.org.au/contactus.htm

Israel, B. A., Schulz, A. J., Parker, E., & Becker, A. B. (2001). Community-based participatory research: Policy recommendations for promoting a partnership approach in health research. *Education for Health*, *14*(2), 182–197. doi:10.1080/13576280110051055 PMID:14742017

Johnson, J. (2002). A conceptual model for enhancing community competitiveness in the new economy. *Urban Affairs Review*, *37*(6), 763–779. doi:10.1177/107874037006001

Katsikas, S., Lopez, J., & Pernul, G. (2008). The challenge for security and privacy services in distributed health settings. *Studies in Health Technology and Informatics*, *134*, 113–125. PMID:18376039

Kipfer, S., & Keil, R. (2002). Toronto Inc? Planning the competitive city in the new Toronto. *Antipode a radical journal of Geography, 34*(2), 227–264.

Kluge, E. H. (2007). Secure e-health: Managing risks to patient health data. *International Journal of Medical Informatics*, *76*(5-6), 402–406. doi:10.1016/j.ijmedinf.2006.09.003 PMID:17084665

Lawton, P., Meczynski, M., & Barber, A. (2013). Policies towards Place Attraction and Policies for Place Retention. In S. Musterd & Z. Kovacs (Eds.), *Place-making and policies for competitive cities* (pp. 105–148). Chichester, West Sussex, United Kingdom: Wiley Blackwell. doi:10.1002/9781118554579.ch8

Maeng, D., & Nedovic-Budic, Z. (2010). Relationship between ICT and urban form in knowledge-based development: Empirical analysis of Washington, DC metro region. *International Journal of Knowledge-Based Development*, *1*(1-2), 97–117. doi:10.1504/IJKBD.2010.032588

Minkler, M. (2000). Using Participatory Action Research to build Healthy Communities. *Public Health Reports*, *115*(2-3), 191–197. doi:10.1093/phr/115.2.191 PMID:10968753

Minkler, M., & Wallerstein, N. (2003). Introduction to community based participatory research. In M. Minkler & N. Wallerstein (Eds.), *Community Based Participatory Research for Health* (pp. 3–26). San Francisco, CA: Jossey-Bass.

Mooney, G., & Fohtung, N. G. (2008). Issues in the measurement of social determinants of health. *Health Information Management Journal*, *37*(3), 26–30. PMID:18941263

Moutinho, J. (2006). From Technological Determinism to Regional Development: Lessons Learned from the Portuguese Digital Cities Program (1998-2006). In P. Cunningham & M. Cunningham (Eds.), *Exploiting the Knowledge Economy: Issues, Applications, Case Studies*. Amsterdam, The Netherlands: IOS Press.

Musterd, S., & Kovacs, Z. (Eds.). (2013). *Place-making and policies for competitive cities*. Chichester, West Sussex, United Kingdom: Wiley Blackwell. doi:10.1002/9781118554579

Musterd, S., & Murie, A. (Eds.). (2010). *Making competitive cities*. Oxford: Wiley-Blackwell.

Northridge, M. E., Sclar, E. D., & Biswas, P. (2003). Sorting out the connections between the built environment and health: A conceptual framework for navigating pathways and planning healthy cities. *Journal of Urban Health*, *80*(4), 556–568. doi:10.1093/jurban/jtg064 PMID:14709705

Perlmutt, D. (2001). Bank of America executive to retire after 23 years. *Charlotte Observer*. Retrieved January 31, 2001, from http://www.charlotte.com/mld/charlotte/archives/

Porter, M. E. (1995). The Competitive Advantage of the Inner City. *Harvard Business Review*, *74*, 61–78.

Ridley, J., & Jones, L. (2002). *User and Public Involvement in Health Services: A Literature Review*. Edinburgh, Scotland: Partners in Change, SHS Trust.

Rowe, G., & Frewer, L. J. (2009). Public Participation Methods: A framework for evaluation. *Science, Technology & Human Values*, *25*(1), 3–29. doi:10.1177/016224390002500101

Schulz, A., & Northridge, M. E. (2004). Social determinants of health: Implications for environmental health promotion. *Health Education & Behavior*, *31*(4), 455–471. doi:10.1177/1090198104265598 PMID:15296629

Shim, J. P., Warkentin, M., Courtney, J. F., Power, D. J., Sharda, R., & Carlsson, C. (2002). Past, present, and future of decision support technology. *Decision Support Systems*, *33*(2), 111–126. doi:10.1016/S0167-9236(01)00139-7

Stern, E., Gudes, O., & Svoray, T. (2009). Web-Based Traditional Public Participation Comprehensive Planning: A Comparative Study. *Environment & Planning B*, *36*(6), 1067–1085. doi:10.1068/b34113

Turban, E. (1993). *Decision support and expert systems: management support systems*. Upper Saddle River, New Jersey, USA: Prentice Hall PTR.

Vajjhala, S. P. (2005, July). Integrating GIS and participatory mapping in community development planning. In *25th Annual ESRI International Users Conference*. San Diego, CA.

Vision, S. (2010). *Spatially Enabling Government – 'Healthtracks' wins 2010 WA Spatial Excellence*. Retrieved November 30, 2010, from http://www.spatialvision.com.au/index.php/latest-news-spatially-enabling-government.html

Warschauer, M. (2003). *Technology and Social Inclusion: Rethinking the Digital Divide*. Cambridge, MA: MIT Press.

Webster, D., & Muller, L. (2000). *Urban Competitiveness Assessment in Developing Country Urban Regions: The Road Forward.* Paper presented at the Urban Group, INFUD, World Bank. Washington, DC: World Bank.

WHO [World Health Organisation]. (1999). Health: creating healthy cities in the 21st century. In D. Satterthwaite (Ed.), *The Earthscan Reader in Sustainable Cities* (pp. 137-172). London, UK: Earthscan.

WHO [World Health Organisation]. (2008). Framework and Standards for Country Health Information Systems. *Health Metrics Network*. Retrieved March 12, 2009, from http://www.who.int/healthmetrics/documents/framework/en/

Wickramasinghe, N. S., Fadlalla, A. M. A., Geisler, E., & Schaffer, J. L. (2005). A Framework For Assessing E-Health Preparedness. *International Journal of Electronic Healthcare*, *1*(3), 316–334. doi:10.1504/IJEH.2005.006478 PMID:18048213

ADDITIONAL READING

Ashton, J. R. (2009). From Healthy Towns 1843. *Public Health*, *123*(1), 11–13.

Baker, G. (Ed.). (2004). *The effects of synchronous collaborative technologies on decision making: A study of virtual teams*. Hershey, PA: IGI Global.

Birkin, M., Clarke, G. P., Clarke, M., & Wilson, A. (1996). *Intelligent GIS: Location Decisions and Strategic Planning*. New York, NY: John Wiley & Sons Inc.

Cromley, E. K., & Mclafferty, S. L. (2011). *GIS and Public Health*. New York, NY: Guilford Press.

Dooris, M. (1999). Healthy Cities and Local Agenda 21: The UK experience—challenges for the new millennium. *Health Promotion International*, *14*(4), 365–375.

Duffy, H. (1995). *Competitive cities: succeeding in the global economy*. London, UK: Routledge.

Forester, J. (1989). *Planning in the face of power*. Berkeley, CA: University of California Press.

Hancock, T., & Duhl, L. (1988). *Promoting health in the urban context*. Copenhagen, Denmark: WHO Regional Office for Europe.

Healey, P. (2003). Collaborative planning in perspective. *Planning Theory*, *2*(2), 101–123.

Higgs, G., & Gould, M. (2001). Is there a role GIS in the 'New NHS'? *Health & Place*, *7*(3), 247–259.

Igbaria, M., & Guimaraes, T. (1994). Empirically Testing the Outcomes of User Involvement in DSS Development. *Omega*, *22*(2), 157–172.

Ishida, T. (2000). Understanding digital cities. In T. Ishida & K. Isbister (Eds.), *Digital Cities: Experiences* (pp. 7–17). Berlin, Germany: Technologies & Future Perspectives.

Kushner, J. A. (2007). *Healthy Cities: the Intersection of Urban Planning, Law and Health*. Durham, NC: Carolina Academic Press.

Liu, Y., Wong, S. Y., & Jin, T. (2009). Equality of Spatial Access to Primary Health Services for Singapore's Baby Boomers. *Asian Population Studies*, *5*(2), 171–188.

Murray, D. J. (2006). *A Critical Analysis of Communicative Planning Theory as a Theoretical Underpinning for Integrated Resource and Environmental Management*. (Unpublished doctoral dissertation). Griffith University, Brisbane, Australia.

Musterd, S., & Kovacs, Z. (Eds.). (2013). *Placemaking and policies for competitive cities*. Chichester, West Sussex, United Kingdom: Wiley Blackwell.

Philips, R. L., Kinman, E. L., Schnitzer, P. G., Lindbloom, E. J., & Ewigman, B. (2000). Using Geographic Information Systems to Understand Health Care Access. *Archives of Family Medicine*, *9*(10), 971–978.

Rushton, G. (2003). Public Health, GIS, and Spatial Analytic Tools. *Public Health*, *24*(1), 43–56.

Scott, A. J. (2006). Creative cities: Conceptual issues and policy questions. *Journal of Urban Affairs*, *28*(1), 1–17.

Smith, L. T., Johnson, D. B., Lamson, E., & Sitaker, M. (2006). A Framework for developing Evaluation Tools Used in Washington State's Healthy Communities Projects. *Preventing Chronic Disease Public Health research. Practice, And Policy*, *3*(2), A64.

Theseira, M. (2002). Using Internet GIS technology for sharing health and health related data for the west Midlands region. *Health & Place*, *8*(1), 37–46.

Zwarenstein, M., & Reeves, S. (2000). What's so great about collaboration? We need more evidence and less rhetoric. *British Medical Journal*, *320*(7241), 1022–1023.

KEY TERMS AND DEFINITIONS

Competitive Cities: Competitive cities sustain and offer its residents high standards of quality of life and place. As a result, it attracts more financial capital and business opportunities, which in turn, can be invested back into improving the city infrastructure and society well-being.

Decision Support Systems: Decision support systems are information communication technology tools, including spatial-based information systems (e.g. GIS) that provide the mechanisms to help decision-makers, policy makers and related stakeholders to assess complex problems and solve these in a meaningful and effective way.

E-Health: E-health encompasses a range of medical informatics applications based on Information and Communication Technology. Utilisation of e-health, is considered to be one of the trendiest ways to increase accessibility to health information.

Geographic Information Systems: Geographic Information Systems is a decision support tool for making informed decisions by stakeholders, policymakers and decisions-makers. The tool uses a mix of spatial and attributes data, queries, analytical procedures and analysis methods to leverage end-users' spatial knowledge.

Healthy Cities: Healthy cities are associated with the following characteristics: Creating and improving those physical and social environments conditions; strengthening community resources; and achieving its maximum potential. The healthy cities approach is based on the process, not just the outcome. Healthy cities are committed to health and have the structure and capacity to execute the necessary health planning processes.

Participatory Action Research: Participatory action research is an application of a research method where the researcher is also a co-learner in the research process in conjunction with the community being researched. One of the most important characteristics of participatory action research is the fact that participants whose lives are affected by the research initiative take an active role of its design.

Spatial-Based Collaborative Technologies: Spatial-based collaborative technologies are based on geographical information. Their primary purpose is to enhance the collaborative practice, debate and decision-making processes. These technologies are being used predominantly by urban planners, policy makers, city leaders and stakeholders.

ENDNOTES

1 Reprinted with permission from Gudes, O., Kendall, E., Yigitcanlar, T., Pathak, V., & Scott, B. (2010). Rethinking health planning: A framework for organising information to underpin collaborative health planning. Health Information Management Journal, 39(2), 18-29.

2 Reprinted with permission from Gudes, O., Kendall, E., Yigitcanlar, T., Pathak, V., & Scott, B. (2010). Rethinking health planning: A framework for organising information to underpin collaborative health planning. Health Information Management Journal, 39(2), 18-29.

Chapter 4
Sustainability Strategies and Projects of Turkish Municipalities

Seda H. Bostancı
Okan University, Turkey

ABSTRACT

Municipalities have variety of tools for improving environmental sustainability. The effects of climate change increase the renewable projects developed by municipalities and public private sectors. Turkish municipalities practiced the early steps of sustainability projects, some of which were small-scale projects. In addition, Turkish municipalities have gained experience in LA 21 Process since the late 1990s. Some of the city models for sustainability, such as CittaSlow and healthy city projects developed by Turkish Municipalities. The work in this chapter represents research about variety of issues for environment and sustainability in Turkish Municipalities. Visions, strategies and projects of these municipalities have been analysed to attain this goal. A literature review and SWOT analysis were used for the methodology to determine the Turkish municipalities' potential for sustainability.

INTRODUCTION

Nowadays the awareness of environmental issues is spreading out to many countries. These multi-disciplinary issues have global and local backgrounds. Some of the local environmental projects have become models for other countries. International organizations like ICLEI (International Council for Local Environmental Initiatives) help the proliferation of this type of successful practices carried out by various countries to become widespread. Municipalities have a wide range of issues, such as urban planning, social responses, participation strategies, infrastructure, health, cultural services, and transportation. Many of these issues are also related to the environment. Sustainability and environmental problems are now playing a vital role in political visions of the countries. The collaborative participation policies for environmental issues are related to ecosystem management and environmental policy. "There has been a relatively recent push in the environmental policy community to decentralize the management of resources and encourage stakeholder

DOI: 10.4018/978-1-4666-8433-1.ch004

collaboration through ecosystem-management approaches" (Campbell & Corley, 2012). The application area of these political decisions is found in municipalities. Therefore, municipalities worldwide create innovative projects and models for the environment.

The main areas of sustainability approaches of Turkish Municipalities can be divided into two parts. These are strategy and policy-based applications and project-based applications as shown in Figure 1.

In Figure 1, the tools for strategy and policy-based applications are LA 21 and Local Councils, strategies from Directorate of Environment, Sister Municipalities, EU Funds for sustainability, International Municipal Organizations for sustainability, social activities for environmental sustainability, and emission reduction strategies. The tools for project-based applications are sustainable urban planning, green transportation planning, waste management and recycling projects, sustainable urban transformation projects, renewable energy projects for sustainability, green public building projects, energy efficiency projects for buildings, and water efficiency projects.

Municipalities are strategic decision-making organs for cities. However, they have to act in a collaborative manner in this decision-making process with the inhabitants and other actors for more democratic and participatory management. When discussing the relations between environmental issues and municipalities in participatory process, the most well-known relation is Local Agenda 21 and local councils, which are parts of the LA 21 process. "A positive implementation of LA 21 presupposes a relatively high degree of local authority. LA 21 was labelled as the whole set of discussions around immediate surroundings and sustainable issues, and on the formulation of assessable local goals and concrete local actions" (Coenen, 2001). The visions and expectations of NGOs and municipalities may sometimes differ to a great extent. If Local Councils formed by LA 21 are democratic and transparent, they will provide opportunities to communicate with municipalities and groups or NGOs who have different political and social visions from the authorities of municipalities.

Figure 1. Sustainability applications of Turkish municipalities

Municipalities have departments about environmental issues, with the main departments usually named Directorate of Environment. The sub-units for these departments are about, climate change, environment, clean environment, energy and recycling, waste management. These departments and issues change from country to country as well as municipality. The Directorate of Disaster Management is usually a separate unit.

Sister municipalities are international participatory processes for municipalities and these international relations pave the way for understanding the management process of other nations' municipalities and sharing their experiences with each other. Some of these experiences and strategic visions are related to environmental issues, and this situation provides an opportunity to make international and innovative environmental projects between countries.

EU funds are economic tools for sustainable future of cities and municipalities. EU policies are strongly concerned with environmental issues. "The integration of environmental and sustainable development objectives into all areas of EU policy-making is a challenging task Institutional arrangements, economic interests and models, political strategies and cultural values are at stake, and profound changes and needed to implement such a task" (Liberatore, 1997).

The problems about sustainable future are global contents, and the solutions can be created by international organizations and commissions. "The past decade has witnessed a growing interest among scholars of international relations, and global environmental governance in particular, in the role of transnational networks within the international arena. While the existence and potential significance of such networks have been documented, many questions concerning the nature of governance conducted by such networks and their impact remain" (Betsill & Bulkeley, 2004). There are some international local organizations about municipalities, such as ICLEI (International Council for Local Environmental Initiatives) and EEA (European Environmental Agency). "Thousands of nongovernmental organizations and cities and towns throughout the world have endorsed the Earth Charter and are working to implement its principles. Among these groups are national and international environmental organizations, educational institutions and associations, religious groups, peace initiatives, and local government councils, including the United States Conference of Mayors and the International Council for Local Environmental Initiatives" (Initiative, 2000).

One of the application areas of municipalities is organizing social and cultural events. Certain cultural events are also related to the environment, such as environment week, which is organized by some municipalities in different countries. This kind of events increases public participation and the social responsibility of the inhabitants.

Emission reducing strategies are a significantly important area for central and local governments. "Local governments can have a large effect on carbon emissions through land use zoning, building codes, transport infrastructure investments, and support for transportation alternatives. Local governments would be assigned an emissions "budget", and would be required to keep annual local transport and buildings emissions within this budget. This policy framework could be implemented and managed by a higher-level government, or might be used in awarding funds to developing country cities from international climate funds" (Salon et al., 2010).

The main project areas of municipalities are urban planning and transportation planning. "Urban planning is a kind of eco-conservation and development tool for creating sustainable cities" (Bostancı, 2012). These tools together shape cities and develop life quality. Sustainable urban planning is related to green areas and green transportation. "The selection of a proper pattern for urban transportation development is necessary for supporting sustainable urban development" (Jiang & Guo, 2009). Sustainable urban planning is one of the critical issues for environmental applications of the municipalities because this process shapes cities. "It is important to understand that city planning does not happen in a vacuum.

For the most part it happens as a part of local government. It is an activity of government in the sense that city planning is done by a government or its agents, and in the sense that government is intimately involved in encouraging, permitting, denying, modifying, or putting conditions on what individuals, groups, or institutions plan and build" (Jacobs, 1980). "The use of ecological information in the urban land use planning process to preserve green spaces and ecosystem services for urban residents has gained acceptance. Local participation with regards to urban nature has the potential to enhance the sustainable development of communities and their green environments especially if participants connected to the green spaces become integrated in planning" (Yli-Pelkonen & Kohl, 2005). Transportation planning and decisions taken related to transportation can cause significant urban problems in metropolises, such as air pollution.

Waste management and recycling are critical areas in sustainable development and quality of life. "The increasing awareness of the environment has contributed to concerns regarding our life styles and our indiscriminate disposal of wastes. The goal of any sustainable growth should be that the efficiency of energy utilization in every step of the system, from the production of the goods to the disposal of the wastes, be maximized. Today, over 19 000 communities are involved in some form of recycling" (Subramanian, 2000).

Urban transformation is a challenging area in many of the developing and populated metropolises. "Nevertheless, as cities grow, managing them becomes increasingly complex. The speed and sheer scale of the urban transformation of the developing world presents formidable challenges. Of particular concern are the risks to the immediate and surrounding environment, to natural resources, to health conditions, to social cohesion, and to individual rights" (Cohen, 2006). Thus, municipalities have to find a balance between urban transformation and sustainable development.

"Renewable energy will play an important role in the transition to a sustainable energy system. With an increased maturity of renewable energy technologies, issues concerning implementation are becoming more important. The decisions and actions of municipalities and other local actors have a significant influence on the implementation of renewable energy" (Khan, 2004).

"Green buildings have less negative impact on the environment than standard buildings. Their construction minimizes on-site grading, saves natural resources by using alternative building materials, and recycles construction waste rather than sending truck after truck to landfills" (Lockwood, 2006). Acquired as a result of meeting certain criteria, green certification systems such as BREEAM and LEED have started to attract the attention of the public sector. In parallel with this, there is a tendency to get this certificate for newly constructed public buildings. Municipalities try to encourage investors to get green certificates for their buildings. "Green building practices can be encouraged by establishing standards to guide design and construction of new and renovated properties, including public buildings, to improve energy efficiency, water and landscape conservation, indoor air quality, use of recycled and durable materials, and locational qualities that promote sustainability" (Frumkin, 2009). The most basic issues in order to keep cities more green and sustainable for future generations are the conservation of natural thresholds and the determination of conservation limits in accordance with the rules and regulations. In the process of green certification, the criteria for green buildings include the buildings' location decisions as well. "If a building or a business campus is going to be truly green, it cannot be constructed on prime farmland, parkland, a historic or prehistoric site, or the habitat of an endangered species, nor can it be built within 100 feet of wetlands" (Lockwood, 2006).

Green buildings are successful in energy efficiency but other buildings can also provide energy efficiency with some supplements and regulations. "The global effort to combat climate change will inevitably rely on improving the energy efficiency of buildings in the coming decades with buildings responsible for one-third of global CO_2 emissions. A holistic approach should be adopted by integrating the quality of energy infrastructure, building design and efficiency optimisation and public policies to remove the barriers to implementation of energy efficiency in buildings" (Li & Colombier, 2009). In order to enable the energy efficiency in buildings and industrial zones, municipalities have to implement a variety of regulations and sanctions.

"A range of sustainable water strategies to address twenty-first-century water challenges have emerged that reach far beyond the conventional water sector. Growing attention is being given to sustainable measures such as low-impact development, water reuse, watershed restoration, water conservation and efficiency, and many other proven and promising practices" (Moore et al., 2014). "Historically water and energy conservation have been approached separately. Although progress has been made to improve efficiencies in both energy use and water use, greater coordination between the two sectors is needed. Acknowledging and accounting for the energy component of water production and use will strengthen the impact of conservation efforts and encourage a more efficient use of our water resources" (Smith, 2012). Municipalities have to make some regulations on water conservation and the use of grey water in buildings.

This chapter focused on sustainability vision, strategies, applications, projects and models for sustainability. These subjects are of vital importance to the future of Turkish cities like the other countries. If sustainable development becomes the main strategy for these municipalities, quality of life in Turkey will increase. Once this process is completed, municipalities will become more participatory, environmentally friendly, innovative and transparent.

BACKGROUND

Sustainability approaches of municipalities are related to sustainable development, sustainable projects and environmental justice. Municipalities are responsible for conservation of the environment. "For municipalities to fulfil their role in a nation's work for a healthy environment, and ultimately for sustainability, there is a need for better information about the pressures society puts on the environment, as well as about the underlying causes of these pressures" (Burström, 1999). "Municipalities can significantly advance community sustainability by developing infrastructure that meets green building standards, creating regulatory incentives which promote a sustainable economy, passing zoning by-laws that establish sustainable patterns of land use and procuring good and services that meet environmentally and socially responsible standards. In addition, local government can maximise the resource efficiency of the environmental services for which they are typically charged with providing— e.g. water treatment, waste management and natural resource management" (Quaid, 2002). "Municipalities have, in playing their traditional roles as authorities and providers of technical and social services, rather limited capacities to successfully manage environmental issues themselves; at least when it comes to issues related to other than administrative aspects of municipal environmental management" (Burström, 2000).

"Sustainability requires that the Earth and its resources be regarded not only as a consumption opportunity, but as a 'planetary trust', passed on to us by our ancestors to be enjoyed and passed on to our descendants for their use. Such an understanding conveys both rights and responsibilities" (Keleş, 1997). "Sustainable development is development that meets the needs of the present without compromising the ability of future generations to meet their own needs" (WCED, 1987). "While the primary objective of the 1992 Earth Summit was to generate new commitments from national governments on global environmental issues, one of the most tangible outcomes of the summit was to focus international attention on the role of cities as central actors in the Earth's ecosystem. As a result, UN Conference on Human Settlements (Habitat II) extended its focus, originally on housing only, to sustainable human settlements. The final product of the meeting, the Habitat Agenda, provides the greatest recognition ever offered by the United Nations to the role of local governments in the sustainable development process. The success of the Habitat Agenda will be defined by the ability of local governments to effectively adopt its recommendations" (Brugmann, 1996).

In environmental policy, sustainable development has to be balanced with environmental justice. "Within the field of urban environmental policy, though, there is a particular issue of justice that has arisen over the last few decades: the distribution of what are often called environmental bads or disamenities" (Campbell & Corley, 2012). Environmental justice and healthy city approaches have some connections to sustainability applications of municipalities.

SUSTAINABILITY APPLICATIONS OF TURKISH MUNICIPALITIES

The municipal system of Turkey has local and central relations. "The Governor represents the central administration at the provincial level and is responsible, among other duties, for overseeing the implementation of government policy at the province level. The Governors are appointed by the government and subordinated to the Ministry of Interior. At the district level, District Governors are subordinated to the Governors and have powers and responsibilities corresponding to those of the Governor. Mayors are elected by universal suffrage every 5 years and so are their Municipal Councils. Villages have a Village Head who chairs an executive committee. There are 3 types of municipalities in Turkey: metropolitan municipalities, district municipalities (within metropolitan areas), and other municipalities" (Bahloul & Özcan, 2006).

Turkish municipalities have different experiences about sustainability issues. Some of them are strategy and policy-based, while some of them are project-based, as topic which has been discussed in the introduction part of this chapter. In this part, these two applications will be introduced through some examples of Turkish municipalities.

Strategy and Policy-Based Applications

The main sustainability strategy of Turkish municipalities is Local Agenda 21 (LA 21) process. "Local Agenda 21 applications in Turkey started in 1997 with the support of UNDP, and the first project was "The Promotion and Development of Local Agenda 21s in Turkey", conducted by the IULA-EMME – International Union of Local Authorities, Eastern Mediterranean and Middle East" (Emrealp, 2005). "One of the first examples for Local Agenda 21 process is founded in Antalya which is called the City Council of Antalya in 1997" (Atvur, 2009). "In 1997, participatory platforms of LA 21 were established at municipal level. There are mainly two LA 21 models. These are the model led by the municipality and the model led by the city council. For the first model, the city of Izmir can be given as an example. The key role in the coordination of LA 21 process in the city belongs to the Execution Board. This board is assigned by the municipality but its role is limited to keep contact among the municipality and other stakeholders. In Antalya, LA 21 process started just after the Habitat Summit in İstanbul. In this model, city council constitutes the participatory platform of the city. The city council includes both assemblies for main groups and Working Committees, and it is the primary institution to establish cooperation and common understanding among municipality, governorship and civil society" (Herguner, 2012).

Sister municipalities, or international municipal partnerships (twinning's), have advantages inclusive of experience sharing of environmental strategies and issues between municipalities. "The importance the government of Turkey gives to international municipal partnerships (twinning's) is motivated by the desire to bring the Turkish communities, businesses and local institutions closer to those of Europe and to improve the management and public service delivery practices of the Turkish local authorities by bringing them closer to the practices of the EU member states. The practice of twinning's (partnership between Turkish and foreign municipalities) exists in Turkey, and it is to a large extent already oriented towards municipalities from European countries" (Bahloul & Özcan, 2006).

"Strategic planning processes, which are commonly used as a tool for region development and territorial structuring, can be harnessed by politicians and public administrations, at the local level, to redesign the regional energy system and encourage renewable energy development and environmental preservation" (Terrados et al., 2007). "The first legal regulation in renewable energy systems for sustainability is law number 5346 in 2005 which is called a Law about Using Renewable Energy Resources for Generating Electrical Energy" (Talu, 2007). Recently in metropolitan municipalities in Turkey, Directorates of Renewable Energy have been opened. Similarly in district municipalities, it is possible to see the opening of these units, which work under Directorate of Environment. Still, it can be said that these attempts are not widespread countrywide.

Municipalities are responsible for creating social public spaces for social activities. "The Municipality of Nilüfer, in Bursa, not only provided a modern city environment for everybody to do sports activities free of charge by arranging 180 parks and playgrounds, 35 runways and equipping them with outdoor sports equipment together with Misi and Balat picnic sites, but also rearranged Atatürk City Forest, which is an area of 150 hectares, with bicycle trails, playfields, and picnic sites and opened them for public use. The purpose of this project is to give possibilities to the inhabitants of Nilüfer to spend their spare times with natural beauties and accordingly to raise people's life quality and make the area more liveable by equipping it with sports facilities and social facilities. In order to strengthen the love of nature, a drawing and poetry competition on the subject 'Environment and Nature' is organized every year, and children and all participants ranking high in the competition are given awards. In order to train students about gardening, Nilüfer organizes ''the most beautiful garden'' competitions among home-sites, even factories and arranges hobby gardens where citizens can make organic farming and enjoy the nature" (Nilüfer Municipality, 2014).

Project Based Applications

"One way local governments incorporate sustainability into their communities is through regional or national agreements to reduce greenhouse gas emissions and waste, promote energy efficiency, encourage the use of alternative and renewable technologies, and recycle" (Browne & Knodel, 2008).

"Solid waste recovery and recycling has been a long-standing commercial activity in Turkey. Glass and paper recycling have been conducted at industrial scales since the 1950s" (Metin et al., 2003). According to the research made by Metin (2003) "The review of municipal and household solid waste statistics in Turkey indicates that average household waste generation per capita is 0.6 kg/day and average municipal solid waste is 0.95 kg/day. The composition of municipal solid waste varies by the source of waste; however in all cases organic constituents accounts for more than 50% of municipal solid waste. Public participation is an important element of all municipal separate collection and recovery operations" (Metin et al., 2003). "Solid waste management is a complex and multidisciplinary problem that should be considered from technical, economic and social aspects on a sustainability basis. For a healthy environment, both municipal and industrial wastes should be managed according to the solid waste management hierarchy" (Banar et al., 2009).

One of the waste management processes in Turkey can be explained with the example of Denizli Municipality. "Local Authority (Denizli Municipality) was responsible for waste collection, transportation and street sweeping until 2005. After this year, collection and transportation were carried out by a private company. The solid waste collection method used in Denizli was curbside collection without source separation. Containers 0.4 m^3 in size were used for interim storage in Denizli. The dimensions and numbers of containers varied according to the waste quantity and population. Solid waste in containers was collected and transported to an unsanitary landfill by trucks with capacities of 11 or 13.5 m^3. Hospital waste was collected by non-specialized trucks which belonged to Denizli Municipality. Contaminated and non-contaminated (municipal-like-waste) medical waste in Denizli was stored and collected together" (Ağdağ, 2009).

There are lots of renewable energy projects of Turkish municipalities but many of them are small-scale projects. Kadıköy is a district municipality in İstanbul, and it has the same variety of small-scale renewable energy projects. "Kadıköy Municipality has been involved in many energy efficiency activities at institutional scale since 2010 aiming to meet the environmental objectives. Municipality signed the Covenant of Mayors which was formed within the scope of European Commission in 2012. The municipality intended to decrease the greenhouse gas emissions by at least 20% until year 2020 in their jurisdiction" (Kadıköy Municipality, 2013).

Nowadays, the applications of green certification in buildings such as BREEAM and LEED have become an item in the agenda of municipalities. Küçükçekmece and Sarıyer municipalities, two district municipalities in İstanbul, have applied for these certificates for their municipality buildings. The process has been completed in the case of Küçükçekmece municipality. Turkey's first green public building, Küçükçekmece Municipality Building, has opened in İstanbul. The Mayor said: 'the building will generate its own energy and will be environmentally friendly. With our savings in water, power and others, the building will be returning the investment in 3 years. The materials used in the building are natural and recyclable. The rain water – which will be collected in the 250 m^3 cistern at the top of the roof will be used for irrigation. Ice storage system will produce ice during cheapest electricity hours, and ice will be used for cooling function in the air conditioning system during hot summer days. Photovoltaic modules will also be installed at the roof-top in the very near future" (Alternatif Enerji, 2013). Küçükçekmece municipality building has BREEAM certificate. The new building of Sarıyer Municipality was also designed as a green building, but its construction process has not finished yet. "Sarıyer Municipality's Main Service Building is being constructed using all the means of contemporary building technologies and the construction will be completed in a short period of time" (Sarıyer Municipality, 2012).

These strategic and project-based applications of Turkish Municipalities are some of the innovative examples of this area. Many of the Turkish Municipalities have LA 21 process and city councils, and nearly all the metropolitan and district municipalities have environment departments. As well as, having projects about green areas, many of them are successful in waste management, and some of them have recycling fields. But also some big projects and urban regeneration plans have negative effects for the green natural areas of the cities and the environment.

SOLUTIONS AND RECOMMENDATIONS

The strategic decisions of the municipalities are strongly related to welfare of the citizens. The expectations of the citizens affected the projects of the municipalities. When municipalities come up with solutions for social welfare, housing, ownership, they gain more advantages for focusing on environmental problems. However, in some of the countries, the effects of climate change strongly threaten cities' future so they put environmental issues on top of the agenda. Also nowadays, many countries are aware of the important effects of environmental issues on disaster management, health and life quality of the cities. Thus, numerous countries have applications related to these environmental areas. The key to a successful sustainable development is that municipalities have to make holistic and collaborative studies, and these studies should be regularly applied by models. The models for sustainable development have some criteria which the municipalities have to perform. Table 1 shows some of these models for sustainability which Turkish Municipalities implement.

"Embedded within the slow living ideology of Cittaslow is the assumption that the "better" life it advocates involves heightened sensory experience and concomitant pleasure" (Pink, 2007). CittaSlow or slow city movement is a kind of sustainable living in a city. "The Citta`slow movement was established in Italy in 1999. In response to what its founders perceive as the "fast" and globally homogenising times we inhabit, Citta`slow emphasises local distinctiveness in a context of globalisation and seeks to improve quality of life locally. It aims to achieve this by globally disseminating a model for local governance which is adopted by its accredited members. To be accredited a town must score over 50% in a self-assessment process, against criteria concerning its environmental and infrastructure policies, the quality of urban fabric, encouraging local produce, hospitality and community and creation of Citta`slow awareness" (Pink, 2008). "Seferihisar residents, as the first representative of the slow city in Turkey. Research findings, shows that two years' experience of Seferihisar as a cittaslow, has been reflected positively on the local cuisine. It seems that it is very common that in the town, the cittaslow movement has been considerably adopted and the movement was the opportunity for protection and promotion of local cuisine. It is effective in raising the city residents (especially students) awareness about disadvantages of fast food-style feeding and the advantages of feeding that produced by local, organic and traditional methods. Among the opportunities offered by the cittaslow movement for the farmers of Seferihisar there are acceleration of the process of transition to organic farming, production by natural methods and in season and directly selling of products to consumers at the village markets, without the need for the agent" (Görkem & Öztürk, 2014).

Table 1. City models of Turkish municipalities for sustainability

Model	Examples from Municipalities of Turkey
CittaSlow (Slow City Movement)	Seferihisar Municipality – İzmir
Healthy City	Bursa Metropolitan Municipality
Participatory Sustainability Model and LA 21 Process	İzmir Metropolitan Municipality
Project based Environmental Municipality	Nilüfer Municipality – Bursa

"A healthy, active city recognizes the value of active living, physical activity and sport. It provides opportunities for physical activity and active living for all. The built and social environments are key focal points. The built environment includes land-use patterns, transport systems, urban design, green spaces and all buildings and spaces that are created by people including schools, homes, workplaces and recreation areas. Elements in the social environment that influence participation in physical activity include income, equity, culture and social support" (Edwards & Tsuorus, 2006). "Bursa, which is called the "green city", is mainly located at the outskirts of the Mountain Uludag. The City of Bursa faced unhealthy circumstances because of the detonation in the population. Transportation in the city was overloaded. All these negative effects draw a picture of unsustainable lifestyle. Starting from the 1990's the city took initiates to take safety measures to deal with the problems and form a healthy city as it was before. Bursa Healthy City initiative has launched the approach of healthy city concept originated from World Health Organization (WHO) to provide all healthy conditions for the city. The vision of Bursa for a healthy city consists of: engaging communities in meaningful and active dialogue on health issues, and reflect the results of this dialogue in concrete actions by public bodies and others, increasing public participation, promoting local capacity in order to satisfy the increasing needs of the maximum health potential" (Tepecik & Anderson, 2006).

Participation strategies have become a critical area of Turkish municipalities, and Local Agenda 21 process with city councils and stakeholder councils has been given remarkable contribution for participatory sustainability model. "In October 2nd 1996, the mayor of Izmir Metropolitan Municipality called for a new meeting after HABITAT II. This call intended to update activities started in 1995. Furthermore, the mayor of Izmir, the governor of Izmir, and the Local Agenda 21 Executive Council invited new participants. Local governments, agencies of central government, universities, non-governmental organisations, some of private sectors' representatives and citizens all took part in this new initiative. The first task was to establish work groups to draw a picture of urban and environmental problems of Izmir under the co-ordination of Local Agenda 21 the Executive Council. Three topics, urbanisation, environment and migration were considered within this framework. Izmir experience produces a guidance to help to create "regional Habitat" (Toprak & Palabıyık, 2000).

Many of the Turkish municipalities do environmental projects in different areas. Some of the applications carried out in these municipalities act as a guide for other municipalities. For example Nilüfer Municipality, which is a district municipality in Bursa, is not only a member of the healthy city association but it also develops various environmental projects in accordance with sustainable city vision. "Nilüfer is surrounded by traces of history, and the cultural and natural heritage that carries these traces takes the history of the region back to ancient ages. Elaborating on increasing the green zones in urban planning and creating an urban environment at peace with nature, the municipality of Nilüfer attempts to create awareness through organizing afforestation campaigns annually. Nilüfer Municipality has been making dedicated efforts for environment protection. In the framework of environmental training activities, Nilüfer Municipality publishes instructive brochures and posters as well as using billboards to inform the public about the issues of air pollution, water conservation, collecting domestic waste herbal oil, electromagnetic field pollution. Nilüfer Municipality, which supports the public-oriented management, has opened the door of municipal council to Nilüfer inhabitants who volunteer to participate in the decision-making process. Having the motto of "health in every area of life", Nilüfer Municipality has accomplished to be the one of the 7 cities in Turkey which has been approved as a member of the 5th Phase of the World Health Organization (WHO) Healthy Cities Network, through its efforts on urban development, environmental and public health" (Nilüfer Municipality, 2014). Nilüfer Municipality is a symbolic example of strategic and technical approaches by municipalities in sustainability issues.

Eco-cities are the cities that have been designed in accordance with the holistic environmental values of the 21st century. "Now in the 21st century, the realization of an eco-city requires the integration of multiple environmental objectives such as climate change mitigation, bio-diversity conservation, and sound material cycles with the objectives of economic growth and liveability in cities" (Imura, 2010). Eco-cities are also on the agenda of the municipalities. These kinds of approaches need multi actor participatory processes. Gaziantep Metropolitan Municipality has an eco-city project in a development area of Gaziantep. "Gaziantep Metropolitan Municipality was supported by AFD (Agence Française & Development) Gaziantep Metropolitan Municipality in its groundbreaking approach to establish a territorial climate/energy plan, which defines the strategy and implements the city's priorities for climate change adaptation" (AFD, 2012). Because of this project has not been completed, this is not added to Table 1 as an eco city example. But in Turkey eco cities will be developed in the future. This is an important example for this aim.

These examples show that Turkey has some attractive environmental studies, although they have not spread to all the cities and districts. However, in spite of the fact that the decision process in city councils founded by LA 21 is rarely applied, the most extensive sustainability area of Turkish Municipalities is LA 21 process.

FUTURE AND EMERGING TRENDS

The main trend of Turkish cities nowadays is urban transformation in different scales. For the sustainable future of this process, some concepts can be effective. These concepts are resilience, green transformation and green retrofitting. In this part, these concepts will be discussed in terms of their potentials for the sustainable development by Turkish Municipalities.

"The world is today searching for interdisciplinary approaches to find holistic solutions to the problems that threaten the environment" (Bostancı, 2012). Municipalities can be mediators in interdisciplinary and multi-actor environmental projects. Some different approaches about sustainable urban planning for Turkish municipalities can be analysed through the effects of urban transformation process. The major challenge of many Turkish cities is natural disasters, especially earthquakes, which causes the increase of urban transformation and transition processes. "Governments have tended to neglect the social aspects of the socio-ecological context and there is lack of understanding of system behavior in high-risk cities" (Yalçıner-Erçoşkun, 2012). These risk management systems creates resilient cities. "A resilient city is committed, processing the necessary resources and organizational capacity for before, during and after disaster" (Yalçıner-Erçoşkun, 2012). "Nowadays, urban transition process in Turkey densely comes to life with multi-dimensional urban renewal projects at neighbourhood scale. These projects mostly concentrate on increasing urban resilience against earthquake risk. Today, urban renewal implementations in Turkey have been practiced within two different application fields that are the historical and informal sites" (Oktay & Çetin, 2013).

Some of the municipalities make some strategic and technical studies for creating green transformation process. Fikirtepe green transformation process is an example done by Kadıköy Municipality. "The project was started in 2012 in order to provide urban sustainability. Especially in urban renewal areas like Fikirtepe and newly planned areas; criteria were brought together in a 'green planning guidebook' for their local initiative. This guidebook, which contains green building and green neighborhood criteria, was shared with the relevant associations that work actively in the district" (Kadıköy Municipality, 2013). Bu these projects have not started yet and Fikirtepe Regeneration project have variety of problems.

Retrofitting is an alternative way to decrease the demolition process of big urban areas. "The importance of greening existing buildings lies in two key facts: existing buildings constitute the vast majority of the energy-using building stock

Table 2. SWOT table for sustainability potential of Turkish municipalities

	Internal Factors	External Factors
Favorable Factors	**Strengths**	**Opportunities**
	• LA 21 process has been started in most of the Turkish Municipalities. • Related to LA 21 Process, the number of city councils in municipalities is increasing day by day. • The geographical situation of Turkey is suitable for the development of renewable energy sources.	• The environment projects of Turkish municipalities are supported by EU funds. • Municipalities attach importance to environmental projects and use them for publicity. • Urban transformation process creates an opportunity for the sustainable development of cities. • Some of the sustainable city models like healthy cities have been applied by Turkish municipalities.
Unfavorable Factors	**Weaknesses**	**Threats**
	Environmental subjects are not the prior expectations of inhabitants from municipalities. Municipalities have a great variety of expenditure areas.	• Climate change. • Earthquakes. • Rapid urban transformation. • Migration to urban areas and irregular housing. • Infrastructure problems of the cities as a result of population growth. • Mass housing lack of green areas.

at any given time, and they have huge impacts not only on energy and water use, but also on the lives of people who occupy them. The perceived high costs of greening an existing building is probably one of the main reasons why owners are reluctant to carry out retrofit. These costs include not only the capital expenditure but also the "losses" resulting from having to shut the building down during retrofitting" (Yu et al., 2011). Municipalities can encourage stakeholders to have their buildings retrofitted.

METHODOLOGY

The methodology of the study is literature review, a thorough search about municipalities' news on web sites and SWOT analysis as a result of this information. "SWOT is an abbreviation including the capital letters of the words Strengths, Weaknesses, Opportunities, and Threats. With this method that, as the base, has the principle of analyzing the four parameters regarding the present structures (Polat, 2012). "SWOT analysis, which inquiries into strengths, weaknesses, opportunities, and threats, is the traditional means of searching for insights into ways of realizing the desired alignment" (Valentin, 2001).

The environmental projects, sustainability issues, agendas and future trends of municipalities in Turkey have been determined after searching the web for the news about municipalities and doing literature review. These assumptions have been used in SWOT analysis. The findings of the research done in the methodology part have been stated. Table 2 shows the SWOT table for sustainability potential of Turkish Municipalities.

CONCLUSION

It can be stated that the main agenda of Turkish municipalities focus on the urban transformation process and social welfare. Newly established metropolises in accordance with the legislation, disaster risks, and dense urbanization trends have made the urban transformation process gain utmost priority in government policies. As a result of the research, it can be seen that variety of environmental issues have been added to the agenda of Turkish Municipalities, associated partly with participation strategies, partly with innovative projects, to a great extent with urban transformation process. If this process is analysed well, it is possible to make considerable gains from the transformation process in terms of sustainability. But the realized projects usually did not represent this situation. Eco-city models can be performed in Turkey. Apart from this, there are some pioneering district municipalities like Nilüfer and Seferihisar which choose environmental issues as their area of focus. Approaches like resilience, green transformation and green retrofitting have provided innovative solutions for the urban transformation process of Turkey.

When SWOT analysis is examined, it can be seen that the biggest challenges municipalities face are disaster risks and infrastructure problems. Social problems resulting from the unequal distribution of income are the major determinant in the relationships between citizens and municipalities. This process caused the citizens not to show great interest in the environmental problems unless they are affected by them. However, when the environmental problems threaten their life quality, citizens join social movements and defend their democratic rights. Although it is considered a positive step that Turkish Municipalities have been applying LA 21 process since the late 1990s, when the city councils are examined, it is found that the decisions taken by these councils are rarely applied when the cost of these projects are high. The increase in the number of NGOs and their acceptance by the citizens result in more participation in environmental issues.

The application of Cittaslow and healthy city models by Turkish municipalities is considered a big potential for sustainable development. In this study, the conditions of Turkish municipalities in terms of administration and application in sustainable and environmental areas have been determined. Consequently, in Turkey, there is a need to start the holistic sustainable municipality model with its strategic and technical tools.

REFERENCES

AFD. (2012). *4th Focus Area: Supporting municipalities in their sustainable development*. Retrieved March 24, 2014, from http://www.afd.fr/lang/en/home/pays/mediterranee-et-moyen-orient/geo/turquie/tr-axes-strategiques-strategie-Turquie-strateji-turkiye/axe-4-accompagner-les-municipalites-dans-leur-developppement-urbain-durable

Ağdağ, O. N. (2009). Comparison of old and new municipal solid waste management systems in Denizli, Turkey. *Waste Management (New York, N.Y.)*, *29*(1), 456–464. doi:10.1016/j.wasman.2008.01.012 PMID:18346887

Alternatif Enerji Web Sitesi. (2013). *Turkey's First Green Public Building in Küçükçekmece*. Retrieved March 24, 2014, from http://www.alternatifenerji.com/turkeys-first-green-public-building-at-kucukcekmece.html

Atvur, S. (2009). Yerel Gündem 21 ve Çevre: Anltalya Kent Konseyi Örneği. *Sosyal Bilimler Dergisi*, *33*(2), 231–241.

Bahloul, H. & Özcan, Ü. (2006). *Municipal Partnership in Turkey: Situation Analysis*. Report Supported by UNDP.

Banar, M., Cokaygil, Z., & Ozkan, A. (2009). Life cycle assessment of solid waste management options for Eskisehir, Turkey. *Waste Management (New York, NY)*, *29*(1), 54–62. doi:10.1016/j.wasman.2007.12.006 PMID:18280731

Betsill, M. M., & Bulkeley, H. (2004). Transnational networks and global environmental governance: The cities for climate protection program. *International Studies Quarterly*, *48*(2), 471–493. doi:10.1111/j.0020-8833.2004.00310.x

Bostancı, S. H. (2012). Eco-Municipalities and Municipal Applications for Sustainability. In Ö. Yalçıner-Ercoşkun (Ed.), *Green and Ecological Technologies for Urban Planning: Creating Smart Cities* (pp. 310–328). Hershey, PA: IGI Global. doi:10.4018/978-1-61350-453-6.ch017

Browne, R., & Knodel, M. (2008). *Sustainability in Hanover*. Hanover: PRS Policy Brief 0708-08.

Brugmann, J. (1996). Planning for sustainability at the local government level. *Environmental Impact Assessment Review*, *16*(4), 363–379. doi:10.1016/S0195-9255(97)81658-7

Burström, F. (1999). Materials accounting and environmental management in municipalities. *Journal of Environmental Assessment Policy and Management*, *1*(3), 297–327. doi:10.1142/S1464333299000247

Burström, F. (2000). *Environment and Municipalities: Towards a Theory on Municipal Environmental Management*. Stockholm, Sweden: KTH/Högskoletryckeriet.

Campbell, H. E., & Corley, E. A. (2012). *Urban Environmental Policy Analysis*. Armonk, NY: M.E. Sharpe.

Coenen, F. (2001). Probing the Essence of LA21 as a Value-Added Approach to Sustainable Development and Local Democracy. In W. M. Lafferty (Ed.), *Sustainable Communities in Europe* (pp. 153–179). London, UK: Earthscan.

Cohen, B. (2006). Urbanization in developing countries: Current trends, future projections, and key challenges for sustainability. *Technology in Society*, *28*(1), 63–80. doi:10.1016/j.techsoc.2005.10.005

Earth Charter Initiative. (2000). *The Earth Charter*. Retrieved May 6, 2006, from http://www.earthcharterinaction.org/

Edwards, P., & Tsuorus, A. D. (2006). *A Healthy City is an Active City: A Physical Activity Planning Guide*. World Health Organization.

Emrealp, S. (2005). *Yerel Gündem 21 Uygulamalarına Yönelik Kolaylaştırıcı Bilgiler El Kitabı. Türkiye- İstanbul: IULA-EMME (UCLG-MEWA)*. Yayını.

Frumkin, H. (2009). Healthy Communities, Green Communities. In S. Piedmont-Palladino & T. Mennel (Eds.), *Green Community* (pp. 118–125). APA Planners Press.

Görkem, O., & Öztürk, Y. (2014). Gastronomic Reflections of Cittaslow Movement on Local Cuisine: The Case Study of Seferihisar (İzmir, Turkey). *Turizam*, *18*(1), 11–21.

Herguner, B. (2012). Local Administrative Reforms in Turkey and the Philippines with regard to Agenda21: Profiling Contexts, Parallelisms, and Contrasts. *International Journal of Business and Social Science*, *3*(19), 107–116.

Imura, H. (2010). Eco-Cities: Re-Examining Concepts and Approaches. In L. L. Fook & C. Gang (Eds.), *Towards a Liveable and Sustainable Urban Environment: Eco-Cities in East Asia*. Singapore: World Scientific. doi:10.1142/9789814287777_0002

Jacobs, A. B. (1980). *Making City Planning Work*. Chicago, IL: American Planning Association.

Jiang, Y. H., & Guo, X. C. (2009). Urban traffic development strategies based on the concept of green transportation. *Journal of Hefei University of Technology*, *7*, 1086–1090.

Kadıköy Municipality. (2013). *Kadıköy Municipality Actions Against Climate Change and Energy Efficiency Operations*.

Keles, R. (1997). *The common heritage of mankind and the new concepts of responsibility*. Retrieved March 12, 2010, from http://biopolitics.gr/biowp/b-i-o-e-library/sociology/

Khan, J. (2004). *Local politics of renewable energy: project planning, siting conflicts and citizen participation*. Lund, Sweden: Lund University.

Li, J., & Colombier, M. (2009). Managing carbon emissions in China through building energy efficiency. *Journal of Environmental Management, 90*(8), 2436–2447. doi:10.1016/j.jenvman.2008.12.015 PMID:19344996

Liberatore, A. (1997). The Integration of Sustainable Developemnt Objectives into EU Policy-Making: Barriers and Prospects. In S. Baker, M. Kousis, D. Richardson, & S. Young (Ed.), The Politics of Sustainable Development: Theory, Policy and Practice Within the European Union. Routledge.

Lockwood, C. (2006). Building the green way. *Harvard Business Review, 84*(6), 129–137. PMID:16770900

Metin, E., Eröztürk, A., & Neyim, C. (2003). Solid waste management practices and review of recovery and recycling operations in Turkey. *Waste Management (New York, N.Y.), 23*(5), 425–432. doi:10.1016/S0956-053X(03)00070-9 PMID:12893015

Moore, E., Cooley, H., Christian-Smith, J., & Donnelly, K. (2014). Sustainable Water Jobs. In E. Moore, H. Cooley, J. Christian-Smith, & K. Donnelly (Eds.), *The World's Water* (Vol. 8, pp. 35–61). Island Press/Center for Resource Economics. doi:10.5822/978-1-61091-483-3_3

Nilüfer Municipality. (2014). *Useful Information*. Retrieved May 2, 2014, from http://www.nilufercity.eu/index.php?s=i&id=12

Oktay, S. Ö., & Çetin, N. İ. (2013). *Proposal of A Local-Specific Environmental Assessment Method for Yedikule Neighbourhood, İstanbul*. Dublin, Ireland: AESOP-ACSP Joint Congress.

Pink, S. (2007). Sensing Cittàslow: Slow living and the constitution of the sensory city. *The Senses and Society, 2*(1), 59–77. doi:10.2752/174589207779997027

Pink, S. (2008). Sense and sustainability: The case of the Slow City movement. *Local Environment, 13*(2), 95–106. doi:10.1080/13549830701581895

Polat, E. (2012). An Approach for Land-Use Sustainability Assessment Using Decision Support Systems, AHP and GIS. In Ö. Yalçıner-Ercoşkun (Ed.), *Green and Ecological Technologies for Urban Planning: Creating Smart Cities* (pp. 310–329). Hershey, PA: IGI Global.

Quaid, A. (2002). The Sustainability inventory: A tool to assist US Municipalities advance towards sustainability. *Local Environment, 7*(4), 447–452. doi:10.1080/1354983022000027545

Salon, D., Sperling, D., Meier, A., Murphy, S., Gorham, R., & Barrett, J. (2010). City carbon budgets: A proposal to align incentives for climate-friendly communities. *Energy Policy, 38*(4), 2032–2041. doi:10.1016/j.enpol.2009.12.005

Sarıyer Municipality. (2012). *Two green investments in the future of Sarıyer*. Retrieved March 22, 2014, from http://en.sariyer.bel.tr/news/654/two-green-investments-in-the-future-of-sariyer.aspx

Smith, M. G. (2012). *Enhancing Water Conservation Strategies in NYC: Saving Water to Save Energy*. (Unpublished master's thesis). School of Architecture, Pratt Institute, New York, NY.

Subramanian, P. M. (2000). Plastics recycling and waste management in the U.S. *Resources, Conservation and Recycling, 28*(3), 253–263. doi:10.1016/S0921-3449(99)00049-X

Talu, N. (2007). *Sürdürülebilir kalkınma durum değerlendirme raporu, Sürdürülebilir Kalkınmanın Sektörel Politikalara Entegrasyonu Projesi*. Retrieved March 27, 2010, from http://www.bayindirlik.gov.tr/turkce/kentlesme/skdurumdegerlendirmeraporu.pdf

Tepecik, A., & Anderson, E. (2006). *Sustainable Development within the Region: Strategies and the Complex Social System- What Turkey and the U.S.A. Can Learn from Skåne, Sweden*. Retrieved May 3, 2014, from http://www.bth.se/tks/esp.nsf/

Terrados, J., Almonacid, G., & Hontoria, L. (2007). Regional energy planning through SWOT analysis and strategic planning tools: Impact on renewables development. *Renewable & Sustainable Energy Reviews*, *11*(6), 1275–1287. doi:10.1016/j.rser.2005.08.003

Toprak, Z., & Palabıyık, H. (2000). Participation and civil society: The experiences of Izmir local agenda 21 (1995–2000). *Turkish Public Administration Annual, 24-26*(1).

Valentin, E. K. (2001). SWOT analysis from a resource-based view. *Journal of Marketing*, *9*(2), 54–68.

WCED. (1987). *Our common future*. Oxford, UK: Oxford University Press.

Yalçıner – Erçoşkun, Ö. (2012). A Paradigm Shift towards Urban Resilience. In Ö. Yalçıner-Ercoşkun (Ed.), Green and Ecological Technologies for Urban Planning: Creating Smart Cities (pp. 1-17). Hershey, PA: IGI Global.

Yli-Pelkonen, V., & Kohl, J. (2005). The role of local ecological knowledge in sustainable urban planning: perspectives from Finland. *Sustainability: Science, Practice, & Policy*, *1*(1), 3–14.

Yu, S. M., Tu, Y., & Luo, C. (2011). *Green Retrofitting Costs and Benefits: A New Research Agenda*. IRES Working Paper Series, 22.

KEY TERMS AND DEFINITIONS

CittaSlow: CittaSlow is a kind of sustainable lifestyle focusing on conserving the uniqueness of the city, protecting the environment, improving life quality. It has been founded in Italy and has a membership system. In order to apply to be a member, cities have to meet the required criteria.

Green Transformation: Green transformation is one of the urban transformation processes. It is a system which puts emphasis on the use of renewable energy sources and green areas for the sustainable future of cities.

Healthy City: A healthy city is a city which is designed and developed for health-supportive environment and improves quality of life.

Local Agenda 21: Local Agenda 21 is a participatory process for creating sustainable development visions and objectives together with the inhabitants.

Sustainability: Sustainability has environmental, social, economic and technical backgrounds, and it's about a kind of living with limits and prevention of natural resources with a view to transferring natural qualities to future generations.

Chapter 5
Recommendations for Natural Resources Conservation in the Influence Areas of Cities: A Case Study of Bucharest, Romania

Mihai Răzvan Niţă
University of Bucharest, Romania

Maria Pătroescu
University of Bucharest, Romania

Mihăiţă Iulian Niculae
University of Bucharest, Romania

Gabriel Ovidiu Vânău
University of Bucharest, Romania

Diana Andreea Onose
University of Bucharest, Romania

Cristiana Maria Ciocănea
University of Bucharest, Romania

ABSTRACT

As urban development has become an increasing problem, urban planning is required to integrate social and economical needs with the sustainable use of natural resources. Since the urban development is favoured by the amount and diversity of the natural resources (land, mineral resources, green areas, aquatic surfaces) available in the area of influence of the cities and its negative externalities aren't limited inside the urban limits the conservation of those resources became an important issue in the scientific circles. Lately planners have been using GIS techniques and remote sensing, based on international and local databases, in finding the most probable scenarios and the best available solutions in order to promote a sustainable development of urban areas. Four models of natural resources conservation have proved effective in the influence areas of cities: protected areas, yellow-green belts, regional parks and oxygen generating surfaces. The establishment and management of these can be better realised by GIS techniques, because of their efficiency and ease of use, the suitability and general availability of data.

DOI: 10.4018/978-1-4666-8433-1.ch005

INTRODUCTION

Natural capital is defined by (Costanza et al., 1997) as a physical form of the capital stock consisting of all environmental components (lithosphere, atmosphere, hydrosphere, and biosphere) and their interactions materialized in natural ecosystems that represent the basis for human welfare. In other approaches, natural capital includes three components: the actual land, our natural resources – the physical amounts of renewable and non-renewable resources, as well as ecosystems sustaining life and providing goods and services to the population (Olewiler, 2006). Natural resources can be divided according to their usage in two main categories (Figure 1). Renewable resources, are either unconditionally renewable (in the case of abiotic resources flows: solar energy, wind, geothermal energy etc.) or conditioned by a certain period of renewing time and an adequate degree of exploitation (the main cycles of elements, vegetation, fauna, ecosystems, soils). Minerals (metallic and non-metallic) and fossil fuels (oil, coal, and natural gas) are among the non-renewable resources.

Ecosystems are being continually aggressed by urbanization, which affects in the same time habitat structure and quality, as well as processes that control its functionality (Alberti, 2008). De facto, cities are considered by ecologists to be heterotrophic ecosystems (Odum, 1971), strongly dependent on external inputs of energy and materials, and requiring spaces which will absorb their emissions and wastes. Urban ecosystems (Duvigneaud, 1974) modify their periphery land uses and concentrate, on limited territory, human communities with different cultural levels and with a spatially variable demographical and ethnical structure.

The area of influence or sphere of influence is referring to the territory polarized by an urban centre on the basis of a set or category of relations

Figure 1. Natural resources classification
(Adapted from Cogălniceanu (1999)).

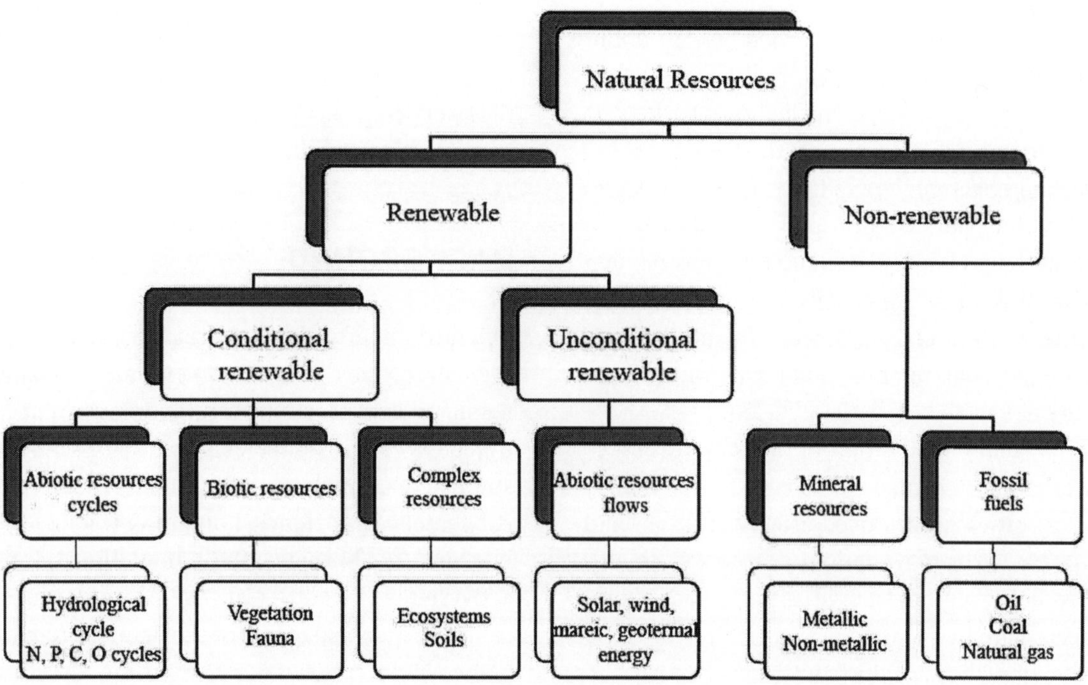

(economical, cultural and/or commercial relations, population mobility and/or environmental externalities) (Pumain & Saint-Julien, 1997). The specific area of influence of a city varies accordingly with the importance of the urban centre and the relations taken into account. This chapter focuses on the influence areas of cities determined from an environmental and economical point of view, as these areas handle the immediate inputs and externalities related to the urban cores.

Urban landscapes are characterised by a high spatial and temporal heterogeneity, consisting of a mosaic of patches with different roles and structures, determined by natural favourability and restrictiveness, but also by social elements (Newman & Thornley, 1996). There are various models of how cities develop which assess social and economic impacts, but few evaluating the impacts on the preservation of ecosystems and natural resources (Williams, McDonnell, & Seager, 2005). Most of the urban development models concentrate on sprawl as a specific form of urban development with low-density, dispersed, auto-dependent and environmentally and socially-impacting characteristics (Hasse & Lathrop, 2003).

A very important aspect when talking about urban planning and the conservation of natural resources in the area of influence of cities is represented by the legislation that regulates the territorial development and planning. The legislation in this field isn't properly standardized in the European Union so each country has its own system of regulations according to the levels of administrative units, the degree of centralization and the national, regional and local politics they promote.

Four main modalities of natural resources conservation and management in the influence areas of cities have proved effective: urban and periphery oxygen generating surfaces, green-yellow belts, regional activities parks and natural protected areas.

The objectives of this study are:

1. Assessing the importance of natural resources encountered in the influence areas of towns, and the factors affecting their balance;
2. Identifying the advantages of the main instruments used in the sustainable management of natural resources in influence areas (oxygen generating surfaces, yellow-green belts, natural protected areas and regional activities parks); and
3. Presenting solutions for an integrated management of natural resources in the influence areas of cities.

This chapter, evidencing natural resources conservation strategies using GIS techniques is structured into four sections. In the introduction, the theoretical general framework illustrates the concept of natural resources conservation. The Background section emphasize different conservation approaches, the historical trends on natural resource conservation awareness, and offer a glimpse into the use of GIS techniques in nature conservation. The main section of the chapter contains four approaches used in the natural resources conservation, with examples from the Bucharest Metropolitan Area. In the last section are presented future research areas for increasing the knowledge on the natural resources conservation – GIS techniques relation.

BACKGROUND

Scientific approaches on urban planning – ecological changes – urban development – natural resources conservation correlations were concentrated especially on the elaboration of sequential studies concerning urban planning (Ahem, Ciliers & Niemela, 2014; Ianoş, Pumain, & Racine, 2000; Newman & Thornley, 1996), modelling of urban ecosystems (Pickett et al., 2001), infrastructure of urban green spaces (Jones, Beebe, Tohme, & Galwey, 1997; Schaffler & Swilling, 2013), the role of urban parks in the sustainable development of a city (Giorgi & Dimitriou, 2010; Iojă, Pătroescu, Vânău, & Iojă, 2007), or urban forests and environmental services.

Within the broader concept of sustainable development, and considering that urban population is continually increasing world-wide, a correct use of urban planning instruments is necessary, as it integrates ecological changes, natural resource conservation and urban development. Achieving the sustainable use of natural resources has become a global issue (Smith & Zollner, 2005), and is fundamental especially in the case of large urban ecosystems which require an important amount of natural resources to properly function and exercise a great impact on the surrounding areas.

The relationship between processes specific to urbanisation and natural environments was analysed from multiple perspectives. Positive effects induced by natural elements upon the quality of urban environments are present in studies with general purpose. Of significant importance are considered green spaces as one of the factors creating an equilibrium inside cities through their ecological (air and water purification, reducing noise), social and psychological functions and services (Chiesura, 2004). As the importance of green spaces has been reassessed in the past years, it has become necessary to identify universal assessment parameters (James et al., 2009). Other approaches evidence relationships between terrestrial ecology and physical or socio-economic components of metropolitan areas (Pickett, et al., 2001; Yli-Pelkonen & Niemelä, 2005). Due to the correlation existing between urban green spaces and quality of life, methods have been developed for evaluating the role of urban green in the quality of life (Alberti, 2008; Van Leeuwen, Vreeker, & Rodenburq, 2006).

The number of studies focusing on punctual assessments of positive effects induced by natural components in urban environments is significant. The potential for noise reduction of urban green spaces is the theme of several studies (Iojă, et al., 2007; Tratalos, Fuller, Warren, Davies, & Gaston, 2007). Another direction is the analysis of aesthetical improvements of landscapes or the amelioration of the physical and psychical state of inhabitants (Fuller, Irvine, Devine-Wright, Warren, & Gaston, 2007; Grahn, 1994). Another important aspect is the manner in which ecological changes determined by urbanisation and metropolisation influence the quality of life in spaces where changes are a common problem. The conservation of natural resources in the framework of urban expansion has represented also an important target in the relationship between urban planning and environment (Allen, 2003). Biodiversity in urban and metropolitan areas represents a research theme which concerns at the same time biologists, ecologists and urban planners (Breuste, Niemelä, & Snep, 2008; Breuste, 2010; Strohbach, Haase, & Kabisch, 2009).

The conservation of natural resources is best reflected by international Conventions and legislative regulations established at national and international level. These conventions regard different aspects of natural resources, examples being the Convention on Biological Diversity, Convention on International Trade in Endangered Species of Wild Fauna and Flora, Convention on the Conservation of Migratory Species of Wild Animals, The International Treaty on Plant Genetic Resources for Food and Agriculture, Convention on Wetlands - known as the Ramsar Convention, World Heritage Convention.

The use of geographical information systems in the conservation of natural resources has been the subject of numerous studies (Beardsley, Thorne, Roth, & Gao, 2009; Jones et al., 1997; Pedersen, Nyhuus, Blindheim, & Werlgeland Krog, 2004) as an effective tool to solve the struggle of accommodating urban growth while simultaneously conserving natural resources. GIS techniques as instruments used in planning are considered as essential in order to preserve and manage natural habitats in highly pressured urban areas. Remote sensing, landscape ecological analysis and geographic information system (Yang et al., 2008) can be combined in order to develop a spatial analyzing system for resources conservation. Initially, multiple thematic paper maps (hydrological, vegetation, soil, etc.) were used but these have been replaced by RS and GIS technology, as it automates cartographic and spatial analysis functions, making the manipulation process more efficient (Barnes & Adams, 1999). GIS has become a technology, an industry and a method of completing tasks (Wikle & Finchum, 2003) as the simple structure of GIS systems (hardware, software and data) make it easy to use and the spatial analysis can reduce significantly the time and money allocated to a research activity. An important aspect of using a GIS system is choosing an adequate work scale, as a small scale can miss out punctual natural resources, or those of small dimensions, while a large scale can ignore processes and phenomena visible only as integers. Databases at different levels (global, European, national) can provide useful information in the conservation of natural resources for the sustainable development of localities. Many of these databases contain numerous free data, which can be accessed and used by researchers and planners.

Eurostat is the statistical office of the European Union providing statistic at European level useful for comparisons between different countries and regions. Eurostat (http://epp.eurostat.ec.europa.eu) offers users free access to its databases and all of its publications (Eurostat yearbooks, regional yearbooks, statistical books and also methodologies and working papers) (European Commission, 2010). OECD (Organization for Economic Co-operation and Development) – an international organization dealing with the economic, social and governance challenges of a globalised economy (OECD, 2009), has a dedicated statistic section (http://www.oecd.org/statsportal), containing dynamic maps and charts, raw data (and the possibility of expressing them graphically), indicators expressing different attributes and publications from over 24 domains, and a series of national economical projections. EUNIS (http://eunis.eea.europa.eu) represents a database created by the European Topic Centre on Biological Diversity containing a description of over 200 000 species, habitats, sites present in international conventions relevant for biodiversity. Corine (Coordination of Information on the Environment) Land Cover represents a compilation of land cover information from all the EU countries and several non-members states, with 44 land cover classes, grouped into three levels, the main level representing: artificial surfaces, agricultural areas, forests and semi-natural areas, wetlands and water bodies. The U.S. Geological Survey (http://earthexplorer.usgs.gov/) represents a 125 years old science organization which provides a large variety of cartographical materials including aerial images, satellite images, raw data for land cover, vegetation and climate analysis. The European Forest Institute offers free online databases (available at http://www.efi.int/portal/virtual_library/databases/) which contain information on different aspects of European forests, forestry and forest research. National statistic institutes can provide useful information for natural resources management. A comprehensive database of these institutes can be found at http://www.freestatistics.info/en/ along with free statistical software which can be used in manipulating data and materials explaining the main statistical concepts. Digital databases present the possibility of preserving a large volume and information and to connect them with spatial information, leading to the creation of more realistic digital images of the land. The main on-line databases, with free access, used in the management of natural resources are SRTM and GDEM (presenting a 3D image of the relief), CLC (land-uses), WORLD CLIME (climatic data which can be used for modelling the vulnerability of different natural resources to climatic risks), spatial databases for NATURA 2000 sites, etc.

NATURAL RESOURCES CONSERVATION

Oxygen generating surfaces are natural and semi-natural areas which sequester Carbon from the atmosphere and eliminate oxygen. There are two main categories of oxygen generating surfaces: green spaces and aquatic surfaces, which can be classified according to their geographical position and their usage (Pătroescu, Iojă, Necşuliu, & Brăilescu, 2004). Oxygen generating surfaces can be found inside the built-up perimeter (parks, public gardens, squares, graveyards, street alignments, fountains, urban lakes, rivers) and in the influence areas of cities (forests, leisure facilities, plantations, lakes, rivers). Urban green spaces present a large variety of forms, from areas of indigenous vegetation to formal urban parks (Gill, Waitt, & Head, 2009). According to their usage, they can be accessible to all visitors (parks, recreation zones, urban lakes), of limited access (green spaces and fountains around institutions, private gardens and pools) and with a specialised profile (botanical gardens, protective plantations, stock ponds). Scientific researchers and urban planners are increasingly using landscape ecology principles to develop green spaces, better their connectivity and restore biodiversity (Konga, Yin, Nakagoshi, & Zong, 2010). Oxygen generating surfaces reduce the impact of carbon emissions, remove air pollutants and reduce noise, contributing to an improvement of environmental quality (Jim & Chen, 2009).

Aquatic ecosystems and urban forests are a valuable resource for the urban environment as they represent natural or semi-natural ecosystems located in an anthropic landscape. The management and conservation efficiency of natural resources in oxygen generating surfaces depend on their surface and number, their location and their degree of connectivity. In addition, an important part is played by the ecosystems health state, which can influence the success of management and conservation measures. Efficiency assessments are realised using a set of parameters, measured at regular intervals, values being compared with the initial state and the targets set in documents at local, regional or national level, international conventions or national legislation.

Communist cities are characterized by a centralized development for which land price doesn't represent a factor of restrictiveness or favourability. Land-uses were strictly controlled, especially as most of the land was public property. Spaces with forests and other types of vegetation, aquatic surfaces or agricultural fields were mostly protected as state property. Forests from the influence areas of large cities were considered extremely important, as it was in the case of Moscow, Budapest, Bucharest or Prague.

In Bucharest's urban development, the transition to the capitalist era determined an expansion directed on certain axes, according to land prices. Suburban areas, characterized by lower land prices, are therefore in the post-communist era the main areas of insertion for new residential projects. Areas with forests or water bodies were mainly affected by urban development, as they were considered extremely attractive for residential projects. The fragmentation of oxygen generating surfaces in the influence area of post-communist cities is present in numerous studies (Boentje & Blinnikov, 2007; Hirt & Kovachev, 2006; Pătroescu, Niţă, Iojă, & Vânău, 2009; Sykora & Ourednícekin, 2007).

In the Bucharest Metropolitan Area, the forests have diminished very much in surface in the last century. One of the best examples of forest surface diminution recorded in the post-communist era in the metropolitan area of Bucharest is encountered in the north-east of the city, where the residential development accompanied by services has driven to an important loss of natural habitat (ex: Voluntari administrative unit – Figure 2). In the case of Bucharest we can't speak of urban forest, as most of the forests are peri-urban and therefore included in the green-yellow belt. Another land-use highly affected by the transition from the consumption patterns characterizing a centralized economy

Figure 2. Residential and services expansion in Voluntari administrative unit (north-east of Bucharest)

to those specific to a market based one is represented by agricultural areas. They have drastically diminished in the area of influence of Bucharest as a result of the urban development due to the proximity to the biggest and most dynamic urban centre in the country and to the politics applied at national and local level which favoured the fragmentation of agricultural surfaces.

Green-Yellow Belts

Osborn (1969, p. 182) defined Green Belts as being "a narrow strip of parkland more or less encircling part of a built-up metropolitan or large urban area". The concept of Green Belt emerged in Britain, where the separation between town and countryside by Green Belts has been a central tendency in planning in the second part of the 20th century, but similar concepts can be encountered in many European (Berlin, Vienna, Barcelona), American (Washington, Chicago) and Asian (Seoul, Tokyo) cities. The "green belt" concept was used to settle the competition between urban and rural land uses and activities by creating a protective "garden" against urban expansion, but also to serve as an area for agriculture and recreation (Gant, Robinson, & Faza, 2011). For areas in which agricultural land uses prevail in the proximity of urban centres, the concept of "green-yellow belts" was introduced, expressing the variety of vegetation cover and town planning conservation easements on agricultural land around the city. In some cases, these belts were viewed initially as passive recreation spaces; subsequently they become residual development spaces, and nowadays are perceived as conservation spaces (Tang, Wong, & Lee, 2007).

Initially Green Yellow Belts had three main purposes: controlling the spread of urban development, preventing neighbouring towns from merging with the central city, and preserving their special characters (Amati, 2008). Subsequently, new objectives were added, such as safeguarding the countryside from encroachment, providing opportunities for outdoor recreation and sport to the population from urban areas, enhancing landscape values, to retain a certain type of land use (agricultural, forestry) and to secure nature conservation interest. The preservation of intact habitats for different biological communities is considered by some authors (Primack, Pătroescu, Rozylowicz, & Iojă, 2008) to be the most efficient way of protecting and sustainable using resources. A model of Metropolitan Green Belt is London, which was first proposed by the Greater London Regional Planning Committee in 1935. After the Town and Country Planning Act from 1947, the Government proposed policies and principles for the development of belts, with general provisions against inappropriate development, unless it can be demonstrated that development will bring more benefits to local communities that the harm caused to the green belts. In France, the Green Belt of Ile-de-France is considered to be representative for regional actions concentrated on protecting the environment. It combines the urban development of Paris and the other five towns, as well as the Roissy cluster, with the preservation of open spaces from the countryside ("campaign").

The effectiveness of the Green belt policies will be dependent on the spatial organization and functions adopted in the Regional Master Plan of the regions, on the partnership between institutions and landowners. In many cases these belts can be eroded by components of the urban-rural fringe. In other cases, urban development doesn't find an obstacle in them, and even though the belts aren't destroyed, they are "jumped", and development continues in the influence areas of cities. By their role of preventing urban sprawl, and therefore the expansion of urban environments in areas with natural resources, green-yellow belts represent an excellent manner of safeguarding land for recreation, forestry or agriculture, although in some places, areas of the green belt have suffered through illegal dumping or through inadequate management measures (Amati, 2008).

In the case of Bucharest, the yellow green belt encircles the capital starting from its outer limits on a radius of approximately 20 km (Figure 3). The yellow green belt includes also numerous protected areas, especially from the North area where it contrasts with the objectives of three new emerging cities (Buftea, Otopeni, and Voluntari). The municipality of Bucharest has a project of planting large surfaces of trees in seven villages encircling the capital adding to the already existing peri-urban forests to generate a new green belt. The existence and characteristics of the yellow green belt aren't regulated through a legislative act in the case of Bucharest, this being the main reason for the problems affecting this structure and its functionality. In other countries, like the United Kingdom where the green-yellow belt is included through the modern planning guidelines promoted by the Town and Country Planning Act and its updated versions, the efficacy of this instrument in conserving natural resources is highly improved.

Regional activities parks represent a sustainable instrument in the management and conservation of natural resources. The structure of regional activities parks consists of a number of villages with certain territorial cohesion, presenting important natural and human resources, together with a natural and cultural patrimony (Pătroescu, Dragomirescu, Iojă, & Niţă, 2008). In this concept, development is based on the existing potential and voluntary cooperation relationships between the territorial administrative units.

The prime role of the regional activities parks is to induce organization and a new sustainable development model in the influence areas of cities. Concepts like "urban region" and "urban landscape" (Kühn, 1999) have gained much weight in the last few decades because of the explosive urban sprawl that converted large surfaces of traditional landscape in an urban characteristic one. (Sieverts, 1999) has proposed the term "in-between city" for these areas which although being rural through economic pattern and standard of living, have important insertions of urban landscape. Although regional

Figure 3. Green Yellow Belt in the metropolitan area of Bucharest
(Adapted from Intergraph (2006)).

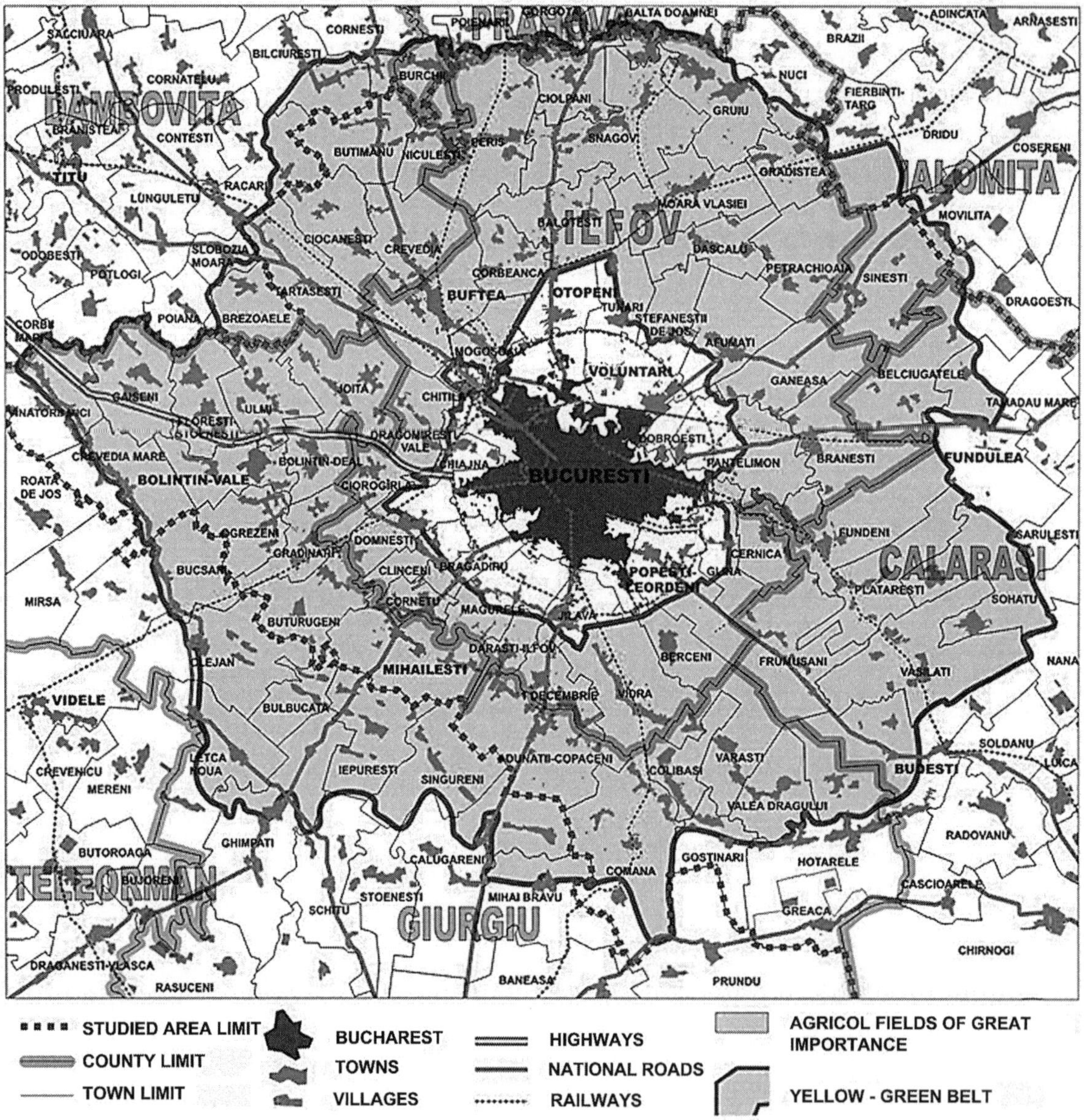

activities parks aim to protect landscapes qualities, this doesn't necessary require the establishment of new conservation areas. Regional activities parks don't extract areas from the economic circuit but promote a sustainable economic development by creating a balance between the usage and the preservation of natural resources.

The efficiency of regional activities parks is determined by the degree of cooperation that exists between different local actors (from residents to local and regional authorities). If this cooperation is non-existent, or of little importance, the regional activities parks are not serving their purpose. Also, between two regional activities parks found at the same level of implementation, the one corresponding to a bigger city will have an increased efficiency because of the number of persons that beneficiate of its services. The efficiency of regional activities parks is measured through the sustainability of the component areas and can be quantified through different indicators.

An example of using regional parks in the management of natural resources is represented by the case of Berlin and Brandenburg (Germany) which recognised in the 90's the necessity of co-ordinated planning as an instrument of fighting against the unplanned sprawl deteriorating natural resources (Gotting-Frosinki & Grigoleit, 2000). These "regional parks" promoted planning measures with success, as the measures were better supported by the citizens, who considered themselves not only participants, but also actors able to take initiative in the processes. Among these are the Regional Parks from Berlin and Brandenburg (Gemeinsame Landesplanung Berlin und Brandenburg, 2001), Saar Regional Park (Hartz, 2006), Rheine-Main Regional Park (Rautenstrauch, 1995), Emscher Landscape Park. Outside Germany, the term "regional park" often applies to areas which in Germany are referred to as "nature parks" (e.g., the parcs naturels régionaux in France and the parchi regionali in Italy). But the basis for comparison and mutual learning processes is provided by urban-regional development strategies like the "green belts" in English urban agglomerations and the Randstad "Green Heart" in the Netherlands.

In the Bucharest Metropolitan Area (Romania), 7 regional activities parks were identified, named after their most important locality: Bolintin, Braneşti, Budeşti, Buftea, Comana, Mihaileşti and Snagov-Vlasia (Figure 4). These regional activities parks were delimited in order to ensure their relative homogeneity which will involve an adequate function, following diverse criteria, such as: possibilities and capacity of villages association to implement the sustainable development programs and access the European Union structural funds in the period 2007-2013 and afterwards; relative balance of economic activities, land use and human resource qualification; accessibility to Bucharest's transport and services infrastructure; common needs of human and quality of life development; harmonizing interests in the sustainable management of protected areas; relative homogeny or complementary tourism potential.

Regional Activities Parks in Bucharest's metropolitan area need to be effective, not only at project level, because they represent convergence spaces in economic and social development, opportunities for public – private partnerships in the management of natural patrimony and favourable settings for establishing national and international plans and projects.

Natural Protected Areas

A dynamic urban area represents a real threat to biodiversity, and therefore is necessary to develop strategic approaches to conservation planning in urban environments and their influence areas, based on clear principles which require understanding of development pressures, landscape patterns and species requirements (Gordon, Simondson, White, Moilanen, & Bekessy, 2009). For better results in the influence areas of cities a systematic conservation planning must be used (Margules & Pressey, 2000) consisting of a suite of methods used to determine, implement and manage a number of areas in which conservation can be achieved with a minimum expenditure of monetary and human resources. The establishment of natural protected areas has as the main purpose the protection and conservation of biological diversity, corroborated with the associated natural and cultural resources preservation, through legal or other means (IUCN, 1994). Natural protected areas are classified into six categories, based on the degree of human intervention in the habitats. Their enforcement is an efficient mechanism in maintaining terrains and resources in good condition (Bruner, Gullison, Rice, & da Fonseca, 2001). Rational exploitation of natural resources

Figure 4. Regional activities parks in the Bucharest Metropolitan Area

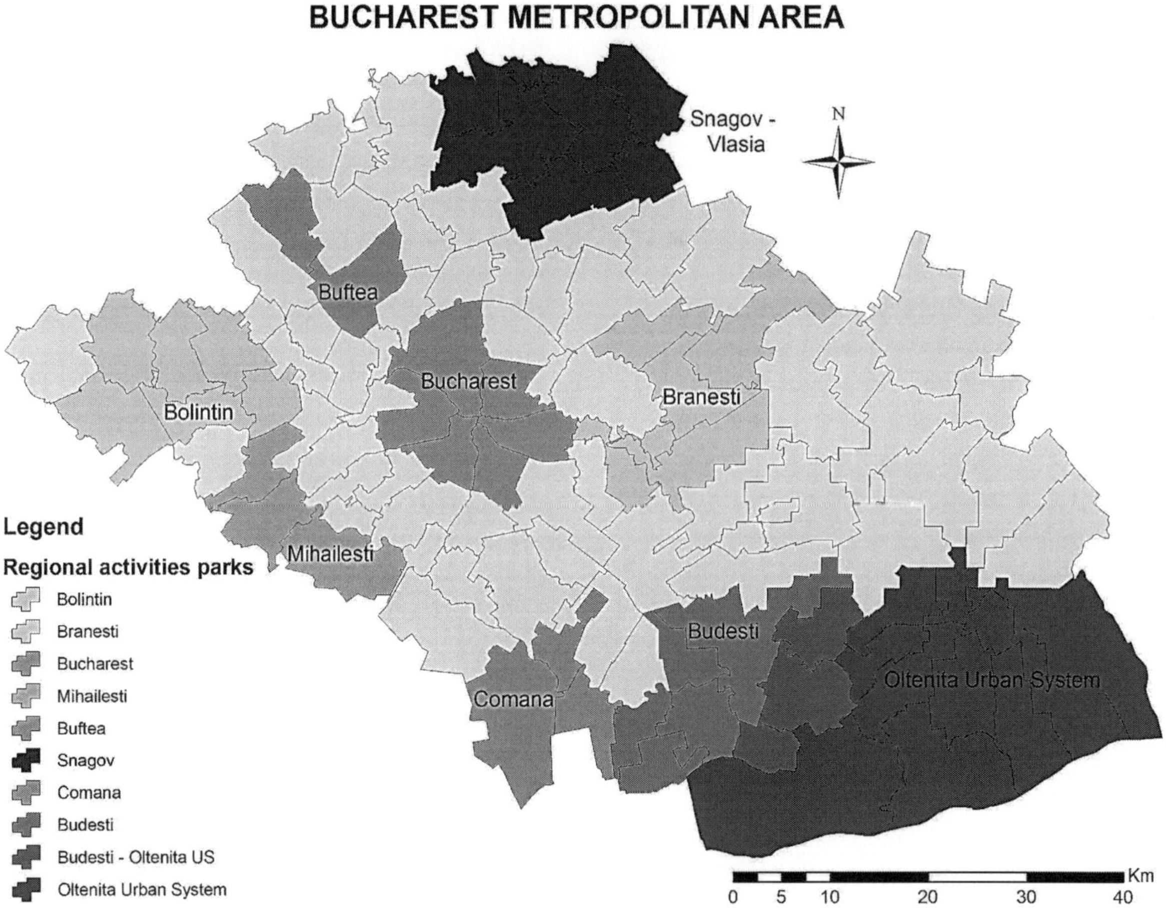

reveals the efficiency of natural protected areas administration (Primack, et al., 2008), which is based on the establishment and enforcement of a long-term and viable management plan, including specific conservation and valorisation actions. The main problems of protected areas in human dominated landscapes arise from political pressure for development, the high economic value of land, the fragmentation of parcels and the priority of creating recreation areas.

An important instrument in the sustainable use of natural resources is the Natura 2000 network, as it is the cornerstone of conservation politics within the European Union. The network includes SPA - Special Protected Areas, (79/409/EEC, 1979) and SCI - Sites of Community Importance (92/43/EEC, 1992), transformed after the letter of advice from the European Commission in SAC (Special Areas of Conservation) (European Commission, 2009). The enforcement of the Natura 2000 network appeared as a necessity in fulfilling the objectives of reducing species and habitats loss (Pullin et al., 2009). However, the vision of the Natura 2000 network as a social rather than ecological network limits its potential for conserving biodiversity to its full potential (Iojă et al., 2010). Results of studies effectuated in the past years show that the establishment of new protected areas hinders the development of residential spaces (Kramer & Doran, 2008), with major effect on the population number (Wittemyer, Elsen, Bean, Burton, & Brashare, 2008) and on the environmental components. Establishing protected areas in the influence areas of cities, where the real estate market is well developed, determines land prices to increase, especially for residential spaces (Armsworth, Dally, Karelva, & Sanchirico, 2006). The existence of protected areas can also influence negatively local communities, as they lose certain facilities and their access to natural resources (Wittemyer, et al., 2008). For some rural spaces, the establishment of protected areas facilitates the access to roads, generates work places and offer the possibility of accessing European financed projects. In developed countries, the emphasis is situated on the agreement value of protected areas (Kramer & Doran, 2010). The complexity of nature determines a difficulty in conservation assessment of ecological communities and in projects regarding the impacts of different management scenarios in natural protected areas (Beissinger & Westphal, 1998).

For example, the protected areas network of the Bucharest Metropolitan Area (Figure 5) consists of one natural park (Comana), five natural reserves, as well as five Sites of Communitarian Importance (SCI): Scroviştea (ROSCI0224), Padurea Bolintin (ROSCI0138), Lunca Mijlocie a Argeşului (ROSCI0106), Comana (ROSCI0043), Olteniţa- Mostiştea- Chiciu (ROSCI0131) and four Special Protection Areas (SPA): Gradiştea-Caldaruşani- Dridu (ROSPA0044), Comana (ROSPA0022), Valea Mostiştea (ROSPA0105) şi Dunare- Olteniţa (ROSPA0038). The existence in the Bucharest Metropolitan Area of important natural reserves (Ciornuleasa Forest, Snagov Forest, Snagov Lake, etc.), determined a land prices

Figure 5. Spatial distribution of protected areas categories in the Bucharest Metropolitan Area, Romania

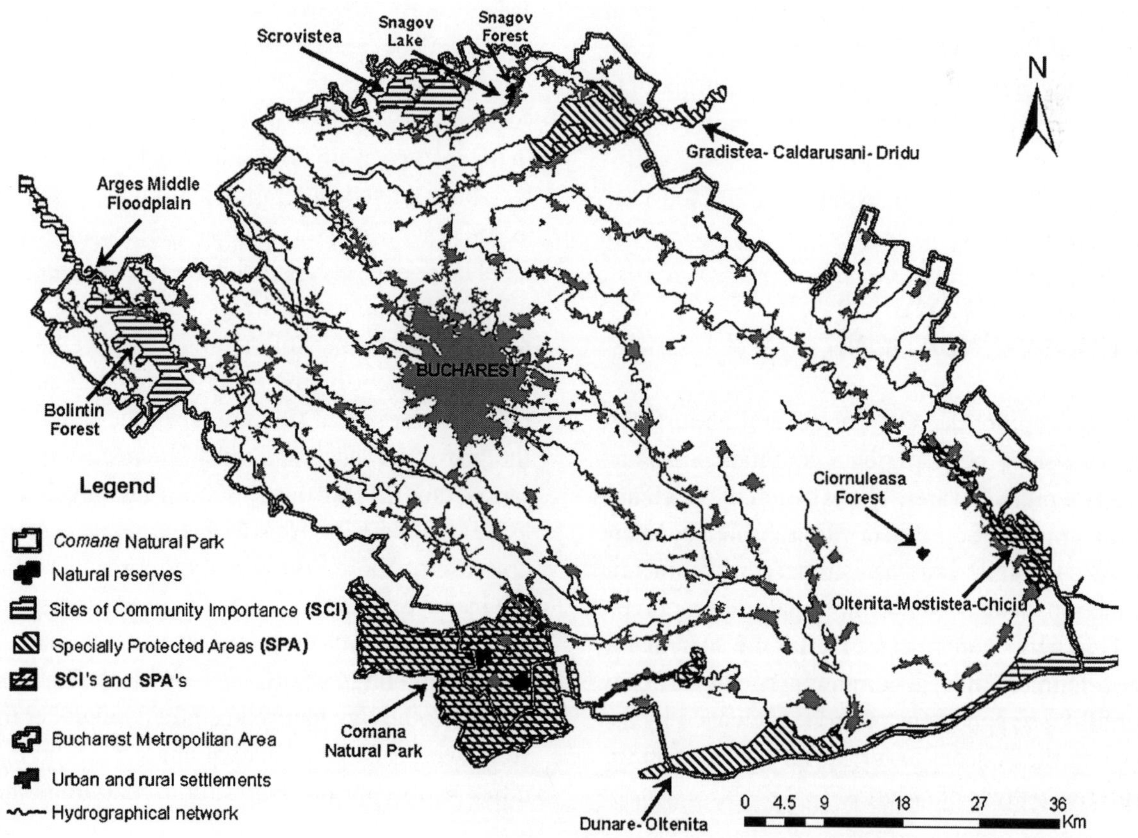

Table 1. Modalities of natural resources conservation in the influence areas of cities

	Oxygen Generating Surfaces	Green Yellow Belts	Regional Activities Parks	Natural Protected Areas
Position	Inside the city and in the influence area	Surrounding the city or parts of it	In the influence area	In the influence area
Natural resources	• Biotic (vegetation, fauna) • Water • Air	• Biotic (vegetation, fauna) • Air	• Mineral resources • Ecosystems • Soils • Land use	• Biotic (vegetation, fauna) • Water • Soil • Mineral Resources
Administrative status	Municipality land owners	Municipality land owners	Voluntary co-operation of localities	Administrations of the areas
Environmental function	• Improving air quality • Biodiversity conservation	• Biodiversity conservation • Improving air quality	Sustainable use of resources	Biodiversity conservation
Economical function	Increasing the value of properties	Increasing the value of properties	• Promoting local economy • Traditional products	• Recreational activities • Traditional products

increase and an explosion of residential spaces, generating a high pressure upon biodiversity and other environmental components. Another pole of attraction is the Comana Natural Park, where economical activities are perceived different by local communities from proximity. Natural protected areas from the Bucharest Metropolitan Area are redistributed at periphery and have an important touristic function, especially for Bucharest inhabitants, but also for foreign tourists.

SOLUTIONS AND RECOMMENDATIONS

The four approaches (oxygen generating surfaces, green yellow belts, regional activities parks and natural protected areas) have different efficiency in natural resources conservation and management (Table 1). While some have stronger environmental functions and conserve more natural resources, others may be more effective for the sustainable development of local communities. The efficacy of all these approaches may be increased by applying the concept of territorial cohesion in the influence areas of cities.

Large scale land-use planning usually requires the development of certain alternative management scenarios for the future use of resources in a long period of time (Smith & Zollner, 2005), scenarios varying from a “no action” alternative to one which poses a strong emphasis on provision of goods and services for the urban environment. Areas with restriction in the use of space situated in the influence areas of cities can be determined by taking into consideration natural factors (such as areas with marshes, lands affected by suffusion, landslides etc., which have been avoided by urban development in the first phases, but as the need for space became stronger were included in development plans) or by factors induced by urban development (including spaces situated in the proximity, such as industrial spaces, animal farms, landfills, airports, nuclear facilities etc.).

Urban planning tries to integrate the sustainable use of these conservation approaches with the increasing requirements of human society, as population density, the proximity of roads, markets and urban centres are driving forces in the land-use changes affecting natural resources, all under the framework of current global changes. Although cities evolve in varying natural conditions and under the pressure of different social factors (the cultural level of resident population), presently there is a tendency towards uniformity in planning, favoured by the explosion of information, with original solutions which rapidly become norms if they are proved efficient. Subsequently, material elements generated by the human pressure, respectively infrastructure and supra-structure or human actions effects upon environmental components, are increasing among the factors which condition urban planning (Nijkamp, 2008).

Besides natural conditions, which remain a central element of the planning process, in the case of ex-communist cities a large and various spectre of particular socio-economical and historical characteristics, express in the cities' morphology and mentality of inhabitants. Certain factors with role in urban planning can be identified for the large cities of Central and Eastern Europe, such as Bucharest: residential buildings of large dimension (blocks) with high constructions and population density and low density of green spaces, commercial units and parking places; the recent development of logistic and commercial spaces located on former industrial platforms, with a central or peripheral position; a more centralized administrative structure (Koch, 2006; Rufat & Suditu, 2008). Smaller cities suffered more dramatic changes, by orientation towards new economical activities (industry, tourism, services), or by involution (as a result of the disappearance of the centralized economical system). These processes introduce new premises in the planning process of the respective city. Globalization imposes to cities a competition for attracting resources and identifying means of economical performance (Newman & Thornley, 1996). Environmental services offered by oxygen generating surfaces (Pătroescu & Iojă, 2004) from the inner city and peri-urban area (Forest, Konijnendijk, & Randrup, 1999), as well as natural protected areas and regional activities parks (Pătroescu et al., 2008) should be studied in their spatial dynamics and temporal diversity. In post communist countries such as Romania, the expansion of industrial surfaces was followed by their restructuration (Ianoş, 2004) and by a residential expansion (Pătroescu et al., 2009) which generated major ecological changes. The metropolisation of large cities, especially in post communist capitals, induced a spatial re-organisation inclusively for the polarised towns from the influence area. The creation of metropolitan areas, valid form a juridical and administrative point of view is very beneficial for the conservation of natural resources since it provides the legal framework in order to apply and obtain European funds directed to sustainable development, conservation and research.

Trying to integrate sustainable urban development with natural resources conservation in relation with all the above problems can be addressed using various GIS techniques, which allow complex analyses and present expert based solutions.

GIS techniques allow the use of models which cover deficiencies in spatial and temporal data and thus the realisation of thematic maps as well as future evolution scenarios. They can facilitate the correlation of several parameters, generating complex analyses. This is the case of maps revealing the exposure to different natural risks, resulting susceptibility maps, vulnerability maps, or maps with different land-use restrictions. Using GIS techniques, land planners can have a simultaneous view of multiple attributes (land-use, patch size and shape, water courses, transportation infrastructure, housing, economical activities) and explore the existing spatial relationships between them. Also, in the analysis process can be introduced specific objectives of management, which will prevail in front of other planning activities.

Among the methods used in analysing natural resources distribution and their management are the spatio-temporal interpolation, which estimates the unknown values at un-sampled locations (Li & Revesz, 2004), revealing a more correct distribution of natural resources in the territory, the spatial proximity analysis, deriving the probability of urban growth towards natural resources by using the distance to transportation and existing built-up areas, land-use change trajectory analysis, revealing the probability of transformations from a natural and semi-natural land-use category into a urban one, multivariate spatial models integrating numerous variables and deriving an overall probability for a certain query.

The components of a strategic management system using GIS techniques can be separated on three levels: land management, patrimony management and environmental management (Marull, Pino, Mallarach, & Cordobilla, 2007). These levels can be transposed in GIS by using a series of indexes and quantitative measurements. Per example, Land management can be expressed through a Land vulnerability index (calculated from the vegetation, substratum and hydrological vulnerability); Patrimony management could consist of a Natural patrimony index, determined as a synthetic result from landscape metrics; Environmental management can be expressed through the Ecological connectivity index, having as main determinant ecosystem services.

Another approach evaluates the input parameters which are necessary in the integrated analyse of natural resources management (Figure 6). In this case, the input could be maps representing vegetation, soil, water, mineral resources, and land use. From these maps are extracted natural resources and terrain complexity. An ancillary database is used (representing roads, railroads and settlements) for the analyse level.

GIS techniques can develop a spatially explicit urban growth model to project seven different growth scenarios that represent a range of public policies (Beardsley et al., 2009) and the impact of each projected urban growth output can be compared with layers representing resources which require conservation.

When GIS analyses use as input information extracted from international databases a high level of generalization is generated, thus eliminating local particularities. On the other hand, by using data generated at local level a detailed analysis is obtained which can better identify factors influencing the management and use of natural resources at local level. GIS techniques represent a useful instrument in identifying spaces with land use restrictions and spaces with functional incompatibilities; in establishing safety areas around natural resources sites according to relief, climate, hydrological conditions; planning green-yellow

Figure 6. Integrated management of natural resources using GIS

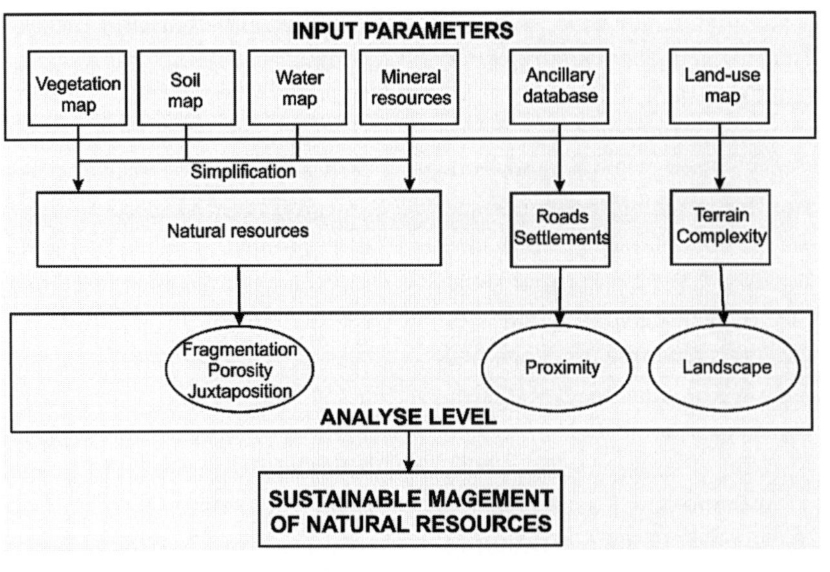

belts to maximize their efficiency regarding the sanitary-ecologic, protective and aesthetic role; designing different urban functions while maintaining a territorial equilibrium. The main barrier of using GIS techniques in the management of natural resources is represented the large volume of work necessary for creating a local database with a suitable detail level, which can present realistic and optimal solutions in resources conservation and sustainable territorial management.

International databases presented in the Background section have the benefit of the uniform methodology used in their development, regardless of national particularities. Therefore, they can be used in comparison studies, but also as basis layers in developing national and regional databases. The main data can be represented by Landsat or Ikonos satellite images, SRTM and GDEM for relief features, CLC in the case of land use, World Clime or spatial databases for the NATURA 2000 network, which can be complementary used.

FUTURE RESEARCH DIRECTIONS

In the framework of present urban development the necessity for a detailed analyse of the modalities in which natural resources conservation and management can be realised, as they represent support for a certain lifestyle. The present chapter illustrates a few solutions used in natural resources management (oxygen generating surfaces, yellow-green belts, regional activities parks, natural protected areas) and analyses their role and efficiency in the current scientific and urban planning framework. An increase of awareness for local authorities and public would be necessary for an efficient application of these concepts into the effective urban planning. A large number of programs can be developed having as objectives natural resources management and conservation in different areas. Detailed studies of natural resources distribution in the influence areas of cities, or in the inner city, are necessary as a first step in projects aimed at generating equilibrium between environmental components and human pressure.

Future studies could concentrate on a holistic approach of the relationship between urban planning (as a determinant of urban development) and natural resources or ecological changes, rather than the present sequential approaches. GIS techniques represent useful tools in the decision-making process, increasing efficiency and effectiveness, by their capacity of comprehension and integration of large data volumes.

CONCLUSION

The accelerated urbanisation, which characterised the last decades of the previous century and the beginning of the present one, had an obvious impact upon natural resources from the cities influence areas. The integration of natural habitats in the urban space and the adaptation of species used in parks and public gardens apparently maintained large values for the biodiversity index, but that was not due to sustainable urban planning, neither had the purpose of conserving natural resources or preserving an equilibrium between components of the initial ecosystems in which the city developed. In order to preserve the natural resources in the influence areas of cities the local, regional and national authorities should encourage the implementation of the optimum approaches and better regulate the aspects related with territorial planning. Because of their efficiency and ease of use, the suitability and general availability of data, GIS techniques could be used in all regions where landscapes are affected negatively by urban development.

ACKNOWLEDGMENT

We would like to thank the editor, and two anonymous reviewers for their suggestions which significantly improved the quality of the chapter.

REFERENCES

79/409/EEC. (1979). *Council Directive 79/409/EEC of 2 April 1979 on the conservation of wild birds*. (Vol. 79/409/EEC): Official Journal L 103, 25/04/1979.

92/43/EEC. (1992). *Council Directive 92/43/EEC of 21 May 1992 on the conservation of natural habitats and of wild fauna and flora*. (Vol. 92/43/EEC): Official Journal of E.U., L 206, 22.7.1992.

Ahern, J., Cilliers, S., & Niemelä, J. (2014). The concept of ecosystem services in adaptive urban planning and design: A framework for supporting innovation. *Landscape and Urban Planning*, *125*(0), 254–259.

Alberti, M. (2008). *Advances in Urban Ecology. Integrating Humans and Ecological Processes in Urban Ecosystems*. New York, NY: Springer.

Allen, A. (2003). Environmental planning and management of the peri-urban interface: Perspectives on an emerging field. *Environment and Urbanization*, *15*(1), 135–147.

Amati, M. (2008). *Urban Green Belts in the Twenty-first Century*. Sydney, Australia: Ashgate.

Armsworth, P. R., Dally, G. C., Karelva, P., & Sanchirico, J. N. (2006). Land market feedbacks can undermine biodiversity conservation. *The National Academy of Sciences of the SUA*, *103*(14), 5403–5408.

Barnes, T. G., & Adams, L. (1999). *A guide to Urban Habitat Conservation Planning*. Lexington, KY: University of Kentucky. Retrieved from College of Agriculture; http://www.ca.uky.edu/agc/pubs/for/for74/for74.htm

Beardsley, K., Thorne, J. H., Roth, N. E., & Gao, S. (2009). Assessing the influence of rapid urban growth and regional policies on biological resources. *Landscape and Urban Planning*, *93*(3-4), 172–183.

Beissinger, S. R., & Westphal, M. I. (1998). On the use of demographic models of population viability in endangered species management. *The Journal of Wildlife Management*, *62*(3), 821–841.

Boentje, J. P., & Blinnikov, M. S. (2007). Post-Soviet forest fragmentation and loss in the Green Belt around Moscow, Russia (1991–2001): A remote sensing perspective. *Landscape and Urban Planning*, *82*(4), 208–221.

Breuste, J., Niemelä, J., & Snep, R. P. H. (2008). Applying landscape ecological principles in urban environments. *Landscape Ecology*, *23*(10), 1139–1142.

Breuste, J. H. (2010). Allotment Gardens as Part of Urban Green Infrastructure: Actual Trends and Perspectives. In N. Müller, P. Werner, & J. G. Kelcey (Eds.), *Central Europe. Urban Biodiversity and Design*. Oxford, UK: Wiley-Blackwell.

Bruner, A. G., Gullison, R. E., Rice, R. E., & da Fonseca, G. A. B. (2001). Effectiveness of parks in protecting tropical biodiversity. *Science*, *291*(5501), 125–128.

Chiesura, A. (2004). The role of urban parks for the sustainable city. *Landscape and Urban Planning*, *68*(4), 129–138.

Cogălniceanu, D. (1999). *Managementul capitalului natural*. Bucureşti: Ars Docendi.

Costanza, R., d'Arge, R., de Groot, R., Farber, S., Grasso, M., Hannon, B., & van den Belt, M. et al. (1997, May). The value of the world's ecosystem services and natural capital. *Nature*, *387*, 253–260.

Duvigneaud, P. (1974). *La synthèse écologique*. Paris, France: Doin.

European Commission. (2009). *Natura 2000 barometer - December 2008*. Natura 2000. European Commission DG ENV Nature Newletter, 8-9.

European Commission. (2010). *Europe in figures - Eurostat yearbook 2010*. Luxembourg: Publications Office of the European Union.

Forest, M., Konijnendijk, C. C., & Randrup, T. B. (Eds.). (1999). *COST action E12 research and development in urban forestry in Europe*. Luxembourg: Office for Official Publications of the European Communities.

Fuller, R. A., Irvine, K. N., Devine-Wright, P., Warren, P. H., & Gaston, K. J. (2007). Psychological benefits of greenspace increase with biodiversity. *Biology Letters*, *3*(4), 390–394.

Gant, R., Robinson, G., & Faza, S. (2011). Land-use change in the 'edgelands': Policies and pressures in London's rural–urban fringe. *Land Use Policy*, *28*(1), 266–279.

Gemeinsame Landesplanung Berlin und Brandenburg. (2001). *Regionalparks in Brandenburg und Berlin*. Potsdam: Ministerium für Landwirtschaft. Umweltschutz und Raumordnung des Landes Brandenburg/Senatsverwaltung für Stadtentwicklung des Landes Berlin.

Georgi, J. N., & Dimitriou, D. (2010). The contribution of urban green spaces to the improvement of environment in cities: Case study of Chania, Greece. *Building and Environment*, *45*(6), 1401–1414.

Gill, N., Waitt, G., & Head, L. (2009). Local engagements with urban bushland: Moving beyond bounded practice for urban biodiversity management. *Landscape and Urban Planning*, *93*(3-4), 184–193.

Gordon, A., Simondson, D., White, M., Moilanen, A., & Bekessy, S. (2009). Integrating conservation planning and landuse planning in urban landscapes. *Landscape and Urban Planning*, *91*(4), 183–194.

Gotting-Frosinki, J., & Grigoleit, B. (Eds.). (2000). *Regionalparks in Brandenburg and Berlin – Strategies for Sustainable Development in the Metropolitan Area*. Berlin, Germany: Saladruck.

Grahn, P. (1994). Green structures—the importance for health of nature areas and parks. *European Regional Planning*, *56*, 89–112.

Hartz, A. (2006). Der Regionalpark Saar – Zwischenbilanz, Projekte, Masterplan. In Ministerium für Umwelt des Saarlandes (MfU), Akademie für Raumforschung und Landesplanung (ARL), & LAG-Hessen/Rheinland-Pfalz/Saarland (Eds.), Kooperation als Erfolgsfaktor für Regionen im Wandel (pp. 42-45). Saarbrücken.

Hasse, J. E., & Lathrop, R. G. (2003). Land resource impact indicators of urban sprawl. *Applied Geography (Sevenoaks, England)*, *23*(2-3), 159–175.

Hirt, S., & Kovachev, A. (2006). The changing spatial structure of post-socialist Sofia. In S. Tsenkova & Z. Nedović-Budić (Eds.), *The Urban Mosaic of Post-Socialist Europe, Contributions to Economics, Part II* (pp. 113–130). Heidelberg, Germany & New York, NY: Physica-Verlag.

Ianoş, I. (2004). *Dinamica urbană. Aplicaţii la oraşul şi sistemul urban românesc*. Bucureşti: Tehnică.

Ianoş, I., Pumain, D., & Racine, J. B. (Eds.). (2000). *Integrated Urban Systems and Sustainability of Urban Life*. Bucureşti, Romania: Editura Tehnică.

Intergraph. (2006). P.A.T.Z.-Zona Aglomeratiei Urbane si Zona Metropolitana ale Municipiului Bucuresti.

Iojă, I. C., Pătroescu, M., Rozylowicz, L., Popescu, D. V., Vergheleţ, M., Zotta, M. I., & Felciuc, M. (2010). The efficacy of Romania's protected areas network in conserving biodiversity. *Biological Conservation*, *143*(11), 2468–2476.

Iojă, I. C., Pătroescu, M., Vânău, G., & Iojă, A. (2007). Noise pollution in Bucharest urban parks. Paper presented at the SECOTOX Conference and the International Conference on Environemental Management, Engineering, Planning and Economics (CEMEPE), Salonic.

IUCN. (1994). *Guidelines for Protected Area Management Categories*. Gland, Switzerland: IUCN.

James, P., Tzoulas, K., Adams, M. D., Barber, A., Box, J., Breuste, J., & Ward Thompsons, C. et al. (2009). Towards an integrated understanding of green space in the European built environment. *Urban Forestry & Urban Greening*, *8*(2), 65–75.

Jim, C., & Chen, W. (2009). Ecosystem services and valuation of urban forests in China. *Cities (London, England)*, *26*(4), 187–196.

Jones, P. G., Beebe, S. E., Tohme, J., & Galwey, N. W. (1997). The use of geographical information systems in biodiversity exploration and conservation. *Biodiversity and Conservation*, *6*(7), 947–958.

Koch, F. (2006). Housing markets and urban regimes – The case of Warsaw. In F. Eckardt & I. Elander (Eds.), *Urban Governance. Future Urban Research in Europe*. Berlin, Germany: Berliner Wissenschaftsverlag.

Konga, F., Yin, H., Nakagoshi, N., & Zong, Y. (2010). Urban green space network development for biodiversity conservation: Identification based on graph theory and gravity modelling. *Landscape and Urban Planning*, *95*(1-2), 16–27.

Kramer, D., & Doran, P. (2008). Protected area establishment and the endogenous effect of residential. Paper presented at the the annual meeting of the International Congress for Conservation Biology, Convention Center. Chattanooga, TN.

Kramer, D., & Doran, P. (2010). Land conversion at the protected area's edge. *Conservation Letters*, *3*(5), 349–358.

Kühn, M. (1999). Kulturlandschaften zwischen Schutz und Nutzung. Modellhafte Planungsansätze einer nachhaltigen Freiraum- und Landschaftsentwicklung. REGIO Beiträge des IRS, 14.

Li, L., & Revesz, P. (2004). Interpolation methods for spatio-temporal geographic data. *Computers, Environment and Urban Systems*, *28*(3), 201–227.

Margules, C. R., & Pressey, R. L. (2000). Systematic conservation planning. *Nature*, *405*(6783), 243–253.

Marull, J., Pino, J., Mallarach, J. M., & Cordobilla, M. J. (2007). A Land Suitability Index for Strategic Environmental Assessment in metropolitan areas. *Landscape and Urban Planning*, *81*(3), 200–212.

Newman, P., & Thornley, A. (1996). *Urban planning in Europe: international competition, national systems, and planning projects*. London: Routledge.

Nijkamp, P. (2008). XXQ factors for sustainable urban development: A systems economics view. *Roumanian Journal of Regional Science*, *2*(1), 1–34.

Odum, E. P. (1971). Fundamental of ecology (Third Edition). Philadelphia, London, & Toronto: W. B. Saunders.

OECD. (2009). *Annual Report 2009*. Paris, France: OECD.

Olewiler, N. (2006). Sustainability for urban areas: The role of natural capital indicators. *Cities (London, England)*, *23*(3), 184–195.

Osborn, F. J. (1969). *Green Belt Cities*. London: Evelyn, Adams & Mackay.

Pătroescu, M., Dragomirescu, Ş., Iojă, I. C., & Niţă, M. R. (2008). Regional activities parks – partenership opportunities in environmental protection. *Present Environment and Sustainable Development*, *1*(1), 71–81.

Pătroescu, M., & Iojă, C. (2004). The role of the parks in Bucharest city ecosystem. Paper presented at the Lucrarile simpozionului Dimitrie Cantemir 25.

Pătroescu, M., Iojă, C., Necşuliu, R., & Brăilescu, C. (2004). The quality of oxygenating surfaces. The green areas of Bucharest. A case studies. *Revue Roumaine de Geographie*, *47-48*, 205–216.

Pătroescu, M., Niţă, M. R., Iojă, I. C., & Vânău, G. (2009). New residential areas in Bucharest Metropolitan Area - location, type and characteristics. Paper presented at the 14th International Conference on Urban Planning, Regional Development and Information Society REAL CORP 2009. Barcelona, Spain.

Pedersen, A. O., Nyhuus, S., Blindheim, T., & Werlgeland Krog, O. M. (2004). Implementation of a GIS-based management tool for conservation of biodiversity within the municipality of Oslo, Norway. *Landscape and Urban Planning*, *68*(4), 429–438.

Pickett, S. T. A., Cadenasso, M. L., Grove, J. M., Nilon, C. H., Pouyat, R. V., Zipperer, W. C., & Costanza, R. (2001). Urban ecological systems: Linking terrestrial ecological, physical, and socioeconomic components of metropolitan areas. *Annual Review of Ecology Evolution and Systematics*, *32*, 127–157.

Primack, R. B., Pătroescu, M., Rozylowicz, L., & Iojă, I. C. (2008). *Fundamentele conservării diversităţii biologice*. Bucureşti: AGIR.

Pullin, A. S., Baldi, A., Can, O. E., Dieterich, M., Kati, V., Livoreil, B., & Sousa-Pinto, I. et al. (2009). Conservation Focus on Europe: Major Conservation Policy Issues That Need to Be Informed by Conservation Science. *Conservation Biology*, *23*(4), 818–824.

Pumain, D., & Saint-Julien, T. (1997). *L'analyse spatiale. 1. Localisation dans l'espace*. Paris: Arman Colin.

Rautenstrauch, L. (1995). Funktionsverteilung zwischen Stadt und Umland. *Das Bauzentrum*, *3/1995*, 15–26.

Rufat, S., & Suditu, B. (2008). Bucarest, faire la ville entre héritages et mimétisme. *L'Espace Geographique*, *4*(37), 327–337.

Schäffler, A., & Swilling, M. (2013). Valuing green infrastructure in an urban environment under pressure — The Johannesburg case. *Ecological Economics*, *86*(0), 246–257.

Sieverts, T. (1999). *Zwischenstadt*. Braunschweig, Wiesbaden: Zwischen Ort und Welt, Raum und Zeit, Stadt und Land.

Smith, W. P., & Zollner, P. A. (2005). Sustainable management of wildlife habitat and risk of extinction. *Biological Conservation*, *125*(3), 287–295.

Strohbach, M. W., Haase, D., & Kabisch, N. (2009). Birds and the city: Urban biodiversity, land use, and socioeconomics. *Ecology and Society*, *14*(2), 31.

Sykora, L., & Ourednícekin, M. (2007). Sprawling post-communist metropolis: Commercial and residential suburbanization in Prague and Brno, the Czech Republic. In E. Razin, M. Dijst, & C. Vázquez (Eds.), *Employment Deconcentration in European Metropolitan Areas* (pp. 209–233). Dordrecht: Springer.

Tang, B., Wong, S., & Lee, A. K. (2007). Green belt in a compact city: A zone for conservation or transition? *Landscape and Urban Planning*, *79*(3-4), 358–373.

Tratalos, J., Fuller, R. A., Warren, P. H., Davies, R. G., & Gaston, K. J. (2007). Urban form, biodiversity potential and ecosystem services. *Landscape and Urban Planning*, *83*(4), 308–317.

Van Leeuwen, E. S., Vreeker, R., & Rodenburq, C. A. (2006). A framework for quality of life assessment of urban green areas in Europe: An application to District Park Reudnitz Leipzig. *International Journal of Environmental Technology and Management*, *6*(1-2), 111–122.

Wikle, T. A., & Finchum, A. (2003). The emerging GIS degree landscape. *Computers, Environment and Urban Systems*, *27*(2), 107–122.

Williams, N., McDonnell, M., & Seager, E. (2005). Factors influencing the loss of an endangered ecosystem in an urbanising landscape: A case study of native grasslands from Melbourne, Australia. *Landscape and Urban Planning*, *71*(1), 35–49.

Wittemyer, G., Elsen, P., Bean, W. T., Burton, A. C., & Brashare, J. S. (2008). Accelerated human population growth at protected area edges. *Science*, *321*(5885), 123–126.

Yang, F., Zeng, G., Du, C., Tang, L., Zhoua, J., & Li, Z. (2008). Spatial analyzing system for urban land-use management based on GIS and multi-criteria assessment modeling. *Progress in Natural Science*, *18*(10), 1279–1284.

Yli-Pelkonen, V., & Niemelä, J. (2005). Linking ecological and social systems in cities: Urban planning in Finland as a case. *Biodiversity and Conservation*, *14*(8), 1947–1967.

ADDITIONAL READING

Andrusz, G., Harloe, M., & Szelenyi, I. (1996). *Cities after Socialism*. New York: Blackwell Publishing. doi:10.1002/9780470712733

Beinat, E., & Nijkamp, P. (Eds.). (1998). *Multicriteria Analysis for Land-Use Management*. Dordrecht: Kluwer Academic Publisher. doi:10.1007/978-94-015-9058-7

Bhatta, B., Saraswati, S., & Bandyopadhyay, D. (2010). Urban sprawl measurement from remote sensing data. *Applied Geography (Sevenoaks, England)*, *30*(4), 731–740. doi:10.1016/j.apgeog.2010.02.002

Botequilha Leitão, A., & Ahern, J. (2002). Applying landscape ecological concepts and metrics in sustainable landscape planning. *Landscape and Urban Planning*, *59*(2), 65–93. doi:10.1016/S0169-2046(02)00005-1

Carter, S. K., Pohlman, J. D., Bergeson, T. L., Hamilton, C. M., Pidgeon, A. M., & Radeloff, V. C. (2014). Improving the utility of existing conservation plans using projected housing development. *Landscape and Urban Planning*, *126*(0), 10–20. doi:10.1016/j.landurbplan.2014.03.002

Daniels, T. (1999). *When City and Country Collide. Managing Growth in the Metropolitan Fringe*. Washington: Island Press.

De Lara, M., & Doyen, L. (2008). *Sustainable Management of Natural Resources. Mathematical Models and Methods*. Berlin: Springer-Verlag.

Douglas, L. R., & Alie, K. (2014). High-value natural resources: Linking wildlife conservation to international conflict, insecurity, and development concerns. *Biological Conservation*, *171*(0), 270–277. doi:10.1016/j.biocon.2014.01.031

Downton, P. (2009). *Ecopolis. Architecture and Cities for a Changing Climate*. Dordrecht: Springer.

Dutrieux, E., & Guélorget, O. (1988). Ecological planning: A possible method for the choice of aquacultural sites. *Ocean and Shoreline Management*, *11*(6), 427–447. doi:10.1016/0951-8312(88)90024-0

Economou, A., & Mitoula, R. (2013). Management of natural resources and protection of the coastal urban area of Glyfada. *Land Use Policy*, *35*(0), 204–212. doi:10.1016/j.landusepol.2013.05.006

Enlil, Z. M., & Vaggione, P. (Eds.). (2006). Cities between integration and disintegration: Opportunities and Challenges. The Hague: International Society of City and Regional Planners (ISOCARP).

Gant, R., Robinson, G., & Faza, S. (2011). Land-use change in the 'edgelands': Policies and pressures in London's rural–urban fringe. *Land Use Policy*, *28*(1), 266–279. doi:10.1016/j.landusepol.2010.06.007

Gordon, A., Simondson, D., White, M., Moilanen, A., & Bekessy, S. A. (2009). Integrating conservation planning and landuse planning in urban landscapes. *Landscape and Urban Planning*, *91*(4), 183–194. doi:10.1016/j.landurbplan.2008.12.011

Hasse, J. E., & Lathrop, R. G. (2003). Land resource impact indicators of urban sprawl. *Applied Geography (Sevenoaks, England)*, *23*(2-3), 159–175. doi:10.1016/j.apgeog.2003.08.002

Haufler, J. B., & Kernohan, B. J. (2009). *Landscape Considerations for Conservation Planning on Private Lands Models for Planning Wildlife Conservation in Large Landscapes* (pp. 153–176). San Diego: Academic Press. doi:10.1016/B978-0-12-373631-4.00006-X

Ismail, S., Hoe, K. W., & Ramli, M. (2013). Sustainable Aggregates: The Potential and Challenge for Natural Resources Conservation. *Procedia: Social and Behavioral Sciences*, *101*(0), 100–109. doi:10.1016/j.sbspro.2013.07.183

Jim, C. Y. (2011). Holistic research agenda for sustainable management and conservation of urban woodlands. *Landscape and Urban Planning*, *100*(4), 375–379. doi:10.1016/j.landurbplan.2011.01.006

Konijnendijk, C. C., Nilsson, K., Randrup, T. B., & Schipperijn, J. (Eds.). (2005). *Urban Forests and Trees. Verlag-Berlin Heidelberg*. Springer. doi:10.1007/3-540-27684-X

Kowarik, I., & Korner, S. (Eds.). (2005). *Wild Urban Woodlands. New Perspectives for Urban Forestry. Verlag-Berlin Heidelberg*. Springer.

Kurian, M., & McCarney, P. (Eds.). (2011). *Peri-Urban Water and Sanitation Services. Policy, Planning and Method*. Dordrecht: Springer.

Margules, C., & Sarkar, S. (2007). *Systematic Conservation Planning*. Cambridge, UK: Cambridge University Press.

Maruani, T., & Amit-Cohen, I. (2007). Open space planning models: A review of approaches and methods. *Landscape and Urban Planning*, *81*(1-2), 1–13. doi:10.1016/j.landurbplan.2007.01.003

McPherson, G., & Esparza, A. (Eds.). (2009). *The Planner's Guide to Natural Resource Conservation. The Science of Land Development Beyond the Metropolitan Fringe*. Dordrecht: Springer.

Mitsova, D., Shuster, W., & Wang, X. (2011). A cellular automata model of land cover change to integrate urban growth with open space conservation. *Landscape and Urban Planning*, *99*(2), 141–153. doi:10.1016/j.landurbplan.2010.10.001

Moughtin, C., & Shirley, P. (2005). *Urban Design - Green Dimensions* (2nd ed.). Oxford: Architectural Press.

Pauleit, S., Slinn, P., Handley, J., & Lindley, S. (2003). Promoting the natural greenstructure of towns and cities: English Nature's Accessible Natural Greenspace Standards Model. *Built Environment*, *29*(2), 157–170. doi:10.2148/benv.29.2.157.54469

Reilly, J., Maggio, P., & Karp, S. (2004). A model to predict impervious surface for regional and municipal land use planning purposes. *Environmental Impact Assessment Review*, *24*(3), 363–382. doi:10.1016/j.eiar.2003.10.022

Sasaki, L. (2006). Change and continuity: The history of a rural landscape in southern Romania. *Geographical Reports of Tokyo Metropolitan University*, *41*, 113–124.

Steiner, F. R., & Butler, K. (Eds.). (2007). *Planning and Urban Design Standards*. New Jersey: John Willey & Sons Inc.

Taleai, M., Sharifi, A., Sliuzas, R., & Mesgari, M. (2007). Evaluating the compatibility of multifunctional and intensive urban land uses. *International Journal of Applied Earth Observation and Geoinformation*, *9*(4), 375–391. doi:10.1016/j.jag.2006.12.002

Termorshuizen, J. W., Opdam, P., & van den Brink, A. (2007). Incorporating ecological sustainability into landscape planning. *Landscape and Urban Planning*, *79*(3-4), 374–384. doi:10.1016/j.landurbplan.2006.04.005

White, R. (2002). *Building the Ecological City*. New York: CRC Press.

KEY TERMS AND DEFINITIONS

Area of Influence of a City: Referring to the territory polarized by an urban centre on the basis of a set or category of relations (economical, cultural and/or commercial relations, population mobility and/or environmental externalities).

Conservation: A management option which implies the protection, preservation and restoration, if needed, of spaces designated as natural protected areas because of their high importance form an environmental point of view.

Green-Yellow Belts: Represent narrow strips of natural areas (forests, parkland) and/or agricultural land which encircle a large urban area.

Natural Capital: Represents the physical form of the capital stock consisting of all environmental components (lithosphere, atmosphere, hydrosphere, and biosphere) and their interactions materialized in natural ecosystems that represent the basis for human welfare. Natural capital includes three components: the actual land, our natural resources – the physical amounts of renewable and non-renewable resources, as well as ecosystems sustaining life and providing goods and services to the population.

Natural Protected Areas: Areas which have as the main purpose the protection and conservation of biological diversity, corroborated with the associated natural and cultural resources preservation, through legal or other means.

Natural Resources: All goods and services supplied by the environment which contribute to assuring human welfare. Natural resources can be divided according to their usage in two main categories: renewable resources (abiotic resources flows: solar energy, wind, geothermal energy etc. and the main cycles of elements, vegetation, fauna, ecosystems, soils) and non-renewable resources (metallic and non-metallic minerals and fossil fuels).

Oxygen Generating Surfaces: Natural and semi-natural areas (green spaces and aquatic surfaces) which sequester Carbon from the atmosphere and eliminate oxygen.

Regional Activities Parks: Represent structures consisting of a number of villages with certain territorial cohesion, presenting important natural and human resources, together with a natural and cultural patrimony. They are based on the existing potential and voluntary cooperation relationships between the territorial administrative units.

Section 2

Energy Options for a Sustainable Future

Chapter 6
Energy Sustainability of Countries

Evangelos Grigoroudis
Technical University of Crete, Greece

Vassilis S. Kouikoglou
Technical University of Crete, Greece

Yannis A. Phillis
Technical University of Crete, Greece

ABSTRACT

The provision of adequate, reliable, and affordable energy, in conformity with social and environmental requirements is a vital part of sustainable development. Currently, countries are facing a two-fold energy challenge: on the one hand they should assure the provision of environmentally sustainable energy, while, on the other, energy services should be reliable, affordable, and socially acceptable. To evaluate such aspects of energy services one needs energy sustainability barometers, which provide the means to monitor the impacts of energy policies and assist policymakers in relevant decision making. Although sustainability is an ambiguous, complex, and polymorphous concept, all energy sustainability barometers incorporate the three major sustainability dimensions: social, economic, and environmental. In this chapter, we review three models for assessing the sustainability of energy development of countries: ESI, SAFE, and EAPI. We also present a brief discussion of the results, the applied methodologies, and the underlying assumptions of these sustainability barometers.

INTRODUCTION

The Brundtland Report recognizes sustainable development as distinct from environmental protection, and suggests that economic development should be ecologically viable and that environmental protection does not preclude economic development. In this context, the report defines sustainable development as "development which meets the needs of the present without compromising the ability of future generations to meet their own needs" (UNEP, 1987).

DOI: 10.4018/978-1-4666-8433-1.ch006

The provision of adequate, reliable, and affordable energy, in conformity with social and environmental requirements has been key to economic well-being. It is key for relieving poverty, improving human welfare and raising living standards. However, energy, despite its crucial role to development, is only a means to an end. The end is good health, high living standards, a sustainable economy, and a clean environment (see for example IAEA, 2005).

The overall energy production and use had been increased more than 50 times between 1850 and 2005, from a global total of approximately 0.2 billion tons of equivalent oil (toe) to 11.4 billion toe (IEA, 2007). Currently, non-renewable, carbon emitting fossil fuels provide approximately 80% of the global primary energy needs (IEA, 2007). At the same time, as noted in TWAS (2008), a large fraction of the world's population still lacks access to one or several types of basic energy services, including electricity, clean cooking fuels and adequate means of transportation. Also, global demand for primary energy is expected to rise by between 27% and 61% by 2050 (WEC, 2013). Thus, both developed and developing countries face a two-fold energy challenge. On the one hand, countries should assure the provision of environmentally sustainable energy, and, on the other, energy services should be reliable, affordable, and socially acceptable. The present overwhelming reliance on fossil fuels is unsustainable primarily because it destroys the climate.

Figure 1. Framework for energy indicators of sustainable development

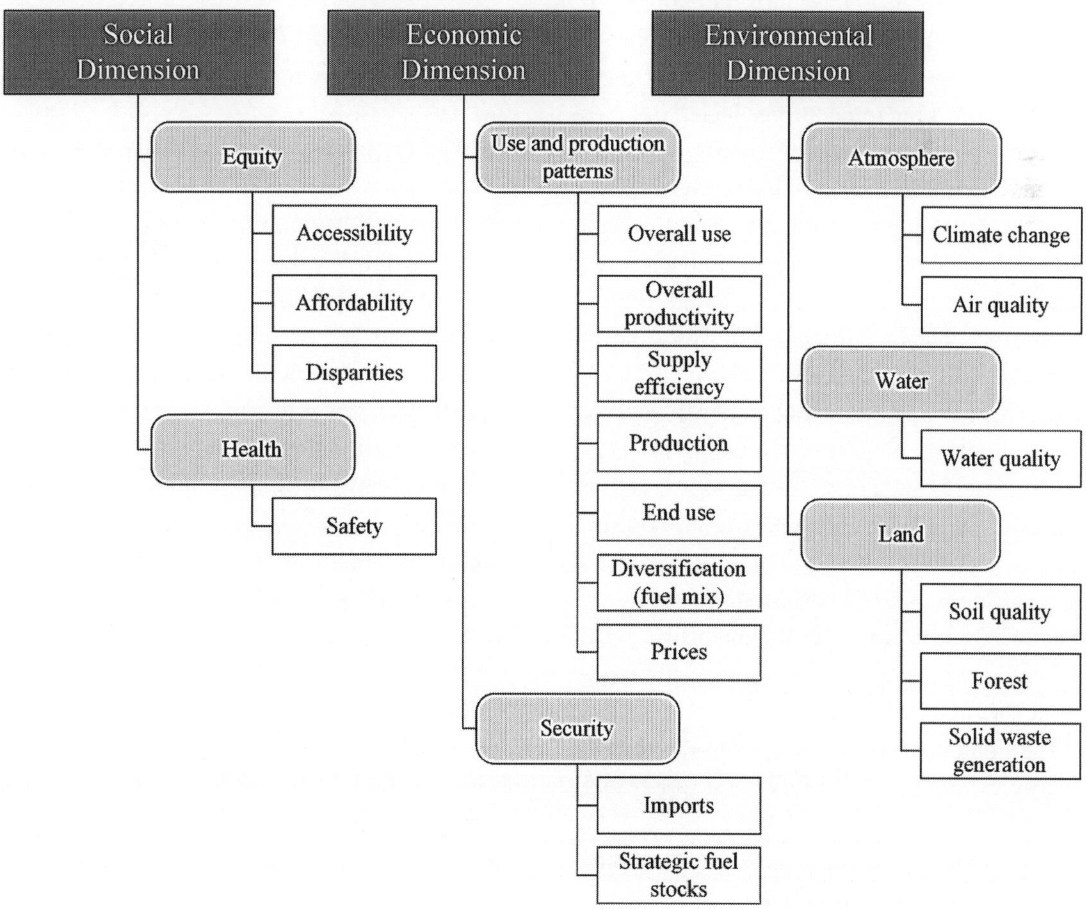

One of the most important efforts towards assessing energy sustainability is the interagency program led by the International Atomic Energy Agency (IAEA), in cooperation with various other international organizations, including the International Energy Agency (IEA), the United Nations Department of Economic and Social Affairs (UNDESA), and a few member states of the IAEA. The aim of the program is to eliminate duplication and provide users with a single set of energy indicators applicable in every country. The proposed framework consists of three main sustainability dimensions, social, economic, and environmental, which are further classified into 7 themes and 19 sub-themes (Figure 1). Although a set of 30 indicators is proposed in the IAEA report, it is emphasized that no set of energy indicators can be final and definitive, since they should evolve over time to fit country-specific conditions, priorities and capabilities (IAEA, 2005).

Regardless of the adopted measurement framework, the primary objective of all energy sustainability barometers is to provide a strategic tool that monitors the impacts of selected policies in order to examine whether they improve sustainable development or they should be adjusted. As well as this, sustainable economic development on a global scale may be achieved only through the appropriate use of resources, technologies, economic incentives and strategic policies at the local and national levels. Moreover, energy projects require long-term planning that justify the necessity of evaluating their potential impacts[1]. Energy sustainability barometers will assist policymakers in the following major domains (IAEA, 2005):

1. Examine a country's current status regarding energy and economic sustainability, what needs to be improved, and how improvements can be achieved.
2. Understand the implications of selected energy, environmental and economic programs, policies and plans, and their impacts on development and the feasibility of making this development sustainable.
3. Analyze trade-offs of potential policies, investments, and corrective actions.

In this chapter we review some major energy sustainability barometers. The main objective is to discuss their methodologies and assumptions and to compare results. To evaluate energy sustainability these alternative barometers adopt the aforementioned framework of social, economic, and environmental indicators. However, different emphasis on the evaluation of components may result in different country rankings.

The remainder of this chapter is organized as follows. The next section presents three major energy sustainability indices, followed by a section with a brief comparison and discussion of these alternative approaches. Concluding remarks are stated in the last section.

ENERGY SUSTAINABILITY BAROMETERS

World Energy Council's Index

The Energy Sustainability Index (ESI) was introduced by the World Energy Council (WEC) in 2011, as a comparative measure of the capability of countries to provide stable, affordable, and environmentally-friendly energy. The annual ESI reports give separate country profiles in order to highlight national relative energy performances, contextual attributes, and future challenges. The 2013 ESI (WEC, 2013) includes a total of 129 countries which, apart from being ranked, are also assigned a "balance score" highlighting the trade-offs between the different energy sustainability dimensions.

The calculation of the energy performance index is based on three dimensions which represent different and often conflicting goals of energy sustainability, called "energy trilemma" by WEC (WEC, 2013):

1. **Energy Security:** Refers to the effective management of primary energy supply from domestic and external sources, the reliability of energy infrastructure, and the ability of energy providers to meet current and future demand.
2. **Energy Equity:** Contains indicators about the accessibility and affordability of energy supply across the population.
3. **Environmental Sustainability:** Is related to energy efficiency at the supply and demand ends as well as energy supply from renewable and other low-carbon sources.

The structure of ESI, as shown in Table 1, consists of two main indicator types: energy and contextual performance. Although the index is weighted in favor of the energy performance, the contextual indicators measure broader aspects of energy performance that have to do with the political, societal, and economic strength of a country. ESI depends on a total of 23 indicators, which are developed using 60 different datasets. All indicators in each group are considered of equal importance and carry equal weight.

Using the indicators and weights of Table 1, an index normalized in [0, 10] is calculated for each dimension. Indices are then weighted in order to

Table 1. ESI dimensions and indicators

Indicator Type	Dimension	Indicators
1. Energy performance (75%)	1.1 Energy security (25%)	1.1.1 Ratio of total energy production to consumption
		1.1.2 Diversity of electricity generation
		1.1.3 Distribution losses as a percentage of generation
		1.1.4 Five year CAGR of the ratio of TPEC to GDP
		1.1.5 Days of oil and oil product stocks
		1.1.6a For importers – Net fuel imports as a percentage of GDP
		1.1.6b For exporters – Fuel exports as a percentage of GDP
	1.2 Energy equity (25%)	1.2.1 Affordability of retail gasoline
		1.2.2 Affordability and quality of electricity relative to access
	1.3 Environmental sustainability (25%)	1.3.1 Total primary energy intensity
		1.3.2 CO_2 intensity
		1.3.3 Effect of air and water pollution
		1.3.4 CO_2 grams/kWh from electricity generation
2. Contextual performance (25%)	2.1 Political strength (8.3%)	2.1.1 Political stability
		2.1.2 Regulatory quality
		2.1.3 Effectiveness of government
	2.2 Societal strength (8.3%)	2.2.1 Control of corruption
		2.2.2 Rule of law
		2.2.3 Quality of education
		2.3.4 Quality of health
	2.3 Economic strength (8.3%)	2.3.1 Cost of living expenditure
		2.3.2 Macroeconomic stability
		2.3.3 Availability of credit to the private sector

(WEC, 2013).

provide an overall ranking of the countries. By its nature, however, this ranking does not indicate how well a country is meeting the energy trilemma challenge balance across the three dimensions. For this reason, WEC introduced a balance score based only on the energy performance dimensions (WEC, 2013). The score uses three-letter labels, similar to the financial crediting scoring systems, where high performers receive a score of "AAA", while countries that do not yet perform well receive a "DDD" score. The scores are assigned by splitting the normalized 0-10 results of the energy performance dimensions into four categories, using the following rules: The best score "A" is given for results higher than 8, while countries with normalized results higher than 5 are given score "B"; average results of between 2.51 and 5 are given a "C", and finally the score "D" is given for underperformance. It should be noted that the sequence of letters does not correspond to a specific energy dimension, but presents the letter scores in descending alphabetical order. The highest score of "AAA" is given to countries which balance the score dimensions of the "energy trilemma" extremely well and achieve high comparative performance in each dimension.

Table 2 shows the 2013 results of ESI, which include the overall sustainability ranking of countries and the individual scores of the three energy performance dimensions. The index reflects data from 2010-2012. According to the 2013 ESI report, the following country groups are identified:

- Pack leaders,
- Fossil-fuelled,
- Highly-industrialized,
- Hydro-powered,
- Back of the Pack.

Countries in each group share common energy characteristics and challenges. The recent ESI results (WEC, 2013) show that "Pack Leaders", including Switzerland and Denmark, have improved their energy security and environmental sustainability by raising the percentage of renewables in their electricity fuel mix. "Fossil-Fuelled" countries such as Saudi Arabia or Malaysia struggle to manage the environmental impact of their secure and affordable energy services. The priority of "Highly-Industrialized" countries (e.g., India, Mexico) is to provide accessible and environmentally-sensitive energy, while maintaining high levels of economic growth. "Hydro-Powered" countries (e.g., Brazil, Colombia) provide environmentally-sensitive energy, which, however, is less accessible and affordable. Finally, "Back of the Pack" nations (e.g., Zimbabwe, Nicaragua) are characterized by a lack of energy investments and thus show poor performance in all three energy performance dimensions.

Although the main objective of ESI is to reveal an aggregate effect of energy policies over time, it should be emphasized that the index is relative, because a country's ranking depends on the data points of the others. Thus, ESI broadly measures the aggregate outcome of energy policies in comparison with countries having similar energy profiles.

Sustainability Assessment by Fuzzy Evaluation

Sustainability Assessment by Fuzzy Evaluation (SAFE) is a model for the numerical assessment of sustainability. It was introduced in Phillis & Andriantiatsaholiniaina (2001) and developed further in Phillis et al. (2003), Andriantiatsaholiniaina et al. (2004), Kouloumpis et al. (2008), and Phillis et al. (2011). SAFE is a hierarchical fuzzy inference system that uses knowledge encoded into 'if-then' rules, fuzzy logic reasoning, and a large set of basic indicators. The model is amended by an imputation procedure to fill in missing data. The model's rule bases are compiled algebraically and the sustainability thresholds are defined so as to reflect expert opinion and international agreements and norms. SAFE was first developed to measure human, ecological,

Table 2. ESI 2013 results

	Country	ESI	ESE[a]	EQ[b]	ESU[c]		Country	ESI	ESE[a]	EQ[b]	ESU[c]
1	Switzerland	AAA	8.59	9.60	10.00	40	Hong Kong	ABD	2.34	8.20	5.54
2	Denmark	AAA	9.84	8.12	9.29	41	Mexico	BBC	7.81	6.40	4.21
3	Sweden	AAA	8.20	8.98	9.60	42	Lithuania	ABC	2.81	6.48	8.04
4	Austria	AAB	7.50	9.53	9.53	43	Latvia	ABD	2.42	5.85	8.98
5	UK	AAA	9.21	9.45	8.59	44	UAEs	BBD	6.25	7.18	2.10
6	Canada	AAB	10.00	9.92	5.39	45	Peru	ABC	8.43	2.57	6.71
7	Norway	AAB	6.09	9.29	9.45	46	Uruguay	ACC	2.89	4.84	9.68
8	New Zealand	AAB	8.90	8.04	7.18	47	Singapore	BBD	0.39	6.71	6.09
9	Spain	AAA	8.35	8.82	8.28	48	Poland	BBC	7.10	7.03	2.73
10	France	AAB	6.64	9.68	9.37	49	El Salvador	ABC	4.76	5.07	9.21
11	Germany	ABB	7.65	9.21	7.73	50	Barbados	ABD	0.85	6.87	8.12
12	Netherlands	ABB	6.79	8.28	7.34	51	Saudi Arabia	ABD	6.56	9.14	0.39
13	Finland	ABB	7.18	8.43	6.56	52	Romania	ACC	9.37	4.60	3.20
14	Australia	AAD	9.29	9.84	2.50	53	Mauritius	ABD	1.56	5.39	8.82
15	USA	AAC	9.14	10.00	3.35	54	Russia	ABD	9.92	5.31	2.34
16	Japan	ABB	6.32	8.75	7.50	55	Bolivia	ACC	9.76	3.51	4.53
17	Belgium	ABB	5.15	9.06	7.42	56	Gabon	ABC	7.34	2.89	9.14
18	Qatar	AAC	9.45	9.37	2.65	57	Chile	BCC	3.04	5.70	4.45
19	Luxembourg	ABD	1.71	9.76	7.81	58	Kazakhstan	ABD	9.60	7.34	1.01
20	Ireland	ABC	3.67	7.73	8.90	59	Angola	ABD	9.45	1.95	7.65
21	Costa Rica	ABB	5.62	6.56	9.92	60	Albania	ACC	3.28	4.14	9.84
22	Slovakia	ABB	8.51	7.10	6.32	61	Guatemala	BBC	6.95	4.21	7.26
23	Portugal	ABB	5.78	5.93	8.51	62	Oman	ACD	3.98	8.51	0.70
24	Colombia	AAC	9.68	3.43	9.76	63	Cyprus	BCD	1.95	7.26	3.82
25	Slovenia	BBB	5.39	7.96	6.79	64	Korea (Rep.)	BCD	2.03	6.25	3.43
26	Argentina	ABB	8.98	7.50	7.10	65	Philippines	BBC	7.03	2.81	5.85
27	Taiwan	ABC	4.53	8.35	5.46	66	Kuwait	BCD	4.37	7.89	0.54
28	Italy	ABC	4.68	7.42	8.20	67	Israel	BCD	2.10	7.81	3.59
29	Panama	ABB	5.93	5.54	8.67	68	Estonia	BCD	5.00	6.09	0.93
30	Croatia	ABC	4.92	7.65	8.43	69	Sri Lanka	BCC	4.45	3.82	6.95
31	Hungary	BBB	6.48	6.79	6.64	70	Bulgaria	ACD	8.04	4.06	1.64
32	Czech Rep	ABC	8.82	7.57	3.04	71	Malta	BCD	0.07	6.32	5.00
33	Iceland	ABC	2.57	8.90	6.87	72	Georgia	ACD	1.79	4.92	8.35
34	Brazil	ABC	7.96	3.35	8.75	73	Indonesia	ACD	8.75	3.59	1.95
35	Ecuador	ABB	8.12	5.23	7.89	74	Paraguay	ACD	3.51	2.34	9.06
36	Tunisia	BBB	7.89	5.62	5.70	75	Turkey	BCC	5.07	3.67	4.60
37	Malaysia	BBC	7.42	6.95	2.89	76	Egypt	BBC	6.40	5.46	3.51
38	Bahrain	AAD	8.28	8.59	0.31	77	Venezuela	BBC	6.87	5.78	3.67
39	Greece	ABC	5.85	8.67	3.75	78	China	ADD	8.67	2.18	0.23

continued on following page

Table 2. Continued

	Country	ESI	ESE[a]	EQ[b]	ESU[c]		Country	ESI	ESE[a]	EQ[b]	ESU[c]
79	South Africa	BCD	6.71	3.98	0.07	105	Morocco	CCD	1.48	3.90	2.57
80	DR Congo	BBD	7.73	0.62	7.96	106	Serbia	CDD	2.18	5.00	0.78
81	Azerbaijan	BCD	7.57	4.29	2.42	107	Tajikistan	BCD	3.75	1.56	5.31
82	Cameroon	BBD	5.23	1.71	7.03	108	Kenya	BCD	3.20	1.17	5.15
83	Montenegro	BCD	1.09	4.53	5.62	109	Lebanon	CCD	0.15	3.20	3.12
84	Nigeria	ACD	9.06	1.40	3.90	110	Dominican R	BDD	1.17	1.79	5.78
85	Armenia	CCC	2.65	4.68	4.37	111	Nepal	BDD	0.31	0.54	6.48
86	FYR Maced.	BCD	3.12	6.17	1.79	112	Ethiopia	BDD	2.50	0.78	6.40
87	Syria	BBD	6.01	6.01	1.25	113	Nicaragua	CCD	2.26	2.96	3.28
88	Algeria	CCC	3.35	4.76	4.29	114	Pakistan	BDD	5.70	2.03	2.26
89	Thailand	CCD	2.96	3.20	2.18	115	India	CDD	4.14	1.48	0.62
90	Namibia	BCD	0.46	2.73	6.25	116	Tanzania	BDD	0.93	0.31	5.85
91	Iran	BCD	4.21	6.64	0.78	117	Libya	CCD	4.60	4.45	0.46
92	Swaziland	BCD	5.31	2.42	4.14	118	Cambodia	CDD	0.62	1.25	4.84
93	Côte d'Ivoire	BCD	7.26	1.64	4.76	119	Mauritania	BDD	5.54	0.93	1.32
94	Malawi	BCD	4.29	0.00	7.57	120	Zambia	BDD	1.64	0.70	5.07
95	Mongolia	BDD	6.17	2.26	0.00	121	Jamaica	CDD	1.01	3.75	1.48
96	Jordan	BDD	0.78	5.15	1.71	122	Niger	CCD	3.82	0.15	2.96
97	Ukraine	BCD	5.46	4.37	1.17	123	Bangladesh	CDD	1.25	1.09	3.98
98	Trin. & Tob.	CCD	3.90	2.65	1.09	124	Madagascar	CDD	1.87	0.23	4.68
99	Botswana	BDD	0.23	2.50	5.23	125	Moldova	CDD	0.54	3.12	1.56
100	Honduras	BCD	1.40	3.04	6.01	126	Senegal	CDD	0.70	0.85	2.81
101	Vietnam	CDD	4.06	2.10	1.87	127	Yemen	CDD	2.73	1.32	1.40
102	Ghana	CCD	3.43	1.87	4.06	128	Benin	DDD	0.00	1.01	2.03
103	Mozambique	CCD	4.84	0.39	4.92	129	Zimbabwe	DDD	1.32	0.07	0.15
104	Chad	BCD	3.59	0.46	6.17						

(WEC, 2013).
[a]ESE: Energy Security;[b]EQ: Energy Equity; [c]ESU: Energy sustainability.

and overall sustainability based on indicators of environmental integrity, economic efficiency and social welfare (see Grigoroudis et al., 2013b, 2014 for the latest results). However, the model has been applied also for the assessment of corporate sustainability (Phillis & Davis, 2009), material recyclability (Phillis et al., 2010), and energy sustainability (Grigoroudis et al., 2013a).

The SAFE model developed for the sustainability evaluation of energy systems assumes that the overall energy sustainability (OSUS) of a country is a combination of two primary components: ecological sustainability (ECOS) and human sustainability (HUMS). The ecological input comprises two secondary components: air quality (AIR) and soil quality (LAND), while the human components of energy sustainability are social (ACCESSIBILITY) and economic (PRODUCTION, CONSUMPTION, SECURITY). As shown in Table 3, each secondary component is assessed using certain basic indicators which are the inputs of the system.

Table 3. Components and indicators in the SAFE model for energy systems

Components	Basic Indicators[a]	Type[b]	Data Sources
AIR	GHG (tons of CO_2 equivalent per capita)	SB	United Nations Environment Programme
	NO_2 (μg/m3 of air)	SB	Esty et al. (2005); Environmental Sustainability Index
	SO_2 (μg/m3 of air)	SB	Esty et al. (2005); Environmental Sustainability Index
	PM10 (μg/m3)	SB	United Nations Environment Programme
LAND	Nuclear waste (tons of heavy metals per capita)	SB	OECD (2005); United Nations Environment Programme
ACCESSIBILITY	Access to electricity (percent of population)	LB	IEA (2002, 2010); World Resources Institute (2006)
PRODUCTION	Renewable energy production (percent of total primary energy supply)	LB	IEA; Human Development Report
	Electricity from oil, gas, and coal sources (percent of total electricity production)	SB	IEA (2011a, 2011b, 2011c, 2011d); World Bank
CONSUMPTION	Energy intensity (kg of oil equivalent per $1,000 GDP, constant 2005 PPP)	SB	World Bank
	Energy use (kg of oil equivalent per capita)	SB	IEA
SECURITY	Imports (percent of energy use)	SB	IEA

(Grigoroudis et al., 2013a).

[a]Measurement units in an annual basis;[b]SB = smaller is better; LB = larger is better;

The main steps of SAFE for calculating the overall energy sustainability are the following (Phillis & Kouikoglou, 2009; Phillis et al., 2011; Grigoroudis et al., 2012, 2013a):

1. **Data Collection:** From the sources shown in Table 3, a database for the assessed 11 basic indicators is developed. The database covers 128 countries and a period of 22 years (1990-2011).
2. **Normalization of Data:** Available data are normalized in [0, 1], where the value 0 is assigned to the least desirable indicator values and the value 1 to the most desirable indicator values or targets. Normalization is necessary in order to make indicators comparable and to facilitate analysis. The normalization procedure is based on linear interpolation between sustainable and unsustainable indicator values, which are specified by international agreements and norms, laws and regulations, and expert opinion.
3. **Exponential Smoothing:** The most recent indicator data are used to estimate the human components of energy sustainability. However, in the case of environmental components, it is important to take into account the cumulative effect of past indicator values. For this reason, an exponential smoothing approach is applied to time series of data.
4. **Data Imputation:** Since the problem of data unavailability is common in many sustainability studies, a data imputation procedure is necessary in order to avoid

possible exclusion of important indicators. The data imputation approach is similar to a hot deck imputation procedure and consists of three main steps (Phillis et al., 2011): (a) Countries are grouped by similarity according to geographic, economic, and cultural criteria; (b) A distance matrix is calculated that measures how different the available data of a country are from those of another similar country; and (c) The missing value of an indicator is calculated by the average of this indicator over all countries with maximum similarity and minimum distance. Data imputation is applied separately to each sustainability component.

5. **Fuzzification:** The normalized basic indicators are fuzzified using triangular membership functions and three fuzzy sets with linguistic values: Weak, Medium, and Strong. For composite indicators five linguistic values are used: Very Bad, Bad, Average, Good, and Very Good. In cases where components depend only on a single basic indicator, this indicator is represented by five fuzzy sets. The overall sustainability is measured using nine fuzzy sets: Extremely Low, Very Low, Low, Fairly Low, Intermediate, Fairly High, High, Very High, and Extremely High.
6. **Fuzzy Assessment of Sustainability:** Each inference stage, or inference engine of the SAFE model has its own rule base and combines input indicators into composite output indicators. A detailed description of the applied "if-then" linguistic rules is given in Grigoroudis et al. (2013a). The inference engines compute the membership grades of each output indicator which is input to the next stage and so on until OSUS is assessed. It is important to note the use of product-sum algebra in inference engines, which ensures the monotonicity of the hierarchical fuzzy system, that is, if a basic indicator improves, OSUS is also improves or, at least, does not decrease (see details in Kouikoglou and Phillis, 2009).
7. **Sensitivity Analysis and Decision Making:** The sensitivity analysis is based on the computation of the gradients of ECOS, HUMS, and OSUS with respect to each basic indicator. The scenarios developed through this approach identifies the indicators that affect sustainability critically. Thus, sensitivity analysis could aid decision makers to formulate sustainable policies by assessing sustainability for different scenarios of development.

The results of the SAFE model for 2011 are presented in Table 4. It can be observed that European and South American countries occupy the top places of the ranking whereas the bottom places are occupied by East European countries and South Korea. As noted by Grigoroudis et al. (2013a), ecological and human sustainability of energy development are not necessarily compatible, since HUMS and ECOS are not strongly correlated.

Based on the results of sensitivity analysis, Table 5 shows the most important indicators that improve energy sustainability. The most important problems of energy systems in China, Russia, and Belgium are mainly ecological, while the problems of South Korea, Italy, and Greece are mainly human. It can also be observed that the most critical factors for the USA, Germany, and Spain are both ecological and human (Grigoroudis et al., 2013a).

ENERGY ARCHITECTURE PERFORMANCE INDEX

The Energy Architecture Performance Index (EAPI) is an initiative by the World Economic Forum (WEF) focusing on evaluating energy architectures[2] that delivers a secure, affordable, and environmentally sustainable energy supply (WEF, 2013). Although EAPI focuses on energy architecture, its main evaluation components are similar to other relevant energy sustainability indices.

Table 4. SAFE results for energy sustainability

	Country	OSUS	ECOS	HUMS		Country	OSUS	ECOS	HUMS
1	Albania	0.8870	0.8582	0.9158	40	Niger	0.7196	0.7500	0.6892
2	Paraguay	0.8631	0.7500	0.9761	41	Malaysia	0.7186	0.7890	0.6483
3	Norway	0.8504	0.8090	0.8918	42	Indonesia	0.7185	0.7500	0.6871
4	Brazil	0.8465	0.7500	0.9429	43	Angola	0.7151	0.7552	0.6750
5	Colombia	0.8426	0.7500	0.9352	44	Nigeria	0.7136	0.8131	0.6141
6	Latvia	0.8123	0.9133	0.7114	45	Nicaragua	0.7132	0.8526	0.5738
7	Vietnam	0.7986	0.7903	0.8069	46	Austria	0.7096	0.8047	0.6145
8	Tajikistan	0.7892	0.8182	0.7601	47	Mozambique	0.7073	0.8889	0.5256
9	Kyrgyzstan	0.7804	0.9072	0.6536	48	Rwanda	0.7005	0.8903	0.5107
10	New Zealand	0.7798	0.7673	0.7924	49	Algeria	0.6994	0.7522	0.6465
11	Peru	0.7795	0.7464	0.8126	50	Sudan	0.6987	0.7500	0.6474
12	Nepal	0.7785	0.8477	0.7094	51	Sri Lanka	0.6975	0.7500	0.6450
13	Papua NG	0.7670	0.8500	0.6840	52	Estonia	0.6949	0.8183	0.5715
14	Denmark	0.7664	0.7735	0.7594	53	China	0.6923	0.6724	0.7123
15	Tunisia	0.7616	0.8186	0.7046	54	Zambia	0.6874	0.8013	0.5734
16	Venezuela	0.7609	0.7499	0.7720	55	Panama	0.6854	0.7957	0.5751
17	Ecuador	0.7576	0.7662	0.7490	56	Pakistan	0.6851	0.7500	0.6202
18	Lithuania	0.7564	0.9100	0.6028	57	Thailand	0.6841	0.7509	0.6172
19	Switzerland	0.7541	0.7737	0.7345	58	Honduras	0.6840	0.7905	0.5775
20	Chad	0.7501	0.7500	0.7502	59	FYR Maced.	0.6837	0.8123	0.5552
21	Ghana	0.7496	0.8186	0.6806	60	Azerbaijan	0.6831	0.7986	0.5676
22	Georgia	0.7476	0.8238	0.6714	61	Malawi	0.6828	0.8559	0.5097
23	Bolivia	0.7463	0.7500	0.7425	62	Laos	0.6823	0.7829	0.5817
24	Sierra Leone	0.7456	0.8019	0.6892	63	Egypt	0.6810	0.6711	0.6908
25	Cameroon	0.7452	0.7587	0.7316	64	India	0.6810	0.7571	0.6050
26	Gabon	0.7427	0.8226	0.6629	65	Kazakhstan	0.6795	0.8524	0.5067
27	Congo	0.7401	0.7550	0.7251	66	Chile	0.6754	0.7500	0.6008
28	El Salvador	0.7324	0.7500	0.7148	67	Madagascar	0.6747	0.8006	0.5487
29	Argentina	0.7309	0.7500	0.7118	68	Syria	0.6731	0.7500	0.5961
30	Philippines	0.7304	0.7667	0.6942	69	Croatia	0.6712	0.7783	0.5642
31	Mexico	0.7296	0.7479	0.7113	70	Australia	0.6700	0.7500	0.5901
32	Zimbabwe	0.7288	0.8188	0.6389	71	Burundi	0.6692	0.8278	0.5107
33	Guatemala	0.7253	0.7500	0.7005	72	Togo	0.6665	0.8210	0.5121
34	Sweden	0.7242	0.7048	0.7436	73	Uganda	0.6665	0.8233	0.5097
35	Uruguay	0.7240	0.7499	0.6980	74	Tanzania	0.6600	0.8104	0.5096
36	Guinea	0.7225	0.7558	0.6892	75	Armenia	0.6584	0.8031	0.5136
37	Cote d'Ivoire	0.7201	0.7976	0.6426	76	Centr Afr R	0.6584	0.8167	0.5000
38	Mali	0.7196	0.7500	0.6892	77	Czech Rep	0.6570	0.7587	0.5553
39	Mauritania	0.7196	0.7500	0.6892	78	South Africa	0.6570	0.7711	0.5429

continued on following page

Table 4. Continued

	Country	OSUS	ECOS	HUMS		Country	OSUS	ECOS	HUMS
79	Iran	0.6550	0.7500	0.5600	104	Saudi Arabia	0.6244	0.7487	0.5000
80	Cambodia	0.6546	0.8171	0.4920	105	Greece	0.6241	0.7491	0.4991
81	Ethiopia	0.6529	0.7592	0.5466	106	Kuwait	0.6241	0.7482	0.5000
82	Uzbekistan	0.6481	0.7865	0.5097	107	Yemen	0.6241	0.7500	0.4983
83	Poland	0.6462	0.7598	0.5326	108	Senegal	0.6200	0.7500	0.4901
84	Portugal	0.6444	0.7715	0.5174	109	Benin	0.6198	0.7770	0.4626
85	Slovakia	0.6426	0.7586	0.5267	110	Morocco	0.6194	0.7784	0.4605
86	Netherlands	0.6425	0.7471	0.5380	111	Spain	0.6169	0.7357	0.4981
87	Kenya	0.6424	0.7774	0.5074	112	Italy	0.6133	0.7500	0.4765
88	DR Congo	0.6421	0.7843	0.5000	113	Belgium	0.6116	0.7275	0.4958
89	Bangladesh	0.6417	0.7500	0.5335	114	Israel	0.6103	0.7810	0.4395
90	Germany	0.6415	0.7825	0.5004	115	USA	0.5973	0.6658	0.5289
91	Lebanon	0.6404	0.8544	0.4265	116	Ireland	0.5932	0.7483	0.4380
92	Hungary	0.6398	0.7624	0.5172	117	Japan	0.5912	0.7127	0.4698
93	France	0.6377	0.6858	0.5896	118	Canada	0.5849	0.4123	0.7576
94	UK	0.6335	0.7275	0.5394	119	Romania	0.5748	0.4401	0.7096
95	Namibia	0.6334	0.7817	0.4851	120	Jordan	0.5724	0.7705	0.3744
96	Guinea-Bissau	0.6286	0.7547	0.5025	121	Finland	0.5716	0.5231	0.6201
97	Burkina Faso	0.6281	0.7500	0.5061	122	Slovenia	0.5421	0.5370	0.5471
98	Botswana	0.6280	0.7644	0.4917	123	South Korea	0.5394	0.6571	0.4218
99	Mongolia	0.6275	0.7500	0.5051	124	Ukraine	0.4655	0.4184	0.5126
100	Gambia	0.6263	0.7500	0.5025	125	Bulgaria	0.3927	0.2465	0.5389
101	Turkey	0.6263	0.7500	0.5026	126	Moldova	0.3863	0.3899	0.3827
102	UAE	0.6250	0.7500	0.5000	127	Russia	0.3603	0.1932	0.5273
103	Oman	0.6247	0.7495	0.5000	128	Belarus	0.3554	0.3185	0.3923

(Grigoroudis et al., 2013a).

Table 5. Sensitivity analysis for selected countries

Country	Most Important Indicators
USA	Renewable energy production, Nuclear waste, Imports, GHG emissions
Germany	NO_2 emissions, Imports, Consumption/cap, GHG emissions
Spain	Imports, NO_2 emissions, Nuclear waste, PM10 emissions
China	NO_2 emissions, SO_2 emissions, Electricity production from oil, gas, and coal, PM10 emissions
Russia	Nuclear waste, SO_2 emissions, Renewable energy production, NO2 emissions
Belgium	Nuclear waste, NO_2 emissions, Consumption/cap, GHG emissions
South Korea	Imports, Electricity production from oil, gas, and coal, Renewable energy production, Nuclear waste
Italy	Imports, Renewable energy production, Electricity production from coal etc., Consumption/cap
Greece	Imports, Electricity production from oil, gas, and coal, Renewable energy production, NO_2 emissions

(Grigoroudis et al., 2013a).

Figure 2. Energy architecture conceptual framework
(Adapted from WEF, 2013).

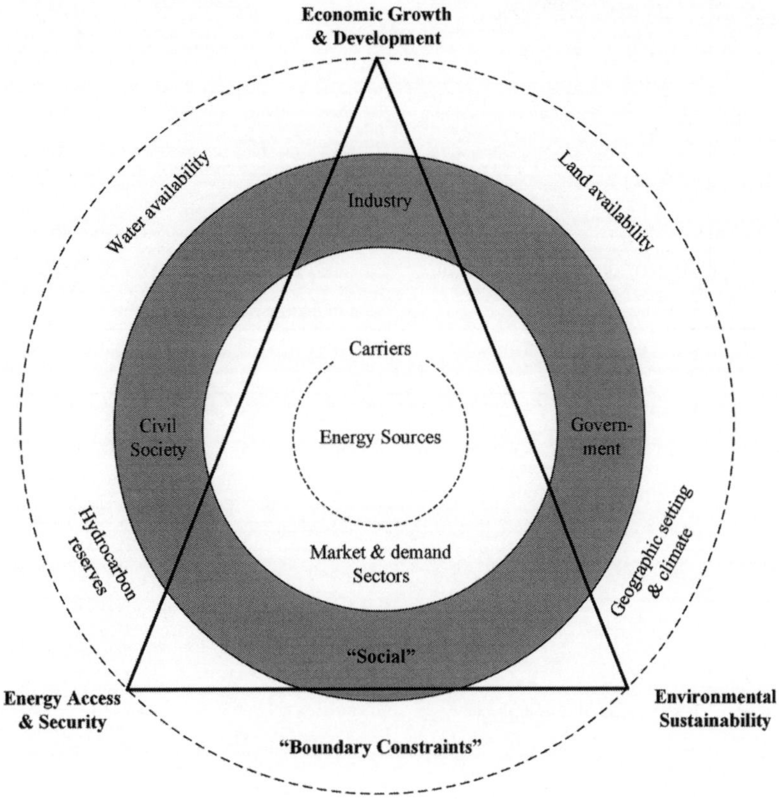

The conceptual framework of EAPI is presented in Figure 2, where the physical and social elements of energy architecture are shown as concentric circles. Moreover, the "energy triangle" represents the main objectives of energy architecture (WEF, 2013):

- Promote economic growth and development;
- Ensure environmental sustainability;
- Provide universal energy access and security.

EAPI is a composite index that measures the performance of global energy systems based on three dimensions (Table 6):

1. **Economic Growth and Development:** It measures the extent to which energy architecture supports economic growth and development. Several indicators of this dimension are connected with price signals that reflect the true costs of energy production in order to ensure that energy consumption is economically viable. It is assumed that reliable energy promotes economic and social development by boosting productivity and generating income.
2. **Environmental Sustainability:** It measures the extent to which energy architecture is designed to minimize the negative impact of external environmental factors. EAPI considers sustainability as a critical energy

Table 6. EAPI indicators and weights

Objective	Measure	Indicator	Weight
Economic growth and development	Efficiency	Energy intensity (GDP per unit of energy use (PPP US$ per kg of oil equivalent))	0.250
	Lack of distortion/affordability	Degree of artificial distortion to gasoline pricing (index)	0.125
		Degree of artificial distortion to diesel pricing (index)	0.125
		Electricity prices for industry (US$ per kWh)	0.250
	Supportive/detracts from growth	Cost of energy imports (% GDP)	0.125
		Value of energy exports (% GDP)	0.125
Environmental sustainability	Share of low-carbon fuel sources in the energy mix	Alternative and nuclear energy (% of total energy use, incl. biomass)	0.200
	Emissions impact	CO_2 emissions from electricity production, total/ kWh	0.200
		Methane emissions in energy sector (10^3 metric tons of CO_2 equivalent)/total population	0.100
		Nitrous oxide emissions in energy sector (10^3 metric tons of CO_2 equivalent)/total population	0.100
		PM10, country level (micrograms per m^3)	0.200
		Average fuel economy for passenger cars (l/100 km)	0.200
Energy access and security	Level and quality of access	Electrification rate (% of population)	0.200
		Quality of electricity supply (1-7)	0.200
		Percentage of population using solid fuels for cooking (%)	0.200
	Self-sufficiency/multi-lateral markets	Import dependence (energy imports, net % energy use)	0.200/0.100
		Diversification of import counterparts (Herfindahl index)	0/0.100
	Diversity of supply	Diversity of total primary energy supply (Herfindahl index)	0.200

(WEF, 2013).

architecture priority, since significant negative environmental externalities are associated with the production, transmission, and consumption of energy. The environmental sustainability indicators are mostly related to renewables and emissions.

3. **Energy Access and Security:** It measures the extent to which energy architecture is at risk of a security disruption, and whether adequate access to energy is provided to all strata of a population.

EAPI was developed in 2013 with the collaboration of World Economic Forum, Accenture[3], and a group of energy experts from across the value chain. The 2014 version of EAPI covers 124 countries through 18 indicators. EAPI is calculated by the average of the main dimensions, since all three objectives receive equal priority and weighting. In exceptional cases basic indicators are combined with equal weights to form a new indicator that is combined with the remaining ones. As shown in Table 6, the exceptions are:

Table 7. EAPI global rankings

	Country	EAPI	EGD[a]	ES[b]	EAS[c]		Country	EAPI	EGD[a]	ES[b]	EAS[c]
1	Norway	0.75	0.69	0.60	0.96	40	Poland	0.58	0.61	0.36	0.77
2	New Zealand	0.73	0.63	0.70	0.85	41	Israel	0.58	0.61	0.40	0.73
3	France	0.72	0.63	0.73	0.81	42	Greece	0.58	0.59	0.41	0.74
4	Sweden	0.72	0.59	0.73	0.85	43	Croatia	0.58	0.63	0.34	0.75
5	Switzerland	0.72	0.73	0.59	0.82	44	El Salvador	0.57	0.52	0.53	0.67
6	Denmark	0.71	0.71	0.54	0.88	45	Bulgaria	0.57	0.53	0.46	0.73
7	Colombia	0.70	0.74	0.50	0.84	46	Argentina	0.57	0.64	0.40	0.68
8	Spain	0.67	0.69	0.55	0.78	47	Turkey	0.57	0.53	0.45	0.73
9	Costa Rica	0.67	0.68	0.56	0.77	48	Panama	0.56	0.64	0.45	0.60
10	Latvia	0.66	0.58	0.65	0.77	49	Italy	0.56	0.46	0.48	0.75
11	UK	0.66	0.60	0.56	0.83	50	Ecuador	0.56	0.56	0.43	0.68
12	Romania	0.66	0.63	0.60	0.75	51	South Korea	0.55	0.55	0.38	0.74
13	Austria	0.66	0.62	0.55	0.82	52	Azerbaijan	0.55	0.44	0.43	0.79
14	Canada	0.66	0.60	0.48	0.88	53	Congo	0.55	0.53	0.58	0.55
15	Germany	0.65	0.64	0.52	0.80	54	South Africa	0.54	0.59	0.38	0.64
16	Portugal	0.65	0.62	0.57	0.77	55	Thailand	0.53	0.49	0.39	0.73
17	Ireland	0.65	0.64	0.56	0.75	56	Albania	0.53	0.52	0.45	0.63
18	Peru	0.65	0.78	0.46	0.70	57	Dominican R	0.53	0.58	0.45	0.56
19	Finland	0.65	0.54	0.55	0.84	58	Georgia	0.53	0.37	0.57	0.66
20	Slovakia	0.64	0.46	0.66	0.81	59	Armenia	0.53	0.33	0.57	0.69
21	Hungary	0.64	0.53	0.61	0.78	60	Tunisia	0.53	0.36	0.45	0.77
22	Brazil	0.64	0.54	0.57	0.79	61	Tajikistan	0.52	0.32	0.65	0.60
23	Uruguay	0.64	0.65	0.53	0.73	62	Singapore	0.52	0.58	0.37	0.61
24	Paraguay	0.63	0.66	0.62	0.61	63	Indonesia	0.52	0.45	0.41	0.69
25	Slovenia	0.63	0.53	0.53	0.82	64	Philippines	0.51	0.51	0.51	0.62
26	Australia	0.63	0.67	0.35	0.87	65	Venezuela	0.51	0.25	0.57	0.70
27	Luxembourg	0.63	0.66	0.52	0.69	66	Algeria	0.50	0.34	0.40	0.76
28	Russia	0.62	0.59	0.49	0.79	67	Cyprus	0.49	0.55	0.39	0.54
29	Czech Rep	0.60	0.50	0.48	0.84	68	Guatemala	0.49	0.35	0.54	0.58
30	Belgium	0.60	0.47	0.56	0.79	69	India	0.48	0.49	0.41	0.54
31	Iceland	0.60	0.28	0.72	0.79	70	Sri Lanka	0.48	0.43	0.48	0.53
32	Chile	0.60	0.61	0.44	0.74	71	Malaysia	0.48	0.26	0.34	0.83
33	Netherlands	0.60	0.49	0.47	0.83	72	Bolivia	0.48	0.33	0.42	0.68
34	Lithuania	0.60	0.56	0.53	0.69	73	Kyrgyzstan	0.47	0.20	0.60	0.62
35	Estonia	0.59	0.54	0.50	0.72	74	Belarus	0.47	0.26	0.48	0.67
36	Mexico	0.59	0.60	0.41	0.75	75	Vietnam	0.47	0.30	0.43	0.66
37	USA	0.59	0.57	0.34	0.84	76	Nicaragua	0.46	0.40	0.48	0.51
38	Japan	0.58	0.58	0.43	0.74	77	Ukraine	0.46	0.23	0.39	0.77
39	Kazakhstan	0.58	0.56	0.40	0.79	78	Malta	0.46	0.48	0.36	0.54

continued on following page

Table 7. Continued

	Country	EAPI	EGD[a]	ES[b]	EAS[c]		Country	EAPI	EGD[a]	ES[b]	EAS[c]
79	Morocco	0.46	0.36	0.38	0.64	102	Iran	0.42	0.25	0.25	0.76
80	Cameroon	0.46	0.35	0.63	0.40	103	Nepal	0.42	0.31	0.63	0.33
81	Egypt	0.46	0.24	0.43	0.71	104	Bosnia & Her.	0.42	0.34	0.24	0.68
82	Namibia	0.46	0.45	0.51	0.41	105	Kuwait	0.42	0.33	0.12	0.80
83	Ghana	0.45	0.34	0.59	0.42	106	Mozambique	0.42	0.29	0.71	0.26
84	Uzbekistan	0.45	0.28	0.41	0.66	107	Eritrea	0.41	0.35	0.55	0.33
85	China	0.45	0.35	0.35	0.65	108	Syria	0.41	0.27	0.27	0.69
86	Libya	0.45	0.33	0.29	0.72	109	Kenya	0.41	0.28	0.63	0.31
87	FYR Maced.	0.45	0.37	0.31	0.66	110	Moldova	0.40	0.31	0.28	0.60
88	UAE	0.44	0.35	0.21	0.77	111	Oman	0.39	0.28	0.12	0.79
89	Honduras	0.44	0.31	0.50	0.51	112	Jamaica	0.39	0.25	0.36	0.56
90	Qatar	0.44	0.35	0.17	0.80	113	Ethiopia	0.39	0.26	0.71	0.19
91	Saudi Arabia	0.44	0.32	0.19	0.81	114	Bangladesh	0.38	0.39	0.39	0.37
92	Zambia	0.44	0.35	0.71	0.27	115	Jordan	0.38	0.25	0.28	0.60
93	Nigeria	0.44	0.38	0.61	0.33	116	Haiti	0.38	0.37	0.52	0.23
94	Trin. & Tob.	0.44	0.42	0.22	0.68	117	Mongolia	0.37	0.29	0.24	0.58
95	Botswana	0.44	0.48	0.37	0.46	118	Bahrain	0.37	0.18	0.21	0.72
96	Pakistan	0.43	0.33	0.44	0.54	119	Togo	0.37	0.25	0.65	0.20
97	Cote d'Ivoire	0.43	0.29	0.59	0.41	120	Cambodia	0.36	0.36	0.45	0.28
98	Iraq	0.42	0.37	0.19	0.72	121	Tanzania	0.36	0.26	0.65	0.17
99	Senegal	0.42	0.37	0.49	0.42	122	Benin	0.35	0.32	0.49	0.25
100	Turkmenistan	0.42	0.25	0.27	0.75	123	Lebanon	0.33	0.33	0.25	0.41
101	Brunei	0.42	0.36	0.21	0.70	124	Yemen	0.32	0.33	0.26	0.38

(WEF, 2013).
[a]EGD: Economic Growth and Development Basket;[b]ES: Environmental Sustainability Basket; [c]EAS: Energy Access and Security Basket.

- The super gasoline and diesel pricing distortion indicators are averaged into a mini-index which is assigned the same overall weight as the other indicators in the economic growth and development dimension. Within the same dimension, the indicators for fuel imports and exports also form a combined index.
- The average of methane and nitrous-oxide emissions indicators is given equal weight as the other indicators in the environmental sustainability dimension.
- In the energy security and access dimension, the energy imports indicator for countries that are net importers is combined with the score for the diversification of import counterparts to form a mini-index, with equal weight as the other indicators of the group.

The normalization of raw data in EAPI is based on targets specified according to international norms or policies. When there are no data available for target setting, thresholds are mainly based on the performance distribution of 2012. EAPI also includes a simple data imputation procedure, where the latest available data point is extrapolated forward when a value is missing for a particular year within an indicator.

The EAPI 2014 overall country scores and the scores for the three EAPI dimensions are shown in Table 7. The top 10 performers are mostly European and/or OECD nations, with the exception of Costa Rica and Colombia.

The differences observed across countries and dimensions show that there is no single pathway to achieving a balanced energy system. However, as emphasized by WEF (2013), the results do underline the importance of economic development on energy performance.

Other Approaches

A large number of sustainability indicators for energy development may be found in the literature, but only a limited number of studies provide aggregate results in the form of an energy sustainability index (IAEA, 2005; UNDESA, 2007). Below we present three approaches to analyzing energy sustainability proposed in Brown & Sovacool (2007), Sovacool & Brown (2010), and Sovacool & Mukherjee (2011). The first two approaches use different suites of indicators which, in contrast to the methods reviewed in the previous sections, aren't aggregated into a single numerical value. The corresponding overall indexes are assessed in linguistic terms by expert knowledge and information from indicator time series data measuring the progress towards energy sustainability.

The, so-called, energy sustainability index (Brown & Sovacool, 2007) aims at informing policymakers, investors, and analysts about the status of energy conditions and educating the public about energy issues. This index uses 12 indicators that belong to the following main groups:

1. **Oil Security:** Oil imports, oil prices, availability of non-petroleum transportation fuels, fuel economy of vehicles.
2. **Electricity Reliability:** Natural gas imports, natural gas prices, electricity retail prices, investments in electric transmission and distribution.
3. **Energy Efficiency:** Energy intensity, energy use per capita.
4. **Environmental Quality:** SO_2 emissions from electric generators, CO_2 emissions from energy consumption.

The method does not provide aggregated results but each indicator gives a sense of where an energy system might be heading. In the US, for example, between 1970 and 2004, the majority of the energy indicators exhibit an unfavorable trend since the country has failed to make real progress in solving some of its most pressing energy problems. As noted by the authors, the proposed index is preliminary and requires further refinement.

In the context of their previous work, Sovacool & Brown (2010) proposed an Energy Security Performance Index (ESPI) in order to study energy security challenges related to climate change, growing dependence on fossil fuels, population growth, and economic development. ESPI uses 10 indicators belonging to the following four groups:

1. **Availability:** oil import dependence, natural gas import dependence, availability of alternative fuels.
2. **Affordability:** retail electricity prices, retail gasoline/petrol prices.
3. **Energy and Economic Efficiency:** energy intensity, electricity use per capita, average fuel economy for passenger vehicles.
4. **Environmental Stewardship:** SO_2 emissions, CO_2 emissions.

ESPI provides results for 22 OECD countries, over a period from 1970 to 2007. In order to study the trends of ESPI, the authors analyzed the relative progress for each country, and, assuming equal weights across all indicators, they found that only four countries (Belgium, Denmark, Japan, and the UK) have made progress towards improving energy security.

Table 8. Energy security dimensions and components

Dimensions	Explanation	Components
Availability	Having sufficient supplies of energy. Being energy independent. Promoting a diversified collection of different energy technologies. Harnessing domestically available fuels and energy resources. Ensuring prudent reserve to production ratios.	1. Security of supply and production 2. Dependency 3. Diversification
Affordability	Producing energy services at the lowest cost, having predictable prices for energy fuels and services, and enabling equitable access to energy services.	4. Price stability 5. Access and equity 6. Decentralization 7. Affordability
Technology Development and Efficiency	Capacity to adapt and respond to the challenges from disruptions, researching and developing new and innovative energy technologies, making proper investments in infrastructure and maintenance. Delivering high quality and reliable energy services.	8. Innovation and research 9. Safety and reliability 10. Resilience 11. Efficiency and energy intensity 12. Investment and employment
Environmental and Social Sustainability	Minimizing deforestation and land degradation, possessing sufficient quantity and suitable quality of water, minimizing ambient and indoor pollution, mitigating GHG emissions associated with climate change, adapting to climate change.	13. Land use 14. Water 15. Climate change 16. Pollution
Regulation and Governance	Having stable, transparent, and participatory modes of energy policymaking, competitive markets, promoting trade of energy technology and fuels, enhancing social and community knowledge about education and energy issues.	17. Governance 18. Trade and regional interconnectivity 19. Competition and markets 20. Knowledge and access to information

(Sovacool & Mukherjee, 2011).

In the same context, Sovacool & Mukherjee (2011) proposed another framework to analyze national energy security policies and performance. Based on research interviews, survey results, a focused workshop, and an extensive literature review, the authors proposed that energy security ought to be comprised of five dimensions. As shown in Table 8, the five dimensions consist of 20 components. The proposed framework breaks down these components into 320 simple and 52 complex indicators.

This work did not present analytical country results, but provided a general methodological framework for developing aggregated energy security indices. The authors note that their main aim was to propose a framework that policymakers and scholars could use to analyze, measure, track, and compare national performance on energy security.

COMPARISON AND DISCUSSION

Sustainable development encompasses environmental, social and economic dimensions (Voinov & Smith, 1994; Adams, 2006). The energy sustainability indices examined in this chapter share these measurement dimensions. However, their focus and their calculation techniques (e.g., aggregation procedure, data imputation, weighting schemes) differ significantly.

A comparison of the main characteristics of the examined energy sustainability models is presented in Table 9. ESI focuses on measuring energy performance and evaluating a country's contextual performance (political, societal, and economic strength). EAPI puts emphasis to energy architectures and transitions to new energy architectures for countries. Finally SAFE applies sophisticated data process techniques and fuzzy

Table 9. Comparison of major energy sustainability indices

Index	Components	Coverage	Advantages	Weaknesses
ESI	1. Energy security 2. Energy equity 3. Environmental sustainability 4. Political strength 5. Societal strength 6. Economic strength	129 countries 23 indicators	• Measures not only energy but also contextual country performance • Provides an overall balance score • Enhanced methodology for measuring energy security and environmental sustainability • Provides analytical country profiles and trends	• Equal weighting scheme • No sensitivity analysis • Relative results
SAFE	1. Air quality 2. Soil quality 3. Accessibility 4. Production 5. Consumption 6. Security	128 countries 11 indicators	• Fuzzy logic models well uncertain and polymorphous concepts, can process quantitative as well as qualitative information, and does not require an explicit mathematical model • Includes a data imputation procedure • Takes into account the time dimension	Subjectivity in modeling (e.g., sustainability thresholds, rule bases, membership functions)
EAPI	1. Efficiency 2. Lack of distortion/affordability 3. Supportive/detracts from growth 4. Share of low-carbon fuel sources in the energy mix 5. Emissions impact 6. Level and quality of access 7. Self-sufficiency/multi-lateral markets 8. Diversity of supply	124 countries 18 indicators	• Provides overall aggregate results as well as a detailed profile for each country • Provides analytical results per region or economic cluster • Includes a data imputation procedure	• Emphasis on energy architecture • Equal weighting scheme • No sensitivity analysis

Table 10. Top 10 countries according to major energy sustainability indices

ESI (2013)	SAFE (2011)	EAPI (2013)
Switzerland	Albania	Norway
Denmark	Paraguay	New Zealand
Sweden	Norway	France
Austria	Brazil	Sweden
UK	Colombia	Switzerland
Canada	Latvia	Denmark
Norway	Vietnam	Colombia
New Zealand	Tajikistan	Spain
Spain	Kyrgyzstan	Costa Rica
France	New Zealand	Latvia

logic to avoid the shortcomings of simple additive aggregation approaches. Since there is no universally accepted definition and measuring technique of sustainability, these different models lead to different assessments.

Table 10 compares the three major energy sustainability models in terms of their top-ten rankings. The observed differences may be justified by the different rationale of their indices. For example, ESI includes political, societal, and economic indicators and thus rich countries with stable political systems often score higher. Indeed all 10 top ranking countries are OECD members. As mentioned in WEC (2013), the contextual dimension often gives an advantage to developed countries, while penalizing developing countries. EAPI gives priority to nuclear energy production among low-carbon fuel sources, while SAFE does the exact opposite on environmental grounds. SAFE is more favorable to countries with hydropower production (e.g., Albania or Latin American countries). However, Norway and New Zealand receive high scores in all major energy sustainability indicators and rank highly in all models.

CONCLUSION

Human development relies on sustainable supply and use of energy. However, the energy sources which are exploitable with current technology are finite, and come mostly from fossil fuels and nuclear fission which cause severe environmental problems. Indicators and assessment methods of energy sustainability can be used by policymakers to monitor, compare, and improve the performance of national energy systems.

Three major energy sustainability barometers are reviewed in this chapter. They are all based on the use of indicators covering three dimensions of the national energy systems: social, economic, and environmental. However the models differ in the choice of indicators and the methods used to combine indicators into an overall energy sustainability index. ESI uses the largest number of indicators among all models and combines energy sustainability with societal and political country performance. The indicators in each group or dimension have equal weights. SAFE uses a relatively small number of indicators in the form of time series or single values, which are combined into more composite ones and, finally, the overall index using fuzzy logic. An imputation scheme can be used to fill in missing data. Although fuzzy logic avoids the use of crisp weights, the choice of appropriate membership functions and rule bases requires expert knowledge. Finally, EAPI is methodologically similar to ESI, using equally weighted indicators, and its rankings have the most similarities with the other two models.

As emphasized by several scholars, there is no universally accepted definition or assessment technique of sustainability, and thus all alternative approaches lead to different assessments (see Grigoroudis et al., 2012 for a discussion). More work remains to be done to refine several aspects of the applied calculation techniques (e.g., weights) and mostly to overcome the problem of data availability and enrich the set of sustainability indicators.

REFERENCES

Adams, W. M. (2006). *The future of sustainability: Re-thinking environment and development in the twenty-first century*. IUCN. Retrieved May 1, 2011, from http://cmsdata.iucn.org/downloads/iucn_future_of_sustanability.pdf

Andriantiatsaholiniaina, L., Kouikoglou, V. S., & Phillis, Y. A. (2004). Evaluating strategies for sustainable development: Fuzzy logic reasoning and sensitivity analysis. *Ecological Economics*, *48*(2), 149–172. doi:10.1016/j.ecolecon.2003.08.009

Brown, M. A., & Sovacool, B. K. (2007). Developing an energy sustainability index to evaluate energy policy. *Interdisciplinary Science Reviews*, *32*(4), 335–349. doi:10.1179/030801807X211793

Esty, D. C., Levy, M., Srebotnjak, T., & de Sherbinin, A. (2005). *Environmental Sustainability Index: Benchmarking national environmental stewardship*. New Haven, CT: Yale Center for Environmental Law & Policy.

Grigoroudis, E., Kouikoglou, V. S., & Phillis, Y. A. (2012). Approaches for measuring sustainability. In P. Olla (Ed.), *Global sustainable development and renewable energy systems* (pp. 101–130). Hersey, PA: IGI Global. doi:10.4018/978-1-4666-1625-7.ch006

Grigoroudis, E., Kouikoglou, V. S., & Phillis, Y. A. (2013a). A fuzzy paradigm for the sustainability evaluation of energy systems. In F. Cavallaro (Ed.), *Assessment and simulation tools for sustainable energy systems: Methodology and applications* (pp. 205–224). New York, NY: Springer. doi:10.1007/978-1-4471-5143-2_10

Grigoroudis, E., Kouikoglou, V. S., & Phillis, Y. A. (2013b). SAFE 2013: Sustainability of countries updated. *Ecological Indicators*, *38*, 61–66. doi:10.1016/j.ecolind.2013.10.022

Grigoroudis, E., Kouikoglou, V. S., & Phillis, Y. A. (2014). Corrigendum to "SAFE 2013: Sustainability of countries updated.". *Ecological Indicators*, *41*, 216–217. doi:10.1016/j.ecolind.2014.02.001

IAEA. (2005). *Energy indicators for sustainable development: Guidelines and methodologies*. Vienna: International Atomic Energy Agency.

IAEA. (2005). *Energy indicators for sustainable development: Guidelines and methodologies*. Vienna: International Atomic Energy Agency. Retrieved July 27, 2014, from http://www-pub.iaea.org/MTCD/ publications/PDF/Pub1222_web.pdf

IEA. (2002). *World energy outlook: Energy and poverty*. Paris: International Energy Agency. Retrieved July 31, 2012, from http://www.iea.org// textbase/nppdf/free/2000/weo2002.pdf

IEA. (2007). *Key energy statistics 2007*. Paris: International Energy Agency.

IEA. (2010). *World energy outlook 2010*. Paris: International Energy Agency. Retrieved July 31, 2012, from http://www.iea.org/publications/ freepublications/publication/weo2010.pdf

IEA. (2011a). *Energy balances of non-OECD countries*. Paris: International Energy Agency.

IEA. (2011b). *Energy balances of OECD countries*. Paris: International Energy Agency.

IEA. (2011c). *Energy statistics of Non-OECD countries*. Paris: International Energy Agency.

IEA. (2011d). *Energy statistics of OECD countries*. Paris: International Energy Agency.

Kouikoglou, V. S., & Phillis, Y. A. (2009). On the monotonicity of hierarchical sum-product fuzzy systems. *Fuzzy Sets and Systems*, *160*(24), 3530–3538. doi:10.1016/j.fss.2009.02.001

Kouloumpis, V. D., Kouikoglou, V. S., & Phillis, Y. A. (2008). Sustainability assessment of nations and related decision making using fuzzy logic. *IEEE Systems Journal*, *2*(2), 224–236. doi:10.1109/ JSYST.2008.925256

OECD. (2005). *OECD Factbook 2005*. Paris: OECD Publications.

Phillis, Y. A., & Andriantiatsaholiniaina, L. (2001). Sustainability: An ill-defined concept and its assessment using fuzzy logic. *Ecological Economics*, *37*(3), 435–456. doi:10.1016/S0921-8009(00)00290-1

Phillis, Y. A., & Davis, B. J. (2009). Assessment of corporate sustainability via fuzzy logic. *Journal of Intelligent & Robotic Systems*, *55*(1), 3–20. doi:10.1007/s10846-008-9289-3

Phillis, Y. A., Grigoroudis, E., & Kouikoglou, V. S. (2011). Sustainability ranking and improvement of countries. *Ecological Economics*, *70*(3), 542–553. doi:10.1016/j.ecolecon.2010.09.037

Phillis, Y. A., Kouikoglou, V. S., & Andriantiatsaholiniaina, L. (2003). Sustainable development: A definition and assessment. *Environmental Engineering and Management Journal*, *2*(4), 345–355.

Phillis, Y. A., Kouikoglou, V. S., & Zhu, X. (2010). Fuzzy assessment of material recyclability and its applications. *Journal of Intelligent & Robotic Systems*, *55*(1), 21–38. doi:10.1007/s10846-008-9290-x

Sovacool, B. K., & Brown, M. A. (2010). Competing dimensions of energy security: An international perspective. *Annual Review of Environment and Resources*, *35*(1), 77–108. doi:10.1146/annurev-environ-042509-143035

Sovacool, B. K., & Mukherjee, I. (2011). Conceptualizing and measuring energy security: A synthesized approach. *Energy*, *36*(8), 5343–5355. doi:10.1016/j.energy.2011.06.043

TWAS. (2008). *Sustainable energy for developing countries*. Trieste: The Academy of Sciences for the Developing World.

UNDESA. (2007). *Energy indicators for sustainable development: Country studies on Brazil, Cuba, Lithuania, Mexico, Russian Federation, Slovakia and Thailand*. New York: United Nations. Retrieved July 31, 2012, from http://www.un.org/esa/sustdev/publications/energy_indicators/chapter2.pdf

UNEP. (1987). *Our common future: The world commission on environment and development*. Oxford: Oxford University Press.

Voinov, A., & Smith, C. (1994). *Dimensions of sustainability*. Paper presented at the 1st International Symposium of Ecosystem Health & Medicine. Ottawa, Canada. Retrieved May 1, 2011, from http://www.uvm.edu/~gundiee/AV/PUBS/DS/Sust_Dim.html

WEC. (2013). *World energy scenarios: Composing energy futures to 2050*. London: World Energy Council. Retrieved July 25, 2014, from http://www.worldenergy.org/wp-content/uploads/2013/09/World-Energy-Scenarios_Composing-energy-futures-to-2050_Full-report.pdf

WEC. (2013). *World energy trilemma: Time to get real – The case for sustainable energy investment*. London: World Energy Council. Retrieved July 25, 2014, from http://www.worldenergy.org/wp-content/uploads/2013/09/2013-Time-to-get-real-the-case-for-sustainable-energy-investment.pdf

WEF. (2013). *The Global Energy Architecture Performance Index Report 2014*. New York: World Economic Forum and Accenture. Retrieved July 25, 2014, from http://www3.weforum.org/docs/WEF_EN_NEA_Report_2014.pdf

World Resources Institute. (2006). *EarthTrends: Environmental information*. Washington, D.C.: World Resources Institute. Retrieved July 31, 2012 from http://earthtrends.wri.org

ADDITIONAL READING

Bell, S., & Morse, S. (1999). *Sustainability indicators: Measuring the immeasurable*. London: Earthscan.

Mayer, A. L. (2008). Strengths and weaknesses of common sustainability indices for multidimensional systems. *Environment International*, *34*(2), 277–291. doi:10.1016/j.envint.2007.09.004 PMID:17949813

Phillis, Y. A., & Kouikoglou, V. S. (2009). *Fuzzy measurement of sustainability*. New York: Nova Science Publishers.

Seth, S. (2009). Inequality, interactions, and human development. *Journal of Human Development and Capabilities*, *10*(3), 375–396. doi:10.1080/19452820903048878

KEY TERMS AND DEFINITIONS

Energy Architecture Performance Index (EAPI): An index similar to ESI using somewhat different indicators.

Energy Equity: It evaluates the accessibility and affordability of energy within a country or region.

Energy Security: It evaluates the reliability of a given energy infrastructure and its ability to meet demand.

Energy Sustainability Index (ESI): An index that ranks countries according to their ability to provide stable, affordable and environmentally-friendly energy.

Fuzzy Logic: A type of mathematical logic that handles incomplete knowledge and inexact data via propositions that are true with varying degrees, ranging from totally true to totally false.

Sustainability Assessment by Fuzzy Evaluation (SAFE): A model that numerically assesses the sustainability of a country, region, corporation or other entity using fuzzy logic.

Sustainability Indicators: Variables related to and used in the assessment of sustainability. They are measured numerically or linguistically.

ENDNOTES

1 The United Nations hope that by 2030 there will be universal access to modern energy services, a doubling of the share of renewable energy sources in the global energy mix, and a doubling of the global rate of improvement in energy efficiency.

2 Energy architecture is defined as the integrated physical system of energy sources, carriers and demand sectors that are shaped by government, industry and civil society (WEF, 2013).

3 Accenture plc is a multinational management consulting, technology services, and outsourcing company with more than 293,000 employees and offices, and operations in more than 200 cities in 56 countries.

Chapter 7
Energy and Sustainability in the European Region:
The Russian Factor

Anatoly Zhuplev
Loyola Marymount University, USA

Dmitry A. Shtykhno
Plekhanov Russian University of Economics, Russia

ABSTRACT

This chapter examines European energy security in the EU-Russian context. Europe is extremely dependent on Russian energy imports. This dependency requires sustainable energy solutions. Russian economy is characterized by high energy consumption and intensity. Russian energy sector needs massive investments, technological and management improvements. They become problematic due to the nation's poor investment climate, stagnating economy, and isolationist foreign policy. These, along with Russia's emerging reorientation of its energy exports toward Asia tend to worsen European energy security. The chapter explores trends in the global energy and analyses the dynamics and outlook for sustainable energy security in Europe in the context of import dependency in energy. It looks at the drivers, constrains and trends in the Russian energy sector in the Eurasian regional context. Despite technological advances, policies toward sustainable development and renewable energy, in the next two decades Europe will predominantly depend on fossil fuels and Russian energy imports.

INTRODUCTION

Globalization, economic growth, and growing political-economic interdependency among nations after WWII have changed an easy access to energy and the whole energy security equation. There is an increasing realization of limited mineral resources and environmental capacity to absorb the consequences of human economic activity in sustainable development. Economic pressures, social and environmental concerns, and development goals set energy access as key priority and subject of acute competition. Emerging global players like China and India have dramatically boosted their energy demand over the past few decades adding urgency to sustainable energy development worldwide.

DOI: 10.4018/978-1-4666-8433-1.ch007

European region critically depends on imported fossil energy. The region's chronic energy dependency is fraught with complex relationships between energy suppliers, transit countries, and recipients. This complexity is often amplified by political-economic relationships on cross-national and regional level – current Russian-Ukrainian standoff and its strategic implications is the case in point. Ensuring European energy security and sustainable growth by simply switching from importing oil and gas to nuclear energy or local coal is problematic due to environmental, nuclear security, economic constrains, and public concerns. Renewable sources of energy, although growing at robust rates, will still be playing relatively limited long-term role in the overall energy supply.

The chapter opens by the exploration of trends and dynamics in the global energy sector. The long-term global energy demand will continue to rise with the developing nations, notably China and India, playing increasingly prominent role in global energy consumption. Despite robust rates of growth in renewable sources of energy, fossils, specifically oil and natural gas, will continue to dominate the global energy mix. Recent advances in global shale oil and gas exploration may signify a new paradigm for global energy. That may create a potential ground for mitigating European energy import dependency and erode Russian monopoly as the region's critical energy supplier. Meantime, Russian domestic energy sector itself faces the growth and development challenges that require technological innovations, capital investment, large-scale social and environmental policies and improvements in management. By extension, it implies large-scale international cooperation, while Russia's current policies of self-isolation are heading in the opposite direction.

After introducing and deliberating the concept of sustainable energy development framework by Munsinghe (2004) the discussion focuses on how the dynamics in the global energy sector impact European energy sector and energy security. In particular, the forces and dynamics of demand and supply, energy intensity, and renewable energy perspectives are explored in the sustainability context. Although OECD Europe demonstrates patterns of high energy efficiency compared to many other regions and countries, the absolute levels of energy consumption in Europe remain among the highest in the world propagating energy security as top political priority. Under limited access to own fossil energy, high energy import dependency, particularly acute with the Russian oil and gas imports, as well as limited share of renewable energy now and in three decades to come, European regional energy security and dependency on Russia imports of oil and gas will remain a critical strategic issue. To a degree these political-economic factors form political dilemmas for sustainable development and growth in the European region.

Russian domestic energy sector and its role in the overall domestic and foreign policy exert critical impacts on European energy security. In this context, the chapter discusses trends, driving forces and dynamics in the Russian domestic energy sector. Under these drivers and constraints Russian energy sector is facing its own strategic development challenges. One of them is renewable energy: it plays very limited current role in the overall energy supply that is not going to change in the long-term perspective. Addressing those sectorial challenges, meeting energy commitments fulfilling the needs of domestic economic growth as well as sizeable export commitments may prove paramount for both European energy security and Russian energy sector. One relatively new strategic geo-regional trend discussed in the chapter is Russia's latest energy doctrine envisioning a large scale shift in oil and natural gas shipments from Europe to Asian region.

Figure 1. Energy system

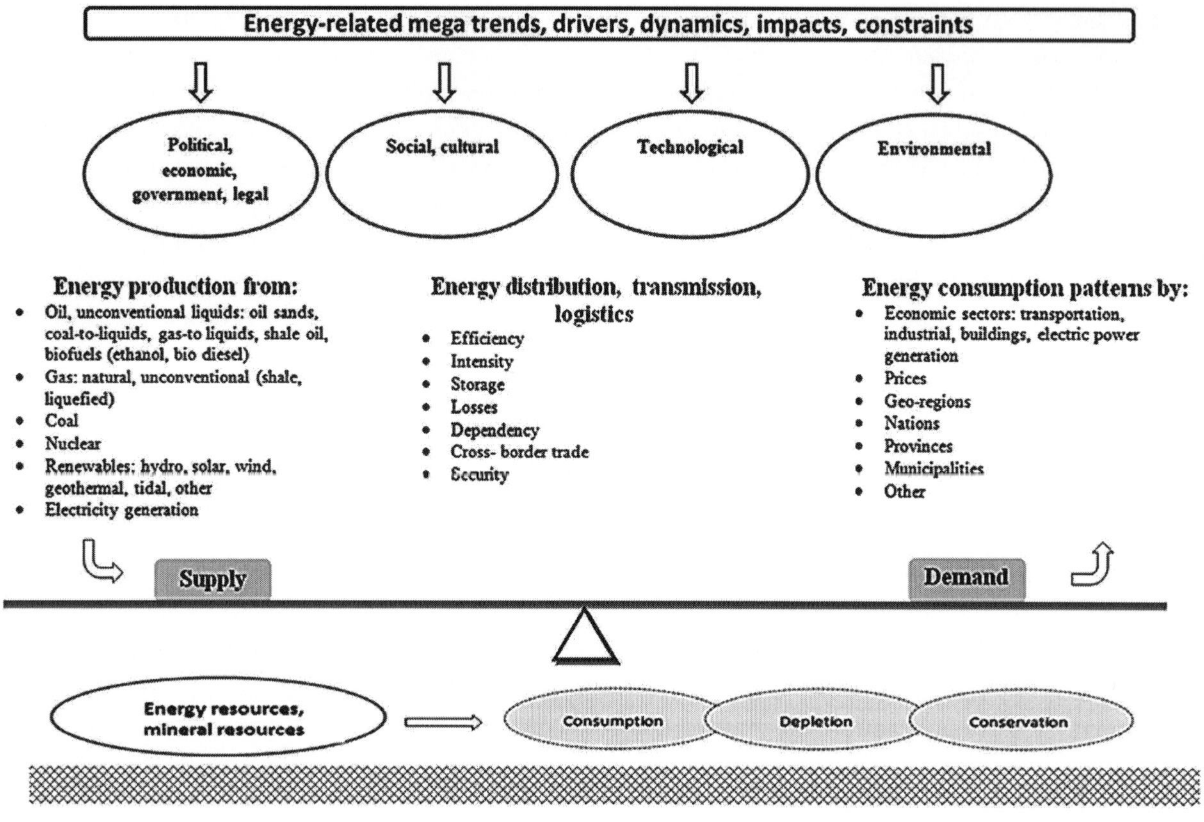

MEGATRENDS AND DYNAMICS IN THE GLOBAL ENERGY SECTOR

Globalization intensifies geo-regional and international strategic interdependency that has critical implications for economic, social, and environmental aspects of sustainable development. With the advent of industrial revolution and technological discovery of the industrial kerosene distillation from crude oil in the second half of the 19th century petroleum as a source of energy has been playing premier political-economic role. By the early 20th century petroleum had become one of the most valuable commodities traded on world markets.

Global energy sector is driven by complex dynamics (Figure 1): supply, demand, economics, technology, logistics, strategic risks, policies and politics play elaborate and often controversial roles in sustainable development. According to the annual World Energy Outlook by the International Energy Agency, main impact factors in global energy include government policy and action, level of economic activity, demographics, energy prices, and technological advances.

There are several key trends reflecting and affecting the dynamics of global energy markets between 2010 and 2035:

1. Energy demand will continue rising long-term with a projected global economy's expansion of almost 140% and a 1.7 billion increase in the world population over the twenty-five year projection period. Under the "New Policies" scenario, world energy demand increases over the projection period by 35%, or 1.2% per year on average.

2. The dynamics of energy markets will be largely determined by emerging economies and by sharpening global competition for global access to energy resources. Developing nations, particularly China and India, play increasingly prominent role, reshaping the competitive landscape in energy demand that was previously dominated by developed nations. The non-OECD share of global primary energy demand, which has already increased from 36% in 1973 to 55% in 2010, continues to rise. That reflects their faster rates of growth in population, economic activity and saturation effects that curb energy demand in the mature economies.
3. Fossil oil, coal, and natural gas will continue to play dominant role in global energy supply. Fossils that represented 81% of the primary fuel mix in 2010 will experience by 2035 only modest reduction of their share to 75.5%.
4. Persistent failure to provide universal energy access to the world's poor; currently almost 1.3 billion people, about 1/5 of the global population, lack access to electricity, while 2.6 billion people rely on traditional biomass for cooking.
5. Continuing increase in CO_2 causing global greenhouse emissions, political and public action is yet another impact factor (World Energy Outlook, 2012).
6. Limited access to mineral resources available for exploration brings about shrinking time horizons within which non-renewable sources of energy worldwide become scarcer physically, unsustainable economically, socially, or environmentally - thus pushing extraction farther into inhospitable territories and deeper underground, constraining growth, undermining sustainability, and creating political-economic anxiety worldwide. Limited physical availability of fossil energy depresses supply and strengthens global suppliers' bargaining positions; on the other hand, it facilitates efficiency in fossils and advances alternative energy sources.
7. Tepid and sporadic economic recovery, particularly in developed world, following the recent global economic slump is another impact factor. Slow economic growth moderates energy demand, but at the same time limits vital investments in the highly capital intensive energy sector (globalEDGE. Energy, 2014).
8. Renewable energy is gradually emerging as an alternative to fossils being driven by conflicting forces. On the one hand, despite technological advances, growing public interest worldwide, and their robust growth outlook, renewables' share in the world's overall energy consumption in the next two-three decades will remain limited - renewables are not cost-competitive against fossils without subsidies and other forms of government support. On the other hand, technological advances and political factors provide increasing support toward renewables on social and environmental grounds. The share of renewables in primary energy use in the New Policies Scenario rises from 13% in 2011 to 18% in 2035, resulting from rapidly increasing demand for modern renewables to generate power, produce heat and make transport fuels. Containing this rapid growth is the sustained shift from the use of traditional biomass in developing countries in favor of modern energy services. Renewable energy technologies are becoming more competitive compared to wholesale electricity prices, but their continued growth hinges on subsidies to facilitate deployment and drive further cost reductions. Subsidies to renewables reached $101 billion in 2012, up 11% relative to 2011. Almost 60% of these were paid in the EU that is going through a period of economic stagnation and facing a dilemma cutting the

subsidies. Global subsidies to renewables increase to over $220 billion by 2035. Wind becomes competitive in a growing number of regions, as does solar photovoltaic, but only in a limited number of markets (World Energy Outlook, 2013). Most of this growth will occur in the power sector where renewables' share in total generation grows from 20% to 31%. Under these dynamics fossils, especially oil and natural gas will remain the main sources in the global energy supply mix in the medium range, thus strengthening fossil producing/exporting countries' leverage over import-dependent energy consuming nations. Europe, and the broader Eurasian region, is strategically vulnerable because of its high dependency on imported energy and limited sustainable alternatives to fossils. Meantime, contingent on the outcome of the conflicting driving forces, long-term outlook may turn positive for renewables.

9. Yet another impetus in the global energy sector is brought about by reservations toward nuclear energy spreading across the world. Currently nuclear energy holds a sizeable share in the final energy consumption, but progressively comes under public scrutiny in many countries, facing pressures on the social and environmental sides of sustainable development. Those have been amplified by the 2011 Fukushima nuclear power plant disaster in Japan. All things considered, in 2035 nuclear power will supply 12% electricity worldwide - almost flat against today's level. In stark contrast, Russia's share of nuclear energy in power generation increases under the International Energy Agency's forecast from 12% in 2010 to 17% in 2035.
10. Over the past decade, technological progress, economic developments, and public interest around the world spurred the development of unconventional natural gas and unconventional oil, especially shale gas and oil. The current glut in the global natural gas supply together with the continuing tepid economic post-recession recovery depressing energy demand, increased output of the liquefied natural gas (LNG) as well as sharp increase in the shale gas output facilitated by the use of hydraulic fracturing ("fracking") technology have brought about drastic changes in the global gas market. A 2009 study concluded that increased shale gas production in the US and Canada could help prevent Russia and Persian Gulf countries from dictating higher prices for the gas they export to European countries (Rice, 2009). The "shale revolution" in the U.S. has had profound impacts on global energy markets. Just a few years ago, the U.S. was expected to become a major importer of LNG. Instead, LNG imports have shrunk to a tiny proportion of demand, and the U.S. and Canada are set to become LNG exporters once the infrastructure is in place in the middle of this decade. That change puts a downward pressure on global gas prices and presents challenge to gas suppliers like Russia (World Energy outlook, 2012, p. 77). Additionally, cheap and widely available natural gas depresses global coal prices and market demand in renewable energy. Interest toward alternative fossil energy sources in the European region as well as other regions around the world has been propagated by the Russian takeover of the Crimea from Ukraine in 2014 and its continuous use of energy as strategic weapon in foreign policy. Adding complexity, there are substantial uncertainties, logistical, social and environmental concerns associated with hydraulic fracturing, such as high water supply requirements, potential contamination of ground water and air, potential migration of gases and chemicals used in hydraulic fracturing to the surface, the waste, and the related health effects.
11. Finally, Russia itself is a critical player in the global energy sector on both supply and consumption side. Internal dynamics in the

Russian energy sector - its macroeconomic environment and policy shifts - may have deep implications for the Eurasian energy security. Russian economics are often driven by politics where energy sector is the main engine playing critical role in Russian domestic decisions and foreign policy.

Sustainability and Renewable Energy Developments

From the time of industrial commencement of oil in the 19th century the global energy sector has been dominated by fossil fuels - petroleum, natural gas, and coal. As of late, energy production across subsectors has been characterized by high level of concentration, automation, and capital intensity with energy demand primarily driven by economic activity and population growth. The energy sector's key profitability drivers lie in increasing production from existing wells, achieving high success rate of new wells drilled, creating the best mixture of products, controlling the short term demand cycle, managing risk, and increasing efficiency of operations (globalEDGE Energy, 2014).

Driven by interdependent forces in the economic, environmental, and social triad, sustainability has been gaining momentum worldwide over the past two-three decades. Energy sector plays paramount and often controversial role in the sustainability context being a foundation of socio-economic development and at the same time exerting negative environmental impacts from the energy producing sector itself and across energy consuming sectors.

Munasinghe (2004) proposed sustainable energy development framework that integrates economic, social, and environmental perspectives. Each perspective in this concept plays its own dynamics with energy emerging as a core resource interacting with three dimensions ("pillars") of sustainable development. Munasinghe developed two analytical and assessment tools for sustainability. The Action Impact Matrix prioritizes economic, environmental, and social interactions and sectorial development policies; advanced cost-benefit analysis, including economic valuation of environmental and social impacts, and multicriteria analysis, especially in cases where impacts cannot be easily quantified in monetary terms. The second tool, Sustainable Development Assessment (SDA), focuses on balanced analysis of development and sustainability in specific policies and projects. SDA's economic component is based on conventional economic and financial analysis, including cost-benefit analysis. SDA also incorporates environmental, social, and poverty assessment.

Munasinghe's matrix model categorizes interactions between energy use and sustainable development into energy-economy and energy-environment-society linkages functioning on national, geo-regional, transnational, and global levels. Specific goals for sustainable energy development on national level might be ensuring: economic efficiency in energy supply and use to maximize growth, including energy efficiency-related objectives such as energy conservation; raising sufficient revenues from energy sales to finance sector development; addressing socio-economic concerns such as meeting basic energy needs of the poor and developing special regions (particularly rural or remote areas) and priority sectors of the economy; preserving the environment; diversifying supply, reducing dependence on foreign sources, saving scarce foreign exchange, and meeting national security requirements; ensuring price stability; etc. (Figure 2).

THE DYNAMICS IN GLOBAL ENERGY AND THEIR IMPACT ON EUROPE

Supply and Demand

As national economies and regions embrace globalization their interdependency increases. Energy sector is closely intertwined with socio-economic development and environmental priorities across global regions and industries.

Figure 2. Framework for sustainable energy development
(Adapted from Encyclopedia of Energy Ed. by Robert Ayres et al. Elsevier. ISBN: 978-0-12-176480-7 March 2004, p. 800.)

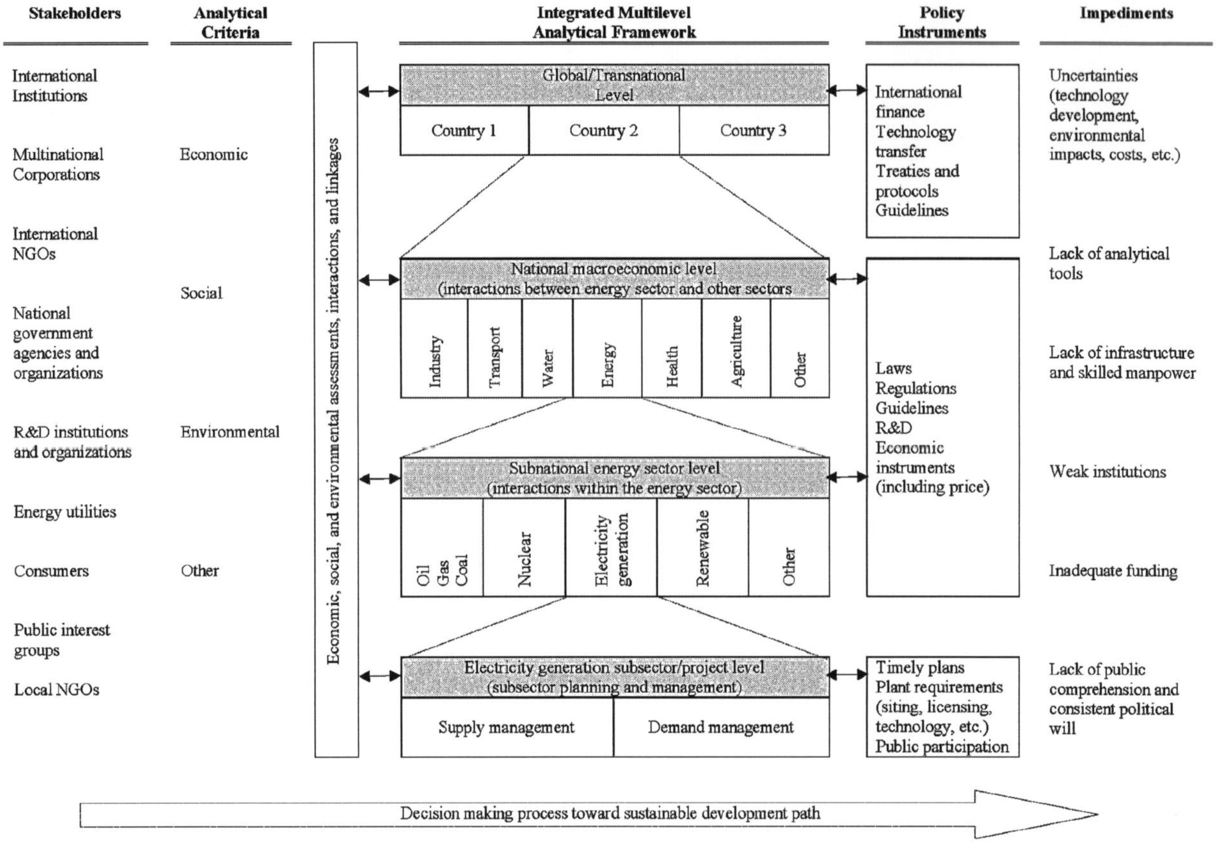

The bi-annual International Energy Outlook 2013 (IEO2013) (Energy Information Administration, 2013) Reference case scenario (Reference case scenario will be used throughout further discussion in this chapter unless otherwise specified) projects that between 2010 and 2040 world energy consumption will grow by 56% or 1.5% per year on average. Total world energy use rises from 524 quadrillion British thermal units (Btu) in 2010 to 820 quadrillion Btu in 2040. Much of the growth in energy consumption occurs in countries outside the OECD, where demand is driven by strong, long-term economic growth. Energy use in non-OECD countries over the projection period increases by 90%, or 2.2% per year on average) compared to just 17% in OECD countries, or 0.5% per year on average.

Renewable energy and nuclear power are projected as the world's fastest-growing energy sources, each increasing by 2.5% per year on average. However, fossil fuels continue to supply a dominant share - almost 80% - of world energy use through 2040. Natural gas is the fastest-growing fossil fuel: global natural gas consumption increases by 1.7% per year. Increasing supplies of tight gas, shale gas, and coalbed methane support growth in projected worldwide natural gas use. Coal use grows faster than petroleum and other liquid fuel use until after 2030, mostly because of increases in China's consumption of coal and tepid growth in liquids demand attributed to slow growth in the OECD regions and high sustained oil prices.

The world industrial sector continues to account for the largest share of delivered energy consumption: it still consumes over half of global delivered energy in 2040. Due to the current policies and regulations limiting fossil fuel use, worldwide energy-related carbon dioxide emissions rise in 2040 by 46% (Energy Information Administration, 2013).

A definite trend affecting global energy on both the supply and demand side is a soaring demand and fierce global competition for energy access from China and India that are rapidly emerging as powerful global players. In contrast to the OECD nations, developing non-OECD economies, particularly in non-OECD Asia, have led the global recovery from the 2008-2009 recession. China and India have been among the world's fastest growing economies for the past two decades. From 1990 to 2010, China's economy grew by an average of 10.4% per year and India's by 6.4% per year. Although the two countries' economic growth remained strong through the global recession, both slowed in 2012 to rates much lower than analysts had predicted at the start of the year. In 2012, real GDP in China increased by 7.2%, its lowest annual growth rate in 20 years. India's real GDP growth slowed to 5.5% in 2012. In 2015, China's GDP growth is projected at +6.9% and India's at +6.4% compared to 2014 (The Economist, 2014).

Even with slower than average growth in China and India in the short-term, medium- and long-term prospects, they continue to lead both world economic growth and energy demand growth. Since 1990, energy consumption in both countries as a share of total world energy use has increased significantly; together, they accounted for about 10% of total world energy consumption in 1990 and nearly 24% in 2010. From 2010 to 2040, their combined energy use more than doubles, and they account for 34% of projected total world energy consumption in 2040. China, which recently became the world's largest energy consumer, is projected to consume more than twice as much energy as the U.S. in 2040 (Energy Information Administration, 2013). These trends are particularly worrisome for the European region characterized by high energy consumption on the demand side and lack of its own fossil energy resources on the supply side.

The IEO2013's 2009-2040 projections show that the world GDP measured in constant 2005 dollars in purchasing power parity will grow on average at 3.6% annually while the annual average marketed energy consumption growth is estimated at only 1.5% (Tables 1 & 2). Under these dynamics, a 1% growth in global GDP is supported by a 0.42% growth in energy consumption. An average rate of GDP growth for non-OECD countries is projected to be 2.53 times higher compared to OECD countries, while energy consumption growth among non-OECD countries exceeds that of OECD by the order of 4.4.

Structural changes in the world energy consumption from 1973 to 2011 are profiled in Figure 3. During this time span the share of oil in the world's total primary energy supply dropped by 14.4 percentage points, natural gas – increased by 5.3 percentage points, coal/peat – increased by 4.2 percentage points, nuclear – increased by 4.2 percentage points, with the shares of remaining groups of fuels undergoing only insignificant fluctuations. In the long term, the *IEO2013* Reference case projects increased world consumption of marketed energy from all fuel sources through 2040 (Figure 4). Under this dynamic, fossil fuels are expected to continue supplying much of the energy used worldwide. Although liquid fuels—mostly petroleum-based—remain the largest source of energy, the liquids share of world marketed energy consumption falls from 34% in 2010 to 28% in 2040, as projected high world oil prices lead many energy users to switch away from liquid fuels when feasible. The fastest growing sources of world energy in the Reference case are renewables and nuclear power. In the Reference case, the renewables share of total energy use rises from 11% in 2010 to 15% in 2040, and the nuclear energy's share grows from 5% to 7% (Energy Information Administration, 2013).

Table 1. World Gross Domestic Product (GDP) by region, purchasing power parity, 2009-2040, $US billion 2005

Region	History		Projections						Average Annual Percent Change, 2010-2040
	2009	2010	2015	2020	2025	2030	2035	2040	
OECD									
Americas	15,498	15,929	18,079	20,833	23,589	26,663	30,250	34,441	2.6
United States (*)	12,758	13,063	14,679	16,859	18,985	21,355	24,095	27,277	2.5
Canada	1,165	1,202	1,349	1,519	1,684	1,850	2,053	2,285	2.2
Mexico/Chile	1,575	1,664	2,050	2,455	2,921	3,458	4,102	4,879	3.7
Europe	14,262	14,618	15,589	17,353	19,224	21,002	22,939	25,080	1.8
Asia	5,791	6,062	6,723	7,386	8,019	8,563	9,139	9,720	1.6
Japan	3,776	3,948	4,215	4,424	4,608	4,687	4,741	4,716	0.6
South Korea	1,244	1,323	1,598	1,951	2,295	2,642	3,024	3,467	3.3
Austral/New Zealand	771	790	910	1,011	1,116	1,234	1,374	1,537	2.2
Total OECD	**35,551**	**36,609**	**40,391**	**45,572**	**50,832**	**56,227**	**62,328**	**69,241**	**2.1**
Non-OECD									
Europe and Eurasia	4,346	4,502	5,463	6,841	8,323	9,918	11,749	13,681	3.8
Russia	1,938	2,022	2,433	2,965	3,474	3,911	4,338	4,618	2.8
Other	2,408	2,480	3,030	3,876	4,850	6,007	7,411	9,063	4.4
Asia	16,628	18,206	25,623	34,632	45,417	58,549	73,472	89,127	5.4
China	8,299	9,167	13,715	18,906	25,203	32,829	40,977	48,404	5.7
India	3,364	3,661	5,112	7,277	9,894	13,124	17,046	21,731	6.1
Other	4,965	5,379	6,796	8,449	10,320	12,597	15,449	18,991	4.3
Middle East	2,263	2,292	2,781	3,316	3,662	3,967	4,241	4,427	2.2
Africa	3,780	3,963	4,868	6,165	7,732	9,725	12,224	15,348	4.6
Central and South America	4,623	4,927	6,016	7,194	8,398	9,711	11,207	12,954	3.3
Brazil	1,833	1,971	2,365	2,860	3,319	3,859	4,522	5,328	3.4
Other	2,790	2,955	3,651	4,334	5,079	5,853	6,685	7,626	3.2
Total Non-OECD	**31,640**	**33,889**	**44,750**	**58,147**	**73,532**	**91,870**	**112,893**	**135,537**	**4.7**
Total World	**67,192**	**70,498**	**85,141**	**103,719**	**124,364**	**148,097**	**175,221**	**204,779**	**3.6**

(Source: Energy Information Administration, 2013, p. 182)

(*)Includes the 50 States and the District of Columbia.

Note: Totals may not equal sum of components due to independent rounding.

Table 2. World total primary energy consumption by region, 2009-2040; reference case, quadrillion Btu

Region	History				Projections				Average Annual Percent Change, 2010-2040
	2009	2010	2015	2020	2025	2030	2035	2040	
OECD									
Americas	117.0	120.2	121.3	126.1	129.7	132.9	137.2	143.6	0.6
United States (*)	94.9	97.9	97.3	100.5	101.8	102.3	103.9	107.2	0.3
Canada	13.7	13.5	14.2	14.8	15.6	16.5	17.3	18.2	1.0
Mexico/Chile	8.4	8.8	9.9	10.9	12.3	14.1	16.0	18.2	2.5
Europe	80.0	82.5	82.1	85.5	88.6	90.9	92.8	94.6	0.5
Asia	37.7	39.6	40.6	43.0	44.3	45.4	46.1	46.4	0.5
Japan	21.0	22.1	21.7	22.5	23.0	23.0	22.9	22.2	0.0
South Korea	10.1	10.8	11.8	13.0	13.8	14.7	15.3	15.9	1.3
Australia/ New Zealand	6.7	6.7	7.0	7.4	7.5	7.7	8.0	8.2	0.7
Total OECD	**234.7**	**242.3**	**244.1**	**254.6**	**262.7**	**269.2**	**276.1**	**284.6**	**0.5**
Non-OECD									
Europe and Eurasia	43.7	47.2	49.8	53.3	56.8	60.8	64.6	67.1	1.2
Russia	27.0	29.6	31.0	33.3	35.7	38.0	39.9	40.5	1.0
Other	16.7	17.6	18.9	20.0	21.1	22.8	24.7	26.6	1.4
Asia	148.1	159.0	194.3	230.3	261.6	290.4	317.2	337.5	2.5
China	93.1	101.2	132.2	159.0	180.9	198.9	213.3	219.9	2.6
India	23.1	24.4	27.5	32.1	37.2	42.6	48.7	55.0	2.7
Other	31.8	33.4	34.6	39.2	43.5	48.9	55.2	62.6	2.1
Middle East	26.6	27.8	33.1	36.6	39.5	42.5	45.7	48.8	1.9
Africa	18.4	18.9	19.6	21.9	24.4	27.4	31.0	35.0	2.1
Central and South America	26.9	28.7	31.0	33.2	35.5	38.8	42.5	46.6	1.6
Brazil	12.7	13.7	14.9	16.5	17.8	19.9	22.3	25.4	2.1
Other	14.3	15.0	16.1	16.7	17.6	19.0	20.2	21.3	1.2
Total Non-OECD	**263.7**	**281.7**	**327.9**	**375.3**	**417.7**	**460.0**	**501.0**	**535.1**	**2.2**
Total World	**498.4**	**523.9**	**572.0**	**629.8**	**680.4**	**729.2**	**777.1**	**819.6**	**1.5**

(Source: Energy Information Administration, 2013, p. 179).
(*) Includes the 50 States and the District of Columbia.
Note: Totals may not equal sum of components due to independent rounding.

In 2009, the summary energy consumption in OECD countries was slightly higher than that of non-OECD countries. As a result of structural changes over 2009-2040, non-OECD countries led by China and India will outpace OECD in their energy demand growth by the order of 2.2.

Structural shifts in global energy consumption and supply by the source constitute another set of trends. Despite wide public interest, technological innovations, and other factors supporting renewable energy, fossil sources in the forthcoming 25 years will remain the leading source of primary energy worldwide. Under the IEO2013 forecast a

*Figure 3. World's fuel shares of total primary energy supply in 1973 and 2011, %; *others include geothermal, solar, wind, heat, etc.*
(Source: Key World Energy Statistics, 2013, p. 6).

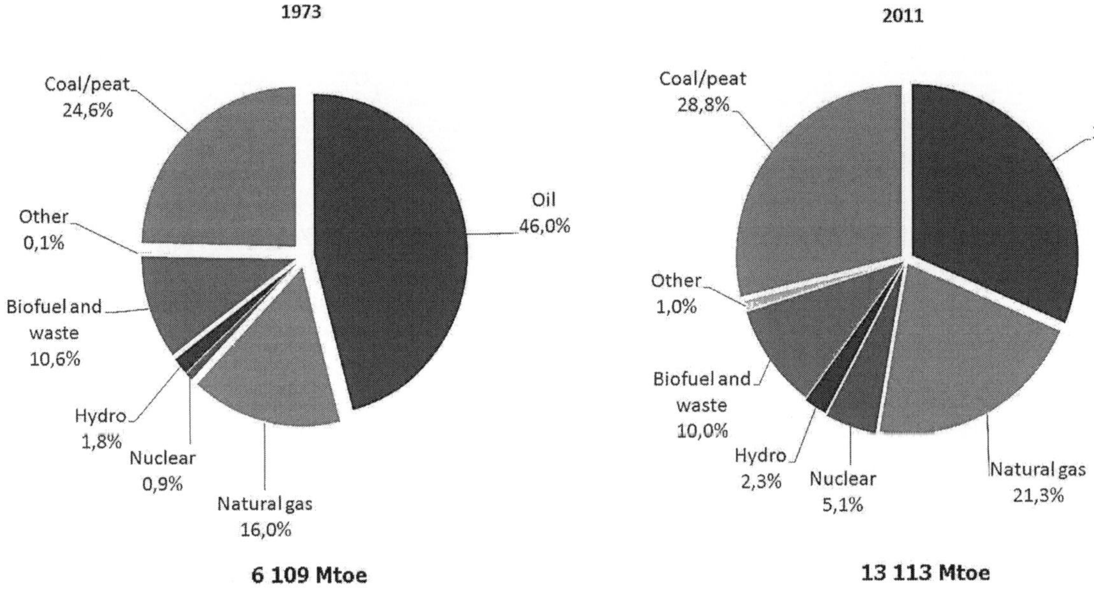

summary share of fossils (liquids, natural, gas and coal) in the overall world marketed energy use will drop only by 6 percentage points from 84.1% in 2009 to 78.5% in 2040. With total energy demand increasing by 1.5% on average annually, liquid fuel consumption will experience the slowest growth at 0.9%; natural gas - 1.7%; coal – 1.3%; nuclear energy – 2.5%; and renewables will experience the highest average annual growth (Energy Information Administration, 2013, p. 181).

As noted earlier, oil is expected to retain its dominant share as a premier energy source worldwide. Advances in technology make liquids production in previously inaccessible regions increasingly feasible, while higher oil prices make production in those regions economically viable. An important example of the potential impact of technological advances is the rapid growth of U.S. shale oil production in recent years, a development that has the potential to change the structure of oil markets worldwide. Although the extent of the world's shale oil resources is not yet fully understood and plenty remaining environmental and social public concerns, there is potential for shale oil production to increase non-OPEC supplies of liquid fuels substantially over the course of the *IEO2013* projection. A study commissioned by EIA to assess shale oil resources in 41 countries outside the U.S., taken in conjunction with EIA's own assessment of resources within the U.S., indicate worldwide technically recoverable resources of 345 billion barrels of shale oil resources, which would add considerable non-OPEC liquid fuels production potential if the resources became economically competitive with other sources of liquids supply (Energy Information Administration, 2013).

Energy Intensity as Sustainability Driver: Cross-Country Comparisons

Apart from the country's economic size, growth rate and specific conditions in energy supply and demand, efficiency in energy consumption at the economy at large also plays role, particularly crucial in sustainability perspective. Although general energy consumption is loosely correlated with the GDP dynamics, it varies across regions and even across nations with comparable GDP per capita.

Figure 4. World energy consumption by fuel type, 1990-2040, quadrillion Btu (Source: Energy Information Administration, 2013, p. 2).

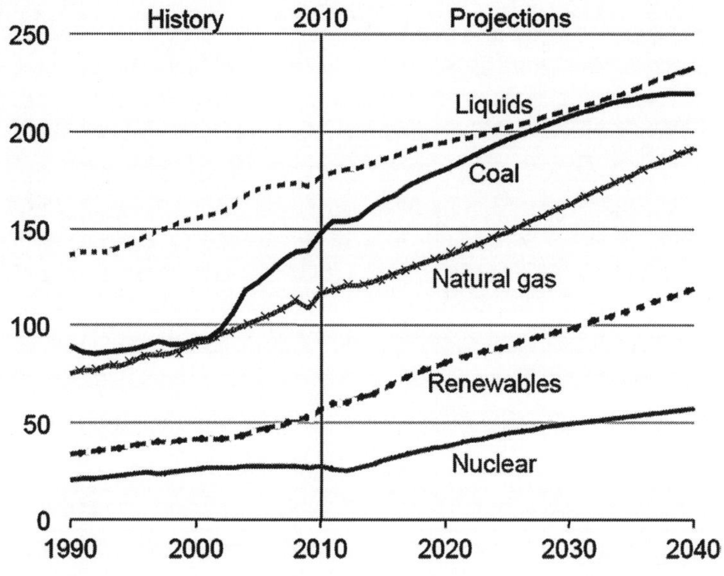

Energy intensity measures the amount of energy required to produce one dollar of GDP (Energy Information Administration, 2014). Table 3 containing the energy intensity summary suggests three important energy related implications for sustainable development for the forthcoming quarter of century. First, energy intensity worldwide drops over projection period, albeit insignificantly, just 2% overall. Second, the rate of energy intensity reduction in non-OECD countries, particularly in China and India, the two leading global energy consuming nations, is higher compared to OECD countries.

Third, significant variations in energy intensity across OECD countries worldwide will remain in place in the long term perspective: by 2040 some OECD countries are expected to register the following levels of energy intensity expressed in Btu per 2005 dollar of GDP: U.S. - 3.9 thousand Btu/$, Japan – 4.7, and Australia/New Zealand – 5.4 thousand Btu/$. In contrast, some illustrations of the 2040 energy intensity level projections among non-OECD countries include: India – 2.5 and Brazil – 4.8 thousand Btu/$. Meanwhile, the Middle East will remain characterized as the world region with the highest energy intensity at 11.0 thousand Btu per 2005 US dollar of GDP (Energy Information Administration, 2013).

In 2010, EU-27's total primary energy consumption as a whole was 5.427 thousand Btu per dollar of GDP (measured in 2005 US dollars, purchasing power parity). In 2011, energy intensity for several major EU-27 economies was as follows: Germany – 4.837, France - 5.385, and UK – 3.952 thousand Btu/$. This indicator for Russia stood at 15.624, compared to 7.329 in the U.S, 10.661 in Canada, Russia's counterpart in cold weather, and 10,842 thousand Btu/$ in China with which Russia has relative commonalities in communist history, territorial proximity, and geographic-economic proximity (Energy Information Administration, 2014). From this standpoint, Russia's energy use per dollar of GDP in 2010/2011 was 2.8 times higher compared to EU-27 as a whole, 3.2 times higher compared to Germany, 2.1 times higher compared to the U.S., 1.5 times higher compared to Canada, and 1.4 times higher compared to China.

Table 3. World energy intensity by region, reference case, 2009-2040; thousand Btu per 2005 dollar of GDP

Region	History		Projections						Average Annual Percent Change, 2010-2040
	2009	2010	2015	2020	2025	2030	2035	2040	
OECD									
Americas	7.6	7.5	6.7	6.1	5.5	5.0	4.5	4.2	-2.0
United States (*)	7.4	7.5	6.6	6.0	5.4	4.8	4.3	3.9	-2.1
Canada	11.7	11.2	10.5	9.7	9.3	8.9	8.4	8.0	-1.1
Mexico/Chile	5.3	5.3	4.8	4.4	4.2	4.1	3.9	3.7	-1.1
Europe	5.6	5.6	5.3	4.9	4.6	4.3	4.0	3.5	-1.3
Asia	6.5	6.5	6.0	5.8	5.5	5.3	5.0	4.8	-1.0
Japan	5.6	5.6	5.2	5.1	5.0	4.9	4.8	4.7	-0.6
South Korea	8.1	8.2	7.4	6.7	6.0	5.6	5.1	4.6	-1.9
Australia/New Zealand	8.7	8.4	7.7	7.3	6.7	6.3	5.8	5.4	-1.5
Total OECD	**6.6**	**6.6**	**6.0**	**5.6**	**5.2**	**4.8**	**4.4**	**4.1**	**-1.6**
Non-OECD									
Europe and Eurasia	10.1	10.5	9.1	7.8	6.8	6.1	5.5	4.9	-2.5
Russia	13.9	14.7	12.7	11.2	10.3	9.7	9.2	8.8	-1.7
Other	6.9	7.1	6.2	5.1	4.4	3.8	3.3	2.9	-2.9
Asia	8.9	8.7	7.6	6.6	5.8	5.0	4.3	3.8	-2.7
China	11.2	11.0	9.6	8.4	7.2	6.1	5.2	4.5	-2.9
India	6.9	6.7	5.4	4.4	3.8	3.2	2.9	2.5	-3.2
Other	6.4	6.2	5.1	4.6	4.2	3.9	3.6	3.3	-2.1
Middle East	11.7	12.1	11.9	11.0	10.8	10.7	10.8	11.0	-0.3
Africa	4.9	4.8	4.0	3.5	3.2	2.8	2.5	2.3	-2.4
Central and South America	5.8	5.8	5.2	4.6	4.2	4.0	3.8	3.6	-1.6
Brazil	6.9	7.0	6.3	5.8	5.4	5.1	4.9	4.8	-1.3
Other	5.1	5.1	4.4	3.9	3.5	3.2	3.0	2.8	-2.0
Total Non-OECD	**8.3**	**8.3**	**7.3**	**6.5**	**5.7**	**5.0**	**4.4**	**3.9**	**-2.5**
Total World	**7.4**	**7.4**	**6.7**	**6.1**	**5.5**	**4.9**	**4.4**	**4.0**	**-2.0**

(Sources: U.S. Energy Information Administration (EIA). *Annual Energy Outlook* 2013. DOE/EIA-0383(2013) (Washington. DC: April 2013); AEO2013 National Energy Modeling System, run REF2013.D102312A www.gia.pov/aeo; and World Energy Projection System Plus (2013).

(*) Includes the 50 States and the District of Columbia.

Note: Totals may not equal sum of components due to independent rounding.

On the energy use side, the highest energy consumption worldwide occurs in industrial sector (including manufacturing and nonmanufacturing sub-sectors – agriculture, mining, and construction), buildings sector (places where people live, reside, work, and buy goods and services – excluding industrial facilities used for producing, processing, or assembling goods) and transportation sector (road, rail, air, water, pipeline). In 2010, industrial users consumed 200 quadrillion Btu of delivered energy worldwide or 38% of the world total energy consumption. The share of renewable energy in the overall industrial energy consumption was 7.6%. The 2010 energy consumption in the buildings sector was 81 quadrillion Btu or 15% of the world total energy consumption. Energy consumption in the transportation sector stood at 101 quadrillion Btu or 19% of the world total energy consumption. According to the International Energy Outlook, over the projection period through 2040 the above shares in delivered energy consumption by major consuming sectors are not expected to experience any noticeable change (Energy Information Administration, 2013).

Renewable Energy

Renewables are steadily expanding their share in the global energy mix. This trend is particularly noticeable in the power sector and in regions that have put in place measures to promote their deployment. European Union is the case in point. Double-digit growth rates have been observed in the last decade for some renewable energy technologies and renewables are projected to continue to grow strongly over the projection period, provided that the necessary support measures are kept in place. However, the situation varies across the three top energy consuming subsectors: electricity, heat and transport.

Under the International Energy Agency's forecast till 2035 (World Energy Outlook, 2013) electricity generation from renewable sources is growing rapidly for most technologies, while renewable energy use for heat is growing more slowly and remains under-utilized. After a period of rapid expansion, the rate of growth of biofuels use has recently slowed, largely due to adverse weather conditions that reduced harvests and increased feedstock prices, as well as sustainability concerns. Investment in renewable power generation has also been rising steadily but it fell, for the first time, in 2012. In part, this reflects falling unit costs, but it is perhaps also a sign that the prospects for renewables are becoming more complex.

In Europe, rapid expansion of renewable power generation, particularly wind and solar, has occurred in recent years, driven by the requirements of the EU's Renewable Energy Directive and national targets. However, low rates of power demand growth and an economic slowdown raise doubts about the timelines of future investments and policymakers in several countries have started to express concerns about the affordability of high shares of certain types of renewable power generation. Particularly, these concerns relate to higher than anticipated rates of deployment of solar photovoltaic (PV) systems, driven, in some countries, by over generous government subsidies. Spain and some other European countries with strong traditions in environmentally and socially oriented political agendas represent examples of those lavish government subsidies that, after being discontinued under the pressure of economic downturn in the region, led to the implosion of the whole PV manufacturing sector. Another factor is the rapidly falling PV system cost driven to large extent by massive global supply from the low cost PV manufacturing industry in China propped by government subsidies and other forms of support. Meanwhile, difficulties about integrating high levels of variable renewables into the electricity system are also emerging in some European countries.

In the U.S., the market for renewables has been growing strongly, in large part due to the continuation of stimulus policies directed at renewable energy, such as the provision of cash grants (instead of a tax credit) of up to 30% of investment costs for eligible renewable energy projects (US Treasury 1603 Program). While this program expired in late 2012, many projects were able to pre-qualify and will continue receiving this support if completed by the end of 2016. An investment tax credit and production tax credits also provided support for renewables in the U.S., despite uncertainty over the future of the programs. 1

With rapidly growing power demand and concerns over energy security and local pollution, deployment of renewables has been accelerating and is expected to continue to do so in non-OECD countries, particularly China and India. In China, the energy development plan, announced in January 2013 as part of the 12th Five-year Plan, sets ambitious renewables goals with mandatory 2015 targets for non-fossil energy use, energy intensity, carbon intensity and particulate emissions. India's 12th Five-year Plan foresees an increase in grid-connected renewable generation capacity of 11 GW from large hydropower and 30 GW from other renewable sources by 2017. Major increases in renewables capacity are planned in the coming years in Brazil, led by hydropower, bioenergy and onshore wind. Tendering schemes in South Africa, the United Arab Emirates and Morocco are prompting investment in wind, solar PV and concentrating solar power (a massive-scale, industrial type solar technology), and many other countries with rising power demand are also embarking on large-scale deployment.

After global biofuels production more than doubled between 2006 and 2010, driven by supportive policies in Brazil, the U.S. and the EU, its growth in 2011and 2012 stagnated, despite high oil prices. Ethanol output in Brazil and the U.S. was affected by poor sugarcane and corn harvests, leading to a shortfall of feedstock supply creating demand pressures and high prices. In Europe, high feedstock prices and poor margins, as well as strong competition from non-European producers, posed challenges for biodiesel producers. Provision for the blending of more than 10% ethanol in the gasoline pool in the U.S. has raised technical and economic challenges, while doubts about the sustainability of biofuels production in the EU have led to a proposal to limit the use of food-crop derived biofuels to 6% of transport fuel. The production of advanced biofuels – which offer the prospect of requiring less land, improving greenhouse-gas balances and lower competition between food and fuel – has been expanding, but only slowly.

The share of modern renewable energy for heat in total final heat demand worldwide has risen only slowly and is currently just above 10%. Most of this contribution comes from bioenergy, although solar thermal and geothermal are playing an increasing part as they become progressively more cost competitive in a number of markets and circumstances. However, these technologies face distinct market and institutional challenges to deployment, with renewable heat energy receiving less policy attention than electricity from renewables or biofuels. To date, only 35 countries have policy frameworks supportive of renewable heat – most of them within the EU stemming from the Renewables Directive (World Energy Outlook, 2013). The world renewable energy current use and projections are profiled in Table 4.

EUROPEAN ENERGY SECURITY AND RUSSIA

Further discussion of European energy security will focus on the EU-27 that continues to be a key part of the global political-economic "triad."

Table 4. World renewable energy: current use and projections by type and scenario

		New Policies		Current Policies		450 Scenario	
	2011	**2020**	**2035**	**2020**	**2035**	**2020**	**2035**
Primary Energy Demand (Mtoe)	1 727	2 193	3 059	2 130	2 729	2 265	3 918
United States	140	196	331	191	282	215	508
Europe	183	259	362	250	326	270	452
China	298	392	509	373	445	405	690
Brazil	116	148	207	146	204	150	225
Share of global TPED	13%	15%	18%	14%	15%	16%	26%
Electricity Generation (TWh)	4 482	7 196	11612	6 844	10 022	7 528	15 483
Bioenergy	424	762	1477	734	1250	797	2 056
Hydro	3 490	4 555	5 827	4 412	5 478	4 667	6 394
Wind	434	1 326	2 774	1 195	2 251	1 441	4 337
Geothermal	69	128	299	114	217	142	436
Solar PV	61	379	951	352	680	422	1 389
Concentrating solar power	2	43	245	35	122	56	806
Marine	1	3	39	3	24	3	64
Share of total generation	20%	26%	31%	24%	25%	28%	48%
Heat demand*(Mtoe)	343	438	602	432	551	446	704
Industry	209	253	316	255	308	248	328
Buildings * and agriculture	135	184	286	177	243	198	376
Share of total final demand	8%	10%	12%	9%	11%	10%	16%
Biofuels (mboe/d) **	1.3	2.1	4.1	1.9	3.3	2.6	7.7
Road transport	1.3	2.1	4.1	1.9	3.2	2.6	6.8
Aviation ***	-	-	0.1	-	0.1	-	0.9
Share of total transport	2%	4%	6%	3%	4%	5%	15%
Traditional biomass (Mtoe)	744	730	680	732	689	718	647
Share of total bioenergy	57%	49%	37%	50%	40%	47%	29%
Share of renewable energy demand	43%	33%	22%	34%	25%	32%	17%

(Source: World Energy Outlook, 2013).

*Excludes traditional biomass; **Expressed in energy-equivalent volumes of gasoline and diesel; *** Includes international bunkers.

Note: Mtoe = million tonnes of oil equivalent; TPED = total primary energy demand; TWh = terawatt-hour; mboe/d = million barrels of oil equivalent per day.

European Energy Consumption

In the 2000s, the EU-27 energy consumption has grown moderately: between 2000 and 2007, an average annual growth rate in inland energy consumption was 0.7% against 0.6% in the previous decade. Recently this rate was further moderated by the current global economic slump. Under a steady growth in the overall energy consumption, the EU-27 energy consumption structure has seen some changes in recent years, notably a decrease of the coal consumption and increase in renewables and natural gas (Mäkinen, 2010).

The EU-27's latest overall energy flow profile is presented in Figure 5. In 2011, 40.3% of the overall EU-27 mix in final energy consumption was comprised of petroleum and petroleum products, 21.9% - gas, 21.6% - electricity, 7% - renewables, 4.4% - delivered heat, 4.4% - solid fuels, and 0.5% - waste, non-renewables. Major economic sectors comprised the following shares in the overall energy balance: transport – 33%, industry – 26%, households – 24.7%, agriculture – 2.1%, fishing – 0.1% and other – 1.3% (European Commission, 2013a).

Historically, EU-27's gross inland energy consumption has been considerably higher than primary energy production (Figure 5) creating a sizeable deficit gap that has to be covered by imports – in 2011 this gap reached 951 Mtoe. EU-27's total import dependency in 2011 grew to 53.8% compared to just 43.2% in 1995. In 2011, petroleum and petroleum products were characterized by the highest level of import dependency across EU-27 at 84.9%, followed by gas (67%), and solid fuels, where EU-27 registered overall import dependency at 41.4%. In contrast, EU-27's import dependency in renewable energy was in low single digits and close to zero for electricity. As a result, over 1995-2011, energy import dependency in the region has been steadily rising for every energy source except renewables (Figure 6).

High energy consumption coupled with limited renewable energy share across EU-27 stands in stark contrast with lack of its own fossil resources, particularly acute in oil and gas. Other severe constrains include limited development potential for hydropower and wide-spread social and environmental public reservations toward nuclear power as renewable alternatives to the fossils creating dilemmas in policy making and regional politics. With the EU-27's current import dependency in energy as high as 53.8%, 16 out of 27 countries satisfy more than half of their energy needs by imports, and for the ten remaining countries energy dependency ranges from 10% to 50%. Denmark is the only energy independent EU-

Figure 5. EU energy flow in 2011, Mtoe
(Source: European Commission, 2013a).

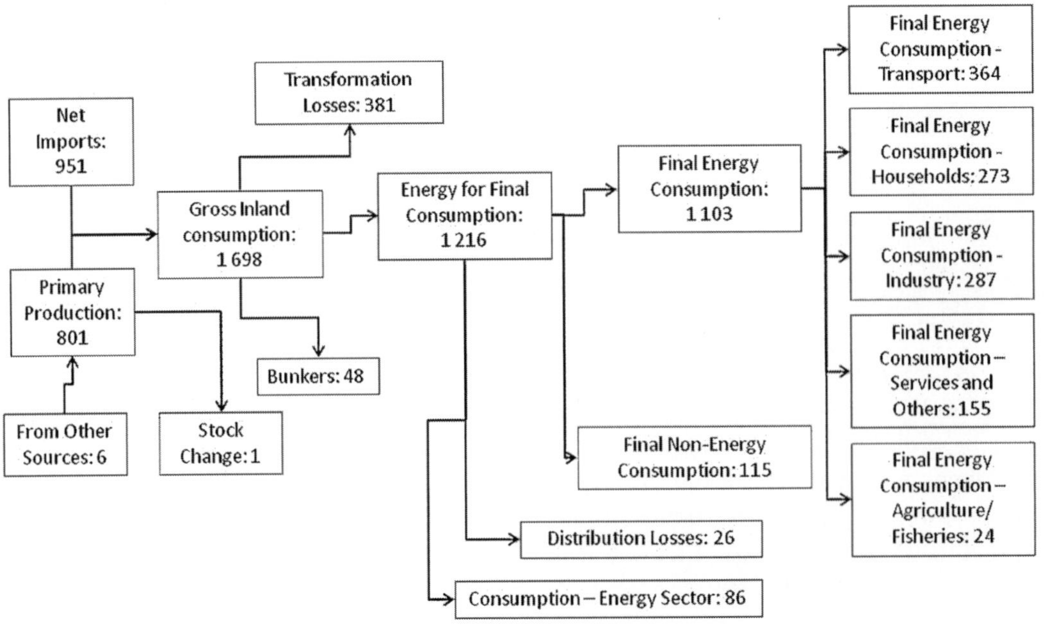

Figure 6. EU-27 import dependency in energy by the source, 1995-2011 (%)
(Source: European Commission, 2013a).

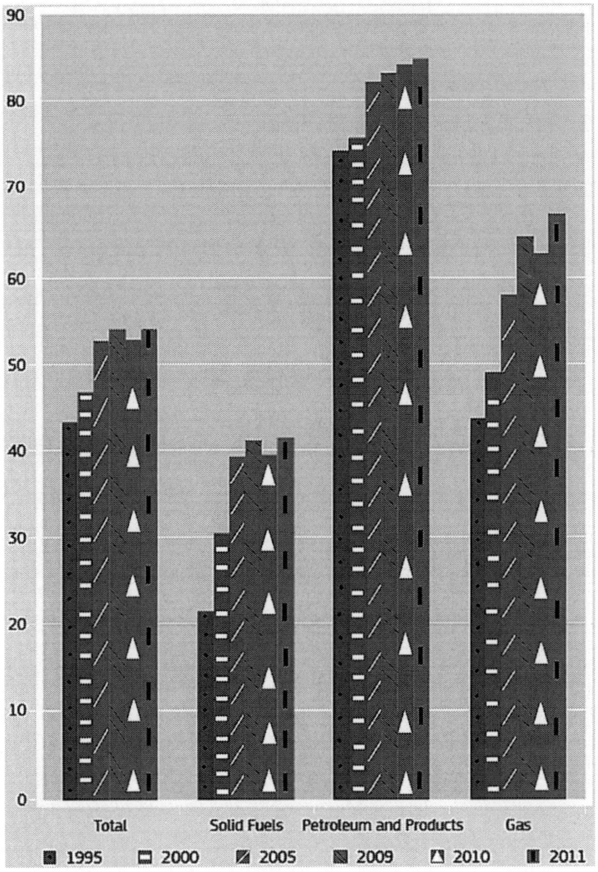

27 member country. Table 5 provides more details on energy dependence on a country by country basis.

In 2011, EU-27's top crude oil and natural gas suppliers were Russia with 35% of EU-27's total oil imports and 30% of natural gas imports and Norway with 12% of EU-27's oil imports and 20% gas imports (European Commission, 2013a). Putting this into a long term perspective, Norway's 2009 share in world's proved total oil reserves was 0.4% against Russia's 5.2%. As for the natural gas, in 2009 Norway's 1.1% share of the world's total proved reserves stood against Russia's 17.6%. Additionally, Russia held 18.2% of the world proved reserves in coal (BP Statistical Review of the World Energy, 2013, pp. 6, 20, & 30).

Meanwhile, there are some positive trends across EU-27 mitigating the region's import dependency on the energy consumption side. In 2011, EU-27's energy intensity (gross inland energy consumption/GDP) was 5.426 thousand Btu per year per 1 US dollar (in 2005 U.S. dollars, purchasing power parities) or 74% of the world average level and 72% of the U.S. level. (Energy Information Administration, 2014). Over the past two decades, EU-27 energy intensity has been declining in all major economic sectors. From 1995 through 2008 it dropped by approximately 65% overall, including 40% in industry, 50% in transport, and 50% in the service sectors (European Commission, 2010). Another positive trend is an increasing, albeit, moderately, share of renewables in the EU-27 overall energy balance. Renewables are projected to experience growth with their share projected to account by 2020 for 20% of the EU's final energy consumption against 13% in 2011 (European Commission, 2013a, p. 25).

Furthermore, the Renewable Energy Directive 2009/28/ by the European Commission ("the Directive") established a European framework for the promotion of renewable energy, setting mandatory national renewable energy targets for achieving a 20% share of renewable energy in the final energy consumption and a 10% share of energy from renewable sources in transport by 2020. These goals are headline targets of the European 2020 strategy for growth, since they contribute to Europe's industrial innovation and technological leadership as well as reducing emissions, improving the security of Europe's energy supply and reducing its energy import dependence. The Directive also requires the simplification of the administrative regimes faced by renewable energy, together with improvements to the electricity grid, to improve access for electricity from renewable energy. It established a comprehensive sustainability scheme for biofuels

Table 5. EU-27 import dependency in energy by the member country, 1995-2011 (%)

%	1995	2000	2005	2009	2010	2011
EU-27	43.2	46.7	52.4	53.8	52.6	53.8
Index 1995	100	108	121	124	122	125
BE	80.9	78.1	80.1	74.3	76.8	72.9
BG	57.2	46.5	47.5	45.3	40.1	36.6
CZ	20.6	23.0	28.3	27.1	25.6	27.9
DK	33.3	-35.3	-50.9	-20.4	-16.9	-8.5
DE	56.8	59.5	61.2	61.5	59.8	61.1
EE	32.4	32.0	25.4	21.4	13.1	11.7
IE	69.2	84.6	89.3	88.2	85.6	88.9
EL	66.7	69.5	68.6	67.8	69.1	65.3
ES	71.7	76.7	81.4	79.2	76.8	76.4
FR	48.0	51.6	51.7	51.0	49.1	48.9
IT	82.0	86.5	84.4	818	83.8	81.3
CY	100.4	98.6	100.7	96.3	100.7	92.4
LV	70.4	59.7	63.0	58.8	41.6	59.0
LT	63.4	59.8	57.0	50.3	82.0	81.8
LU	97.7	99.6	97.3	97.4	97.0	97.2
HU	48.0	55.2	63.2	58.7	58.3	52.0
MT	104.8	100.3	100.0	101.1	99.1	100.6
NL	18.3	38.7	38.4	36.5	30.7	30.4
AT	66.6	65.6	71.4	65.0	62.1	69.3
PL	0.0	10.6	17.6	31.7	31.6	33.7
PT	85.4	84.9	88.5	81.0	75.4	77.4
RO	30.8	22.0	27.6	20.2	21.7	21.3
SI	50.8	52.6	52.3	48.1	49.4	48.4
SK	68.9	65.0	65.4	66.4	63.0	64.2
FL	53.9	55.3	54.2	54.0	48.3	53.8
SE	37.6	39.2	37.7	37.1	36.7	36.8
UK	-16.2	-17.0	13.4	26.2	28.1	36.0

(Source: European Commission, 2013a).

and bioliquids with compulsory monitoring and reporting requirements. All biofuels used for compliance with the 10% target and that benefit from national support are required to comply with the scheme (European Commission, 2013b).

In March 2014, the EU heads of government requested the European Commission to produce a plan for reducing energy dependency (European Energy Secutiry, 2014). Given high complexity and interdependency of the energy system (Figure 1), energy sector's critical impacts on the three "pillars" of sustainability as well as political, economic, social, technological and other multiple constraints in reducing European energy dependency is a daunting task. Finding solutions balancing economic, environmental, and social aspects of sustanable development is likely to be a tradeoff in which some components of the triad will be given a priority at the expense of other components.

Under the flat projections for energy demand growth and limited share of renewable and nuclear energy in the overall consumption across Europe fossil fuels are destined to retain their premier role in the forthcoming decades. Lacking its own fossil energy resources, notably oil and gas, having high aspirations in the robust economic dynamics, while simultaneously emphasizing sustainability, and yet striving to reduce import dependency in energy leave Europe with limited "green" options. These options are somewhat more flexible in diversifying oil imports in which Europe has the highest import dependency compared to natural gas (Figure 6). Oil shipments are not as rigidly tied to stationary pipeline networks and can be diversified more easily. Natural gas imports have been historically tied to the existing gas pipeline networks and long-term contracts. Diversification in natural gas supply is much harder to accomplish due to the limitations in global sources of supply alternatives and enormous capital intensity involved in constructing pipelines. Only recently, over the past few years, there have been a noticeable global trend toward building liquified natural gas (LNG) facilities to mitigate Europe's import dendency on Russian gas in the midium to long term perspective (European Energy Security, 2014). Meanwhile, with the stagnant and even declining natural gas production potential in Norway and UK, two major gas suppliers after Russia (BP Statistical Review of World Energy, 2013), Europe is destined to remain dependent on Russian natural gas imports. Put in other words, unless there are drastic improvements in energy efficiency and/or transition to alternative energy sources. Russia is poised to retain its key strategic role as Europe's energy supplier.

EU-Russia Relationships

Europe and Russia have had complex interdependent relationships. Both parties have many areas of vital mutual interest. Russia is EU's third largest trade (exports + imports) partner that plays extraordinary role in regional oil and gas supply. In turn, EU is Russia's #1 trade partner, distantly followed by China, Ukraine, Belarus and the U.S. (European Union, 2014b). From the EU perspective, strategic cooperation with Russia concentrates on four key priorities: economy and environment; freedom, security, and justice; external security; and research and education, including cultural aspects (European Union, 2014a). In some of these areas EU and Russia's interests are converging, in others – diverging. Energy tends to play a common denominator and often a bone of content in this complex political-economic relationship. The Russian-Ukrainian crisis unfolding since spring 2014 has complicated EU-Russian political relationships, aggravated European energy security issue in the sustainability context and placed it to the forefront of the EU-Russian interdependency debate and foreign policy (Barroso, 2014).

Since 1997 the Partnership and Cooperation Agreement between the EU and Russia has been the framework of the EU-Russia relations. It regulates the political and economic relations between the two parties. Trade between the two economies showed steep growth rates until mid-2008 when the trend was interrupted by the economic crisis and unilateral measures adopted by Russia, which had a negative impact on EU-Russia trade. Since 2010 mutual trade has resumed its growth reaching record levels in 2012. EU exports to Russia are dominated by machinery and transport equipment, chemicals, medicines and agricultural products. EU imports from Russia are dominated by raw materials, in particular, oil (crude and refined) and gas. The EU is the most important investor in Russia. It is estimated that up to 75% of Foreign Direct Investment stocks in Russia come from EU Member States, including Cyprus (European Commission, 2014a).

More specifically, European-Russian economic relations can be illustrated by trade and investment statistics. In 2012, Russian exports in goods to EU-27 constituted 45.0% of its total exports worldwide against 34.1% in Russian imports from EU-27 of its total imports worldwide. The absolute level of EU-Russia trade in services is relatively low: in 2012 EU-27 exports of services to Russia were €28.2 billion and imports of services from Russia were twice as low at €15.2 b billion.

Product wise, EU's top exports of goods to Russia were, in billions of €: (#1) machinery and transport equipment – €61.0 billion (49.6% of the EU total exports to Russia), (#2) chemicals and related products - €19.4 billion (15.8% of the total), (#3) miscellaneous manufactured articles - €14.7 billion (11.9% of the total), and (#4) food and live animals - €8.3 billion (6.7% of the total).

Russia's top exports of goods to EU-27 were, billions of €: (#1) mineral fuels, lubricants and related materials - €162.4 (76.3% of the Russia's total exports to EU), manufactured goods classified chiefly by material - €13.5 billion (6.4% of the total), chemicals and related products – €6.6 billion (3.0% of the total), and various commodities and transactions – €5.9 billion (2.8% of the total) (European Commission, 2014a).

Clearly, Russian exports of goods to EU-27 are dominated by mineral fuels, lubricants and related materials, while its imports from EU-27 are largely machinery and transport equipment, chemicals, miscellaneous manufactured articles and food items.

In 2012, Russia's inward foreign direct investment (FDI) stocks in EU-27 were €53.1 billion compared to €166.8 billion in EU-27's outward FDI stocks in Russia (European Commission, 2014a).

Strategically, Russia's dependency on European imports in machinery, agricultural products and food stuff can be relatively easy neutralized by shifting to alternative sources of supply in other global regions and countries. In case of FDI such a strategic shift would be more difficult for Russia to achieve, especially in high-tech or sophisticated product manufacturing sectors: viable alternatives in these sectors outside EU can be found largely in the U.S. and Japan with which Russia has frosty relationships. In contrast, European dependence on Russian oil and gas is critical and has no plausible alternatives (Mäkinen, 2010; Liuhto, 2010), making it extremely difficult for Europe to find substitutes to Russian energy supply. Meantime, Europe's drive for a large-scale shift to renewable energy sources is beginning to take root but, as discussed earlier, is not likely to reach its "critical momentum" soon. That reinforces Russia's strategic energy-based leverage over Europe. Furthermore, observers (Helm, 2007; Roettger, 2007; Perovic, 2007; Hadfield, 2008; Baev, 2009) argue that Russia has been successfully advancing its strategic position in energy-dependent Europe through building gas pipelines, equity participation in European energy companies and other forms of expansion.

European integration, unprecedented expansion and the post-Cold War political-economic dynamics brought about the Energy Charter Treaty (ECT) adopted with an original idea of integrating the energy sectors of the U.S.S.R. and Eastern Europe into the broader European and world markets (Energy Charter Secretariat, 2010). Signed in 1994, the ECT, along with the Protocol on Energy Efficiency and Related Environmental Aspects (PEEREA), came into effect in 1998. The ECT covers four broad areas: -the protection of foreign investments, based on the extension of national treatment or most-favored nation treatment and protection against key non-commercial risks; -non-discriminatory conditions for trade in energy materials, products and energy-related equipment based on WTO rules, and provisions to ensure reliable cross-border energy transit flows through pipelines, grids and other means of transportation; -the resolution of disputes between participating states, and - in the case of investments - between investors and host states; and -the promotion of energy efficiency minimization of environmental impact of energy production and use.

The ECT includes an obligation of signatory countries to facilitate energy transit across their territory, in line with the principle of freedom of transit, and an obligation to secure established transit flows. At the same time, it does not require any signatory to introduce mandatory third party access. While the ECT stresses that international investments and technologies in the energy sector are mutually beneficial, national sovereignty over energy resources is its core principle. The ECT strives to promote transparency and operational efficiency in the energy markets, but governments define the structure of their national energy sectors. To date, the ECT has been signed or acceded to by fifty-two states with all members having ratified the Treaty except for five countries, Australia, Belarus, Iceland, Norway, and Russia.

Russia has signed but failed to ratify the ECT, tying up the ratification of the ECT to negotiations on the Energy Charter Transit Protocol. The Protocol would amplify and strengthen ECT provisions on energy transit issues in order to mitigate some specific operational risks that continue to affect energy transit flows.

The progress in the EU-Russian cooperation under the ECT has been deteriorating, so in 2000 the EU proposed establishing the energy dialogue. It aims at enhancing European energy security by binding Russia and the EU into a closer relationship where issues of mutual concern in the energy sector can be addressed, ensuring, at the same time, opening and integrating energy markets. With strong mutual dependency and special common interest in the energy sector, this was a key area of EU-Russia relations. The proposed energy partnership is intended at improving the investment opportunities in Russia's energy sector to: upgrade and expand energy production and transportation infrastructure and improve their environmental impact; encourage the ongoing opening up of energy markets; facilitate the market penetration of more environmentally friendly technologies and energy resources; and promote energy efficiency and energy savings (European Commission, 2006; European Commission, 2007).

Several rounds of ECT negotiations were complicated by the tie-up with Russia's WTO accession provisions initiated by Europeans. After Russia and EU agreed on the terms of the Russian WTO accession, further EU-Russian consultations have been held since 2004. In 2006, Russia indicated that the ratification of the ECT was unlikely due to the provisions requiring a third-party access to Russia's pipelines. Responding to this demand, in 2007, the European Parliament determined that the EU should only support Russian WTO membership if Russia adheres to the ECT. In 2009 Prime Minister Putin announced his decision not to sign the ECT that has in effect resulted in Russia's termination of its provisional application of the ECT and the PEEREA (Energy Charter Secretariat, 2010; Romanova, 2008). For many commentators and political analysts this has been viewed as a crass attempt at evasive unilateralism by a Russia anxious to avoid the implications of the ongoing Yukos arbitration. But even if Russia formally withdrew from the ECT on 19 October 2009, it is still bound in its governmental capacity to uphold the proprietary rights of the oil and gas investors under Article 45 ECT until 2029 even after it has withdrawn from the charter (Josh Mak LLP, 2012).

Early discussions on the Energy Dialog were driven by Russia's sector-specific goals under the domestic protectionism-foreign expansion agenda. It was geared toward securing long-term markets, exporting processed goods, such as electricity and nuclear material to Europe, channeling European investments and technologies into depleted Russian fields and outdated processing facilities and yet preserving Moscow's autonomy under non-binding energy supply arrangements. Russia's long-term conceptual vision of the Energy Dialogue has been formulated at the end of 2000s. It can be broken down into three issues: - separation of energy issues from the overall economic relations, including the WTO support, - mutual guarantees for suppliers and consumers, and - reciprocity in access to the market (Romanova, 2008).

Russia's WTO membership finally materialized in August 2012 and in essence has signified a removal of one of EU's levers in the energy dialog. Among other measures, Europe has been contemplating steps challenging Russia's policy of using energy to influence selected EU countries. Lately, some EU members have been calling for the establishment of a European energy union. This union would, among other things, stipulate that EU member states will have enter natural gas supply negotiations with Russia -- Europe's premier energy supplier -- as a single bloc. Forming a European energy union, conceptually similar to the Euroatom agency of the 1950s, has come up before without moving forward, but it is likely to be considered more seriously this time around in light of difficult relations with Moscow amplified by the Russian-Ukrainian hostilities in 2014. Certain aspects of the energy union proposal will probably advance but others will meet resistance. In response to Russia's actions regarding the Ukraine crisis, the European Union will probably make greater political and financial efforts to integrate the physical energy infrastructure in the bloc. As a result, Russia will have less ability in the longer term to influence European countries' foreign policy through natural gas pricing (Iržikevičius, 2014).

Another strategy that EU-27 has adopted in order to mitigate its import dependency on Russian natural gas is the development of a network of the gas pipe interconnectors across the member countries. Similar to any electric grid, a network of interconnectors installed in EU-27 countries with various degrees of import dependency in natural gas format should provide Europe with a strategic tool to reverse the gas flows or redirect them through the network of member countries' pipelines making the whole gas supply system more flexible and knocking down Russian leverage in import monopoly (European Energy Security, 2014).

EUROPEAN ENERGY SECURITY AND EMERGING SUSTAINABLE ALTERNATIVES

Under the pressures of high energy consumption, limited availability of own fossil energy, and critical dependency on imported oil and gas from Russia with which Europe's relations have been tenuous, the EU has been developing policy initiatives to address the situation. In 2000 the European Commission published the "Green Bible." It admits EU's energy dependency in excess of 50%, and predicts that if measures are not being taken that percentage would rise to 70% by 2025 as the latest. Furthermore, it recognizes the importance of the Middle East (oil) and Russia (natural gas), in meeting Europe's energy needs. The Green Bible mentions the need for paying attention to renewable energy, biofuel production, reduction of energy consumption and overview of the current energy efficiency so as not to waste any. For the time being the media hype on the environmental threats and the "climate change" serves Europe's original schemes in reducing its energy consumption and proceed with the projects involving alternative energy productions. What is also needed though is the understanding that the economic system by which the West function nowadays favoring overwhelming consumption trends. That makes it difficult to overcome the antithesis between sustainable development and mass consumerism (Michaletos, 2007).

Among the most prominent European initiatives on improving its energy security is the ambitious 10-year trillion-euro energy investment plan for a single EU energy network to cut fossil fuel imports and fight climate change - this proposal was discussed by EU leaders at the bloc's first ever energy summit in February 2011. Regarding efforts to combat climate change, the Energy Commissioner Guenther Oettinger said the bloc could realistically achieve its 2020 goals of slicing carbon emissions by 20% and increasing the use of renewable energies such as wind and solar power by 20% under the "20-20 initiative." But EU leaders failed to confront the fact that they are on track to fall halfway short of a 20 percent energy efficiency goal by 2020. Leaders agreed that funding should be found for those strategically useful gas links that industry has ignored in its quest for profits -- for example a link across the Pyrenees to carry northwards Spain's glut of natural gas from Algeria. "No EU member state should remain isolated from the European gas and electricity networks after 2015 or see its energy security jeopardized by lack of the appropriate connections," the accord reads (Harrison, 2011).

In recent years, renewable energy sources across the EU have been heavily supported with fixed tariffs. This has enormously driven the growth of renewables in the energy mix and has put Europe on track for meeting its 2020 renewables target. However, this type of support has also sheltered them from price signals and has led to market distortions. In particular, renewables installations have generated electricity irrespective of the actual demand and they have out-competed other electricity generation which has to rely solely on the market price to operate economically. As technologies mature and their production reaches a substantial share of the market, renewable energy production can and should react to market signals, and aid amounts should respond to falling production costs.

In April 2014, the European Commission has adopted new Guidelines on State Aid for Environmental Protection and Energy 2014-2020 (European Commission, 2014). The document is designed to guide and support EU member states in reaching their 2020 climate targets, while addressing the market distortions that may result from subsidies granted to renewable energy sources. To this end, the guidelines promote a gradual move to market-based support for renewable energy. They also provide criteria on how member states can relieve energy intensive companies that are particularly exposed to international competition from charges levied for the support of renewables. Furthermore, the guidelines include new provisions on aid to energy infrastructure and generation capacity to strengthen the internal energy market and ensure security of supply.

The new guidelines therefore aim to better integrate renewables into the internal electricity market in a gradual way, limiting support to what is truly necessary. Competition between different technologies is introduced in a cautious manner so as not to undermine the development of less mature technologies and investment in innovation. The system gives member states flexibility to take account of national circumstances, and even allows them to depart from competitive processes when the outcome might not be optimal. To facilitate the better functioning of the internal electricity market, the guidelines also promote the use of co-operation mechanisms to facilitate cross-border support of renewable energy where possible and appropriate.

Charges levied to fund renewable energy support make up for an increasing proportion of the energy bill for households and industry. One of the main objectives of the guidelines is to make support to renewable energy more cost-effective, which should eventually reduce energy costs. Additionally, some support is allowed for energy intensive sectors, such as the manufacturing of chemicals, paper, ceramics or metals. These sectors support a very high burden from levies charged for renewables support because they are heavy intensive users of electricity. Moreover, the exposure of these sectors to global trade puts them at a disadvantage towards competitors from outside the EU where electricity prices are lower (European Commission, 2014).

RUSSIAN ENERGY SECTOR: INTERNAL DYNAMICS

Following the dissolution of the U.S.S.R., economic reforms in Russia in the 1990s privatized most industry, with notable exceptions in the energy and defense-related sectors. In this context Russia's manufacturing sector is generally uncompetitive on world markets and is geared toward domestic consumption. Russia's political-economic reliance on commodity exports makes it vulnerable to boom and bust cycles that follow the volatile swings in global prices. The economy, which had averaged 7% growth during 1998-2008 as oil prices rose rapidly, was one of the hardest hit by the 2008-09 global economic crisis as oil prices plummeted and the foreign credits that Russian banks and firms relied on dried up. Slowly declining oil prices over the past few years and difficulty attracting foreign direct investment have contributed to a noticeable slowdown in GDP growth rates. In late 2013, the Russian Economic Development Ministry reduced its growth forecast through 2030 to an average of only 2.5% per year, down from its previous forecast of 4.0 to 4.2% (CIA, 2014). Russia's latest yearly GDP growth forecasts for 2015 have been reduced to just +1.2% for 2014 and +1.8% (The Economist, 2014).

Trends, Driving Forces, and Dynamics in the Russian Energy Sector

Russia enjoys top global rankings in energy: it holds #2 in natural gas production and consumption, #1 in natural gas exports and proved reserves; #3 in crude oil production, #2 in crude oil exports and #8 in proved crude oil reserves; #4 in electricity production and #11 in electricity exports (CIA, 2014). Russia is the third-largest generator of nuclear power in the world and fourth-largest in terms of installed capacity. With ten nuclear reactors currently under construction, Russia is the second country in the world in terms of number of reactors under construction in 2012 (Russia. Country Report/Energy Information Administration, 2013).

Historically, energy and commodities, particularly oil, natural gas, metals, and timber have played strategic paramount role in Russia, its domestic and foreign policy. Illustrative of this, in 2011 the product composition of the Russian principal exports was as follows: oil fuel and gas - 69.8% of the total, metals – 11%, chemicals – 6%, machinery and equipment – 4.5%, and other items – 8.7% (Russia/Country report/Economist Intelligence Unit, 2014). The combined oil and gas revenues account for more than 50% of the federal budget revenues (Energy Information Administration, 2013).

A mixture of highly centralized governance, sheer military power inherited from the U.S.S.R. and the nation's historically important role in the region, especially in the "near abroad," explain a supreme significance of the energy sector in shaping and maintaining Russian national identity, domestic and foreign policy, as well as inner power and politics.

As of January 2013, Russia's proven oil reserves were 80 billion barrels. Most of Russia's resources are located in Western Siberia, between the Ural Mountains and the Central Siberian Plateau and in the Volga-Urals region, extending into the Caspian Sea. Eastern Siberia holds some reserves, but the region has had little exploration. In 2012, Russia produced an estimated 10.4 million bbl/d of total liquids (of which 9.9 million bbl/d was crude oil), and it consumed roughly 3.2 million bbl/d. Russia exported over 7 million bbl/d in 2012, including roughly 5 million bbl/d of crude oil and the remainder in products. Russia's pipeline oil exports fall under the jurisdiction of Transneft, the state owned pipeline monopoly (Russia. Country report. Energy Information Administration, 2013).

Apart from being a world's supreme oil and gas supplier, Russia is also a major energy consumer. Russia's primary energy consumption structure is profiled in Figure 7.

According to the MarketLine, a consultancy, after a substantial decline in 2009, Russian oil and gas market recovered the next year and continued to accelerate until 2012. The market is expected to decline in 2013, followed by a return to mod-

Figure 7. Russia's primary energy consumption, 2011
(Source: Energy Information Administration, 2013, p. 2).

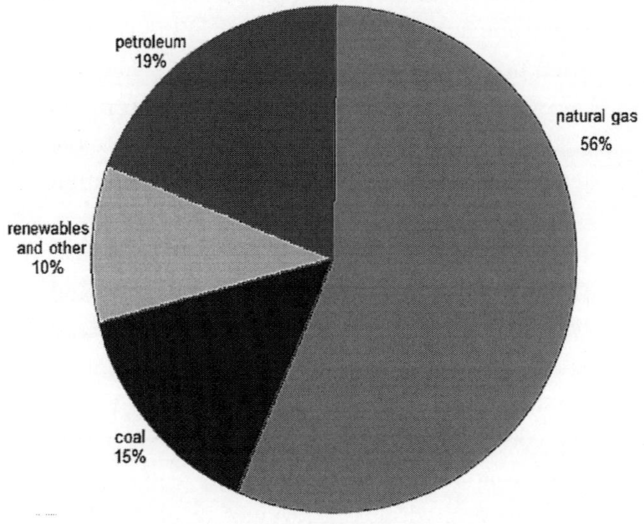

est growth over the remainder of the forecast period to 2017. In 2012, the Russian oil and gas market had total revenues of $160.7 billion, representing a compound annual growth rate (CAGR) of 2% between 2008 and 2012. Market consumption volume increased with a CAGR of 1.2% between 2008 and 2012, to reach a total of 3.8 billion barrels equivalent in 2012. The market's volume is expected to rise to 3.8 billion barrels equivalent by the end of 2017, representing a CAGR of just 0.2% for the 2012-2017 period. Natural gas consumption had the highest volume in the Russian oil and gas market in 2012, with total consumption of 2.6 billion barrels equivalent, translating into 68.5% of the market's overall volume. In comparison, consumption of crude oil had a volume of 1.2 billion barrels equivalent in 2012, equating to 31.5% of the market total. The performance of the market is forecast to decelerate, with an anticipated CAGR of 1.1% for the five-year period 2012 - 2017, which is expected to drive the market to a value of $170.billion by the end of 2017 (Oil and Gas in Russia, 2013).

Oil and gas are characterized by high energy, labor, and capital intensity (Oil and Gas in Russia, 2013; globalEdge. Energy, 2014). Back in the U.S.S.R. and later in the post-Soviet Russia the production potential of major oil and gas fields with the best geological and techno-economic conditions has been largely depleted (Energy Information Administration, 2013). As an illustration, in 2012, more than 60% of the Russian oil production was generated in Western Siberia. Similarly, the bulk of the country's natural gas reserves under development and production are in the upper Western Siberia (Energy Information Administration, 2013).

Increasing or even maintaining steady oil and gas output means going deeper underground, farther North/East and/or using expensive state-of-the-art imported technology or know-how to continue extracting energy from depleted fields. New frontier energy regions in the Russian vastness are typically located far from civilization and major energy markets, suffer from harsh climate and unlivable conditions, and often lack basic industrial and social infrastructure (roads, communications, childcare centers, schools, medical/social care, etc.). Large-scale needs for investments, technological and human/social developments in the energy sector and supporting industries in Russia are particularly acute in the long term perspective as the country continues to experience demographic decline (Russia. Economist Intelligence Unit, 2014), environmental degradation and other socio-economic problems domestically (CIA, 2014) as well as stagnant or deteriorating positions in international ratings (Zhuplev, 2013). That makes attracting foreign direct investment or even marshalling domestic investment difficult.

Aside from the inhospitable investment climate, inadequate legislative framework, and heavy-handed government control and political meddling (The Economist Intelligence Unit Limited, 2013), attracting investment in Russian fossil energy is complicated by the rapid rise in the costs of new oil and gas worldwide that have more than doubled over the last four years. Every dollar of investment buys only half of what it would have bought four years ago. Put in other way, companies have to budget twice what they would have for the same project four years ago. Some examples are even more extreme: a deepwater drillship that would have rented for $125,000 per day four years ago now costs $650,000 per day (Yergin, 2008). In case of Russia the effects of rising costs are likely to be more dramatic due to its vast territories and harsh climate, operational inefficiencies, mismanagement, pervasive cronyism, and rampant corruption permeating the investment process.

Under these conditions, renewables seem like an attractive alternative both as an energy source and from the environmental viewpoint. It is estimated that Russia's renewable energy potential could provide up to 30% of the total potential energy supply (Russian Renewables, 2003). As of 2013, 56% of the Russian primary energy consumption was natural gas, 19% - petroleum, 15% - coal and 10% - renewables and other fuels (Figure 7). According to the Economist Intelligence Unit, by 2020 Russian energy consumption structure will not experience any significant change with fossils to continue holding dominant positions: petroleum products are projected to comprise 21.2% of gross domestic energy consumption, natural gas – 48.4%, coal – 17.7, nuclear – 8.6%, hydro – 2%, geothermal – 1.6%, combustible renewables and waste consumption – 0.9%, and solar, wind and other will stay below one percent (Russia. Economist Intelligence Unit, 2014). Outside hydropower, Russia has not made a meaningful progress in renewable energy and its historical dependence on oil and gas will continue to be the major the political-economic driver.

One formidable force revolutionizing the global energy landscape and critically reshaping Russia's role and position is the shale gas exploitation (for more detail please refer to Probe International, 2013; Baker Institute, 2013). Thanks to relatively recent technological advances, the U.S. is already competing with Russia in natural gas production and global supply. Its production prices are comparatively lower (about 60% cheaper than in Europe), and there are prospects for the U.S. to become a major LNG exporter in the years to come, possibly profoundly changing the global gas landscape. Besides gas itself, the U.S. has broad vested national interests in overcoming its national dependence on energy imports that translates into government action. Before long, U.S. experience, if proved positive, will be replicated by Europe, Russia's major customer in energy supply, and by China, Russia's important potential energy market. In this context, "it is surprising how little Russia seems to take into account the threat shale gas represents to its core energy edge" (Scenarios for Russian Federation, 2013, 15).

Methane hydrates, a product resulting from new emerging technology, is another example of potentially disruptive (in the "creative distraction" context) technological innovation in unconventional energy. If successful on large scale, it may further erode Russia's global leadership in exports and, with the nation's continuing massive strategic dependence on energy exports, undermine domestic growth and political-economic stability.

These emerging changes may eventually give Europe an edge in reducing its dependence on Russia as an external energy supplier and encourage China to pursue even tougher negotiations over prospective agreements with the country. This scenario is particularly unsettling for Russia as it tempers the notion that China could be an alternative market to Europe should energy demand be affected by sluggish growth or political considerations in the latter. In both cases, Russia may be compelled to lowering the prices of its exports, but this would eventually be at odds with its fiscal needs.

Another challenge to the Russian energy-based global strategic edge may be presented by the proliferation of sustainability, efficiency, and the emerging global transition toward low-carbon economies. Although, as shown earlier, fossil fuels are likely to remain a dominant source in global energy consumption, several non-oil and gas supplies (e.g. coal and its derivatives) could at least partially meet global energy demand. Additional factors include the advent of carbon capture and storage, nuclear power, proliferation of renewable energies, and other disruptive innovations. In many ways, these dynamics may prove detrimental to Russia and ultimately diminish its global strategic superiority currently anchored in oil and gas. While Russia could make further use of its coal, nuclear and hydropower resources, its economy remains dependent on a highly energy-intensive and fossil fuel-driven growth model - which is clearly in transition. For long-term sustainability, Russia needs to explore ways in which it can benefit from a global transition towards low-carbon growth (Scenarios for Russian Federation, 2013, p. 16).

Latest Developments in the Russian Energy Sector

In 2009, Russian government adopted the Energy Strategy till 2030 (ES 2030) that envisions three phases. During the initial phase (2013 - 2015) the energy sector will be recovering from the effects of the economic crisis and building a foundation for future development. The second phase (2015 - 2022) will include introduction of modern innovative technologies to the energy sector. The final phase (2022 - 2030) will focus on energy efficiency and serve as a beginning point for Russia's transition to fuels not based on hydrocarbons.

The ES 2030, if fulfilled, might have a profound political economic impact on both European and global energy landscape through the planned re-orientation of Russia's oil and gas exports from Europe to Asia as well as changes in the Russian domestic energy sector itself.

The ES 2030 looks ambitious in its sustainability aspect, especially in its final stage where sustainable solutions are envisioned to flourish. However, evidently to an unbiased observer, such a simplistic linear model bears limited representation of complex realities of the energy sector and pertaining political-economic dynamics. Some authoritative industry forecasts and experts remain skeptical whether this grand vision can be fulfilled. In particular, with the view of Russia's highly publicized and politically loaded grand government spending commitments toward defense, social, education, and other priorities finding themselves in stark contrast with the stagnant domestic economy. Those doubts have been further exacerbated by the 2014 Ukrainian conflict and Western sanctions to follow.

Raising the plank, in November 2012, President Putin approved the "Doctrine of the Energy Security for the Russian Federation" (2012). The document is a set of political-administrative imperatives and prescriptions for the development of the Russian energy sector in the strategic security context. It does not contain any strategies or "road maps" guiding the goal accomplishment process. Since the ES 2030 inception in 2009, there have been some academic discussions and presentations nationwide, internationally (Институт экономической стратегии, 2014) and regionally (Институт систем энергетики, 2014). However, no comprehensive, rigorous independent analytical reviews or even progress reports of the ES 2030 have been available so far. The program was adopted in 2009, when V. Putin was the Prime Minister and Sergey Shmatko was the Minister of Energy of the Russian Federation. By now, both are gone: V. Putin was elevated to the current position of the President and S. Shmatko was replaced (May 2012) as the Energy Minister by Alexander Novak. While ES 2030 at inception looked ambitious in grand intentions and scope, its progress remain an open question.

Meanwhile, the National Human Development Report (United Nations Development Project, 2010) presents three hypothetical scenarios for the Russian energy sector:

- **Inertial Scenario:** Assumes global demand for energy to be strong in the post-crisis recovery. High oil and gas export earnings can support both the Russian energy sector and economy as a whole. Neither the state nor big business is interested in serious innovations. The inertial scenario means the following implications for Russia in the forthcoming decade:
    - Energy efficiency remains at half the developed countries' level; it is accompanied by slow improvements and increased export volume of energy-intensive commodities with low value-added processing.
    - Oil and gas are dominant in the primary energy consumption (75% of the total). Efficiency of the oil and gas industry could be increased somewhat by containing gas flaring. Growth in the hydro and nuclear power industries is relatively slow.
    - Prevalence of the natural gas-fired power stations despite limited shift to coal in some locations.
    - Limited share of higher-grade oil products in exports (2-2.5 times lower compared to the crude oil exports by volume).
    - Government priorities stay focused on increasing the extraction capacities and development of the transport infrastructure for oil and gas. The development of nuclear and hydropower generation driven by government-controlled companies dominant in these segments.
    - Most activities in innovations are limited to the oil and gas sector and supporting industries.
- **Innovative Scenario:** Presumes that due to the worsening of international energy market in the post-world crisis environment or difficulties in developing energy resources, the falling oil and gas export incomes lead to a partial restructuring of the energy sector and the economy as a whole. Government's long-term investment policy integrates latest global trends towards energy efficiency. Innovative scenario leads to the following implications in the forthcoming decade:
    - State and private investments shift from extensive development to modernization of the energy sector. Deeper oil refining and increase in oil product export volumes to the level comparable with crude oil exports.
    - Emphasis on innovations in energy efficiency and energy saving.
    - Development of market institutions in the energy sector, including termination of subsidized energy use and improvement of contract mechanisms.
    - Incentives toward energy efficiency in the industrial sector and households, including flexible pricing, subsidies, exemptions, and other economic instruments to stimulate energy saving.
    - Increasing the share of renewable energy sources (aside from large hydropower stations) to 4-5% of the total electricity generation.
    - Narrowing the gap in energy intensity between Russia and developed countries.
    - Government focus on deploying additional energy resources through improved energy efficiency/savings. Gaining competitive advantages in 'new energy' (energy efficiency and alternative energies).
    - Focus of innovation in the energy sector and related industries as well as defense sector dominated by state-controlled companies.
- **Diversification Scenario:** Assumes that in the post-crisis recovery, after 2020–2025, the government embarks on diversifica-

tion. Positive institutional environment is created for the development of economic sectors beyond energy and defense. Diversification scenario leads to the following implications:

- Energy efficiency of the Russian economy comes closer to that of developed countries, although Russia remains more energy intensive due to its energy intensive manufacturing industries such as paper, fertilizers and metals.
- Domestic energy markets become competitive to facilitate energy efficiency and cost reduction for consumers.
- Government energy policy facilitates competitiveness of other industries. Supporting the 'national energy champions' ceases to be a main policy priority.
- Diversification forces the energy sector to seek private investments, including foreign investment. A share of Russian GDP generated by the energy sector is dramatically reduced.
- Innovation activities spread quickly throughout industry and agriculture.

Russian Energy Sector and Sustainability

Energy has been a foundation of Russia's medium-term macroeconomic stability and a steady source of rent in the 2000s. The National Human Development Report in the Russian Federation (United Nations Development Project, 2010) argued that sustainable progress of the Russian economy could no longer be based on extensive use of energy resources and energy intensity is the key in sustainability both on the country and the energy sector level. The report outlines the following specific directions for sustainable development in energy:

- **Reduced Energy Intensity:** During 2000–2008, energy intensity of the Russian GDP fell by almost 5% annually. It is much faster than in many other countries but its level is still 2.5 times higher than the world average and 2.5-3.5 times higher against developed countries. In a sense, high energy intensity of the Russian GDP is a historical legacy: energy efficiency in the Tsarist Russia was 3.5 times higher against Germany, 3 times higher against France and Japan, 4.4 times higher against the UK and USA and 3.5 times higher against the world average. Although Russia has reduced energy intensity faster than other countries, it remains among the most energy-inefficient countries in the world, since the reductions were mainly due to structural changes and the country has failed to narrow the technological gap with developed countries.
- **Development and Diversification of the Energy Infrastructure:** Oil and gas development in Eastern and Northern regions of Russia, including the Arctic offshore, is to support domestic demand and diversify export directions. The Russian Energy Strategy 2030 (Russian American Business, 2009) proposes considerable geographical reorientation of Russian oil and gas exports: by 2030, 20% of Russian gas exports and 25% of oil exports are expected to go to Eastern markets (Gromov, 2009). Meantime, economic decline in 2008-2009 has weakened demand for gas both in Europe and Russia reducing Russia's energy export earnings. If unfavorable trends continue, they could hinder Russia's ambitious investment plans, including geo-strategically important but extremely complex next-generation gas fields in the Yamal Peninsula, the Barents Sea offshore, the Ob and Taz Bays, Eastern Siberia and Far East. If these fields are not developed as planned, Russia's export

volumes to the EU and CIS can fall significantly (Mäkinen, 2010; Liuhto, 2010). Gazprom, the world's biggest gas producer, controlled by the Russian government and used as government tool in domestic and foreign policy, aims to remain the leading gas supplier to Europe, its key market, Alexander Ivannikov, first deputy head of the company's finance and economics department, said during a conference call with analysts. Growth in Europe will be one of the value drivers this year, according to a presentation on its website. The company didn't disclose its export forecast. In 2013, fuel supplies beyond the former Soviet Union rose to 174.3 billion cubic meters, including volumes traded by the company's European units (Rudnitsky & Mazneva, 2014). With Russia aiming to enter the LNG market and the Gas Exporting Countries Forum (GECF) could turn into a cartel, similar to OPEC, there is a risk that the EU could become dependent on very few suppliers of gas, this time only LNG. Furthermore, increasing LNG trade would involve environmental risks, including heavier maritime traffic and tanker collisions with disastrous environmental impacts.

- **Environmental Consideration:** Russian energy sector, particularly electricity generation, is responsible for the biggest share of man-made greenhouse gas emissions in the country (60% for the energy sector, including 25% for electricity generation). Most emissions come from fossil fuels and related operations in their extraction, storage, transportation, processing and consumption, including emissions from gas flaring and other fuels without useful application of the energy produced. Energy development should take into account environmental conditions and new environmental requirements by international authorities as well as engage modern technologies already widely used in developed countries. Decisions regarding the energy sector expansion should also include health hazard assessments and action plans focusing on risk reduction to acceptable level. Technically, Russia is a global environmental donor because the overall impact of its economy on the environment is much lower than a useful input of Russia's ecosystems to global environmental stability. But Russia could lose this status if negative environmental impact from the energy sector increases. As most renewable energy systems only contribute to greenhouse gas emissions during their construction and produce zero or very little CO_2 emissions during their operation, environmental consideration is closely linked to renewable energy sources.
- **Renewable Energy Sources:** Russia's major problem is that the country is heavily addicted to the raw material exporting dependence and is therefore 'stuck' with the low-tech growth platform that spells long-term stagnation. While Russia has an enormous potential for renewables, their current share in the total electricity production is just 0.9%. There are no statistics available for the amounts of heat produced by using renewables, but experts estimate it at about 4% of the total. 'Technological' potential for generation in Russia by using renewables (i.e. the amount of generation theoretically possible using existing renewable technologies to the utmost) has been estimated at 24 billion tons of fuel equivalent per year (not including the large rivers' potential), that is over 20 times more than Russia's annual domestic primary energy consumption. 'Economic' potential of renewable energy (i.e. the amount of generation which is commercially feasible, including costs for the renewable and fos-

sil fuel generation, etc.) depends on several factors: the current state of economy; cost, availability and quality of the fossil fuel energy resources; electricity and heating prices across the country; distribution of technology capabilities across regions; etc. This potential is changing with time and should be specifically factored in the renewable energy program assessment (United Nations Development Project, 2010).

Some of the Russian technological concepts in renewable energy are competitive with foreign technologies. Russia has significant experience in the construction and use of small hydropower plants ($\leq$ 25 MW capacity), and its technological developments in tidal and geothermal energy are arguably ahead of the EU and U.S. But western countries are superior to Russia in wind turbines, solar cells, and heat pumps. Additionally, Russian technologies are largely at R&D or testing stages, while many similar western technologies are already at various stages of commercialization. Moreover, certain types of renewable energy in the EU and U.S. are already economically competitive with conventional energy while in Russia the gap remains high.

There are areas of mutual interest between EU and Russia that may lead to sustainable energy development if jointly explored and exploited. Russia can draw on the EU and other countries' experiences like government assistance to renewable energy companies. On the top of that, focus on renewable technologies in Russia may facilitate job creation, improve living standards, and mitigate migration of rural population, especially the outflows of people from energy resource rich northern and eastern territories.

Recognizing the importance of renewable energy, the Russian Government has been paying more attention to this issue in recent years. In 2007 Russia adopted a federal law "On the electric power industry" (Federal Law No. 250) introducing the concept and outlining key measures for the development of renewable energy. The Federal Law was followed by regulations in support of renewable energy technology and markets. The 2009 Government decree "Main Directions of the State Policy for Improvement of Electric Energy Efficiency up to 2020 through the Use of Renewables" sets targets for electricity generation through renewable energy sources. Under this decree the share of renewables is to be raised fivefold to 4.5% by 2020. "Energy Strategy until 2030" envisions renewable electricity output of at least 80-100 billion KWh by the end of this period.

RUSSIA'S ROLE IN THE EUROPEAN ENERGY SECURITY

Russian approaches to energy market are characterized by close state monitoring and ad hoc solutions rather than the development of objective impartial regulation, thus presupposing a different notion of private–public partnership and reciprocity. Russian vision in the ECT context is in contrast with the EU's idea of creating a wider European energy market (similar to the EU's common market but extending beyond its borders) based on rules and norms already developed by the EU's institutions (liberalization, energy efficiency, etc.). Moreover, the Russian vision sometimes is expressed in grand political terms, with little attention paid to the technical details. Finally, the Russian vision hinges on the idea of indivisible sovereignty (Romanova, 2008) and "realpolitik" in international relations.

Beyond the macroeconomics and politics, Russia's renewed energy-driven assertiveness in foreign policy is buttressed by windfalls from skyrocketing world energy prices that, after some moderation under the current global downturn, are projected to grow high, further fueling Russia's energy-based political clout. Another force behind Russian assertiveness in foreign policy stems from aspirations to rise "from its knees" and regain the global "superpower" status.

Cohen (2007) describes the Russian tactical toolbox reinforcing its oil and gas grip on Europe:

- **Locking in Demand:** Using long-term contracts separately with European countries to lock in demand.
- **Locking in Supply:** Consolidating control of strategic energy infrastructure throughout Europe and Eurasia, including supply, sale, and distribution of natural gas as well as pipelines, refineries, electric grids, and ports.
- **Derailing Competition:** For example, Russia has pushed the South Stream gas pipeline which competes against the EU's Nabucco pipeline as well as the proposed extension of the EU-backed South Caucasus Pipeline.
- **External Consolidation:** Consolidating control of supply outside Russia, particularly by signing long-term exploration and supply agreements with Turkmenistan, Uzbekistan, and Kazakhstan.
- **Internal Consolidation:** Consolidating Russia's oil and gas sector in the hands of state-controlled entities.
- **A Gas OPEC:** Russia is "stealthily and steadily" developing a "gas OPEC" cartel to control the output and price of gas. The cartel would include major producers, including Argentina, Bolivia, Venezuela, Iran, and Qatar.

There are numerous documented cases illustrating the issue. Larsson in his 2007 study counted over 55 incidents (cut-offs, explicit threats, coercive price policy and certain takeovers) since 1991, most with "both political and economic underpinnings." Another Larsson's study in 2006 concluded that from Europe's perspective, Russia is moving in the wrong direction. It has largely ignored criticism, and has been unwilling to change its behavior. Dependence on Russian energy would not be a problem if Russia played by the same rules as other energy players or European states. Larsson concludes that the core problem is the combination of Russia's perception, intentions, capabilities and track record along with lack of real stability, a high degree of unpredictability and a development away from democracy, rule of law and market norms to the detriment of Europe. Close connections between the Government and the largest Russian companies, whether through executive appointments, the promotions of overseas operations, or financial, legal, and police instruments, demonstrate that foreign policy is closely coordinated. Russian enterprises have been encouraged to gain political influence through involvement with officials, parties, and media outlets in targeted East European states (Larsson, 2006; Liuhto, 2010; Le Cog, 2009; Milov at al., 2006).

The countermeasures debated across Europe include: legal actions against Russian energy companies under the EU and national antitrust and anticompetitive laws; shifting to energy efficient technologies and processes, liquefied gas supply, engaging renewable and nuclear energy sources; legal investigations of energy disruptions in Europe caused by Russian energy companies and economic sanctions against their assets in Europe; legal restrictions on Russian energy companies' asset acquisitions in Europe until they become more transparent in their accounting, operating and other practices in business management; restricting Russian companies' equity participation share in Europe commensurably with the level of restrictions European energy companies face in their equity participation in Russian energy enterprises, and others; creating natural gas pipeline network interconnectors enabling to reverse the flows of gas mitigating disruptions of supply. Experts call for common European foreign policy on energy, including the creation of alternative gas pipelines, such as the West-backed Nabucco project, to circumvent existing Russian energy supply chains (Cohen, 2007; Aslund, 2008; Baev, 2008; Goldthau 2008a, 2008b; Götz, 2008; Roettger, 2007; Woehrel, 2009; Iržikevičius, 2014).

As illustrated, quite often Russian-EU energy relations are described in military terms, such as "energy war" or "energy weapons." Little is said about partnership, despite the fact that Russia is a gas seller and Europe is a gas buyer. Evolution of the European-Russian energy dialog depends on many variables ingrained in this relationship as well as emerging trends in energy technologies, environmental developments, laws, regulations, and ethics, as well as global economic dynamics.

It is clear that EU will develop alternative energy resources sooner or later but still the Russian-EU energy partnership is a long-term one. Currently, Russia is Europe's main reliable gas supplier as it has never breached its obligations, unlike the transit countries. The current tripartite talks between Russia, EU and Ukraine and the new Russian-Polish gas deal are steps towards energy security in the region.

Meanwhile, Gazprom indicated that its profit declined 7% in 2013 as tensions escalate in Ukraine, the transit route for half its natural gas deliveries to Europe. Gazprom faces pressure from the EU and Ukraine as they seek new sources of gas and relations with Russia sink to their worst since the Cold War. The U.S. and EU are targeting executives and officials close to Russian President Vladimir Putin with an expanding series of sanctions. The U.S. added the head of OAO Rosneft, the state-controlled crude producer, to its list at the end of April 2014. "Political and economic tensions between Russia and Ukraine have caused renewed concerns regarding the reliability of gas supplies to Europe," Gazprom said. "Any disputes with Ukraine could potentially lead to a disruption." (Rudnitsky & Mazneva, 2014)

CONCLUSION

Globalization and increasing geo-regional interdependence have serious political-economic impacts and implications for the energy sector and its stakeholders worldwide. While the post-recession economic growth requires energy, global access to traditional fossil sources becomes more competitive. According to latest long-term forecasts, energy demand in developed countries is tapering out. Between 2010 and 2040, the OECD Europe's share in the overall world energy consumption will decline from 15.6% to 11.6%. At the same time, China and India combined are projected to consume about 34% of the total world energy in 2040, compared to just 24% in 2010. Alternatively, renewable energy shows high absolute growth rate, but between 2011 and 2035 its share in the overall energy mix is projected to increase modestly from 13% to 18%. Fossil fuels will continue to play crucial role in the future providing almost 80% of the world total energy supply through 2040. Liquid fuels – mostly petroleum based – will remain the largest sources of energy. However, the liquids share of world marketed energy consumption falls from 34% in 2010 to 28% in 2040. Crude oil prices by that time are expected to reach $163 per barrel under the Reference scenario.

European economies are characterized by high absolute levels of absolute energy consumption but remain energy efficient comparative to other countries. Under severe constraints in availability of their own sources of fossil energy and existing environmental and economic drivers toward renewable energy, while experiencing strong reservations toward nuclear energy, European region is critically dependent on oil and natural gas imports. In 2011, EU-27's overall energy import dependency stood at an astounding 53.8%. Petroleum and petroleum products had the highest level of import dependency across EU-27 at 84.9%, followed by natural gas at 67%. Sixteen out of 27 countries satisfy more than half of their energy needs by imports, for ten remaining countries energy dependency ranges from 10% to 50%. Denmark is the only energy independent EU-27 member country. In 2011, EU-27's main crude oil and natural gas suppliers were Russia (35% of the total oil imports and 30% of gas imports to EU-27) and Norway (12% of oil imports and 20% gas imports).

Energy is a central part of the EU-27-Russian regional political-economic relations and driver of interdependency. While being Europe's premier oil and gas supplier and a major economy in the region, Russia needs vast amounts of energy for its own domestic consumption exacerbated by its high energy intensity. Russia's energy intensity is 2.8 greater compared to EU-27 and 2.1 times greater compared to the U.S. Even under the currently stagnating economy and somewhat improving energy intensity Russia still has high level of absolute energy consumption where oil and gas play prominent role in the energy sector, in the domestic economy at large and foreign policy. That, along with Russia's large scale export oil and gas commitments, the declining domestic energy output and very limited role of renewable energy may be a concern for European energy security and sustainable development. Adding to this concern is Russia's strategic effort in reorientation of its oil and natural gas exports from Europe to Asia driven by political-economic dynamics.

EU-27-Russian political-economic relations are characterized by high and asymmetric interdependency. Russian exports to EU-27 are dominated by mineral fuels, lubricants and related materials whose share to EU-27 in 2012 was 76.3% in the overall exports, while its imports from EU-27 are largely machinery and transport equipment, chemicals, food and live animals (altogether approximately 72.1% of Russia's total imports). Strategically, Russia's dependency on European imports in machinery agricultural and products can be relatively easy mitigated by shifting to alternative sources of supply in other global regions. In contrast, European dependence on imported Russian oil and gas is critical and the region has no plausible substitutes to Russian fossil energy. Although Europe's shift to renewable energy sources is taking root, by 2020 its share in the final energy consumption is projected at 20% against just 7% in 2011, leaving Europeans with limited strategic options mitigating energy import dependency from Russia.

Over the past two decades European energy developments have been evolving under the Energy Charter Treaty (ECT) followed recently by the EU-Russian Energy Dialog. Its view under the European and Russian perspectives differs. EU envisions a wide European energy market (similar to the EU's common market for goods, services, people and capital, but extending beyond its borders). Russian vision is characterized by close state monitoring and pragmatic ad hoc solutions (this style is often categorized in Russian politics as "manual steering") driven by politics rather than the objective impartial regulation. The state, trends and outcomes of the EU-Russian Energy Dialog have been affected by many conditions. Among them is Russia's renewed assertiveness in foreign policy buttressed by its strategic monopoly position in Europe's continuing fossil energy dependency on Russian oil and natural gas. Russian military takeover of the Crimea, current hostilities in Southern and Eastern Ukraine, and ensuing political strife complicate the EU-Russian Energy Dialog.

Energy, commodities and low value added manufacturing products constitute nearly 90% of Russian total export and the oil and gas revenues combined account for more than half of the federal budget revenues. Oil and gas sector, the backbone of Russia's domestic economy and foreign policy, are characterized by high energy, labor, and capital intensity. Maintaining, let alone increasing Russia's oil and gas output in order to support sizeable domestic economy and energy export commitments mandate massive expansion to new frontier regions. In 2012, more than 60% of Russian oil production and the bulk of the country's natural gas reserves under development and production are in the West and upper West Siberia. These developments cannot happen without large-scale investments, technological, human, social and other developments in the energy sector itself and supporting industries. However, Russia's difficult investment climate, capital flight, inadequate legislative framework, corruption, heavy-handed government control and political involvement, rapid rise in the costs of new oil and gas development worldwide and other causes hinder much needed private domestic and foreign investment as well as technology transfer in the Russian energy sector. These negative trends have been exacerbated by Russia's hostilities with Ukraine and deteriorations of political relations with the West at large. Unless those issues are addressed, Russian energy sector is set to continue suffering stagnation or declining production outputs, inefficiency, outdated technology and other problems.

Russian energy sector has been lagging behind in embracing renewable energy. Its role in the current energy mix and future developments are very limited. Although renewable energy could provide up to 30% of the overall potential energy supply outside hydropower, Russia has not made a meaningful progress. By 2020 renewable power is projected to comprise a minor share in the overall energy mix: nuclear – 8.6%, hydro – 2%, geothermal – 1.6%, combustible renewables and waste consumption – 0.9%, and solar, wind and other combined will stay below one percent.

As a formidable potential challenge to the Russian global energy superiority and a boon to European clout in energy security the technological revolution in shale oil and gas and methane hydrates has been unfolding over the past few years. Thanks to these advances the U.S. is already competing with Russia in natural gas production and global supply and there are prospects for the U.S. to become a major LMG exporter, possibly profoundly changing the global gas landscape. Another strategic threat to the Russian energy-based global strategic edge may be presented by the proliferation of sustainability, efficiency, and the emerging global transition toward low-carbon economies, although the pace of change so far has been tepid.

Russian Energy Strategy until 2030 has been adopted in 2009 to set up long and medium term goals and means for the nation's energy sector. Special focus in the Strategy is placed on sustainability, including renewable energy sources and environmental priorities.

The nation's historical dependence on oil and gas has long been Russia's major political-economic driver, lever, and strategic disadvantage. If successful (there are plenty of sceptics both inside and outside Russia), the Energy Strategy 2030 (Russian American Business, 2009) will have major implications for both Russia's domestic energy sector and economy at large as well as across for the EU-27 region. The Strategy proposes drastic geographical reorientation of Russian oil and gas exports: by 2030, 20% of Russian gas exports and 25% of oil exports are expected to go to Eastern markets, notable China, Korea, Japan and other countries.

The recent National Human Development Report identifies three hypothetical scenarios for the Russian energy sector: inertial, innovative, and diversification one. There are indications that in the short to medium range Russian energy sector will evolve between inertial and diversification scenarios gravitating more toward inertia.

Energy security will remain top priority in the European political-economic agenda in the forthcoming decades. Russia is poised to continue being Europe's top oil and natural gas supplier. Russia's domestic energy sector and general economic dynamics tend to impose constraints on its oil and gas exports to Europe. Under its latest geo-regional energy doctrine Russia has initiated a shift of its energy oil and gas exports from Europe to the Asian region where China, Japan and Korea emerge as major recipients while worsening European energy security situation. Europe's ability to act under coherent and effective energy security policy and speak in one voice toward its foreign partners is critical in maintaining EU-Russia asymmetric political-economic interdependency in the energy dialog. Meanwhile, EU states will have to find ways of mitigating their high dependency on imported oil and gas.

Main energy policy implications for EU-27 in the Russian factor context include:

- Shift to energy efficient technologies and processes on both energy generation and consumption sides;
- Geographic diversification of natural gas imports, including LNG;
- Pursuit of shale oil and gas and rebalancing of economic, social and environmental priorities in the overall sustainability context;
- Pursuit of renewable energy sources;
- Enhancement in the application of common European foreign policy as opposed to national level policies on energy both inside and outside the EU;
- Proactive engagement in the EU-Russian energy dialog and issues of mutual interest;
- Comprehensive legal protection against Russian companies under the EU and national antitrust and anticompetitive laws;
- Using reciprocity on wide front of foreign policy issues of mutual interest and priority; and
- Creation of alternative pipelines, cross-border interconnectors, and other energy delivery routes to circumvent existing Russian government monopoly energy supply chains.

Main energy policy implications for Russia in the EU-27 factor context include:

- Shift to energy efficient technologies and processes on both energy generation and consumption sides;
- Pursuit of renewable energy sources, including nuclear energy;
- Wider engagement in the EU-Russian energy dialog and other issues of mutual interest and importance; and
- Borrowing from the EU experience in energy efficiency and sustainability, government assistance in renewable energy solutions, and other best practices.

Although Russia plans to increase its gas supplies to Asia, it's very difficult to replace the supplies and revenues received on the European market. Thus EU-Russia energy relations should be viewed as the business foundation for the future of the bilateral energy dialogue.

REFERENCES

Aslund, A. (2008). *Russian energy and the European Union: Perspectives of Gazprom*. Peter G. Peterson Institute for International Economics. Retrieved May 9, 2014, at http://www.iie.com/publications/papers/aslund0508.pdf

Baev, P. (2008). *The East-West maneuvering in Russia's energy policy: Could oil and gas exports to China endanger Europe's energy security?* Working paper. International Peace Research Institute, Oslo (PRIO). Retrieved May 8, 2014, at http://www.fni.no/russcasp/Russia-China-energy-Baev.pdf

Baev, P. (2009). *Russian energy policy and military power: Putin's quest for greatness*. London: Routledge.

Baker Institute. (2013). *Shale Gas and U.S. National Security*. Baker Institute. Retrieved May 7, 2014, from http://bakerinstitute.org/center-for-energy-studies/shale-gas-and-us-national-security/

Barroso, J. M. (2014). *Letter from President Barroso to President Putin*. Retrieved April 22, 2014, from http://europa.eu/rapid/press-release_STATEMENT-14-132_en.htm

CIA. (2014). World Factbook. Retrieved April 28, 2014, from https://www.cia.gov/library/publications/the-world-factbook/geos/rs.html

Cohen, A. (2007). *Europe's strategic dependence on Russian energy*. Retrieved December 5, 2010, from http://www.heritage.org/research/reports/2007/11/europes-strategic-dependence-on-russian-energy

Cohen, A. (2012). *Doctrine of the Energy Security for the Russian Federation.* Retrieved May 7, 2014, from http://sei.irk.ru/promo/doktrina-energeticheskoy-bezopasnosti-rossii/ - in Russian.

Energy Charter Secretariat. (2010). *Energy Charter.* Retrieved December 5, 2013, from http://www.encharter.org/

Energy Information Administration. (of the U.S. Department of Energy). (2013). *International Energy Outlook 2013.* Retrieved April 7, 2014, from http://www.eia.gov/forecasts/ieo/pdf/0484(2013).pdf

Energy Information Administration. (2013). *Russia Country Report.* Retrieved April 28, 2014, from http://www.eia.gov/countries/cab.cfm?fips=rs

Energy Information Administration. (2014). *Energy Intensity.* U.S. Energy Information Administration. Retrieved April 13, 2014, from http://www.eia.gov/cfapps/ipdbproject/iedindex3.cfm?tid=92&pid=47&aid=2&cid=CG1,&syid=2007&eyid=2011&unit=BTUPUSDM

European Commission. (2006). *EU-Russia Energy Dialog: Eight progress report.* Retrieved April 15, 2014, from http://ec.europa.eu/energy/russia/joint_progress/doc/progress8_en.pdf

European Commission. (2007). *EU-Russia Energy Dialog: Euractive.* Retrieved April 15, 2014, from http://www.euractiv.com/en/energy/eu-russia-energy-dialogue/article-150061

European Commission. (2009). *EU-Russia Energy Dialog: Europa.* Retrieved March 30, 2014, from http://europa.eu/rapid/press-release_MEMO-09-121_en.htm

European Commission. (2013a). *EU energy in figures.* Retrieved May 4, 2014, from http://ec.europa.eu/energy/publications/doc/2013_pocketbook.pdf

European Commission. (2013b). *Renewable Energy Progress Report.* Retrieved April 16, 2014, at http://eur-lex.europa.eu/legal-content/EN/TXT/PDF/?uri=CELEX:52013DC0175&from=EN

European Commission. (2014). *Guidelines on State aid for environmental protection and energy 2014-2020.* Retrieved May 11, 2014 at http://ec.europa.eu/competition/sectors/energy/eeag_en.pdf

European Commission. (2014a). *European Commission*/Trade/Russia. Retrieved April 22, 2014, from http://trade.ec.europa.eu/doclib/docs/2006/september/tradoc_111720.pdf

European Union. (2014a). *European Union/External Service/Russia.* Retrieved April 22, 2014, from http://eeas.europa.eu/russia/index_en.htm

European Union. (2014b). *European Union/Trade in Goods with Russia.* Retrieved April 27, 2014, from http://trade.ec.europa.eu/doclib/docs/2006/september/tradoc_113440.pdf

globalEDGE. Energy. (2014). Michigan State University.

Godzimirski, J. (2009). *Russian Energy Strategy 2030.* Norwegian Institute of international Affairs. Retrieved May 5, 2014, from http://www.fni.no/russcasp/Godzimirski_2009_03_25_Russian_energy_sector_2030.pdf

Goldthau, A. (2008a). Russia's energy weapon. *EU Energy Policy Blog February 17.* Retrieved May 1, 2014, from http://www.energypolicyblog.com/?p=118

Goldthau, A. (2008b). *Resurgent Russia? Rethinking Energy Inc.: Five Myths about the "Energy Superpower."* Hoover Institution. Retrieved May 1, 2014, from http://www.hoover.org/publications/policyreview/14931716.html

Götz, R. (2008). *Managing European-Russian energy independence*. Retrieved September 28, 2013, from http://www.swp-berlin.org/fileadmin/contents/products/arbeitspapiere/Oslo_Dec_13__ks.pdf

Gromov, A. (2009). *Russian energy strategy for the period up to 2030: the Way to the innovative energy development*. Retrieved May 5, 2014, from http://www.iea.org/work/2008/neet_russia/Gromov.pdf

Gromov, A. (2009). *Energy Strategy of Russia for the year 2030: Approaches, priorities and reference points*. Retrieved May 5, 2014, from http://www.energystrategy.ru/ab_ins/source/Gromov_MGIMO-23.10.09.ppt

Hadfield, A. (2008). EU–Russia Energy Relations: Aggregation and Aggravation. *Journal of Contemporary European Studies*, *16*(2), 231–248. doi:10.1080/14782800802309953

Helm, D. (2007). *The Russian dimension and Europe's external energy policy*. University of Oxford. Retrieved May 12, 2014, at http://www.dieterhelm.co.uk/node/655

Institute of Economic Strategy. (2014). Retrieved May 7, 2014, from http://www.energystrategy.ru/ - in Russian.

Institute of Energy Systems. (2014) Retrieved May 7, 2014, from http://sei.irk.ru/index.php - in Russian.

Iržikevičius, R. (2014). *Europe discusses an Energy Union*. Retrieved on May 10, 2014, from http://www.lithuaniatribune.com/67212/europe-discusses-an-energy-union-201467212/

Le Cog, C. (2009). Russian gas suply and common energy policy. *Baltic Rim Economies. Bimonthly Review, Expert Article 330.*

Liuhto, K. (2010). *Energy in Russia's foreign policy: Electronic Publications of Pan-European Institute*. Retrieved April 24, 2014, from http://www.utu.fi/fi/yksikot/tse/yksikot/PEI/raportit-ja-tietopaketit/Documents/Liuhto_final_netti.pdf

Mäkinen, H. (2010). The future of natural gas as the European Union's energy source – risks and possibilities. *Electronic Publications of Pan-European Institute*. 9/2010. Retrieved May 5, 2014, from http://www.utu.fi/fi/yksikot/tse/yksikot/PEI/raportit-ja-tietopaketit/Documents/Mäkinen_final.pdf

Milov, V., Coburn, L., & Danchenko, I. (2006). Russia's energy policy: 1992-2005. *Eurasian Geography and Economics*, *47*(3), 285–313. doi:10.2747/1538-7216.47.3.285

Munasinghe, M. (2004). Sustainable development: Basic concepts and application to energy. In C. Cleveland (Ed.), *Encyclopedia of Energy* (pp. 789–808). New York, NY: Elsevier Academic Press. doi:10.1016/B0-12-176480-X/00441-1

Perovic, J., & Orttung, R. (2007). Russia's energy policy: Should Europe worry? *Russian Analytical Digest*, *18*(7). Retrieved September 27, 2013, from www.russlandanalysen.de

Perovic, J., Orttung, R., & Wenger, A. (Eds.). (2009). *Russian energy power and foreign relationships: Implications for conflict and cooperation*. Oxon, UK: Routledge.

Probe International. (2013). *Shale Oil*. Retrieved May 7, 2014, from http://probeinternational.org/library/wp-content/uploads/2013/02/pwc-shale-oil1.pdf

Roettger, G. (2007). *Over a barrel: Where Russian energy policy leaves Europe with regards to its energy security*. (Unpublished Master's thesis). Naval Postgraduate School, Monterey, CA.

Romanova, T. (2008). The Russian perspective on the energy dialogue. *Journal of Contemporary European Studies*, *16*(2), 219–230. doi:10.1080/14782800802309938

Rudnitsky, J., & Mazneva, E. (2014). *Gazprom Sees Growth in Europe as Net Falls Below Estimates*. Blumberg/Business Week, April 29, 2014. Retrieved May 2, 2014, from http://www.businessweek.com/news/2014-04-29/gazprom-2013-net-falls-to-1-dot-14-trillion-rubles-below-estimates

Russian American Business. (2009). *Energy Strategy 2030*. Retrieved March 5, 2014, from *http://* russianamericanbusiness.org/we*b_CURRENT/ articles/545/1/*Energy-strategy-2030

Russian Government. (2013). *Federal Law No. 250*. Retrieved April 25, 2014, from http://www.minfin.ru/common/upload/library/2013/12/main/FZ349-FZ_ot_021213.pdf

The Economist. (2014). *Output/Prices/Jobs*. Retrieved May 4, 2014, from http://www.economist.com/news/economic-and-financial-indicators/21601526-output-prices-and-jobs

The Economist Intelligence Unit Limited. (2003). *Russian Renewables Business Brief: Power Economics*. Retrieved October 3, 2009, from the Business Source Complete database.

The Economist Intelligence Unit Limited. (2013). *Russia Energy Report*. The Economist Intelligence Unit Limited. Retrieved May 2, 2014, from the Business Source Complete database.

The Economist Intelligence Unit Limited. (2014). *Russia Energy Report*. Moscow, Russia: Economic Intelligence Unit.

United Nations Development Project. (2013). *National human development report in the Russian Federation*. Retrieved May 15, 2014, from http://hdr.undp.org/en/countries/profiles/RUS

United Nations Development Project. (2013). *Oil and gas in Russia: MarketLine industry profile*. Retrieved April 29, 2014, from the Business Source Complete database (Reference code: 0153-2116 (September)).

Woehrel, S. (2009). *Russian energy policy towards neighboring countries*. Congressional Research Service Report for Congress (May 20). Retrieved April 27, 2013, from http://www.fas.org/sgp/crs/row/RL34261.pdf

World Energy Outlook. (2012). *International Energy Agency*. Retrieved April 28, 2014, from http://www.worldenergyoutlook.org/publications/weo-2012/

World Energy Outlook. (2013). *Renewable Energy Outlook*. International Energy Agency. Retrieved April 16, 2014, at http://www.worldenergyoutlook.org/media/weowebsite/2013/WEO2013_Ch06_Renewables.pdf

Yergin, D. (2008). *Oil at the "breakpoint."* Special Report. Testimony before the US Congress Joint Economic Committee in Washington, DC, June 25, 2008. Retrieved October 16, 2009, from http://www2.cera.com/news/DYergin_June2008_Testimony.pdf

Zhuplev, A. (2008). Economic internationalization of Russia: Roots, trends, and scenarios. *International Political Science Review*, *29*(1), 99–119. doi:10.1177/0192512107083449

Zhuplev, A. (2013). Russian Energy Sector: Megatrends, Drivers and Strategic Implications. Paper presented at the Academy of International Business Meeting, Moscow, Russia.

Zhuplev, A., & Shein, V. (2004). Administrative Culture in a Borderless World: Russia. In J. Jabbra & O. Dwivendi (Eds.), Administrative Culture in the Borderless World. Willowdale, Ontario, Canada: de Sitter Publications.

KEY TERMS AND DEFINITIONS

Energy Dependency: A degree of nation's reliance on imported energy resulting from insufficient domestic supply. EU's current import dependency in energy stands at 53.8%. Sixteen EU member nations satisfy more than half of their energy needs by imports, and for the remaining countries energy dependency ranges from 10% to 50%.

Energy Intensity: A measure of the energy efficiency of a nation's economy. It measures the amount of energy required to produce units of energy per unit of GDP (often measured in US dollars).

EU-Russia Energy Dialog: Launched in 2000, the Energy Dialogue provides the overall structure for energy cooperation between the EU and Russia. The Dialogue seeks to facilitate: improving investment opportunities in the energy sector, ensuring secure and adequate infrastructure, increasing the use of environmentally friendly technologies and energy resources, promoting energy efficiency and energy savings on the way to a low-carbon economy, and exchanging information on legislative initiatives.

Geo-Regional Strategic Interdependency: A mutual dependency and strategies of nations in global regions resulting from their actions and interactions in the political, economic, social, environmental, military and other areas of human activity. Interdependency intensifies with the proliferation of globalization, advances in communications, transportation, falling trade and investment barriers, trends in political-economic liberalization and other impact factors.

Hydraulic Fracturing ("Fracking"): The procedure of creating fractures in rocks and rock formations by injecting fluid and sand into cracks to force them further open. The larger fissures allow more oil and gas to flow out of the formation and into the wellbore, from where it can be extracted. Fracking has resulted in many oil and gas wells attaining a state of economic viability, due to the level of extraction that can be reached.

Renewable Energy: Comes from resources which are replenished by power of nature from sunlight, wind, rain, tides, waves, and geothermal heat. Main sources of renewable energy include biofuel, biomass, geothermal energy, hydropower, solar energy, and wind power.

Sustainability Triad: The interplay of economic, social, and environmental factors of development. The interaction of these factors under optimization forms a triad for sustainable development.

Sustainable Energy Development Framework: Integrates economic, social, and environmental perspectives of sustainable development in energy. Includes two analytical/assessment tools for sustainability: the Action Impact Matrix and the Sustainable Development Assessment.

Chapter 8
Renewable Energy Technologies, Sustainable Development, and Environment

Abdeen Mustafa Omer
Energy Research Institute (ERI), UK

ABSTRACT

The move towards a low-carbon world, driven partly by climate science and partly by the business opportunities it offers, will need the promotion of environmentally friendly alternatives, if an acceptable stabilisation level of atmospheric carbon dioxide is to be achieved. This chapter presents a comprehensive review of energy sources, and the development of sustainable technologies to explore these energy sources. It also includes potential renewable energy technologies, efficient energy systems, energy savings techniques and other mitigation measures necessary to reduce climate changes. The chapter concludes with the technical status of the ground source heat pumps (GSHP) technologies. The purpose of this study, however, is to examine the means of reduction of energy consumption in buildings, identify GSHPs as an environmental friendly technology able to provide efficient utilisation of energy in the buildings sector.

INTRODUCTION

Over millions of years ago, plants have covered the earth converting the energy of sunlight into living plants and animals, some of which was buried in the depths of the earth to produce deposits of coal, oil and natural gas (Lin & Chang, 2013; Glaas & Juhola, 2013; Gerald, 2012). The past few decades, however, have experienced many valuable uses for these complex chemical substances and manufacturing from them plastics, textiles, fertiliser and the various end products of the petrochemical industry. Indeed, each decade sees increasing uses for these products. Coal, oil and gas, which will certainly be of great value to future generations, as they are to ours, are however non-renewable natural resources. The rapid depletion of these non-renewable fossil resources need not continue. This is particularly true now as it is, or soon will be, technically and economically feasible to supply all of man's needs from the most abundant energy source of all, the sun. The sunlight is not only inexhaustible, but, moreover, it is the only energy source, which is completely

DOI: 10.4018/978-1-4666-8433-1.ch008

non-polluting (Bendewald & Zhai, 2013). This requires the harnessing and use of natural resources that produce no air pollution or greenhouse gases and provides comfortable coexistence of human, livestock, and plants.

Industry's use of fossil fuels has been largely blamed for warming the climate. When coal, gas and oil are burnt, they release harmful gases, which trap heat in the atmosphere and cause global warming. However, there had been an ongoing debate on this subject, as scientists have struggled to distinguish between changes, which are human induced, and those, which could be put down to natural climate variability. Notably, human activities that emit carbon dioxide (CO_2), the most significant contributor to potential climate change, occur primarily from fossil fuel production. Consequently, efforts to control CO_2 emissions could have serious, negative consequences for economic growth, employment, investment, trade and the standard of living of individuals everywhere.

ENERGY SOURCES AND USE

Scientifically, it is difficult to predict the relationship between global temperature and greenhouse gas (GHG) concentrations. The climate system contains many processes that will change if warming occurs. Critical processes include heat transfer by winds and tides, the hydrological cycle involving evaporation, precipitation, runoff and groundwater and the formation of clouds, snow, and ice, all of which display enormous natural variability. The equipment and infrastructure for energy supply and use are designed with long lifetimes, and the premature turnover of capital stock involves significant costs. Economic benefits occur if capital stock is replaced with more efficient equipment in step with its normal replacement cycle. Likewise, if opportunities to reduce future emissions are taken in a timely manner, they should be less costly. Such a flexible approach would allow society to take account of evolving scientific and technological knowledge, while gaining experience in designing policies to address climate change (Morrow, 2012).

The World Summit on Sustainable Development in Johannesburg in 2002 (Morrow, 2012) committed itself to ''encourage and promote the development of renewable energy sources to accelerate the shift towards sustainable consumption and production''. Accordingly, it aimed at breaking the link between resource use and productivity. This can be achieved by the following:

- Trying to ensure economic growth does not cause environmental pollution.
- Improving resource efficiency.
- Examining the whole life-cycle of a product.
- Enabling consumers to receive more information on products and services.
- Examining how taxes, voluntary agreements, subsidies, regulation and information campaigns, can best stimulate innovation and investment to provide cleaner technology.

The energy conservation scenarios include rational use of energy policies in all economy sectors and the use of combined heat and power systems, which are able to add to energy savings from the autonomous power plants. Electricity from renewable energy sources is by definition the environmental green product. Hence, a renewable energy certificate system, as recommended by the World Summit, is an essential basis for all policy systems, independent of the renewable energy support scheme. It is, therefore, important that all parties involved support the renewable energy certificate system in place if it is to work as planned. Moreover, existing renewable energy technologies (RETs) could play a significant mitigating role, but the economic and political climate will have to change first. It is now universally accepted that climate change is real. It is happening now, and GHGs produced by human activities are significantly contributing to it. The predicted global temperature increase of between 1.5 and 4.5°C could lead to potentially catastrophic environmental impacts (Cantrell & Wepfer, 1984). These include sea level rise, increased frequency of extreme weather events, floods, droughts, disease migration from various places and possible stalling of the Gulf Stream. This has led scientists to argue that climate change issues are not ones that politicians can afford to ignore, and policy makers tend to agree (ASHRAE, 2005). However, reaching international agreements on climate change policies is no trivial task as the difficulty in ratifying the Kyoto Protocol and reaching agreement at Copenhagen have proved.

Therefore, the use of renewable energy sources and the rational use of energy, in general, are the fundamental inputs for any responsible energy policy. However, the energy sector is encountering difficulties because increased production and consumption levels entail higher levels of pollution and eventually climate change, with possibly disastrous consequences. At the same time, it is important to secure energy at an acceptable cost in order to avoid negative impacts on economic growth. To date, renewable energy contributes only as much as 20% of the global energy supplies worldwide (ASHRAE, 2005). Over two thirds of this comes from biomass use, mostly in developing countries, and some of this is unsustainable. However, the potential for energy from sustainable technologies is huge. On the technological side, renewables have an obvious role to play. In general, there is no problem in terms of the technical potential of renewables to deliver energy. Moreover, there are very good opportunities for the RETs to play an important role in reducing emissions of the GHGs into the atmosphere, certainly far more than have been exploited so far. However, there are still some technical issues to address in order to cope with the intermittency of some renewables, particularly wind and solar. Nevertheless, the biggest problem with relying on renewables to deliver the necessary cuts in the GHG emissions is more to do with politics and policy issues than with technical ones (Kavanaugh & Rafferty, 1997). For example, the single most important step governments could take to promote and increase the use of renewables is to improve access for renewables to the energy market. This access to the market needs to be under favourable conditions and, possibly, under favourable economic rates as well. One move that could help, or at least justify, better market access would be to acknowledge that there are environmental costs associated with other energy supply options and that these costs are not currently internalised within the market price of electricity or fuels. This could make a significant difference, particularly if appropriate subsidies were applied to renewable energy in recognition of the environmental benefits it offers. Similarly, cutting energy consumption through end-use efficiency is absolutely essential. This suggests that issues of end-use consumption of energy will have to come into the discussion in the foreseeable future (UN, 2003).

However, the RETs have the benefit of being environmentally benign when developed in a sensitive and appropriate way with the full involvement of local communities. In addition, they are diverse, secure, locally based and abundant. In spite of the enormous potential and the multiple benefits, the contribution from renewable energy still lags behind the ambitious claims for it due to the initially high development costs, concerns about local impacts, lack of research funding and poor institutional and economic arrangements (UNFCCC, 2009). Hence, an approach is needed to integrate renewable energies in a way that meets the rising demand in a cost-effective way.

ROLE OF ENERGY EFFICIENCY SYSTEM

The prospects for development in power engineering are, at present, closely related to ecological problems. Power engineering has harmful effects on the environment, as it discharges toxic gases into atmosphere and also oil-contaminated and saline waters into rivers, as well as polluting the soil with ash and slag and having adverse effects on living things on account of electromagnetic fields and so on. Thus there is an urgent need for new approaches to provide an ecologically safe strategy. Substantial economic and ecological effects for thermal power projects (TPPs) can be achieved by improvement, upgrading the efficiency of the existing equipment, reduction of electricity loss, saving of fuel, and optimisation of its operating conditions and service life leading to improved access for rural and urban low-income areas in developing countries through energy efficiency and renewable energies.

Sustainable energy is a prerequisite for development. Energy-based living standards in developing countries, however, are clearly below standards in developed countries. Low levels of access to affordable and environmentally sound energy in both rural and urban low-income areas are therefore a predominant issue in developing countries. In recent years many programmes for development aid or technical assistance have been focusing on improving access to sustainable energy, many of them with impressive results. Apart from success stories, however, experience also shows that positive appraisals of many projects evaporate after completion and vanishing of the implementation expert team. Altogether, the diffusion of sustainable technologies such as energy efficiency and renewable energy for cooking, heating, lighting, electrical appliances and building insulation in developing countries has been slow. Energy efficiency and renewable energy programmes could be more sustainable and pilot studies more effective and pulse releasing if the entire policy and implementation process was considered and redesigned from the outset (Rees, 1999). New financing and implementation processes, which allow reallocating financial resources and thus enabling countries themselves to achieve a sustainable energy infrastructure, are also needed. The links between the energy policy framework, financing and implementation of renewable energy and energy efficiency projects have to be strengthened and as well as efforts made to increase people's knowledge through training. . The purpose of this study, however, is to examine the means of reduction of energy consumption in buildings, identify GSHPs as an environmental friendly technology able to provide efficient utilisation of energy in the buildings sector, promote using GSHPs applications as an optimum means of heating and cooling, and to present typical applications and recent advances of the DX GSHPs.

Energy Use in Buildings

Buildings consume energy mainly for cooling, heating and lighting. The energy consumption was based on the assumption that the building operates within ASHRAE-thermal comfort zone during the cooling and heating periods (Bos, My, Vu, & Bulatao, 1994). Most of the buildings incorporate energy efficient passive cooling, solar control, photovoltaic, lighting and day lighting, and integrated energy systems. It is well known that thermal mass with night ventilation can reduce the maximum indoor temperature in buildings in summer (Duchin, 1995). Hence, comfort temperatures may be achieved by proper application of passive cooling systems. However, energy can also be saved if an air conditioning unit is used (Givoni, 1998). The reason for this is that in summer, heavy external walls delay the heat transfer from the outside into the inside spaces. Moreover, if the building has a lot of internal mass the increase in the air temperature is slow. This is because the penetrating heat raises the air temperature as well as the temperature of the heavy thermal mass. The result is a slow heating of the building in summer as the maximal inside temperature is reached only during the late hours when the outside air temperature is already low. The heat flowing from the inside heavy walls could be reduced with good ventilation in the evening and night. The capacity to store energy also helps in winter, since energy can be stored in walls from one sunny winter day to the next cloudy one. However, the admission of daylight into buildings alone does not guarantee that the design will be energy efficient in terms of lighting. In fact, the design for increased daylight can often raise concerns relating to visual comfort (glare) and thermal comfort (increased solar gain in the summer and heat losses in the winter from larger apertures). Such issues will clearly need to be addressed in the design of the window openings, blinds, shading devices, heating system, etc. In order for a building to benefit from daylight energy terms, it is a prerequisite that lights are switched off when sufficient daylight is available. The nature of the switching regime; manual or automated, centralised or local, switched, stepped or dimmed, will determine the energy performance. Simple techniques can be implemented to increase the probability that lights are switched off (ASHRAE, 2003). These include:

- Making switches conspicuous and switching banks of lights independently.
- Loading switches appropriately in relation to the lights.
- Switching banks of lights parallel to the main window wall.

There are also a number of methods, which help reduce the lighting energy use, which, in turn, relate to the type of occupancy pattern of the building (UN, 2003). The light switching options include:

- Centralised timed off (or stepped)/manual on;
- Photoelectric off (or stepped)/manual on;
- Photoelectric and on (or stepped), photoelectric dimming; or
- Occupant sensor (stepped) on/off (movement or noise sensor).

Energy Conservation

Likewise, energy savings from the avoidance of air conditioning can be very substantial. Whilst day-lighting strategies need to be integrated with artificial lighting systems in order to become beneficial in terms of energy use, reductions in overall energy consumption levels by employment of a sustained programme of energy consumption strategies and measures would have considerable benefits within the buildings sector. It would perhaps be better to support a climate sensitive design approach that encompasses some elements of the pure conservation strategy together with strategies, which work with the local ambient conditions making use of energy technology systems, such as solar energy, where feasible. In practice, low energy environments are achieved through a combination of measures that include:

- The application of environmental regulations and policy;
- The application of environmental science and best practice;
- Mathematical modelling and simulation;
- Environmental design and engineering;
- Construction and commissioning; and
- Management and modifications of environments in use.

While the overriding intention of passive solar energy design of buildings is to achieve a reduction in purchased energy consumption, the attainment of significant savings is in doubt. The non-realisation of potential energy benefits is mainly due to the neglect of the consideration of post-occupancy user and management behaviour by energy scientists and designers alike. Calculating energy inputs in agricultural production is more difficult in comparison to the industry sector due to the high number of factors affecting agricultural production, as Table 1 shows. However, considerable studies have been conducted in different countries on energy use in agriculture

Table 1. Energy equivalent of inputs and outputs

Energy Source	Unit	Equivalent Energy (MJ)
	Input	
Human Labor	h	2.3
Animal Labor		
Horse	h	10.10
Mule	h	4.04
Donkey	h	4.04
Cattle	h	5.05
Water Buffalo	h	7.58
Electricity	kwh	11.93
Diesel	Litre	56.31
Chemicals Fertilisers		
Nitrogen	kg	64.4
P_2O_5	kg	11.96
K_2O	kg	6.7
Seed		
Cereals and Pulses	kg	25
Oil Seed	kg	3.6
Tuber	kg	14.7
Total Input	kg	43.3
	Output	
Major Products		
Cereals and Pulses	kg	14.7
Sugar Beet	kg	5.04
Tobacco	kg	0.8
Cotton	kg	11.8
Oil Seed	kg	25
Fruits	kg	1.9
Vegetables	kg	0.8
Watermelon	kg	1.9
Onion	kg	1.6
Potatoes	kg	3.6
Olive	kg	11.8
Tea	kg	0.8
Byproducts		
Husk	kg	13.8
Straw	kg	12.5
Cob	kg	18.0
Seed Cotton	kg	25.0
Total Output	kg	149.04

(Kammerud, Ceballos, Curtis, Place, & Anderson, 1984; Shaviv, 1989; Singh, 2000; CAEEDAC, 2000; Yaldiz, Ozturk, & Zeren, 1995; Dutt, 1982) in order to quantify the influence of these factors.

RENEWABLE ENERGY TECHNOLOGIES

Sustainable energy is the energy that, in its production or consumption, has minimal negative impacts on human health and the healthy functioning of vital ecological systems, including the global environment (Baruah, 1995). It is an accepted fact that renewable energy is a sustainable form of energy, which has attracted more attention during recent years. Increasing environmental interest, as well as economic consideration of fossil fuel consumption and high emphasis of sustainable development for the future helped to bring the great potential of renewable energy into focus. Nearly a fifth of all global power is generated by renewable energy sources, according to a book published by the OECD/IEA (Baruah, 1995). "Renewables for power generation: status and prospects" claims that, at approximately 20%, renewables are the second largest power source after coal (39%) and ahead of nuclear (17%), natural gas (17%) and oil (8%) respectively. From 1973-2000 renewables grew at 9.3% a year and it is predicted that this will increase by 10.4% a year to 2010. Wind power grew fastest at 52% and will multiply seven times by 2020, overtaking biopower and hence help reducing greenhouse gases, GHGs, emissions to the environment.

Table 2 shows some applications of different renewable energy sources. The challenge is to match leadership in the GHG reduction and production of renewable energy with developing a major research and manufacturing capacity in environmental technologies (wind, solar, fuel cells, etc.). More than 50% of the world's area is classified as arid, representing the rural and desert part, which lack electricity and water networks. The inhabitants of such areas obtain water from borehole wells by means of water pumps, which are mostly driven by diesel engines. The diesel motors are associated with maintenance problems, high running cost, and environmental pollution. Alternative methods are pumping by photovoltaic (PV) or wind systems. At present, renewable sources of energy are regional and site specific. It has to be integrated in the regional development plans.

Table 2. Sources of renewable energy

Energy Source	Technology	Size
Solar energy	Domestic solar water heaters Solar water heating for large demands PV roofs: grid connected systems generating electric energy	Small Medium-large Medium-large
Wind energy	Wind turbines (grid connected)	Medium-large
Hydraulic energy	Hydro plants in derivation schemes Hydro plants in existing water distribution networks	Medium-small Medium-small
Biomass	High efficiency wood boilers CHP plants fed by agricultural wastes or energy crops	Small Medium
Animal manure	CHP plants fed by biogas	Small
CHP	High efficiency lighting High efficiency electric Householders appliances High efficiency boilers Plants coupled with refrigerating absorption machines	Wide Wide Wide Small-medium Medium-large

Solar Energy

The availability of data on solar radiation is a critical problem. Even in developed countries, very few weather stations have been recording detailed solar radiation data for a period of time long enough to have statistical significance. Solar radiation arriving on earth is the most fundamental renewable energy source in nature. It powers the bio-system, the ocean and atmospheric current system and affects the global climate. Reliable radiation information is needed to provide input data in modelling solar energy devices and a good database is required in the work of energy planners, engineers, and agricultural scientists. In general, it is not easy to design solar energy conversion systems when they have to be installed in remote locations. First, in most cases, solar radiation measurements are not available for these sites. Second, the radiation nature of solar radiation makes the computation of the size of such systems difficult. While solar energy data are recognised as very important, their acquisition is by no means straightforward. The measurement of solar radiation requires the use of costly equipment such as pyrheliometers and pyranometers. Consequently, adequate facilities are often not available in developing countries to mount viable monitoring programmes. This is partly due to the equipment cost as well as the cost of technical manpower. Several attempts have, however, been made to estimate solar radiation through the use of meteorological and other physical parameter in order to avoid the use of expensive network of measuring instruments (Thakur & Mistra, 1993; Wu & Boggess, 1999; OECD/IEA, 2004; Duffie & Beckman, 1980; Sivkov, 1964).

Two of the most essential natural resources for all life on the earth and for man's survival are sunlight and water. Sunlight is the driving force behind many of the RETs. The worldwide potential for utilising this resource, both directly by means of the solar technologies and indirectly by means of biofuels, wind and hydro technologies, is vast. During the last decade interest has been refocused on renewable energy sources due to the increasing prices and fore-seeable exhaustion of presently used commercial energy sources. The most promising solar energy technology are related to thermal systems; industrial solar water heaters, solar cookers, solar dryers for peanut crops, solar stills, solar driven cold stores to store fruits and vegetables, solar collectors, solar water desalination, solar ovens, and solar commercial bakers. Solar PV system: solar PV for lighting, solar refrigeration to store vaccines for human and animal use, solar PV for water pumping, solar PV for battery chargers, solar PV for communication network, microwave, receiver stations, radio systems in airports, VHF and beacon radio systems in airports, and educational solar TV posts in villages. Solar pumps are most cost effective for low power requirement (up to 5 kW) in remote places. Applications include domestic and livestock drinking water supplies, for which the demand is constant throughout the year, and irrigation. However, the suitability of solar pumping for irrigation, though possible, is uncertain because the demand may vary greatly with seasons. Solar systems may be able to provide trickle irrigation for fruit farming, but not usually the large volumes of water needed for wheat growing.

The hydraulic energy required to deliver a volume of water is given by the formula:

$$E_w = \rho_w g V H \quad (1)$$

where E_w is the required hydraulic energy (kWh day^{-1}); ρ_w is the water density (kg m^{-3}); g is the gravitational acceleration (ms^{-2}); V is the required volume of water (m^3 day^{-1}); and H is the head of water (m).

The solar array power required is given by:

$$P_{sa} = \frac{E_w}{E_{sr} \eta F} \quad (2)$$

Table 3. Classifications of data requirements

Criteria	Plant Data	System Data
Existing data	Size Life Cost (fixed and variation operation and maintenance) Forced outage Maintenance Efficiency Fuel Emissions	Peak load Load shape Capital costs Fuel costs Depreciation Rate of return Taxes
Future data	All of above, plus Capital costs Construction trajectory Date in service	System lead growth Fuel price growth Fuel import limits Inflation

where: P_{sa} is the solar array power (kW_p); E_{sr} is the average daily solar radiation (kWhm^{-2} day^{-1}); F is the array mismatch factor; and η is the daily subsystem efficiency.

Substituting Equation 1 in Equation 2, the following equation is obtained for the amount of water that can be pumped:

$$V = \frac{P_{sa} E_{sr} \eta F}{\rho_w g H} \quad (3)$$

$P_{sa} = 1.6\ kW_p$, $F = 0.85$, $\eta = 40\%$.

Table 4. Effective biomass resource utilisation

Subject	Tools	Constraints
Utilisation and land clearance for agriculture expansion	• Stumpage fees • Control • Extension • Conversion • Technology	• Policy • Fuel-wood planning • Lack of extension • Institutional
Utilisation of agricultural residues	• Briquetting • Carbonisation • Carbonisation and briquetting • Fermentation • Gasification	• Capital • Pricing • Policy and legislation • Social acceptability

A further increase of *PV* depends on the ability to improve the durability, performance and the local manufacturing capabilities of *PV*.

Biomass Utilisation

The data required to perform the trade-off analysis simulation of bio-energy resources can be classified according to the divisions given in Table 3, namely the overall system or individual plants, and the existing situation or future development. The effective economical utilisations of these resources are shown in Table 4, but their use is hindered by many problems such as those related to harvesting, collection, and transportation, besides the photo-sanitary control regulations. Biomass energy is experiencing a surge in interest stemming from a

Table 5. Agricultural residues routes for development

Source	Process	Product	End Use
Agricultural residues	Direct Processing Processing Carbonisation Fermentation	Combustion Briquettes Carbonisation (small scale) Briquettes Carbonised Biogas	Rural poor Urban household Industrial use Industrial use Limited household use Rural household (self sufficiency) Urban fuel Energy services Household, and industry
Agricultural, and animal residues	Direct Briquettes Carbonisation Carbonisation Fermentation	Combustion Direct combustion Carbonised Briquettes Biogas	(Save or less efficiency as wood) (Similar end use devices or improved) Use Briquettes use Use

combination of factors, e.g., greater recognition of its current role and future potential contribution as a modern fuel, global environmental benefits, its development and entrepreneurial opportunities, etc. Possible routes of biomass energy development are shown in Table 5. However, biomass usage and application can generally be divided into the following three categories.

1. Biomass energy for petroleum substitution driven by the following factors:
    a. Oil price increase.
    b. Balance of payment problems, and economic crisis.
    c. Fuel-wood plantations and residue utilisation.
    d. Wood based heat and electricity.
    e. Liquid fuels from biomass.
    f. Producer gas technology.
2. Biomass energy for domestic needs driven by:
    a. Population increase.
    b. Urbanisation.
    c. Agricultural expansion.
    d. Fuel-wood crisis.
    e. Ecological crisis.
    f. Fuel-wood plantations, agro-forestry.
    g. Community forestry, and residue utilisation.
    h. Improved stoves, and improved charcoal production.
3. Biomass energy for development driven by:
    a. Electrification.
    b. Irrigation and water supply.
    c. Economic and social development.
    d. Fuel-wood plantations.
    e. Community forestry.
    f. Agro-forestry.
    g. Briquettes.
    h. Producer gas technology.

The use of biomass through direct combustion has long been, and still is, the most common mode of biomass utilisation (Table 5). Examples for dry (thermo-chemical) conversion processes are charcoal making from wood (slow pyrolysis), gasification of forest and agricultural residues (fast pyrolysis – this is still in demonstration phase), and of course, direct combustion in stoves, furnaces, etc. Wet processes require substantial amount of water to be mixed with the biomass. Biomass technologies include:

- Carbonisation and briquetting.
- Improved stoves.
- Biogas.
- Improved charcoal.
- Gasification.

Briquetting and Carbonisation

Briquetting is the formation of a charcoal (an energy-dense solid fuel source) from otherwise wasted agricultural and forestry residues. One of the disadvantages of wood fuel is that it is bulky with a low energy density and therefore requires transport. Briquette formation allows for a more energy-dense fuel to be delivered, thus reducing the transportation cost and making the resource more competitive. It also adds some uniformity, which makes the fuel more compatible with systems that are sensitive to the specific fuel input. Charcoal stoves are very familiar to African societies. As for the stove technology, the present charcoal stove can be used, and can be improved upon for better efficiency. This energy term will be of particular interest to both urban and rural households and all the income groups due to its simplicity, convenience, and lower air polluting characteristics. However, the market price of the fuel together with that of its end-use technology may not enhance its early high market penetration especially in the urban low income and rural households.

Charcoal is produced by slow heating wood (carbonisation) in airtight ovens or retorts, in chambers with various gases, or in kilns supplied with limited and controlled amounts of air. The charcoal yield decreased gradually from 42.6 to 30.7% for the hazelnut shell and from 35.6 to 22.7% for the beech wood with an increase of temperature from 550 to 1,150 K while the charcoal yield from the lignin content decreases sharply from 42.5 to 21.7% until it was at 850 K during the carbonisation procedures (Sivkov, 1964). The charcoal yield decreases as the temperature increases, while the ignition temperature of charcoal increases as the carbonisation temperature increases. The charcoal briquettes that are sold on the commercial market are typically made from a binder and filler.

Improved Cook Stoves

Traditional wood stoves are commonly used in many rural areas. These can be classified into four types: three stone, metal cylindrical shaped, metal tripod and clay type. Indeed, improvements of traditional cookers and ovens to raise the efficiency of fuel saving can secure rural energy availability, where woody fuels have become scarce. However, planting fast growing trees to provide a constant fuel supply should also be considered. The rural development is essential and economically important since it will eventually lead to a better standard of living, people's settlement, and self-sufficiency.

Biogas Technology

Biogas technology cannot only provide fuel, but is also important for comprehensive utilisation of biomass forestry, animal husbandry, fishery, agricultural economy, protecting the environment, realising agricultural recycling as well as improving the sanitary conditions, in rural areas. However, the introduction of biogas technology on a wide scale has implications for macro planning such as the allocation of government investment and effects on the balance of payments. Hence, factors that determine the rate of acceptance of biogas plants, such as credit facilities and technical backup services, are likely to have to be planned as part of general macro-policy, as do the allocation of research and development funds (Barabaro, Coppolino, Leone, & Sinagra, 1978).

Improved Charcoal

Dry cell batteries are a practical but expensive form of mobile fuel that is used by rural people when moving around at night and for powering radios and other small appliances. The high cost of dry cell batteries is financially constraining for rural households, but their popularity gives a good indication of how valuable a versatile fuel like electricity is in rural areas (Table 6). However, dry cell batteries can constitute an environmental hazard unless they are recycled in a proper fashion. Tables 6 & 7 further show that direct burning of fuel-wood and crop residues constitute the main usage of biomass, as is the case with many developing countries. In fact, biomass resources play a significant role in energy supply in all developing countries. However, the direct burning of biomass in an inefficient manner causes economic loss and adversely affects human health. In order to address the problem of inefficiency, research centres around the world, e.g., Hall & Scrase (1998) have investigated the viability of converting the resource to a more useful form of improved charcoal, namely solid briquettes and fuel gas. Accordingly, biomass resources should be divided into residues or dedicated resources, the latter including firewood and charcoal can also be produced from forest residues (Table 7). Whichever form of biomass resource used, its sustainability would primarily depend on improved forest and tree management.

Gasification

Gasification is based on the formation of a fuel gas (mostly CO and H_2) by partially oxidising raw solid fuel at high temperatures in the presence of steam or air. The technology can use wood chips, groundnut shells, sugarcane bagasse, and other

Table 6. Energy carrier and energy services in rural areas

Energy Carrier	Energy End-Use
Fuel-wood	Cooking Water heating Building materials Animal fodder preparation
Kerosene	Lighting Ignition fires
Dry cell batteries	Lighting Small appliances
Animal power	Transport Land preparation for farming Food preparation (threshing)
Human power	Transport Land preparation for farming Food preparation (threshing)

Table 7. Biomass residues and current use

Type of Residue	Current Use
Wood industry waste	Residues available
Vegetable crop residues	Animal feed
Food processing residue	Energy needs
Sorghum, millet, and wheat residues	Fodder, and building materials
Groundnut shells	Fodder, brick making, and direct fining oil mills
Cotton stalks	Domestic fuel considerable amounts available for short period
Sugar, bagasse, and molasses	Fodder, energy need, and ethanol production (surplus available)
Manure	Fertiliser, brick making, and plastering

similar fuels to generate capacities from 3 kW to 100 kW. Many types of gasifier designs have been developed to make use of the diversity of fuel inputs and to meet the requirements of the product gas output (degree of cleanliness, composition, heating value, etc.) (Pernille, 2004).

Biomass and Sustainability

A sustainable energy system includes energy efficiency, energy reliability, energy flexibility, fuel poverty, and environmental impacts. A sustainable biofuel has two favourable properties, which are availability from renewable raw material, and its lower negative environmental impact than that of fossil fuels. Global warming, caused by CO_2 and other substances, has become an international concern in recent years. To protect forestry resources, which act as major absorbers of CO_2, by controlling the ever-increasing deforestation and the increase in the consumption of wood fuels, such as firewood and charcoal, is therefore an urgent issue. Given this, the development of a substitute fuel for charcoal is necessary. Briquette production technology, a type of clean coal technology, can help prevent flooding and serve as a global warming countermeasure by conserving forestry resources through the provision of a stable supply of briquettes as a substitute for charcoal and firewood.

There are many emerging biomass technologies with large and immediate potential applications, e.g., biomass gasifier/gas turbine (BGST) systems for power generation with pilot plants, improved techniques for biomass harvesting, transportation and storage. Gasification of crop residues such as rice husks, groundnut shells, etc., with plants already operating in China, India, and Thailand. Treatment of cellulosic materials by steam explosion which may be followed by biological or chemical hydrolysis to produce ethanol or other fuels, cogeneration technologies, hydrogen from biomass, striling energies capable of using biomass fuels efficiently, etc. Table 8 gives a view of the use of biomass and its projection worldwide.

However, a major gap with biomass energy is that research has usually been aimed at obtaining supply and consumption data, with insufficient attention and resources being allocated to basic research, to production, harvesting and conservation processes. Biomass has not been closely examined in terms of a substitute for fossil fuels compared to carbon sequestration and overall

Table 8. Final energy projections including biomass (Mtoe)

Region	Biomass	Conventional Energy	Total	Share of Biomass (%)
1995				
Africa	205	136	341	60
China	206	649	855	24
East Asia	106	316	422	25
Latin America	73	342	416	18
South Asia	235	188	423	56
Total developing countries	825	1632	2456	34
Other non-OECD countries	24	1037	1061	1
Total non-OECD countries	849	2669	3518	24
OECD countries	81	3044	3125	3
World	930	5713	6643	14
2020				
Africa	371	266	631	59
China	224	1524	1748	13
East Asia	118	813	931	13
Latin America	81	706	787	10
South Asia	276	523	799	35
Total developing countries	1071	3825	4896	22
Other non-OECD countries	26	1669	1695	1
Total non-OECD countries	1097	5494	6591	17
OECD countries	96	3872	3968	2
World	1193	9365	10558	11

environmental benefits related to these different approaches. To achieve the full potential of biomass as a feedstock for energy, food, or any other use, requires the application of considerable scientific and technological inputs (D'Apote, 1998). However, the aim of any modern biomass energy systems must be:

1. To maximise yields with minimum inputs;
2. Utilise and select adequate plant materials and processes;
3. Optimise use of land, water, and fertiliser; and
4. Create an adequate infrastructure and strong research and development (R&D) base.

An afforestation programme appears an attractive option for any country to pursue in order to reduce the level of atmospheric carbon by enhancing carbon sequestration in the nation's forests, which would consequently mitigate climate change. However, it is acknowledged that certain barriers need to be overcome if the objectives are to be fully achieved. These include the followings.

- Low level of public awareness of the economic/environmental benefits of forestry.
- The generally low levels of individuals' income.
- Pressures from population growth.

- The land tenural system, which makes it difficult (if at all possible) for individuals to own or establish forest plantations.
- Poor pricing of forest products especially in the local market.
- Inadequate financial support on the part of governments.
- Weak institutional capabilities of the various Forestry Departments as regards technical manpower to effectively manage tree plantations.

However, social policy conditions are also critical. This is still very much lacking particularly under developing countries conditions. During the 1970s and 1980s different biomass energy technologies were perceived in sub-Saharan Africa as a panacea for solving acute problems. On the account of these expectations, a wide range of activities and projects were initiated. However, despite considerable financial and human efforts, most of these initiatives have unfortunately been a failure.

Therefore, future research efforts should concentrate on the following areas:

- Directed R and D in the most promising areas of biomass to increase energy supply and to improve the technological base.
- Formulate a policy framework to encourage entrepreneurial and integrated process.
- Pay more attention to sustainable production and use of biomass energy feedstocks, methodology of conservation and efficient energy flows.
- More research aimed at pollution abatement.
- Greater attentions to interrelated socio-economic aspects.
- Support R and D on energy efficiency in production and use.
- Improve energy management skills and take maximum advantage of existing local knowledge.
- Closely examine past successes and failures to assist policy makers with well-informed recommendations.

Combined Heat and Power (CHP)

District Heating (DH), also known as community heating can be a key factor to achieve energy savings, reduce CO_2 emissions and at the same time provide consumers with a high quality heat supply at a competitive price. Generally, DH should only be considered for areas where the heat density is sufficiently high to make DH economical. In countries like Denmark for example, DH may today be economical even to new developments with lower density areas, due to the high level of taxation on oil and gas fuels combined with the efficient production of DH.

Most of the heat used for DH can be produced by large CHP plants (gas-fired combined cycle plants using natural gas, biomass, waste or biogas) as shown in Table 2. DH is energy efficient because of the way the heat is produced and the required temperature level is an important factor. Buildings can be heated to a temperature of 21°C and domestic hot water (DHW) can be supplied at a temperature of 55°C using energy sources other than DH that are most efficient when producing low temperature levels (<95°C) for the DH water (David, 2000). Most of these heat sources are CO_2 neutral or emit low levels. However, only a few of these sources are available to small individual systems at a reasonable cost, whereas DH schemes because of the plant's size and location can have access to most of the heat sources and at a low cost. Low temperature DH, with return temperatures of around 30-40°C can utilise the following heat sources:

- Efficient use of CHP by extracting heat at low calorific value (CV).
- Efficient use of biomass or gas boilers by condensing heat in economisers.
- Efficient utilisation of geothermal energy.

- Direct utilisation of excess low temperature heat from industrial processes.
- Efficient use of large-scale solar heating plants.

Heat tariffs may include a number of components such as a connection charge, a fixed charge and a variable energy charge. Also, consumers may be incentivised to lower the return temperature. Hence, it is difficult to generalise but the heat practice for any DH company, no matter what the ownership structure is, can be highlighted as follows:

- To develop and maintain a development plan for the connection of new consumers.
- To evaluate the options for least cost production of heat.
- To implement the most competitive solutions by signing agreements with other companies or by implementing own investment projects.
- To monitor all internal costs and with the help of benchmarking, improve the efficiency of the company.
- To maintain a good relationship with the consumer and deliver heat supply services at a sufficient quality.

Also, installing DH should be pursued to meet the objectives for improving the environment through the improvement of energy efficiency in the heating sector. At the same time DH can serve the consumer with a reasonable quality of heat at the lowest possible cost. The variety of possible solutions combined with the collaboration between individual companies, the district heating association, the suppliers and consultants can, as it has been in Denmark, be the way forward for developing DH in the United Kingdom.

Fuel Cells

Platinum is a catalyst for fuel cells and hydrogen-fuelled cars presently use about two ounces of the metal. There is currently no practicable alternative. Reserves are in South Africa (70%), and Russia (22%). Although there are sufficient accessible reserves in South Africa to increase supply by up to 5% per year for the next 50 years, there are significant environmental impacts associated with its mining and refining, such as groundwater pollution and atmospheric emissions of sulphur dioxide ammonia, chlorine and hydrogen chloride. The carbon cost of platinum use equates to 360 kg for a current fuel cell car, or 36 kg for a future car, with the target platinum loading of 0.2 oz, which is negligible compared to the CO_2 currently emitted by vehicles (IHA, 2003). Furthermore, Platinum is almost completely recyclable. At current prices and loading, platinum would cost 3% of the total cost of a fuel cell engine. Also, the likely resource costs of hydrogen as a transport fuel are apparently cheapest if it is reformed from natural gas with pipeline distribution, with or without carbon sequestration. However, this is not as sustainable as using renewable energy sources. Substituting hydrogen for fossils fuels will have a positive environmental impact in reducing both photochemical smog and climate change. There could also be an adverse impact on the ozone layer but this is likely to be small, though potentially more significant if hydrogen was to be used as aviation fuel.

Hydrogen Production

Hydrogen is now beginning to be accepted as a useful form for storing energy for reuse on, or for export off, the grid. Clean electrical power harvested from wind and wave power projects can be used to produce hydrogen by electrolysis of water. Electrolysers split water molecules into its constituent parts: hydrogen and oxygen. These are collected as gases; hydrogen at the cathode and oxygen at the anode. The process is quite simple. Direct current is applied to the electrodes to initiate the electrolysis process. Production of hydrogen is an elegant environmental solution. Hydrogen is the most abundant element on the planet, it cannot be destroyed (unlike hydrocarbons) it simply changes state (water to hydrogen and back to water) during consumption. There is no CO or CO_2 generation in its production and consumption and, depending upon methods of consumption, even the production of oxides of nitrogen can be avoided too. However, the transition will be very messy, and will take many technological paths to convert fossil fuels and methanol to hydrogen, building hybrid engines and so on. Nevertheless, the future of hydrogen fuel cells is promising. Hydrogen can be used in internal combustion engines, fuel cells, turbines, cookers gas boilers, road-side emergency lighting, traffic lights or signalling where noise and pollution can be a considerable nuisance, but where traffic and pedestrian safety cannot be compromised.

Hydrogen is already produced in huge volumes and used in a variety of industries. Current worldwide production is around 500 billion Nm^3 per year (EWEA, 2003). Most of the hydrogen produced today is consumed on-site, such as at oil refineries, at a cost of around \$0.70/kg and is not sold on the market (Steele, 1997). When hydrogen is sold on the market, the cost of liquefying the hydrogen and transporting it to the user adds considerably to the production cost. The energy required to produce hydrogen via electrolysis (assuming 1.23 V) is about 33 (kWh/kg). For 1 mole (2 g) of hydrogen the energy is about 0.066 (kWh/mole) (Sitarz, 1992). The achieved efficiencies are over 80% and on this basis electrolytic hydrogen can be regarded as a storable form of electricity. Hydrogen can be stored in a variety of forms:

- Cryogenic; this has the highest gravimetric energy density.
- High-pressure cylinders; pressures of 10,000 psi are quite normal.
- Metal hydride absorbs hydrogen, providing a very low pressure and extremely safe mechanism, but is heavy and more expensive than cylinders, and
- Chemical carriers offer an alternative, with anhydrous ammonia offering similar gravimetric and volumetric energy densities to ethanol and methanol.

Hydropower

Hydropower has a valuable role as a clean and renewable source of energy in meeting a variety of vital human needs. Water is a basic requirement for survival: for drinking, for food, energy production and for good health. As water is a commodity, which is finite and cannot be created, and in view of the increasing requirements as the world population grows, there is no alternative but to store water for use when it is needed. However, the major challenges are to feed the increasing world population, to improve the standards of living in rural areas and to develop and manage land and water in a sustainable way. Hydropower plants are classified by their rated capacity into one of four regimes: micro (<50kW), mini (50-500 kW), small (500 kW-5 MW), and large (>5 MW) (Agnew & Duncan, 1989).

The total world installed hydro capacity today is around 1000 Giga Watts (GW) and a lot more are currently planned, principally in developing countries in Asia, Africa and South America as shown in Table 9, which is reproduced from (Okkan, 1993). However, the present production of hydroelectricity is only about 18 per cent of the technically feasible potential (and 32 per cent of the economically feasible potential); there is no doubt that a large amount of hydropower development lies ahead (Okkan, 1993).

Table 9. World hydro potential and development

Continent	Africa	Asia	Australia and Oceania	Europe	North and Central America	South America
Gross theoretical hydropower potential (GWhy^{-1})	4x10^6	19.4x10^6	59.4x10^6	3.2x10^6	6x10^6	6.2x10^6
Technically feasible hydropower potential (GWhy^{-1})	1.75x10^6	6.8x10^6	2x10^6	10^6	1.66x10^6	2.7x10^6
Economically feasible hydropower potential (GWhy^{-1})	1.1x10^5	3.6x10^6	90x10^4	79x10^4	10^6	1.6x10^6
Installed hydro capacity (MW)	21x10^3	24.5x10^4	13.3x10^4	17.7x10^4	15.8x10^4	11.4x10^4
Production by hydro plants in 2002 or average (GWhy^{-1})	83.4x10^3	80x10^4	43x10^3	568x10^3	694x10^3	55x10^4
Hydro capacity under construction (MW)	> 3024	>72.7x10^3	>177	>23x10^2	58x10^2	>17x10^3
Planned hydro capacity (MW)	77.5x10^3	>17.5x10^4	>647	>10^3	>15x10^3	>59x10^3

Wind Energy

Water is the most natural commodity for the existence of life in the remote desert areas. However, as a condition for settling and growing, the supply of energy is the close second priority. The high cost and the difficulties of mains power line extensions, especially to a low populated region can focus attention on the utilisation of different and more reliable and independent sources of energy like renewable wind energy. Accordingly, the utilisation of wind energy, as a form of energy, is becoming increasingly attractive and is being widely used for the substitution of oil-produced energy, and eventually to minimise atmospheric degradation, particularly in remote areas. Indeed, utilisation of renewables, such as wind energy, has gained considerable momentum since the oil crises of the 1970s. Wind energy, though site-dependent, is non-depleting, non-polluting, and a potential option of the alternative energy source. Wind power could supply 12% of global electricity demand by 2020, according to a report by the European Wind Energy Association and Greenpeace (Njeru, 2013).

Wind energy can and will constitute a significant energy resource when converted into a usable form. As Figure 1 illustrates, information sharing is a four-stage process and effective collaboration must also provide ways in which the other three stages of the 'renewable' cycle: gather, convert and utilise, can be integrated. Efficiency in the renewable energy sector translates into lower gathering, conversion and utilisation (electricity) costs. A great level of installed capacity has already been achieved. Figure 2 clearly shows that the offshore wind sector is developing fast, and this indicates that wind is becoming a major factor in electricity supply with a range of significant technical, commercial and financial hurdles to be overcome. The offshore wind industry has the potential for a very bright future and to emerge as a new industrial sector, as Figure 3 implies.

Figure 1. The renewable cycle

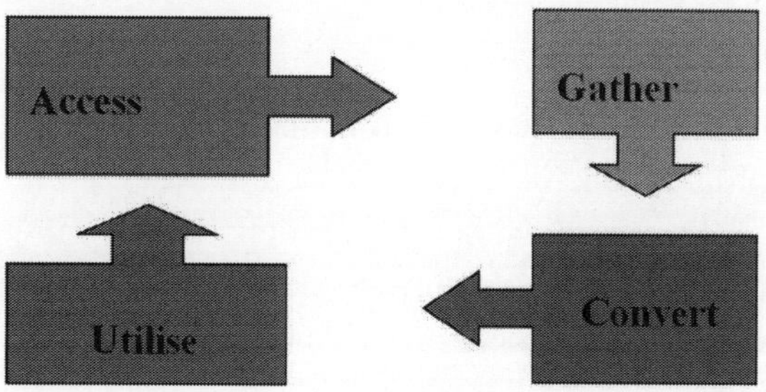

Figure 2. Global prospects of wind energy utilisation by 2003-2010

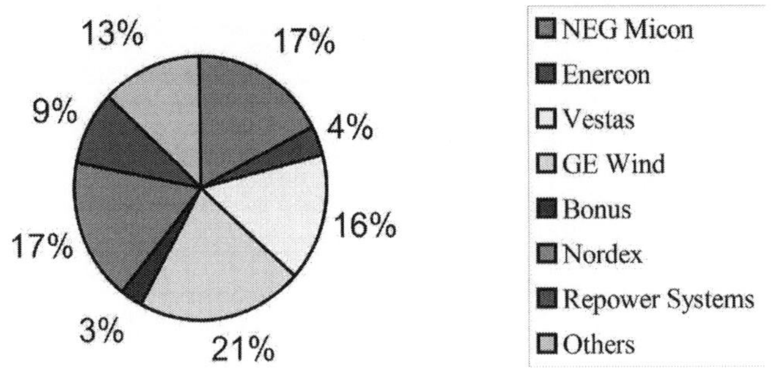

Figure 3. Prospect turbines share for 2003-2010

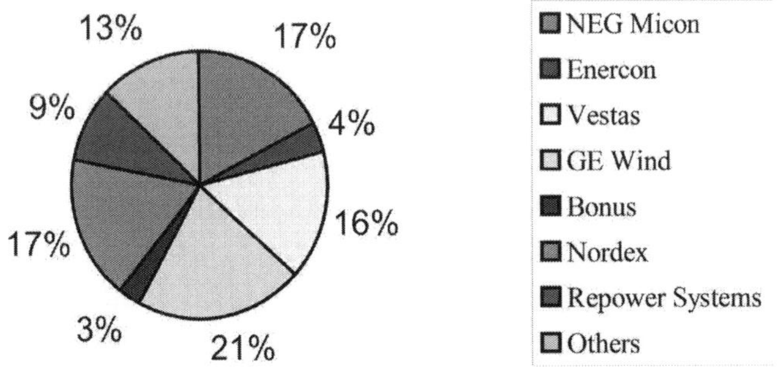

The speed of turbine development is such that more powerful models would supersede the original specification turbines in the time from concept to turbine order. Levels of activities are growing at a phenomenal rate (Figure 4), new prospects developing, new players entering, existing players growing in experience; technology evolving and, quite significantly, politics appear to support the sector.

Figure 4. Average windfarm capacity 2003-2010

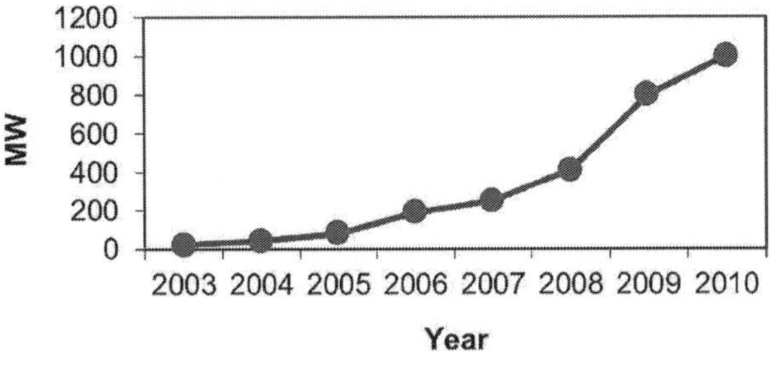

ENERGY AND SUSTAINABLE DEVELOPMENT

Sustainability is defined as the extent to which progress and development should meet the need of the present without compromising the ability of the future generations to meet their own needs (Odeku, Maveneka, & Konanani, 2013). This encompasses a variety of levels and scales ranging from economic development and agriculture, to the management of human settlements and building practices. Tables 10, 11 & 12 indicate the relationship between energy conservation, sustainable development and environment.

The following issues were addressed during the Rio Earth Summit in 1992 (Abdeen, 2009):

Table 10. Energy and sustainable environment

Technological Criteria	Energy and Environment Criteria	Social and Economic Criteria
Primary energy saving in regional scale	Sustainability according to greenhouse gas pollutant emissions	Labour impact
Technical maturity, and reliability	Sustainable according to other pollutant emissions	Market maturity
Consistence of installation and maintenance requirements with local technical known-how	Land requirement	Compatibility with political, legislative and administrative situation
Continuity and predictability of performance	Sustainability according to other environmental impacts	Cost of saved primary energy

Table 11. Classification of key variables defining facility sustainability

Criteria	Intra-System Impacts	Extra-System Impacts
Stakeholder satisfaction	• Standard expectations met • Relative importance of standard expectations	Covered by attending to extra-system resource base and ecosystem impacts
Resource base impacts	• Change in intra-system resource bases • Significance of change	• Resource flow into/out of facility system • Unit impact exerted by flow on source/sink system • Significance of unit impact
Ecosystem impacts	• Change in intra-system ecosystems • Significance of change	• Resource flows into/out of facility system • Unit impact exerted by how on source/sink system • Significance of unit impact

- The use of local materials and indigenous building sources.
- Incentive to promote the continuation of traditional techniques, with regional resources and self-help strategies.
- Regulation of energy-efficient design principles.
- International information exchange on all aspects of construction related to the environment, among architects and contractors, particularly non-conventional resources.
- Exploration of methods to encourage and facilitate the recycling and reuse of building materials, especially those requiring intensive energy use during manufacturing, and the use of clean technologies.

And, the following action areas for producers were recommended:

- **Management and Measurement Tools:** Adopting environmental management systems appropriate for the business.
- **Performance Assessment Tools:** Making use of benchmarking to identify scope for impact reduction and greater eco-efficiency in all aspects of the business.
- **Best Practice Tools:** Making use of free help and advice from government best practice programmes (energy efficiency, environmental technology, resource savings).
- **Innovation and Eco-Design:** Rethinking the delivery of 'value added' by the business, so that impact reduction and resource efficiency are firmly built in at the design stage.

Table 12. Positive impact of durability, adaptability, and energy conservation on economic, social, and environment systems

Economic System	Social System	Environmental System
Durability	Preservation of cultural values	Preservation of resources
Meeting changing needs of economic development	Meeting changing needs of individuals and society	Reuse, recycling and preservation of resources
Energy conservation and saving	Savings directed to meet other social needs	Preservation of resources, reduction of pollution and global warming

- **Cleaner, Leaner Production Processes:** Pursuing improvements and savings in waste minimisation, energy and water consumption, transport and distribution, as well as reduced emissions.
- **Supply Chain Management:** Specifying more demanding standards of sustainability from 'upstream' suppliers, while supporting smaller firms to meet those higher standards.
- **Product Stewardship:** Taking the broadest view of 'producer responsibility' and working to reduce all the 'downstream' effects of products after they have been sold on to customers.
- **Openness and Transparency:** Publicly reporting on environmental performance against meaningful targets; actively using clear labels and declarations so that customers are fully informed; building stakeholder confidence by communicating sustainability aims to the workforce, the shareholders and the local community (Figure 5).

This is the step in a long journey to encourage progressive economy, which continues to provide people with high living standards, but, at the same time helps reduce pollution, waste mountains, other environmental degradation, and environmental rationale for future policy-making and intervention to improve market mechanisms. This vision will be accomplished by:

- 'Decoupling' economic growth and environmental degradation. The basket of indicators illustrated in Table 13 shows the progress being made. Decoupling air and water pollution from growth, making good headway with CO_2 emissions from energy, and transport. The environmental impact of our own individual behaviour is more closely linked to consumption expenditure than the economy as a whole.

Figure 5. Link between resources and productivity

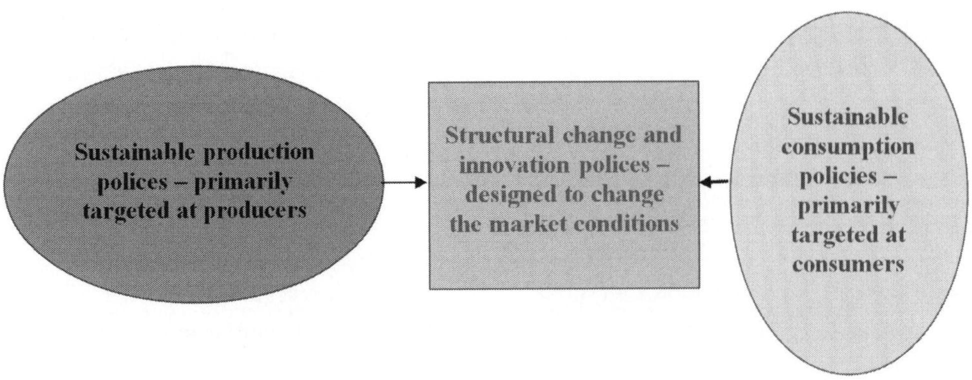

- Focusing policy on the most important environmental impacts associated with the use of particular resources, rather than on the total level of all resource use.
- Increasing the productivity of material and energy use that are economically efficient by encouraging patterns of supply and demand, which are more efficient in the use of natural resources. The aim is to promote innovation and competitiveness. Investment in areas like energy efficiency, water efficiency and waste minimisation.
- Encouraging and enabling active and informed individual and corporate consumers.

Chemicals

Humans and wildlife are being contaminated by a host of commonly used chemicals in food packaging and furniture, according to the World Wildlife Federation (WWF) and European Union (Abdeen, 2008). Currently, the chemical industry has been under no obligation to make the information public. However, the new proposed rules would change this. Future dangers will only be averted if the effects of chemicals are exposed and then the dangerous ones are never used. Indeed, chemicals used for jacket waterproofing, food packaging and non-stick coatings have been found in dolphins, whales, cormorants, seals, sea eagles and polar bears from the Mediterranean to the Baltic. The European Commission has adopted an ambitious action plan to improve the development and wider use of environmental technologies such as recycling systems for wastewater in industrial processes, energy-saving car engines and soil remediation techniques, using hydrogen and fuel cells (Abdeen, 2012). The legislation, which has not been implemented in time, concerns the incineration of waste, air quality limit, values for benzene and carbon monoxide, national emission ceilings for sulphur dioxide, nitrogen oxides, volatile organic compounds and ammonia and large combustion plants.

Wastes

Waste is defined as an unwanted material that is being discarded. Waste includes items being taken for further use, recycling or reclamation. Waste produced at household, commercial and industrial premises are control waste and come under the waste regulations. Waste Incineration Directive (WID) emissions limit values will favour efficient, inherently cleaner technologies that do not rely heavily on abatement. For existing plant, the requirements are likely to lead to improved control of:

- NO_x emissions, by the adoption of infurnace combustion control and abatement techniques.
- Acid gases, by the adoption of abatement techniques and optimisation of their control.
- Particulate control techniques, and their optimisation, e.g., of bag filters and electrostatic precipitators.

Table 13. The basket of indicators for sustainable consumption and production

Economy-Wide Decoupling Indicators
1. Greenhouse gas emissions 2. Air pollution 3. Water pollution (river water quality) 4. Commercial and industrial waste arisings and household waste not cycled
Resource Use Indicators
5. Material use 6. Water abstraction 7. Homes built on land not previously developed, and number of households
Decoupling Indicators for Specific Sectors
8. Emissions from electricity generation 9. Motor vehicle kilometres and related emissions 10. Agricultural output, fertiliser use, methane emissions and farmland bird populations 11. Manufacturing output, energy consumption and related emissions 12. Household consumption, expenditure energy, water consumption and waste generated

The waste and resources action programme has been working hard to reduce demand for virgin aggregates and market uptake of recycled and secondary alternatives. The programme targets are:

- To deliver training and information on the role of recycling and secondary aggregates in sustainable construction for influences in the supply chain, and
- To develop a promotional programme to highlight the new information on websites.

Global Warming

This results in the following requirements:

- Relevant climate variables should be generated (solar radiation: global, diffuse, direct solar direction, temperature, humidity, wind speed and direction) according to the statistics of the real climate.
- The average behaviour should be in accordance with the real climate.
- Extremes should occur in the generated series in the way it will happen in a real warm period. This means that the generated series should be long enough to capture these extremes, and series based on average values from nearby stations.

On some climate change issues (such as global warming), there is no disagreement among the scientists. The greenhouse effect is unquestionably real; it is essential for life on earth. Water vapour is the most important GHG; followed by carbon dioxide (CO_2). Without a natural greenhouse effect, scientists estimate that the earth's average temperature would be –18°C instead of its present 14°C (Raphael, 2012). There is also no scientific debate over the fact that human activity has increased the concentration of the GHGs in the atmosphere (especially CO_2 from combustion of coal, oil and gas). The greenhouse effect is also being amplified by increased concentrations of other gases, such as methane, nitrous oxide, and CFCs as a result of human emissions. Most scientists predict that rising global temperatures will raise the sea level and increase the frequency of intense rain or snowstorms. Climate change scenarios sources of uncertainty and factors influencing the future climate are:

- The future emission rates of the GHGs (Table 14).
- The effect of this increase in concentration on the energy balance of the atmosphere.
- The effect of these emissions on GHGs concentrations in the atmosphere, and

Table 14. West European states GHG emissions

Country	1990	1999	Change 1990-99	Reduction Target
Austria	76.9	79.2	2.6%	-13%
Belgium	136.7	140.4	2.8%	-7.5%
Denmark	70.0	73.0	4.0%	-21.0%
Finland	77.1	76.2	-1.1%	0.0%
France	545.7	544.5	-0.2%	0.0%
Germany	1206.5	982.4	-18.7%	-21.0%
Greece	105.3	123.2	16.9%	25.0%
Ireland	53.5	65.3	22.1%	13.0%
Italy	518.3	541.1	4.4%	-6.5%
Luxembourg	10.8	6.1	-43.3%	-28.0%
Netherlands	215.8	230.1	6.1%	-6.0%
Portugal	64.6	79.3	22.4%	27.0%
Spain	305.8	380.2	23.2%	15.0%
Sweden	69.5	70.7	1.5%	4.0%
United Kingdom	741.9	637.9	-14.4%	-12.5%
Total EU-15	4199	4030	-4.0%	-8.0%

- The effect of this change in energy balance on global and regional climate.

It has been known for a long time that urban centres have mean temperatures higher than their less developed surroundings. The urban heat increases the average and peak air temperatures, which in turn affect the demand for heating and cooling. Higher temperatures can be beneficial in the heating season, lowering fuel use, but they exacerbate the energy demand for cooling in the summer times.

Neither heating nor cooling may dominate the fuel use in a building in temperate climates, and the balance of the effect of the heat is less. As the provision of cooling is expensive with higher environmental cost, ways of using innovative alternative systems, like the mop fan will be appreciated. The solar gains would affect energy consumption. Therefore, lower or higher percentages of glazing, or shading devices might affect the balance between annual heating and cooling loads. In addition to conditioning energy, the fan energy needed to provide mechanical ventilation can make a significant further contribution to energy demand. Much depends on the efficiency of design, both in relation to the performance of fans themselves and to the resistance to flow arising from the associated ductwork. Figure 6 illustrates the typical fan and thermal conditioning needs for a variety of ventilation rates and climate conditions.

Figure 6. Energy impact of ventilation

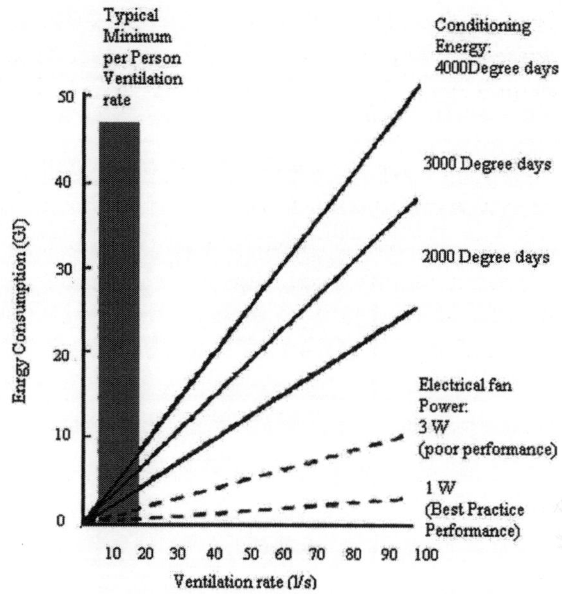

Ground Source Heat Pumps

The term "ground source heat pump" has become an all-inclusive term to describe a heat pump system that uses the earth, ground water, or surface water as a heat source and/or sink. Some of the most common types of ground source ground-loop heat exchangers configurations are classified in Figure 7. The GSHP systems consist of three loops or cycles as shown. The first loop is on the load side and is either an air/water loop or a water/water loop, depending on the application. The second loop is the refrigerant loop inside a water source heat pump. Thermodynamically, there is no difference between the well-known vapour-compression refrigeration cycle and the heat pump cycle; both systems absorb heat at a low temperature level and reject it to a higher temperature level. However, the difference between the two systems is that a refrigeration application is only concerned with the low temperature effect produced at the evaporator, while a heat pump may be concerned with both the cooling effect produced at the evaporator and the heating effect produced at the condenser. In these dual-mode GSHP systems, a reversing valve is used to switch between heating and cooling modes by reversing the refrigerant flow direction. The third loop in the system is the ground loop in which water or an antifreeze solution exchanges heat with the refrigerant and the earth.

The GSHPs utilise the thermal energy stored in the earth through either vertical or horizontal closed loop heat exchange systems buried in the ground. Many geological factors impact directly on site characterisation and subsequently the design and cost of the system. The solid geology of the United Kingdom varies significantly. Furthermore there

Figure 7. Common types of ground-loop heat exchangers

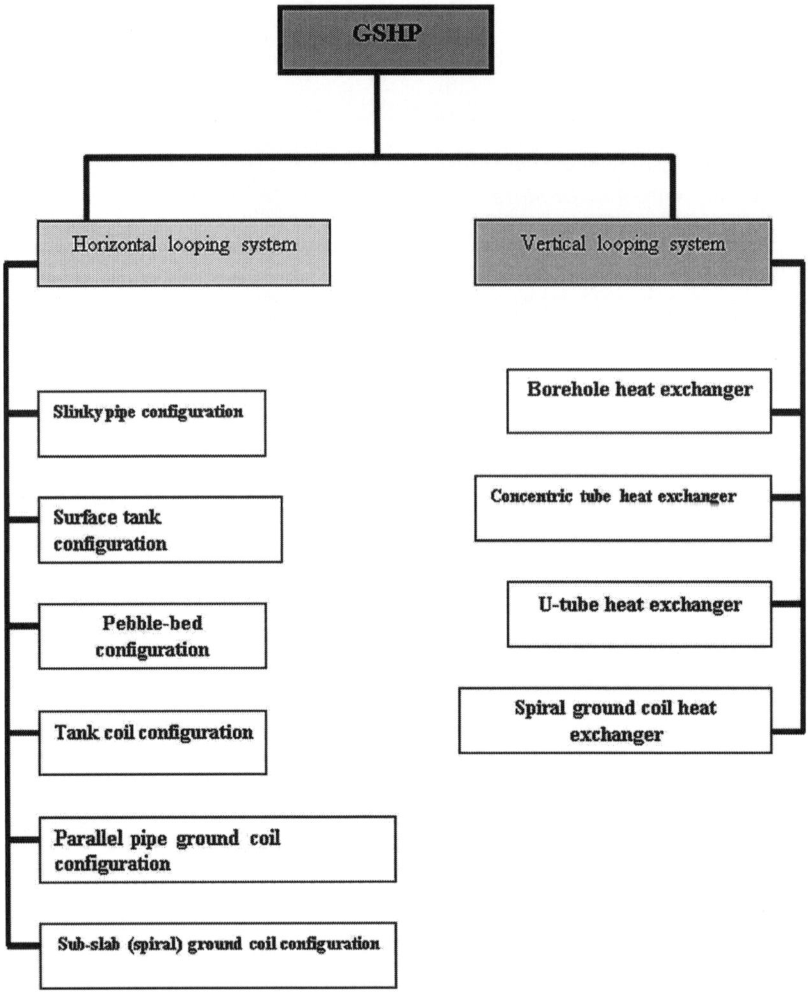

is an extensive and variable rock head cover. The geological prognosis for a site and its anticipated rock properties influence the drilling methods and therefore system costs. Other factors important to system design include predicted subsurface temperatures and the thermal and hydrological properties of strata. The GSHP technology is well established in Sweden, Germany and North America, but has had minimal impact in the United Kingdom space heating and cooling market. Perceived barriers to uptake include geological uncertainty, concerns regarding performance and reliability, high capital costs and lack of infrastructure. System performance concerns relate mostly to uncertainty in design input parameters, especially the temperature and thermal properties of the source. These in turn can impact on the capital cost, much of which is associated with the installation of the external loop in horizontal trenches or vertical boreholes. The climate in the United Kingdom makes the potential for heating in winter and cooling in summer from a ground source less certain owing to the temperature ranges being narrower than those encountered in continental climates. This project will develop an impartial GSHP function on the site to make available information and data on site-specific temperatures and key geotechnical characteristics.

The GSHPs are receiving increasing interest because of their potential to reduce primary energy consumption and thus reduce emissions of greenhouse gases. The technology is well established in North Americas and parts of Europe, but is at the demonstration stage in the United Kingdom. The information will be delivered from digital geoscience's themes that have been developed from observed data held in corporate records. This data will be available to the GSHP installers and designers to assist the design process, therefore reducing uncertainties. The research will also be used to help inform the public as to the potential benefits of this technology.

The GSHPs play a key role in geothermal development in Central and Northern Europe. With borehole heat exchangers as heat source, they offer de-central geothermal heating with great flexibility to meet given demands at virtually any location. No space cooling is included in the vast majority of systems, leaving ground-source heat pumps with some economic constraints. Nevertheless, a promising market development first occurred in Switzerland and Sweden, and now also in Austria and Germany. Approximately 20 years of R and D focusing on borehole heat exchangers resulted in a well-established concept of sustainability for this technology, as well as in sound design and installation criteria. The market success brought Switzerland to the third rank worldwide in geothermal direct use. The future prospects are good, with an increasing range of applications including large systems with thermal energy storage for heating and cooling, ground-source heat pumps in densely populated development areas, borehole heat exchangers for cooling of telecommunication equipment, etc.

Loops can be installed in three ways: horizontally, vertically or in a pond or lake. The type chosen depends on the available land area, soil and rock type at the installation site. These factors help to determine the most economical choice for installation of the ground loop. The GSHP delivers 3-4 times as much energy as it consumes when heating, and cools and dehumidifies for a lower cost than conventional air conditioning. It can cut homes or business heating and cooling costs by 50% and provide hot water free or with substantial savings. The GSHPs can reduce the energy required for space heating, cooling and service water heating in commercial/institutional buildings by as much as 50%.

Efficiencies of the GSHP systems are much greater than conventional air-source heat pump systems. A higher COP (coefficient of performance) can be achieved by a GSHP because the source/sink earth temperature is relatively constant compared to air temperatures. Additionally, heat is absorbed and rejected through water, which is a more desirable heat transfer medium because of its relatively high heat capacity. The GSHP systems rely on the fact that, under normal geothermal gradients of about 0.5°F/100 ft (30°C/km), the earth temperature is roughly constant in a zone extending from about 20 ft (6.1 m) deep to about 150 ft (45.7 m) deep. This constant temperature interval within the earth is the result of a complex interaction of heat fluxes from above (the sun and the atmosphere) and from below (the earth interior). As a result, the temperature of this interval within the earth is approximately equal to the average annual air temperature (Roriz, 2001). Above this zone (less than about 20 feet (6.1 m) deep), the earth temperature is a damped version of the air temperature at the earth's surface. Below this zone (greater than about 150 ft (45.7 m) deep), the earth temperature begins to rise according to the natural geothermal gradient. The storage concept is based on a modular design that will facilitate active control and optimisation of thermal input/output, and it can be adapted for simultaneous heating and cooling often needed in large service and institutional buildings (Strauss, 2013). Loading of the core is done by diverting warm and cold air from the heat pump through the core during periods with excess capacity compared to the current need of the building (Tukahirwa, 2013; Valkila & Saari, 2012; Vargas-Parra, 2013). The cool section of the core can also be loaded directly with air during the night, especially in spring and fall when nights are cold and days may be warm.

DISCUSSION

Peoples rely upon oil for primary energy and this for a few more decades. Other conventional sources may be more enduring, but are not without serious disadvantages (Vargas-Parra, 2013). The renewable energy resources are particularly suited for the provision of rural power supplies and a major advantage is that equipment such as flat plate solar driers, wind machines, etc., can be constructed using local resources and without the advantage results from the feasibility of local maintenance and the general encouragement such local manufacture gives to the build up of small-scale rural based industry. This communication comprises a comprehensive review of energy sources, the environment and sustainable development. It includes the renewable energy technologies, energy efficiency systems, energy conservation scenarios, energy savings in greenhouses environment and other mitigation measures necessary to reduce climate change. This study gives some examples of small-scale energy converters, nevertheless it should be noted that small conventional, i.e., engines are currently the major source of power in rural areas and will continue to be so for a long time to come. There is a need for some further development to suit local conditions, to minimise spares holdings, to maximise interchangeability both of engine parts and of the engine application. Emphasis should be placed on full local manufacture. It is concluded that renewable environmentally friendly energy must be encouraged, promoted, implemented and demonstrated by full-scale plant (device) especially for use in remote rural areas.

The communication reviews various options of renewable energy sources that are possibly be applied to rural based energy needs which may wholly or partly replace the conventional sources of energy. Sustainable energy is a prerequisite for development. Energy-based living standards in developing countries, however, are clearly below standards in developed countries. Low levels of access to affordable and environmentally sound energy in both rural and urban low-income areas are therefore a predominant issue in developing countries. In recent years many programmes for development aid or technical assistance have been focusing on improving access to sustainable energy, many of them with impressive results. Apart from success stories, however, experience also shows that positive appraisals of many projects evaporate after completion and vanishing of the implementation expert team. Altogether, the diffusion of sustainable technologies such as energy efficiency and renewable energy for cooking, heating, lighting, electrical appliances and building insulation in developing countries has been slow. Energy efficiency and renewable energy programmes could be more sustainable and pilot studies more effective and pulse releasing if the entire policy and implementation process was considered and redesigned from the outset. New financing and implementation processes, which allow reallocating financial resources and thus enabling countries themselves to achieve a sustainable energy infrastructure, are also needed. The links between the energy policy framework, financing and implementation of renewable energy and energy efficiency projects have to be strengthened and as well as efforts made to increase people's knowledge through training. Different sources of energy, which can be used for different final uses. Those sources are wind power, solar energy, geothermal energy, the existing electricity production system and the conventional fuels with direct use (Figure 8). The main categories of final uses are: transportation, space heating, water heating and electricity for other uses.

Figure 8. Energy sources their final uses

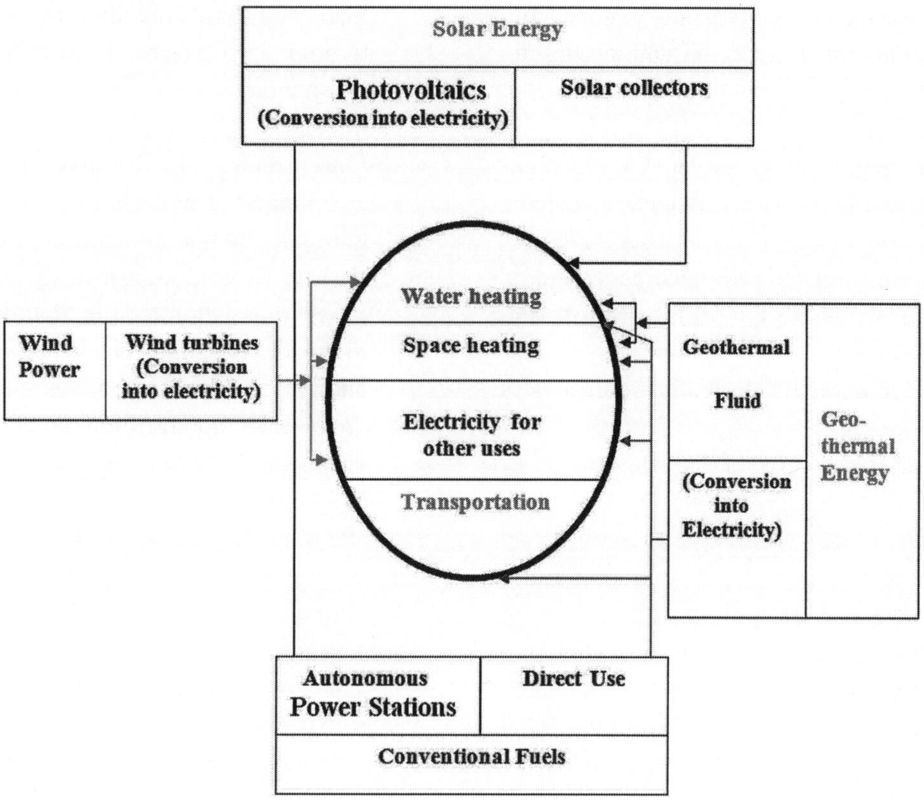

CONCLUSION

There is strong scientific evidence that the average temperature of the earth's surface is rising. This is a result of the increased concentration of carbon dioxide and other GHGs in the atmosphere as released by burning fossil fuels. This global warming will eventually lead to substantial changes in the world's climate, which will, in turn, have a major impact on human life and the built environment. Therefore, effort has to be made to reduce fossil energy use and to promote green energy, particularly in the building sector. Energy use reductions can be achieved by minimising the energy demand, rational energy use, recovering heat and the use of more green energy. This study was a step towards achieving this goal.

The adoption of green or sustainable approaches to the way in which society is run is seen as an important strategy in finding a solution to the energy problem. The key factors to reducing and controlling CO_2, which is the major contributor to global warming, are the use of alternative approaches to energy generation and the exploration of how these alternatives are used today and may be used in the future as green energy sources. Even with modest assumptions about the availability of land, comprehensive fuel-wood farming programmes offer significant energy, economic and environmental benefits. These benefits would be dispersed in rural areas where they are greatly needed and can serve as linkages for further rural economic development.

However, by adopting coherent strategy for alternative clean sustainable energy sources, the world as a whole would benefit from savings in foreign exchange, improved energy security, and socio-economic improvements. With a nine-fold increase in forest – plantation cover, every nation's resource base would be greatly improved while the international community would benefit from pollution reduction, climate mitigation, and the increased trading opportunities that arise from new income sources.

The non-technical issues related to clean energy, which have recently gained attention, include:

1. Environmental and ecological factors, e.g., carbon sequestration, reforestation and revegetation;
2. Renewables as a CO_2 neutral replacement for fossil fuels;
3. Greater recognition of the importance of renewable energy, particularly modern biomass energy carriers, at the policy and planning levels;
4. Greater recognition of the difficulties of gathering good and reliable renewable energy data, and efforts to improve it; and
5. Studies on the detrimental health efforts of biomass energy particularly from traditional energy users.

The chapter is one effort in touching all these aspects.

RECOMMENDATIONS

- Launching of public awareness campaigns among local investors particularly small-scale entrepreneurs and end users of the RET to highlight the importance and benefits of renewable, particularly solar, wind, and biomass energies.
- Amendment of the encouragement of investment act, to include furthers concessions, facilities, tax holidays, and preferential treatment to attract national and foreign capital investment.
- Allocation of a specific percentage of soft loans and grants obtained by governments to augment budgets of the (R&D) related to manufacturing and commercialisation of the RET.
- Governments should give incentives to encourage the household sector to use renewable energy instead of conventional energy. Execute joint investments between the private sector and the financing entities to disseminate the renewable information and literature with technical support from the research and development entities.
- Availing of training opportunities to personnel at different levels in donor countries and other developing countries to make use of their wide experience in application and commercialisation of the RET particularly renewable energy.
- The governments should play a leading role in adopting renewable energy devices in public institutions, e.g., schools, hospitals, government departments, police stations, etc., for lighting, water pumping, water heating, communication and refrigeration.
- Encouraging the private sector to assemble, install, repair and manufacture renewable energy devices via investment encouragement and more flexible licensing procedures.

ACKNOWLEDGMENT

The financial support for this research work is from the Energy Research Institute (ERI). Thanks to my wife Kawthar Abdelhai Ali for her warmth and love. Her unwavering faith in me, her intelligence, humour, spontaneity, curiosity and wisdom added to this article and to my life.

REFERENCES

Abdeen, M. O. (2008). Green energies and environment. *Renewable & Sustainable Energy Reviews*, *12*(7), 1789–1821. doi:10.1016/j.rser.2006.05.009

Abdeen, M. O. (2009). Principle of low energy building design: Heating, ventilation and air conditioning. *Cooling India: India's Premier Magazine on the Cooling Industry*, *5*(4), 26–46.

Abdeen, M. O. (2012). Clean and green energy technologies: Sustainable development and environment. *Sky J. Agric. Res.*, *1*(2), 28–50.

Agnew, J. A., & Duncan, J. S. (Eds.). (1989). *The power of place: bringing together geographical and sociological imaginations*. Boston, MA: Unwin Hyman.

ASHRAE. (2003). Energy efficient design of new building except new low-rise residential buildings. BSRIASHRAE proposed standards 90-2P-1993. Atlanta, GA: American Society of Heating, Refrigerating, and Air Conditioning Engineers Inc.

ASHRAE. (2005). Commercial/Institutional Ground Source Heat Pump Engineering Manual. Atlanta, GA: American Society of heating, Refrigeration and Air-conditioning Engineers, Inc.

Barabaro, S., Coppolino, S., Leone, C., & Sinagra, E. (1978). Global solar radiation in Italy. *Solar Energy*, *20*(5), 431–438. doi:10.1016/0038-092X(78)90163-9

Baruah, D. (1995). Utilisation pattern of human and fuel energy in the plantation. *Journal of Agriculture and Soil Science*, *8*(2), 189–192.

Bendewald, M., & Zhai, Z. J. (2013). Using carrying capacity as a base line for building sustainability assessment. *Habitat International*, *37*(1), 22–32. doi:10.1016/j.habitatint.2011.12.021

Bos, E., My, T., Vu, E., & Bulatao, R. (1994). *World population projection: 1994-95*. Baltimore, MD & London, UK: World Bank by the John Hopkins University Press.

CAEEDAC. (2000). *A descriptive analysis of energy consumption in agriculture and food sector in Canada*. Final Report, February 2000.

Cantrell, J., & Wepfer, W. (1984). Shallow Ponds for Dissipation of Building Heat: A case Study. *ASHRAE Transactions*, *90*(1), 239–246.

D'Apote, S. L. (1998). IEA biomass energy analysis and projections. In *Proceedings of Biomass Energy Conference: Data, Analysis and Trends*. Paris, France.

David, J. M. (2000). Developing hydrogen and fuel cell products. *Energy World*, *303*(0), 16–17.

Duchin, F. (1995). *Global scenarios about lifestyle and technology, the sustainable future of the global system*. Tokyo: United Nations University.

Duffie, J. A., & Beckman, W. A. (1980). *Solar Engineering of Thermal Processes*. New York, NY: J. Wiley and Sons.

Dutt, B. (1982). Comparative efficiency of energy use in rice production. *Energy*, *6*(0), 25.

EWEA. (2003). *Wind force 12*. Brussels: EWEA.

Gerald, S. (2012). Why we disagree about climate change: A different viewpoint. *Energy & Environment*, *23*(8), 76–95.

Givoni, B. (1998). *Climate consideration in building and urban design*. New York, NY: Van Nostrand Reinhold.

Glaas, E., & Juhola, S. (2013). New levels of climate adaptation policy: Analysing the institutional interplay in the Baltic Sea Region. *Sustainability*, *1*(0), 56–122.

Hall, O., & Scrase, J. (1998). Will biomass be the environmentally friendly fuel of the future? *Biomass and Bioenergy*, *15*(4-5), 357–367. doi:10.1016/S0961-9534(98)00030-0

IHA. (2003). *World Atlas & Industry Guide*. United Kingdom: The International Journal Hydropower & Dams.

Kammerud, R., Ceballos, E., Curtis, B., Place, W., & Anderson, B. (1984). Ventilation cooling of residential buildings. *ASHRAE Trans Part 1B*, *90*(1), 226–252.

Kavanaugh, S., & Rafferty, K. (1997). Ground source heat pumps. Design of Geothermal Systems for Commercial and Institutional Buildings. Atlanta, GA: American Society of heating, Refrigeration and Air-conditioning Engineers, Inc.

Lin, K., & Chang, T. C. (2013). Everyday crises: Marginal society livelihood vulnerability and adaptability to hazards. *Progress in Development Studies*, *13*(1), 45–78. doi:10.1177/146499341201300101

Morrow, K. (2012). Rio+20, the green economy and re-orienting sustainable development. *Environmental Law Review*, *14*(4), 15–23.

Njeru, J. (2013). 'Donor-driven' neoliberal reform processes and urban environmental change in Kenya: The case of Karura Forest in Nairobi. *Progress in Development Studies*, *13*(1), 17–25. doi:10.1177/146499341201300105

Odeku, K. O., Maveneka, A., & Konanani, R. H. (2013). Consequences of Country's Withdrawal from Climate Change Agreements: Implications for Carbon Emissions Reduction. *Journal of Human Ecology (Delhi, India)*, *41*(1), 17–24.

OECD/IEA. (2004). *Renewables for power generation: status and prospect*. UK: OECD.

Okkan, P. (1993). Reducing CO_2 emissions-How do heat pumps compete with other options? *IEA Heat Pump Centre Newsletter*, *11*(3), 24–26.

Pernille, M. (2004). Danish lessons on district heating. *Energy Resource Sustainable Management and Environmental, March/April*, 16-17.

Raphael, A. T. (2012). Energy and Climate Change: Critical reflection on the African Continent; Is There an Ideal REDD+ Program? An Analysis. *Journal Sustainable Development in Africa*, *14*(6), 25–36.

Rees, W. E. (1999). The built environment and the ecosphere: A global perspective. *Building Research and Information*, *27*(4), 206–220. doi:10.1080/096132199369336

Roriz, L. (2001). *Determining the potential energy and environmental effects reduction of air conditioning systems*. Commission of the European Communities DG TREN.

Shaviv, E. (1989). The influence of the thermal mass on the thermal performance of buildings in summer and winter. In T. C. Steemers & W. Palz (Eds.), *Science and Technology at the service of architecture* (pp. 470–472). Dordrecht: Kluwer Academic Publishers.

Singh, J. (2000). *On farm energy use pattern in different cropping systems in Haryana, India*. Unpublished master's thesis, International Institute of Management-University of Flensburg, Germany.

Sitarz, D. (1992). *Agenda 21: The Earth Summit Strategy to save our planet*. Boulder, CO: Earth Press.

Sivkov, S. I. (1964). To the methods of computing possible radiation in Italy. *Trans. Main Geophys Obs*, *160*(0), 1–20.

Sivkov, S. I. (1964). On the computation of the possible and relative duration of sunshine. *Trans. Main Geophys Obs*, *160*(0), 21–39.

Steele, J. (1997). *Sustainable architecture: principles, paradigms, and case studies*. New York, NY: McGraw-Hill Inc.

Strauss, J. (2013). Does housing drive state-level job growth? Building permits and consumer expectations forecast a state's economic activity. *Journal of Urban Economics*, *73*(1), 77–93. doi:10.1016/j.jue.2012.07.005

Thakur, C., & Mistra, B. (1993). Energy requirements and energy gaps for production of major crops in India. *Agricultural Situation of India*, *48*(10), 665–689.

Tukahirwa, J. T., Mol, A. P. J., & Oosterveer, P. (2013). Comparing urban sanitation and solid waste management in East African metropolises: The role of civil society organisations. *Cities (London, England)*, *30*(0), 204–211. doi:10.1016/j.cities.2012.03.007

United Nations (UN). (2003). World urbanisation project: the 2002 revision. New York, NY: The United Nations Population Division.

United Nations Framework Convention on Climate Change (UNFCCC). (2009). *The draft of the Copenhagen Climate Change Treaty* (pp. 3–181).

Valkila, N., & Saari, A. (2012). Perceptions Held by Finnish Energy Sector Experts Regarding Public Attitudes to Energy Issues. *J. Sustainable. Dev.*, *5*(11), 23–45.

Vargas-Parra, M. V., Villalba, G., & Gabarrell, X. (2013). Applying exergy analysis to rainwater harvesting systems to assess resource efficiency. *Resources, Conservation and Recycling*, *72*(0), 50–59. doi:10.1016/j.resconrec.2012.12.008

Wu, J., & Boggess, W. (1999). The optimal allocation of conservation funds. *Journal of Environmental Economics and Management*, *38*(3), 302–332. doi:10.1006/jeem.1999.1091

Yaldiz, O., Ozturk, H., & Zeren, Y. (1993). *Energy usage in production of field crops in Turkey*. Paper presented at 5th International Congress on Mechanisation and Energy Use in Agriculture. Kusadasi, Turkey.

ADDITIONAL READING

Abdeen, M. O. (2008a). Renewable building energy systems and passive human comfort solutions. *Renewable & Sustainable Energy Reviews*, *12*(6), 1562–1587. doi:10.1016/j.rser.2006.07.010

Abdeen, M. O. (2008b). People, power and pollution. *Renewable & Sustainable Energy Reviews*, *12*(7), 1864–1889. doi:10.1016/j.rser.2006.10.004

Abdeen, M. O. (2008c). Energy, environment and sustainable development. *Renewable & Sustainable Energy Reviews*, *12*(9), 2265–2300. doi:10.1016/j.rser.2007.05.001

Abdeen, M. O. (2008d). Focus on low carbon technologies: The positive solution. *Renewable & Sustainable Energy Reviews*, *12*(9), 2331–2357. doi:10.1016/j.rser.2007.04.015

Abdeen, M. O. (2008e). Development of integrated bioenergy for improvement of quality of life of poor people in developing countries. In F. L. Magnusson & O. W. Bengtsson (Eds.), *Energy in Europe: Economics, Policy and Strategy* (pp. 341–373). New York, NY: NOVA Science Publishers, Inc.

Abdeen, M. O. (2009a). *Environmental and socio-economic aspect of possible development in renewable energy use*. Paper presented at the 4th International Symposium on Environment. Athens, Greece.

Abdeen, M. O. (2009b). *Energy use, environment and sustainable development*. Paper presented at the 3rd International Conference on Sustainable Energy and Environmental Protection (SEEP 2009). Dublin, Republic of Ireland.

Abdeen, M. O. (2009c). Energy use and environmental: impacts: a general review. *Journal of Renewable and Sustainable Energy*, *1*(0), 1–29.

Abdeen, M. O. (2009d). Energy use, environment and sustainable development. In R. T. Mancuso (Ed.), *Environmental Cost Management* (pp. 129–166). New York, NY: NOVA Science Publishers, Inc.

Aroyeun, S. O. (2009). Reduction of aflatoxin B1 and Ochratoxin A in cocoa beans infected with *Aspergillus* via Ergosterol Value. *World Review of Science, Technology and Sustainable Development*, *6*(1), 75–90.

Barton, A. L. (2007). *Focus on Sustainable Development Research Advances*. New York, NY: NOVA Science Publishers.

Brain, G., & Mark, S. (2007). Garbage in, energy out: Landfill gas opportunities for CHP projects. *Cogeneration and On-Site Power*, *8*(5), 37–45.

Commission of the European Communities (CEC). (2000). *Towards a European strategy for the security of energy supply.* Green Paper, Brussels, 29 November 2000 COM (2000) 769.

DeCarlo, F., & Bassano, A. (Eds.). (2010). *Freshwater Ecosystems and Aquaculture Research*. New York, NY: Nova Science Publishers, Inc.

Farm Energy Centre (FEC). (2000). *Helping agriculture and horticulture through technology, energy efficiency and environmental protection*. Warwickshire.

Fowler, P. D. (2001). *Indoor hydroponics: A guide to understanding and maintaining a hydroponic nutrient solution*. UK: Highdro Publishing.

Hindsworth, M. F., & Lang, T. B. (Eds.). (2009). *Community Participation and Empowerment*. New York, NY: NOVA Science Publishers, Inc.

Huttrer, G. (2001). The status of world geothermal power generation 1995-2000. *Geothermics*, *30*(1), 1–27. doi:10.1016/S0375-6505(00)00042-0

IEA. (2008). *Combined heat and power: evaluating the benefits of greater global investment*. 2008.

Jeremy, L. (2005). The energy crisis, global warming and the role of renewables. *Renewable Energy World*, *8*(2), 1–3.

Kowalczyk, L., & Piotrowski, J. (Eds.). (2009). *Energy Costs: International Developments and New Directions*. New York, NY: NOVA Science Publishers, Inc.

Lam, J. C. (2000). Shading effects due to nearby buildings and energy implications. *Energy Conversion and Management*, *47*(7), 47–59.

Lund, J. W., Freeston, D. H., & Boyd, T. L. (2005). Direct application of geothermal energy: 2005 Worldwide Review. *Geothermics*, *34*(6), 691–727. doi:10.1016/j.geothermics.2005.09.003

Omer, A. M. (2010). *The crux of matter: water in the Republic of the Sudan*. New York, NY: NOVA Science Publishers, Inc.

REN21. (2007). Renewables (2007) global status report. Retrieved from www.ren21.net

Reddy, A., Williams, R., & Johansson, T. (2007). Energy after Rio: prospects and challenges. New York, NY: United Nations Development Programme (UNDP).

Roriz, L. (2001). *Determining the potential energy and environmental effects reduction of air conditioning systems*. Commission of the European Communities DG TREN.

Shao, S., Lin, R. S., & Zhejiang, D. X. (2002). *Thermodynamic analysis on heat pumps with economiser for cold regions* (pp. 23–28). China.

United Nations. (UN). (2001). World Urbanisation Prospect: The 1999 Revision. New York, NY: The United Nations Population Division.

United Nations. (UN). (2002a) *Science and Technology as a Foundation for SD*. Commission on SD acting as the preparatory committee for the World Summit on Sustainable Development Fourth Preparatory Session, May 21–June 7, 2002.

United Nations. (UN). (2002b). Global challenge global opportunity: trends in sustainable development. In Proceedings of World Summit on Sustainable Development. Johannesburg, South Africa: UN Department of Economics and Social Affairs.

United Nations Economic Commission for Africa (UNECA). (2002). Address by Josué Dioné: science and technology policies for sustainable development and Africa's global inclusion. In *Proceedings of the Sustainable Development Division ATPS Conference*. Abuja, Nigeria: UNECA.

United Nations Economic Commission for Africa (UNECA). (2003a). *Making Science and Technology Work for the Poor and for Sustainable Development in Africa*. Addis Ababa, Ethiopia: UNECA.

United Nations Economic Commission for Africa (UNECA). (2003b). *The state of food security in Africa: Progress Report of the 3rd Meeting of the Committee on Sustainable Development, 7–10 October, 2003*. Addis Ababa, Ethiopia: UNECA.

United Nations Economic Commission for Europe (UNECE). (2004). Note by the ECE Secretariat, Steering Group on Sustainable Development. In *Proceedings of the Second Meeting of the 2003/2004 Bureau at the Conference of European Statisticians*. Geneva, Switzerland: UN Statistical Commission.

United Nations Environment Programme (UNEP). (2003). *Handbook for the International Treaties for the Protection of the Ozone Layer*. Nairobi, Kenya: United Nations Environment Programme.

United Nations Under-Secretary General & United Nations Environment Programme (UNEP). (2000). *Global Environment Outlook: Overview, outlook and recommendations*. London, UK: Earthscan.

Vilinac, D. (2008). Plant medicines: An herbalist's perspective. *World Review of Science. Technology and Sustainable Development*, *5*(2), 140–151.

White, J. R., & Robinson, W. H. (Eds.). (2008). *Natural Resources: Economics, Management and Policy*. New York, NY: NOVA Science Publishers, Inc.

Witte, H., van Gelder, A. J., & Serrão, M. (2002). *Comparison of design and operation of a commercial UK ground source heat pump project*. In *Proceedings of the 1st International Conference on Sustainable Energy Technologies* (pp. 1-6). Porto, Portugal: World Society of Sustainable Energy Technologies.

World Bank. (WB). (2003a). World Development Report. Oxford University Press, New York.

World Bank. (WB). (2003b). Global economic prospects: realising the development promise of the Doha agenda. Washington, DC: The International Bank for Reconstruction and Development, The World Bank.

World Bank. (WB). (2004). World Development Report 2004: Making Services Work for Poor People. Washington, DC: The World Bank.

World Bank. (WB). (2006). Sustainable Development in the 21st Century. Washington, DC: The World Bank.

World Bank. (WB). (2007). World Bank Sustainable Development Reference Guide. Washington, DC: The World Bank.

KEY TERMS AND DEFINITIONS

Biomass Energy: The energy embodied in organic matter ("biomass") that is released when chemical bonds are broken by microbial digestion, combustion, or decomposition. Biofuels are a wide range of fuels, which are in some way derived from biomass. The term covers solid biomass, liquid fuels and various biogases. Biofuels are gaining increased public and scientific attention, driven by factors such as oil price spikes and the need for increased energy security.

Environment: The natural environment, commonly referred to simply as the environment, encompasses all living and non-living things occurring naturally on Earth or some region thereof. The biophysical environment is the symbiosis between the physical environment and the biological life forms within the environment, and includes all variables that comprise the Earth's biosphere.

Geothermal Energy: Geothermal power (from the Greek roots geo, meaning earth, and thermos, meaning heat) is power extracted from heat stored in the earth. This geothermal energy originates from the original formation of the planet, from radioactive decay of minerals, and from solar energy absorbed at the surface. Heat transferred from the earth's molten core to underground deposits of dry steam (steam with no water droplets), wet steam (a mixture of steam and water droplets), hot water, or rocks lying fairly close to the earth's surface.

Greenhouse Gases: Greenhouse gases are gases in an atmosphere that absorb and emit radiation within the thermal infrared range. This process is the fundamental cause of the greenhouse effect. The main greenhouse gases in the Earth's atmosphere are water vapour, carbon dioxide, methane, nitrous oxide, and ozone. Changes in the concentration of certain greenhouse gases, due to human activity such as fossil fuel burning, increase the risk of global climate change.

Hydropower: Hydropower, hydraulic power or waterpower is power that is derived from the force or energy of moving water, which may be harnessed for useful purposes. Hydropower is using water to power machinery or make electricity. Water constantly moves through a vast global cycle, evaporating from lakes and oceans, forming clouds, precipitating as rain or snow, and then flowing back down to the ocean.

Renewable Energy: Renewable energy is energy generated from natural resources such as sunlight, wind, rain, tides, and geothermal heat, which are renewable (naturally replenished). Energy obtained from sources that are essentially inexhaustible (unlike, for example the fossil fuels, of which there is a finite supply). Energy sources that are, within a short time frame relative to the Earth's natural cycles, sustainable, and include non-carbon technologies such as solar energy, hydropower, and wind, as well as carbon-neutral technologies.

Resource Management: Efficient incident management requires a system for identifying available resources at all jurisdictional levels to enable timely and unimpeded access to resources needed to prepare for, respond to, or recover from an incident. Resource management is the efficient and effective deployment for an organisation's resources when they are needed. Such resources may include financial resources, inventory, human skills, production resources, or information technology (IT).

Solar Energy: Energy from the sun that is converted into thermal or electrical energy; "the amount of energy falling on the earth is given by the solar constant, but very little use has been made of solar energy". Energy derived ultimately from the sun. It can be divided into direct and indirect categories. Most energy sources on Earth are forms of indirect solar energy, although we usually do not think of them in that way. Solar energy uses semiconductor material to convert sunlight into electric currents. Although solar energy only provides 0.15% of the world's power and less than 1% of USA energy, experts believe that sunlight has the potential to supply 5,000 times, as much energy as the world currently consumes.

Sustainable Development: Development, which seeks to produce sustainable economic growth, while ensuring future generations' ability to do the same by not exceeding the regenerative capacity of the nature. In other words, it is trying to protect the environment. A process of change in which the resources consumed (both social and ecological) are not depleted to the extent that they cannot be replicated. Environmentally friendly forms of economic growth activities (agriculture, logging, manufacturing, etc.) that allow the continued production of a commodity without damage to the ecosystem (soil, water supplies, biodiversity or other surrounding resources).

Wind Energy: Kinetic energy present in wind motion that can be converted to mechanical energy for driving pumps, mills, and electric power generators. Wind power is the conversion of wind energy into a useful form of energy, such as using wind turbines to make electricity, wind mills for mechanical power, wind pumps for pumping water or drainage, or sails to propel ships.

Chapter 9
A Regional Energy Planning Approach:
An Integrated Framework and Its Application to Jeju Island's Renewable Roadmap

Wei-Ming Chen
National Taiwan University of Science and Technology, Taiwan

Young-Doo Wang
University of Delaware, USA

Jong Chul Huh
Jeju National University, South Korea

Youn Cheol Park
Jeju National University, South Korea

ABSTRACT

Augmenting recent coverage of the topic of regional energy planning, this chapter introduces an Integrated Regional Energy Policy and Planning Framework (IREPP), which is conceptually comprehensive and also enhances feasibility of implementation. This framework contains important concepts of sustainable energy planning, including integrated resource planning, soft energy path, distributed generation using decentralized energy technologies, and energy-environment-economy-equity balance (E^4). The IREPP also includes implementation feasibility analysis and highlights the importance of monitoring and evaluation. In the second part of this chapter, the IREPP is applied to the case of Jeju. Jeju's "Mid- and Long-Term Roadmap of Renewable Energy Planning" intends to promote renewable energy applications in order to build a carbon free energy system. This chapter evaluates Jeju's overall Roadmap via the lens of IREPP, assesses the rationale and feasibility of achieving its individual renewable target set for 2050, and, additionally, reviews progress made in some individual targets as of 2014.

DOI: 10.4018/978-1-4666-8433-1.ch009

INTRODUCTION

A fossil fuel-based economy triggers a variety of problems including economic instability, energy insecurity, social inequity, environmental pollution, and global warming. These problems point to an urgent need to seek a new energy system based on the concept of sustainability. Through decentralized applications of locally-endowed renewable sources and efficiency improvements, fossil fuel-based long supply chains can be shortened, and the adverse impact can be within the tolerance limit of local environment. In these regards, sustainability is enhanced, along with local viability (Sheer, 2004; Brown, 2009; Li, 2005).

The importance of a regional initiative in developing an energy plan cannot be overlooked. It is because decisions at the regional level may be able to consider the unique pattern of local energy needs and mix of local energy resources. The decisions made at the regional level also may represent the interests of local government, stakeholders, and communities, appropriately meeting long-term local energy needs. Energy planning which integrates regional energy demand and supply, based on regional circumstances, is important and necessary for creating positive impacts for a region, including but not limited to environmental quality, regional employment, and standard of life (Domac et al., 2011).

Regional energy planning is especially important for renewable energy development that is a site-specific and multi-dimensional task (Brandoni & Polonara, 2012). Regional authorities/governments have better chance to estimate the real potential for regional renewable energy, evaluate local environmental impacts, identify any business opportunities created from utilizing renewable energy, and integrate regional energy planning into national energy policies (Montis, 2014; Domac et al., 2011).

The purpose of this chapter is to construct a comprehensive regional energy policy and planning framework and to evaluate a regional energy plan based on this framework. Thus we introduce the Integrated Regional Energy Policy and Planning (IREPP) framework, which is considered to be conceptually comprehensive in its approach. Based on the IREPP framework, we evaluated a renewable master plan, "Jeju's Mid- and Long-Term Roadmap of Renewable Energy Planning" (hereinafter called the Roadmap), and also the feasibility of the specific target of each renewable option identified in the Roadmap.

This chapter is composed of five sections. In the sections which follow, we first review the existing regional energy planning approaches as part of developing the IREPP. Then we outline the conceptual framework of the IREPP. In the third section, the Jeju's overall renewable energy plan to meet a 50 percent energy from renewable sources in 2050 (the Roadmap) is evaluated on the basis of the IREPP. Thereafter, we review individual renewable energy technology introduced in the Roadmap and assess its feasibility of achieving individual target. Renewable experiences by US and EU are important guidelines for the assessment of the target. In the final section, we offer some policy suggestions for Jeju Island to obtain its 50 percent target of renewable applications by 2050.

REGIONAL ENERGY PLANNING APPROACHES

The importance of regional energy planning for regional development has been recognized, especially in the triangular relationship of regional development, energy planning and environmental management (Nijkamp & Volwahsen, 1990). Many times regional energy planning can capture specific development goals that are not achievable through national-level policies. That is because policy makers at the local level have concerns which are typically very specific, and which include the precise set of measures (techno-economic as well as political) that would achieve some desired target at minimum cost (Domac et al., 2011; Cai et al., 2009; Kanudia & Loulou, 1999).

In many areas of the world, regional energy plans have been under development for decades, and they are getting a significant academic interest recently. Research on regional energy planning has shown various foci, including decision-making and planning method. Ramachandra (2009) treated regional energy planning as a constrained optimization problem, which means policy makers need to satisfy local energy need with an optimal manner (least cost or most efficiency) under the availability of local sources. Ramachandra developed a computer program, named "decision support systems (DSS)" to assist policy makers to find the best mix of energy resources at least economic and environmental cost.

Tsioliaridou et al. (2006) introduced a simulation computer model, called INVERT, to support the design of regional energy planning in order to efficiently promote renewable energy technologies in the electricity sector. The basic idea of INVERT is to compare the cost with the corresponding CO_2 reduction and evaluate the most effective way to promote renewable energy in the regional level. Beccali et al. (2003) showed a multi-criteria decision support approach, called Electre III, to assess an action plan for the diffusion of renewable energy technologies at regional scale. The purpose of Electre III is to help energy planners choose the most innovative technologies in the energy sector. Tsoutsos et al. (2009) also exploited a multi-criteria methodology for the sustainable energy planning and applied the methodology to the island of Crete in Greece.

To enhance the integration of renewable energy sources and technologies into energy systems, Cormio et al. (2003) developed a bottom-up energy system optimization model to support planning policies for promoting the use of renewable energy sources in the regional level, detailing the description of the industrial cogeneration system scheme. Lam et al. (2011) used regional energy clustering (REC) and regional resources management composite curve (RMC) to analyze the trade-off between land use and biomass generation at the regional level. Deshmukh & Deshmukh (2009) used multi-objective goal programming approach to do the scenario analysis for optimal allocation of local resources for various end-uses.

In addition to the quantitative approach of a regional energy planning, many regional energy planning approaches adopted by Hawaii, San Diego and California highlight practical concerns of regional energy issues such as how to integrate renewable energy into current energy systems. Domac et al. (2011) illustrated a set of regional energy planning concept, based on integrated energy planning (IRP) approach to enhance renewable energy utilization on the regional level. The concept set includes existing energy balance, future energy supply and demand, and environmental concerns.

The Worldwatch Research Institute (WRI) has developed the "Sustainable Energy Roadmaps" to assist regions, as well as other geographic and political levels, shifting from fossil fuels-based energy systems to renewable and efficient systems. The Roadmaps provide data and analysis of:

1. Energy efficiency opportunities;
2. Renewable energy potentials;
3. Grid integration and technical needs;
4. Socioeconomic impacts;
5. Best-practice policy framework and recommendations; and
6. Domestic and international financing options (WRI, 2012).

Table 1 compares the major components of theoretical and actual regional energy planning models. The components include

1. Demand-supply analysis and target setting;
2. Renewable energy integration;
3. End-use efficiency and conservation;
4. Power generation, transmission and distribution (T&D) efficiency;
5. Distributed generation;

Table 1. Comparison of dimensions in various regional energy models

	Target Setting	Integrated Resource Planning							Regional Sustainability				Implementation Feasibility					Monitoring and Evaluation
		Demand-Side		Supply-Side														
		Conservation	End-Use Efficiency	Renewable	CHP/DHC	DG	Efficiency	T&D	Energy	Environment	Economy	Equity	Fiscal	Technical	Political	Administrative/ Legal	Cultural/ Ethical	
RIEP (Ramachandra, 2009)	√	√	√	√	√	√	√		√	√	√	√		√		√		
INVERT (Tsioliaridou et al., 2006)	√		√	√	√		√		√	√	√			√		√		
Electre III (Beccali et al., 2003)	√	√	√	√	√		√		√	√	√		√	√	√	√		
PROMETHEE (Tsoutsos et al., 2009)	√			√					√	√	√		√	√	√			
REP based on EFOM (Cormio et al., 2003)	√			√	√		√			√			√					
REC & RMC (Lam et al., 2011)	√								√	√								
Micro-level energy planning (Deshmukh & Deshmukh, 2009)	√			√						√	√	√						
Regional Energy Planning Methodology (Domac et al., 2011)	√			√					√	√	√			√		√		
Sustainable Energy Roadmaps (WRI, 2012)			√	√	√	√	√	√	√	√	√	√	√	√	√	√	√	
Hawaii Clean Energy Initiative	√		√	√		√	√		√	√	√		√	√	√	√		
Integrated Energy Policy Report California	√	√	√	√				√	√	√	√							
San Diego Regional Energy Strategy	√	√	√	√	√	√	√	√	√	√	√	√	√		√	√		

Note: RIEP: Regional integrated energy plan/ INVERT: the name of planning model used in this reference/ Electre III: the name of model used in this reference/ PROMETHEE: the name of sustainable energy planning model used in this reference/ REC: Regional energy clustering/ RMC: Regional resources management composite curve/ REP: Regional energy planning/ EFOM: Energy flow optimization model (the name of planning model used in this reference).

6. Combined heat and power (CHP) and district heating and cooling;
7. Sustainability with respect to energy, environment, economy and equity (E^4); and
8. Policy implementation and evaluation.

Nearly all these models include the application of renewable energy resources in their energy mix with specific targets and consideration of environmental impacts. Most models focus on methodologies for regional energy decision making process and planning (ex. Lam et al., 2011; Deshmukh & Deshmukh, 2009; Ramachandra, 2009; Tsoutsos et al., 2009; Tsioliaridou et al., 2006; Beccali et al., 2003; Cormio et al., 2003) while others highlight the integration of alternative energy sources in local environmental, economic, and social circumstances (ex. RIEP, WRI Roadmaps, Hawaii Clean Energy Initiative, Integrated Energy Policy Report California). Many models, however, do not consider certain components, which lay between the target setting and the policy implementation and evaluation.

In terms of integrated resource planning (IRP), the benefits derived from energy conservation (demand-side planning) and potential energy savings from transmission and distribution efficiency (supply-side planning) are only mentioned in a couple of models including California and San Diego energy plans and WRI Roadmaps. In terms of regional sustainability, almost all models consider the relationship among energy, economy, and environment but the fourth "E" (social equity) is neglected. For implementation feasibility, fiscal, technical, and administrative feasibility receive attention while the feasibility related to cultural and ethical aspects is seldom discussed. Monitoring and evaluation is a missing component in most models. IRP (D'Sa, 2005) covers a broad range of components, but it is mainly used for power sector instead of regional energy plan. IREPP meanwhile is a framework which covers a regional energy planning procedure from the beginning (energy target setting) to the end (monitoring and evaluation).

INTEGRATED REGIONAL ENERGY POLICY AND PLANNING (IREPP) FRAMEWORK

The IREPP is a comprehensive conceptual framework designed to assist policy makers and planners at regional levels in developing and evaluating sustainable energy programs and policies. The IREPP is constructed on the basis of the following energy concepts and planning components (Figure 1):

- One basic component of the IREPP is to set a clear target year and objective(s) of the regional energy plan. Depending on the target year established, a plan can be characterized as short-term or long-term,[1] and policy makers are able to link the energy objective with regional economic, environmental and social goals;
- Integrated resource planning to pursue an optimal combination of demand- and supply-side options to meet energy service needs within an energy region on equal footing (D'Sa, 2005; Yilmaz et al., 2008; Ramachandra, 2009);
- Soft energy path focusing on soft energy technologies and combining a serious commitment to efficient use of energy, rapid development of available renewable energy sources, and transitional use of fossil fuels (Lovins, 1977);
- Distributed generation using decentralized energy technologies to reduce needs for costly peak power generation and greenhouse gas (GHG) emissions (Iannucci, 1994; Feinstein et al., 1997; Kelley, 2008; Mitchell, 2008; Sauter & Bauknecht, 2009; Carley, 2009);
- Enhanced sustainability based on energy-environment-economy-equity balance (E^4), emphasizing social equity aspects (especially in relation with poverty and women) in addition to intergenerational, geographical,

Figure 1. Integrated Regional Energy Policy and Planning (IREPP) framework

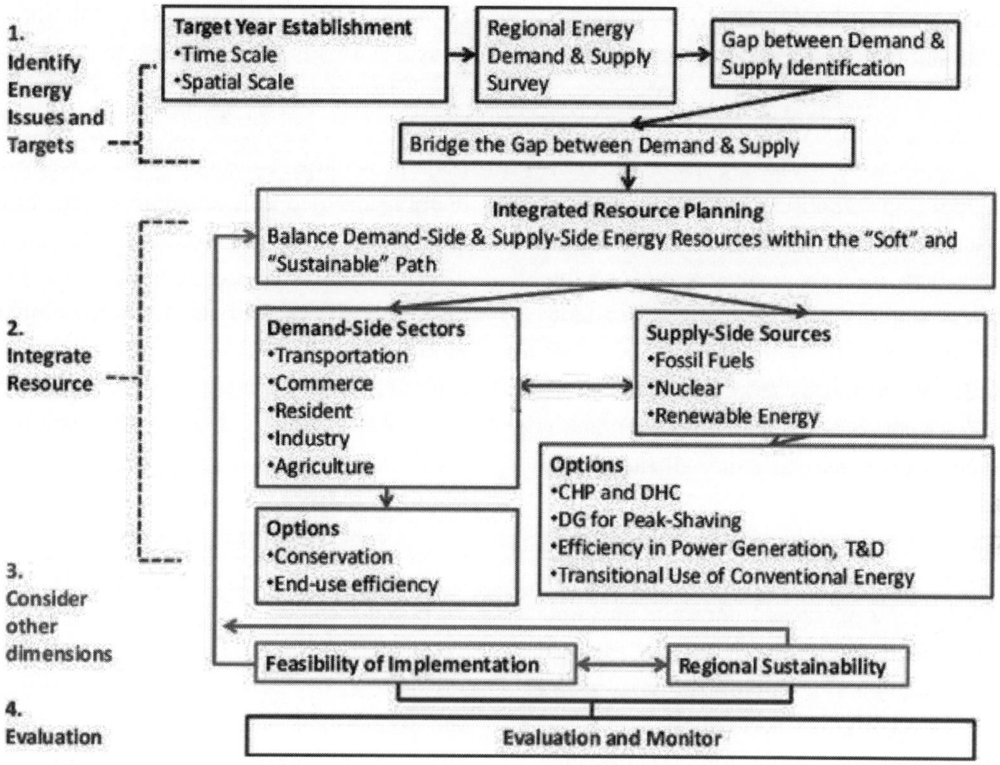

inter-species and procedural equity issues (Wang et al., 1996; UNDP, 2000; Hopwood et al., 2005; Dorian et al., 2006);

- Implementation feasibility in terms of financial, technological, political, cultural, etc., along with partnerships of national or even global organizations[2] to facilitate and accelerate the successful implementation of a regional energy policy and program (Cooper & Vargas, 2004); and
- Monitoring and evaluation to explore the effectiveness of policies to provide performance information for the reset of energy targets or redesign and improved adaptation of policy instruments (D'Sa, 2005; Yue et al., 2006; Vine, 2008)

The IREPP differs from the most conventional regional energy approaches in which the IREPP considers such energy planning issues as resource, sustainability, implementation, and evaluation in a holistic way. The IREPP highlights potential for increasing regional energy supply (i.e., renewables) and decreasing energy demand (i.e., efficiency and conservation) to close the demand-supply gap. The IREPP enhances sustainability by contributing the potential co-benefits of energy policy and planning to environment, economies, and social equity (such as improve air quality, job creation, and equitable access to energy). The IREPP places the emphasis on successful policy implementation by not just fiscal and technical feasibility but also assessing political and cultural feasibility. Thus, the IREPP is a process not an end product, addressing the crucial role of monitoring and evaluation of the plan for its continuing success. Other specific differences are listed in the following:

- Focus of the planning shifts from supply of energy to provision of energy services based on the least-cost options from both supply- and demand-side resources;

- Development of local energy resources such as wind, solar, biomass, ocean energy, etc. rather than outside energy resources to meet local energy needs efficiently;
- Energy services are provided as a form of energy efficiency improvements throughout energy production to consumption;
- Consumer-sited small-scale distributed generation including diverse sustainable energy options that are most available and affordable in the region, such as CHP, wind, PV, biomass, ocean energy, etc.;
- Energy agenda is expanded to include social equity, environmental sustainability and economic development;
- Successful implementation is an important consideration. The planning is based on the principles of transparency and accountability of the government as well as local participation and collaborative partnership with the community and nation.
- Monitoring and evaluation are included as a final and important procedure. The effectiveness of regional energy planning implementation need to be examined as the fuel for future planning direction.

RENEWABLE ENERGY ROADMAP OF JEJU ISLAND

Jeju, the southernmost island of South Korea, covers an area of 1,848 km^2 approximately 41 km long and 73 km wide. At the end of 2012, Jeju's population stood at 592.5 thousand. Jeju's gross regional domestic product (GRDP) was US$ 11,767 million and its per capita GRDP was US$ 21,800 in 2012. The main industrial structure is heavily relied on the service industry including tourism, accounting for 67.2 percent. The agriculture, forestry and fisheries industries account for 17.4 percent, the construction industry accounts for 9.2 percent, and the mining and manufacturing industries, only 4.2 percent. In 2012, Jeju's primary energy supply is 1,425 thousand tons of oil equivalent (TOE) and the total final energy consumption is 1,095 thousand TOE (MOTIE & KEEI, 2013). Petroleum was the dominant source of energy at 65.9 percent, natural gas 1.2 percent, and electricity 30.4 percent. Renewable energy provided 2.6 percent of energy as of 2012 (MOTIE & KEEI, 2013).

The provincial government of Jeju Island has developed the Roadmap to promote renewable energy applications and develop energy industries in order to build a sustainable and carbon free energy system. For this purpose, Jeju's Roadmap has set a target of 50 percent of energy from renewable sources by 2050, with a long-term goal of becoming completely carbon-free. Renewable energy will account for 10 percent in 2013, 20 percent in 2020, 30 percent in 2030, and 50 percent in 2050. As shown in Table 2, by 2050, wind energy will account for 30 percent of total renewable generation, solar will account for 7.5 percent, concentrated solar thermal plants will account for 2.5 percent, geothermal 15 percent, bioenergy 10 percent, and fuel cells 35 percent.

In order to achieve these goals, Jeju's Roadmap outlines a number of specific promotional strategies for renewable energy development and applications. The Roadmap includes the overall institutional level of planning and the specific planning for each individual renewable technology.

Overall institutional plan:

- Build "Renewable Energy Promotion Center" and "Solar Theme Park".
- Establish leading energy companies specialized in renewable energy.
- Install renewable energy facilities in the public sector.
- Construct a Renovation City based on renewable energy.
- Implement a 1 million Green Home project including fuel cells for homes.

Table 2. New and renewable energy supply targets by energy source (Unit: 1,000 TOE)

		2007	2013	2020	2030	2050
Total		17.7	194.6	444.0	761.7	1,469.5
Wind		16.0(90.4%) 34 MW	136.2(70%) 289 MW	266.4(60%) 565.8 MW	380.8(50%) 808.8 MW	440.8(30%) 936.2 MW
Solar Power		0.34(1.9%) 1.36 MW	17.4(8.9%) 71.1 MW	56.6(12.7%) 231.2 MW	60.9(8.0%) 248.7 MW	110.1(7.5%) 449.7 MW
Solar Thermal		0.046(0.2%) 848m^2	2.1(0.1%) 38,889m^2	10.0(2.3%) 185,185m^2	15.2(2.0%) 281,482m^2	36.8(2.5%) 681,482m^2
Geothermal		0	7.7(4.0%) 4.5 MW	44.4(10%) 26.2 MW	114.3(15%) 67.4 MW	220.5(15%) 130.1 MW
Bio	Total	1.3(7.3%)	30.2(15.5%)	44.4(10%)	76.1(10%)	146.9(10%)
	Biofuel	0	27.2 32,000kℓ	39.4 46,000kℓ	66.1 77,000kℓ	136.9 161,000kℓ
	Biogas	1.3 1,232 Nm^3	3 2,840 Nm^3	5 4,739 Nm^3	10 9,479 Nm^3	10 9,479 Nm^3
Fuel Cells		0	1.0(0.5%) 0.88 MW	22.2 (5%) 19.6 MW	114.3(15%) 101.1 MW	514.4(35%) 455 MW

- Develop Jeju as a hub for renewable energy research, development, and deployment (RD&D).
- Establish a comprehensive business center.
- Introduce renewable portfolio standards (RPS).
- Implement a GHG reduction project.

Technology specific plan:

- Develop private and public sector investment projects for wind power.
- Select sites for geothermal, solar thermal, and ocean thermal development.
- Increase PV installations including Green Home project.
- Supply biofuel for the transportation sector, including replacement of diesel by 25 percent from biodiesel.
- Utilize potential bioenergy sources including biogas from livestock manure.
- Commercialize alternative fuels including hydrogen with fuel cells.

EVALUATION OF OVERALL JEJU'S RENEWABLE ROADMAP

The government of Jeju Island developed this Roadmap for the mid- and long-term energy planning in order to diversify energy sources and achieve a sustainable future. The Roadmap is evaluated based on the concepts identified in the IREPP framework.

Integrated Resource Planning

The Roadmap has identified the energy demand and supply up to the target year 2050. Supply-side resource planning with regard to renewable energy resources has only been emphasized because of its objective to develop renewable energy development and applications. It is noteworthy, however, that the proposed rates of renewable development are proportional to each decade as shown in Table 3: 20 percent renewable energy share in 2020; 30 percent in 2030; and 50 percent in 2050. These seem to be normatively-driven targets rather than the ones based on rigorous resource analyses.

Table 3. Overview of renewable energy supply targets in Jeju (Unit: 1,000 TOE)

	2007	2013	2020	2030	2050
Primary energy demand	1,708	1,946	2,220	2,539	2,939
Renewable energy	17.7	194.6	444.0	761.7	1,469.5
Renewable share (%)	1%	10%	20%	30%	50%

The paralleled consideration of demand-side resource planning is necessary. In most cases, demand-side resources through efficiency improvements are much cheaper than the supply-side resource options. The average costs of demand-side options lie between 2.1 and 3.2 cents/kWh compared to around 5 cents/kWh in conventional power generation options (Sovacool et al., 2009). In the current short-term approach, most renewable options are expensive compared to conventional supply-side options. However, if we consider including social and environmental costs in our lifecycle evaluation, most renewable options are better positioned than conventional options (Sovacool et al., 2009).

Soft Energy Path

As shown in Table 3, the contribution of renewable energy to Jeju's energy needs is only 1 percent in 2007, but is planned to increase to 50 percent in 2050. Achieving a 50 percent renewable energy contribution will require aggressive and smartly-crafted policy intervention. This is an ambitious plan, but is on par with the renewable energy development plans of some European countries[3] and the US state of Hawaii. Hawaii is a particularly relevant case because it is a state composed of islands which has similar physical conditions and renewable energy resource endowments. Hawaii intends to supply 40 percent of its energy needs from renewable energy sources by 2030 (Busche et al., 2010).[4]

The Roadmap intends to fully utilize Jeju's renewable resources in wind, geothermal, PV, solar thermal, bio-diesel, bio-ethanol, and animal wastes, but it has not identified the potentials for each individual renewable resource. It is not customary to estimate each renewable contribution without knowing its total potential. Matching of a specific energy end-use application (i.e. golf course or resort) with a specific renewable technology (i.e. wind, geothermal, or PV) is well conceived.

Supply-side and demand-side efficiency improvements are critically important in soft energy path. There is potential to enhance efficiency improvements in fossil-fuel power generation, transmission and distribution. Significant potential still exists in end-use efficiency improvements. The Roadmap includes a 15 percent reduction in electricity demand through the development of power line communications (PLC) over internet protocol-ubiquitous sensor networks (IP-USN) or wireless internet (WiFi). Demand-side management could also include utility-initiated efficiency and conservation programs, peak shaving strategy, and demand response programs, but these options are not explicitly explored.[5]

A study published by Center for Energy and Environmental Policy at University of Delaware shows almost 28 percent efficiency improvement potential in South Korea (Byrne, Wang, Kim, Lee, & Kim, 2004). Hawaii's Clean Energy Initiatives aims to raise energy efficiency by 30 percent in 2030 (DBEDT, 2014). Many researchers strongly suggest that without efficiency improvements, renewable applications are less attractive options (Mancisidor et al., 2009; Yalcintas & Kaya, 2009).

Distributed Generation

The Roadmap includes distributed generation options to meet the energy demand of a specific area in the Jeju Island, including combined heat and power (CHP), district heating and/or cooling (DHC), and heat pumps, in addition to the onsite generation from renewable sources. An integrated system of fuel cells and hydrogen is also introduced in the Jeju Roadmap. CHP, DHC, and heat pump significantly improve efficiency because the need for energy inputs is reduced, and in some cases lost heat can be utilized (Morgan et al., 2005). Hydrogen with fuel cells has many applications for the building and transportation sectors, but the Roadmap's target for hydrogen's contribution to Jeju's renewable economy (35 percent in 2050) is too ambitious, viewed in terms of the current maturity of the technology and the limitations of input fuels whether it is natural gas or renewable sources (McDowall & Eames, 2006).

There are several examples of district heating and cooling using water as heat source/sink and heat pumps. In Stockholm, Sweden, for example, both Baltic heat water and aquifers are used. Also, a project of district cooling using deep ocean water is ongoing in Hawaii, and in Geneva, Switzerland lake water is used for both heating and cooling with heat pumps. The ground itself can be used, taking benefit from the fact that ground temperature below 10 meters depth is roughly equal to the average annual air temperature. Transferring this application at the district level is even more helpful since the efficiency of the heat pump increases with its size (Butera, 2008). Small-scale combustion turbine (CT) is another application of distributed generation. According to the Energy Information Administration (EIA), small-scale CT generated 1,964 MW in the US in 2007 and the capacity continues growing (EIA, 2009).

At the urban level, the so-called Merton Rule is applied in the UK. The Borough of Merton was the first council in the UK to pass legislation according to which developers of new commercial buildings above 1,000 square meters are obliged to satisfy 10 percent of their energy needs from on-site renewable energy systems. A number of UK councils have followed suit (SolarCentury, 2009). Barcelona's Solar Thermal Energy Capture went into force in August 2000 for regulating the incorporation of solar thermal energy systems for the production of sanitary hot water in the city's buildings. The Solar Ordinance is applied to newly built, or rehabilitated and fully reformed buildings, and those seeking to implement a change of use, with a forecasted volume of sanitary hot water demand equal to an average annual energy consumption of over 292 net megajoules (MJ). Barcelona was the first city in Europe to pass such legislation (BEA, 2009).

Enhancement of Sustainability

A successful regional energy plan could enhance sustainability in terms of energy security, environmental protection, economic development, and social equity (E^4). Usually economic concern is a dominant issue, followed by environmental concern, but equity issue should be also considered fairly. Of course, balancing of E^4 is a challenge but must be one goal within any regional energy planning. The Jeju Roadmap enhances E^4, but some of the factors are not clearly indicated. By promoting renewable industries Jeju will create additional jobs, enhancing economic development. By replacing half of fossil fuel consumption with renewable energy sources, Jeju will reduce GHG emissions and air pollution, enhancing environmental protection. Furthermore, the reduction of fossil fuel consumption will reduce or eliminate energy imports from off-island sources, thus enhancing energy security as well as promoting economic development. Significant positive economic impacts to be derived from a 50 percent renewable application are not elaborated fully in the Roadmap.

Generally, the Jeju's Roadmap enhances equity in terms of inter-generational, geographical, and inter-species by introducing 50 percent of energy needs from renewable energy sources. The Roadmap could also fully consider intra-generational equity (social equity) and procedural equity (open and fair participation in decision-making). In regard to Jeju's goal of increasing farmer's income by selling energy crops, Jeju must be wary of the impact on equity that such actions may have due to influence on other commodities, especially food.[6] Thus, as Jeju seeks to enhance sustainability there should be attention paid to potential unintended externalities, especially those that affect social equity, brought on by the policies.

Feasibility of Implementation

The feasibility of any energy plans need to be evaluated through the lenses of technical, fiscal, political, administrative, institutional, and cultural feasibility before policy implementation occurs (Cooper & Vargas, 2004). The Roadmap considers most of the dimensions, but some of the components could be addressed in further detail. Even though the target year of Jeju's Roadmap is 2050, its implementation and fiscal plans end before 2013.[7] However, without a sound long-term fiscal plan supported by strong policies, the plan could be subject to future uncertainties. Table 4 shows a total budget of US$718.9 million (833 billion Won) by year and source. More than 75 percent of funding will come from private investment.

Public participation not only improves procedural equity, but also is a key component to enhancing political feasibility. The implementation of Jeju's Roadmap will require the will and cooperation of a broad spectrum of local residents and other interest groups, especially because it deals with the characteristics of decentralized renewable energy options. As a part of this effort, Jeju's Roadmap needs to include a well-conceived public education and outreach program for its successful implementation. Building of a renewable energy promotional center and construction of the theme park planned in the Roadmap will be helpful in this regard.

Although Jeju's regional energy plan is based on the national "Energy Basic Law" enacted in 2006, the detailed legislative regulations and measures conforming with the national law are not fully illustrated in the energy planning in the Roadmap. Jeju's action plan should not violate any legalities with the central government's superior law, national energy plan, relevant other central ministries' regulations, or civil rights. Therefore, because the implementation of energy plans will be especially related to economic development, social equity, and environmental protection, energy plans should be founded on a solid, and well-designed legal foundation.

Even if a sustainable energy policy meets the tests of fiscal, technical, and political feasibility, it is also essential to evaluate whether the proposed action plan is administratively feasible. The issues of administrative feasibility are related to the organizations and managerial capability to implement sustainable energy policies. Jeju's Roadmap also plans to establish a comprehensive business center that will develop and diffuse renewable energy under the Jeju's energy policy. To ensure successful implementation, the center should be professionally staffed and managed by personnel that can carry out the various mandates, along with properly maintaining essential administrative processes.

Table 4. Jeju's annual investment plan (Unit: million US$)

	Total	2008	2009	2010	2011	2012	2013
Total	718.9	87.7	179.1	49.2	154.3	128.6	120.0
Central Government	45.8	4.9	24.0	4.1	4.1	4.3	4.3
Jeju Province	38.1	6.7	19.8	2.8	2.8	3.0	3.0
Private Investment	541.3	26.3	124.1	35.4	138.8	112.6	104.0
Research Institutes	93.7	49.7	11.2	6.9	8.6	8.6	8.6

Monitoring and Evaluation

Monitoring and evaluation is the step to close the loop of IREPP. It is important to monitor and evaluate the implementation of an energy plan. It can be used as a basis for further target set up and policy development. However, monitoring and evaluation were not mentioned in Jeju's Roadmap. In order to successfully implement the Roadmap, the explicit consideration of comprehensive procedures and methods of monitoring and evaluation should be recognized and planned.

In Jeju's Roadmap, each renewable energy technology has an explicit quantitative target. These targets are clearly divided into short-term (10 percent in 2013), medium-term (20 percent in 2020 and 30 percent in 2030), and long-term (50 percent in 2050) goals. Therefore, monitoring and evaluation can be conducted in different time-frame. The evaluation results of short-term targets can act as the reference for medium- and long-term policy adjustment. In the case of the balance between energy-economic-environment-equity, sustainability indicators could be constructed to evaluate E^4 performance.

EVALUATION OF SPECIFIC SUSTAINABLE ENERGY TECHNOLOGIES

In the previous section, we evaluated the Jeju's Roadmap based on major concepts of IREPP. Sustainable energy technologies use local renewable energy resources and are a key strategy in Jeju's Roadmap. This section intends to evaluate each of sustainable energy technologies identified in the Roadmap to achieve a 50 percent renewable target in 2050. We first evaluate whether the specific target set up for each individual sustainable technology is achievable and then introduce policy options to address any barriers to the target based on experiences with renewable energy polices in the EU and in the US. Before evaluating each option, we review South Korean government's renewable policy as well as its official report on the economic prospects of sustainable energy technologies, because both influence Jeju's renewable energy plan and implementation.

RPS and Technological Prospects

The Korean government is scheduled to adopt Renewable Portfolio Standard (RPS) to increase the distribution of renewable energy from 2012. As Table 5 shows, RPS will require large-scale energy plants to supply new and renewable energy, and the required supply share will be increased annually up to 10 per cent by 2022 (TFCCPMO, 2008). It is expected that RPS will contribute to expanding the foundation for an emerging renewable energy market in South Korea and promote a favorable environment for the implement of renewable energy deployment plan of the Roadmap.

According to the Korean government, renewable energy technologies that harness renewable sources such as wind, solar, geothermal, and bioenergy are expected to become economically comparative with fossil fuel energy as shown in Table 6 (MKE, 2008). Each technology becomes economically competitive with fossil fuels by the end of 2020. These technological development combined with a RPS will be a factor in facilitating renewable energy deployment in Jeju Island.

Table 5. Mandatory renewable energy supply share

	2012	2013	2014	2015	2016	2017	2018	2019	2020	2021	2022
Supply Share (%)	2.0	2.5	3.0	3.5	4.0	5.0	6.0	7.0	8.0	9.0	10.0

Table 6. Prospects for economic feasibility of each renewable technology compared to fossil fuel energy in South Korea

		'10	'11	'12	'13	'14	'15	'16	'17	'18	'19	'20
PV	1st generation solar cell						●					
	2nd generation solar cell						●					●
	3rd generation solar cell											
Solar Thermal	10kW system: Dish			●						●		
	25kW system: Dish				●							
	200kW system: Tower											
Wind	Small, mid-sized turbine	●										
	2MW wind turbine	●						●				
	5MW wind turbine											
Bioenergy	Biogas plant with anaerobic digestion				●							
	Biomass to liquid (BTL)									●		
	Biooil									●		
Geothermal	Geothermal pump			●						●		
	Geothermal plant									●		
	EGS excavation technology											
Ocean	500kW wave power system		●									
	500kW tidal power system		●							●		
	1MW ocean thermal energy conversion											

Source: MKE. (2008). *New & Renewable Energy White Paper 2008.*

Wind Power

The Roadmap has outlined the following goal to foster increased wind power development through public and private investment projects:

- Develop 936 MW of wind capacity by 2050, accounting for a 30 percent contribution to total renewable generation (15 percent to total primary energy supply).

The global wind power market has steadily been expanding with the annual growth rate of around 10 percent. China, US, and European led global wind market in 2012, with annual installation of 13.2 GW, 13.1 GW, and 12.4 GW, respectively. The global total wind power installation was 318.1 GW at the end of 2013 (GWEC, 2014). The US National Renewable Energy Laboratory (NREL) developed a scenario that wind power supplies 20 percent of US electricity in 2030 (NREL, 2008). In case of Hawaii, electricity generation from wind power will be 23 percent in 2030 (Busche et al., 2010) (see Table 7). Development of offshore wind power is also growing. European Wind Energy Association (EWEA) statistics show that on average in 2008, over 1 MW of off-shore wind power was installed in Europe per day, reaching a total of 1,471 MW worldwide by the end of the year. Today, more than 90 percent of offshore wind capacity is installed in European (i.e., in the North Sea, Baltic Sea), and in the Atlantic Ocean. The US and some Asian countries, including China, Japan, South Korea, Taiwan, are taking off the offshore wind development as well (GWEC, 2014). Global cumulative offshore installed capacity in 2013 is around 7 GW (GWEC, 2014).

Table 7. Comparison of wind energy target in Jeju and other regions

	Jeju in 2050	South Korea in 2030	US in 2030	Hawaii in 2030	EU in 2020	Germany in 2020
Wind	15% of primary energy	1.4% of primary energy	20% of electricity	23% of electricity	11.7-14.1% of electricity	15% of electricity

Global trends in wind power development and Jeju's excellent wind potential suggest that Jeju could have more than 15 percent of the total primary energy supply from wind power. According to the Ministry of Knowledge and Economy, the technical wind power potential in Jeju is around 1,706 MW/year (MKE, 2008). The Roadmap also shows that 60 percent of South Korea's national wind potential including its offshore power is concentrated at Jeju Island. The potential should be exploited to the fullest extent. Wind power is one of the least expensive forms of renewable energy, and Jeju should pursue this technology as its flagship renewable option. As of 2014, Jeju's wind power capacity is 113 MW. The Jeju Province has formed in 2014 the new task-force team to modify the wind power roadmap, and it expects to have a new wind plan within 6 months.

Concerns over climate change and energy security issues put higher importance on wind power worldwide (Bolinger & Wiser, 2009). A number of countries have outlined specific goals for the development of wind power and have developed ambitious policies. Regarding policies, there are two main tools for the development of wind power: feed-in tariffs (FIT) and green certificates where producers have to generate a certain share of their electricity from renewable energy sources while they have the option of selling or buying certificates to meet the legal target imposed on them. Other possibilities, such as RPS, public tendering, investment incentives such as production tax credit (PTC) or tax exemptions are also applied by a few countries or are combined with one of the two main tools (EWEA, 2009b).[8] Hawaii uses tax incentives to promote wind energy, such as wind energy production tax credit and income tax credits for wind energy systems installation (DBEDT, 2010). In 2013, wind energy became the second most utilized renewable energy in Hawaii, providing 31 percent of total renewable generation (DBEDT, 2014).

Solar Power

The Roadmap has outlined the following basic goals to foster increased solar power development in the province by using roof tops and others including usage of surplus properties from wind farms:

- In 2050, production of 110.1 thousand TOE (449.7 MW) of energy by solar PV power, accounting for 7.5 percent of total renewable energy supply (3.75 percent to total primary energy supply).
- In 2050 production of 36.8 thousand TOE (681,482 square meters) of energy by solar thermal power, accounting for 2.5 percent of renewable energy supply (1.25 percent to total primary energy supply).

On a global scale, installation of solar power systems (especially PV) has been growing at a rapid pace in recent years. The global cumulated installed PV capacity reached 138.9 GW in 2013. China (11.8 GW) was the top PV market in 2013, followed by Europe with 11 GW of PV

Table 8. Comparison of solar energy target in Jeju and other regions

	Jeju in 2050	South Korea in 2030	US in 2035	Hawaii in 2030	EU in 2020	Germany in 2020
PV	3.8% of primary energy	0.5% of primary energy	-	3.5% of electricity	4.4-5.3% of electricity	2.7% of electricity
Solar Thermal	1.3% of primary energy	0.6% of primary energy	0.5% of electricity		1.1-1.3% of electricity	0.2% of electricity

installation (EPIA, 2014). Many nations have set aggressive goals. Spain, for example, seeks the installation of 10 GW of solar power by 2020; the US seeks 70-100 GW by 2030; and Italy seeks 8 GW by 2020. The PV development is under the path especially in EU. As shown in Table 8, the PV electricity target of EU in 2020 is 4.4 to 5.3 percent. Currently, PV already covers 3 percent of the electricity demand and 6 percent of the peak electricity demand in Europe (EPIA, 2014).

Even though the countries like Spain, the US, and Italy may have greater financial capacity of solar investments than Jeju, it could develop solar resources to a greater degree than what is sought in the Roadmap. The technical PV potential in Jeju is estimated to be 14,680 thousand TOE, and solar thermal potential is around 23,074 thousand TOE (MKE, 2008). As shown in Table 8, Hawaii seeks a 3.5 percent contribution of solar power to electricity generation in 2030 (Busche et al., 2010). As of 2014, Jeju's PV and solar thermal capacities are 15.8 MW and 3,448 m^2, respectively.

Many countries have adopted various policies to promote the development of solar power. A typical and one of the most important tools to boost the harnessing of solar power is the tariff paid for electricity from installations of solar power systems, known as a FIT. FIT is commonly used in Europe and are virtually absent in the US.[9] RPS, PTC, and tax incentives are more common inducements in the US. In the United States, 37 states and DC have enacted requirement of PV in RPS (DSIRE, 2014). The addition of around 30 percent state tax to the 10 percent federal tax credit is collected for purchase and installation of residential (electric and water heating) solar energy systems. Soft loan is another type of policy for accelerating solar power deployment. The "GreenSun Hawaii Loan Program" provides loan for all property owners to install solar thermal hot water system and solar electric (PV) system in Hawaii (DBEDT, 2014). In addition to FIT or RPS, a combination of tax incentives and financial incentives used by other countries and the US could apply to the Jeju Roadmap.

Geothermal Power

The Jeju's Roadmap has outlined a basic goal to foster increased geothermal energy development, especially through building geothermal facilities located close to the industrial sites:

- Plan to produce 220.5 thousand TOE (130.1 MW) of energy by geothermal power, accounting for 15 percent of total renewable supply in 2050 (7.5 percent of total primary energy supply).

Geological conditions and economic costs are two crucial limitations for geothermal energy development. Jeju island has abundant geothermal potential and has annual investment plan from year 2008 to 2011 (US$42 million), playing a significant role in Jeju's renewable energy future. However, as of 2014, there has been no additional investment to develop geothermal energy since 2011.

As of August 2013, global geothermal capacity is 11.8 GW and several new geothermal projects are under construction in Indonesia (425 MW),

Table 9. Comparison of geothermal energy target in Jeju and other regions

	Jeju in 2050	South Korea in 2030	US in 2035	Hawaii in 2030	EU in 2020	Germany in 2020	Iceland in 2030
Geothermal	7.5% of primary energy	0.4% of primary energy	0.5% of electricity	5% of electricity	0.8-0.9% of electricity	0.3% of electricity	17% of electricity

Kenya (296 MW), Iceland (260 MW), the US (178 MW), and New Zealand (166 MW) (GEA, 2013). In case of Hawaii, geothermal generated 2 percent of electricity in 2013 (DBEDT, 2014) and will contribute to 5 percent of electricity generation in 2030 (Busche et al., 2010). In Iceland, renewable energy supplies power for all its 300,000 residents, and geothermal energy provides 17 percent of electricity and 87 percent of heating needs (GEA, 2009), and renewable energy is expected to meet a significant portion of energy needs in the near future.

A number of countries have designed specific mechanisms for geothermal power development. In the United States, at the federal level, the Federal Production Tax Credit (PTC) plays a vital role in financing renewable energy projects, including geothermal power projects. At roughly 2 cent per kWh, the credit allows a geothermal energy project to take the benefit during the first ten years of operation. The Geothermal Technologies Program (GTP) develops innovative geothermal energy technologies to find, access, and use the geothermal resources in the United States. In Germany, FIT for geothermal facilities and bonuses for heat cogeneration has been introduced to facilitate the development of geothermal energy. FIT for geothermal energy was also introduced in Italy and in France. Geothermal plants can benefit from a tariff of 20 eurocents per kWh in Italy and 10-12 eurocents per kWh in France. In addition to the feed-in tariffs, a Green Certification has been adopted in Italy to promote geothermal energy. The Indonesian government provided financial support for geothermal development. For example, the government established a US$ 128 million fund for exploring geothermal drilling (WWF, 2012). The government also established the ceiling price for geothermal power as 9.7 cents/kWh (MEMR & NCCC-Indonesia, n.d.). The above policies could be considered as an example for Jeju in its geothermal policy design.

Biogas and Biofuels

Jeju has outlined basic goals to foster increased biogas and biofuels development in the province to increase farmers' income and promote alternative vehicle technology development with support from R&D activities. A summary of the goals, as discussed in Jeju's roadmap, is provided here:

- In 2050, production of a total of 10 thousand TOE (9,479 net cubic meters) of energy by biogas.
- In 2050, production of a total of 136.9 thousand TOE (161,000 kiloliters) of energy by biofuels.
- In total, biomass accounts for 10 percent of renewable energy supply (a 5 percent contribution to total primary energy supply).

Jeju has set the goal of meeting 10 percent of the renewable energy supply (5 percent of total primary energy supply) with biofuels and biogas by 2050 and includes the construction of production facilities for biodiesel, bioethanol, and biogas. The production of bioethanol uses discarded citrus, and biogas is produced from livestock manure and other organic wastes. Similarly, Hawaii has

Table 10. Comparison of bioenergy target in Jeju and other regions

	Jeju in 2050	South Korea in 2030	US in 2035	Hawaii in 2030	EU in 2020	Netherlands in 2030
Bioenergy	5% of primary energy	3.45% of primary energy	5.5% of electricity	19% of electricity	6.1-7.4% of electricity	30% of primary energy

an ambitious plan for bio-energy, targeting a 19 percent contribution to electricity generation in 2030 which includes biomass, municipal solid wastes (MSW), and biofuels (Busche et al., 2010).

A number of countries have outlined specific goals for the development of biomass energy. The Netherlands is one of the most progressive nations in the area of biomass and biofuels. The bio-energy target of the Netherlands is to supply 30 percent of their primary energy with biomass by 2030 (Junginger & Faaij, 2005).[10] It is difficult to say whether Jeju's biomass goals are feasible, but if the goals set by the Netherlands and Hawaii are an indicator of potential for bio-energy development (see Table 10), Jeju could most likely develop even more bio-energy resources than they have currently outlined.

Hawaii plans to replace fossil fuels with biofuels. As a tropical island, Hawaii has great biomass potential, including forest industry residues, agricultural residues, animal waste, and ocean biomass (especially algae). Hawaii government offers a corporate income tax credit for ethanol production and also implements the Bioenergy Master Plan to explore the potential for ethanol production (DBEDT, 2010). The Dutch government uses a policy instrument called "transition management" to expand their biomass and biofuel industries and also adopts FIT to subsidize biomass electricity generation (Junginger & Faaij, 2005).

Hydrogen and Fuel Cells

The Jeju Roadmap has outlined an ambitious goal to build a hydrogen economy, or a clean "enertopia"[11] through concerted efforts to develop hydrogen and fuel cell technology:

- In 2050, production of 514.4 thousand TOE (455 MW) of energy by fuel cells, accounting for 35 percent of renewable energy supply (17.5 percent of total primary energy supply).

A number of countries have outlined specific goals for the development of hydrogen technology. Iceland is perhaps the most successful country in the area of hydrogen for transportation. Iceland captured world attention when in 1999 it declared a national goal to convert its economy totally to hydrogen energy by 2030 (Solomon & Banerjee, 2006). Iceland already makes 2,000 tons of hydrogen a year and hopes to provide sufficient renewable hydrogen for its entire transport sector. Current policy in Iceland focuses on developing hydroelectric and geothermal energy resources with the goal of converting the entire transport system to hydrogen fuel cells in the long-run. Short-term policy goals include promoting methanol fuel cell cars as a stepping-stone to hydrogen technology.

In Japan, commitment to the Kyoto Protocol target of 6 percent GHG reductions by 2010 has spurred the country into action on hydrogen development. The Hydrogen and Fuel Cell Demonstration Project (JHFC) aims to develop the way for widespread use of fuel cell vehicles and hydrogen stations (METI, 2009). Japan has also aggressively pursued stationary fuel cells for residential use. Focusing on 1 kW PEM fuel cells for residential applications, Japan has pursued aggressive R&D and market penetration programs since 2005 with the goals of enticing home-builders to install fuel cell systems (COSPP, 2005).

Jeju's commitment of US$11.6 million (13,300 million Won) to hydrogen development is noteworthy, but may prove to be too little to meet its 35 percent target. Given the lower funding level and technological immaturity, a more concerted effort would be needed by Jeju in the areas of RD&D and innovative financing. It is also important that Jeju not neglect the complementary nature of hydrogen vehicles and the refueling infrastructure, and that it seeks policy measures which balance research and funding initiatives between the vehicle and infrastructure sectors. Neglecting either vehicular or infrastructure development can lead to a severely underdeveloped and fragile hydrogen industry (Meyer & Winebrake, 2009).

Fuel cell vehicles have not been deployed yet, but Jeju is now one of two local governments in Korea that introduced "EV Taxi Pilot Project" in cooperation with Renault-Samsung motors, one of the major automotive manufacturers in Korea (MOE, 2014). Through this project, Jeju will analyze the potential of "EV Taxi" business endeavors, and taxi passengers can have a chance to experience EVs as future potential customers.

Ocean Energy

Jeju's Roadmap has not included any ocean energy development, and as of 2014, the Jeju government does not have any concrete development plan yet. Considering that Jeju has affluence ocean energy resources as an island, Jeju needs to seriously consider launching an ocean energy project.[12] Ocean energy technologies include wave energy, tidal energy, temperature and salinity gradient/osmotic energy, and marine biomass. Despite the diversity of the technology, the current development status of the harnessing of ocean renewable energy resources is at an early stage compared to the development of other renewable energy sources.

British Columbia, Canada, has some implications of value for Jeju's Roadmap. The government of British Columbia has set up a target for tackling climate change and decreasing the dependence on carbon in the province. According to the new energy plan, the government of British Columbia will achieve the status of energy self-sufficient by 2016. This Energy Plan emphasized ocean energy as a "future supply option with great potential" and included mechanisms such as a CDN Innovation Clean Energy Fund valued at US$ 23.3 million (IEA-OES, 2007). As shown in Table 11, Hawaii also has a plan to develop ocean energy, contributing to 1 percent of electricity generation in 2030 (Busche et al., 2010).

Many governments have raised government funding for ocean energy R&D. Some governments adopt market support mechanisms to cover the current cost gap. These policy tools can be categorized into three groups as follows (IEA-OES, 2007): research and innovation policies; market deployment policies; and market-based energy policies. For example, the Natural Energy Laboratory of Hawaii Authority (NELHA), a state agency of Hawaii, is dedicated to promote ocean energy research, education and environmentally sound commercial dissemination activities (HCEI, 2009). The Hawaii National Marine Renewable Center (HINMREC) is one of three US federally-funded centers for marine energy research. The HINMREC cooperated with the US Department of Defense to establish a wave energy test center which will be constructed in 2014 (DBEDT, 2014). Considering that ocean energy technologies are at an early stage of development compared to other renewable and conventional generation technologies (IEA-OES, 2007), the Jeju government should invest in RD&D specific to ocean energy

Table 11. Comparison of ocean energy target in Jeju and other regions

	Jeju in 2050	South Korea in 2030	Hawaii in 2030	EU in 2020
Ocean Energy	-	0.5% of primary energy	1% of electricity	0.1% of electricity

technology to overcome technical barriers through international technical collaboration as well as the close cooperation with the central government.

CONCLUSION

This chapter introduces an integrated regional energy planning framework (IREPP) and then evaluates the mid- and long-term renewable energy roadmap of the Jeju Island on the basis of the IREPP. Individual renewable technology options identified in the Roadmap are also evaluated for their technical feasibility, along with policy suggestions, based on experiences with renewable developments from the EU countries, Japan, and the US states. The IREPP framework is comprehensive in terms of the concept and procedure. Conceptually, it contains major sustainable energy concepts such as integrated resource planning, soft energy, distributed generation, and sustainability. Procedurally, it starts with the target setting through implementation feasibility and ends with monitoring and evaluation.

The IREPP is most applicable in the context of the regional level, because of the homogeneity of its renewable resources, socio-economic characteristics, energy demand and supply, etc. But the adaptation of the IREPP at the national level is also possible because many concepts of the IREPP can also be applicable to national energy planning.

Jeju's overall target of a 50 percent contribution of renewable energy resources to the total primary energy supply is ambitious, but not beyond the range based on our literature review and other experiences including Hawaii's 40 percent target in 2030. Overall, Jeju's Roadmap is comprehensive in the scope and well-conceived in its plan. But after careful consideration of the Jeju Roadmap, as well as review of policy actions taken by OECD nations and the US states, we offer the following recommendations.

First, technical and economic potentials for each renewable resource need to be identified. The Jeju Roadmap provides information on 2050 targets for new and renewable energy development, but their targets are set even without knowledge of each individual resource potential.

Second, the long-term financial and investment plans need to be developed. The Roadmap provides financial and investment targets until only 2013. In order for Jeju to meet long-term renewable development goals of 2050, it must have a reliable financial plan outlined for at least the next couple of decades. Sound financial plan is crucial, especially because most renewable energy technologies are expensive.

Third, the maximum development of wind power potential is necessary in Jeju Island. The Jeju Roadmap has set the goal of meeting 15 percent of the 2050 primary energy supply with wind power (equivalent to only a 5 percent contribution to electricity generation). Given that 60 percent of South Korea's total wind energy potential exists in and around Jeju, the opportunity for on-shore and off-shore wind developments in Jeju is likely immense.

Fourth, it is better to reduce the role of hydrogen fuel cells. A 35 percent contribution of hydrogen to Jeju's renewable energy supply in 2050 (or 17.5 percent to the total primary energy supply) is excessive based on the current immature status of technological development and high input fuel costs for hydrogen generation.

Last but not least, Jeju's government should consider ocean energy as an additional renewable source. Ocean energy is an emerging technology, and a number of countries have begun to pursue it actively. Given that Jeju is an island, Jeju should follow suit, creating a more robust and well-rounded portfolio of renewable energy sources.

ACKNOWLEDGMENT

This work was supported by the Test & Evaluation Research Center for Clean Energy Development (CCED), Jeju National University and the Jeju Special Self-Governing Province.

REFERENCES

Barcelona Energy Agency (BEA). (2009). *Barcelona Solar Thermal Ordinance (OST)*. Retrieved December 11, 2009, from http://www.barcelonaenergia.cat/eng/operations/ost.htm

Beccali, M., Cellura, M., & Mistretta, M. (2003). Decision-making in energy planning. Application of the Electre method at regional level for the diffusion of renewable energy technology. *Renewable Energy*, *28*(13), 2063–2087. doi:10.1016/S0960-1481(03)00102-2

Bolinger, M., & Wiser, R. (2009). Wind power price trends in the United States: Struggling to remain competitive in the face of strong growth. *Energy Policy*, *37*(3), 1061–1071. doi:10.1016/j.enpol.2008.10.053

Brandoni, C., & Polonara, F. (2012). The role of municipal energy planning in the regional energy-planning process. *Energy*, *48*(1), 323–338. doi:10.1016/j.energy.2012.06.061

Brown, L. (2009). *Plan B 4.0: Mobilizing to Save Civilization*. Washington, DC: Earth Policy Institute.

Busche, S., Doris, E., Braccio, R., Lippert, D., Finch, P., O'Toole, D., & Fetter, J. (2010). *Clean Energy Policy Analysis: Impact Analysis of Potential Clean Energy Policy Options for the Hawaii Clean Energy Initiative*. Technical Report. NREL/TP-742-47891.

Butera, F. (2008). Towards the Renewable Built Environment. In P. Droege (Ed.), *Urban Energy Transition: From Fossil Fuels to Renewable Power* (pp. 329–364). Oxford, UK: Elsevier. doi:10.1016/B978-0-08-045341-5.00014-1

Byrne, J., Wang, Y.-D., Kim, J.-D., Lee, H., & Kim, J.-W. (2004). *Energy Revolution: 21 Century Energy and Environmental Strategy*. Maeil Business Newpaper.

Cai, Y., Huang, G., Lin, Q., Nie, X., & Tan, Q. (2009). An optimization-model-based interactive decision support system for regional energy management systems planning under uncertainty. *Expert Systems with Applications*, *36*(2, Part 2), 3470–3482. doi:10.1016/j.eswa.2008.02.036

Carley, S. (2009). Distributed generation: An empirical analysis of primary motivators. *Energy Policy*, *37*(5), 1648–1659. doi:10.1016/j.enpol.2009.01.003

Cogeneration and On-site Power Production (COSPP). (2005). *Stationary fuel cells*. Retrieved January 7, 2010, from http://www.cospp.com/display_article/272983/122/ARTCL/none/TECHS/1/Stationary-fuel-cells/

Cooper, P., & Vargas, C. (2004). *Implementing Sustainable Development: From Global Policy to Local Action*. Lanham, MD: Rowman & Littlefield Publishers, Inc.

Cormio, C., Dicorato, M., Minoia, A., & Trovato, M. (2003). A regional energy planning methodology including renewable energy sources and environmental constraints. *Renewable & Sustainable Energy Reviews*, *7*(2), 99–130. doi:10.1016/S1364-0321(03)00004-2

D'Sa, A. (2005). Integrated resource planning (IRP) and power sector reform in developing countries. *Energy Policy*, *33*(10), 1271–1285. doi:10.1016/j.enpol.2003.12.003

Database of State Incentives for Renewables and Efficiency (DSIRE). (2014) *DSIRE RPS Data Spreadsheet*. Retrieved June 11, 2014, from http://www.dsireusa.org/rpsdata/index.cfm

Department of Business, Economic Development and Tourism, State of Hawaii (DBEDT). (2010). *Hawaii - DOE Clean Energy Initiative*. Retrieved May 10, 2010, from http://hawaii.gov/dbedt/info/energy/hcei/

Department of Business, Economic Development and Tourism, State of Hawaii (DBEDT). (2014). *Hawaii Energy Facts and Figures*. Retrieved June 12, 2014, from http://energy.hawaii.gov/wp-content/uploads/2011/08/HI-Energy-Facts-Figures_May2014.pdf

Deshmukh, S. S., & Deshmukh, M. K. (2009). A new approach to micro-level energy planning--A case of northern parts of Rajasthan, India. *Renewable & Sustainable Energy Reviews*, *13*(3), 634–642. doi:10.1016/j.rser.2007.11.015

Domac, J., Segon, V., Przulj, I., & Rajic, K. (2011). Regional energy planning methodology, drivers and implementation--Karlovac County case study. *Biomass and Bioenergy*, *35*(11), 4504–4510. doi:10.1016/j.biombioe.2011.07.018

Dorian, J. P., Franssen, H. T., & Simbeck, D. R. (2006). Global challenges in energy. *Energy Policy*, *34*(15), 1984–1991. doi:10.1016/j.enpol.2005.03.010

Energy Information Administration (EIA). (2009). *Capacity of Distributed Generators by Technology Type*. Retrieved January 7, 2010, from http://www.eia.doe.gov/cneaf/electricity/epa/epat2p7b.html

European Photovoltaic Industry Association (EPIA). (2014) *2013: Record-year for solar photovoltaics, accelerating market globalisation*. Retrieved June 11, 2014, from http://www.epia.org/fileadmin/user_upload/Press_Releases/Global_Market_Outlook_2014_Press_Release.pdf

European Wind Energy Association (EWEA). (2009a). *Global Statistics-US, China & Spain Lead World Wind Power Market in 2007*. Retrieved 7 January, 2010, from http://www.ewea.org/index.php?id=1487

European Wind Energy Association (EWEA). (2009b). *Legal framework for wind energy*. Retrieved November 24, 2009, from http://www.ewea.org/index.php?id=197

Feinstein, C. D., Orans, R., & Chapel, S. W. (1997). The Distributed Utility: A New Electric Utility Planning and Pricing Paradigm. *Annual Review of Energy and the Environment*, *22*(1), 155–185. doi:10.1146/annurev.energy.22.1.155

Geothermal Energy Association (GEA). (2009). *Geothermal 101: Basics of Geothermal Energy Production and Use*. Washington, D.C.: Geothermal Energy Association.

Geothermal Energy Association (GEA). (2013). *2013 Geothermal Power: International Market Overview*. Retrieved June 11, 2014, from http://geo-energy.org/events/2013%20International%20Report%20Final.pdf

Global Wind Enery Council (GWEC). (2014). *Global Wind Report Annual Market Update 2013*. Retrieved June 11, 2014, from http://www.gwec.net/wp-content/uploads/2014/04/GWEC-Global-Wind-Report_9-April-2014.pdf

Hawaii Clean Energy Initiative (HCEI). (2009). *How can Oahu reach 70% clean energy?: Hawaii Powered*. Hawaii Clean Energy Initiative, and Booz Allen Hamilton.

Hopwood, B., Mellor, M., & O'Brien, G. (2005). Sustainable Development: Mapping Different Approaches. *Sustainable Development*, *13*(1), 38–52. doi:10.1002/sd.244

Iannucci, J. (1994). *The Distributed Utility: Is This the Future?* Paper presented at the 5th National Conference on Integrated Resource Planning. Washington, D.C.

International Energy Agency (IEA). (2008). *Energy Technology Perspectives: Scenarios & Strategies to 2050*. Paris, France: International Energy Agency.

International Energy Agency Implementing Agreement on Ocean Energy Systems (IEA-OES). (2007). Annual Report 2007. Retrieved June 13, 2014 from http://www.oreg.ca/docs/IEA_docs/IEA_Annual_Report_2007.pdf

Jeju Special Self-Governing Province. (2009). *Jeju's Mid- and Long-Term Roadmap of New and Renewable Energy Planning*.

Junginger, M., & Faaij, A. (2005). *IEA Bioenergy task 40-Country report for the Netherlands*. Paris, France: International Energy Agency.

Kanudia, A., & Loulou, R. (1999). Advanced bottom-up modelling for national and regional energy planning in response to climate change. *International Journal of Environment and Pollution, 12*(2/3), 191–216. doi:10.1504/IJEP.1999.002292

Kelley, I. (2008). *Energy in America*. University of Vermont Press, University Press of New England.

Lam, H. L., Varbanov, P. S., & Klemes, J. J. (2011). Regional renewable energy and resource planning. *Applied Energy, 88*(2), 545–550. doi:10.1016/j.apenergy.2010.05.019

Li, X. (2005). Diversification and localization of energy systems for sustainable development and energy security. *Energy Policy, 33*(17), 2237–2243. doi:10.1016/j.enpol.2004.05.002

Lovins, A. (1977). *Soft Energy Paths: Toward a Durable Peace*. San Francisco: Friends of the Earth International.

Mancisidor, I. M. A., Uraga, P. D. B., Mancisidor, I. M. A., & López, P. R. A. (2009). European Union's renewable energy sources and energy efficiency policy review: The Spanish perspective. *Renewable & Sustainable Energy Reviews, 13*(1), 100–114. doi:10.1016/j.rser.2007.07.003

McDowall, W., & Eames, M. (2006). Forecasts, scenarios, visions, backcasts and roadmaps to the hydrogen economy: A review of the hydrogen futures literature. *Energy Policy, 34*(11), 1236–1250. doi:10.1016/j.enpol.2005.12.006

Meyer, P. E., & Winebrake, J. J. (2009). Modeling technology diffusion of complementary goods: The case of hydrogen vehicles and refueling infrastructure. *Technovation, 29*(2), 77–91. doi:10.1016/j.technovation.2008.05.004

Ministry of Economy, Trade and Industry (METI). (2009). *Japan Hydrogen and Fuel Cell Demonstration Project (JHFC) project was launched for the Future of the Earth*. Retrieved October 22, 2009, from http://www.jhfc.jp/e/jhfc/index.html

Ministry of Energy and Mineral Resources-Indonesia & National Council on Climate Change-Indonesia (MEMR & NCCC-Indonesia). (n.d.). *Geothermal in Indonesia Low Carbon Development: Profile, Status and Role of Market Mechanism*. Retrieved June 12, 2014, from http://www.thepmr.org/system/files/documents/Geothermal+in+Indonesia+Low+Carbon+Development+R2.pdf

Ministry of Environment (MOE). (2014). Seminar on promotional policies for electric vehicles. March 20-21, Jeju International Convention Center.

Ministry of Knowledge and Economy (MKE). (2008). *New & Renewable Energy White Paper 2008*. Gwacheon: Korean Ministry of Knowledge and Economy.

Ministry of Trade, Industry and Energy (MOTIE) & Korea Energy Economics Institute (KEEI). (2013) 2013 Year Book of Regional Energy Statistics. Korea: Korea Energy Economics Institute.

Mitchell, D. (2008). *A Note on Rising Food Prices*. Washington, DC: The World Bank. doi:10.1596/1813-9450-4682

Montis, A. D. (2014). Strategic environmental assessment of energy planning tools. A study of Italian regions and provinces. *Environmental Impact Assessment Review*, *46*, 32–42. doi:10.1016/j.eiar.2014.01.006

Morgan, G., Apt, J., & Lave, L. (2005). The US, Electric Power Sector and Climate Change Mitigation. The Pew Center on Global Climate Change, Arlington, VA (June 2005).

National Renewable Energy Laboratory (NREL). (2008). *20% Wind Energy by 2030*. US Department of Energy.

Nijkamp, P., & Volwahsen, A. (1990). New directions in integrated regional energy planning. *Energy Policy*, *18*(8), 764–773. doi:10.1016/0301-4215(90)90029-4

Ramachandra, T. (2009). RIEP: Regional integrated energy plan. *Renewable & Sustainable Energy Reviews*, *13*(2), 285–317. doi:10.1016/j.rser.2007.10.004

San Diego Association of Governments. (2009). *Regional Energy Strategy*. Retrieved November 29, 2010, from http://www.sandag.org/uploads/publicationid/publicationid_1476_10631.pdf

Sauter, R., & Bauknecht, D. (2009). Distributed Generation: Transforming the Electricity Network. In I. Scrase & G. MacKerron (Eds.), *Energy for The Future: A New Agenda* (pp. 147–164). New York, NY: Palgrave MacMillan.

Sheer, H. (2004). *The Solar Economy: Renewable Energy for a Sustainable Global Future*. London, UK: Earthscan.

Soerensen, H. C., & Weinstein, A. (2006). *Ocean Energy: Position paper for IPCC*. Retrieved June 13, 2014, from http://www.eu-oea.com/euoea/files/ccLibraryFiles/Filename/000000000400/Ocean_Energy_IPCC_final.pdf

SolarCentury. (2009). *The Merton Rule*. Retrieved December 11, 2009, from http://www.solarcentury.co.uk/Knowledge-Base/The-Merton-Rule

Solomon, B., & Banerjee, A. (2006). A global survey of hydrogen energy research, development and policy. *Energy Policy*, *34*(7), 781–792. doi:10.1016/j.enpol.2004.08.007

Sovacool, B. K., & Watts, C. (2009). Going Completely Renewable: Is it Possible (Let Alone Desirable)? *The Electricity Journal*, *22*(4), 95–111. doi:10.1016/j.tej.2009.03.011

Task Force on Climate Change Prime Minister's Office. (2008). *Comprehensive Plan on Combating Climate Change*. Seoul: Task Force on Climate Change Prime Minister's Office.

Task Force on Climate Change Prime Minister's Office (TFCCPMO). (2008). *Comprehensive Plan on Combating Climate Change*. Seoul: Task Force on Climate Change Prime Minister's Office.

Terrados, J., Almonacid, G., & Hontoria, L. (2007). Regional energy planning through SWOT analysis and strategic planning tools: Impact on renewables development. *Renewable & Sustainable Energy Reviews*, *11*(6), 1275–1287. doi:10.1016/j.rser.2005.08.003

The California Energy Commission. (2007). *2007 Integrated Energy Policy Report*. Retrieved May 10, 2010, from http://www.energy.ca.gov/2007_energypolicy/

Tsioliaridou, E., Bakos, G., & Stadler, M. (2006). A new energy planning methodology for the penetration of renewable energy technologies in electricity sector: Application for the island of Crete. *Energy Policy*, *34*(18), 3757–3764. doi:10.1016/j.enpol.2005.08.021

Tsoutsos, T., Drandaki, M., Frantzeskaki, N., Iosifidis, E., & Kiosses, I. (2009). Sustainable energy planning by using multi-criteria analysis application in the island of Crete. *Energy Policy*, *37*(5), 1587–1600. doi:10.1016/j.enpol.2008.12.011

United Nations Development Programme (UNDP). (2000). *World energy assessment: energy and the challenge of sustainability*. Retrieved January 20, 2010, from http://www.energyandenvironment.undp.org/undp/indexAction.cfm?module=Library&action=GetFile&DocumentAttachmentID=1020

Vine, E. (2008). Strategies and policies for improving energy efficiency programs: Closing the loop between evaluation and implementation. *Energy Policy*, *36*(10), 3872–3881. doi:10.1016/j.enpol.2008.06.038

Wang, Y., Byrne, J., Boo, K., Yun, S., & Soh, Y. (1996). *A spatially-integrated energy planning model for Korea's sustainable development*. Seoul: Korean Ministry of Commerce, Industry and Energy.

World Wild Fund for Nature (WWF). (2012). *Igniting the Ring of Fire, A Vision for Developing Indonesia's Geothermal Power*. Retrieved June 13, 2014, from http://awsassets.wwf.or.id/downloads/geothermal_report.pdf

Yalcintas, M., & Kaya, A. (2009). Conservation vs. renewable energy: Cases studies from Hawaii. *Energy Policy*, *37*(8), 3268–3273. doi:10.1016/j.enpol.2009.04.029

Yilmaz, P., Hakan Hocaoglu, M., & Konukman, A. E. S. (2008). A pre-feasibility case study on integrated resource planning including renewables. *Energy Policy*, *36*(3), 1223–1232. doi:10.1016/j.enpol.2007.12.007

Yue, C., & Wang, S. (2006). GIS-based evaluation of multifarious local renewable energy sources: A case study of the Chigu area of southwestern Taiwan. *Energy Policy*, *34*(6), 730–742. doi:10.1016/j.enpol.2004.07.003

ADDITIONAL READING

Barnes, D., & Toman, M. (2006). Energy, Equity, and Economic Development. In R. Lopez & M. A. Toman (Eds.), *Economic Development and Environmental Sustainability: New Policy Options* (pp. 245–272). New York: Oxford University Press.

Brown, L. R. (2009). *Stabilizing Climate: An Energy Efficiency Revolution. Plan B 4.0: Mobilizing to Save Civilization* (pp. 79–108). Washington, DC: Earth Policy Institute.

Byrne, J., Hughes, K., Rickerson, W., & Kurdgelashvili, L. (2007). American policy conflict in the greenhouse: Divergent trends in federal, regional, state, and local green energy and climate change policy. *Energy Policy*, *35*(9), 4555–4573. doi:10.1016/j.enpol.2007.02.028

Byrne, J., Martinez, C., & Ruggero, C. (2009). Relocating Energy in the Social Commons: Ideas for a Sustainable Energy Utility. *Bulletin of Science, Technology & Society*, *29*(2), 81–94. doi:10.1177/0270467609332315

Byrne, J., Wang, Y. D., Lee, H., & Kim, J. D. (1998). An Equity- and Sustainability-Based Policy Response to Global Climate Change. *Energy Policy*, *26*(4), 335–343. doi:10.1016/S0301-4215(97)00174-2

Cassedy, E. S. Jr. (2000). *Solar Energy Sources. Prospects for Sustainable Energy: A Critical Assessment* (pp. 19–47). Cambridge: Cambridge University Press.

Christensen, J., Denton, F., Grag, A., Kamel, S., Pacudan, R., & Usher, E. (2006). *Changing Climates: The Role of Renewable Energy in a Carbon-Constrained World*. The United Nations Environment Programms (UNEP). Retrieved August 1, 2010 http://130.226.56.153/rispubl/art/2006_120_report.pdf

Edwards, P. P., Kuznetsov, V. L., & David, W. I. F. (2007). Hydrogen Energy. *Philosophical Transactions of the Royal Society*, *365*(1853), 1043–1056. doi:10.1098/rsta.2006.1965 PMID:17272235

Fox-Penner, P. (2010). *The New Paradigm. Smart Power: Climate Change, the Smart Grid, and the Future of Electric Utilities*. Washington: Island Press.

Geller, H. (2003). *Energy Revolution: Policies for a Sustainable Future*. Washington, DC: Island Press.

Godfrey, B. (2004). *Renewable Energy: Power for a Sustainable Future*. Oxford: Oxford University Press.

Goldemberg, J. (2007). Energy Choices Toward a Sustainable Future. *Environment: Science and Policy for Sustainable Development*, *49*(10), 7–17. doi:10.3200/ENVT.49.10.7-17

Hunt, S. C., Sawin, J. L., & Stair, P. (2006). Cultivating Renewable Alternatives to Oil. In *State of the World 2006* (pp. 61–77). The Worldwatch Institute.

Johansson, T. B. (2005). The Imperatives of Energy for Sustainable Development. In A. J. Bradbrook, R. Lyster, R. L. Ottinger, & W. Xi (Eds.), *The Law of Energy for Sustainable Development* (pp. 46–52). New York: Cambridge University Press. doi:10.1017/CBO9780511511387.005

Makhijani, A. (2007). *Carbon-free and nuclear-free: A roadmap for US energy policy*. Muskegon, MI: RDR Books.

Pasqualetti, M. J. (2004). Wind power: Obstacles and opportunities. *Environment*, *46*(7), 22–38. doi:10.1080/00139150409604395

Romm, J. J. (2004). Fuel Cell Basics and Hydrogen Production. In The Hype about Hydrogen: Fact and Fiction in the Race to Save the Climate. (pp. 23-34, 67-88). Washington, DC: Island Press.

Scheer, H. (2004). Exploiting Solar Energy. In *The Solar Economy: Renewable Energy for a Sustainable Global Future* (pp. 251–284). London: Earthscan.

Simon, C. A. (2007). *Why Alternative Energy and Fuels? Alternative Energy: Political, Economics, and Social Feasibility* (pp. 1–20). New York: Rowman & Littlefield Publishers, Inc.

Simon, C. A. (2007). Studying Public Policy and Alternative Energy/Fuels. In *Alternative Energy: Political, Economics, and Social Feasibility* (pp. 21–38). New York: Rowman & Littlefield Publishers, Inc.

Spees, K., & Lave, L. B. (2007). Demand Response and Electricity Market Efficiency. *The Electricity Journal*, *20*(3), 69–85. doi:10.1016/j.tej.2007.01.006

Strange, T., & Bayley, A. (2008). What is Sustainable Development? Sustainable Development: Linking Economy, Society, Environment. (pp. 20-35). Paris, France: Organization for Economic Co-operation and Development (OECD).

Tester, J. W., Drake, E. M., Driscoll, M. J., Golay, M. W., & Peters, W. A. (2005). *Sustainable Energy — the Engine of Sustainable Development. Sustainable Energy: Choosing Among Options* (pp. 1–50). Cambridge, MA: The MIT Press.

Tester, J. W., Drake, E. M., Driscoll, M. J., Golay, M. W., & Peters, W. A. (2005). *Solar Energy. Sustainable Energy: Choosing Among Options* (pp. 543–571). Cambridge, MA: The MIT Press.

Tietenberg, T. (2009). Reflections – Energy Efficiency Policy: Pipe Dream or Pipeline to the Future? *Review of Environmental Economics and Policy*, *3*(2), 304–320. doi:10.1093/reep/rep004

Tonn, B., Healy, K. C., Gibson, A., Ashish, A., Cody, P., Beres, D., & Ritter, A. J. et al. (2009). Power from Perspective: Potential future United States energy portfolios. *Energy Policy*, *37*(4), 1432–1443. doi:10.1016/j.enpol.2008.12.019

Vine, E. (2008). Breaking down the silos: The integration of energy efficiency, renewable energy, demand response and climate change. *Energy Efficiency*, *1*(1), 49–63. doi:10.1007/s12053-008-9004-z

Wang, Y. D. (2001). Development of an Alternative Energy System: The Challenge and Its Future. In Hyoung-Kook & Kim (Eds.), Energy and Korean Life (pp. 1-13).

Wang, Y. D. (2006). *Energy Efficiency Potentials in European Union and South Korea: Toward less Energy, a Better Economy and a Sustainable Environment. Energy Focus*. Korea: Korea Energy Economics Institute.

Wimberly, J. (2006). *Three Sings of a Ripening Market for Alternative and Distributed Energy* (pp. 1–11). Energy Pulse.

World Commission on Environment and Development. (1987). *Energy: Choices for Environment and Development. Our Common Future* (pp. 168–205). New York: Oxford University Press.

World Energy Council. (2008). *Conclusions and Recommendations. Energy Efficiency Policies around the World: Review and Evaluation* (pp. 93–109). London, UK: World Energy Council.

KEY TERMS AND DEFINITIONS

Carbon Free Island: Carbon Free Island is a goal of the island towards a carbon-free future by realizing a sustainable energy system.

Distributed Generation: Distributed generation uses decentralized small, modular power technologies to generate energy (electricity and heat) at or close to the point of demand.

E^4: E^4 means energy, environment, economy, and equity. They are the four buttresses of sustainable development. For achieving sustainability, regional energy planning should consider the balance of E^4.

Implementation Feasibility: Implementation feasibility is the framework of facilitating and accelerating the successful implementation of a regional energy plan by evaluating whether the plan at hand is fiscally, technologically, legally, politically, administratively, culturally, and ethically feasible.

Integrated Resource Planning: Integrated resource planning pursues an optimal combination of demand- and supply-side options to meet energy service need at the least economic, social and environmental cost.

Jeju Roadmap: Jeju Roadmap is a mid- and long-term renewable energy policy and planning which is developed to establish a regional sustainable energy supply system and to promote new and renewable energy industries throughout Jeju.

Renewable Energy: Renewable energy means environmentally benign and generally carbon-free or carbon neutral energy which is utilized from natural sources such as sun, wind, geothermal heat, ocean, etc.

Soft Energy Path: Soft energy path is the transition from a centralized mega-power oriented hard energy path towards a decentralized soft technology path of renewable energy system and improved energy efficiency.

ENDNOTES

1 Iceland has developed one of the most ambitious long-term regional energy plan in the world, with goals of converting their entire energy economy to a hydrogen economy by 2030 (Solomon & Banerjee, 2006).

2 The state of Hawaii cooperates with the US Department of Energy to form the Hawaii Clean Energy Initiative to transform the energy sectors in Hawaii to a 70 percent renewable energy economy.

3 Denmark intends to continue their aggressive development of renewable energy. By 2025 renewable energy will account for more than 28 percent of total energy consumption.

4 Hawaii's Clean Energy Initiatives has a goal to supply 70 percent of electricity generation from clean energy sources in 2030 such as 30 percent from efficiency improvements and 40 percent from renewable resources.

5 The Hawaiian Island of Oahu is an example. Oahu's government plans to achieve 18.9 percent energy savings by improving efficiency in Oahu's buildings before 2030 (HCEI, 2009). About 7,000 homes and 250 commercial buildings on Oahu are retrofitted each year. Moreover, all new buildings will be qualified as "net zero energy" buildings after 2015. Jeju can take Oahu's target and path as a reference to increase the energy saving target through energy efficiency.

6 In the US, where bioenergy has been aggressively pursued in the last half-decade, the increased usage of crops for the production of energy has led to a considerable increase in the cost of food not only within the US, but in neighboring countries as well. The price of corn, in particular, has had devastating effects on poor families in Mexico and other developing countries who can no longer afford basic sustenance (Mitchell, 2008).

7 The development before 2013 is intended as the first phase (2009-2013), focusing on only 6 most promising projects. This is a sound approach as a first phase, but it still needs additional phase plans up to 2050 supported by manageable investment plans.

8 Due to these efforts, global wind energy capacity grew by 28.8 percent in 2008, even higher than the average over the past decade, to reach total global installations of more than 120.8 GW at the end of 2008. Over 27 GW of new wind power generation capacity came online in 2008, 36 percent more than in 2007 (EWEA, 2009a).

9 Recently, feed-in tariffs have been contemplated in the US, and some states are investigating their implementation—including Indiana, Minnesota, Michigan, and California.

10 Another successful country in the area of bio-energy is Canada. The 2003 federal budget announced $30 million for the development of bio-based technologies. The federal government also has several market-pull programs in place to support utilization of bio-energy technologies.

11 The term enertopia is used mostly in the Korean context to refer to an "energy utopia". In the US and EU context, the term "hydrogen economy" has been more commonly used.

12 Theoretically, the global potential of ocean energy is estimated as follows (Soerensen & Weinstein, 2006): 8,000 - 80,000 TWh/year for wave energy; 800 TWh/year for tidal current energy; 2,000 TWh/year for osmotic energy; and 10,000 TWh/year for ocean thermal energy.

Section 3
The Business of Sustainable Development

Chapter 10
A Holistic Model for Linking Sustainability, Sustainable Development, and Strategic Innovation in the Context of Globalization

David L. Rainey
Renssealer at Hartford, Rensselaer Polytechnic Institute, USA

ABSTRACT

This chapter presents the foundations of a holistic model for connecting the key elements necessary for corporations to adopt sustainability and sustainable development in the context of the global economy and strategic innovation. The complexities of doing business on a global scale have increased dramatically over the last two decades. While sustainability involves many perspectives, strategies, actions, and management constructs, the chapter focuses on how global corporations employ strategic innovations in response to driving forces in the global economy and how they can improve their level of management sophistication in a turbulent business environment. The holistic model focuses on strategic innovations that provide more positve aspects and fewer negative ones since innovations have the potential to create dramatic new solutions with exceptional value and to eliminate or reduce negative effects and impacts. Strategic innovations include radical technological innovations, business model innovations, product developments, and organizational developments that are game changers.

INTRODUCTION

This chapter presents an comprehensive, i.e. holistic, model for adopting sustainability, and sustainable development (SD) in business organizations based on the perspective of the globalization, the management constructs associated with strategic innovations, and the imperative to lead change. Globalization has become one of the most important management considerations as the driving forces of change are shifting from national and regional settings to a more global landscape.

DOI: 10.4018/978-1-4666-8433-1.ch010

Globalization implies that distance and time constraints have become less relevant due to innovative technologies and sophisticated methods that have dramatically improved the efficiency, effectiveness, and costs of production, transportation and telecommunications. Globalization provides new opportunities for global corporations, societies, and individuals around the world to connect with each other and participate in economic, social, political, and technological activities that would have been prohibitively expensive, unprofitable, impractical, and/or very risky in the past. Widespread use of the Internet, fifth generation digital technologies, advanced microprocessors, global positioning systems, biotechnology, and nanotechnologies are just a few of the revolutionary technologies affecting almost every industry and corporation. Technological changes are making the business environment more complex and dynamic than it was just a decade ago. Keeping ahead of the dramatic changes is one of the most significant challenges facing global business leaders today.

The prevalent view pertaining globalization is that the world is shrinking as innovative technologies, advanced manufacturing, and supply chain integration provided new avenues for cost reductions and making products and services more valuable and attractive. Business leaders can obtain parts, components, and even end products from far of places. The focus is on economic exchanges and financial outcomes. However, the business world has also increased considerably as billions of additional people are now engaged in global business transactions. There are billions of additional customers and many more potential ones. There are also many new and emerging competitors in the developing countries that can leverage their comparative advantages like low-cost labor and growing populations.

Strategic innovations refer to technological innovations and high-level product developments that have the potential to change the global competitive landscape by introducing major advancements in the solutions and systems; ones with more positive and fewer negatives. Innovations must provide outstanding results in the short term and ensure sustainable success for the long term. Creating, developing and deploying strategic innovations offer bright prospects for an enhanced global business environment with the greater possibilities for more people worldwide to enjoy the outcomes provided by global corporations. However, the global business environment is full of risks and vulnerabilities.

Leading change is based on the theory that the best approach for meeting the needs, wants, and mandates of the market spaces and business environment is to leap ahead of the prevailing and expected requirements and to exceed the desires and expectations of the people and entities involved (Rainey, 2014). Leading change examines how to stretch beyond the limits of the present possibilities and transform the current strategic positions into more powerful and beneficial realities. Leading change is a critical imperative of strategic leadership. Imperatives are critical mindsets mandates, expectations, and/or constructs that are essential for achieving and sustaining successful; they are the "must do" challenges that provide the foundations for success. While leading change depends on the conditions and trends in the business environment and vary considerably based on context and circumstances, strategic leaders have to envision bold and innovative ways to lead change and manage their companies and enterprises. They have to go beyond the mainstream thinking and explore new theoretical constructs for achieving success. Using popular management constructs may allow strategic leaders to quickly obtain a consensus within the company because everyone understands the methods and techniques. However, many of the old-line strategies and mainstream approaches are no longer adequate in a more turbulent and fast-paced business world. Such approaches may lead to inferior results because they are not in concert with the demands and expectations of the business environment.

Given that globalization is still far from a true reality, sustainability and SD are essential constructs for leading change and sustaining success. Moreover, sustainable success has to be based on having a holistic perspective of the social, economic, ethical, political, technological, and environmental underpinnings that provide opportunities and mitigate challenges and risk. Global businesses have to concentrate on satisfying all of the expectations, requirements and mandates of the external dimensions. The external dimensions include markets, customers, stakeholders, supply networks, related industries, infrastructure and competition. The broadest perspectives involve the well-being of society and the general social, economic, and environmental good.

Sustainability involves meeting the needs of today without disrupting or harming the social and economic well-being of humankind and the natural environment. Sustainability implies that all human and business activities are carried out at rates equal to or less than the Earth's natural carrying capacity to renew the resources used and to naturally mitigate the waste streams generated (Rainey & Araujo, 2014). It inherently means creating a future that enhances the positives and minimizes negatives. It involves the development and deployment of new scientific, technical, and leadership methods and the systematic creation of new-to-the-world technologies, solutions, and systems that are superior to the prevailing ones.

From a business perspective, sustainability is about creating, enhancing, developing, deploying, and sustaining business value. Building trust, improving brand recognition, and enhancing corporate reputation are critical elements. Sustainability involves the quest toward creating more ideal solutions, developing integrated systems, and building solid relationships. It necessitates having the best possible solutions for enhancing the well-being of people, preserving the natural environment, and ensuring social and economic stability. Sustainability involves a transformation to a higher level of sophistication in how business leaders formulate and implement strategies, policies, and actions plans to achieve such outcomes.

SD is a critical element of sustainability that focuses on developing and deploying strategic innovations that exceed the expectations customers, stakeholders, and people. SD focuses on improving the social, economic, ethical, and technological aspects and protecting the natural environment as well as achieving superior strategic, market, and financial results by corporations. SD involves obtaining the best outcomes possible for the present generation and ensuring that future generations can realize their aspirations for social and economic well-being in harmony with the natural world. SD originated in 1987 by the World Commission Environment and Development for the General Assembly of the United Nations that prepared the Brundtland Report, entitled *Our Common Future*. In the report, SD refers to the notion "that it [humankind] meets the needs of the present without compromising the ability of future generations to meet their own needs." (The World Commission of Environment and Development, 1987, p. 8)

Specifying precisely what strategic leaders must do to achieve sustainability, SD and strategic innovation is an arduous task. Given that an all-compassing model linking globalization, sustainability, SD, and strategic innovation may not be possible in the short term, developing and gaining acceptance of a general model that fits global corporations, multinational enterprises (MNEs), and small and medium sized enterprises (SMEs) may take years to realize. Moreover, as more companies from the developing countries play a significant role in the global business environment, the possible variations increase exponentially. Such a model or models have to accommodate the social, cultural, ethical, economic, political, technological, and environmental realities that exist across the world. Most importantly, a holistic model pertaining to sustainability and SD has to recognize and incorporate the differences in mindsets, resources, capabilities, and sophistication between the MNEs and the SMEs, between the companies from the developed countries and those from the developing ones, and the between the old-line corporations and the emerging businesses.

The objective of the chapter is to articulate the basic elements of a holistic model for improving the adoption of sustainability in the context of globalization. The model provides broad guidelines for what is necessary and beneficial from a global perspective. Such guidelines are intended to provide insights and assistance in developing and implementing the requisite methods and mechanisms. The adoption of the model would be voluntary and offer benefits to corporations, governments, business leaders, government officials, and practitioners alike, since they would have a sense of the underlying specifications so that they can more easily determine what needs to be done going forward. Sustainability and SD involve a continuum of strategies, solutions, innovations, and actions that unfold over decades.

The chapter does not provide all of the answers. The holistic model discussed herein cannot include all of the requisite details to fully articulate how to develop and implement the model nor is it possible to discuss all of the aspects in a single article. Moreover, trying to prescribe a single pathway to sustainability and SD would require a model that is so intricate and detailed that it would take many books to spell out all of the variations. The intent herein is to offer insights about what can be done to become more sustainable in a world full of opportunities and challenges.

GLOBAL ASPECTS AND INSIGHTS

The business world has changed dramatically over the last two decades as the scope of the social, economic, political, ethical, technological, and environmental forces impacting businesses has broadened to include not just those pertaining to the developed countries, but those affecting developing countries as well. While there has been much discussion about a shrinking world, it can also be said that the business opportunities have expanded multifold with the inclusion of all people living in the developed and developing countries. This profound change has been supported by numerous strategic innovations including the lowering of the costs of fabricated parts and assembled products, and the related supply chain realities have made the potential integration of the global economy possible, especially from an economic perspective. A quarter of a century ago, most businesses generally served approximately one billion people, those living in the developed countries. Today, the business world is not only global, but it is richer in scope, scale, and diversity. Worldwide, there are approximately 7.1 billion people who play a role in the global economy. While some are active participants in the served markets, many are bystanders who might be considered latent customers waiting for the right solutions to meet their needs and circumstances; ones that are affordable and based on the needs, wants and expectations of the people involved.

Globalization is a complex term that has many meanings from a limited view focusing mainly on the economic exchanges of the global economy to the multi-dimensional perspective involving an interrelated, interactive, innovative and more sustainable business world. Regardless, globalization includes interconnections and interrelationships between business enterprises, national governments, and non-governmental organizations (NGOs) among many others. Most importantly, it is based on the context of all of the social, political, ethical, economic, technological, and environmental forces.

The limited view of globalization is often stated in terms of the merging of national economies into a regional economy and ultimately into a global economy. The European Union (EU) is an example of a regional economy that includes 27 nation states that have linked their economic interests and activities to enjoy economies of scale and more open associations. The intent is to enhance free trade based on a transnational, borderless economic system. On a global basis, the limited view pertains to economic exchanges and activities as the primary forces that drive international trade, business investments, and the global economic system. In the limited perspective, global corporations vie to satisfy customer demand and meet stakeholder expectations based strategic positions and global resources and capabilities. The key factors for achieving success are perceived to be cost-effectiveness, high quality products, and tailored products and services; ones that generate advantages and financial rewards for the entities involved. Economics is perceived to be the overarching factor and markets and customers are viewed as the main driving forces. The underpinnings of the limited view are based on free enterprise and market capitalism combined with compliance with environmental, health and safety (EH&S) laws and regulations and due considerations about powerful stakeholders. Nicholas Ashford and Ralph Hall argue "That major technological, organizational, institutional, and social changes, not just incremental advances, are necessary to achieve sustainability: these changes must be more systematic, multidimensional, and disruptive" (2011).

A multi-dimensional perspective of globalization involves proactive strategies, cutting-edge solutions, sophisticated management systems, and innovative methods that are developed and deployed to enhance the positive aspects and eliminate the negative aspects. It is based on advanced ICT, more effective and efficient means and mechanisms for producing and transporting goods from remote locations to the markets across the world, sophisticated management constructs for decision making and actions, and strategic innovations, especially those pertaining to new-to-the- world technologies and products. The multi-dimensional perspective includes a longer time horizon. While most business leaders, economists, and government officials view five to ten years out to be the long term, the long term in the context of the multi-dimensional perspective is measured in decades; it includes considerations about future generations of people as well. It is also based on the realization that enduring economic success depends on satisfying all entities and individuals engaged in or impacted by business transactions, not just customers. It has to include social factors and forces. It implies that participants and non-participants have to be included in the analysis of what is necessary and appropriate and in the creation of sustainable outcomes. It involves creating, developing, producing and providing innovative solutions and systems for people based on their context and realities, not just the objectives, strategies, and actions of the global corporations. Most importantly, solutions must be dual-sided or multi-sided based disclosing, improving, and deploying all of the positives and the negatives in an open and honesty manner. Such considerations are an integral part of true globalization that has yet to be fully developed.

Openness and honesty play critical roles as internal contributors (management and employees) and external participants (customers and stakeholders) want factual data and information rather than perceptions or assumptions. They want their involvement to be based on trust. It is critical for corporations to avoid being charged with "green wash." Green wash is viewed as painting positive stories about situations or expected outcomes that are not grounded in reality or ones that are single-sided, i.e. they focus on the positive aspects. For instance, corporations are often accused of green wash when they overstate their vision and intentions or actions through misleading corporate communications that suggest something that is not the case. Stakeholders are usually wary of corporations that do not have good track records of achieving positive results. Ravi Fernando discusses the concerns about globalization and sustainability; he argues (2012):

Strategic decisions that impacts sustainability can never be made by leaders in "transit" nor by leaders who focus on delivering the next quarter's results at any cost. Until and unless the global reward system changes from an obsession with the short term and re-calibrates its focus from short term results for survival in both business and politics to Strategic Corporate Sustainability, a tipping point for sustainability will remain a concept at best.

Globalization without sustainability, SD, and strategic innovations may be viewed as a continuation of the "business usual" mindset that has dominated strategic management thinking over the last half century. The business-as-usual mindset represents the line of strategic thinking, in which the main focus is on growing and expanding corporations without significant concerns about their social and environmental underpinnings, effects, and impacts. It presumes that such corporations and their strategic leaders comply with the existing laws and regulations and take due care of their specified EH&S responsibilities, but they are not compelled to go beyond such mandates and requirements. The business-as-usual mindset has positives from an economic perspective, but it is generally limited in terms of the social, ethical, and environmental aspects. The time horizon is relatively short, usually five years or so. Historically, such perspectives resulted in reasonable outcomes in the developed countries, especially if the social and economic forces were stable and enduring. However, difficulties and discontinuities often arise in the long term. For instance, if the effects of oil depletion are the most profound in latter stages of the life cycle of petroleum, then the next several decades may be relatively stable in terms of conventional energy sources, but chaotic thereafter. Moreover, with the addition of many new participants in the global economy and expanding global energy consumption, the business world may become less stable and secure as conflicts arise over obtaining the necessary resources. Under such conditions, there is a significant possibility that the economic and social forces may be overwhelmed by increasing demand for energy; thus, affecting the costs of all materials and goods and leading to significant competition for resources and unsustainable outcomes. Indeed, the recent economic recession may be a harbinger of more challenging times ahead, especially if strategic leaders maintain the business as usual mindset.

Today, many of the strategic leaders focus their efforts on the developed countries because people in those countries have money and can afford to buy the branded products and services. Moreover, many of the same strategic leaders pay little attention to people in the least developed countries because most of the people are poor and seemingly do not have the necessary disposable income to buy the existing products. True globalization has to incorporate the concepts of sustainability, SD and strategic innovation based on a holistic model that include all of the essential elements for achieving broad based outcomes and sustainable success for all people. Globalization based on sustainability, SD, and strategic innovation necessitates a mindset shift in business from exploiting the current situations and selling the prevailing products to customers who have the financial wherewithal to developing and deploying innovative solutions and systems that fit the needs, expectations, and circumstances of people worldwide. The requisite strategic change involves providing people with solutions and systems from their perspectives.

Daniel Esty and Andrew S. Winston (2006) in their book, *Green to Gold*, articulate that "successful, long-lasting companies regularly redefine themselves. Environmental-inspired innovations offer companies a new and exciting way to find fresh expressions for their capabilities" (p. 301). In support of sustainability, Bob Willard (2005) in his book, *The Next Sustainability Wave*, suggests that "sustainability strategies give corporations that choice of getting ahead of the curve, defining the new rules, and being rewarded by their stakeholders for behaving responsibly (p. 1). In Arthur D. Little's book, The Board's

Sustainability Book (2011), businesses have to think big in order to transition to sustainable success (p. 40):

Sustainability requires you to be aware of the whole picture in which the business sits: from one end of the supply chain to the other; the short term and the long term; the complete lifecycle of your products; and the full gamut of risks and opportunities that face your business not just financial and reputational ones, but competitive, legal and regulatory as well as societal, community and environmental ones.

The multi-dimensional perspective of globalization includes the effects and impacts on a much larger scale, including all of the driving forces of change. The management constructs are more complicated because reality and future requirements have to be examined from multiple views involving more intensive analysis of the salient forces and more in-depth understandings of the interactions and interrelationships between the forces. Moreover, such analyses require exploring the possibilities as well as the realities, i.e. what could be or should be not just what is. Thus, it is not just a simply matter of obtaining information and data and discerning what is happening; it also involves getting to the underpinnings of reality and trying to ascertain what could be done instead of just trying to understand what is being done. It involves a mindset shift from exploring "what is" to "what could be."

Sustainability, SD, and strategic innovations are about leading change to create better outcomes and more enduring business value. Proactive business leaders and organization understand that Sustainability, SD, and strategic innovations are among the most important perspectives for the future.

UNDERPINNINGS AND GLOBAL REALITIES

Prevailing Business Situation

The economic crisis of 2007 through 2011 has shed new light on the many difficulties and problems facing business leaders, politicians, government officials, and NGO leaders as they try to right the global economy and develop new mechanisms for dealing with the related challenges. All leaders are being challenged to make dramatic improvements in the ways they manage their responsibilities and achieve desired outcomes. Politicians and government officials focus on setting new policies, providing stimulus, and allocating resources. Business leaders across the spectrum of industries and markets try to develop and implement the most effective brands, products, programs, and platforms to maximize benefits and outcomes and minimize the risks and vulnerabilities.

Today, strategic leaders and senior management of all persuasions have to expand their capabilities and knowledge and adapt innovative management approaches that are in line with the realities of the world. As evidenced by the recent economic crisis with its myriad of causes, effects, impacts, and consequences, the underpinnings and key elements of the global economy are too complicated and intertwined for "old school" approaches to succeed. A major untangling of the turbulence and new understandings of the global economy are necessary for creating the requisite solutions. C. K. Prahalad (2005) in his book, *The Fortune at the Bottom of the Pyramid*, talked about how to handle the global challenges: "What is needed is a better approach to help the poor, an approach that involves partnering with them to innovate and achieve sustainable win-win scenarios where the poor are actively engaged, and at the same time, the companies providing products and service to them are profitable" (pp. 3-4). With all of the uncertainty, there are incredible opportunities for companies to succeed. The great challenge for strategic leaders is not just to "right the mistakes" of the past or cut through the turbulence, but to invent a more sustainable future by creating wonderful new solutions for people everywhere and by eliminating the problems and the underlying risks and vulnerabilities. Innovative strategic leaders have to recognize that they are responsible for assuring that the best solutions possible are devised and implemented.

Unfortunately, most of today's management models are not in synch with the new realities of true globalization and the twenty-first century business world. The world has changed significantly over the past two decades, yet many strategic leaders still follow the theories and practices that were developed during the 1980s and 1990s. While such management constructs may have been innovative methods during the later years of the twentieth century, they are based on the realities of those times. Most of the models viewed the business world in the context of the developed countries and Western business philosophies. They were underpinned by many assumptions that were relevant for the major markets like those in the US, UK, Germany, France, Japan, etc. The underlying assumptions were based on political stability, economic freedom, open exchanges, linear increases in market demand, affluent populations with significant disposable income, and well-established infrastructure. Today, many of those assumptions are questionable, especially on a global basis. The economic, social, political, and environmental conditions and trends are now less predictable and more volatile. Many factors and phenomena play out on a global scale. The global economy with its numerous interconnections and interrelationships brings significant risks and uncertainties. With all of the enhancements in management science, managing global corporations is still an extremely risky venture.

Insights about Global Realities and Possibilities

The global economy includes all of the existing, emerging, and potential markets and customers in the world. One of the most significant primary strategies in the drive to be more successful is to make products and services more affordable through design innovations and incorporating customers' needs and expectations in the solutions. Such methods have been in play for several decades in the developed countries as companies like Walmart, and Toyota have become global giants and great financial successes through innovations to make their products and services both more affordable and their systems more productive and cost-effective.

Globalization requires that businesses and governments become key participants in developing, supporting, and advancing the social, economic, ethical, technological, market, and environmental underpinnings and support the needs and expectations of the global community of nations and people. The underpinnings include assuring that the recipients of the solutions, especially customers, stakeholders, and societies of the world, are provided with right products and services that have been design and delivered from an external perspective and not just those of business leaders and/or high-level government officials, and that everyone's well-being is positively enhanced and not exploited.

Globalization requires global corporations to recognize new responsibilities if they plan to create value and enjoy success. Paul Hawken (2007) in *Blessed Unrest* discusses the challenges of globalization (p. 135).

One of the failures of the arguments opposing market globalization is the visible lack of an alternative economic model that might address the plight of the world's poor. The failure of those making the case for globalized free trade is their inability to adequately address the results of rapid economic change in human and ecological degradation, roughly in equal measure, incomparable through they may seem.

Hawken clearly points out the problems with the prevailing business situation. The present form of globalization is not inclusive. It does not provide the necessary support for the poor of the world nor does it include a scope wide enough to assure that solutions are complete. It still focuses on the economic aspects.

Strategic leaders have to view human developments and the elimination of poverty in the least developed countries as enormous opportunities to transform non-customers into customers. Moreover, strategic leaders in rapidly industrializing countries have to create positive outcomes without overwhelming the social world and the natural environment with pollution and wastes. For instance, strategic leaders in China are expanding their industrial outcomes at incredible rates, but in doing so they are creating wastes streams that may become impossible to mitigate in just a few years. Air and water pollution may be the limiting factor in China's quest to be a global economic power. Such difficulties are much easier to correct and mitigate before the industrial facilities and power plants are built. Once the plants have been designed and constructed, it is often close to impossible to retrofit pollution abatement on a cost-effective basis. With positive actions, strategic leaders have the opportunity to solve future problems at low investments that in the long-term are inconsequential to overall economics of the processes. Failure to do so may result in significant long-term costs, expenditures, and possible failures.

In *Globalization: A Critical Introduction*, J. A. Scholte (2000) identifies five categories that help to articulate what globalization is as follows (pp. 15-17):

- **Internationalization:** The growth of international trade and interdependence among countries and participants.
- **Liberalization:** Reducing government imposed trade restrictions on the movement of goods between countries.
- **Universalization:** Spreading of concepts and experiences to people around the world in harmonizing aspirations and outcomes.
- **Modernization:** Spreading social structures around the world affecting local self-determination and destroying local cultures.
- **Deterritorialization:** Reconfiguring geography so that social space is mapped out in terms of territorial places, territorial distances, and territorial borders.

Scholte's perspective provides a sense of the complexities involved in globalization. Clearly, globalization involves moving away from just economic theories about international trade and exchanges to the more integrated business world in which all of the driving forces are considered and acted upon from a unified perspective. Moreover, there are many positive aspects, but as indicated by Scholte, there are many concerns and issues that have to be dealt with, especially those impacting social structures like the destructions of ingenious cultures and languages.

Globalization today is more than economic forces, political decisions and geography. The expanding physical and informational links between distance markets have spawned a better understanding of cultural and regional similarities and differences among people. Public policy directives in the developed countries to eliminate historic barriers to trade and commerce contribute to common markets and more open communications and travel. However, the evidence about whether globalization is real does not provide a compelling answer. Globalization can be viewed as part of the evolutionary track of expanding opportunities for economic and social activities and interactions. It may be viewed as simply a linear expansion of the economic power that has migrated from just the Western countries, principally the G7, to include new players who are vying for the share in the economic riches. This perspective is not a new paradigm for achieving growth and improvements for all people, but one of simply adding new players to the world elites. The new powerhouses are Brazil, Russia, India, and China (BRIC countries).

The current form of globalization may lead to more intense competition among the key players without regard for the broader social, economic, and environmental factors. New companies in the BRIC countries may focus extensively on economic outcomes and try to gain superior positions against the old line corporations like BMW, DuPont, Ford, IBM, Pfizer, Proctor & Gamble, Shell Oil, Unilever, and thousands of others. Emerging companies may use their strategic advantages of low-cost labor and positive cash flow to grow rapidly. They may quickly become global players. In this scenario, globalization is really a different manifestation of the old world of the economic models of the twentieth century. The main competitors not only seek to dominate customers and markets, they try to monopolize the essential resources for production through whatever means available. For instance, companies in China are trying to secure sources of raw materials around the world from aluminum to zirconium. Moreover, with the numerous examples of toxic substances being used in producing products or incorporated in the products, there are great concerns that Chinese companies in particular are not following prescribed protocols or generally accepted practices for ensuring safeguards, consumer protection, proper work standards, and environmental protection.

True globalization has to be based on a holistic model. It has to include the whole context of reality (inclusiveness), involve providing the best solutions and systems possible (innovativeness), build enduring and trust-based relationships with customers, stakeholders, partners, and people around the world (connectedness), provide the requisite information and data about products, processes, and services to all customers and constituencies (openness), and ultimately ensure that people are successful and that success is enduring over time (effectiveness). To do this, strategic leaders must embrace the importance of the social underpinnings, recognize and respect cultural differences between societies, protect and preserve the natural environment, create and deploy the best technologies and products possible, contemplate non-traditional and countervailing perspectives that reveal ways of doing business more efficiently and effectively, and understand the needs of the future as well as the expectations of the present.

Adil Najam, David Runnalls, and Mark Halle (2005) of the International Institute of Sustainable Development in their article, "Environment and Globalization: Five Propositions", identify several challenges and opportunities associated with globalization (p. 10):

1. The rapid acceleration in global economic activity and our dramatically increased demand for critical natural resources undermine our pursuit of continued economic prosperity.
2. The linked processes of globalization and environmental degradation pose new security threats to an already insecure world. They impact the vulnerability of ecosystems and societies. And the least resilient ecosystems. The livelihoods of the poorest communities are most at risk.
3. The newly prosperous and the established wealthy will have to come to terms with the limitations of the ecological space in which both must operate, and also with the needs and rights of those who have not been as lucky.
4. Consumption-in both the North and South-will define the future of globalization as well as the global environment.
5. Concerns about the global market and global environment will become even more intertwined and each will become increasingly dependent on the other.

These perceptions are very useful when exploring the meaning and future aspects of globalization. It is crucial to realize that globalization is accelerating and that the availability of resources is a significant strategic factor for the sustainable success of global corporations. For most the twentieth century, competition played out in the domain of the markets and the drive for revenue and profits. Today, the availability of natural resources, especially metal ores, petroleum and water, is among the most critical factors for achieving strategic success. Resource vulnerabilities are becoming worrisome. Such vulnerabilities are multifaceted. From a business perspective, vulnerabilities are negatives that could be avoided with careful considerations, proper decision making, and effective actions. Vulnerabilities are often linked to the risks to the businesses; however, there are important distinctions. They include being unable to handle all of the wastes being generated and lacking the capabilities to mitigate, if not eliminate, pollution and hazardous wastes. Failures to resolve such difficulties may limit the overall economic and market potential. As more people around the world expect and demand products and service, the economic realities have to be improved dramatically to satisfy all of the needs and at the same time keep the negative effects and impacts under control and mitigated to the extent possible. The world is more complex and is expected to become more interdependent as emerging markets take their place in the business world of the twenty-first century. Vulnerabilities are often the result making decisions based on the realities of the present situations without significant regard for the future aspects. Think about the issues pertaining to climate change. The business decisions today may produce vulnerabilities in the future unless the actions and outcomes are adaptability to the changing business landscape.

A HOLISTIC MODEL FOR THE ADOPTION OF SUSTAINABILITY AND LEADING CHANGE

The Strategic Logic for the Adoption of the Model

External context in the long term drives change and the opportunities and challenges facing global corporations. In the days when most corporations primarily focused on their home markets, the scope of their enterprises was relatively narrow and the market aspects were easily defined and deployed. For most of the early twentieth century, corporations obtained most of their revenues and profits from their national markets and operations. Some MNEs participated in exporting their products and licensing their know-how and technologies and the largest ones often had subsidiaries or divisions serving a few of the other developed economies. As such corporations expanded internationally during the last century, their external context often became more complicated and difficult to manage as the geographic scope expanded. They usually adapted their business models to recognize the additional factors and forces that required special attention and actions. However, the complexities of the situations were mitigated to a large extent because there were many similarities between the most advanced developed economies. For instance, all of the G7 countries had relatively stable political, social, and economic systems and structures. The markets were generally expanding and customers demanded fairly similar products. Variations in demand were easily accommodated through incremental innovations and relatively simply modifications in marketing methods. While there were major differences based on culturally-based considerations such as the French preferences for their own wines and American preferences for fast food, most MNEs accommodated the market-related expectations with ease and low costs.

As discussed earlier, the business world changed dramatically in the 1990s. Free trade was expanded with the formalization of the European Union (EU) and the North American Free Trade Agreement (NAFTA). The EU enhanced economic exchanges throughout most of Western Europe and NAFTA eliminated many of the trade restrictions between Canada, Mexico and the US. While the underpinnings and implications of the EU and NAFTA are profound and beyond the scope of this discussion, such changes dramatically improved the prospects for trade and business growth by integrating national economies into regional ones. The changes were more compelling in the EU than in North America. The difference might be explained by that fact that the national economies of the leading European countries (Germany, France, UK and Italy) were more or less coequal, whereas the US economy overwhelmed the economies of Canada and Mexico. Moreover, US economy was already interconnected with many other national economies on a global basis.

Regionalization introduces many more variables to the scope of the business environment. As the scope expands, strategic leaders of global corporations have to modify their perspectives of what is necessary for achieving success and adapt new models for including the essential elements. Most importantly, strategic leaders have to shift their strategic thinking from what the company has to do to serve its home market to how it can adapt to the needs and expectations of more complicated market situations and business actions. In a nutshell, they have to become market-centric or enterprise-centric instead of company-centric. They have to transition from basic management constructs like improving their competitiveness in markets, building a large portfolio of products and services, obtaining efficient and effective operations, and maximizing profits to more advanced approaches like achieving strategic leadership, creating cutting-edge solutions and systems that are unique, establishing strategic direction for exceeding expectations, obtaining desirable market outcomes,, and building solid relationships with people.

The logic behind the transition is not based on an "either-or" situation, but a realization that the business models in scope and scale have to become much greater as a corporation moves from national markets to regional ones. This implies that the basic means and mechanisms for serving national markets are still important, except that additional perspectives are also required for achieving success in a much large business environment. It is important to point out that these discussions only cover some of the most salient aspects and that in both cases the requisite models are much more complicated than outlined herein. In many cases, global corporations have made the transition from focusing on national markets to regional or more broadly based markets, especially considering the phenomena and changes in the developed countries. Obviously, some corporations are more successful than others and that outcomes are dependent on circumstances and the capabilities of the organizations involved. However, there is still a long way to go in the pursuit of sustainability and true globalization. Gary Hamel in *The Future of Management* (2007) suggests the "there's little that can be said with certainty about the future except this; sometimes over the next decade your company will be challenged to change in a way for which it has no precedent (p. 41).

Managing in the global economy necessitates more comprehensive and sophisticated management constructs and models for realizing extraordinary performance and achieving long-term success. Globalization introduces many additional forces and factors to the scope of the business environment. Indeed, it requires that strategic leaders consider, analyze, engage, strategize, and execute from the very broad perspectives. While it is impossible to know and manage everything in the world, sophisticated strategic leaders have to be holistic in their thinking and have inclusive strategies, solutions, systems, decision making, and actions if they expect to realize success in a complex and turbulent reality. In a global setting, global corporations have to become enterprise-centric as well as market-centric. They have to recognize that success depends on more than addressing markets and satisfying customers and stakeholders. It involves incorporating all of the driving forces and facets of the global business environment into the strategic direction and the models used for decision making and actions.

Globalization necessitates the adoption of more comprehensive management constructs and business models. The transition and/or transformation to a broader scope using more sophisticated constructs and models does not mean that the conventional constructs and models are no longer appropriate or useful. Some may be embedded within the systems and structures of the more contemporary models; others can be applied in special cases, in which the underpinnings and forces are less complicated. For instance, Southwest Airlines (SWA) is a specialized US airline that successfully serves small markets. Its model is fine-tuned to the US and its business environment is national in scope and nature. While global forces impinge on all corporations, SWA's strategic leaders have chosen to focus on a fairly narrow perspective.

On a more global basis, many large corporations have become more sophisticated over the last two decades. Their strategic leaders know that the business world has changed significantly and that there many more profound opportunities and compelling challenges and risks. They realize that their corporations must be more capable, innovative, responsive, and global. They have made improvements; however, in many cases incremental improvements are simply not good enough to stay ahead of the changes and expectations in the business environment. For instance, for more than a decade many strategic leaders in the developed countries viewed globalization in terms of outsourcing processes and activities to lower their cost structures and improve profits. They were company-centric focusing on improving the sales and profits of their products and services. Such strategic leaders believed that their strategies and actions would lead to positive outcomes and financial success. While such theories and practices were seemingly sound in the short term, they have become less powerful over time as competitors followed the similar lines of thinking and decision making. Such methods have helped consumers in the developed countries obtain more affordable products and services and allowed governments to keep inflation low. However, the hoped for gains in profitability became less and less viable as outsourcing evolved into a global phenomenon. Ultimately, management constructs that can be easily copied are subject to being generic approaches with limited advantages, if any at all. Simple methods have the allure of being easy to understand, develop, and implement, but they also have the risk of being quickly duplicated by competitors. Table 1 provides some of the salient factors involving the transformation from national markets to regional ones and then to global perspectives.

The higher level of sophistication identified under "global" in Table 1 provides strategic leaders with the prospects of realizing more enduring performance and success. While very little in the business world lasts forever, the broader the scope, the more inclusive the model, and the more sophisticated elements, the more difficult it is for others to emulate the strategies, solutions, systems, and actions.

Sustainability is the imperative of the twenty-first century. It implies exactly what the term means, i.e. to support from the foundation, to strengthen the framework, to endure over the course of time, to keep going regardless of the challenges, and to lead change. For instance, it is fool-hardy to create new products, invest in new capital equipment, and develop new ventures among numerous other business initiatives unless they are sustainable over the long term. Sustainability is about realizing ongoing success from every dimension, not just the economic and environmental ones. While there are strategic leaders, practitioners, and scholars who discuss concepts like environmental sustainability, sustainability is really about integrating the social, political, economic, ethical, environmental, technological,

Table 1. Salient factors pertaining to national, regional, and global markets

Scope	National	Regional	Global
Focus	**Company**	**Market**	**Business Environment**
Key Elements	**Salient Aspects of the Internal Context**		
Imperative Means Mechanisms Measures Strategies	Competitiveness Products & Services Operations & Marketing Process Innovations Profitability Competitive Strategies	Market Leadership Cutting Edge Brands Strategic Planning Product Innovations Market Share Market Strategies	Sustainability Sustainable Solutions Sustainable Development Strategic Innovations Sustainable Success Preemptive Strategies
Dimensions	**Salient Factors of the External Context**		
Market	Customers Competitors National Stakeholders	Customers Allies & Partners Regional Stakeholders	Customers & Non-customers Contributors & Recipients All Stakeholders
Social	Communities Employees Shareholders	Civil Society National Identity Social systems	All people Cultural Diversity Social Structure
Economic	Production / Consumption Competitive Positions Revenue & Profits	Value Proposition Market Positions Economic Performance	Value Creation Value Maximization Sustainable Success
Technological	Products/Services Dominant Technologies Incremental Innovation	Innovative Products Advanced Technologies Radical Innovation	Cutting-Edge Solutions Clean Technologies Strategic Innovation
Environmental	Regulatory Compliance Pollution Prevention Waste Management	Beyond Compliance Green Management Waste Minimization	Openness & Transparency Sustainable Enterprise Zero Defects & Wastes
Political	Legal System Political Structure Regulatory Mandates	Political Economy Governmental Structures Directives	International Laws and Policies International Organizations International Treaties
Ethical	Values and ethics Accepted Principles Established Behaviors	World Class Standards Axiomatic Principles Proper Behaviors	Universal Standards Global Compact Profound Respect

and market forces and considerations into a holistic perspective (model), in which success is obtained in every dimension. For instance, outsourcing of jobs from developed countries to developing countries may result in improved cost structures, but in the long term the consumers in the developed countries may not be able to afford the products, if they do have sufficient disposable income; therefore, such approaches may not be sustainable. Sustainability requires an integrated model for decisions, strategies, solutions and actions.

Sustainability is facilitated through sustainable solutions. The construct is based on the realization that customers and stakeholders really want and desire solutions. A sustainable solution is the complete package of everything that is necessary to provide the customers and stakeholders with their own successfully outcomes. It includes the products and services, the support mechanisms, the complementary products, and all of the short-term and long-term requirements to make the solution succeed and endure. Solutions are usually unique since they vary considerable from company to company.

SD involves the mechanisms that are employed to create sustainable solutions, employ innovations, sustain success, and advance sustainability. It is underpinned by strategic innovations. Strategic innovations are particularly powerful when they create extraordinary value for all contributors and recipients and eliminate difficulties and challenges across the business environment. Strategic leaders have to have the confidence and courage to develop new solutions and systems that offer extraordinary value and new-to-the-world outcomes. SD requires preemptive (proactive) strategies for leading change. In my book, *Enterprise-wide Strategic Management: Achieving Sustainable Success through Leadership, Strategies, and Value Creation*, the construct of preemptive strategies is developed and discussed in detail. Preemptive strategies are cutting edge methods for leapfrogging expectations and competitors and achieving sustainable success. The following excerpts provide the main perspectives (Rainey, 2010, pp. 373-376):

Preemptive strategies are proactive approaches for leading change and taking the initiative to aggressively move on opportunities and challenges in the business environment before such actions are expected or become obvious. Preemptive strategies necessitate changing and even disrupting industry or market space norms through fast-paced, hard to duplicate strategic actions that provide distinctive and sustainable advantages for first mover, fast follower, or strategic change leaders. Preemptive strategies eschew the notions of reacting to change or anticipating changes only slightly ahead of a necessity for action. Preemptive strategies imply that strategic leaders seek out every opportunity to forge positive changes and exploit new opportunities before customers or competitors understand the implications.

Preemptive strategies require extremely assertive actions in making dramatic or radical improvements to the external and internal dimensions of [the company and/or] business units... Aggressive does not mean increasing the rivalry among competitors; it does mean taking every opportunity to make profound changes that advance the well-being of customers, the extended enterprise, the organization, and all of the key contributors. Preemptive strategies usually involve the full integration of the whole enterprise into a seamless and highly assertive value delivery system (holistic management system) that is fully capable of planning and executing every action at the highest level of quality and performance. Most importantly, preemptive strategies involve strategic innovations that significantly or radically improve underlying technologies, products and services-the solutions. Such innovations include inventing and validating clean technologies, developing and delivering more valuable solutions, enriching and exploiting improved process capabilities, and reinventing the strategic management system and value delivery system with outstanding intellectual capital, capabilities and resources. Preemptive strategies involve transitions and transformations to the next higher levels of achievements and sustainable outcomes...

[Preemptive strategies] involve out-of-the-box thinking about how to move closer toward perfection and obtain the best solutions for customers and stakeholders, and to build enduring relationships with all of the essential contributors and recipients. Strategic thinking shifts from the competitive spaces of the past to preempting the market spaces and creating the business enterprise of the future. This includes integrating the extended enterprise into a complete system, leading change to secure sustainable advantages, and using all of the capabilities and resources in the most effective and least damaging ways.

Sustainability involves applying the most sophisticated management constructs and business models possible to attain market leadership and value creation. In the context of globalization, it provides the underlying elements and perspectives that make the concept of globalization truly global. Sustainability integrates of all of the external driving forces into a coherent model for creating value and sustainable solutions for the present and future. Sustainability is more than the "triple bottom line" articulated by John Elkington (1997, p. 2). The "triple-bottom line" includes social, economic, and environmental considerations in managing businesses. While Elkington's concept is an important contribution to management theories, preemptive strategies and sustainable solutions necessitate dynamic actions to produce sustainable success, especially from the development and deployment of new-to-the-world technologies and products.

The Model: Sustainability and SD in the Context of Globalization and Strategic Innovation

Sustainability and SD fit well in the context of globalization. They are essential for true globalization. However, sustainability and SD are preeminent management constructs in their own right with or without globalization. Moreover, sustainability and SD are inextirpable linked with strategic innovations. Given the current state of affairs in the business world, global corporations are a long way from achieving the level of sophistication that is necessary to achieve a modicum of sustainability within a decade or two. In my book, *Sustainable Business Development: Inventing the Future through Strategy, Innovation and Leadership*, the important factors for realizing sustainable are detailed. Some of the key underlying concepts include (Rainey, 2006, pp678-680):

Management across the world is engaged in the relentless struggle to keep pace with technological, social, economic and environmental changes that seem to accelerate as time moves forward. Great strides in competitive advantages are marginalized by the gains of peers and competitors, and the changing business environment. Where past breakthroughs led to competitive advantages that lasted for decades, the effects of such achievements today are often measured in months. However, with all of the challenges, there are also enormous opportunities, opportunities to lead change and move beyond the social, economic and environmental mandates. Across the world people want solutions to the problems they face. The opportunities for providing these solutions range from finding ways to expand health care and obliterate hunger to protecting natural resources and eliminating waste streams.

...The penultimate objective is the quest for greatness, the quest for perfection, not perfection itself. It is akin to the building of the great cathedrals of Europe. The architects and builders recognized the daunting nature of such projects. They knew that it would take many generations of skilled and dedicated people to realize the dreams. Nevertheless, they were willing to invest their time and efforts in the process because they believed in the vision. They understood that laying the foundation and building solid walls would provide the means for others to continue building. Moreover, they realized that the succeeding generations of their relatives and compatriots would enjoy the fruits of their labor and that the structures would provide humankind a lasting testimonial of their contributions and achievements.

Sustainability and SD require dedication, ongoing development, and steadfast deployment. While continuous improvement was one of the main management themes of the late twentieth century, the pursuit of sustainability and SD are the critical perspectives driving global corporation in this century. Sustainability and SD involve the relentless pursuit toward perfection through innovativeness, inclusiveness, and connectedness. The requisite model includes the key elements for leading change through innovation, managing the systems and structures across the organization and the extended enterprise, and building enduring relationships with people through social responsibility. The model provides a framework pertaining to how the key elements interrelate. The model is depicted in Figure 1; it is an adaptation of the model presented in my

Figure 1. A holistic model for linking sustainability, SD, and strategic innovation in the context of globalization

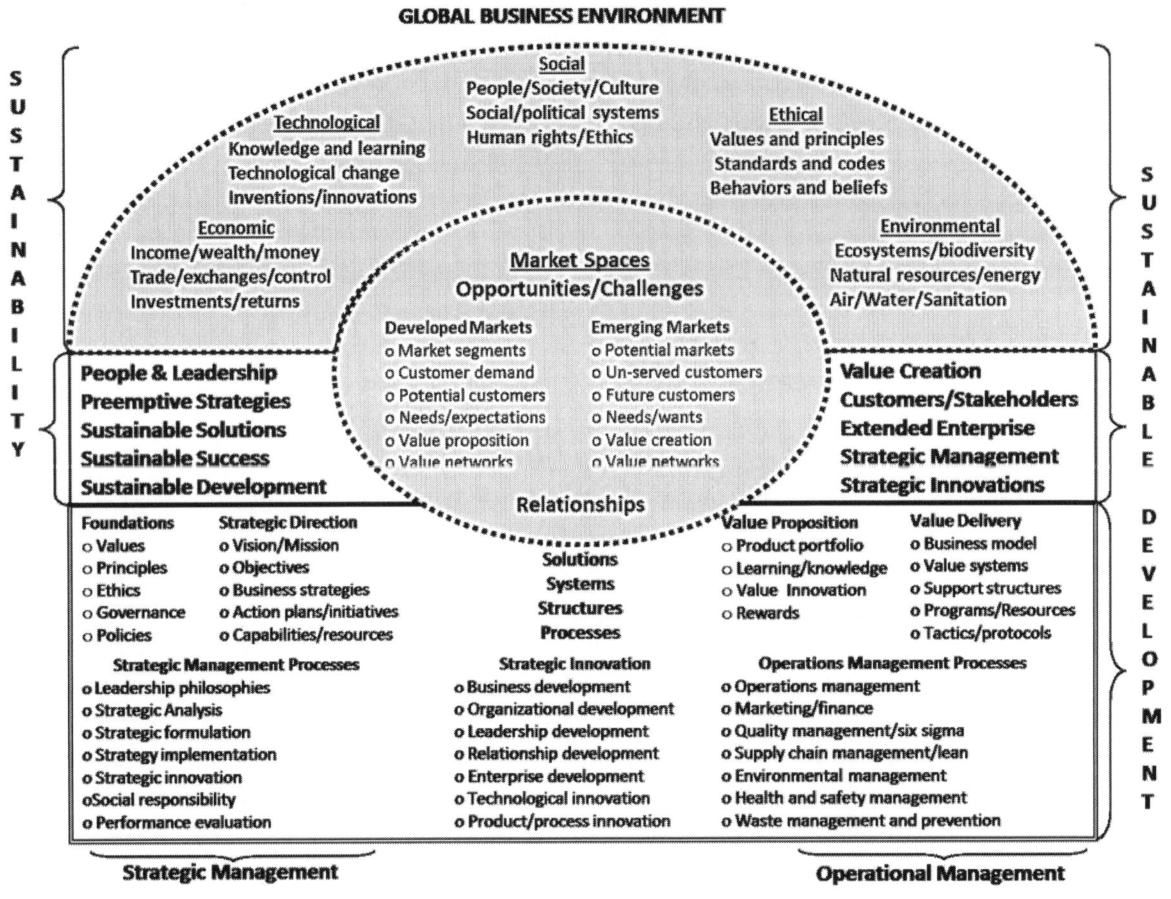

book, *Enterprise-wide Strategic Management: Achieving Sustainable Success through Leadership, Strategies and Value Creation* (Rainey, 2010, p. 160). While the framework maps out the essential elements, it is impossible to articulate all of the details.

The model offers several exciting perspectives and elements:

- The model provides an inclusive, sophisticated, and broader framework for leading change in complex business situations, in which strategic leaders create extraordinary value for all constituents in realizing sustainable success.
- The focus is on the global business environment and market spaces. Market spaces include existing markets, emerging ones, customers, and non-customers. While many existing models are either company-centric based on core competencies or competition-centric based on rivalry, sustainable success focuses on making people the center of strategies and actions and making them successful.
- The underlying aspirations include creating sustainable solutions and achieving sustainable outcomes through SD and strategic innovations, not just making short-term profits at the expense of long-

term success. Sustainability and SD are interconnected and interrelated constructs that link a broad array of people across the extended enterprise. Given that people are central to sustainable success, building enduring relationships is essential for realizing the expected outcomes on an ongoing basis.

- The model has holistic connections with strategic management and operational constructs. It focuses on integrating the corporation's strategies and actions with the external contributions of the extended enterprise and the needs and expectations of the market spaces. This represents a quantum leap forward in connecting the systems, structures, processes, and practices that facilitate developing and deploying the best solutions possible.

The model addresses perspectives and constructs that are in line with 21st century dynamics. It examines the business environment in the context of the whole global landscape, and strategic leadership and management in the context of sustainability and SD. Indeed, it examines the whole perspective rather than focusing on the parts, which is often the prevailing methodology. For instance, the model integrates concepts for dealing with customers and stakeholders and building relationships rather than just focusing on marketing and selling. It recognizes that customers want solutions that exceed their needs and expectations. It discusses solutions in the context of social, economic, technological, ethical, environmental, and market space considerations. It explores not only the prevailing situation but how innovative solutions taken from the market perspective can create new opportunities. It includes the systems, structures, and processes required for obtaining results.

These perspectives are reinforced by the contributions of C. K. Prahalad and M. S. Krishnan (2007) in *the new age of innovation*, in which they state that building relationships with external contributors are a main source of competitive advantage (p. 46). In the article, "Why Sustainability Is Now the Key Driver of Innovation," the authors discuss developing new business models as an advanced stage of corporate development (Nidumolu, 2009). They indicate that sustainability and SD require higher levels of strategizing and executing based on sophisticated frameworks. The holistic model discussed herein meets these requirements.

The Means: Sustainability and Sustainable Development

Sustainability is the overarching constructs that includes the philosophical perspectives, theoretical constructs, and practical approaches for leading positive change in global corporations and managing their businesses, enterprises, and organizations. The intellectual challenges include determining the vision and strategic direction and the strategic leadership philosophies and constructs for leading change. The simple yet most compelling philosophical perspective is putting the business environment or external context first before thinking about internal context. This fits the concept of "people, planet and profit," (Bergmans, 2006, pp. 117-119). It is based on the recognition that people and the natural environment are the overarching considerations and that profit is important for sustaining companies, but profit is really a derivative of good analysis, decision making, strategies and actions.

Sustainability is a continuum of strategic thinking and actions that is internally driven by visionary strategic leadership based on external realities. Strategic leaders have to have the courage, fortitude, and dedication to take on incredible challenges, to think about radical new ways of providing solutions, and to use preemptive strategic for realizing extraordinary outcomes and sustainable success. Without direction from strategic leaders, sustainability and SD do not get traction. They require concerted efforts and significant investments. Strategic leaders have to provide the resources and commitments to implement the revolutionary ways to do more good and less bad as Peter Senge discussed in his book, *The Necessary Revolution* (Senge, 2008, pp. 33-41).

SD is often conceptually accepted by global corporations. While the underpinnings and aspirations are often clear, it involves a complex array of solutions, systems, structures, processes and techniques. Unlike most of the major initiatives of the last century like strategic planning and total quality management, SD cannot be implemented on a project basis, in which significant efforts and funds are allocated to create the systems and then enjoy the results at completion. SD involves a long-term approach for transforming the whole corporation and its enterprise(s) into a fully integrated and innovative entity.

SD requires an embedded structure that is parallel to the salient factors associated with the transition from national and regional markets to global ones as portrayed in Table 1. The key elements for being successful in national markets are also necessary for success in the global economy. As depicted in Figure 1, strategic leaders have to provide all of the key elements for establishing the basic foundation and the strategic direction. They define the values, principles, and ethics of the organization based on the broader social, legal, ethical, and environmental responsibilities. Strategic leaders and the directors of the corporation determine governance structure and company policies. They must articulate the vision and mission and set the objectives. These elements are translated into strategies and action plans that are implemented by the organization and the extended enterprise. Strategic leaders also ensure that the capabilities and resources of the organization are aligned with the strategic direction. Moreover, strategic leaders allocate the resources and provide learning opportunities for employees and contributors across the enterprise.

Operational management engages in the implementation and execution. It includes a myriad of the critical systems and processes that a used to realize outcomes and achieve success. They include but are not limited to, marketing, finance, quality management, supply chain management, environmental management, health and safety management and waste management. Results are accomplished through support systems and structures, programs, protocols, and tactics. While most global corporations have well-functioning operating systems and reasonably effective processes, the management constructs are often based on twentieth century requirements rather than on the current realities or future ones. Like many of the military situations and organizations of the past, strategic leaders are often well prepared to fight the battles of the past, instead of being proactive and contemplating what is necessary for the future. Strategic leaders too often think about what their organizations are instead of what they must be. Understanding the past is important because it gives us insights about the social and economic dimensions, but transforming the corporation and organization to lead change and being ahead of mandates and expectations is the essence of SD.

The Mechanism: Strategic Innovations

The transformation to highly levels of achievement is predicated on strategic innovations. Strategic innovations are radical changes to the corporation, its business units, the extended enterprise, the organization, the leadership, relationships, and the technologies, products, and processes. Strategic innovations involve high-level investments in employees, learning, intellectual property, know-how, business portfolios, technological underpinnings, brands, and product lines. They also involve the tangibles of developing and commercializing new products and creating and building new business ventures and the intangibles of enhancing one's reputation and acquiring new knowledge. Strate-

Table 2. Types of strategic innovations

Categories	Main Types	Salient Aspects
Solutions	Radical technological innovation	Radical technological innovation involves developing new or dramatically improved technologies that change the basis for delivering value. Creating a new-to-the-world solution starts with insights and innovativeness. It incorporates the full spectrum of internal and external ingredients based on inclusiveness and connectedness to create exceptional value and realize sustainable success.
Systems	Business model innovation	Business model innovation involves a conceptual combination of all of the entities and the patterns of interrelationships and interfaces that are linked together in formal and informal arrangements to create and deliver value-producing outcomes that are guided by strategies and actions. Business venture innovation also involves starting new business units that have superior solutions with new technologies.
Structures	Leadership and organizational development	Leadership and organizational development are critical for realizing sustainable success. They involve the development of new competencies and capabilities and the transfer of know-how and management wherewithal between the generations of leaders and practitioners within the corporation and enterprise. Leadership and talent development are crucial for assuring the going commitment to sustainable success.

gic innovations make sustainability and SD real for the people who are tasked with carrying out the actions.

Strategic innovations are a global corporation's answers to how to develop a unique place in today's turbulent and complex business world. Global corporations seek practical approaches to their quests to be competitive and achieve ongoing success. While strategic innovations do not always result in significant advancements in competitiveness and market success, they do offer a greater probability of achieving game changing outcomes that are more difficult for competitors and would be rivals to emulate. However, strategic leaders often view strategic innovations, especially radical innovations, as risky and subject to many perils. While it is clear that strategic innovations are more challenging, they are not necessarily more risky than incremental innovations or doing nothing when all factors are considered. While the potential results of incremental innovations are usually more predictable and successful from a product or process point of view, the actual business outcomes are often less fruitful and enduring. For instance, improving obsolete products may result in additional sales and revenues in the short term, but the resultant business performance and financial outcomes are often unchanged and the products are eventually replaced or eliminated. The investment in incremental innovations may be positive, but the business may lose valuable time and money pursuing marginal outcomes.

Strategic innovations are necessary to assure that global corporations stay ahead of the driving forces and expectations in the business environment. Among the most crucial are strategic innovations that create unique advantages for the corporation through innovative solutions, systems, and structures and build enduring relationships. Table 2 lists some types of strategic innovations.

Innovative solutions engender outstanding combinations of value creation, value innovation, and value delivery expressed and supported using the value systems and extended enterprise. Radical technological innovation is a primary mechanism for effecting strategic innovation. The strategic leaders initiate the development of new technologies using the research and development (R&D) programs and projects. While there are many variations, the corporate R&D generally involves developing new-to-the-world technologies and/or products with potentially exceptional business value.

Radical technological innovations depend on external context. Exploring the global business environment and the market spaces and determining how the corporation and its enterprise(s) fit the needs and requirements for the future are effective ways for initiating the long process of creating new technologies. Francisco Szekely and Heidi Strebel suggest that "radical innovation encompasses a wider sphere of activity and closer interaction with suppliers, regulators, civil society organizations, and other stakeholders (2013)."

Radical technological innovations are based on insights from the business environment and the organization's imagination about what can be accomplished. Global corporations can take a proactive approach and invest into transforming their businesses by developing new technologies that are cleaner and more efficient and effective. Some of the best opportunities are those involving eliminating the negative side of existing technologies. This results in new-to-the-world products that have superior attributes and value. Strategic leaders must allow for risk taking and even failures to occur as the R&D people find new ways of achieving success. Moreover, creating radical innovations that solve problems for people in emerging markets are also great opportunities. Antoine van Agtmael (2007) in his book, *The Emerging Markets Century,* details many of the emerging companies in BRIC countries, Taiwan, South Korea and Mexico are gaining footholds as world-class competitors through brainpower and innovation. He cites the incredible progress made by companies like Embraer of Brazil, Lenovo of China, Samsung of South Korea, and TSMC of Taiwan. These aggressive companies are vying for their place in the world.

Historically, global corporations used simple business models for managing their businesses. The general methodology employed a de-coupled, hierarchical approach that included operations management of the value system on the bottom and strategic business management at the top. Traditional business models limited the scope of the analytical framework to facilitate decision-making and simplify the interactions. Due to the lack of integration at the operating level, strategic leaders had to play a significant role in resolving difficulties within the system. The strength of the approach became the weakness.

During the mid-1980s Michael Porter's models of the value chain and the value system dramatically shifted the management constructs from a vertical organizational approach to a system approach with horizontal processes (Porter, 1985, pp. 33-35). With the rise of globalization, the intensity of competition, and the sophistication of technological innovation, narrow business models become less adequate for understanding and managing the complexities of the business environment. A higher level of sophistication is necessary for incorporating all of the forces impinging on the entire organization and its linkages, partners, stakeholders, and customers. An effective business model is a comprehensive management construct that forms the basis for analysis, understanding, decision-making, continuous improvement, as well as radical innovation. It is a unifying approach that integrates the people, the processes, the practices and the programs into a comprehensive management system. Today, fully integrated business models are pivotal for success as more corporations depend on supply networks, strategic alliances, and external relationships for sustaining success. Business model innovation encompasses the whole, both internal and external, and the present and the future. It is inclusive of all of the essential dimensions in managing and leading an organization. Business model innovation involves the convergence of the solution, systems and the structure.

In *Leading the Revolution*, Gary Hamel (2000) discusses the 'age of revolution'. He suggests that "it is not knowledge that produces wealth, but insights into opportunities for discontinuous innovation" (p. 14). Hamel's business model includes "four major components: core strategy, strategic resources, customer interfaces, value networks" (p. 70). He incorporates into the "new innovation" model the concept of a solution (pp. 283-313). He views innovation as an essential element for achieving strategic success. Sustainability is a key to business model innovation, profitability, and business success. In a recent MIT Sloan Management Review article, the authors cite insights from their research (Kiron, 2013).

According to our 2012 global executive survey on sustainability, an important factor is business model innovation. Managers who say that their company's sustainability activities have added to the company's profits are more than twice as likely to say that sustainability has caused their organization to change their business model than not.

Business model innovation involves integrating all of the critical elements into a framework that facilitates implementations and execution. It ties all of the business objectives together that leads to successes in all categories, including making money. Sustainability is all inclusive.

Given the diversity of the global competitive landscape and the expectations of people and society, the most important part of strategic innovation is the development of talent. Unlike the business world of the early twentieth century that was based on machine-driven methods, twenty-first century corporations are based on intellectual capital. The core competencies and capabilities of the corporations are its true strategic assets. From strategic management and strategic innovation perspectives, people are the innovative force. They create the solutions and the systems. Leadership and organizational development address the needs of the people in the organization and how to enhance their knowledge and capabilities through learning and experience. Leadership and organizational development invoke a spirit to become the best and to build new capabilities and competencies for the emerging technologies and practices of the 21st century. It provides the means and mechanisms for the organization to acquire the new knowledge and skills to perform to the highest standards.

Developing capabilities is important but it is insufficient. Organizations have to promote innovation and lead change on a real-time basis. Successful businesses have to apply their strategies, solutions, and systems. They have to lead. In a recent article on innovation capabilities, Yair Holtzman articulates how "a portfolio of capabilities creates exponential value; he further states (2013):

A vast majority of senior executives we provide consulting services to, say that innovation will be at least one of the top key drivers of growth for their companies in the next three to five years. Other executives see innovation as the most important way for companies to accelerate the pace of change in today's business environment. Leading strategic thinkers are moving beyond a focus on traditional products and service categories to pioneer innovations in business processes, distribution, value chains, business models, and even functions of management.

Businesses have to develop and implement their strategies and solution through people. Building relationships is essential for achieving success. Building relationships with customers and stakeholders is one of the most effective ways for sustaining success. Success is often predicated on the social interactions between people. The closer one is to the people involved in the actual transactions and exchanges, the greater are the opportunities to make contributions to achieve positive outcomes and success and the more likely that success continues.

CONCLUSION

Rapid changes in the business world over the last two decades have made most of the prevailing management constructs obsolete. In a global business environment of limited time and scarce resources, strategic leaders have to seek and develop innovative ways to keep ahead of change. This necessity is especially important for global corporations. Global corporations have to expand their reach and sophistication to create sustainable solutions, integrated systems, and robust structures that are proactive and unique. Good is no longer good enough. Global corporations have to lead change and become sustainable enterprises. They have to incorporate sustainability and SD in their models and ensure that they can exceed customer and stakeholder expectations and outperform competitors.

Strategic leaders have to preemptive the market and competitive situations through strategic innovations that open the doors to new possibilities and success. They have to think about the whole enterprise and ensure that solutions and systems are fully aligned and providing successful outcomes for all contributors and recipients.

Globalization without a multi-dimensional perspective is a prescription for enduring ongoing problems, challenges, and instability. Solutions have to be multifaceted and holistic. They have to produce positive outcomes. They must avoid creating tensions and conflicts among people across the world. For instance, simply shifting jobs to low-wage countries to obtain low-cost products may result in cost-effective products that people in the developed countries cannot afford to buy because they lack employment opportunities and personal income.

The holistic model discussed in the chapter provides a framework for creating win-win outcomes that are balanced in terms of the social, political, ethical, economic, technological, and environmental forces. Balanced solutions require an integrated approach with strategic leaders and contributors working together using strategic innovations. For most global corporations, the focus shifts from "business as usual" approaches to creating sustainable solutions and developing holistic systems and structures to deploy the solutions.

From a strategic perspective, the decision making methodology for strategic innovations has to become more comprehensive and farsighted. Decision makers have to be proactive. They have to use learning and acquire new knowledge to obtain a more comprehensive understanding of the realities. They must be thorough in their assessments of context to obtain insights about what the solutions have to be. Ultimately, they need to use their imaginations to envisions how to create the best strategies, solutions, and outcomes and to use the judgments of all of the participants in the decision making process. Great decisions are based on the collective wisdom and intellectual capital of the people involved.

True globalization may only be possible in the context of sustainability, SD and strategic innovation. Otherwise, short-term successes may turn into complex challenges and difficulties that limit long-term performance and outcomes. For instance, pollution and wastes are critical factors that have to be eliminated via clean technologies and new-to-the-world products, if solutions are to endure. Future developments may be stymied because resources have to be allocated for cleaning up the messes created due to poor decision making or simply not available because of resource depletion. It is critical that business leaders, government officials, and people understand, develop, produce, and deploy sustainable solutions and achieve sustainable success. With true globalization, global corporations have to adopt a more inclusive and comprehensive model of their external and internal context, if they aspire to obtain competitive advantages, achieve outstanding business performance, and enjoy sustainable success. The underpinnings must focus on protecting future generations of people, preserving the natural environment, ensuring that the economic, social, environmental and financial interests of businesses and society continue well into the future.

REFERENCES

Anonymous, . (2011). *The Board's Sustainability Book*. London, UK: Arthur D. Little.

Ashford, N., & Hall, R. (2011). The Importance of Regulation-Induced Innovation for Sustainable Development. *Sustainability*, *3*(1), 270–292. doi:10.3390/su3010270

Bergmans, F. (2006). Integrating People, Planet and Profit. In J. Jonker & M. de Witte (Eds.), *Management Models for Corporate Social Responsibility* (pp. 117–125). Berlin, Germany: Springer. doi:10.1007/3-540-33247-2_14

Elkington, J. (1997). *Cannibals with Forks: The Triple Bottom Line of Sustainable Development*. Oxford, UK: Chapstone Publishing.

Esty, D., & Winston, A. (2006). *Green to Gold: How Smart Companies Use Environmental Strategy to Innovate, Create Value, and Build Competitive Advantage*. New Haven, CT: Yale University Press.

Fernando, R. (2012). Sustainable globalization and implications for strategic corporate and national sustainability. *Corporate Governance*, *12*(4), 579–589. doi:10.1108/14720701211267883

Hamel, G. (2000). *Leading the Revolution*. Boston, MA: Harvard Business School Press.

Hamel, G., & Breen, B. (2007). *The Future of Management*. Boston, MA: Harvard Business School Press.

Hawken, P. (2007). *Blessed Unrest: How the Largest Movement in the World Came into Being and Why No One Saw It Coming*. New York, NY: Viking/Penguin Group.

Holltzman, Y. (2013). A strategy of innovation through the development of a portfolio of innovation capabilities. *Journal of Management Development*, *33*(1), 24–31. doi:10.1108/JMD-11-2013-0138

Kiron, D., Kruschwitz, N., Reeves, M., & Goh, E. (2013, Winter). The Benefits of Sustainability-Driven Innovation. *MIT Sloan Management Review*, *54*(2), 69–73.

Najam, A., Runnalls, D., & Halle, M. (2007). *Environment and Globalization: Five Propositions*. Winnipeg, Canada: International Institute of Sustainable Development.

Nidumolu, R., Prahalad, C. K., & Rangaswami, M. R. (2009). Why Sustainability Is Now the Key Driver of Innovation. *Harvard Business Review*, (September): 2009.

Porter, M. (1985). *Competitive Advantage: Creating and Sustaining Superior Performance*. New York, NY: Free Press.

Prahalad, C. (2005). *The Fortune at the Bottom of the Pyramid: Eradicating Poverty Through Profits*. Upper Saddle River, NJ: Wharton School Publishing.

Prahalad, C. K., & Krishnan, M. (2007). *The new age of innovation: Driving Co-created Value Through Global Networks*. New York, NY: McGraw-Hill.

Rainey, D. L. (2006). *Sustainable Business Development: Inventing the Future through Strategy, Innovation and Leadership*. Cambridge, UK: Cambridge University Press. doi:10.1017/CBO9780511617607

Rainey, D. L. (2010). *Enterprise-wide Strategic Management: Achieving Sustainable Success through Leadership, Strategies and Value Creation*. Cambridge, UK: Cambridge University Press.

Rainey, D. L., & Araujo, R. (2014). *The Pursuit of Sustainability: Creating Business Value through Strategic Leadership, Holistic Perspectives, and Exceptional Performance*. Charlotte, NC: Information Age Publishing.

Scholte, J. A. (2000). *Globalization: The Critical Introduction*. New York, NY: Palgrave.

Senge, P. (2008). *The Necessary Revolution: How Individuals and Organizations Are Working Together to Create A Sustainable World.* New York, NY: Doubleday Publishing Group.

Szekely, F., & Strebel, H. (2013). Incremental, radical and game-changing: Strategic innovation for sustainability. *Corporate Governance, 13*(5), 467–481. doi:10.1108/CG-06-2013-0084

The World Commission of Environment and Development. (1987). *Our Common Future*. Oxford, UK: Oxford University Press.

van Agtmael, A. (2007). *The Emerging Markets Century: How a New Breed of World-Class Companies is Overtaking the World.* New York, NY: Free Press.

Willard, B. (2005). *The Next Sustainability Wave: Building Boardroom Buy-*. Gabriola Island, BC: New Society Publishers.

KEY TERMS AND DEFINITIONS

Business Environment: The business environment includes the external forces impinging upon the corporation. It includes the social, economic, political, technological, environmental, and market forces. It also includes the external dimensions of markets, stakeholders, and competition.

Clean Technology: Clean technology involves advanced technological designs that maximize the positive benefits and minimize the negative defects, burdens, and impacts. It includes systems, processes, equipment and know-how that eliminates, reduces or controls pollution and waste streams better than alternates.

Construct: A construct is a theoretical framework or model used to analyze and determine strategies, systems, structures, and solutions. A construct is intended to be a representation of the dimensions and elements of business situations. It combines information, data and experience with theoretical thinking about how to view the business situation in light of its opportunities, challenges, and constraints.

Context: Context provides the basis for analysis, understanding and decision making. It includes the business environment and the management systems of the organization. Context is framed based on defining the scope of the analysis and the inclusion or exclusion of variables. The context includes both time and space considerations.

Extended Enterprise: The extended enterprise includes the contributors to the solutions and recipients who use the solutions. It includes customers, stakeholders, supply networks, strategic partners, related industries, competition, and infrastructure. It provides a framework for a descriptive, analytical, and structural understanding of the needs, opportunities, challenges, requirements, specifications, and the strategies and action plans.

Globalization: The notion that the world economies are shifting toward a borderless economic structure, in which global corporations vie to satisfy customer demand on a global basis. Space and time are compressed and geography becomes less of a critical factor.

Preemptive Strategies: Preemptive strategies are intended to gain sustainable advantages by significantly improving the solutions, systems and structures. The focus is primarily on leading change and value creation.

Product Innovation: Product innovation includes the initiatives, methods, techniques, and processes for making incremental improvements to existing products and services. It involves making evolutionary changes to the products employing the prevailing technologies and organizational capabilities.

Radical Technological Innovation: Radical technological innovation involves creating new-to-the-world technology that brings about revolutionary changes. It often creates new industry or market structures or involves dramatic changes to the existing ones. It also involve making substantial changes to the existing strategic management system including developing new customers, new markets, new supply networks, and other related entities.

Sustainability: Sustainability implies that all human and business activities are carried out rates equal to or less than the Earth's natural carrying capacity to renew the resources used and naturally mitigate the waste streams generated.

Sustainable Development: Sustainable development is a holistic management construct that includes the entire management business system from the origins of the raw materials to production processes and the customer applications and to the end-of-life solutions. Sustainable development involves making dramatic improves and positive changes to the full scope of relationships and linkages of the supply networks, customers and stakeholders, and support service providers for handling wastes, residuals and impacts.

Chapter 11
Developing Sustainable Governance Systems at the Regional Level:
The Case of Emissions Trading

Tim Cadman
Griffith University, Australia & University of Southern Queensland, Australia

Margee Hume
Central Queensland University, Australia

Tek Maraseni
University of Southern Queensland, Australia

Federico Lopez-Casero
Institute for Global Environmental Strategies, Japan

ABSTRACT

As a consequence of the United Nations' Conference on Environment and Development in 1992, the international community has effectively redefined environmental degradation as a problem that can be addressed by means of sustainable development. In turn, this places an onus on businesses to develop practices that reflect new norms of behaviour. This chapter offers an overview of current implementation of governance systems that relate to regional sustainability programmes and firms' activities. This work offers credibility to the field of sustainability research and practice by identifying and discussing all actors in the business community and how they interact with sustainability. This chapter looks at market-based sustainability initiatives, and, from a quality of governance perspective, investigates the strengths and weaknesses of two emissions trading schemes. It concludes with a series of reflections on market-based approaches to environmental problem solving.

INTRODUCTION

Achieving sustainable consumption and sustainable living is a response to the scientific and international communities' concern that the world is living beyond its ecological systems, facing a potential crisis with regard to its environmental and other resources (Packard, 1960; Daub & Ergenzinger, 2005; Dolan, 2002). Placet, Anderson, & Fowler (2005) argue if goals pertaining to environmental and social responsibility are met, the more likely economic prosperity will follow

DOI: 10.4018/978-1-4666-8433-1.ch011

for the company (Placet, Anderson, & Fowler, 2005; Robins, 1999). The Stern Review (2006) concluded that all individuals, firms and communities, in relation to production of housing, transport and food consumption decisions must unite to develop sustainable change and wellbeing. While solutions to unsustainable consumption involve a diverse stakeholder group they also extend to a diverse range of disciplines and fields including environmental, social and economic paradigms. Consequently, examination into sustainable systems requires a number of different knowledge disciplines to be involved including political science, economics, environmental science, marketing, general business, design, sociology, and consumer behaviour scientists in the design and practice of sustainable living (Tukker et al., 2006; Uiterkamp & Vlek, 2007).

Defining sustainable consumption is difficult because of the multiple perspectives that surround the concept (Peattie & Charter, 1994; Tukker et al., 2006; Christensen, Godskesen, Gram-Hassen, Quitzau, & Ropke, 2007). It is best viewed as an umbrella term that incorporates sustainability's environmental, social and economic dimensions and takes on such ideas as reducing environmental impact, enhancing quality of life, minimising waste, taking a life cycle approach and looking at ecological preservation for future generations (Kemp, 2008; UNEP, 2002). From a business perspective sustainable practice incorporates all elements of business from inputs procurement, manufacture, packaging design, marketing and more. The goal of sustainable living is to ensure that society is able to be maintained over time and can be applied to all layers of community and business. Solutions to sustainable consumption are multidimensional and involve in most part three parties; governments (policy makers); producers (business); and consumers (Tukker et al., 2006; Connolly & Prothero, 2003). The notion of consumption in this context extends beyond the initial purchase of products to include their manufacture, use and disposal – a concept that is wider than a narrow marketing ideology (Peattie & Charter, 1994; McDonald & Oates, 2006). Managing the interactions of these actors (stakeholders) is proving to be complex, particularly with regard to ensuring the legitimacy of the 'green' economy. Close attention needs to be paid to ensuring that the goals of sustainability and good governance are met in business practice on the ground.

The changing social, environmental and economic conditions that have arisen as a consequence of globalisation present some major challenges as to how to structure institutional responses in ways that effectively tackle global problems while supporting local initiative. Sustainable practice is no longer exclusively the domain of the nation-state, and new global processes have generated alternative forums of decision-making, characterised by the interplay between traditional government, the global corporate sector and civil society interacting at with each other from the international to the community level – a process also referred to as 'glocalisation'. With no one single nation state acting as the global political facilitator of sustainable development there has been an evolution in the delegation of authority away from traditional government towards the more abstract concept of governance by independent authorities and bodies. Contemporary social processes transcend boundaries so completely that it has been necessary, from a governance perspective, to rethink current arrangements (Rosenau, 1993; Arts, 2006).

The environment features prominently as a locus for the contemporary interplay between globalisation and governance (Lipschutz & Mayer, 1996). Excessive production and consumption of goods place huge burdens on global natural resources. Currently, while some businesses have developed a systems-wide approach to managing and monitoring their environmental impact, implementation has not been universally adopted (Kilbourne, McDonagh, & Prothero, 1997). Smart organizations are realizing the value of sustainable strategies as a differentiation tool and as an important tool for long-term cost reduction of energy and resource usage, whilst enhancing their image as responsible corporate citizens. Universally adopted schemes and auditing programmes are rare, and sector-wide adoption still seems some way off. This chapter will specifically examine the current implementation of a number of governance systems that relate to regional sustainability programmes and firms' practices. Understanding the current practice will assist in the overall adoption and credibility of the field of sustainability research and practice by all actors in the business community. From a regional perspective innovative primary producers and resource stewards often take up sustainability initiatives with little or no knowledge of the governance quality and legitimacy of the schemes they are seeking to implement. This chapter looks at market-based sustainability initiatives, investigates the strengths and weaknesses of two emissions trading programmes, identifies some key governance requirements and offers some reflections on market-based approaches to environmental problem solving at the global, regional and local levels.

GLOBAL GOVERNANCE SUSTAINABILITY AND THE MARKET

As a consequence of the United Nations Conference on Environment and Development (UNCED) of 1992 (also known as the Rio 'Earth Summit') the international community has effectively redefined the environment as an issue, which can be addressed by means of sustainable development. Rio played an important role in the negotiations over environmental standards (Arts, 2006; Kollman & Prakash, 2002; Chavan, 2005). Although the UN does not function as a government, it is nevertheless true to say that there is still global governance, whereby actors enmeshed in regimes (or more appropriately, less formalised arrangements of norms, rules and procedures) engage in behaviour that is nevertheless regulated and predictable (Held, McGrew, Anthony, Goldblatt, & Perraton, 1999). Emergent contemporary social initiatives and movements around the environment are a response to this lack, and are triggering more inclusive forms of global governance to compensate, which are based on the 'dynamic interplay between civil society, business and public sector' (Ruggie, 2003). The literature identifies a range of types and sub-types of instruments, and there is recognition of a move away from the traditional regulatory approaches dating back to the late 1960s towards newer instruments, with a strong market emphasis (Jordan, Wurzel, & Zito, 2005). These new instruments often hybridise one with another, but for the sake of convenience can be broken down into four main types with these revisited in subsequent section:

1. **Market-Based Instruments (MBIs):** Comprising four main types:
    a. Eco-taxes (charges and levies);
    b. Tradable permit systems;
    c. Subsidies, e.g. fiscal incentive to less polluting products; and
    d. Deposit- refund schemes;
2. **Eco-Labels:** Comprising three sub-types:
    a. Externally (i.e. state) verified, multi issue schemes ('Type I');
    b. Unverified self-declaring schemes ('Type II'); and
    c. Single-issue schemes ('Type III'). They seek to harness market forces by encouraging consumers to make more informed purchasing decisions. That said, in markets where 'green' consumerism is very strong, eco-labels may in practice steer producers in ways similar to traditional regulatory standards;
3. **Environmental Management Systems (EMS):** These include the EU's environmental management and audit system (EMAS) and the International Standardisation Organisation's (ISO) ISO 14000 series of standards, which seek to encourage industry

to behave more responsibly, but whilst differing slightly contain similar provisions for environmental impact auditing, developing international environmental management systems to monitor and (where possible) reduce impacts, and provide stakeholders with a regular statement of activities. In response a company is granted official confirmation (or logo) by a recognised authority, which they can use in public materials. Although voluntary, market pressure can force participation, as can government requirements, which are often linked to another lighter, regulatory regime;

4. **Voluntary Agreements:** These can include negotiated agreements, which are formal contracts, not necessary binding, but requiring public disclosure, negotiated between industry and public authorities to address a specific problem (e.g. pollutant emissions); public voluntary schemes are usually developed by public bodies like ISO and the EU, defining particular performance criteria and other conditions of membership, and which might some EMSs; and unilateral commitments, consisting of general statements and promises made by individual companies or industry associations, increasingly containing social-responsibility elements regarding corporate activities (Jordan, Wurzel, & Zito, 2005).

Since the Rio Earth Summit, a range of global programmes have continued to promote sustainable business practices, including the Global Compact 2000, Millennium Summit 2001, and the 2002 Johannesburg World Summit on Sustainable Development ('Rio Plus Ten'). All of these are based on the normative preference for voluntary, self-regulated standards created by the corporate players themselves (Clapp, 2005). In effect, sustainable practice related to and managed by these programmes is self-managed and self-regulated at the corporate (firm) level. Questions have been asked as to how effective this method of self-governance and regulation is on regulating, managing and ensuring scrupulous practice in particular 'greenwash' and outrageous claims about practice (Parto, 1999). The term greenwash refers to misleading consumers over your business' environmental practices either by unscrupulous and deceptive claims, by non-disclosure of un-environmental practices and by diluting poor practice by using an unrelated claim to promote positive practice and benefit your business. It is also important to note the global trade environment in which such schemes were developed, especially the influence of Uruguay Round of negotiations and the creation of the World Trade Organisation. Here, voluntary process (as opposed to product) standards were encouraged as a means of addressing environmental concerns without violating trade rules. These have been portrayed as seeking to pre-empt the proliferation of national environmental laws, which, it was seen, could act as barriers to trade (Raines, 2003). The problem with the voluntary approach is that it often fails to deal with intractable, or non-compliant, entities (May, 2005). Substantive targets may be watered down during the course of negotiations. In this case, extensive monitoring, reporting and verification are necessary to provide an option for successful implementation (Skjærseth, Stokke, & Wettestad, 2006).

Given the need for monitoring and reporting there is now a growing corporate trend for reporting on environmental and social performance, often referred to as 'sustainability reporting'. In the absence of governmental regulation (often the case in developing countries), global businesses wishing to demonstrate their credentials have come to rely increasingly on the idea of corporate social responsibility (CSR). There are a range of schemes, such as Private Voluntary Organization Standards, the Global Sullivan Principles, the OECD Guidelines for Multinational Enterprises and the International Non-Governmental Organizations Accountability Charter – to name but a few. Then there is the International Standardisation Organisation's (ISO) 26000 series for corporate responsibility, and the competitor Social Accountability International (SAI) SA8000 standards. This vast array of schemes has resulted in a growing consulting industry to assist with implementation. These too vary in organisational type, and are located in both the business and non-profit sectors. There is also a further collection of think tanks, institutions, forums and other associations that seek to lobby, comment, and provide assistance on matters of sustainable development, including investment. There are also watchdogs, and other activist organisations that are seeking to raise awareness regarding the activities of corporations that may or may not have responsibility standards in place, and are simply engaging in 'greenwashing' (Waddock, 2008).

Nevertheless, the move to self-regulation is to be interpreted as not simply due to industry opportunism seeking to undermine regulatory systems to the lowest common denominator. Some companies are in fact developing international standards that exceed the requirements of national legislation. Instead, self-regulation is seen as further evidence of the changing nature of global environmental politics, particularly, as noted before, in the increasing use of collective mechanisms addressing issues of policy. Three discrete actor groups have been associated with self-regulation: civil-society, which favours advocacy initiatives on behalf of specific sectors; industry, which prefers to set its own standards; and traditional government-led regulation at the regional, national and local levels. All three models are in addition to the various international institutions created to deal with common problems among countries. It is therefore important to add the caveat that although self-regulation is seen as having the potential to encourage significant improvements, traditional political approaches continue (Haufler, 2001). So what is the best mechanism for managing and reporting claims of sustainability, and why it is important to advance our knowledge and practice of these systems? The chapter proceeds to offer discussion on the types of governance mechanisms, case practices and green claims requiring monitoring to support the need for further discussion in this area.

Global Environmental Governance Frameworks: Public or Private?

Understanding the nature of governance frameworks can assist in the understanding of the external forces at play and the needs of the green sustainable movement in developing appropriate governance mechanisms. The developments of the 1990s led to revisiting of the 'regime' concept of international policy, away from the commonly-recognised 'hard' law arrangement of a single international legal convention implemented by national governments. Policy scholars now emphasise the role being played by 'soft' law, such as non-legally binding instruments and conclude that private governance has become a reality that few can deny (Humphreys, 2006). Private governance is also to be closely related to processes of economic globalisation and a concurrent restructuring of the functions of the state; whilst corporations continue to lobby governments through traditional processes based around multilateral environmental agreements (MEAs), these firms also interact with each other and other private actors, including civil society, as well as the state, giving rise to governance arrangements that resemble the public governing functions of states and intergovernmental institutions. These interactions which should be distinguished from mere co-operation, which is ad hoc and short-lived, since it has arisen out of a context in which interaction is of a more permanent and institutionalised nature (Falkner, 2003).

Designating all such types of governance as 'private' is over-simplistic, however, as it ignores the rapid development of systems of international authority, which are not driven by the state. The loss of state authority, including the granting of legitimacy to alternative venues of power – particularly market-based instruments – is worthy of examination in its own right. These are referred to as non-state market driven (NSMD) and were introduction in the earlier section. The state does not exercise sovereign authority in requiring adherence to non-state market-driven governance systems. Rather, a whole range of organisations make decisions as to whether to support such schemes. Participants are generally the same as in public policy making (environmental NGOs, business groups, professional and trade associations), and they act as representatives for the broader public, who grant them their authority based on their shared values. Government simply becomes an interest group. This has impacted on traditional notions of authority, which now sit alongside non-state and shared private/public concepts. Whilst it is not yet clear if non-state systems will complement or challenge the nation state, or if the nation-state will seek to simply absorb the phenomenon in some way, non-state systems mark a radical departure from the traditional model of public policy (Cashore, Auld, & Newsom, 2004).

Participants in private governance include the same members as in public policy making (NGOs, business groups, professional and trade associations), and they act on behalf of the broader public, who grant them their authority based on their representational nature and shared values. Government under this system simply becomes an interest group (Warren, 2002; Cashore, Auld, & Newsom, 2004). But the fact that there are now so many players and conflicting standards on the scene is resulting in confusion. Beyond the expectation that corporations should be accountable, responsible, transparent, and ecologically sustainable there is less clarity over what other governance arrangements underpin CSR.

While accountability and transparency are acknowledged as the place to begin the development of stakeholder relations the end point is not yet clear. Perhaps the most important current discussion debate is about who can be seen as a 'stakeholder'. In traditional corporate governance the term is almost the same as 'shareholder'. As the influence of non-government organisations (NGOs) and other interests increases, the definition becomes more encompassing. There is also an acceptance that local the community and citizenry, private businesses, governments, workers, regulatory bodies, and joint venture partners and so forth, all make up a corporation's stakeholder base. Although the first responsibility of a board is to its shareholders, a broader view of stakeholders adds value and helps avoid risk. This level of collaboration model has changed the relationships between businesses, NGOs and governments, and these interactions are generating a new goods and services, of which market-based environmental mechanisms are one such example (GGCF and IFC undated).

The Importance of Accreditation, Certification, and Verification

The most credible way for any firm to communicate their claims regarding sustainability practices is to gain some form of accreditation, often through a process of assessment and the issuing of a certificate attesting to compliance with a set of claims. The aim of certification is to provide assurance that sustainability claims and practices are credible and genuine. Certification has arisen as a means for attesting to the claims made in the market regarding the specific attributes of a given product. It has been described as 'a process, which results in a written quality statement (a certificate) attesting to the origin of [the] material and its status and/or qualifications following validation by an independent third party' (Baharuddin & Simula, as cited in Lammerts van Beuren & Blom, 1997). Certification is often undertaken against standards, which act as a mechanism for demonstrating sustainability and green claims with these standards forming the basis for monitoring and reporting against those claims, and as point of reference for assessment of actual management (Lammerts van Beuren & Blom, 1997).

Certification is a voluntary initiative, and not all companies that make claims are certified. Even ISO, a leader in global management standards has only one standard in the 14000 series, ISO 14001, designed for registration (another term for certification) by a third party. Even with 14001 a company can use the specification for internal guidance only, or for self-declaration purposes, and may choose not to seek third party verification. ISO 14001 has five main sets of requirements: the adoption of an environmental policy supported by top management (commitment and policy); the formulation of a plan to fulfil the policy (planning); allocation of responsibilities and associated training and awareness raising (implementation); development of a system for checking, correcting, monitoring, reporting and preventing environmental impacts (measurement and evaluation); and the establishment of management review and associated continuous improvement processes (Tibor & Feldman, 1996). The provision of a label demonstrating the claims of the certification programme made, and appended to the given products is often part of a certification programme. ISO 14020 (goals and principles of all environmental labelling) was released in 1998 (Parto, 1999).

Is in the forestry sector that some of the most advanced examples of certification exist. It serves as a good example of sustainability certification, and represents a specific form of private governance to address growing public concerns about environmental degradation (Pattberg, 2005). During its development in the 1990s timber certification was forced to confront 'the difficulties with implementing credible certification programmes, as well as the challenges involved in the operation of reliable accreditation systems, capable of efficiently assessing potential certifiers, and of adequately monitoring their activities' (Centeno, as cited in Romeijn, 1999, p. 12). It also typifies the common problem amongst private governance of inconsistency in standards. Firstly, it is quite possible that standards developed for monitoring and reporting environmental performance internationally or nationally, will not be compatible with those, which assess the quality on the ground, for example at the forest management unit (FMU) level in the case of timber certification (or the farm in the case of organic certification). There are competing schemes, and claims over quality of the certification programme used. The requirements imposed by these different types of standard makes the comparison of one with another difficult (Lammerts van Beuren & Blom, 1997). A good example of this is the rivalry between the Forest Stewardship Council (FSC) a timber certification and labelling scheme initiated and supported by non-governmental interests, and the Programme for the Endorsement of Forest Certification, initiated by industry (Cadman, 2011).

Governments and local councils are also offering incentives-based support to sustainable practice through procurement programmes such as ECO-Buy in the Australian state of Victoria, established in 2000 as a recycling alliance among local councils, which has now expanded to encourage other governments and businesses to buy sustainable products. Once a firm has adopted procurement practices, they can then use these to further develop supply chain practices, and develop their own schemes and related quality standards for accreditation (Kanellos & Valos, 2010)

It is often expected that certifiers themselves should be accredited, although this depends on the certification scheme. Accreditation can be by national accreditation bodies, or regionally via such agencies as the European Co-operation for Accreditation (EA), or at the international level via the International Accreditation Forum or other bodies. ISO Guide 61 has been adopted by a number of certification schemes as the standard protocol for third parties seeking accreditation under a given programme (PEFC, 2005). The 'Good Environmental Choice' Organisation as a further example offers accreditation to firms who offer environmentally sound products. The firm first tests the products over the full lifecycle and awards the label/brand the certification. There is a tendency that only 20% of products are awarded with most of the 80 products that have qualified, manufactured by SMEs seeking to differentiate their products from those of competitors. This certification carries a fee for certification and an annual license fee for using the award and label.

A relationship has been established between accountability and transparency of environmental management and the need for independent monitoring, assessment and reporting (Bernstein, 2005). Managing and controlling sustainable practices to ensure quality and legitimacy will therefore be one of the many challenges facing the emerging 'green' economy. Civil society stakeholders in particular have played an essential role in opening up global business practice, and have forced various institutions to increase their visibility by publishing information. They have also pushed for the development and implementation of mechanisms for monitoring and controlling activities, which are essential in view of the current preference for voluntarism (Scholte, 2004). Quality and legitimacy of governance in market-driven systems has consequently become a preoccupation amongst a number of governance scholars (Cadman 2011; 2013).

CASE STUDIES: EMISSIONS TRADING – THE CLEAN DEVELOPMENT MECHANISM AND REDD+

Emissions trading is market-based approach to controlling pollution through economic incentives to achieve reductions in human-induced atmospheric pollution (Stavins, 2001). Carbon trading refers to the trading of emissions of six of the main greenhouse gases including carbon dioxide (CO_2) and is a market-based instrument to mitigate climate change (Perdan & Azapagic, 2011). Emissions Trading Schemes (ETS) differ in scale, coverage and architecture, but a common approach is to 'offset' existing emissions (often in developed countries) by purchasing emissions reductions gained elsewhere (often in developing countries). AS elaborated below, they can be either voluntary, sometimes referred to as a voluntary carbon offset (VCO) or mandatory such as the certified emissions reduction (CER), they all share a general approach: reducing emissions where the cost is the lowest, thereby minimising the overall economic burden associated with combating climate change. In contrast to other approaches to pollution mitigation, ETS require more stringent institutional and regulatory architecture.

As a total system, markets trading in greenhouse gas (GHG) are heavily impacted by uncertainty and change in regulatory frameworks (Mehling, 2009). As the number of voluntary market schemes have increased it appears that a mix of approaches and types of governance systems functioning at different spatial and temporal scales are necessary if markets are to function effectively and deliver emissions reductions (Ingram & Wilkie, 2008). If the operation or features of emissions trading changes in one jurisdiction, this may have consequences for the price discovery and operation of markets in all other jurisdictions (Flachsland, Marschinski, & Edenhofer, 2009). Governance arrangements underlying IET must therefore include regulatory mechanisms that provide assurance that joint systems will remain compatible over time (Mehling, 2009). Although ETS primarily rely on market forces, they also require clearly defined objectives and stringent enforcement if they are to be effective.

The variety of private/public/hybrid sustainability initiatives is investigated here in two case studies: the Clean Development Mechanism (CDM) largely initiated as a consequence of intergovernmental climate negotiations arising from the Kyoto Protocol; and Reducing Emissions from Deforestation and Forest Degradation (REDD+) one of the policy instruments under development for the second commitment period under the Kyoto Protocol of the United Nations

Framework Convention on Climate Change (UNFCCC). CDM and REDD+ are examples of emissions reduction schemes designed to accredit new activities than demonstrably reduce GHG emissions. These case studies both concern themselves with forest-management, although CDM also permits industrial developments, and are reliant on the governmental regulatory frameworks for basic levels of compliance, but they are driven by differing strategic objectives. One of the main challenges confronting market mechanisms such as CDM and REDD+ is whether institutional and operation governance will be given sufficient weight so that the structural and procedural aspects stakeholder involvement are as meaningful as possible (Lederer, 2011). Quality of governance, and institutional legitimacy is ultimately based on the level of collaboration between actors solving collective action problems, in this case, anthropogenic climate change (Cadman, 2013). The following section highlights the specifics of each of the cases.

Clean Development Mechanism (CDM)

In 1992 UNFCCC and the subsequent COP raised concerns about stabilizing GHG concentrations in the atmosphere. The Kyoto Protocol, adopted at the third COP in 1997, was to be a milestone as for the first time the majority of developed countries realised they were responsible for past emissions and accepted legally binding caps on GHG emissions. The Kyoto Protocol set legally binding GHG reduction targets of at least 5.2% of 1990 levels by the first commitment period (2008-2012). To achieve this collective target of 5.2%, each developed country (more appropriately Annex B countries of the Kyoto Protocol) was given a specific GHG emissions target. The European Union agreed to reduce emissions by 8%, Canada and Japan by 6% while Australia was generously allowed to increase GHG emissions by 8% of 1990 levels in the first commitment period. To meet this target in a cost-effective manner, the Protocol adopted three flexible market-based mechanisms: Emissions Trading, Joint Implementation and Clean Development Mechanism (CDM). Of them, CDM was the only mechanism that linked developed and developing countries, and it was the first global environmental investment and credit scheme of its kind. The main objective of CDM is to help developed countries to meet their quantified emission reductions obligations at lower cost, while helping developing countries in achieving sustainable development. The CDM offered an opportunity to make progress simultaneously on climate, development, and local environmental issues for developing countries; otherwise, they may be preoccupied with immediate economic and social needs (UNEP, 2003. 'Annex B' countries and their eligible companies can invest in CDM projects in developing countries, or purchase CERs. As an aspect of meeting a country's overall emissions reduction target under the Kyto protocol, CERs can consequently been seen as being more along the mandatory continuum, while VCOs – often constructed from projects that do not meet the strict requirements of the CDM – are more voluntary. Over 80% of CDM markets investors are United Kingdom (27.68%), Switzerland (20.35%), Netherlands (11.90%), Japan (11.54%), Sweden (6.33%) and Germany (5.77%) (Maraseni, 2013).

CDM projects have historically been highly concentrated in limited countries. About 74% of the total CDM projects are in China, India, Brazil and Mexico). These are the financially highly capable emerging countries that can easily afford emission reduction projects through their own efforts. In fact, in several COPs they are asked to oblige for legally binding targets. Several other developing countries, where CDM projects are badly needed, have insignificant number of CDM projects. In that sense, there is no regional balance and no equitable distribution of CDM projects. Over 70% of the total expected annual CER comes from China and India. The total amount of money invested for all CDM projects is estimated at

Table 1. Comparison of governance quality and institutional legitimacy: CDM, REDD+

Scheme	Criteria of Governance Quality				Legitimacy Rating
	Interest Representation	Organisational Responsibility	Decision Making	Implementation	
CDM	Medium	Low	Medium	Medium	Medium
REDD+	High	Medium	High	High	High

Source: Cadman &Maraseni (2011).

almost US$95 billion, of which China and India accounts US$50.4 billion and US$18.9 billion, respectively (Seres, 2008).

Reducing Emissions from Deforestation and Forest Degradation (REDD+)

REDD addresses the problem of climate change via a range of state and non-state market-based mechanisms to encourage sustainable management of tropical forests via a series of payments from developed to developing countries and thereby reduce GHG. It is now formally referred to as REDD+ in the wake of the UNFCCC COP 15 in Copenhagen, to reflect the initiative's growing emphasis on conserving and enhancing forests on the basis of their value for carbon sequestration, rather than simply reducing emissions (Parker, Mitchell, Trivedi, & Mardas, 2009). It is linked to the Kyoto Protocol (KP) and the Protocol-related CDM as it offers developing countries a means of meeting their emissions targets through reducing GHG emissions and increasing GHG sinks (i.e. forests) in developing countries (CIFOR, 2010).

The concept of REDD+ is still evolving, but Parties to the UNFCCC have agreed that REDD+ will be part of the future global climate framework. While negotiators are still to agree on the funding arrangements for REDD+ activities, most countries appear to be of the view that carbon markets will make an important contribution to REDD+. REDD+ thus seeks to at least partly correct the market failure underlying deforestation (i.e. the failure of markets to value most forest ecosystems services) by putting a value on the role that forests play in stabilising climates. REDD+ aims to deliver performance-based payments to forest owners and managers in developing countries who protect and/or enhance forest carbon stocks. At this stage REDD+ 'pilot' projects consist of a mix of public projects (i.e. funded by developed country governmental donors) and private initiatives (funded by non-governmental organisations and philanthropic ventures). It is important to note that millions of people live in and next to forests worldwide, and their involvement in REDD+ development, implementation and governance is key to its success (Cadman, 2013b).

Comparison of Governance Quality and Institutional Legitimacy: CDM, REDD+

Table 1 depicts a comparison of the schemes, based on four criteria that overall contribute to governance legitimacy. In the absence of clear and overarching sustainability objectives (which have yet to be finalised in REDD+, and which remain disputed in CDM) a governance analysis can provide a useful surrogate method for evaluating institutional performance in the sustainability arena.

CURRENT PRACTICE AND DESIGN: CASE APPLICATION

Business contributes to sustainable consumption through the manufacture of goods and services that are more ecologically efficient and durable, using fair trade practices and ensuring an economic benefit to the community (Tukker et al., 2006; Peattie & Charter, 1994). The integration of sustainable procurement and manufacture into service design is fundamental to firms for creating a 'greenscape' that delivers sustainable products, and also aids promotional claims to consumers (Jones, Hillier, Comfort, & Eastwood, 2005). Service design transects many functional departments including marketing, finance, operations, human resource, research and development and information technology, with the aim of coordinating and delivering ideas to the market place. Environmentally responsible business practice takes into account consumer concerns about conserving the natural environment. In particular, 'green' marketing campaigns highlight the superior environmental protection characteristics of a company's products and services. The sorts of characteristics usually highlighted include such things as reduced waste in packaging, increased energy efficiency of the product in use, reduced use of chemicals in farming, or decreased release of toxic emissions and other pollutants in production. Sustainable design seeks to reduce negative impacts on the environment, and promote the health and comfort of stakeholders in the supply chain.

Coupling this with the distinct objectives of traditional services design, sustainability service design firms can offer efficient, productive and quality products from a 'green' ideology. Although this is not yet mainstream, many big companies are now implementing the triple bottom line into activity reporting and embedding corporate social responsibility requirements across their supply chains. Procurement policies can have a significant impact on a company's environmental footprint, given that somewhere between 50 and 70 percent of a company's overall costs originate from purchasing, procurement policy has become important for firms seeking to demonstrate their commitment to sustainability. A good procurement policy – including aligning with suppliers and intermediaries – integrates sustainably sourced resources into the manufacturing chain (Joyce, Green, & Winch, 2006). Enhancing indoor environments at the individual office/manufactory level further reduces non-renewable energy consumption at all supply chain points; minimising water and using environmentally preferable products in-house are also popular strategic choices. Adopting delivery practices within a sustainability framework also often forms the basis of sustainability claims. Sustainable manufacture and process flow and small incremental changes can make a large difference to the environment and will flow on to other areas of the supply chain. Sustainable distribution is about being efficient, timely and cost effective, and supporting the sustainability agenda with sustainable distribution focusing on storage and movement of goods in a way that supports continued economic growth while protecting the environment and delivering a better quality of life for future generations. Finally, firms are also adopting sustainable retailing as a means of demonstrating good practice with consumers, who are willing to spend more for products from firms retailing 'green' brands (Tukker et al., 2006). Depending on the sector and type of firm product and or service, how the sustainability message is framed will be very diverse in both interpretation and practice.

The case studies discussed in the chapter, demonstrate a diverse approach to governance of claims and practices, and as indicated, how each model conceives of authority and legitimacy is similarly differentiated. It is perhaps worthwhile remembering at this point that both systems arose in the context of UNCED where sustainable development was identified as major objective of *Agenda 21*. In terms of climate change, *Agenda 21* was initially aimed at protection of the atmosphere (Chapter 9), but the means of achieving this objective came to be increasingly couched, particularly through the UNFCCC processes, in terms of mitigating (and subsequently adapting to) climate change. Here, it is possible to see that the sustainable management of forests under REDD+ is seen as including social and environmental, as well as economic considerations.

The examples used offer support for the differences in interpretation and practice and the argument that governance of sustainability claims is a difficult one and that no one system is perfect. The general public should be cautious about initiatives, which promote themselves on the basis of their internally generated values. Rather, they should look to see who was involved in standards setting, and whether there is widespread stakeholder support for the programme in question.

CHALLENGES CONFRONTING MARKET-BASED SUSTAINABILITY INITIATIVES

Divergence in Governance Quality between Sustainability Systems

In the context of the case studies, it might be concluded that REDD+ provides the greatest quality of governance, and that investors should be more cautious about CDM. However, REDD+ is still in its early stages of development, and has not yet been fully tested in the market. What might be observed is the evolution in global environmental instruments over time: CDM is in many ways a 'first generation' scheme, while REDD+ has had the benefit of learning from the governance short-comings of CDM. Here it should be noted that The UNFCCC explicitly recognised the importance of good forest governance for REDD+. In the Cancún Agreements (Decision 1/CP.16) at COP 16 in 2010 UNFCCC acknowledged the need for "transparent and effective…governance structures" (Appendix I, 2.(b)) (UNFCCC, 2011). But it is difficult to draw any definitive conclusions without a large-scale empirical study – particularly if it is to be argued that there is a causal relationship between governance quality and effectiveness on the ground. Any future analytical studies into the legitimacy of sustainable development mechanisms would require a greater number of institutional types to determine if the trends identified here are correct.

Clearly, CDM and REDD+ have opted to address the 'problem' of climate change through the 'solution' of sustainable development in different ways, and with divergent strategic objectives. In the case of CDM, the original aim of reducing emissions by tackling the unsustainable levels of GHG has been partially obscured by a greater level of uptake in the arguably relatively well-developed countries of China and India, compared to the 'ultra poor' countries (such as Bangladesh) where CDM projects are desperately needed. For REDD+, greater emphasis was placed on poorer developed countries, and preliminary funding was targeted more effectively. In the case of CDM, there is a strong link to the industries of the developed world and their governments. This is true for REDD+ as well, but given the greater emphasis on transparency and accountability post COP-15, there is a greater inclusion of, and recognition given to, non-state actors such as civil society organisations, and Indigenous peoples' organisations, not just business. In a sense the two programmes can be seen as 'old' and 'new' examples of global environmental governance. This variability relates also to how each system conceives its contribution to sustainability.

Both CDM and REDD+ also have their own sets of external constraints, the most notable being their market-based orientation, and their location in the developing countries, with all the ethical problems that payments from developed countries to offset their own emissions entail. Whether they will assist or hinder action on reducing emissions and contributing to sustainable development over the longer term is not yet clear.

Reflection 2: Why We Need Controls – Greenwash, Deception, and Its Implications

The perception that the sustainable market place is organised and offers many alternatives for quality management and assurance, is not the case. Overall governance mechanisms are required to assist businesses to make the successful transition to being a sustainable provider, and avoid the detrimental effects of greenwash. Communicating to consumers the truth about a firm's philosophy and how each claim is integrated and beneficial will avoid the greenwash backlash. Overall, good design practice that adopts the philosophy will create both a sustainable market and a profitable and beneficial outcome for the firm.

Regulation of content and green claims applies to all forms of advertising and practice and to all sectors irrespective of diversity, including claims on packaging, labelling and in advertising and promotions in all mediums. If a firm chooses to make environmental claims such as the forestry cases about their business or product, they should be clearly and accurately explained and justified by scientific research. Business should provide enough information to not appear to be not 'telling the whole truth' or be subjective to large disparity across the industry sector. When a firm compares the environmental benefits of competitor products/firms, enough information must be provided to consumers so they can make relevant decisions. The basis for comparison must be sufficiently clear and substantiated by scientific test results. A marketing claim such as 'This bottle contains 20% more recycled content than our previous is preferable to the more ambiguous 'This bottle contains 20% more recycled content than our previous package' is preferable to the more ambiguous 'This bottle contains 20% more recycled content'. The complexity of the audience characteristics, the scientific foundation of environmental practice and the nature of firms to 'spin' away from negative or detrimental practice and emphasize good practice strengthen the practice of greenwash as a tool used by unethical firms, and position verification programmes and trade acts as positive systems to manage sustainability claims. Greenwash is one of the many reasons why examination and development of governance and verification of green practice is warranted.

There is an argument voluntary accreditation programmes are little more than 'greenwash' doing little to improve members' performance (Potoski & Prakash, 2005). These critics suggest there are substantial benefits for industry in adopting externally verifiable standards. Businesses then would have an obligation not to engage in any conduct that is likely to mislead or deceive consumers, with this obligation governed by penalties and breaches (such as losing certification) regulated by the system. The current Trade Practices Act (TPA) in Australia suggests that content does not actually have to mislead anyone; it only needs to appear that it could mislead or deceive. This type of regulated act and terminology can be especially relevant to claims regarding recycled and recyclable content or the environmental impact of components used in the product. The TPA requires that a business's not represent that goods or services have sponsorship, approval, performance characteristics, accessories, uses or benefits they do not have, this can also be interpreted to relate to environmental claims.

With respect to the discussions above and the case studies it is possible that in the absence of clear and overarching sustainability objectives, a governance-based analytical approach could act as a useful surrogate when evaluating institutional performance in the sustainability arena. When consistently formulated and applied such an approach has the potential to be applied at all spatial levels – global, regional, national, and local (Lammerts van Beuren & Blom, 1997). A further advantage of a governance-based evaluation, as summarised in Table 1, is that such an approach allows for the creation of standards that can serve as a reference for monitoring, assessment in a manner that is not merely based on internal claims made by the organisation itself.

Reflection 3: All Claims Should Be Monitored – But Who Watches the Watchdog?

Sustainability claims relate to all areas of the supply chain and product development and these have been raised as areas warranting monitoring and attention. The practices of 'green' seals and logos, recyclable and recycled products, corporate social responsibility (CSR) initiatives, organic textiles and food products, 'natural' products, carbon 'neutral' products, renewable products, chemical free products, green building codes and building products, 'green' packaging products–all should be accredited and regularly audited via third-party certification which itself should also monitored and accredited. Part of the problem is the structural tension inherent in the role of the certification bodies. By being deliberately set apart and independent of the programmes they are accrediting, there is at best a weak link in 'vertical' accountability to scheme members. There are also 'horizontal' accountability issues, since it is questionable how much certification bodies are really answerable to the broader public at large. It could also be argued there is a transparency problem, due to the relationships between the certifiers, their clients and the bodies whose standards they are implementing. The exact nature of the relationship is not always clear to the broader public due to commercial-in-confidence requirements, resulting in the potential for conflicts of interest.

Qualifications and disclosures should be sufficiently clear and prominent to prevent deception with environmental claims clear as to whether they apply to the product, the package, or a component of the business or some other member and practice within the supply chain. Claims need to be qualified with regard to minor, incidental components of the product or package and the degree of compliance and integration into the green design. Environmental claims should not overstate the environmental attribute or benefit and marketers should avoid implying a significant environmental benefit where the benefit is, in fact, negligible. Several countries and industry sectors have produced guides for operation. Such guides suggest campaigns must comply with existing laws and policies. Self-regulatory bodies, consumer groups and trade commissions most often establish these laws and policies. These guides suggest marketers need to develop and review scientific substantiation for advertising claims and conduct a comprehensive review of advertising guidelines, promotional materials, and marketing campaigns to ensure that environmental claims are not deceptive or misleading to consumers. Moreover, most of these guides suggest regulatory developments relating to green issues should occur at local, state, federal, and international levels – and should be monitored by an overarching body.

Reflection 4: The Relevance of Regional Systems

How 'regional' is understood should be seen in the context of contemporary developments around state sovereignty and non-spatial authority. This is particularly the case with trans-boundary pollutants, such as greenhouse gasses. The world order can no longer be conceived as purely state-centric or even primarily state governed, as authority has become increasingly diffused among public and private agencies at the local, national, regional and global levels (Held, McGrew, Goldblatt, & Perraton, 1999). These arrangements are exemplified by the growing number of social-environmental, market-based initiatives built around the concept of sustainable development. A fundamental shift is occurring in the national and international public/private sector balance (Hansen & Schrader, 1997), which is delivering opportunities for civil society and corporations to play a key role.

In the case of emissions trading, there is an inter-relationship between the international (i.e. intergovernmental), regional (supra-national, such as the EU), national and project-specific (often local) levels. Good governance of these various levels and systems are necessary if risks to sellers and buyers in carbon markets are to be avoided. International emissions trading (IET) therefore needs at least some basic level of common understanding regarding governance and regulation, even if these commonalities are expressed differently in various systems. Once ETS are integrated at the international level through some form of common approach, domestic regulations – Community-wide in the case of the EU – will need to accommodate the requirements of the 'higher' system (Jaffe & Stavins, 2007). The very nature of global warming makes it impossible to escape the necessity of multi-level, and multi-stakeholder, collaboration – and acknowledge the importance of all levels, macro, meso, and micro, in solving the problem of human-induced climate change.

CONCLUSION

It is clear that the world is facing a range of pressing environmental problems, and the market is becoming an ever-important mechanism trying to resolve some of these issues. But these mechanisms exist in a competitive environment, where the rules are largely ad-hoc and self-determined – albeit with some recognition of, and compliance with, existing governmental regulation. There is a clear need for the creation of governance standards as a means to demonstrate to consumers how 'kosher' a given environmental product really is. Moreover using these standards will increase consumer confidence when firms make green claims. Such standards will also make it easier for stakeholders to evaluate if they should participate in a given green scheme, or not. This will avert some of the uncertainties amongst key interests as to whether involvement in a particular programme endows it with an undeserved degree of legitimacy. Given the government-to governance transition apparent in market-driven sustainability initiatives, such standards could complement existing national regulatory frameworks, and help avoid potential crises of confidence in the future.

REFERENCES

Arts, B. (2006). Non-state Actors in Global Governance: New Arrangements Beyond the State. In M. Koenig-Archibugi & M. Zürn (Eds.), *New Modes of Governance in the Global System: Exploring Publicness, Delegation and Inclusiveness* (pp. 177–200). Basingstoke, London: Palgrave Macmillan.

Baharuddin, H. G., & Simula, M. (1996). Timber certification in transition. Study on the development in the formulation and implementation of certification schemes for all internationally traded timber and timber products. Yokohama, Japan: International Tropical Timber Organization (ITTO).

Bernstein, J. (2005). Sustainable Development Governance Challenges in the New Millennium. In M. Berglund (Ed.), *International Environmental Law-making and Diplomacy Review 2004* (pp. 31–50). Joensuu: University of Joensuu, Department of Law.

Cadman, T. (2011). *Quality and Legitimacy of Global Governance: Case Lessons from Forestry*. Basingstoke: Palgrave Macmillan. doi:10.1057/9780230306462

Cadman, T. (2013). Applying an Empirical Evaluation to the Governance Legitimacy of Carbon Offset Mechanisms on the Basis of Stakeholder Perceptions. In T. Cadman (Ed.), *Climate Change and Global Policy Regimes: Towards Institutional Legitimacy* (pp. 79–95). Basingstoke: Palgrave Macmillan. doi:10.1057/9781137006127.0012

Cadman, T. (Ed.). (2013b). *Climate Change and Global Policy Regimes: Towards Institutional Legitimacy*. Basingstoke: Palgrave Macmillan. doi:10.1057/9781137006127

Cadman, T., & Marseni, T. (2011). The Governance of Climate Change: Evaluating the Governance Quality and Legitimacy of the United Nations' REDD-plus Programme. *International Journal of Climate Change: Impacts and Responses*, *2*(3), 103–124.

Cashore, B., Auld, G., & Newsom, D. (2004). *Governing Through Markets: Forest Certification and the Emergence of Non-State Authority*. New Haven, London: Yale University Press.

Chavan, M. (2005). An appraisal of environment management systems. *Management of Environmental Quality*, *16*(5), 444–463. doi:10.1108/14777830510614321

Christensen, T. H., Godskesen, M., Gram-Hassen, K., Quitzau, M., & Ropke, I. (2007). Greening the Danes? Experience with consumption and environment policies. *Journal of Consumer Policy*, *30*(2), 91–116. doi:10.1007/s10603-007-9029-2

CIFOR. (Centre for International Forestry research) (2010). *Simply REDD: CIFOR's Guide to Forests, Climate Change and REDD*. Bogor: CIFOR. Retrieved October 1, 2010, from www.cifor.cgiar.org/publications/pdf_files/.../Media-Guide_REDD.pdf

Clapp, J. (2005). Global Environmental Governance for Corporate Responsibility and Accountability. *Global Environmental Politics*, *5*(3), 23–34. doi:10.1162/1526380054794916

Connolly, J., & Prothero, A. (2003). Sustainable Consumption: Consumption, Consumers and the Commodity Discourse. *Consumption Markets & Culture*, *6*(4), 275–291. doi:10.1080/1025386032000168311

Daub, C., & Ergenzinger, R. (2005). Enabling sustainable management through a new multi-disciplinary concept of customer satisfaction. *European Journal of Marketing*, *39*(9/10), 998–1217. doi:10.1108/03090560510610680

Dolan, P. (2002). The Sustainability of 'Sustainable Consumption'. *Journal of Macromarketing*, *22*(2), 170–181. doi:10.1177/0276146702238220

Falkner, R. (2003). Private Environmental Governance and International Relations: Exploring the Links. *Global Environmental Politics*, *3*(2), 72–87. doi:10.1162/152638003322068227

Flachsland, C., Marschinski, R., & Edenhofer, O. (2009). To link or not to link: Benefits and disadvantages of linking cap-and-trade systems. *Climate Policy*, *9*(4), 358–372. doi:10.3763/cpol.2009.0626

Hansen, U., & Schrader, U. (1997). A Modern Model of Consumption for a Sustainable Society. *Journal of Consumer Policy*, *20*(4), 443–468. doi:10.1023/A:1006842517219

Haufler, V. (2001). *A Public Role for the Private Sector: Industry Self-regulation*. Washington, DC: Carnegie Endowment for International Peace.

Held, D., McGrew, A. G., Goldblatt, D., & Perraton, J. (1999). *Global Transformations: Politics, Economics and Culture*. London: Polity Press.

Humphreys, D. (2006). *Logjam: Deforestation and the Crisis of Global Governance*. London: Earthscan.

Ingram, J. C., & Wilkie, D. (2008). Governance of the Global Carbon Market: Does Scale Matter? WCS Working Paper Series. In K. Redford & C. Grippo (Eds.), *WCS Working Paper 36, Protected Areas, Governance and Scale*. Bronx, NY: Wildlife Conservation Society.

International Institute for Sustainable Development (IISD) Reporting Services. (N.D.). *GEF STAP Considers REDD, Forest Conservation and Sustainable Forest Management*. Retrieved October 1, 2010, from http://climate-l.org/news/gef-stap-considers-redd-forest-conservation-and-sustainable-forest-management/

Jaffe, J., & Stavins, R. N. (2007). *Linking Tradable Permit Systems for Greenhouse Gas Emissions: Opportunities, Implications, and Challenges. Report prepared for the International Emissions Trading Association*. IETA.

Jones, P., Hillier, D., Comfort, D., & Eastwood, I. (2005). Sustainable Retailing and Consumerism. *Management Research News*, *28*(1), 34–33. doi:10.1108/01409170510784760

Jordan, A., Wurzel, R., & Zito, A. (2005). The Rise of 'New' Policy Instruments in Comparative Perspectives: Has Governance Eclipsed Government? *Political Studies*, *53*(3), 441–469. doi:10.1111/j.1467-9248.2005.00540.x

Joyce, P., Green, R., & Winch, G. (2006). A new construct for visualizing and designing e-fulfilment systems for quality healthcare delivery. *The TQM Magazine*, *18*(6), 638–651. doi:10.1108/09544780610707129

Kanellos, T., & Valos, M. (2010). *Green Marketing and the Green Consumer: Integrating Environmental Marketing into the Firm's Overall Business Strategy*. Faculty of Business and Law, Deakin University.

Kilbourne, W., McDonagh, P., & Prothero, A. (1997). Sustainable Consumption and Quality of Life: A Macromarketing Challenge to the Dominant Social Paradigm. *Journal of Macromarketing*, *17*(2), 4–24. doi:10.1177/027614679701700103

Kollman, K., & Prakash, A. (2002). EMS-based Environmental Regimes as Club Goods: Examining Variations in Firm-level Adoption of ISO 14001 and EMAS in U.K., U.S. and Germany. *Policy Sciences*, *35*(1), 43–67. doi:10.1023/A:1016071810725

Lammerts van Beuren, E. M., & Blom, E. M. (1997). *Hierarchical Framework For The Formulation Of Sustainable Forest Management Standards*. Leiden: The Tropenbos Foundation.

Lederer, M. (2011). From CDM to REDD+—What do we know for setting up effective and legitimate carbon governance? *Ecological Economics*, *70*(11), 1900–1907. doi:10.1016/j.ecolecon.2011.02.003

Lipschutz, R., & Mayer, J. (1996). *Global Civil Society and Global Environmental Governance: The Politics of Nature from Place to Planet*. New York: State University of New York Press.

Maraseni, T. N. (2013). Evaluating the clean development mechanism. In T. Cadman (Ed.), *Quality and Legitimacy of Global Governance: Case Lessons from Forestry* (pp. 96–110). Basingstoke: Palgrave Macmillan.

May, P. (2005). Regulation and Compliance Motivations: Examining Different Approaches. *Public Administration Review, 34*(65/1), 31-44.

McDonald, S., & Oates, C. J. (2006). Sustainability: Consumer perceptions and marketing strategies. *Business Strategy and the Environment*, *15*(3), 157–170. doi:10.1002/bse.524

Mehling, M. (2009). *Global Carbon Market Institutions: An Assessment of Governance Challenges and Functions in the Carbon Market*. Climate Strategies.

Packard, V. (1960). The Waste Makers. Penguin, Harmondsworth. In Robins, N. (1999). Making sustainability bite: Transforming global consumption patterns. *The Journal of Sustainable Product Design*, *10*, 7–15.

Parker, C., Mitchell, A., Trivedi, M., & Mardas, N. (2009). *The little REDD+ book*. Oxford: Global Canopy Programme.

Parto, S. (1999). Aiming Low. In R. B. Gibson (Ed.), *Voluntary Initiatives: The New Politics of Corporate Greening* (pp. 182–198). Peterborough, Canada: Broadview Press.

Pattberg, P. H. (2005). The Forest Stewardship Council: Risk and Potential of Private Forest Governance. *Journal of Environment & Development, 14*(3), 356–374. doi:10.1177/1070496505280062

Peattie, K., & Charter, M. (1994). Green marketing. *The Marketing Book, 5*, 726–755.

PEFC. (2005). *Certification and Accreditation Procedures*. Annex 6, version 11 April 2005.

Perdan, S., & Azapagic, A. (2011). Carbon trading: Current schemes and future developments. *Energy Policy, 39*(10), 6040–6054. doi:10.1016/j.enpol.2011.07.003

Placet, M., Anderson, R., & Fowler, K. M. (2005). Strategies for Sustainability. *Research Technology Management, 48*(5), 32–41.

Potoski, M., & Prakash, A. (2005). Green Clubs and Voluntary Governance: ISO 14001 and Firms' Regulatory Compliance. *American Journal of Political Science, 49*(2), 235–248. doi:10.1111/j.0092-5853.2005.00120.x

Raines, S. S. (2003). Perceptions of Legitimacy and Efficacy in International Environmental Management Standards: The Impact of the Participation Gap. *Global Environmental Politics, 3*(3), 47–78. doi:10.1162/152638003322469277

Robins, N. (1999). Making sustainability bite: Transforming global consumption patterns. *The Journal of Sustainable Product Design, 10*, 7–15. http://www.poptel.org.uk/iied/smg/pubs/susbite.html Retrieved July 2, 2007

Romeijn, P. (1999) *Green Gold: on Variations in Truth in Plantation Forestry*. Heelsum: Treemail.

Rosenau, J. (2003). *Distant Proximities: Dynamics Beyond Globalization*. Princeton, Oxford: Princeton University Press.

Ruggie, J. G. (2003). Taking Embedded Liberalism Global: The Corporate Connection. In D. Held & M. Koenig-Archibugi (Eds.), *Taming Globalisation: Frontiers of Governance* (pp. 93–129). Cambridge: Polity Press.

Scholte, J. A. (2004). Civil Society and Democratically Accountable Global Governance. *Government and Opposition, 39*(2), 211–233. doi:10.1111/j.1477-7053.2004.00121.x

Seres, S. (2008). *Analysis of technology transfer in CDM projects*. Bonn: UNFCCC Secretariat.

Skjærseth, J. B., Stokke, O. S., & Wettestad, J. (2006). Soft Law, Hard Law, and Effective Implementation. *Global Environmental Politics, 6*(3), 104–120. doi:10.1162/glep.2006.6.3.104

Stavins, R. N. (2001). *Experience with Market-Based Environmental Policy Instruments*. Discussion Paper 01-58. Washington, DC: Resources for the Future.

Stern, N. (2006). *Stern Review: The economics of climate change*. London: HM Treasury.

Tibor, T., & Feldman, I. (1996). *ISO 14000: A Guide to the New Environmental Management Standards*. Chicago: Irwin Professional Publishing.

Tukker, A., Cohen, M. J., de Zoysa, U., Hertwich, E., Hofstetter, P., Inaba, A., & Stø, S. et al. (2006). The Oslo Declaration on Sustainable Consumption. *Journal of Industrial Ecology, 10*(1-2), 9–14. doi:10.1162/108819806775545303

Uiterkamp, A. J. M. S., & Vlek, C. (2007). Practice and Outcomes of Multidisciplinary Research for Environmental Sustainability. *The Journal of Social Issues, 63*(1), 175–197. doi:10.1111/j.1540-4560.2007.00502.x

UN-REDD. (2010). *The UN-REDD Programme*. Retrieved March 23, 2010, from http://www.un-redd.org/UNREDDProgramme/tabid/583/language/en-US/Default.aspx

UNFCCC. (2011). Addendum. Part Two: Action taken by the Conference of the Parties at its sixteenth session. In *Proceedings of the Conference of the Parties on Its Sixteenth Session*. Retrieved from http://unfccc.int/resource/docs/2010/cop16/eng/07a01.pdf

Waddock, S. (2008). Building a New Institutional Infrastructure for Corporate Responsibility. *The Academy of Management Perspectives*, *22*(3), 87–108. doi:10.5465/AMP.2008.34587997

Warren, M. (2002). What Can Democratic Participation Mean Today? *Political Theory*, *30*(5), 677–701. doi:10.1177/009059102030005003

ADDITIONAL READING

Global Corporate Governance Forum and International Finance Corporation. (N.D.). *Stakeholder Engagement and the Board: Integrating Best Governance Practices*. Washington, DC: Global Corporate Governance Forum and International Finance Corporation.

Global Witness. (2009). *Building Confidence in REDD, Monitoring Beyond Carbon*. London: Global Witness. Retrieved February 22, 2011, from http://www.ecosystemsclimate.org/Portals/22/Reports/Building%20Confidence%20in%20REDD%20Final(En).pdf

Kjaer, A. M. (2004). *Governance*. Cambridge & Malden, MA: Polity Press.

Lopez-Casero, F., Cadman, T., & Maraseni, T. (2013). *Quality-of-governance standards for carbon emissions trading: developing REDD+ governance through a multi-stage, multi-level and multi-stakeholder approach. Discussion paper*. IGES.

Quazi, A. M. (2002). Managerial views of consumerism: A two-country comparison. *European Journal of Marketing*, *36*(1/2), 36–50. doi:10.1108/03090560210412692

KEY TERMS AND DEFINITIONS

Accreditation: The process of recognising bodies responsible for overseeing or evaluating activities against standards.

Certification: The issuing of a written document (certificate) by a recognised body attesting to compliance with a given standard.

Clean Development Mechanism: A market mechanism under the Kyoto Protocol (1997-2012) for certifying and trading in carbon emissions reduction activities in developing countries.

Governance: The structures and processes by which institutions, programmes and projects are steered or coordinated.

Market-Based Mechanisms: Policy programmes, which use the market to solve environmental problems (such as selling reductions in carbon emissions to bring down greenhouse gasses in the atmosphere; or 'eco-labelling' to encourage the purchase of 'green' products).

Reducing Emissions from Deforestation and Forest Degradation: A programme under the United Nations Framework Convention on Climate Change (UNFCCC) which provides finance for activities in developing countries aimed at reducing emissions arising from deforestation (removal of forests by land clearing and clear-fell logging) and forest degradation (reducing the quality of forests through selective clearing and logging).

Standards: Rules and guidelines for ongoing use agreed to by consensus, and approved by a recognised body, subject to periodic review.

Sustainability: Meeting the social, environmental and economic needs of present generations, without impacting negatively on future generations.

Verification: The process of ensuring that activities are compliance with standards.

Chapter 12
Development and Progress of the Mining Association of Canada's Towards Sustainable Mining Program

Michelle Edith Jarvie-Eggart
Barr Engineering, USA & University of Maryland University College, USA

ABSTRACT

Early efforts to address sustainability within the mining industry (GMI and ICMM) did not create a common set of protocols by which individual operations could be clearly ranked on their performance. Although the Global Reporting Initiative (GRI) does provide protocols for the reporting of sustainability indicators for mining operations, GRI-based reports include a letter grade based on report completeness, not performance on the actual indicators. The Mining Association of Canada's Towards Sustainable Mining (TSM) program provides protocols to address biodiversity, tailings management, crisis management, safety and health, energy/GHGs, and Aboriginal/community engagement. The TSM-based reports grade mining operation performance at implementing programs and systems to address each of these topics. Progress along these indicators tells us how well the industry is doing at addressing sustainability along each concept, and where further progress is still needed.

INTRODUCTION

Increasingly the mining industry is faced with demands to address their triple bottom line throughout the lifecycle of a mining operation. Public outcry against poor environmental and social performance in the industry can stymie the permitting process, preventing new mines from developing. Both the industry and public can benefit from an honest and realistic assessment of the social, environmental, and economic impacts of mining, and attempts to reduce and mitigate the most significant impacts. In response to public concerns surrounding the impacts of the mining industry, the Mining Association of Canada (MAC) developed a program called Towards Sustainable Mining (TSM), including sustainability indicators on which member companies of MAC are required

DOI: 10.4018/978-1-4666-8433-1.ch012

to report. This chapter provides a summary of the program, reporting results across the mining industry within Canada, the progress made by the industry since the inception of the program, and opportunities for further improvement.

BACKGROUND

With increasing global population comes ever more competition for the Earth's finite mineral resources. Unfortunately, minerals are not distributed evenly on the planet, leaving some countries comparatively richer in minerals than others. Canada is among the leading mining countries in the world. With over 3,000 companies mining in Canada, its main products include potash, sulfur, uranium, aluminum, cobalt, gem-quality diamonds, refined indium, nickel, platinum-group metals, sodium sulfate, and zinc (USGS 2011). As the world's second largest country by area, Canada has vast amounts of wilderness and roadless areas (CIA, 2009). Through Canada's Aboriginal populations of the First Nations, Inuit, and Métis, Canada also has a unique cultural heritage and connection to its natural environment. Canada's diverse society, expansive wilderness environment, and vast mineral resources have all contributed to the need for efforts to balance the social, environmental, and economic impacts of the mining industry. To better understand how these impacts can be addressed through sustainability programs, we must first revisit what it is that sustainability means.

Definitions of Sustainability

In 1983, to answer the global community's questions on how to best guide development, the United Nations convened the World Commission on Environment and Development (WCED). As the Commission was chaired by Gro Harlem Brundtland, the Prime Minister of Norway, it came to be known as the Brundtland Commission. The Brundtland Commission was created to address the growing concern "about the accelerating deterioration of the human environment and natural resources and the consequences of that deterioration for economic and social development." The Brundtland Commission's 1987 report, Our Common Future, defined sustainable development as "development that meets the needs of the present without compromising the ability of future generations to meet their own needs." This definition is considered the original, and is probably the most quoted, definition of sustainable development. It also begs the questions of whether extractive industries can ever be truly sustainable.

The act of mining a finite resource results in an ever dwindling amount available for future generations to consume. Some mined materials can be reused. Recycling of metals can help to maintain the amount of total metal available for the use of future generations. But mined fuels are consumed in their use, such as coal and bituminous oil sands, leaving less available for future needs. It is obvious that the extraction of finite resources cannot continue indefinitely. At some theoretical point in time, all available mineral resources could be mined. How then, can the term sustainability, be applied to the mining industry? The answer lies in the evolution of the concept of sustainability, as it is applied to the business world.

John Elkington is often credited with the integration of sustainability concerns into the business world. Traditionally, business has only concerned itself with the economic bottom line as a measure of success. In his 1998 book, Cannibals with Forks: the Triple Bottom Line of 21st Century Business, John Elkington coined the phrase "Triple Bottom Line" (TBL) as a new means of accounting. Elkington advised for an expansion of the traditional accounting framework to consider environmental and social performance in addition to the traditional business metric of financial performance. The triple bottom line includes the three elements (or pillars) of sustainability as environment, economy, and society, which must all be considered for truly sustainable development to occur. As the world must live with the social, environmental, and economic impacts of mining, there is a need for the industry to address these impacts through programs and efforts which move us towards more sustainable mining.

The Global Mining Initiative has been credited with the original use of the term *sustainable mining* in 1998 (Whitmore, 2006). The phrase *sustainable mining* has been criticized as an oxymoron (Kirsch, 2010), but use of the term *sustainable* in extractives is not meant to invoke the Brundtland definition of sustainability. Clearly, extractive industries leave fewer non-renewable resources for future generations by their very nature. The term *sustainability* applied to extractive industries utilizes Elkington's Triple Bottom Line concept of accounting for economic, social, and environmental impacts and risks. Sustainable mining implies that companies can identify and rank the most relevant social, economic, and environmental risks and plan strategies to manage potential impacts. However, some prefer to use other terms, such as responsible mining or corporate social responsibility (CSR), to avoid implication of the Brundtland definition. The term CSR has been documented to encompass a wide range of activities by mining companies, including regulatory compliance, environmental rehabilitation, social action, health care, providing fresh water, building roads, addressing educational needs, and supporting local charities. CSR activities in the mining industry have been noted to lack a uniform global measure or statutory enforcement (Weaver, 2012).

Diffusion of Sustainability Concepts into the Mining Industry

In the late 1990s, concerns for sustainability in mining began to be addressed by both private citizens and the mining industry. Growing public concern about sustainability in the mining industry resulted in the 1999 formation of the non-profit group Mining Watch Canada, which established the goals of insuring that mineral development occurs in a manner which provides for sustainable communities and ecological health, increasing the technical and strategic skills of communities faced with the impacts of mineral development, imposing appropriate terms and conditions on mining, and advocating for policies which reduce the risks of mineral development (Mining Watch Canada, 2010).

Mining Watch Canada joined forces with several other organizations focusing on the economic, social, and environmental impacts of mining on indigenous and land based peoples around the globe by participating in the Mines and Communities' London Mining Declaration, originally published in 2001. This declaration demanded, among other things, mandatory standards in all mining, and that land rights of indigenous peoples and mining affected communities be respected and enforced. In effect, it was insisting that the social and environmental impacts of the industry be addressed.

In addition to the calls by NGOs for the social and environmental impacts to be addressed by the industry, a business case can be made for addressing CSR. It has been documented that social responsibility related news events have a direct impact on the share price of a company (Casault, 2011). In response to NGO shareholder concerns, The Global Mining Initiative (GMI) was started by nine of the largest mining and metals companies in response to the public criticism of the environmental and social damages of mining to surrounding communities, and is credited with creating the concept of "sustainable mining" in 1998 (Whitmore, 2006). Although the term sustainable mining is often criticized as a corporate oxymoron, an example of Orwellian doublethink (Kirsch, 2010), "sustainable mining" is not meant to imply the Brundtland definition of sustainability. It does not imply that mining can be performed in a way which allow for enough resources to meet the needs of future generations. Extractive industries, by their very nature, leave less of a finite resource for future generations. Sustainability, as it applies to mining, becomes an exercise in economic, social and environmental risk management. It requires companies and communities to identify the most significant risks to the environment, society, and even the local economy, and plan actions to address stakeholder concerns. It even requires considering and honoring a decision not to go forward with a project.

GMI formed the International Council of Mining and Metals (ICMM) in 2001 to address sustainable development performance in the mining industry, and is composed of major mining and metals companies, as well as national and regional mining associations. As the same time, from 2000-2002, the Mining, Minerals, and Sustainable Development (MMSD) project met with stakeholders to address key issues relating to mining and sustainable development, the results of which were included in Johannesburg at the 2002 World Summit on Sustainable Development (Mudd, 2007). The MMSD effort has been continually developed, and lead to the development of ICMM's Sustainable Development Framework, based on ten principles for sustainable development released in 2003.

ICMM requires its members to integrate the ten principles into their corporate policies and report on them. The ten principles include:

- Ethical business practices and sound corporate governance.
- Sustainable development considerations in corporate decision making.
- Upholding human rights, respecting cultures.
- Risk management.
- Health and safety continual improvement.
- Biodiversity conservation.
- Encourage product reuse and recycling of products.
- Contributing to the social, economic, and institutional development of communities in which they operate.
- Effective stakeholder engagement and reporting (ICMM, 2003).

The principles focus more on company policies than providing any measurable indicators which can be tracked over time. Since 2008, ICMM has committed to using the Global Reporting Initiative's (GRI) standards, including the mining and metals sector supplement (developed in 2005). However, GRI grades its reports based on the number of indicators a company reports on and whether they are externally verified. GRI does not grade member reports based on performance on a specific indicator. In fact, a company can report on many indicators, with poor performance on all of them, and still receive their top rating. The GRI system does not provide an overall ranking of company performance which can be compared between mining operations.

Many companies produce voluntary sustainability reports, which are often also referred to as corporate social responsibility (CSR) reports in the mining industry, which may or may not follow GRI guidelines based on company choice. A study of the ten largest mining companies' voluntary corporate social responsibility (or sustainability) reports found that they varied so much in sophistication of reporting and the types of metrics used that companies could not be compared against each other. The study concluded that there was no real measure for overall performance and progress towards sustainability in the global mining industry (Jenkins, 2006). Although no global program yet exists which does this, there is one program in Canada which does provide ranking on mining company performance with regards to sustainability. From 1998 to 2002, the Mining Association of Canada investigated and defined public sustainability concerns through social research, which included meeting with community leaders across Canada to determine their concerns with regards to sustainability in the mining industry. An earlier effort by MAC, the 1993 Whitehorse Mining Initiative, also tried to provide a national

Figure 1. Timeline of diffusion of sustainability concepts into the mining industry

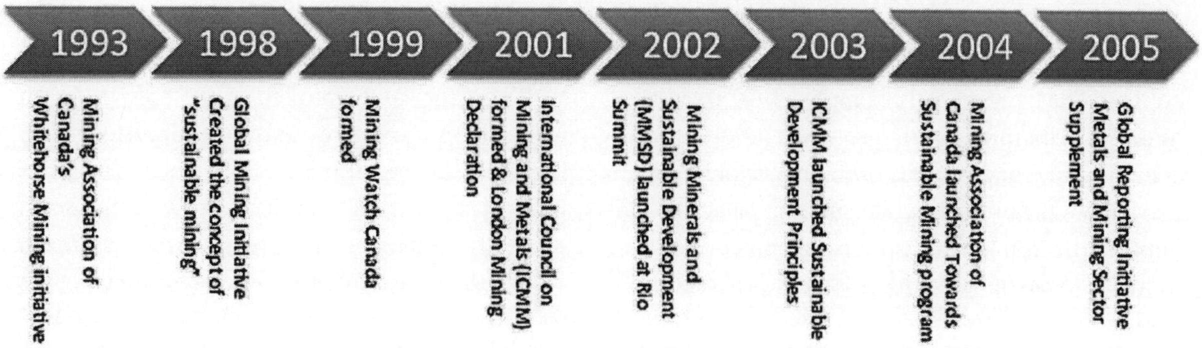

roundtable for miners, regulators, environmental groups, Aboriginal groups, and labor groups, but lacked any elements of monitoring, verification, and reporting on performance (Fitzpatrick, 2011).

In response to these concerns, in 2004, the Towards Sustainable Mining (TSM) program was launched by the Mining Association of Canada. A timeline of events leading up to the launch of the TSM program is shown in Figure 1. The original TSM program began with four protocols: tailings management, energy and greenhouse gas (GHG) emissions management, external outreach, and crisis management planning. The TSM program was established as a living, dynamic program, with the intent that protocols would be revised periodically and new protocols could be added as necessary. As such, indicators for biodiversity conservation management, and safety and health were added for member reporting to MAC in 2010. Also in that year, the protocol for external outreach was revamped and launched as to address Aboriginal and community of interest engagement, which was revised again in May of 2012 as the Aboriginal and Community Outreach Protocol. In June of 2013, the Energy Use and GHG Emissions Management Protocol; the Biodiversity Conservation Management Protocol; and the Safety and Health Protocol were revised. In March of 2014, the Crisis Management Planning Protocol was also revised; while the accompanying Crisis Management Planning Reference Guide was updated in January of 2013.

As of 2014, additional protocols are planned to address mine closure and water issues. The development of new indicators over time is intended to provide the program with the flexibility to respond to emerging concerns in the industry. In fact, water as a human right and local rights to water are one of the emerging issues which mining companies are just beginning to face (Kemp et al., 2010). In addition to these protocols, it has also been suggested that for mining to occur sustainably at the operational level, the rate of commodity extraction should be addressed to maximize mine life, and minimize boom-bust scenarios (Laurence, 2011). The TSM program does not currently have any protocols existing or planned to address mining at rates to maximize the life of mine.

TOWARDS SUSTAINABLE MINING PROGRAM DEVELOPMENT

Although membership in MAC is voluntary, implementation of the TSM program is mandatory for MAC members at their Canadian operations. Many MAC members also have mining operations outside of Canada. MAC encourages, but does not require, members to implement the TSM program at their operations beyond Canada. Although, research suggests that home-country factors should play an important role in shaping effective CSR approaches (Webb, 2012). Thus, the TSM program, developed for use in Canada, may yet have to be proven effective for use in developing countries with very different social and governmental structures in place.

The TSM program is composed of a set of guiding principles, with protocols addressing specific issues and guidance documents for how to implement the protocols. The guiding principles, published in 2004, establish MAC members' commitment to sustainable development including:

- Involving communities of interest in the design and implementation of the TSM program.
- Proactively seeking, engaging and supporting dialogue regarding member operations.
- Fostering leadership throughout member companies to achieve sustainable resource stewardship wherever they operate.
- Conducting all facets of business with excellence, transparency and accountability.
- Protecting the health and safety of employees, contractors and communities.
- Contributing to global initiatives to promote the production, use and recycling of metals and minerals in a safe and environmentally responsible manner.
- Seeking to minimize the impact of member operations on the environment and biodiversity, through all stages of development, from exploration to closure.
- Working with communities of interest to address legacy issues, such as orphaned and abandoned mines.
- Practicing continuous improvement through the application of new technology, innovation and best practices in all facets of member operations (MAC, 2004).

MAC member companies also commit to respect human rights, respect local cultures (including Aboriginal), conduct business ethically, comply with laws and regulations, be responsive to community needs, and provide lasting benefits to communities. These guiding principles provide a context of overarching values for the TSM program. Specific issues are addressed through protocols for specific performance elements.

To put the values into action, the TSM program has developed six protocols that detail performance requirements regarding:

- Aboriginal and Community Outreach (originally called External Outreach);
- Biodiversity Conservation Management;
- Tailings Management;
- Energy Use and Greenhouse Gas Emissions Management;
- Safety and Health;
- Crisis Management planning.

MAC provides details on the implementation of each of these protocols, as well as scoring for self-reporting. The requirements for each protocol are discussed in greater detail later in this chapter.

Program Oversight

The TSM program is overseen by both MAC members and external stakeholders. The MAC Board of Directors sets the overall objectives for the program. The Board approves all MAC positions, including the TSM guiding principles, strategy documents, frameworks, protocols, indicators, budgets, and work plans. Essentially, the Board must give final approval to all the elements of the program. MAC also has a TSM Governance Team, a subcommittee of the MAC Board, which meets three times a year. The Governance Team makes recommendations to the Board on all program elements, acts as an arbitrator in cases of dispute between a verification service provider and a MAC member, and provides directions to initiative leaders at MAC member companies. Initiative leaders are the individuals within each MAC member company responsible for implementing the TSM program and annually reporting on TSM progress for their companies.

MAC operates a Community of Interest Advisory Panel for the TSM program. The Advisory Panel includes approximately 20 representatives from communities where mining or mineral processing occurs, the financial community, labor organizations, environmental organizations, Aboriginal communities, and the mining community, including members of the MAC Board. The Advisory Panel meets twice a year to provide MAC with a platform for open dialogue with external stakeholders. The Panel may provide input on developing protocols, or review the progress in implementing protocols. As an additional check on reporting, the panel also provides an annual review of a few of the MAC member's externally verified reports.

The Mining Association of Canada continues to consult the public on its program through its Community of Interest Advisory Panel. The 2014 panel was composed of 18 representatives from Aboriginal (including Metis National Council, Seine River First Nation, and Cree Regional Authority), labor (United Steelworkers), communities (Campbell River Economic Development Corporation), environmental conservation (Canadian Boreal Initiative and My Sustainable Canada), investors (Caisse de Dépôt et Placement du Québec), Universities (the Institute for the Study of International Development at McGill University), religious community (Canadian Council of Churches), and companies (Sandoz Canada Inc., Noront Resources, Agnico Eagle Mines Ltd., De Beers, Syncrude Canada Ltd., and Vale), and the MAC board. The panel meets twice a year to monitor progress of the TSM Program and offer advice to the MAC on the program. The panel also performs an annual review of two to three member companies' externally verified reports.

Reporting

For each of the TSM protocols, there are several performance indicators for which the mining operation reports a letter grade. For example, the tailings management protocol has five performance indicators:

1. Tailings management policy and commitment.
2. Tailings management system.
3. Assigned accountability and responsibility for tailings management.
4. Annual tailings management review.
5. Operation, maintenance and surveillance (OMS) manual.

For each of these performance indicators, the protocol provides assessment criteria for assigning a grade, answers to frequently asked questions, guidelines for interpretation of the performance indicator, definitions of key terms, and self-assessment check lists. For all TSM protocols the performance indicators target institutional systems and management practices, not environmental or social outcomes. Good grades indicate that the company has established systems and practices that meet TSM standards.

The lowest possible performance level in the MAC scoring system is a C, and the highest is AAA. Although specific guidelines are provided for each performance indicator, the general scoring system is as follows:

Level C: No systems in place; activities tend to be reactive; procedures may exist but they are not integrated into policies and management systems.

Level B: Procedures may exist but they are not documented, not consistent, or do not meet MAC's requirements; systems/processes planned and being developed.

Level A: Systems/processes are developed and implemented in accordance with MAC requirements.

Level AA: Integration of the protocol requirements into management decisions and business functions.

Level AAA: Excellence and leadership.

A level must be assigned for each performance indicator. There are no plus or minuses, only whole letter grades. The company earns the highest grade for which it meets all the criteria. For each performance indicator, assessors begin with level C criteria, and work their way up until a specific requirement for a given level is not met. For example, if the performance indicator for tailings management policy and commitment were being assessed, and all the criteria for levels C, B, and A were met, but only some of the criteria for level AA were met, the company would report an A grade for tailings management policy and commitment.

Once a grade has been assigned for each performance indicator within a protocol, the *lowest* indicator score determines the overall score for the protocol. For example, the Tailings Management Protocol has fiver performance indicators (tailings management policy and commitment; tailings management system; assigned accountability and responsibility for tailings management; annual tailings management review; and operation, maintenance and surveillance manual). If a mining operation is assessed at a B level of implementation for tailings management system, but AAs are assessed for all of the other indicators, the highest score that operation can receive for tailings is a B.

The TSM program encourages MAC members to strive for a minimum performance level of A for every protocol at each Canadian operation, indicating compliance with MAC requirements. However, the required programs can take time to develop. New members of MAC are given three years to implement the TSM program before they must begin publicly reporting on performance. Existing members are also given three years to implement any new protocols developed by MAC. Each MAC member uses the evaluation criteria provided in the protocols to self-assess their performance at each operating site within Canada and reports the results to MAC. As a check on self-reporting, every three years the self-assessments must be verified by a MAC trained TSM verification service provider. Each year, MAC publishes an overall performance report for the public, providing a break-down of performance by protocol for each operation by company. The next sections will describe in detail the requirements of each protocol (Aboriginal and community outreach, biodiversity conservation management, tailings management, energy and GHG management, safety and health, and crisis management).

Aboriginal and Community Outreach Protocol

The concept of free prior and informed consent (FPIC) requires that communities affected by a mining project be identified and dealt fairly with from the point of conception of the project (Whitmore, 2006). Today, mining companies recognize the need for social license to operate and often work towards negotiated agreements with stakeholders to maximize their own certainty of being able to mine a resource while guaranteeing benefits to local communities (Fidler, 2012). Where communities are not engaged, confrontation and opposition to the operation may occur (Laurence, 2011). Even when Aboriginal engagement occurs proactively for mining operations in Canada, these efforts have been criticized for the unequal power relationship between big companies, the government, and Aboriginal peoples. Within Canada, "free mining" has been noted to occur, where land is treated as property of the federal government, and businesses may acquire ownership rights of minerals, including the rights to explore and extract mineral resources. Free mining has been criticized as prioritizing business interests over those of local and Aboriginal communities, creating an unequal relationship which affects the ability of local and Aboriginal communities to give consent to mining projects (Hall, 2013). In fact, because of these unequal relationships, it is even more important that companies act proactively to engage with local and Aboriginal communities regarding mine development and operations. This approach to mining is a result of a shift in industry perspective. In the early years of sustainable development efforts, avoiding harm was often the objective. Increasingly, mining companies are investing in communities in ways in which they want and need. Outreach efforts can help companies to identify these community needs and wants through connective engagement based on a mutual understanding of each other. The ultimate goal of connective engagement is to develop a project that creates shared value for mining companies and communities (Haddow, 2013). Each protocol in the Towards Sustainable Mining program has associated support documents which establish the commitments member companies are expected to make surrounding that protocol. For Aboriginal and community outreach, the *Towards Sustainable Mining Framework: Mining and Aboriginal Peoples* is a one page document which details the commitments MAC members are expected to make with regards to their relationships with Aboriginal peoples. These commitments include:

- Respect Aboriginal and Treaty rights and seek to understand local perspectives on those rights;
- Acknowledge and respect the social, economic, environmental and cultural interests of Aboriginal Peoples;
- Engage with Aboriginal Peoples, in accordance with the TSM Guiding Principles, to develop open and effective relationships throughout the mining lifecycle. This includes:
    - Building cross-cultural understanding so that company personnel understand Aboriginal Peoples' culture, values and aspirations, and Aboriginal Peoples understand the company's principles, objectives, operations and practices;
    - Undertaking early, timely and culturally appropriate engagement with Aboriginal Peoples, including within the environmental assessment process, to ensure their interests in a project and its potential impacts are understood;
    - consideration of traditional knowledge to minimize or mitigate potential adverse environmental and social impacts. and enhance positive benefits, of mining and related activities;
    - Developing agreements for participation, where appropriate, either directly with local Aboriginal communities or in conjunction with governments;
    - Working with governments and communities to support and encourage community development programs, which may include education, training, health, culture, employment and business development or other community needs and priorities, such as capacity building;
    - Supporting and encouraging Aboriginal involvement in environmental monitoring, closure planning and reclamation and other environmental activities that may be of interest to them; and
- Develop and implement company policies and systems that support these commitments and encourage suppliers of goods and services to the industry to do the same (MAC, 2008).

Protocols assess the way that individual mining operations adhere to and implement the required MAC commitments provided through frameworks and/or guides on that subject. The TSM protocol for Aboriginal and community outreach (MAC, 2012) includes four indicators: community of interest (COI) identification, effective COI engagement and dialogue, COI response mechanism, and reporting. The protocol sets the standard for assessing Aboriginal and community outreach efforts of mining companies.

Aboriginal and Community Outreach Protocol

Indicator 1: Community of Interest Identification.

The *Aboriginal and Community Outreach Protocol's* first indicator, Community of Interest (COI) Identification, was established to make sure that companies have standardized and documented efforts to identify communities of interests (COIs), including Aboriginal peoples and First Nations. COIs include more than just native and other local neighbors. In fact, within the TSM program a COI is anyone who has an interested in, or believes they are affected by, the decisions and management of mining operations. Level A criteria for this indicator requires a formal system is documented for identifying COI, including the consideration of a wide range of COIs, such as those whose interests or concerns may challenge the operation. Level A for this indicator also requires that Aboriginal and First Nations traditional lands and treaty rights which may be affected by the operation have been researched and documented, including any on-going traditional use of the land for hunting, fishing, trapping, and harvesting (MAC, 2012). Once the appropriate COIs have been identified for a specific mining operation, the TSM program requires engagement and dialogue with COIs, as detailed in the second indicator of this protocol.

Indicator 2: Effective COI Engagement and Dialogue.

The *Aboriginal and Community Outreach Protocol's* second indicator, Effective COI Engagement and Dialogue, was established to make sure that companies have processes for engaging COIs in dialogue on issues of concern to them, identifying how the issues might be addressed by the company, transparently informing COIs on activities and performance, and understanding COI viewpoints. Level A criteria for this indicator includes the following:

- A formal and documented COI engagement and dialogue system is in place.
- Assistance is provided to ensure COI are able to participate in these systems, where appropriate.
- Written communications using the local COI language (where required) and in a manner that is clear and understandable to COI.
- Clear accountability is established for the engagement and dialogue systems, as well as any consultation requirements of governments.
- Appropriate time is built into the system to allow for meaningful reviews by COIs, and relevant materials are provided in a timely manner.

In addition to formal and documented systems for COI engagement and dialogue, the TSM program requires that negotiated agreements with Aboriginal peoples are in place for the operations or projects where appropriate (MAC, 2012).

Indicator 3: COI Response Mechanism.

The *Aboriginal and Community Outreach Protocol's* third indicator, COI Response Mechanism, was established to make sure that companies have a system in place for receiving and responding to complaints and concerns. Level A requirements for this indicator include the following:

- A formal system is in place for receiving, documenting, and responding to complaints, including follow-up and tracking.
- The mining operation has a good understanding of COI concerns.
- Decisions about the operation consider COI input.

In addition to engagement and dialogue activities, and formal complaint and response systems, the TSM program also requires that issues of mutual concern are addressed collaboratively (MAC, 2012).

Indicator 4: Reporting.

The *Aboriginal and Community Outreach Protocol's* fourth and final indicator addresses reporting on engagement and dialogue activities. The level A requirements include that a formal system is in place to report on the COI engagement and dialogue activities internally (within the company), and that the reporting system assures that responses are provided to the COI on issues they raised (MAC, 2012).

Aboriginal and Community Outreach Protocol Progress

As previously indicated, in 2010 the *External Outreach Assessments Protocol* was revised to the *Aboriginal and Community Outreach Protocol, which was again revised in 2012*. Results from the revised indicator were first reported in 2013. Although the revised protocol does have a new focus on including Aboriginal populations within engagement efforts, the indicator topics of COI Identification, Effective COI Engagement and Dialogue, COI Response Mechanism, and Reporting remained the same. In fact, MAC member companies have been publicly reporting on these indicators since 2006. As detailed in the *Towards Sustainable Mining: Progress Report* 2013, progress has been achieved on all indicators within this protocol among the members of the MAC from 2006 to 2012.

In 2006, 52% of reporting facilities received a level A for COI identification. By 2012, 95% were achieving the A level ranking (MAC, 2013). The significant increase in adaptation of this indicator indicates how important proper COI identification is to the mining industry. By establishing documented procedures and methods that are used to identify COIs, an operation sets the foundation for fairness and neutrality in the selection of those parties with whom they will engage. A more inclusive engagement is likely to be established. Claims and perceptions of neglect of one group or favoritism towards another can be avoided.

In this same time frame (2006 to 2012) the amount of facilities receiving a Level A for Effective COI Engagement and Dialogue jumped from 54% to 88% (MAC, 2013). Progress on this indicator isn't as great as that for the identification of COIs. However, engagement systems are more complex to establish and maintain than identification systems.

In 2006, 59% of the facilities ranked a Level A for COI Response Mechanism, with a jump to approximately 93% by 2012 (MAC, 2013). This indicator requires documented systems for receiving complaints/concerns and responding to them. Companies benefit from these systems by having a record and history of issues of concern to COIs, allowing them to better manage their operations in a manner which is more acceptable to their stakeholders.

The percentage of facilities achieving a Level A for Reporting went from52% in 2006 to 92% in 2012 (MAC, 2013). However, the name of this protocol can be misleading, as the level A requirements include that a formal system is in place to report on the COI engagement and dialogue activities internally, and it is only at the AA level where responses to COI concerns must be reported publicly (MAC, 2012). Thus, those achieving a level A may not be reporting their efforts outside their organization.

Biodiversity Conservation Management Protocol

Biodiversity conservation management is guided by the MAC *Biodiversity Conservation Management Framework,* which details MAC's commitment to the conservation of biodiversity on mining sites. MAC members commit to "positively contribute" to biodiversity conservation throughout a mine's life cycle, transparently report on their efforts to conserve biodiversity, comply with requirements of legally protected areas, not explore/mine in World Heritage Sites, and promoting the biodiversity framework. Member companies also commit to:

- Integrate biodiversity conservation into mine planning, including examining the option of not mining.
- Perform biodiversity assessment and monitoring through the mine's lifecycle.
- Avoid, minimize, mitigate, and compensate for adverse impacts to biodiversity.
- Share information and research to enhance understanding of biodiversity conservation and within mining, including the use of partnerships and traditional knowledge.
- Recognizing that mining can permanently alter the land scape, perform reclamation that turns post-mining sites into viable and diverse ecosystems, considering desirable land uses (MAC, 2007).

Implementation of this framework is assessed by MAC's *Biodiversity Conservation Management Protocol,* which was most recently updated in 2013 and includes indicators for assessing a corporate commitment to biodiversity conservation, mine level planning and implementation, and reporting (MAC, 2013b).

Biodiversity Conservation Management Protocol

Indicator 1: Corporate Biodiversity Conservation Commitment, Accountability, and Communications.

The first *Biodiversity Conservation Management Protocol*'s indicator, Corporate Biodiversity Conservation commitment, Accountability, and Communications, is meant to assess whether or not companies are requiring biodiversity conservation management through an established commitment by senior management. The level A criteria requires that senior management endorse a biodiversity policy in accordance with MAC's *Biodiversity Conservation Management Framework*; that the policy be communicated to all staff and local COIs, and appropriate roles and resources are identified to implement the policy. To appropriately manage biodiversity impacts, site level plans are required in the second indicator of this protocol (MAC, 2013b).

Indicator 2: Facility-Level Biodiversity Conservation Planning and Implementation.

The second indicator within the *Biodiversity Conservation Management Protocol* is Facility-Level Biodiversity Conservation Planning and Implementation, which provides the criteria to rank how well a mining operation is managing its biodiversity impacts. The level A criteria require that each mining operation (including tailings basins and any associated plants) have a formal facility level plan or management system for biodiversity aspects at that site. Activities should include:

- Assessment of potential impacts or risks to biodiversity.
- Action plans for reaching targets for identified biodiversity aspects.
- Staff at the facility are assigned responsibility for biodiversity conservation management.
- Training is provided on the subject to facility staff.
- The mining operation consults with COIs (including Aboriginals) about biodiversity conservation management.
- Plan implementation and progress towards targets are regularly tracked and reported internally.

Once a facility is managing biodiversity, reporting requirements are addressed in the last indicator of this protocol (MAC, 2013b).

Indicator 3: Biodiversity Conservation Reporting.

The final *Biodiversity Conservation Management Protocol* indicator is Biodiversity Conservation Reporting. The A level requirements for this indicator include the establishment of a formal system for both internal and external biodiversity conservation performance reporting. Internal reporting should be designed in a way which supports management decision making (MAC, 2013b).

Biodiversity Conservation Management Protocol Progress

As previously stated, the *Biodiversity Conservation Management Protocol* was new to the TSM program in 2010. Facilities first publicly reported on this protocol in the *Towards Sustainable Mining: Progress Report* 2013. This report details the progress made on this indicator as of 2012, when 33% of reporting facilities achieved a level A for the first indicator on corporate commitment, accountability, and communications (MAC, 2013). This indicator assesses whether corporate commitments to biodiversity conservation are contestant with MAC's Mining and Biodiversity Policy Framework. The low level of implementation of the protocol may not be due to lack of commitment to biodiversity conservation on behalf of companies, but due to lack of alignment of that commitment with MAC's framework.

For the second indicator in this protocol, addressing planning and implementation, 39% of reporting facilities achieved a level A (MAC, 2013). However, it should be noted that 19% of facilities were assessed at a level B, indicating that a facility level biodiversity conservation plan or management system has been developed with baseline data and monitoring, but may not include all the level A requirements, such as action plans, targets, COI engagement, and internal reporting. Considering the level B facilities, 58% of reporters had some sort of facility level biodiversity conservation plan or management system in place.

For the final biodiversity indicator, which covers reporting, 47% of reporting facilities achieved a level A (MAC, 2013). The A level requires a formal internal system for biodiversity conservation reporting and public reporting on performance (MAC, 2013b). The comparatively high achievement at the A level for this indicator is likely reflected by the fact that many mining companies report on biodiversity conservation activities within external sustainability reports. An additional 27% achieved a level B, indicating regular internal reports on biodiversity conservation (MAC, 2013). Thus, a total of 74% of facilities are at least reporting biodiversity conservation performance internally.

Tailings Management Protocol

The requirements for tailings management by MAC members are detailed in three supporting documents to the *Tailings Management Protocol* (MAC, 2011)*; A Guide to the Audit and Assessment of Tailings Facility Management* (MAC, 2011b)*; Developing and Operation, Maintenance, and Surveillance Manual for Tailings and Water Management Facilities* (MAC, 2011c); *and A Guide to the Management of Tailings Facilities* (MAC, 2011d). The *A Guide to the Management of Tailings Facilities,* details the requirements of a tailings management system. The guide focuses on the management of tailings throughout the life cycle of project, from planning through final closure. It includes a tailings management framework and associated checklists. The framework requires a policy and commitment to locate, design, and operate all tailings facilities in a manner that all structures are stable, and solids and water are managed within designated areas. Tailings structures must also comply with all company, MAC, regulatory and COI commitments. There are also requirements for managing risk with respect to tailings facilities, including emergency preparedness and response, as an annual review of tailings management systems, including corrective actions (MAC, 2011d). The *Guide to the Audit and Assessment of Tailings Facility Management* provides the framework and checklists for auditing and assessing tailings facilities. *Developing and Operation, Maintenance, and Surveillance Manual for Tailings and Water Management Facilities* details the elements which should be in included in an operation, maintenance and surveillance (OMS) manual for tailings facilities. Together, these three documents lay out the requirements for MAC members' tailings management, which is assessed through the application of the *Tailings Management Protocol*. The protocol includes indicators on tailings policies, management systems, accountability/responsibility, annual review, and *OMS manuals*.

Tailings Management Protocol

Indicator 1: Tailings Management Policy and Commitment.

The first indicator of the *Tailings Management Protocol* is Tailings Management Policy and Commitment. It is meant to confirm that a company establishes its commitment with regards to tailings management. The level A requirements include that senior management endorse a tailings policy, which is both consistent with MAC requirements and developed or reviewed with COI. Once the policy is in place, each tailings facility is required to have a tailings management system, as explained in the next indicator.

Indicator 2: Tailings Management System.

The second indicator of the *Tailings Management Protocol* is Tailings Management System. Tailings management systems should provide a structure for assessing facility risks, assuring proper management, and consulting with COIs on issues surrounding tailings facilities. The level A criteria requires an MAC compliant tailings management system, which is developed or reviewed in consultation with COIs. Once a tailings management system is in place, this protocol also requires annual review of the management system within indicator three.

Indicator 3: Assigned Accountability and Responsibility for Tailings Management.

The third indicator of the *Tailings Management Protocol* is Assigned Accountability and Responsibility for Tailings Management. The level A requirements include that an executive officer of the company be assigned responsibility for tailings management. They also require that responsibility for implementing and reporting on the tailings management system be appropriately delegated. Once responsibility for tailings management and review has been properly assigned, the fourth indicator can be used to assess the annual tailings management review requirements.

Indicator 4: Annual Tailings Management Review.

The fourth indicator of the *Tailings Management Protocol* is Annual Tailings Management Review. The level A criteria requires a that an MAC compliant annual corporate review of tailings management be reported to the accountable executive officer.

Indicator 5: OMS Manual.

The final indicator of the *Tailings Management Protocol* is OMS Manual. The level A requirements include the establishment of an MAC compliant OMS manual for tailings facilities, including standard operating procedures, maintenance and inspection procedures, and documented emergency preparedness and response plans.

Tailings Management Protocol Progress

Progress has been made on the implementation of each of the five indicators of the *Tailings Management Protocol* since reporting began in 2006. The number of facilities reporting a level A for Tailings Management Policy & Commitment jumped from 44% in 2006 to 79% in 2012, an increase of 35% (MAC, 2013). In the same time period, those achieving a level A for Tailings Management Systems progressed from 39% to 77%, an increase of 38%. Facilities with a level A for Assigned Accountability & Responsibility for Tailings Management rose from 61% to 92%, an increase of 31%. Reporters earning a level A for Annual Tailings Management Review rose from 56% to 92%, an increase of 36%. Those with level A for OMS Manual went from 47% to 92%, an increase of 45%.

The indicator requiring an OMS Manual showed the most increase over time (45 percentage points for level A achievement). The indicators requiring an OMS Manual, annual tailings management review, and assigned accountability and responsibility for tailings management were the best implemented, with all three achieving 92% for level A.

Energy and Greenhouse Gas Management Protocol

Energy use is a significant cost of business for the mining industry. For this reason, most companies are motivated to manage energy consumption as a good business practice. The industry also has growing interest in managing its GHG emissions, as climate change has been recognized as a significant business risk to the mining sector. As climate change occurs, transportation routes and mining infrastructure are likely to become more susceptible to damage and failure from increased flooding and extreme weather events (Pearce et al., 2011). Thus, the industry has an interest in managing their own contribution to climate change.

The *Energy and GHG Emissions Management Guidance Document* provides guidance for companies on energy and GHG emissions management criteria; assists members with qualifying and reporting energy use and GHG emissions to regulators; leads those applying the guidance to energy cost and GHG emissions reductions; and highlights the best practices for energy management within the industry (MAC, 2009). The *Energy and GHG Emissions Management Protocol* provides criteria for assessing performance through the use of indicators on energy management systems, energy reporting systems, energy intensity targets, GHG management systems, GHG reporting systems, and GHG intensity targets (MAC, 2013c). When this protocol was originally released, it included six indicators for energy use and GHG management (tracked and managed separately). In 2013, this protocol was revised so that energy metrics and management may be used as a proxy for GHG metrics and management, recognizing that most companies already track energy use due to the costs involved, and manage GHG emissions through energy management. Currently, the protocol includes three indicators: energy use and GHG emissions management systems, energy use and GHG emissions reporting systems, and energy and GHG emissions performance targets.

Energy and Greenhouse Gas Management Protocol

Indicator 1: Energy Use and Greenhouse Gas Emissions Management Systems.

The first indicator within the *Energy and Greenhouse Gas Management Protocol* addresses energy use and GHG emissions management systems. Energy and GHG emissions management systems ensure that data is tracked at the facility and company level, and integrated into decision making. At the A level, it requires an energy use and GHG emissions management system with standardized quantification methods for data, that operational managers be clearly assigned the responsibility for energy use and GHG emissions management, that energy data is regularly reviewed and integrated into operator actions, and annual review of which energy and emissions sources are material (MAC, 2013c). Once the energy use and GHG emissions management system is developed and in place, the next indicator addresses how energy data is reported.

Indicator 2: Energy Use and Greenhouse Gas Emissions Reporting Systems.

The second indicator within the *Energy and Greenhouse Gas Management Protocol* addresses energy use reporting systems. This indicator ensures that energy use and GHG emissions are reported beyond the facility level, to the parent company and the public. The A level requires the establishment of an energy use and GHG emissions reporting system in which the performance results of each facility are reported to management on a regular basis to support decision making, and the public reporting of energy data (MAC, 2013c). Once mines are regularly reporting their energy consumption to management, the next indicator requires that energy goals be established for each facility.

Indicator 3: Energy and Greenhouse Gas Emissions Performance Targets.

The third indicator within the *Energy and Greenhouse Gas Management Protocol* addresses energy and GHG emissions performance targets. At the A level, a facility has energy and GHG emissions performance targets which are met (MAC, 2013c). If the targets are not met, the facility can only achieve a level B. In this way, greater scores are given to those facilities that actually reach their targets.

Energy and Greenhouse Gas Management Protocol Progress

The initial implementation at the level A level in 2006 along the *Energy and Greenhouse Gas Management Protocol* was the lowest of all those reported. The original protocol tracked energy use and GHG emissions management separately, which was revised in 2013. The 2013 progress report calls out energy use and GHG emissions management separately.

Energy use management systems were implemented at the A level for only 23% of reporters in 2006, rising to 58% by 2012. Energy use reporting systems at the A level went from 35% to 68% in the same time; while energy performance targets increased from 18% to 52% (MAC, 2013). Compared to tailings management, energy management has a lower implementation at the A level. This may be due to the cost of managing and identifying multiple sources for energy use on a site. Where smart metering equipment exists, energy management systems are likely already being implemented. However, cost of retrofitting equipment with smart meters necessary for process level breakdown of data must be considered. Without a regulatory driver, operations may not be likely to voluntarily incur the cost and process downtime to install this equipment.

GHG emissions management systems implemented at the A level increased from 13% in 2006 to 50% in 2012. GHG emissions reporting systems were implemented at the A level for 28% of facilities in 2006, increasing to 55% by 2012. GHG emissions performance targets at the A level increased from 23% to 43% (MAC, 2013). GHG emissions indicators had even less success in implementation at the A level than those for energy management. This is likely due to the fact that the indicators currently reported on are for a previous version of the protocol, which recommends tracking of GHG emissions at the process level. Most facilities track GHGs or major components for reporting purposes. GHGs must be reported to Environment Canada, but not all provinces currently have cap and trade systems. GHG emissions management and intensity target related indicators may be more likely to be implemented at facilities operating in provinces with cap and trade programs where there is a regulatory driver for these programs.

Safety and Health Protocol

The requirements assessed in MAC's *Safety and Health Protocol* are laid out in *Safety and Health Framework*. The framework is a one-page document which details the commitments MAC member companies make with regards to safety and health, with the belief that all work place related illnesses and injuries can be prevented. Members commit to:

- Providing healthy and safe work places through the establishment and support of appropriate behavior and controls to maintain a safe workplace.
- Establish clear accountability and responsibility for safety and health within senior management.
- Implement and review safety and health related policies, standards, and metrics, making sure all workers understand and can meet them.
- Implement management systems around safety and health to proactively prevent incidents and improve performance.
- Provide effective injury prevention and disability management programs to address wellness at work and at home.
- Encourage and support those with whom a company does business to address safety, including contractors and suppliers.
- Engage governments with regards to safety and health.
- Integrate performance targets into business and risk management. Report on worker and contractor performance for established metrics (MAC, 2011e).

Implementation of programs to address these commitments is assessed through the protocol's five indicators on policy and commitments, planning and implementation, training and behavior, monitoring and reporting, and performance. The protocol was most recently updated in 2013.

Safety and Health Protocol

Indicator 1: Policy, Commitment, and Accountability.

The first indicator of the *Safety and Health Protocol* addresses a company's safety and health policy, commitment, and accountability. This indicator ensures that member companies are committing to the agreed upon MAC commitments with regards to safety and health. At the A level, a company's safety and health policy should be authorized by senior management and include the commitments made within the *Safety and Health Framework*. The policy must also be communicated to all who work at the facility, including contractors and suppliers. Responsibility and accountability must be documented and understood at all levels of the company (MAC, 2013d). Once a company has clearly committed to managing these issues and has assigned responsibility for health and safety, management systems must be developed to ensure proper management is occurring, as explained in the second indicator of this protocol.

Indicator 2: Planning, Implementation, and Operation.

The second indicator of the *Safety and Health Protocol* addresses a company's safety and health related planning, implementation, and operation. This indicator requires a safety and health management system. Management systems focus on documentation, clear metrics for success and progress, and continual review and improvement. A well-developed management system also provides a handbook for everything that should be done, so that as new people step into roles at a site, procedures and processes do not get lost in the transition.

The A level for this indicator requires the establishment of a formal safety and health management system which includes objectives and targets with associated plans, hazard identification, risk assessment and control, safety standards and procedures, roles and responsibilities defined, workplace inspections, safety and health records maintenance, and the allocation of appropriate resources to the management system. The required safety standards and procedures do a company no good unless workers are aware of and use them (MAC, 2013d). Thus, the next indicator addresses safety and health training.

Indicator 3: Training, Behavior, and Culture.

The third indicator of the *Safety and Health Protocol* addresses a company's safety and health training, behavior, and culture. The A level requires:

- A documented training program which includes training needs analysis, risk-based training, and orientation for all who visit and work at the site.
- The training program must be implemented, tracked, and updated yearly.
- Appropriate resources must be assigned to the program and trainers should be assessed for competency.
- Training should focus being proactive when it comes to safety and health and should address reporting and hazard identification programs.
- A formal job/worker identification program should be in place (MAC, 2013d).

Once those at the site are trained in safety and health measures, progress of these programs must also be tracked through monitoring and reporting, as detailed in the fourth indicator of this protocol.

Indicator 4: Monitoring and Reporting.

The fourth indicator of the *Safety and Health Protocol* addresses a company's safety monitoring and reporting. The A level requires a formal safety and health monitoring and reporting program which includes:

- Regular assessed and reported performance metrics with clear definitions.
- Internal reporting and tracking of both leading (before an accident/incident) and lagging (after an accident/incident) indicators, safety and health inspection and surveillance, and follow up on all safety incidents.
- A formal audit program and annual facility assessments of the management system with follow up on needed improvements and management review.
- Regular management review and annual public reporting of safety and health performance.
- Regular posting of results of workplace monitoring and inspection at the facility.
- Annual public performance reporting (MAC, 2013d).

This indicator requires tracking and reporting of performance with regards to safety and health. Under this protocol, facilities must also attempt to improve performance through targets as explained in the next indicator.

Indicator 5: Performance.

The fifth indicator of the *Safety and Health Protocol* addresses a company's safety and health performance. At the A level, annual performance targets are set for both workers and contractors through the involvement of site management, which also reviews targets and works to improve performance. The targets are regularly tracked, assessed, and communicated (MAC, 2013d).

Safety and Health Protocol Progress

As previously indicated, the *Safety and Health Protocol* was added to the TSM program in 2010. The first reporting on the implementation of this protocol was made public in the 2013 progress report. As safety is a significant and highly regulated issue for the mining industry, it is no surprise that at first reporting, this protocol is relatively well implemented. For the first indicator on policy, commitment, and accountability, 96% of facilities reported implementation at the A level in 2012. The second indicator covering planning, implementation, and operation, had 90% implementation at level A in 2012. The third indicator on training, behavior, and culture had 84% implementation at the A level in the same year. The fourth indicator covering monitoring and reporting was the least implemented, at 75% achieving a level A. The last indicator on performance had 92% implementation at the A level (MAC, 2013).

Crisis Management Protocol

The *Crisis Management Planning Protocol* (MAC, 2014) assesses the implementation of the *Crisis Management Planning Reference Guide* (MAC, 2013e). The guide is meant to assist companies in developing site-specific crisis plans, and includes a sample crisis plan. The guide covers criteria for initiating a crisis plan, site-specific crisis vulnerability assessments, development of plan objectives, crisis management team organization (including structure, responsibilities, roles, and reporting), criteria and protocols for plan activation (including a crisis control center), communication during a crisis, debriefing, training, and review. The guide can be used at the facility level during the establishment, assessment, or revision of a crisis management plan. Once the plan is established, crisis planning is assessed using the three indicators of the *Crisis Management Planning Protocol*, which address preparedness, review, and training. For this protocol, a letter grade is not assigned, and facilities are assessed on the basis of a yes or no answer as to whether or not they meet the requirements for each indicator.

Crisis Management Protocol

Indicator 1: Crisis Management Preparedness.

The first indicator of the *Crisis Management Planning Protocol* assesses whether or not a facility is prepared for a crisis (MAC, 2014). It requires that a facility have a crisis management plan in place which complies with all the requirements set out in the *Crisis Management Planning Guide*, as explained in the previous section. The plan is meant to be a living document, and must be regularly updated and reviewed, as required by the following indicator.

Indicator 2: Review.

The second indicator of the *Crisis Management Planning Protocol* assesses whether or not a facility regularly reviews, and accordingly updates, its crisis management plan (MAC, 2014). The plan should be assessed regularly to make sure it meets the needs of the parent company and the individual facility it addresses, and reflects the facility's risks and industry best practices. Not only must plans be reviewed and updated to ensure they remain relevant, but companies must also train their employees on crisis plan implementation, as required by the next indicator.

Indicator 3: Training.

The final indicator of the *Crisis Management Planning Protocol* assesses whether or not a facility and its parent company appropriately train employees with regards to the implementation of the crisis plan (MAC, 2014). It requires appropriate training on the plan, as well as annual crisis simulation exercises. These exercises are meant to assure that, in the event of a crisis, the plan will be implemented smoothly.

Crisis Management Protocol Progress

The crisis management preparedness indicator was implemented at a level A for 53% of the reporters in 2006. By 2012, 82% were achieving a level A for this indicator (MAC, 2013). Although the reporting facilities showed great progress in developing crisis management plans, they did not show as much progress at reviewing and updating those plans. In 2006, 59% of the reporting facilities achieved a level A, which increased to 73% in 2012. In the same time, implementation of the training indicator jumped from 40% to 80%. This large increase in level A implementation for training indicates that facilities are concerned that their crisis management plans be carried out as written, which can only occur if individuals involved are appropriately trained.

REVIEW OF PROGRESS AND FURTHER ACTIONS

Progress on the indicators within the protocols shows which programs are under development, and highlight areas where further efforts will be required. The protocol related to aboriginal and community outreach showed the highest implementation at level A or above, with an average of 92% level A implementation across all indicators. This was followed by the protocol for safety and health, which averages 87% level A implementation across all indicators, and the protocol for tailings management, which averages 86% The protocol for crisis management exhibited an average of 78% level A implementation across all indicators. The protocol for energy/GHGs averaged 55%, the lowest level A implementation across all indicators. Results for the protocols related to biodiversity and safety were reported publicly for the first time in 2013. Member companies have been reporting on the protocol addressing outreach efforts, as well as those related to tailings, crisis, and energy/GHGs, for several years.

Of the protocols which had reported data back to 2006, the protocol for aboriginal and community outreach showed the most progress, increasing an average of 38 percentage points for level A implementation across all indicators, followed by closely by the protocol for tailings management, which increased 37 percentage points for level A implementation across all indicators. The protocol for energy and GHGs increased average of 35 percentage points for level A implementation across all indicators. The protocol for crisis management showed the least improvement, but still increased an average of 28 percentage points for level A implementation across all indicators.

The protocol related to Aboriginal and community outreach displayed the best implementation progress of all the protocols. Like most of the TSM protocols, the indicators within this protocol build upon one another. When commencing engagement efforts, companies must begin with identifying COIs, the first indicator. As engagement efforts begin with this step, it is not surprising that the most progress had been documented on COI identification than any other indicator in the TSM program, a 43 percentage point increase from 2006 to 2012. Once COIs are identified, a company can begin engaging and dialoging with them, the second indicator, which shows a 34 percentage point increase over the six years. Once a company interacts with COIs, and knows its concerns, it can begin to respond to them, the third indicator, showing a 33 percentage point increase from 2006 to 2012. After all of these efforts have been developed, a company may begin reporting on them, the fourth indicator, showing a 40 percentage point increase. This protocol shows both the highest level of implementation and the most progress over time, demonstrating the importance the mining industry places on aboriginal and community outreach. These efforts help companies to build trust and gain consent and acceptance of developing projects.

The protocol with the second-best implementation was that addressing safety and health, averaging 87% for level A implementation across all indicators. It is not surprising that at the first public reporting of progress on this indicator, such great success is met. The industry has long recognized the importance of safety at mining operations and continually works to address it. The least implemented of the indicators for this protocol was the fourth indicator, covering monitoring and reporting, with 75% achieving a level A. According to MAC, "a comprehensive monitoring program will track performance against leading and lagging indicators" (MAC, 2013). Although lagging indicators (after an incident occurs) can be easy to track, meaningful leading indicators for safety can be difficult to develop. In fact, the International Council on Mining and Metals has recently been working with the industry on this issue.

Progress of the implementing the indicators of the protocol addressing tailings management show a logical sequence in their implementation. To address this issue, most companies will develop a tailings policy, indicator one, and assign accountability within the organization, indicator three. To assure proper operation of tailings systems, a company must develop an OMS manual, indicator five, before it can develop a full tailings management system, indicator two. As it is the last step in this process, the second indicator has the lowest level-A implementation of the tailings indicators, at 77%. Following this sequence of implementation, it may be confusing that indicator one is the second-least implemented tailings indicator, at 79%, with the remaining indicators implemented ay 92%. However, the level A requirements for the first indicator include that senior management endorse a tailings policy, which is both consistent with MAC requirements and developed or reviewed with COI. Thus, company policies may exist, but not exactly meet all MAC requirements, including COI review.

The protocol addressing crisis management had an overall implementation of 78% level A. It showed the greatest increase in training, indicator three, increasing 40 percentage points from 2006 to 2012. The indicator requires appropriate training on the plan, as well as annual crisis simulation exercises. Although the development of a plan is important, it is the crisis simulations which test the plan and really prepare staff for responding to an actual crisis.

The indicators of the energy/GHG protocol build on one another. Energy/GHG management systems (indicator one) are required before reporting (indicator 2) can occur or energy/GHG intensity targets can be developed (indicator 3). It should be noted that greater progress has been made on the energy related indicators, an average of 34 percentage points increase over 2006-2012, than on the GHG indicators, increasing on average by 28 percentage points. This is likely due to the fact that companies can see a direct economic benefit for energy management in the form of reduced energy bills, which means it is more likely to be addressed. Additionally, many view GHG management systems as redundant when a company is already managing energy. Energy management is viewed as indirectly managing the release of GHGs.

The protocol with the lowest level A implementation is biodiversity, at 36% on average across all indicators. Like safety and health, results of implementing this protocol were first reported in 2013. However, safety and health averaged 87% level A implementation. The difference in progress exemplifies how prepared the industry was to address these issues through existing efforts. Clearly, the industry has long been aware of safety concerns, and is just beginning to address biodiversity impacts. Reclamation efforts as mines have often included the planting of monocultures for the purpose of soil stabilization and dust control, and have not historically focused on biodiversity. Further progress is needed on implementing this protocol. In particular, appropriate metrics for base lining and measuring the progress of biodiversity management have yet to be standardized. Biodiversity can be measured in the macro scale, such as by ecosystem function, or the micro scale, such as counting the number of a particular species on a site. Much leeway is given to reporters of this protocol to determine how biodiversity will be measured and managed. Lacking clear guidelines for implementation, it is difficult for companies to accurately determine appropriate metrics for biodiversity management at a specific site.

CONCLUSION

Only a couple of decades ago mainly academics and environmental organizations were concerned with sustainability within the mining industry. That the mining industry within Canada is addressing sustainability concepts has been touted as worth recognition and a sign of progress (Fitzpatrick, 2011). TSM program was developed so that the mining industry could better respond to the concerns of the public regarding the social and environmental impacts of the industry. It is clear that great progress is being reported on Aboriginal and community outreach. But further efforts need to be made on biodiversity conservation management. Without clear metrics for measuring and managing biodiversity, efforts will not be standardized across the industry and results may not be comparable. Great progress has been made on tailings management, and safety and health efforts were very well implemented in their first reporting cycle. Of all the protocols, biodiversity conservation management has been implemented at the lowest level. Clear guidelines for measuring and monitoring biodiversity would be useful for the industry (MAC, 2014b). Overall, progress has been occurring on the protocols in the TSM program, and new protocols have been established. This program demonstrates how an industry can document and respond to public concerns regarding social and environmental impacts as they emerge over time. These efforts directly affect the public perception of the industry in Canada. In a 2014 public opinion survey commissioned by MAC, one in three respondents indicated that their impression of mining is improving (MAC, 2014b). This improved public image of the industry is a result of organized efforts to address the public's concerns.

REFERENCES

Canadian Business for Social Responsibility. (2010). *CSR Governance Guidelines*. Toronto, Canada: Canadian Business for Social Responsibility.

Casault, K. (2011). Publication of Social Responsibility News and its Impacts on Mining Sector Investors' Behavior. *Proceedings of the 2011 Northeast Decision Sciences Institute Conference* (pp. 201-206). Houston, TX: Decision Sciences Institute.

Central Intelligence Agency. (2009). *The World Factbook 2009*. Washington, DC: Central Intelligence Agency. Retrieved August 6, 2012, from https://www.cia.gov/library/publications/download/download-2009/index.html

Elkington, J. (1998). *Cannibals with Forks: the Triple Bottom Line of 21st Century Business*. Gabriola Island, British Columbia: New Society Publishers.

Fidler, C. (2010). Increasing the Sustainability of a Resource Development: Aboriginal Engagement and Negotiated Agreements. *Environment, Development and Sustainability*, *12*(2), 233–244. doi:10.1007/s10668-009-9191-6

Fitzpatrick, P., Fonseca, A., & McAllister, M. L. (2011). From the Whitehourse Mining Initiative Towards Sustinable Mining: Lessons Learned. *Journal of Cleaner Production*, *19*(4), 376–384. doi:10.1016/j.jclepro.2010.10.013

Haddow, K. H. (2013). Consultation, the Way Forward. *Journal of Energy & Natural Resources Law*, *31*(1), 81–91.

Hall, R. (2013). Diamond Mining in Canada's Northwest Territories: A Colonial Continuity. *Antipode*, *45*(2), 376–393. doi:10.1111/j.1467-8330.2012.01012.x

International Council on Mining and Metals. (2003). *10 Principles*. London, UK: International Council on Mining and Metals. Retrieved August 6, 2012, from http://liveassets.iucn.getunik.net/downloads/minicmmstat.pdf

Jenkins, H., & Yakovleva, N. (2006). Corporate Social Responsibility in the Mining Industry: Exploring Trends in Social and Environmental Disclosure. *Journal of Cleaner Production*, *14*(3-4), 271–284. doi:10.1016/j.jclepro.2004.10.004

Kemp, D., Bond, C., Franks, D., & Cote, C. (2010). Mining, Water and Human Rights: Making the Connection. *Journal of Cleaner Production*, *18*(15), 1553–1562. doi:10.1016/j.jclepro.2010.06.008

Kirsch, S. (2010). Sustainable Mining. *Dialectical Anthropology*, *34*(1), 87–93. doi:10.1007/s10624-009-9113-x

Laurence, D. (2011). Establishing a Sustainable Mining Operation: An Overview. *Journal of Cleaner Production*, *19*(2-3), 278–284. doi:10.1016/j.jclepro.2010.08.019

Mines and Communities. (2001). *London Declaration*. Retrieved August 6, 2012, from http:www.minesandcommunities.org/article.php?a=8470

Mining Association of Canada. (2004). *Towards Sustainable Mining Guiding Principles*. Ottawa, Ontario: Mining Association of Canada.

Mining Association of Canada. (2007). *Biodiversity Conservation Management Framework*. Ottawa, Ontario: Mining Association of Canada.

Mining Association of Canada. (2008). *Towards Sustainable Mining Framework: Mining and Aboriginal Peoples*. Ottawa, Ontario: Mining Association of Canada.

Mining Association of Canada. (2008). *Aboriginal and Community Outreach Framework*. Ottawa, Ontario: Mining Association of Canada.

Mining Association of Canada. (2009). *Energy and GHG Emissions Management Guidance Document*. Ottawa, Ontario: Mining Association of Canada.

Mining Association of Canada. (2011). *Tailings Management Protocol*. Ottawa, Ontario: Mining Association of Canada.

Mining Association of Canada. (2011b). *A Guide to the Audit and Assessment of Tailings Facilities Management*. Ottawa, Ontario: Mining Association of Canada.

Mining Association of Canada. (2011c). *Developing an Operation, Maintenance, and Surveillance Manual for Tailings and Water Management Facilities*. Ottawa, Ontario: Mining Association of Canada.

Mining Association of Canada. (2011d). *A Guide to the Management of Tailings Facilities*. Ottawa, Ontario: Mining Association of Canada.

Mining Association of Canada. (2011e). *Safety and Health Framework*. Ottawa, Ontario: Mining Association of Canada.

Mining Association of Canada. (2012). *Aboriginal and Community Outreach Protocol*. Ottawa, Ontario: Mining Association of Canada.

Mining Association of Canada. (2013). *Towards Sustainable Mining: Progress Report 2013*. Ottawa, Ontario: Mining Association of Canada.

Mining Association of Canada. (2013b). *Biodiversity Conservation Management Protocol*. Ottawa, Ontario: Mining Association of Canada.

Mining Association of Canada. (2013c). *Energy and GHG Emissions Management Protocol*. Ottawa, Ontario: Mining Association of Canada.

Mining Association of Canada. (2013d). *Safety and Health Protocol*. Ottawa, Ontario: Mining Association of Canada.

Mining Association of Canada. (2013e). *Crisis Management Planning Reference Guide*. Ottawa, Ontario: Mining Association of Canada.

Mining Association of Canada. (2014). *Crisis Management Planning Protocol*. Ottawa, Ontario: Mining Association of Canada.

Mining Association of Canada. (2014b). *Research Findings: Public Opinion Tracking Study*. Complied by Abacus Data.

Mining Watch Canada. (2011). *About Us*. Retrieved December 10, 2011, from http://www.miningwatch.ca/about-us-1

Mudd, G. (2007). Global trends in Gold Mining: Towards Quantifying Environmental and Resource Sustainability? *Resources Policy*, *32*(1-2), 42–56. doi:10.1016/j.resourpol.2007.05.002

Pearce, T. D., Ford, J. D., Prno, J., Duerden, F., Pittman, J., Beaumier, M., & Smit, B. et al. (2010). Climate Change and Mining in Canada. *Mitigation and Adaptation Strategies for Global Change*, *16*(3), 347–368. doi:10.1007/s11027-010-9269-3

United States Geological Service. (2011). *2009 Minerals Yearbook: Canada*. Washington, DC: United States Department of the Interior, United States Geological Survey.

Weaver, M. (2012). Canadian Mining and Corporate Social Responsibility: Advancing Corporate Interest and Community Engagement. *Global Conference on Business and Finance Proceedings*, *7*(2), 582-592.

Webb, K. (2012). Multi-level Corporate Responsibility and the Mining Sector: Learning from the Canadian Experience in Latin America. In V. K. Aggarwal (Ed.), *Business and Politics* (pp. 1–43). Boston, MA: De Gruyter. doi:10.1515/bap-2012-0022

Whitmore, A. (2006). The Emperor's New Clothes: Sustainable Mining? *Journal of Cleaner Production*, *14*(3-4), 309–314. doi:10.1016/j.jclepro.2004.10.005

World Commission on Environment and Development. (1987). *Our Common Future*. Oxford: Oxford University Press.

KEY TERMS AND DEFINITIONS

Aboriginal: As used in Canada, this term refers to all indigenous peoples.

Biodiversity: Refers to the variation of organisms within an area or ecosystem.

Corporate Social Responsibility: Voluntary efforts by companies to address provide positive economic, social and environmental benefits to the communities in which they operate.

Greenhouse Gasses: Gasses that cause a heating effect in the earth's atmosphere, including carbon dioxide, methane, nitrous oxide and ozone.

Sustainable Development: "Development that meets the needs of the present without compromising the ability of future generations to meet their own needs" as defined by the Brundtland Commission.

Tailings: Waste rock remaining (often in pulverized liquid slurry form) after ore has been processed to recover valuable minerals.

Triple Bottom Line: Refers to the expansion of the traditional business accounting framework to consider environmental and social performance in addition to the traditional business metric of financial performance, a term coined by John Elkington.

Chapter 13
Smart Sustainable Marketing of the World Heritage Sites: Teaching New Tricks to Revive Old Brands

Deepak Chhabra
Arizona State University, USA

ABSTRACT

This chapter revisits the author's earlier findings that scrutinized online marketing strategies employed by the world heritage sites (WHS) based on a predetermined set of sustainability indicators. Recent data shows that, for the most part, the WHS continue to lack behind in sustainable initiatives to promote their sites in a responsible manner. Only slight improvement is noted in terms of efforts to seek host community views on how the local heritage should be showcased and the manner on which culturally appropriate representations can be promoted. In the light of unexpected decreased visitation levels at most of the WHS, as reported by literature, a retro brand marketing strategy is suggested which strives to marry the rich historical past of the sites with the present need. A smart sustainable marketing agenda is proposed to improve brand equity and facilitate coordination between different stakeholders of the heritage sites and to attract increased visitations.

INTRODUCTION

In the recent years, nations are making an enormous effort to place their historic sites on the world heritage list because they believe that the international recognition can serve as a powerful engine to attract different kinds of visitors, diminish seasonality, and offer international recognition thereby enabling them to promote extended stays in their regions (Patuelli, Mussoni, & Candela, 2013; Weidmann, Hennings, Schmidt, & Wuestefeld, 2011). The UNESCO (United Nations Educational, Scientific and Cultural Organization) strives to facilitate the identification for the WHS list and conservation of cultural and natural heritage considered unique to humanity. The UNESCO's World Heritage mission aims to:

- Encourage countries to sign the World Heritage Convention and to ensure the protection of their natural and cultural heritage;

DOI: 10.4018/978-1-4666-8433-1.ch013

- Encourage States Parties to the Convention to nominate sites within their national territory for inclusion on the World Heritage List;
- Encourage States Parties to establish management plans and set up reporting systems on the state of conservation of their WHS;
- Help States Parties safeguard World Heritage properties by providing technical assistance and professional training; provide emergency assistance for WHS in immediate danger;
- Support States Parties' public awareness-building activities for World Heritage conservation;
- Encourage participation of the local population in the preservation of their cultural and natural heritage; and
- Encourage international cooperation in the conservation of our world's cultural and natural heritage (UNESCO 2010).

Despite the emerging significance of world heritage and increasing number of site entries on the WHS list, tension continues to exist with regard to negative impacts associated with the international valorization of heritage for tourism purpose. From a tourism perspective, heritage is a commodity purposefully designed to satisfy the needs of contemporary audience. In line with this view, Taylor (2001) maintains that heritage tourism is motivated by monetary benefits. World heritage recognition, therefore, continues to share a dialectic and complex relationship with tourism (Boyd & Butler, 1997; Cesari, 2010). A divide exists between scholars of cultural heritage and their counterparts of tourism and marketing. According to Lyon, the "practitioners involved in the design of heritage as a visitor attraction face professionals whose interest is focused on the resource and its protection rather than on the question of public access" (2007, p. 62). Several studies have argued that the coveted UNESCO honor is extensively tapped by the world heritage site managers as a key marketing tool to attract tourists (Lyon, 2007; Rakic & Leask, 2006; Rakic & Chambers, 2007). This has brought to light concerns that the concept of 'World Heritage' has deviated from its original path in that the designation is being exploited to "either to serve the purposes of the tourism industry or for the purposes of nation building" (Rakic & Chambers, 2007, p. 146).

In other words, although the original intention was to bestow unique and universal value to selected heritage and garner support for its conservation, these motivations have extended to nation building, global identity and economic benefits. It is feared that the conservation of heritage sites is being shadowed by the need to seek financial numerations (Bregalia, 2005; Chhabra, 2010, 2013; Drost, 1992; Hede, 2007; Winter, 2007). Much blame has rested on the tourism industry. Several authors postulate that the world heritage has become commodified and exploited for contemporary hedonistic pursuits (Lyon, 2007). A dialectic relationship, therefore, between tourism and heritage needs to be nurtured through the use of strategic tools such as sustainable certifications and sustainable marketing (Chhabra, 2010; Lyon, 2007). Galla (2012) argues that a sustainable perspective is crucial for safeguarding the unique universal value accorded to the WHS which can be compromised by commodification.

For viable use of heritage sites, it is therefore important that sustainable marketing strategies are devised. The sustainable perspective calls for a holistic, unbiased, and responsible view of marketing (Haywood, 1990; Walle, 1998) which takes current and potential impacts of tourism into consideration. According to Kilbourne, responsible marketing needs to extend beyond microenvironments and promote "sustainable consumption and quality of life and expand the domain of inquiry to include technological, political and economic benefits and costs of consumption, thus challenging the paradigm itself" (1998, p. 642). It is implied that marketing strategies should be guided by consideration towards natural, social, and cultural environments. Sustainable tourism marketing can be defined as a form of marketing that considers cultural, social, economic and environmental perspectives (Chhabra, 2010; Fullerton et al., 2010; Sirakaya, Jamal, & Choi, 2001) to enhance marketing competitiveness in heritage tourism

In the light of the emerging significance of an integrated perspective of sustainability in heritage tourism, the previously published version of my chapter sought to use an integrated sustainable marketing paradigm. The purpose was to determine if a predetermined set of sustainable marketing important indicators are visibly implemented by the world heritage sites (WHS). The paper examined sustainable marketing efforts of different WHS across the globe by evaluating mission statements and signature websites. The mission statement is important because responsible strategies have to form the foundation of any organization that supports tourism (Aguilar, 2009) and they serve as a starting point to highlight the key functions of an organization. Therefore, a list of sustainable development indicators can help gauge effectiveness of sustainable promotion efforts in the mission statement and the textual content of the signature websites.

The aim of my chapter, therefore, was to identify gaps between mission statements and the website marketing content and suggest how WHS can use website marketing in a sustainable manner to achieve viable economic, cultural, and social benefits for the sites and the host communities. It is extensively recognized that online information can generate awareness and sensitivity towards a visited heritage site (Chhabra, 2010; Heuermann & Chhabra, 2014). In fact, the effect of online digital information on image formation is increasingly recognized by the heritage tourism industry (Choi, Lehto, & Morrison, 2007). Current trends have shifted towards the use of website texts and pictures to promote and advertise destinations. Thus, the underlying purpose of my study was to advocate sustainable development of tourism through the use of marketing tools. The study scrutinized marketing strategies utilized by the WHS based on a predetermined set of sustainable indicators.

Although sustainability was at the forefront of the ideology behind the world heritage movement in the early twenty-first century (Aas, Ladkin, & Fletcher, 2005), it initially offered limited value due to its somewhat narrow focus on conservation and authenticity thereby denying a broader and integrated approach. However, most recent literature (associated with WHS and tourism) has called for a need for a holistic and integrated perspective to sustain the unique cultural/heritage value of such sites and their surrounding environments for current and future generations. According to Galla, "an integrated approach that transcends boundaries, including those maintained between the environmental, economic and cultural aspects of sustainability as well as community and political boundaries" (2012, p. 91). When the first version of this chapter was penned down, only a few studies had examined the impact of WHS recognition on visitation numbers, brand equity and economic impact. Most studies were busy touting perceived benefits or highlighting perceived costs of the WHS endorsement or discussing a range of benefits for different stakeholders (Poria, Reichal, & Cohen, 2010). However, several recent studies report that visitation numbers at most heritage sites across the globe have not exponentially grown, as predicted, despite official recognition.

Given the new insights reported in recent literature, I argue that a smart sustainable marketing agenda has become all the more crucial to address the concerns and needs of different stakeholders and also to attract visitors and their spending in the region. One key contribution is suggestions on how to enhance brand equity and formulate strategies to increase visitations and spending. A retro branding perspective is suggested to build a strong WHS brand identity. That is, relaunch of WHS using a mix of historical essence (to foster a longing for a nostalgic past or community) and updated innovations to address the needs of contemporary markets (Brown, Kozinets, & Sherry, 2003). The updated version revisits a purposeful sample of websites of spatially dispersed WHS across the globe to identify trends associated with sustainable marketing initiatives.

BACKGROUND

It cannot be denied that globally endorsed heritage has received unprecedented attention in heritage tourism, more so, because it brings with it a celebrity status to the heritage site. The accolade has become a reference point and "a measure of quality, trademark, and an authenticity stamp for heritage tourists" (Rakic & Chambers, 2007, p. 146). Mixed results regarding benefits of WHS recognition are reported by documented literature. This section first offers a summary of studies focusing on issues associated with WHS. Next, studies focusing on marketing of WHS are examined using a sustainability perspective. The section concludes with a discourse on contemporary marketing strategies reported in general tourism literature which can be embraced to promote sustainable use of WHS.

A plethora of issues examine WHS from a heritage tourism perspective. Documented literature reports that heritage shares a problematic relationship with tourism (Hede, 2007; McKercher & du Cros, 2004). One reason is attributed to conflicting aims between the two (Drost, 1992). For instance, the goal of a heritage organization is to protect and preserve whereas tourism objectives are slanted towards commercial gains. Conservation and maintenance efforts are affected by wear and tear of increased tourist visitations (Lyon, 2007). Other issues include increased site deterioration, inconvenience and intrusion for the surrounding host communities (Breglia, 2005). Also, misuse of heritage has been reported in terms of tension between the universal and the national, which implies that there is a conflict between local values bestowed on the site versus universal values imposed by the United Nations and international tourism (Cesari, 2010; Timothy, 2011).

Several issues are associated with "archaeological preservation, urban growth, and tourism development" (Winter, 2007, p. 32). Winter reported that the political elite were eager to maximize the World Heritage Listing status as a 'cash cow' for tourism development (2007, p. 32). Cesari (2010) questions the advocacy of liberal multi-culturism agenda by UNESCO. He examines the function of heritage n Palestine/Israel' and argues that "multicultural heritage policies not only risk affirming and solidifying cultural differences, but also the asymmetries between them" (Cesari, 2010, p. 299). The author condemns language used to promote heritage as a global commodity and calls it 'contaminated universalism.' In doing so, he points to the friction between the desire to be placed on the global map while at the same time striving to maintain local cultural identity. His view can be evidenced in the following:

... erasure of politics and 'locality' from UNESCO's representation of itself- a silencing of the necessarily dialogic nature of its universalism and rootedness in a multiplicity of different contexts and histories- helps reproduce the rule of international experts and authorize global heritage. World Heritage also facilitates and in fact sponsors the extension of the reach and control of the state over heritage, often at the expense of the grassroots. Paradoxically, the heritage of humanity reinforces the nation-state (2010, p. 318).

Conway (2014) examined two aspects of showcased heritage at a WHS: tangible/public and intangible/local. Public heritage stresses on historical authenticity as determined by professional heritage brokers where as private heritage refers to the manner in which past is connected with present in a dynamic manner, based on values that are selected and deemed important by the local community or custodians rather than the culture brokers (Chambers, 2009). Conway brought to light issues faced by local custodians who are driven by the need to seek economic benefits; the most recurrent ones existed in their efforts to position their intangible heritage within frozen cultural heritage offerings designed by elites and professional heritage brokers. Based on interviews with local ranchers, the author suggested a shared/coordinated heritage construction process to assist the local community in defining their heritage and identifying the manner in which they value it so that selected features could be carefully commodified to showcase to tourists. An important issue is associated with stakeholder coordination because of the interest of a wide range of stakeholders; this implies that it is not an easy task to plan a unified heritage tourism offering. It is crucial to separate "stakeholders whose claim on the heritage is both locally based "perceived 'heirs' from stakeholders whose claims are more remote" (Conway 2014, pp. 153-154). The author further notes that isolated locations of recently recognized WHS offer local communities more time to develop their preferred heritage tourism offerings and juxtapose their product on the world heritage tourism map.

Winter (2007) stresses on the need for an integrated holistic examination perspective to promote sustained use of heritage sites. Parallel to the aforementioned concerns and impacts has emerged an established need for alternative measures to plan, develop and promote sustainable use of the sites and their surrounding environments. Evidence also exists of efforts to seek a compromise between heritage and tourism and use of tourism as a tool to promote and conserve heritage (Coetzee et al., 2006; Nuryunti, 1996). Sustainable development and management of WHS can assist in resolving the issues identified in documented literature. One way to accomplish this is to use marketing as a tool to promote sustainable management and use of WHS. Therefore, sustainable marketing needs to address issues associated with global and local views of heritage, partnerships with host communities, contaminated universalism, and tension between conservation and commodification. Despite the fact that extant literature recognizes the power of strategic sustainable marketing agenda to strike a compromise between various conflicts, it is of surprise to note that literature on sustainable marketing is still meager.

Only a handful of studies have examined WHS from a marketing perspective. McKercher et al. (2004) report a conflict between strategies needed to developing a heritage site (based in China) for locals versus western tourists. There existed a disparity between tourism and cultural management because the sites relied on funding from local and government agencies; it was noted that the sites were more slanted towards satisfying local needs than those of the tourists. One study examined motivations to heritage sites and found most visitors sought educational and diversity-based experiences (Poria, Butler, & Airey, 2004). Emotions were also an important factor and association between emotions and overall experience at the site was found to be significant (Poria et al., 2004).

Some studies report that the political elite are eager to maximize the World Heritage Listing status as a 'cash cow' for tourism development (Winter, 2007, p. 32). Patuelli, Mussoni, & Candela (2013) studied effects of world heritage sites on domestic tourism. The authors examined the relationship between domestic tourism and cultural endowment for 20 regions with WHS in Italy and found that a strong relationship exists; regions with endowed WHS attract a large number of tourists. Also, they report that addition of one WHS endowment results in a 4% increase in 'in-tourist flows.' That said, this economic benefit does not appear to be a universal phenomenon. For instance, Cellini's (2011) conducted an econometric analysis and questioned "the degree to which UNESCO accreditation generates the economic returns from tourism that may have prompted the original applications" (2011, p. 452). Empirical evidence, in this case, states the opposite: "Effects of inclusion of sites on UNESCO WHL are far from being clear-cut and robust- inclusion in WHL exerts insignificant effect on tourism. Myth- notion if cultural heritage is properly managed, it will draw tourists" (Cellini, 2011, p. 453).

Heritage and tourism are mutually dependent partners in that "operators and destinations can use them to add value to their products and local services which, in turn, generates greater income from tourists while the heritage sites achieve higher revenues" (Fyall & Rakic, 2006, p. 162). The use of such 'iconic' sites is often deemed indispensable to the marketing of destinations. The WHS can be used as a landmark to enhance destination image by marketing managers to lure both domestic and international tourists. Also, such images characterize dominant and reminiscent symbols of a country's identity. Nevertheless, the application of tools to promote WHS such as tourism marketing has been condemned for its partial approach towards growth and neglect of externalities on natural, social, and cultural environments (Jamrozy, 2007). Although authors such as Guerin (2000) hold that heritage practitioners are skeptical about the usefulness of marketing in the promotion and preservation of authentic heritage, more recent literature embraces the concept of marketing as a tool to promote sustainable use of heritage resources (Chhabra, 2010; Wiedmann et al., 2011).

Recent literature has progressed in the context of clearly visualizing key elements associated with sustainable marketing of heritage tourism. Fullerton, McGettigan, & Stephens (2010) call for marketers to balance visitation impacts and preservation of cultural and heritage resources. Fullerton et al. (2010) suggest demarketing strategies to attract selected group of tourists or reduce visitations to protect the heritage sites. Chhabra (2010) has proposed a strategic sustainable marketing model for heritage tourism comprising of local community involvement/benefits, economic viability, partnership and collaboration, authenticity and conservation, creating mindful visitors, and interpretation on the outer circle. The inner circle consists of core marketing elements which need to be taken into consideration to design an effective/sustainable communication mix: mission, market segmentation, research, and environment analysis. Chhabra tested her modified model on museums, historic houses, heritage hotels, and festivals and made further additions to the model associated with enterprise management and civic engagement. Fullerton et al. (2010) have explored the potential role of marketing in visitor management. The authors opine that careful management of tourists through marketing can minimize impacts and help to retain authenticity of heritage. Sadiki (2012) suggests three core marketing dimensions for the WHS: political contributions, visitor management, and brand equity. With regard to political contributions, Sadiki (2012) reports that degree of democracy has a significant effect on the manner in which the WHS title is promoted. A strong relationship is noted between marketing and visitor management.

Responsible marketing strategies are thus required for long term heritage health of sites (McKercher et al., 2004; Chhabra, 2009, 2010). It is argued that sustainability emphasis can make an organization competitive. Additionally, a perusal of literature identifies multiple indicators that help to gauge sustainability levels: cultural, economic, ecological, social, partnership, and heritage (in the context of conservation and authenticity). It has been noted that the traditional heritage institutions continue to use the objective version of authenticity (Chambers, 2009; Chhabra, 2010, 2013; Timothy, 2011). Objective authenticity is often described as traditional, genuine, pristine, "flow of life, not interfered with by the 'framing' of sights, sites, objects, and events for touristic purposes, by various overt markers" (Cohen, 2007, p. 76); and 'cool' (Selwyn, 1996). It is argued that the heritage suppliers should embrace sustainable development by using a strategic marketing perspective. Furthermore, Chhabra (2010) pointed out the significance of a holistic approach to promote both intergenerational and intra-generational equity. Use of sustainable indicators is one way to gauge sustainability and suggest future course of action.

Although not directly tied to heritage environments, Pomering, Noble, & Johnson's (2011) sustainable tourism marketing model is worthy of note as inferences can be drawn for heritage sites. It embraces sustainability at each step of the marketing process. The authors suggest a 30 cell matrix encompassing a check list with a set of ten marketing indicators, namely product, price, promotion, place, participants, process, physical evidence, partnership, packaging and programming. According to Pomering et al. (2011):

Tourism marketing is a cooperative activity, as consumers rarely use just one brand in consuming the overall experience. Packaging permits different products and brands to be combined synergistically to deliver clear and superior benefits, or a whole that is greater than the sum of its parts. Alliances, or partnerships, are needed in optimally bundling different brands' ingredients, and these are often combined in ways and at times to efficiently manage demand and capacity usage. Programming and packaging at times of low demand will not only help deal with the perishability characteristic of tourism service products that is so important to financial management but also allow uneven tourist loads to be spread more consistently. Packaging, programming and partnerships can help tourism organizations optimize profitable inventory and sustainability management (2011, p. 965).

Sustainable Indicators

Sustainable indicators are important in that they can serve as a pathway for principles that form the core mission of the heritage sites and their sustained use in tourism. According to the United Nations-World Tourism Organization, the indicator development process can help respond to risks triggered by the negative impacts of tourism. Aguilar (2009) maintains that indicators are a response to the anticipated risks associated with the key assets of a destination and provide summary information on the levels of effort being made to plan or protect the destination (Manning, 1999 as cited in Aguilar, 2009). According to Manning (2007), indicators should have the following characteristics: specific, objective, reliable and replicable, and sensitive to visitor use as level of use changes. Additionally, their measurement must be easy and cost effective and be monitored regularly.

Specific guidelines for indicators were suggested by Sirakaya et al. (2001) and these include all levels of society to enable consideration of a broad range of socio-economic, cultural, natural and political environments; manageable and easy application to diverse environments; reflection of local community views and involvement; strategic vision, that is, taking long term benefits in to consideration; organized development of indicators to ensure that they are "strong, quantifiable, affordable and capable of providing and integrated analysis of definite and general conditions of the sustainability of the destination and its natural and cultural resource" (Aguilar, 2009, p. 21).

A plethora of studies have confirmed that the majority of the externalities because of tourism attractions occur in the social, cultural, ecological, and economic environments (Manning, 1999; Carbone, 2005; Choi & Sirakaya, 2006). A sub-set of indicators for each externality category can help measure extent of impacts in an ongoing manner. Ecological indicators relate to a diverse set of items which define environmental sustainability centered on efforts to reduce negative impacts on the environment (Carbone, 2005) by ensuring compatibility with the vital ecological processes and biological processes (Mill & Morrison, 2006).

According to Aguilar (2009), social and cultural sustainability refers to efforts to conserve and protect traditional rituals and customs, so they are not impacted by demonstration effects such as tourist lifestyles. Also, is included the need to reduce any possible conflicts that may arise from unequal distribution of tourism benefits (Carbone, 2005). Although culture evolves and is

Figure 1. An integrated sustainable marketing model

not static, it is important to control harmful effects, and educate tourists to behave in a responsible manner so that the local culture is not vulnerable to demonstration effects. The underlying efforts of social and cultural sustainability are to ensure that tourism development strengthens community identity (Mill & Morrison, 2006) in addition to improving the tourist and host relationships and interactions. Retaining authenticity and conservation of heritage belongs to the heritage category of indicators. Economic sustainability advocates equity of economic benefits both for the current and future generations (Mill & Morrison, 2006).

METHODOLOGY

Approximately 981 heritage sites currently exist in the world (70 sites more were added to the list in the last five years) and these are marked on UNESCO's World Heritage List. Of these, 759 are cultural sites, 193 are natural sites and 29 are mixed. These are distributed between 160 countries (State Parties) across the globe and include internationally renowned sites such as the Taj Mahal in India, Statue of Liberty in the United States, Uluru in Australia, and Stonehenge in the UK. The previous version of this chapter examined signature websites and mission statements of approximately 130 WHS to determine the extent to which sustainable measures are pursued and visibly implemented. Efforts were made to include at least one from each country. The end data had resulted in 100 countries. The mission statements and signature websites of the WHS were examined using the content analysis method and evaluated based on four fundamental tenets of sustainability: socio-economic benefits, heritage and cultural integrity, environmental integrity and institutional benefits (see Figure 1). Also, certification documents of the WHS were scanned to identify sustainable marketing indices. This enhanced version selects thirty spatially dispersed WHS from the previously examined list and revisits the content of their signature websites and mission statements to determine if sustainable marketing initiatives have improved since the time they were reviewed (five years ago).

Indicators

Mission Statement Indicators

As pointed in documented literature, a mission statement is a brief statement defining the core purpose of a business or organization. It is an important statement because it defines the business and provides an overview of its objectives. For an organization to be sustainable, it is crucial for the mission statement to emphasize on sustainable contributions. Literature has suggested the inclusion of following terms to reinforce a promise and commitment towards sustainability (Aguilar, 2009; Chhabra, 2009; Lyon, 2007):

heritage, cultural, social, economic, and environmental. This study defines a mission statement as promoting sustainability if it strives to make contributions towards the local economy and the host community in addition to producing viable social, cultural and environmental impacts and promoting site heritage in the context of conservation and authenticity and striving to use effective interpretation to inform the audience so that they can behave in a sustainable manner.

Website Indicators

- **Ecological Indicators:** A variety of environmental indicators are presented by previous literature such as biodiversity; maintenance of natural state; maintaining carrying capacity, and adopting recycling practices (Choi & Sirakaya, 2006; Manning 1999). The previous and enhanced versions of this study employ following ecological indicators: carrying capacity and recycling practices.
- **Economic Indicators:** Tangible measures of economic sustainability have included assessment of employment opportunities and income distribution (Nelson & Payne, 1993). Carbone (2005) also refers to the extent additional income is provided to locals as compensation for intrusion and inconvenience due to tourist presence. Harris & Nelson's (1993) list of economic indicators include local ownership, gender equity, ethnic equity, local employment and training and support, emphasis on strong linkages. Choi & Sirakaya (2006) identified a similar set of indicators such as local employment including employment growth and unemployment rate, income distribution/capital leakage and linkage, capital formation in the community/investment, percentage of repeat tourists, seasonal nature of tourist visitation, economic well-being in terms of comparable wages, new GDP (measure of economic welfare), economic stability of the hosts, nature of labor and labor conditions and income earned by the local government. Following economic indicators are used in this study: increase in local wage; generate income for locals and produce employment benefits; and promote investment in the local region.
- **Heritage and Cultural Indicators:** Both versions of the chapter use the following site heritage sustainability indicators: maintain authenticity; conservation of cultural heritage; interpretation for cultural education. Cultural indicators are defined by the following measures: respect for local community heritage; and advocacy of culturally appropriate activities and behavior.
- **Social Indicators:** Several social sustainability measures are proposed by documented literature such as aligned with the community vision, community control and plans to check intrusion, maintaining spiritual and aesthetic values, and quality of life (Harris & Nelson, 1993). Other indicators include monitoring of social relations and changes in subsistence activities, family structures and decision making strategies in the allocation of resources (Nelson & Payne, 1993). Choi & Sirakaya (2006) also present an extensive list of indicators such as social cohesion, community health and safety and quality of life.
- **General/Institutional Indicators:** In addition to the foregoing indicators, some indicators cross over to multiple categories and hence are often grouped under 'Institutional' indicators. Most recurring measures of sustainable tourism in documented literature as summarized by Miller (2001) are the ones which: maximize economic benefit, self-regulatory, observe carrying capacity, promote intergenerational equality, make efficient use of resources, utilize the technology based approach, take

> a long term view, enable local involvement, encourages local revitalization, improve level of natural capital stock, ensure resident satisfaction, ensure customer satisfaction, maintain levels of natural capital stock, and contain well developed tourism plans. Aguilar (2009) stressed on five priorities based on Miller's study: strategic view, carefully planned tourism development, efficient use of local resources, facilitate local community involvement and maintain existing levels of natural capital stock.

Hassan (2000) also advocated cooperation and partnership between the public and private sectors as a core purpose of a sustainable model and emphasized on building relationships and alliances to strengthen local community resources and produce viable economic benefits in a way suitable to the local environment. The underlying objectives of Hassan's model were: (1) to educate all stakeholders of tourism of the significant relationship between tourism development and environment sustainability; (2) to promote equitable opportunities between local and non-local tourism developers; (3) to strive to provide best quality service to the tourists; (4) to generate support for the host community; (5) to enhance local quality of life and life style; (6) to ensure a balanced approach by taking into consideration the economic, social and environmental necessities in the tourism planning and development programs; (7) to determine thresholds of social and environmental carrying capacity of the destination; (8) to measure impacts on the ecology in an ongoing manner; (9) to conserve the local culture and support local heritage and values; and (10) to develop training and educational programs so that human resource skills are enhanced. In this study, the following institutional indicators are used: long term view/ survival; well-developed tourism plans; intergenerational equity; stakeholder collaboration/partnerships; local community involvement; customer satisfaction; local resident satisfaction; emphasis on ongoing research; code of ethics for tourists; and educating/training the local community.

FINDINGS

Mission Statement

Approximately half a decade ago, the WHS were found to actively embrace the vision laid down by the World Heritage Convention. Important highlights were the need for enhanced training and expertise of site personnel, strategic management plans, protection and conservation of culture and heritage, and international outreach. Most of the examined mission statements of the WHS endorsed the core principles of the World Heritage Convention by striving to promote conservation and cultural sustainability.

As Table 1, from the original chapter shows, approximately 50% also stressed about maintaining objective authenticity of their sites. Evidence followed of initiatives to promote social and environmental sustainability by minimizing social externalities and reducing other negative impacts of tourism on the site environment. Almost 30% of the mission statements highlighted the need for effective interpretation. Least consideration was given to local community-related issues and promotion of viable economic benefits. Stakeholder collaborations were not noted. Based on these findings, the vision and mission of the majority of the WHS was best described as predominantly site-centric in terms of protection, conservation, authenticity, proficiency, and international networking efforts. More recent review of the WHS websites shows similar patterns with regard to minimum emphasis on stakeholder collaborations, mitigation of social and environmental costs, and economic benefits for the host communities. However, more mission statements (70%) now emphasize on authenticity and inclusion of host community views in the decision making process.

Table 1. Mission statement indicators (2009)

Indicator	Frequency N=130
Social	41.0
Economic	13.8
Local Community	20.7
Conservation	65.5
Authenticity	48.3
Interpretation	31.0
Cultural	70.0
Environmental	40.0

Signature Website Indicators

- **Economic and Ecological:** Earlier, approximately 86 of the 130 WHS featured economic and/or ecological indicators. As Table 2 reveals, with regard to the presence of economic measures on the signature websites, approximately 60% emphasized on increasing investment through donations. However, this interest was found to be site-centric, focused on accumulating economic enumerations for the site only, and did not extend to secure funds for the benefit of the surrounding host communities. More recent content analysis shows traces slight increase in efforts on the part of some WHS to garner economic benefits for local communities. That said, these efforts are not noted to be universal across all WHS.

Table 2. Economic and ecological indicators (2009)

Economic	Frequency (N=86)
Generate income for locals	39.5
Employment benefits	9
Increase in investment	60.6
Ecological	**Frequency (N=86)**
Recycling practices	13.9
Carrying capacity	12.8

A substantial percentage, although less than half, of the websites demonstrated efforts to generate income for the local community through tourism and less than 10% illustrated evidence of providing employment benefits for the surrounding communities. As evidenced in Table 2, least emphasis was given to recycling practices and carrying capacity. It appears that economic viability measures were still in their infancy stage. Coetzee et al. (2006) concurred with these results and suggested that the economic health of the host communities should be taken into consideration for successful sustainable efforts. However, more recent data shows slight shift towards efforts to enhance employment for local communities. Initiatives towards recycling practices, carrying capacity strategies, and interpretation techniques have declined.

Next, as pointed out earlier, visible adherence to a variety of ecological indicators is required to obtain a harmonious equilibrium between use of the sites and surrounding areas which provide a passage to their entry. It is feared that increased visitation sites and their peripheral areas will continue to impose a drain on the natural resources (Li et al., 2008). Early results found the WHS mostly lacking in this regard. As point out earlier, more recent data shows a visible decline towards advocacy of ecological efforts such as showcasing of recycling initiatives and minimizing of crowding effects.

- **Cultural:** Cultural indicators are defined as measures that promote authenticity and conservation of cultural heritage presented at the WHS. Also, under this category are markers which promote reverence for the host culture and showcase activities sensitive to the local culture for the host communities. Authenticity and conservation were emphasized in 90% of the websites in 2009. Also, other cultural indicators were significantly highlighted throughout the website content. Similar patterns are noted in the recent data with objective authenticity being showcased in approximately 95% of the websites.

Table 3. Cultural indicators (year-2009)

Indicator	Frequency N=130
Authenticity	93.0
Conservation of cultural heritage	90.7
Respect cultural heritage	80.2
Culturally appropriate	80.2

As Table 3 shows, maximum emphasis has been placed on cultural preservation indicators because these form the underpinnings of the WHS nomination criteria (Hede, 2007; Winter, 2007). Similar patterns continue to be noted in the recent data as well. However, although more visible in recent data, majority of the WHS websites continue to lend less attention towards the responsible promotion of host community culture because most fail to mention code of behavior or information about the host community culture.

- **Social:** With regard to social indicators, the majority of the websites failed to feature concern or efforts to minimize social costs generated by tourism on the host communities. Only 21% of the evaluated websites mentioned one or more of the listed social indicators. Only 16% highlight the need to generate local employment to enhance quality of life or seek to advocate increase in local wage so that the standard of living of the host community may be enhanced. These results confirmed the lack of social sustainability attempts reported by previous studies (Wager, 1995; Li et al., 2008). Content analysis of recent data shows that minimal progress is reported on these indicators although several of the analyzed websites are noted to offer opportunities for social interactions within the site and between the site and the surrounding communities through volunteer opportunities, both for the tourists and the locals.
- **Institutional:** The previous findings reported pronounced emphasis on stakeholder collaboration and partnerships. A further analysis of the website content showed that the majority of the websites promote stakeholders associated with the tourism businesses such as lodging, transportation, restaurants, and retail (see Table 4). Also, a substantial number (50%) of the websites mention coordination or partnerships with stakeholders with interests focused on conservation, education, architecture, and research. More recent data shows similar emphasis on stakeholder partnerships. It is also important to note that visibility of education and training has declined across the WHS.

Well-developed tourism plans were found to be site-centric. That is, the documents downloaded from the website showed that management strategies focused on visitor traffic and site management issues. Although other sustainability criteria were emphasized, they were mostly concerned with the site resources and interests associated with micro management. In recent data, similar patterns with regard to most of the institutional

Table 4. Institutional indicators (year – 2009)

Indicator	Frequency N=125
Stakeholder collaboration/ partnership	83.7
Well-developed tourism plans	74.4
Local community involvement at the site	73.2
Intergenerational equity	70.9
Long term survival	69.8
Customer satisfaction	61.6
Education/training for the community	61.6
Emphasis on ongoing research	58.1
Local resident satisfaction	38.4
Code of ethics for tourists	19.8

indicators are noted. Slight increase is evidenced in opportunities for the local communities and more host community representations especially in a culturally appropriate perspective. Involvement of the host community in decision making processes has slightly improved. However, code of ethics for tourists, as a guide to appropriate behavior, is mostly missing from the websites.

Further Explorations

The previous version also took an initiative to identify the WHS with the highest and lowest level of adherence to the majority of the sustainability measures under consideration. Most of the content in this section is borrowed from the previous chapter. Efforts were made to obtain information on the political environments, other site-specific particularities and type of stakeholder involvement at the premises. For example, an insight was gained into the political status of the country, the urban or rural nature of the site location, type of ownership, and specific characteristics of the surrounding community.

The sites that ranked high on the overall sustainability index (in order) were Škocjan Caves (Slovenia), Tongariro National Park (New Zealand), Kizhi Pogost, (Russia), and the Historic Centre (Old Town) of Tallinn (Estonia). The Škocjan Caves have gained worldwide recognition and the state has committed itself to doing everything in its power to conserve and protect this outstanding natural site. In addition to crafting programs for the protection and development of the Park, the site authorities monitor and analyze the status of natural and cultural heritage in an ongoing manner. Other tasks include promotion of the caves, research, education, and infrastructure maintenance. Co-operation with local residents is considered important. Location specific attributes include being in a developed and democratic country, mixed nature of stakeholders, and active involvement of the local community. Content analysis of these sites showed consistency in commitment towards high quality sustainable tourism.

Tongariro National Park was established in 1887 and became the first national park in New Zealand. It is recognized as a dual World Heritage area because of its unique cultural and natural value. It is a living evidence of Maori culture, has outstanding volcanic features and is also home to many native creatures. Its distinct characteristics showcased in 2010 included location in a developed and democratic country, mixed nature of the stakeholders, and evidence of active involvement of the Maori community. Recent data shows further improvement in the manner

Kizhi Pogost is an open air museum located in Russia which has a democratic government now. This WHS has received paramount attention because of its efforts to preserve its prized collections. Education and research are also emphasized by the site managers and recent data endorses continued dedication in this regard. The next WHS, Tallinn is famous for its historic center and was nominated as the European Capital of Culture for 2011. This honor is part the European Union initiative to provide European cities with an opportunity to showcase their cultural offerings at an international level. Tallinn is well known for its creative works, ecological souvenirs and spiritual/cultural connections with the seashore. It is located in a democratic and developed country. Evidence also exists of pronounced emphasis on learning and advancement in technology. The host community also plays a prominent role in the planning of events in the old town. Stakeholders listed on the website were found to predominantly belong to the tourism industry. The site continues to obtain a high rank in terms of its sustainability efforts.

Minimum sustainability emphasis was noted earlier from the following sites (in order): Historic Centres of Berat and Gjirokastra (Albania), Sewell Mining Town (Chile), Port, Fortresses and Group of Monuments in Cartagena (Columbia), and Old Havana and its Fortifications (Cuba). The two historic towns of Berat and Gjirokastra are located in central Albania and are recognized as a rare example of Ottoman style of architecture.

Berat is witness to the coexistence of various religious and cultural communities. It features a castle, citadel, and several mosques. Gjirokastra features a collection of unique two-story houses, a bazaar, a mosque and two churches. They bear witness to the wealth and immense variety of urban and architectural heritage. The cultural integrity and authenticity of the two towns is retained but a series of illegal constructions in the late 1990s has compromised its sanctity. More commercial emphasis appears to shadow sustainable planning. Recent data on the websites shows meager progress towards sustainability.

Sewell Mining Town has the largest copper mine in the world and was built by the Braden Copper Company in 1905. The town was constructed terrain which is very steep for vehicles and accessible through rail only. Next, Fortresses and Group of Monuments Cartagena is a large city seaport located on the coast of Colombia. It was founded in 1533 and was a main center of early Spanish settlements in the Americas. It is known for its defense strategy - a walled military fortress to protect the city from pirates. The Cuban capital Havana was founded by the Spanish and is recognized as one of the oldest cities in the contemporary world. It is known for its trading port and its strong fortifications. It also contains an important shipyard. Common finding from these aforementioned sites is that they are all located in developing countries, lack evidence of host community involvement, and emphasize engagement with tourism stakeholders only. Similar results are noted in the recent data.

CONCLUSION

The World Heritage Convention supports an exhaustive list of site-centric heritage sustainability issues associated with conservation and objective authenticity. However, less attention appears to be directed to the other crucial aspects of sustainability and issues that arise with regard to how heritage is selected, interpreted, and presented to the global audience. Recent literature reports that views of local communities do not resonate with the manner the heritage sites and their heritage are showcased. Content analysis of mission statements, website content, and certification documents show that more often than not, the host communities are not part of the decision making process. Host community concerns, stakeholder collaborations, social and viable economic impact (in regard to generating employment for locals) considerations continue to receive comparatively less or inequitable attention in most of the reviewed WHS websites although positive initiatives by some of the WHS are noted. The previous paper analyzed mission statements and signature websites to gauge visible efforts of sustainable management based on presupposed indicators related to social, economic, and environmental accountability. Additionally, it looked at the certification documents of the WHS. It was unique in its academic contribution as it used an integrated approach and highlighted apparent hiatus to stir further scholarly inquiries (McCool, Moisey, & Nickerson, 2001). That said, it was also subject to several limitations with regard to the measurement technique and its inability to evaluate other promotional collateral beside the signature websites. However, the study made an important effort and offered useful inferences for future investigation. The enhanced version of that chapter revisits a purposeful sample of the WHS across the globe to track progress in sustainable marketing initiatives and also to offer a new perspective in the light of recent literature and issues associated with the WHS.

Review of mission statement content had earlier showed that the World Heritage Convention trains its members to conform judiciously to the heritage conservation and authenticity guidelines whereas other indicators of sustainability fail to feature prominently in the sustainability equation. Moreover, insofar as the website analysis reflects, the themes continue to be visibly nested within the priorities set by the convention. Few websites advocate links with NGOs, social and community interest groups in addition to demonstrating weak sustainable supply chain initiatives and extended stakeholder collaborations and partnerships between the public and private sectors (Aas, Ladkin, & Fletcher, 2005; Saipradist & Staiff, 2007; Hede, 2007). Majority of the sites continue to lack in evidence in terms of ongoing research to monitor visitor impacts, support of ecological practices, and offering of programs to educate tourists, stakeholders and the host communities. Overall, a decline in integrated sustainable marketing initiatives is noted. On a positive note, some success stories are also noted. For instance, more websites are showcasing efforts to showcase object authenticity of their site. Also, more are seeking views of host communities and are demonstrating support for culturally appropriate representations.

Although symbiosis between heritage management and tourism development is besotted with inherent challenges, efforts can be made to strike an equilibrium between protection and conservation and planned development of heritage tourism so that a level-playing field can be designed (Wager, 1995). A discussion of development issues is also required to raise the knowledge and understanding of varied stakeholder views and constraints, "which in turn can lead to a wider collaboration and formulation of alliances" (Aas, Ladkin, & Fletcher, 2005, p. 45). Also, mounting pressures such as lower visitations, budget deficit and political ambitions need to be handled in a strategic manner. Each WHS is a separate entity and is bestowed with distinct features specific to its location and host community environment. Hassan argues that "it is crucial for future tourism development plans to be compatible with the environment to main its market competitiveness" (2000, p. 242). It is also tremendously impacted by the political and cultural values and other related particularities of the host country. Hence capturing its essence and magnitude, through a limited set of heritage and intangible indices, can restrict the existing and future value of its brand. Its purpose needs to extend beyond the guidelines set by the World Heritage Convention and build a strong sense of brand identity that resonates both with the past and the present. A glocal (a mix of global and local) perspective was suggested in the earlier chapter to understand and gauge successful growth and vitality of heritage tourism initiatives, while at the same time, striving to promote a value-laden educational experience. However, in the light of more recent findings, 'glocalization' of heritage is a phenomenon that brings with it serious challenges (Cesari, 2010; Conway, 2014; Rakic & Chambers, 2007). Hence, a smart retro brand marketing agenda is needed to avoid pitfalls associated with the marriage of global with local.

Heritage tourism planning should focus on a themed tourism environment which is complimentary to the world heritage site and its host community culture. In my previous chapter, I had stressed the need to attract appropriate target markets to the WHS to help reinforce carrying capacity agenda and keep a check on visitation impacts. Strategies such as high price theory or demarketing can be pursued to attract selected audience seeking meaningful and sustained experiences. One point, worthy of note, is that recent literature has reported that visitations to several WHS across the globe have not increased as anticipated. Several studies also share that brand equity of a heritage site has not improved or benefited only to a moderate extent, as a result of official recognition by UNESCO. Clearly, at this point, scholars need to revisit anticipated benefits and costs associated with the WHS status. While, the status offers political impetus to nations, the universally touted justification in the form of economic benefits lacks clout today.

It has been extensively suggested that integrated and strategic sustainability of heritage tourism is crucial to maintain the destination attractiveness and enhance prospects and competitiveness in the long term (Chhabra, 2010; Wager, 1995). Sadiki (2012) stresses on three elements for sustainable marketing of the WHS: conservation, visitation numbers, and expanding facilities for visitors. Also, is emphasized, crucial coordination between local and government agencies and strategies such as "demarketing, promotion, developing brand awareness, agency collaboration, cooperation between benefiting parties, price strategy and marketing sustainability, and list of WHS in danger (2014, pp. 20-21). Possible demarketing tools include: educating potential visitors, focusing on desired markets, publicizing alternate sites, informing of substitute sites, and restricting access to fragile area by making them difficult to reach.

More recent literature also emphasizes on ethical production and consumption of heritage. However, in the light of disappointing economic returns at some WHS, it is evident that several factors contribute to transform a heritage site into a successful tourism attraction. As an instance, it was noted in Italy, geographic location and clusters draw visitors. In sum, this enhanced version supports earlier suggestions to avoid site- centric perspectives to accomplish successful integrated sustainable development. Integrated sustainable marketing plan is needed to assist in promoting cultural, social, economic and environmental integrity of the heritage site and its surrounding host community resources to successfully manage the growing tourism demand. Pomering et al.'s (2011) ten marketing indices (integrating the 4 Ps, consumer needs, process, physical evidence, partnerships, bundling and packaging, and value added programming) lends support to this perspective. A smart marketing perspective inclusive of retrobranding tactic is required, for smart commodification of heritage resources, to attract visitors.

Brown et al. (2008) opine that "brands are symbolic creations and are experiential in nature," hence their meaning needs to be strategically managed to improve brand equity (2003, p. 30). Retro brand marketing strategic can help relaunch the WHS and enhance their brand identity and equity. Retro brand narratives are drawn partially from "meanings and associations emanating from advertisers and marketers; however, they are also constructed by the mass media, press releases, news stories, and related celebrities. Most importantly, for retro brands, they are redolent of historical periods; temporal connections; and their attendant national, regional, and political associations" (Brown et al., 2008, p. 30). In a nutshell, retro branding strategy can serve as an effective mechanism to improve the brand equity of the WHS, since they have an authentic product that holds potential to instill a strong sense of nostalgia for the bygone era or place; they offer an ideal setting to present the past in a form that is received favorably by the contemporary audience. According to Brown et al. (2008), for a retro brand marketing strategy to be effective, it is important to build a "schismatic core that facilitates emotional investment on the part of the consumers. Retro brands can offer a simultaneous presence of old and new, tradition and technology, primitivism and progress, same and different" (2008, p. 21).

Moving forward, I suggest a smart marketing agenda which can help design a retrobranding strategy to attract target markets, while at the same time, keeping a check on how heritage resources are used so that externalities may be minimized. Smart marketing means marrying past and present resources while embracing intelligent online and traditional communication mix initiatives to maximize both online and off line presence of heritage in a way that connections are established harmoniously with key stakeholders of heritage tourism and conservation (Brown et al., 2008; Chhabra, 2010; Pomering et al., 2011). What is required is a hybrid (mixed) approach to set up a smart marketing agenda that co-creates brand essence of the WHS supported by ethical principles and that which is resilient in the face of different crisis situations, strives to promote increased visitations, and offers equitable socio-economic benefits to the different stakeholders, especially the host communities.

REFERENCES

Aas, C., Ladkin, A., & Fletcher, J. (2004). Stakeholder Collaboration and Heritage Management. *Annals of Tourism Research*, *32*(1), 28–48. doi:10.1016/j.annals.2004.04.005

Aguilar, M. (2009). *Examining Destination Marketing from the Lens of Sustainability*. Unpublished master's thesis. Arizona State University, Phoenix, AZ.

Boyd, S., & Butler, R. (1997). Sustainable Tourism Development in Protected Areas. *International Journal of Heritage Studies*, *10*(3), 309–319.

Bregalia, L. (2005). Keeping World Heritage in the Family: A Geneology of Maya Labour at Chichen Itza. *International Journal of Heritage Studies*, *8*(3), 247–265.

Carbone, M. (2005). Sustainable Tourism in Developing Countries: Poverty Alleviation, Participatory Planning, and Ethical Issues. *European Journal of Development Research*, *17*(3), 559–565. doi:10.1080/09578810500209841

Cellini, R. (2011). Is UNESCO Recognition Effective in Fostering Tourism? A Comment on Yang, Lin and Han. *Tourism Management*, *32*(2), 452–454. doi:10.1016/j.tourman.2010.01.018

Cesari, C. (2010). World Heritage and Mosaic Universalism: A View from Palestine. *Journal of Social Archaeology*, *10*(3), 299–324. doi:10.1177/1469605310378336

Chambers, E. (2009). From Authenticity to Significance: Tourism on the Frontier of Culture and Place. *Futures*, *41*(6), 353–359. doi:10.1016/j.futures.2008.11.003

Chhabra, D. (2009). Proposing a Sustainable Marketing Framework for Heritage Tourism. *Journal of Sustainable Tourism*, *17*(3), 313–320. doi:10.1080/09669580802495758

Chhabra, D. (2010). *Sustainable Marketing of Cultural and Heritage Tourism*. London: Routledge.

Chhabra, D. (2012). Authenticity of the objectively authentic. *Annals of Tourism Research*, *39*(1), 499–502. doi:10.1016/j.annals.2011.09.005

Choi, H., & Sirakaya, E. (2006). Sustainability Indicators for Managing Community Tourism. *Tourism Management*, *27*(6), 1274–1289. doi:10.1016/j.tourman.2005.05.018

Choi, S., Lehto, X., & Morrison, A. (2007). Destination image representation on the web: Content analysis of Macau travel related websites. *Tourism Management*, *28*(1), 118–129. doi:10.1016/j.tourman.2006.03.002

Coetzee, W., Nierkel, M., & Saayman, M. (2006). Applying Economic Guidelines for Responsible Tourism in a World Heritage Site. *Koedoe*, *50*(1), 54–60.

Cohen, E. (2007). Authenticity in Tourism Studies. *Tourism Recreation Research*, *32*(2), 75–82. doi:10.1080/02508281.2007.11081279

Conway, F. (2014). Local and Public Heritage at a World Heritage Site. *Annals of Tourism Research*, *44*(30), 143–155. doi:10.1016/j.annals.2013.09.007

Drost, A. (1992). Developing Sustainable Tourism for WHS. *Annals of Tourism Research*, *23*(2), 479–492. doi:10.1016/0160-7383(96)83345-7

Farrell, B., & Ward, L. T. (2005). Seven Steps towards Sustainability: Tourism in the Context of New Knowledge. *Journal of Sustainable Tourism*, *13*(2), 109–122. doi:10.1080/09669580508668481

Fullerton, L., McGettigan, K., & Stephens, S. (2010). Integrating Management and Marketing Strategies at Heritage Sites. *International Journal of Culture, Tourism, and Hospitality Research*, *4*(2), 108–117. doi:10.1108/17506181011045181

Fyall, A., & Rakic, T. (2006). The Future Market for WHS. In A. Leask & A. Fyall (Eds.), *Managing World Heritage Sites*. New York: Butterworth Heinemann.

Galla, A. (Ed.). (2012). *World Heritage: Benefits Beyond Borders*. Cambridge, UK: Cambridge University Press. doi:10.1017/CBO9781139567657

Guerin, H. (2000). Marketing: Complement or Compromise. In N. Buttimer, C. Rynee, & H. Guerin (Eds.), *The Heritage of Ireland*. Cork, Ireland: The Collins Press.

Harris, J., & Nelson, J. (1993). Monitoring Tourism from a Whole Economy Perspective: A Case from Indonesia. In J. Nelson, R. Butler, & G. Wall (Eds.), *Tourism and Sustainable Development: Monitoring, Planning and Managing* (pp. 179–196). Waterloo, Canada: Department of Geography Publications Series, University of Waterloo.

Hassan, S. (2000). Determinants of Marketing Competitiveness in an Environmentally Sustainable Tourism Industry. *Journal of Travel Research*, *38*(3), 239–245. doi:10.1177/004728750003800305

Haywood, M. (1990). Revisiting and Implementing the Marketing Concept as It Applies to Tourism. *Tourism Management*, *11*(3), 195–206. doi:10.1016/0261-5177(90)90042-8

Hede, A. (2007). World Heritage listing and the Evolving Issues Related to Tourism and Heritage: Cases from Australia and New Zealand. *Journal of Heritage Tourism*, *2*(3), 133–144. doi:10.2167/jht055.0

Heuermann, K., & Chhabra, D. (2014). The Darker Side of Dark Tourism: An Authenticity Perspective. *Tourism Analysis*, *19*(2), 213–225. doi:10.3727/108354214X13963557455766

Jamerozy, U. (2007). Marketing of Tourism: A Paradigm Shift towards Sustainability. *International Journal of Culture. Tourism and Hospitality Research*, *1*(2), 117–130.

Kilbourne, W. (1998). Green Marketing, a Theoretical Perspective. *Journal of Marketing Management*, *14*(6), 641–655.

Kivenzor, G. (2007). Brand Equity Aberrations: Heritage Brand Perception Effects in Russian Markets. *Academy of Marketing Science Review*, *10*, 1–20.

Lyon, S. (2007). Balancing Values of Outstanding Universality with Conservation and Management at the Three United Kingdom Cultural WHS. *Journal of Heritage Tourism*, *2*(1), 53–63. doi:10.2167/jht028.0

Manning, T. (1999). Indicators of tourism sustainability. *Tourism Management*, *20*(1), 179–181.

Marsh, J. (1993). The Potential Organization and Components of a Tourism Sustainability Index. In J. Nelson, R. Butler, & G. Wall (Eds.), *Tourism and Sustainable Development: Monitoring, Planning and Managing* (pp. 234–238). Waterloo, Canada: Department of Geography Publications Series, University of Waterloo.

McKercher, B., Ho, P., & du Cros, H. (2004). Attributes of Popular Culture Attractions in Hong Kong. *Annals of Tourism Research*, *31*(2), 393–407. doi:10.1016/j.annals.2003.12.008

Mill, R., & Morrison, A. (2006). *The Tourism System* (pp. 143–147). Dubuque, IA: Kendall Hunt Publishing Company.

Miller, G. (2001). The Development of indicators for sustainable tourism: Results of a Delphi survey of tourism researchers. *Tourism Management*, *22*(4), 351–362. doi:10.1016/S0261-5177(00)00067-4

Nelson, J., & Payne, R. (1993). An Introduction to Tourism and Sustainable Development with Special Reference to Monitoring. In J. Nelson, R. Butler, & G. Wall (Eds.), *Tourism and Sustainable Development: Monitoring, Planning and Managing* (pp. 3–19). Waterloo, Canada: Department of Geography Publications Series, University of Waterloo.

Nuryunti, W. (1996). Heritage and Postmodern Tourism. *Annals of Tourism Research, 23*(2), 249–260. doi:10.1016/0160-7383(95)00062-3

Patuelli, R., Mussoni, M., & Candela, G. (2013). *The Effects of World Heritage Sites on Domestic Tourism: A Spatial Interaction Model for Italy.* The Rimini Centre for Economic Analysis. Retrieved April 20, 2014, from http://link.springer.com/article/10.1007/s10109-013-0184-5#page-1

Pomering, A., Noble, G., & Johnson, L. (2011). Conceptualizing a Contemporary Marketing Mix for Sustainable Tourism. *Journal of Sustainable Tourism, 19*(8), 953–969. doi:10.1080/09669582.2011.584625

Rakic, T., & Chambers, D. (2007). World Heritage: Exploring the Tension between the Universal and the National. *Journal of Heritage Tourism, 2*(3), 145–155. doi:10.2167/jht056.0

Rakic, T., & Leask, A. (2006, June). *World Heritage List: historical development, current status and future scenarios*. Paper presented at the Cutting Edge Research in Tourism Conference-New Directions Challenges and Applications Conference. Surrey, UK.

Sadiki, F. A. (2012). *Sustainable Tourism Marketing Strategies at UNESCO World Heritage Sites (UNLV Theses/Dissertations/Professional Papers/Capstones; Paper 1477)*. Las Vegas, NV: University of Las Vegas University Libraries.

Saipradist, A., & Staiff, R. (2007). Crossing the Cultural Divide: Western Tourists and Interpretation at Ayutthaya World Heritage Site, Thailand. *Journal of Heritage Tourism, 2*(3), 211–224. doi:10.2167/jht061.0

Selwyn, T. (1996). Introduction. In T. Selwyn (Ed.), *The Tourist Image: Myths and Myth Making in Tourism* (pp. 1–33). Chichester, UK: John Wiley and Sons, Ltd.

Sirakaya, E., Jamal, T., & Choi, H. (2001). In Search of Sustainable Tourism Indicators. In D. Weaver (Ed.), *Encyclopedia of Ecotourism* (pp. 411–432). Oxford, UK: Oxford University Press.

Taylor, J. (2001). Authenticity and Sincerity in Tourism. *Annals of Tourism Research, 28*(1), 7–26.

Timothy, D., & Boyd, S. (2006). Heritage Tourism in the 21st Century: Valued Traditions and New Perspectives. *Journal of Heritage Tourism, 1*(1), 1–16.

Timothy, D. J. (2011). *Cultural heritage and tourism: An introduction.* Bristol, UK: Channel View Publications.

UNESCO. (2002). *Operational Guidelines for the Implementation of the World Heritage Convention.* Paris, France: UNESCO.

Wager, J. (1995). Developing a strategy for the Angkor world heritage site. *Tourism Management, 16*(7), 515–523. doi:10.1016/0261-5177(95)00069-Z

Walle, A. H. (1998). *Cultural tourism: a strategic focus*. Boulder, CO: Westview Press, Inc.

Weidmann, K., Hennings, N., Schmidt, S., & Wuestefeld, T. (2011). The Importance of Brand Heritage as a Key Performance Driver in Marketing Management. *Journal of Brand Management, 19*(3), 182–194. doi:10.1057/bm.2011.36

Winter, T. (2007). Rethinking tourism in Asia. *Annals of Tourism Research*, *34*(1), 27–44. doi:10.1016/j.annals.2006.06.004

KEY TERMS AND DEFINITIONS

Heritage Tourism: A form of tourism that focuses on inheritance and past legacies. It manages past to showcase it to visitors and offers opportunities to experience local traditions.

Retro Brand Marketing: Focused on enhancing brand identity and equity of a heritage product while keeping a check on sustainable use of heritage resources to minimize externalities. This form of marketing helps negotiate and adapt old notions to new environments and changing demand.

Stakeholders of Heritage Tourism: Refer to those organizations and businesses that have an interest and personal stake in heritage tourism.

Sustainable Indicators: Factors that tangibly measure social, cultural, economic, and environment impacts of tourism.

Sustainable Tourism Marketing: Focuses on marketing strategies that take into consideration negative impact on natural, social, and cultural environments. It strives to minimize externalities on host communities.

Chapter 14
Considering Sustainability in Project Management Processes

Gilbert Silvius
LOI University of Applied Sciences, The Netherlands & Van Aetsveld, The Netherlands

ABSTRACT

Sustainability is one of the most important challenges of our time. How can prosperity be developed without compromising the life of future generations? Companies are integrating sustainability in their marketing, corporate communication, annual reports and in their actions. The concept of sustainability has more recently also been linked to project management. Sustainability needs change of business models, products, services, resources, processes, etc. and projects are a frequently used practice of realizing change. Several studies explored how the concept of sustainability impacts project management. This chapter elaborates on the impact of sustainability found in literature and analyses the most influential standards of project management processes for their coverage of this impact. The study concludes that the most important standards of project management processes still fail to refer convincingly to sustainability considerations. Based on the author's analysis, this chapter also provides guidance for the further development of the process standards towards a 'sustainable project management' process.

INTRODUCTION

In the last 10 to 15 years, the concept of sustainability has grown in recognition and importance (Silvius et al., 2012). How can humans develop prosperity without compromising the future? The pressure on companies to broaden reporting and accountability from economic performance for shareholders, to sustainability performance for all stakeholders has increased substantially (Visser, 2002). Industry leaders realize that 'greenwashing' of current business practices is not a solution. The 2012 BSR/Globe Scan study concludes that "The most important leadership challenge facing business today is the integration of sustainability into core business functions" (BSR/GlobeScan, 2012).

The concerns about sustainability indicate that the current way of producing, organizing, consuming, living, etc. may have negative effects on the future. In short, the current business processes of organizations are not sustainable. This conclusion outlines the need for re-thinking, re-designing and re-developing of business practices in a more sustainable way. Sustainability therefore means

DOI: 10.4018/978-1-4666-8433-1.ch014

change. Change of business models, products, services, resources, processes, reporting, and behavior (Silvius et al., 2012). A frequently used practice of realizing change in organizations is by initiating and performing projects: temporary, task oriented organizations (Lundin & Söderholm, 1995; Turner & Muller, 2003).

The concept of sustainability has therefore also been linked to project management (Gareis et al., 2009; Silvius et al., 2012). Association for Project Management (past-) chairman Tom Taylor recognizes that "the planet earth is in a perilous position with a range of fundamental sustainability threats" and "Project and Programme Managers are significantly placed to make contributions to Sustainable Management practices" (Association for Project Management, 2006). Also in academic research, the relationship between project management and sustainability is explored (e.g. Gareis et al., 2009; Brent & Labuschagne, 2006; Silvius et al., 2009) as one of the (future) developments in project management. However, Eid (2009) concludes in his study on sustainable development and project management that the standards for project management "fail to seriously address the sustainability agenda" (Eid, 2009).

This chapter explores the integration of the concepts of sustainability in project management processes as identified by the most-prominent standards for project management. It aims to identify the relationship between sustainability and project management and to provide guidance on how the processes and standards of project management should integrate the concepts and principles of sustainability.

THE DIMENSIONS OF SUSTAINABILITY

The balance between economic growth and social wellbeing has been around as a political and managerial challenge for over 150 years (Dyllick & Hockerts, 2002). Also the concern for the wise use of natural resources and our planet emerged already many decades ago, with Carson's book "Silent Spring" (Carson, 1962) as a launching hallmark. In 1972 the 'Club of Rome', an independent think tank, published its book "The Limits to Growth" (Meadows et al., 1972). In the book, the authors concluded that if the world's population and economy would continue to grow at their current speeds, our planet's natural resources would approach depletion. The Limits to Growth fuelled a public debate, leading to installation of the UN 'World Commission on Development and Environment', named the Brundtland Commission after its chair. In their report, the Brundtland commission defines sustainable development as "development that meets the needs of the present without compromising the ability of future generations to meet their own needs" (World Commission on Environment and Development, 1987). By stating that "In its broadest sense, sustainable development strategy aims at promoting harmony among human beings and between humanity and nature", the report implies that sustainability requires also a social and an environmental perspective, next to the economical perspective, on development and performance.

The visions that none of the development goals, of economic growth, social wellbeing and a wise use of natural resources, can be reached without considering and effecting the other two, got widely accepted (Keating, 1993). In his book "Cannibals with Forks: the Triple Bottom Line of 21st Century Business", identifies John Elkington, this as the 'triple bottom line' or 'Triple-P (People, Planet, Profit)' concept: Sustainability is about the balance or harmony between economic sustainability, social sustainability and environmental sustainability (Elkington, 1997).

However, several publications consider more dimension or 'principles' of sustainability that are relevant to project management. For example, Gareis et al. (2011) define sustainability with the principles: economic, social and ecologic orientation; short-, mid- and long-term orienta-

Table 1. Additional dimension of sustainability relevant to project management

Additional Dimensions	Considered By
A values dimension	Eid (2009), Gareis et al. (2009, 2011, 2013), Silvius et al. (2012, 2013), Eskerod & Huemann (2013), Goedknegt (2012), Keeble et al. (2003), Khalfan (2006), Keeys (2012), Prieto (2011), Schieg (2009), Silvius & Nedeski (2011), Russell (2008)
A time dimension	Eid (2002, 2009), Gareis et al. (2009, 2011, 2013), Haugan (2012), Silvius et al. (2012, 2013), Taylor (2010), Al-Saleh & Taleb (2010), Badiru (2010), Brent & Labuschagne (2006), Eskerod & Huemann (2013), Goedknegt (2012), Herazo et al. (2010), Khalfan (2006), Keeys (2012), Labuschagne & Brent (2005, 2007), Pade et al. (2008), Prieto (2011), Schieg (2009), Silvius & Nedeski (2011)
A geographical dimension	Gareis et al. (2009, 2011, 2013), Haugan (2012), Silvius et al. (2012), Taylor (2010), Badiru (2010), Edum-Fotwe & Price (2009), Eskerod & Huemann (2013), Goedknegt (2012), Prieto (2011), Schieg (2009), Silvius & Nedeski (2011)
A performance dimension	Eid (2009), Craddock (2013), Maltzman & Shirley (2010, 2013), Tiron-Tudor & Ioana-Maria (2013), Thoumy & Vachon (2012)
A participation dimension	Ding (2008), Klotz & Horman (2010), Goedknegt (2012), Eskerod & Huemann (2013)
A waste (reduction) dimension	Eid (2002), Ma (2011), Maltzman & Shirley (2010, 2013), Khalfan (2006)
A transparency dimension	Silvius et al. (2012), Khalfan (2006), Silvius & Nedeski (2011), Achman (2013)
A accountability dimension	Silvius et al. (2012), Silvius & Nedeski (2011), Achman (2013)
A cultural dimension	AlWaer et al. (2008)
A risk (reduction) dimension	Goedknegt (2012), Gareis et al. (2009), Turner (2010)
A political dimension	Pade et al. (2008)

tion; local, regional and global orientation; value orientation. The last dimension, value orientation, refers to sustainability as a normative concept that requires specific values underpinning the attitudes and behaviors of individuals. This dimension can also be found with Eskerod & Huemann (2013), Eid (2009), and Schieg (2009). Other dimensions or principles of sustainability that are mentioned include risk reduction (Gareis et al., 2009; Goedknegt, 2012), transparency (Silvius et al., 2012; Khalfan, 2006) and performance (Eid, 2009; Craddock, 2013; Maltzman & Shirley, 2010). Table 1 summarizes the additional dimensions, next to the social, environmental and economic dimensions of the triple bottom line, which are mentioned in the publications in our sample. These dimensions provide additional insight as to how sustainability is considered in the context of project management.

After the analysis of the dimensions of sustainability found in the publications on sustainability in project management, those dimensions were then synthesized. It was concluded that the following dimensions of sustainability are relevant to the understanding of sustainability in the context of project management.

- *Sustainability is about balancing or harmonizing social, environmental and economical interests.* In order to contribute to sustainable development, a company should satisfy all 'three pillars' of sustainability: social, environment and economic (Elkington, 1997). The dimensions are interrelated, that is, they influence each other in various ways.
- *Sustainability is about both short-term and long-term orientation.* A sustainable company should consider both short-term and long-term consequences of their actions, and not only focus on short-term gains (Gareis et al., 2011). The dimension of both short-term and long-term orientation focuses the attention to the full lifespan of the matter at hand (Brent & Labuschagne, 2006).

- *Sustainability is about local and global orientation.* The increasing globalization of economies affects the geographical area that organizations influence. Intentionally or not, many organizations are influenced by international stakeholders whether these are competitors, suppliers or (potential) customers. The behaviour and actions of organizations therefore have an effect on economic, social and environmental aspects, both locally and globally. "In order to efficiently address these nested and interlinked processes sustainable development has to be a coordinated effort playing out across several levels, ranging from the global to the regional and the local" (Gareis et al., 2011, p. 61).
- *Sustainability is about values and ethics.* As argued by Robinson (2004) and Martens (2006), sustainable development is inevitably a normative concept, reflecting values and ethical considerations of society. Part of change needed for more sustainable development, will therefore also be the implicit or explicit set of values that professionals, business leaders or consumers have and that influence or lead our behavior.
- *Sustainability is about transparency and accountability.* The principle of transparency implies that an organization is open about its policies, decisions and actions, including the environmental and social effects of those actions and policies (International Organization for Standardization, 2010). This implies that organizations provide timely, clear and relevant information to their stakeholders so that the stakeholders can evaluate the organization's actions and can address potential issues with these actions. Complementing the principle of transparency, is the principle of accountability. This principle implies that an organization is responsible for its policies, decisions and actions and the effect of them on environment and society. The principle also implies that an organization accepts this responsibility and is willing to be held accountable for these policies, decisions and actions.
- *Sustainability is about stakeholder participation.* Considering and respecting the potential interests of stakeholders is key to sustainability. ISO 26000 emphasizes the behavioral side of this principle, by mentioning "proactive stakeholder engagement" as one of its principles (International Organization for Standardization, 2010). Stakeholder participation therefore requires "a process of dialogue and ultimately consensus-building of all stakeholders as partners who together define the problems, design possible solutions, collaborate to implement them, and monitor and evaluate the outcome" (Goedknegt & Silvius, 2012, p. 3).
- *Sustainability is about risk reduction.* The so-called precautionary principle is based on the understanding that in environment-society system interactions, the complexity, indeterminacy, irreversibility and non-linearity has reached a level in which it is more efficient to prevent damage, rather than ameliorate it (Turner, 2010). The recent Deepwater Horizon oil-spill disaster has fuelled the discussion on the suitability of financial risk management techniques for societal and environmental risks.
- *Sustainability is about eliminating waste.* The importance of eliminating waste is mentioned by several authors, including Maltzman & Shirley (2010, 2013). They refer to "The Seven Wastes" as identified in the Toyota production system. These seven wastes are: overproduction, waiting, transporting, inappropriate processing, unnecessary inventory, unnecessary or excess motion and defects. The principle of

eliminating waste can also be found in the cradle-to-cradle concept (McDonough & Braungart, 2002) that builds upon the idea that waste equals food.

- *Sustainability is about consuming income, not capital.* Sustainability implies that nature's ability to produce or generate resources or energy remains intact. The 'source and sink' functions of the environment should not be degraded. Meaning that the extraction of renewable resources should not exceed the rate at which they are renewed and the absorptive capacity of the environment to assimilate waste should not be exceeded (Gilbert et al., 1996). The principle may also be applied to the social perspectives (Silvius et al., 2012). Organizations should also not 'deplete' people's ability to produce or generate labour or knowledge by physical or mental exhaustion. In order to be sustainable, companies have to manage not only their economic capital, but also their social and environmental capital.

These dimensions of sustainability provide the context of considering the concepts of sustainability in project management and project management processes and in the following paragraphs.

THE IMPACT OF SUSTAINABILITY ON PROJECT MANAGEMENT

The dimensions of sustainability identified earlier have an impact on the way projects are performed and managed. For example, Maltzman and Shirley (2010), Silvius et al. (2012) and Tharp (2013) specify the impact of sustainability on project management in 'impact areas', such as the identification of relevant stakeholders, the recognition of benefits in the business case, the assessment of risks, etc. Based on a structured analysis of 164 publications on sustainability in project management, Silvius & Schipper (2014) conclude the following 'areas of impact'.

- **Recognition of the Context of the Project:** A starting point for all aspects of a project and its management is the recognition of the context of the project. Integrating the dimensions of sustainability into project management inevitably implies a broader consideration of the context (Silvius et al., 2012; Tharp, 2013) of the project. Both the time and the spatial boundaries of the context are stretched when considering sustainability. Especially the sustainability dimensions 'both short and long term' and 'local and global' impact the project context. In an increasingly global business world, more and more projects also touch upon the geo-economic challenges as part of the project team may be located in emerging economies like India or China, and suppliers may be all over the world. Or customers benefitting from the project's deliverable. It is clear that the globalizing business world also includes globalized projects and project management. Within the project management community, the discussion about globalization aspects of the result or deliverable of the project still has to emerge. Van den Brink (2009) illustrates the recognition of the broader context of 'Sustainable Project Management', compared to traditional or modern project management (Figure 1), by mentioning local and global society and an enlarged time scale, in a visual illustration of the scope of sustainable project management. In sustainable project management, the context of the project is addressed in relationship to the organization's strategy, but also in relationship to society as a whole.

Figure 1. Sustainable project management
(Based on Van den Brink, 2009).

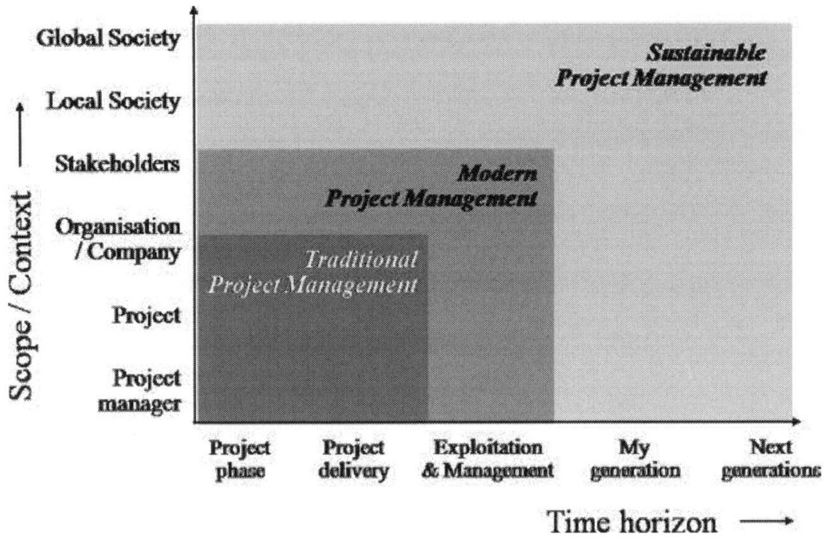

- **Identification of Stakeholders:** The dimensions of sustainability, more specific the principles 'balancing or harmonizing social, environmental and economical interests', 'both short term and long term' and 'both local and global', will likely increase the number of stakeholders of the project (Tharp, 2013; Eskerod & Huemann, 2013). Typical 'sustainability stakeholders' may be environmental protection pressure groups, human rights groups, nongovernmental organizations, etc. (Silvius et al., 2012).
- **Project Specifications/Requirements/Deliverable/Quality Criteria:** Integrating the principles of sustainability will influence the specifications and requirements of the project's deliverable or output, and the criteria for the quality of the project (Eid, 2009; Maltzman & Shirley, 2010; Taylor, 2010). For example the inclusion of environmental or social aspects in the project's objective and intended output and outcome (Silvius et al., 2012). Integrating sustainability into project management suggests that the content, intended output/outcome and quality criteria are based on a holistic view of the project (Gareis et al., 2013) including sustainability dimensions as 'economical, environmental and social', 'short term and long term' and 'local and global', and developed together with a broad group of stakeholders (Eskerod & Huemann, 2013).
- **Business Case/Costs/Benefits:** The influence of the principles of sustainability on the project content, will need to be reflected also in the project justification (Silvius & Schipper, 2012). The identification of costs, benefits and the business case of the project may need to be expanded to include also non-financial factors that refer to for example social or environmental aspects (Gareis et al., 2011, 2013). Considering the concepts of sustainability in project management implies that the business case of a project addresses the triple bottom line of economic, social and environmental benefits. Silvius & Schipper (2012) conclude that this implies a multi-criteria approach

to investment evaluation, with consideration of both financial and non-financial criteria.

- **Dimensions of Project Success:** Shenhar et al. (2001) relate the criteria and perception of project success to a time scale. In their model, the perception of success develops from the short term criterion of 'project efficiency' to the medium-term criterion of 'business success' and eventually the long term criterion of 'prepare for the future'. Given the sustainability dimension 'short term and long term', it has to be concluded that integrating sustainability in the dimensions implies that also criteria that refer to the development of future capabilities of the organization are included in the dimensions of project success, next to the traditional 'iron triangle' or project efficiency. This also implies that the success of the project is assessed based on the life cycle of the project and its outcome (Pade et al., 2008; Craddock, 2013). Taking into account the sustainability dimension 'economical, environmental and social', implies that the criteria of project success refer to both economic, social and environmental benefits.
- **Selection and Organization of Project Team:** Another area of impact of sustainability is the project organization and management of the project team. Especially the social aspects of sustainability, such as equal opportunity and personal development, can be put to practice in the management of the project team (Tharp, 2013), but also aspects such as commuting distance and work-life balance may be considered in the organization and management of the team. Van den Brink (2013) applies the principles of positive psychology to project management in order to manage the project team in a sustainable way.
- **Project Sequencing and Schedule:** Taylor (2010) recognizes the opportunities for considering sustainability in project planning, scheduling and sequencing. Het challenges project managers to think beyond 'how things are normally done', and provides several examples. One of the examples being offsite fabrication rather than onsite. This provides possible sustainability advantages of less waste, reduced delivery costs, better use of resources, opportunities to increase labor skills, opportunities for job creation in poorer locations, economies of mass production, etc. Sustainable project management also implies performing the project as efficient as possible, thereby minimizing waste. Waste can occur in materials, but also in idle resources or waiting times (Maltzman & Shirley, 2010). These last two types of waste typically relate to scheduling and sequencing.
- **Materials Used:** An obvious impact area for sustainability in project management is the selection of materials used in the project (Akadiri et al., 2013; Silvius et al., 2012). Logical considerations are use of hazardous substances, pollution and energy use, both in the production process as in the use and remaining life cycle of the materials. However, the most important sustainability insight regarding materials, might be applying a life cycle perspective (Brent & Petrick, 2007). This implies considering the production supply chain, but also durability, reusability and recyclability at the decommission stage of the project's deliverable.
- **Procurement:** Not just the materials used, but also the processes concerned with procurement and selection of suppliers provide a logical opportunity to integrate considerations of sustainability. For example appreciating the sustainability performance of potential suppliers in supplier selection

(Taylor, 2010), but also in fighting bribery and non-ethical behavior in procurement (Tharp, 2013), both by participants in the project or organization and by potential suppliers or authorities.

- **Risk Identification and Management:** Risk management, including risk mitigation, is a well-known concept in project management. In project management standards, a risk is defined as an uncertain event or set of events that, should it occur, will have an effect on the achievement of objectives (Office of Government Commerce, 2010). However, when considering this definition from a sustainability perspective, some question may come up. For example, which objectives are being considered in the identification of potential risks? Are these the triple-constraint objectives of the projects or the desired outcomes of the project's deliverable? And whose objectives are being considered? The objectives of the project sponsor or the objectives of all stakeholders? With the inclusion of the concepts of sustainability in project management, the assessment of potential risks will need to evolve (Winnall, 2013). Logically in the identification of risks, also environmental and social risks are to be considered. And, following the life cycle approach, these risks need to be assessed for the project's resources, processes, deliverables and effects (Silvius et al., 2012). However, considering sustainability in risk identification and management does not only apply to the kind of risks considered. It also implies that risks are considered from the different points of views and interests of all stakeholders, not just the project sponsor. This also suggests that in sustainable project management, the stakeholders are participating in the identification, assessment and management of risks (Silvius, 2013).
- **Stakeholder Involvement:** Several authors (For example Pade et al., 2008; Gareis et al., 2009; Perrini & Tencati, 2006) emphasize the importance of stakeholder participation in projects. This principle logically impacts the stakeholder management and the communication processes in project management. However, the intention behind 'participation' goes beyond the identification of some specific processes. Stakeholder participation isn't so much a specific process, as it is an attitude with which all project management processes are performed. According to the ISO 26000 guideline, proactive stakeholder engagement is one of the basic principles of sustainability (International Organization for Standardization, 2010). Also Eskerod & Huemann (2013) link sustainable development, projects and the role of stakeholders, and conclude that there is a need "to incorporating stakeholders and their interests in more project management activities" (Eskerod & Huemann, 2013, p. 45).
- **Project Communication:** Following the principle of transparency and accountability, incorporating sustainability into project management processes and practices would imply proactive and open communication about the project, that would also cover social and environmental effects, both short-term and long-term (Khalfan, 2006; Taylor, 2010; Silvius et al., 2012).
- **Project Reporting:** As the project progress reports logically follow the definition of scope, objective, critical success factors, business case, etc. also the project reporting processes will be influenced by the inclusion of sustainability aspects (Perrini & Tencati, 2006).
- **Project Handover:** The different studies show a more diverse picture of the opportunities to integrate sustainability aspects.

For example, the respondents in Eid's study (2009) suggest that the closing phase of a project offers the least appealing opportunities for integrating sustainability (Eid, 2009). However, Pade et al. (2008) and Silvius et al., (2012) point out the importance of also the closing processes for a more sustainable project result. The closing processes typically include hand-over to the permanent organization. The success of this hand-over and the acceptance of the project result are important aspects of a project's sustainability. Failed or non-accepted projects can hardly be considered sustainable, given the waste of resources, materials and energy they represent.

- **Organizational Learning:** A final area of impact of sustainability is the degree to which the organization learns from the project. Sustainability also suggests minimizing waste. Organizations should therefore learn from their projects in order to not 'waste' energy, resources and materials on their mistakes in projects (Eid, 2009; Silvius et al., 2012).

These impact areas of sustainability in project management will be out analysis framework when analyzing the consideration of sustainability in project management processes.

PROJECT MANAGEMENT PROCESSES

In this chapter project management processes are considered based on the most influential standards of project management. Standards form an important building block of any profession (Crawford, 2007). They capture the body of knowledge that provides guidance for individuals and organizations practicing the profession and for the development of professionals. For projects and project management, several standards can be identified. Some relate to the process of performing or managing projects, some to the competences or qualifications of the project manager and some to the organization that commissions projects.

For the purpose of this chapter, two broadly used standards of project management processes were selected, and one developing standard, as the object of analysis. The two broadly used standards are the Project Management Institute's project management body of knowledge (PMBOK® Guide) and the Axelos' PRojects IN Controlled Environments (PRINCE2®). These two standards were selected on the criteria:

1. **Usage:** Frequently and internationally used;
2. **Endorsement:** By an international organization;
3. **Recognition:** As a project management standard.

In Europe, PRINCE2® is the leading standard for management of projects (Zoete, 2009), whereas the PMBOK® Guide may be the globally the most recognized standard for project management. The third standard considered in this chapter is the recently released ISO 21500:2012 Guidance on project management (International Organization for Standardization, 2012).

The PMBOK® Guide (Project Management Institute, 2013) is often considered as the most influential standard on project management, because of the distribution of the Guide and the popularity of the related Project Management Professional (PMP®) certification process. The first version of the PMBOK® Guide was published in 1987, making it one of the first standards for project management. A second version followed in 2000, a third in 2004 and a fourth in 2008. The current version of the PMBOK® Guide, version 5, was published early 2013. The PMBOK® Guide describes 'best practices' of project management, structured in ten 'knowledge areas' and 47 processes.

PRINCE2® (Office of Government Commerce, 2009) is a structured approach to project management, originally developed as the 'PRINCE' methodology in 1989 for the government of the United Kingdom. The second release, 'PRINCE2®'was released in 1996 as a generic project management methodology. The original PROMPT methodology, which evolved into the PRINCE methodology, with IBM's PRINCE2® combined MITP (managing the implementation of the total project) methodology. PRINCE2® provides a methodology for managing projects within a clearly defined framework. It describes project management principles, themes and processes (Office of Government Commerce, 2009).

ISO 21500:2012 (International Organization for Standardization, 2012) was published as the result of a five year development process to create a "common frame of reference and a process standard, that is intended to be overarching for all standards and concepts of project management." (Legerman et al., 2013, p.1). This standard was selected because of its potential to provide a universal and common language for project management.

Project management processes logically refer to the processes required for the management of the projects. A common misunderstanding is that project management processes therefore refer to all processes in the project. That is not the case, but is also not very clearly stated by all project management standards. ISO 21500 clearly distinguishes three types of processes within a project:

- **Project Management Processes:** Those processes required for planning, organizing, managing, monitoring, controlling and reporting the project activities and the realization of the project's output.
- **Product Processes:** Those processes that actually create the project's output.
- **Support Processes:** Those processes that enable the product processes and the project management processes, by providing support services.

The standards discussed in this chapter are project management standards, which refer to the project management processes, and sometimes to the support processes. In this chapter does not explicitly discuss the sustainability aspects of the product processes, although the project management processes logically refer to these product processes.

The PMBOK® Guide recognizes five project management process 'groups':

- Initiating Processes;
- Planning Processes;
- Executing Processes;
- Closing Processes;
- Monitoring & Controlling Processes.

And although these process groups suggest a project life cycle, they do not necessarily represent the phasing of the project. Projects appear in many variations and "there is no single way to define the ideal structure for a project" (Project Management Institute, 2013). The project management process groups may therefore depict a full project life cycle or the nature of the project management processes in a certain stage or phase of the project. The 5 process groups are detailed in 47 processes.

In contrast to the PMBOK® Guide, PRINCE2®, does base its identification of project management processes on the project life cycle. The processes describe a step by step progression throughout the project lifecycle, from getting started till project closure. Each process provides checklists and formats of recommended activities, products and related responsibilities. The eight project management process groups that PRINCE2® recognizes are:

- Starting Up a Project;
- Initiating a Project;
- Planning;
- Managing Project Delivery;
- Controlling a Stage;

- Managing Stage Boundaries;
- Directing a Project;
- Closing a Project.

These eight process groups are detailed in 45 (sub) processes.

ISO 21500 also selected a life cycle approach to identifying project management processes. The process groups identified in the ISO 21500 resemble those of the PMBOK® Guide: Initiating; Planning; Implementing; Controlling; and Closing. The term 'Implementing' was preferred above 'Executing', as the corresponding PMBOK® Guide process group is labeled, because 'executing' translates quite harsh in various other languages. Within the five process groups, a total of 39 project management processes are identified.

When comparing these standards, the process groups show great similarity. Table 2 presents an overview of the process groups. Especially in the process groups 'Initiating', 'Controlling' and 'Closing', the three standards are almost identical. For the 'Planning' and 'Executing / Managing / Implementing' process groups, the differences between the standards appear to be more notable, but the nature of these processes, a iterative cycle of planning, managing and executing, is shared by all three standards.

Given the similarities of the three standards, a generic project life cycle was used. The method based identification of process groups (initiating, planning, executing, controlling, and closing) as our baseline for analyzing the impact of sustainability on project management processes.

Table 2. Comparison of project management process groups as identified by the standards for project management processes considered in this chapter

PM BOK® Guide	PRINCE®	ISO 21500
Initiating Processes	Starting Up a Project	Initiating
	Initiating a Project	
Planning Processes	Planning	Planning
Executing Processes	Managing Project Delivery	Implementing
	Managing Stage Boundaries	
	Directing a Project	
Monitoring & Controlling Processes	Controlling a Stage	Controlling
Closing Processes	Closing a Project	Closing

(Silvius, 2013).

INTEGRATING SUSTAINABILITY INTO PROJECT MANAGEMENT PROCESSES

In the study by Eid (2009), a forum of project management practitioners was asked about their assessment of the impact of sustainable development on project management processes. More specifically, for each project management process group (initiating, planning, executing, controlling, closing) the study asked their views on the area of integration of sustainability aspects. The questions asked were:

- To which account do the scope and objectives of the project (more or less the project content) provide opportunities for integrating sustainability?
- To which account do the actual processes of delivering and managing the project (the project process) provide opportunities for integrating sustainability?

Figure 2 shows the result of Eid's study.

From this study it can be concluded that the respondents see opportunities for the integration of sustainability in all process groups of project management. The area of integration of sustainability aspects, however, differs:

- The initiating and planning stages of the project provide opportunities for integrating sustainability into the content of the project.

Figure 2. The best areas to integrate sustainable development into project management (Based on Eid, 2009).

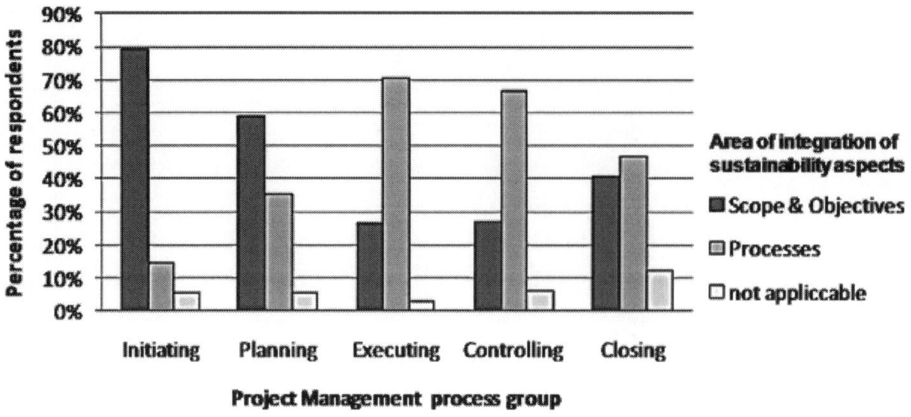

- The executing and controlling stages of the project provide opportunity for integrating sustainability in the process of the project.

This outcome is not unexpected, as the dimensions of sustainability are best integrated from the origins of the process, system or asset that is defined as the intended project result.

A more specific assessment of the impact of sustainability on the project management processes is presented in the following section. In this section, the consideration of the impact areas of sustainability in project management, as identified earlier, in the three standards of project management processes, PMBOK® Guide, PRINCE2® and ISO 21500, is discussed. Based on this discussion a suggestion for the development of the processes towards the processes of 'sustainable project management' is made.

Recognition of the Context of the Project

In the PMBOK® Guide, Section 2.1.5, Enterprise Environmental Factors, mentions the organization's human resources and marketplace conditions as "internal or external environmental factors that surround or influence a project's success" (Project Management Institute, 2013). However, the section fails to more explicitly identify potential social or environmental interest resulting from sustainability policies as factors of influence.

PRINCE2® addresses the project context in several processes during the start-up and initiation stages of the project. For example, the business case and intended project result may logically be linked to the context of the project in terms of organizational goals and strategy. However, also here no mentioning is made of a larger societal context of the project (Office of Government Commerce, 2009).

Also in ISO 21500, clause 3 describes the context and concepts of projects mainly from an organizational strategy realization perspective. However, section 3.5 mentions the 'Project Environment', including "factors outside the organizational boundary such as socio-economic, geographical, political, regulatory, technological and ecological". It is stated that the project team should consider these factors.

On this impact area, it should be concluded that the standards of project management processes consider a project predominantly within the context of an organization and the strategy or goals of that organization. The larger societal context is only explicitly recognized in ISO 21500. Sustainable project management would require that the context of the project is addressed in relationship to the organization's strategy, but also in relationship to society as a whole.

Identification of Stakeholders

In the listing of examples of project stakeholders, in paragraph 2.2.1, the PMBOK® Guide lacks any reference to typical 'sustainability' stakeholders, such as environmental protection interest groups, human rights groups or non-governmental organizations. Also chapter 13, Project Stakeholder Management, fails to recognize these potential stakeholders when it discusses the identification, analysis and management of stakeholders of the project.

In PRINCE2®, the identification of stakeholders is mentioned in different processes of the initial stages of the project and in the theme 'Organization' (Office of Government Commerce, 2009). In this section, an explicit mentioning is made of 'pressure and interest groups', 'charities' and 'NGO's as potential stakeholders.

ISO 21500 uses a broad definition of potential stakeholders, a "person, group or organization that has interests in or can affect, be affected by, or perceive themselves to be affected by any aspect of the project" and makes an explicit reference to "Special Interest Groups" as potential stakeholders, without elaborating on this in the text of the guideline.

It can be concluded that all three standards use abroad definition of stakeholders, as people or organizations that could be impacted by, or themselves could impact, the project. In the examples of stakeholders, ISO 21500 and PRINCE2® refer explicitly to potential stakeholders that potentially would represent social or environmental interests.

On this impact area, sustainable project management would require that in the identification of potential stakeholders, explicit notion is made of potential stakeholders representing the environmental and/or social aspects of the project. Sustainable project management also implies that the project communicates proactively with all, identified and potential, stakeholders.

Project Specifications/Requirements/Deliverable/Quality Criteria

In the PMBOK® Guide, the specifications, requirements, deliverables and quality of the project, as formulated by the requesting organization, logically play a central role in the project. For example, in the project charter's 'statement of work' these specifications and/or requirements are frequently referred to as the project's scope. The PMBOK® Guide does not suggest any criteria for the aspects or dimensions in which the project scope is defined.

PRINCE2® defines the specifications, requirements, scope and quality of the project foremost in terms of the products of the project: the deliverables and partial deliverables. The criteria for this are stated in terms of business goals and benefits. No specific reference to environmental or social aspects is made.

Also ISO 21500 positions the content, goal and outcome of the project in the context of the organizational strategy. No reference is made to the content of this strategy or the project.

In line with the conclusion derived on the impact area 'Recognition of the context of the project', it should be concluded that the current project management standards consider a project predominantly within the context of an organization and the strategy or goals of that organization.

On this impact area, sustainable project management would require that the specifications, requirements, deliverables and quality criteria are based on a holistic view of the project, including sustainability perspectives as 'economical, environmental and social', 'short term and long term' and 'local and global'. And that the requirements or interests of other stakeholders are considered to the degree that they may interfere with the requirements of the sponsor (Eskerod & Huemann, 2013).

Business Case/Costs/Benefits

The PMBOK® Guide, in section 4.1.1. 'Develop Project Charter', recognizes ecological impacts and social needs as potential benefits of a project when it discussed the business case (Project Management Institute, 2013).

In PRINCE2®, the business case the business case has a central role. In all stages of the project, specific project management processes are identified to define or update the business case. These processes address benefits and the business case in general, without specifically addressing potential social or environmental benefits (Office of Government Commerce, 2009).

Section 3.4.2 of the ISO 21500 mentions the business case as the justification for the investment in the project. Reference to a holistic view on justification is made by stating that the evaluation "may include multiple criteria including financial investment appraisal techniques and qualitative criteria such as strategic alignment, social impact, and environmental impact."

None of the standards mention the consideration of ecological or social costs.

On this impact area, sustainable project management would require that the business case addresses the 'triple bottom line' of economic, social and environmental benefits, both on the short and the long term. Investment evaluation would need to be based on a multi-criteria approach of both quantitative and qualitative criteria (Silvius & Schipper, 2012).

Dimensions of Project Success

In paragraph 2.2.3, the PMBOK® Guide mentions that "the success of the project should be measured in terms of completing the project within the constraints of scope, time, cost, quality, resources and risk as approved between the project managers and senior management" (Project Management Institute, 2013, p. 35). This 'definition' of project success focuses on the short term and medium term criteria for project success, as identified by Shenhar et al. (2001). The longer term perspective on project success is lacking in the PMBOK® Guide. And although the criterion 'quality' can cover all sorts of aspects, when defined by the requesting organization, the explicit mentioning of 'cost' as a measurement of project success, inevitably emphasizes the economical perspective of the project (Silvius et al., 2012).

PRINCE2® mentions six project performance variables: 'costs', 'timescales', 'quality', 'scope', 'risk' and 'benefits'. Also here sustainability dimensions may be included in the performance variables 'quality' and 'benefits', but they are not mentioned explicitly. In fact, Barbone et al. (2011) suggest that 'sustainability' is added as a seventh project performance variable (Barbone et al., 2011, p. 52).

ISO 21500 mentions "comply with requirements to satisfy the project sponsor, customers and other stakeholders" as an important criterion for project success. Following the 'broad' definition of stakeholders mentioned earlier, this statement may support a holistic view on project success.

On this impact area, the conclusion of our analysis should be that the standards for project management fail to explicitly recognize sustainability as a dimension of project success. Sustainable project management would require that the definition and perception of project success take into account the 'triple bottom line' of economic, social and environmental benefits as laid out in the business case, both in the short term as in the long term. This implies that the success of the project is assessed based on the life cycle of the project and its result.

Selection and Organization of Project Team

The PMBOK® Guide, in chapter 9 Project Human Resource Management, shows little consideration of social sustainability aspects such as life-work balance, equal opportunity, part time job opportunities, etc. Paragraph 9.2.2., however, pays attention to virtual teams and links this to team members working from home offices, potentially with mobility limitations or disabilities (Project Management Institute, 2013). Also the personal development of team members is addressed. However, the objective for this development is the performance of the project team, without considering the effectiveness of team members in their professional life after the project.

PRINCE2® pays ample attention to the management and development of the project team. The theme 'Organization' is largely dedicated to the management and governance structure of the project. Where the project team is mentioned, some references are made to diversity of roles and personalities of team members and to the development of team members, but these social aspects of the projects are not elaborated upon.

ISO 21500 Process 4.3.15 'Establish Project Team' mentions that "the project manager, when possible, should take into consideration factors such as skills and expertise, different personalities, and group dynamics when establishing the project team". No reference is made social sustainability aspects such as life-work balance, equal opportunity, part time job opportunities, etc. Process 4.3.18 does mention the development of the project team.

On this impact area, sustainable project management would require that the management and development of project team members is aimed at preparing them for their role in the project and keeping them fit for this role. However, in the management of the project, also the effectiveness of team members in their personal and professional life after the project would be considered. These aspects are only marginally covered in the standards for project management processes.

Project Sequencing and Schedule

The PMBOK® Guide describes the planning and scheduling of the project in Chapter 6, Project Time Management. This chapter discusses different techniques for the development of the project schedule and the optimization of the project schedule. However, the chapter does not include criteria for the quality of the project schedule, other than 'fitting the project constraints'. Obvious criteria to for the prevention of 'waste' in the form of idle time or waiting time are not mentioned as considerations, although 'leveling' of resources is discussed.

In PRINCE2®, 'planning' is one of the themes, and the planning of activities / work packages is included in 'plans', for example project plan, stage plan and team plan. Also here, several scheduling techniques are presented, but no criteria for the quality of the planning / schedule are discussed, except for leveling of resources.

ISO 21500 includes a subject group 'time' with processes on sequencing and planning of activities. Also in this standard, no criteria for the quality of the planning / schedule are discussed, other than the development of an achievable time schedule, in relation to the desired project output.

On this impact area, sustainable project management would require that project activities are sequenced and scheduled with consideration of minimizing transport movements, idle time, waste, safety hazards and nuisance for the project's stakeholders.

Materials Used

Processes related to the selection of materials and/or procurement can be found in different sections of the PMBOK® Guide. For example paragraph 3.4.20 Plan procurements, paragraph 3.5.8. Conduct procurements, chapter 12 Project Procurement Management. None of these sections include any references to sustainability aspects in the selection of materials.

In PRINCE2®, materials and procurement are implicitly included in work-packages. No reference is made to the selection of materials, based on sustainability criteria.

In ISO 21500, references to materials, procurement and suppliers are all related to a controlled execution of the project. In process 4.3.36 Select Suppliers, no reference is made to social or environmental criteria that may be considered in supplier or materials selection.

On this impact area, sustainable project management would require that in the selection of materials for the project, environmental and social criteria are applied.

Procurement

As described in the previous impact area, materials used, the current standards of project management logically include processes related to procurement and the selection of suppliers. However, none of these standards include any references to sustainability considerations, such as working conditions, human rights and 'fair' pricing, in these processes (Silvius, 2013).

On this impact area, sustainable project management would require that selection of suppliers for the project is done with consideration of economic, environmental and social criteria, and that this process is done in a fair and ethical manner.

Risk Identification and Management

Chapter 11, Project Risk Management, of the PMBOK® Guide, risk is defined as "an uncertain event or condition that, if it occurs, has a positive or negative effect on one or more project objectives such as scope, schedule, cost and quality." (Project Management Institute, 2013:310). Except for the general objective 'quality', this definition focuses on the short term aspects of the project, without recognizing the longer term risks that may be related to the project. The rest of the chapter discusses several a processes and techniques to identify and manage risks, however, these techniques do not mention the possibility of environmental and/or social risks.

In PRINCE2®, risk, as one of the central themes, is addressed in many processes throughout the project life cycle (Office of the Government Commerce, 2009). However, also here no explicit reference is made to environmental and/or social risks.

In ISO 21500, section 3.5 'Project Environment' mentions risks imposed by factors outside the organizational boundary. And section 3.11 'Project Constraints' mentions that consensus on the "level of acceptable risk exposure "should be reached among key project stakeholders. However, no explicit reference is made to environmental and/or social risks.

On this impact area, sustainable project management would require that the risk identification and risk management processes include the identification and management of environmental and/or social risks. These processes consider risks in relation to the objectives and goals of the project, but also in relation to the interests of stakeholders.

Stakeholder Involvement

The PMBOK® Guide recognizes that stakeholders can be actively involved in the project (Project Management Institute, 2013); however, the processes related to stakeholders imply a perspective of stakeholders as external actors. Sustainable project management would imply to involve stakeholders proactively in project activities, such as the definition of requirements, assessment of costs and benefits, project planning and scheduling, identification and assessment of risks, handling of issues and project reporting.

PRINCE2® in general is more product oriented, describing *what* has to be delivered, than activity oriented, describing *how* the project management processes need to be executed. Therefore, a potential participation of stakeholders in project activities is not suggested.

ISO 21500 suggest that "Stakeholders may be actively involved in the project" (International Organization for Standardization, 2012, p. 25), without specifying in any of the other processes, where this would be appropriate or how this could be organized.

On this impact area, it should be concluded that the standards of project management processes do not propagate a proactive stakeholder engagement, as is suggested by the ISO 26000 guideline. Sustainable project management would on this aspect require that stakeholders are invited to participate in activities such as benefits identification, risk identification, scheduling, etc. as also suggested by Eskerod & Huemann (2013).

Project Communication

Chapter 10 of the PMBOK® Guide, Project Communications Management, discusses project communication in relation to the identification and management of stakeholders. And although the sustainability dimensions of transparency and accountability are not explicitly mentioned, the chapter takes the "stakeholder's information needs and requirements" as starting point of the planning of communication actions. However, the statement that the project manager should provide "only the information that is needed" (Project Management Institute, 2013, p. 290), reflects a more reactive and less transparent approach.

Also PRINCE2® discusses the project's 'Communications Management Strategy' in relationship to the engagement of stakeholders. It is mentioned that communication with external stakeholders, for example about risks, should be done cautiously, which may be considered not completely in line with the transparency that sustainability requires.

Also ISO 21500 recognizes 'Communications' as a subject group with related processes. Again the stakeholder's information needs are taken as a starting point for communications planning, and it is recognized that organizational factors and multiple cultures may affect communication requirements.

On this impact area, sustainable project management would require a more explicit recognition of the principles of transparency and accountability in the planning and management of communication with stakeholders.

Project Reporting

Project reporting processes can be found in the PMBOK® Guide in paragraph 10.2.2.5 Performance Reporting. In this section, project reporting focuses on progress and changes in the areas scope, schedule, cost and quality of the project. Reporting on sustainability aspects is not explicitly addressed, nor is the principle of transparency.

The 'Report highlights' process as part of 'Controlling a stage' of PRINCE2®, reports the progress of the project in terms of the work packages, issues and changes. Reporting on sustainability aspects is not addressed, nor is the principle of transparency.

In ISO 21500, progress reports and inspection reports are frequently mentioned as inputs or outputs of processes without being detailed. Reporting on sustainability aspects is not addressed, nor is the principle of transparency.

On this impact area, sustainable project management would require that project reporting is pro-active and transparent. Project progress is reported on different aspects of the project, including environmental and social aspects.

Project Handover

The PMBOK® Guide pays ample attention to the handover of the project deliverables to the requesting organization and the acceptance of these deliverables. The processes of the 'Closing' process group mention the transition of project deliverables, but do not discuss the organizational change aspects of this transition.

PRINCE2®, in the process Closing a Project' puts more emphasis on the acceptance of the project deliverables and provides guidance for practices that may facilitate this acceptance.

ISO 21500 lacks adequate attention to the handover of the project deliverables in the closing processes of the project.

On this impact area, sustainable project management would require that a successful handover of the project's deliverables, and their acceptance by the permanent or requesting organization, is considered in all stages of the project, as this is a condition for a sustainable project result (Pade et al., 2008; Silvius et al., 2012).

Organizational Learning

In the PMBOK® Guide, Section 2.4.3 mentions 'Historical information and lessons learned' as part of the 'Corporate Knowledge Base' of the organization (Project Management Institute, 2013). However, this section lacks a more explicit reference to organizational learning or knowledge management in order to improve an organization's competence in doing projects.

In PRINCE2®, the 'Lessons log' and the 'Lessons report' explicitly capture the lessons learned in a project. These lessons are explicitly addressed in the starting up stage of a project in the process 'Capture previous lessons' (Office of Government Commerce, 2009).

In ISO 21500, Process 4.3.8 'Collect lessons learned', covers the capturing, compiling, formalizing, storing and dissemination of experiences to benefit current and future projects. The planning processes mention lessons learned as an input.

On this impact area, sustainable project management would require that lessons learned and previous experiences are explicitly captured during project execution and closing and are made to use in the initiation and start-up of new projects. This is done to improve an organization's competence in doing projects.

Reflecting on the analysis above, it should be concluded that, on the logical areas of impact of sustainability, the most important standards of project management processes (*PMBOK® Guide*, PRINCE2® and ISO 21500) fail to refer convincingly to sustainability considerations. Identification of environmental and social aspects, if any, is mostly implicit. Furthermore, the standards of project management place emphasis on the processes of project management and consider the content of the project (objective, intended result, deliverable) as given. Integrating the concepts of sustainability, however, suggests that not just the process of delivering the project is considered, but also the content of the project itself. The integration of sustainability in projects and project management therefore requires an elaborated view of the profession.

This more elaborated view is provided by the PMI 'Code of Ethics and Professional Conduct' (Project Management Institute, 2010). This code addresses the increased awareness of business ethics as well as the differentiation of ethical values in different cultures. The code addresses four values: responsibility, respect, fairness, and honesty; that should be guiding the work and the profession of the project manager.

The code strongly relates the profession of project management to sustainability, by stating that is the project managers' duty to "make decisions and take actions based on the best interest of society, public safety, and the environment".

The explicit recognition of the relationship between sustainability and project management in the PMI Code of Ethics and Professional Conduct is what is missing in the standards of project management processes.

And despite of the proposal by about 200 members of PMI, the latest of the standards discussed in this paper, the PMBOK® Guide Fifth edition, did not show more consideration of sustainability dimensions, as the Fourth edition that was discussed in earlier publications (Silvius, 2013). Most of the 'sustainability changes' that the PMI members proposed (Maltzman et al., 2010) were 'deferred' to a future Sixth edition.

CONCLUSION

Projects can make a contribution to the sustainable development of organizations. It should therefore be expected that the concepts and principles of sustainability are reflected in projects and project management and their standards. Reflecting on the analysis, it can concluded that on the logical areas of impact, the standards of project management processes (PMBOK® Guide, PRINCE2® and ISO 21500) fail to refer convincingly to sustainability considerations. Identification of environmental and social aspects, if any, is mostly implicit. The explicit recognition of the relationship between sustainability and project management in the PMI Code of Ethics and Professional Conduct is missing in the standards of project management processes.

And, since the standards of project management place emphasis on the processes of project management, the content of the project (objective, intended result, deliverable) is mostly considered as given. Integrating the concepts of sustainability, however, suggests that not just the process of delivering the project is considered, but also the content of the project itself.

It is clear that still a lot of work has to be done on the implications of Sustainable Project Management and that there is a growing need of expertise, criteria and concepts to practically implement the concept in the management of projects.

FUTURE RESEARCH DIRECTIONS

Future research may elaborate on the impact of sustainability on the project management processes by providing process descriptions, formats and enhanced standards. However, as with many standards, it should be taken into account that the integration of sustainability concepts may be specific to the context of the project. The fact that most standards for sustainability indicators developed context specific or industry specific sets of indicators, supports this view. It is for that reason that there is a demand for in depth case studies to understand what the implications are for integrating sustainability into project management processes.

REFERENCES

Achman, R. (2013). Stakeholders' Perspectives on Sustainability in Project Management. In A. J. G. Silvius & J. Tharp (Eds.), *Sustainability Integration for Effective Project Management* (pp. 321–336). Hershey, PA: IGI Global Publishing. doi:10.4018/978-1-4666-4177-8.ch020

Akadiri, P. O., Olomolaiye, P. O., & Chinyio, E. A. (2013). Multi-criteria evaluation model for the selection of sustainable materials for building projects. *Automation in Construction*, *30*(2), 113–125. doi:10.1016/j.autcon.2012.10.004

Al-Saleh, Y. M., & Taleb, H. N. (2010). The integration of sustainability within value management practices: A study of experienced value managers in the GCC countries. *Project Management Journal*, *41*(2), 50–59. doi:10.1002/pmj.20147

AlWaer, H., Sibley, M., & Lewis, J. (2008). Different Stakeholder Perceptions of Sustainability Assessment. *Architectural Science Review*, *51*(1), 48–59. doi:10.3763/asre.2008.5107

Association for Project Management. (2006). *APM supports sustainability outlooks.*

Badiru, A. B. (2010). The many languages of sustainability. *Industrial Engineer*, *42*(11), 30–34.

Barbone, S., Groot, J., Horam, R., Liuni, S., & Imerti, V. (2011). *Project Management for European Sustainable Development*. Foundation for European Sustainable Tourism.

Brent, A. C., & Labuschagne, C. (2006). Social indicators for sustainable project and technology life cycle management in the process industry. *International Journal of Life Cycle Assessment*, *11*(1), 3–15. doi:10.1065/lca2006.01.233

Brent, A. C., & Petrick, W. (2007). Environmental Impact Assessment (EIA) during project execution phases: Towards a stage-gate project management model for the raw materials processing industry of the energy sector. *Impact Assessment and Project Appraisal*, *25*(2), 111–122. doi:10.3152/146155107X205832

BSR/GlobeScan. (2012). *2012 BSR/GlobeScan State of Sustainable Business Poll*. Retrieved January 8, 2013, from http://www.globescan.com/commentary-and-analysis/press-releases/press-releases-2012/244-new-poll-of-business-leaders-highlights-sustainability-priorities-for-global-companies.html

Carson, R. (1962). *Silent Spring*. Boston, MA: Houghton Mifflin.

Craddock, W. T. (2013). How Business Excellence Models Contribute to Project Sustainability and Project Success. In A. J. G. Silvius & J. Tharp (Eds.), *Sustainability Integration for Effective Project Management* (pp. 1–19). Hershey, PA: IGI Global Publishing. doi:10.4018/978-1-4666-4177-8.ch001

Crawford, L. (2007). Global Body of Project Management Knowledge and Standards. In P. W. G. Morris & J. K. Pinto (Eds.), *The Wiley Guide to Managing Projects*. Hoboken, NJ: John Wiley and Sons, Inc. doi:10.1002/9780470172391.ch46

Ding, G. K. C. (2008). Sustainable construction—The role of environmental assessment tools. *Journal of Environmental Management*, *86*(3), 451–464. doi:10.1016/j.jenvman.2006.12.025 PMID:17289255

Dyllick, T., & Hockerts, K. (2002). Beyond the business case for corporate sustainability. *Business Strategy and the Environment*, *11*(2), 130–141. doi:10.1002/bse.323

Edum-Fotwe, F. T., & Price, A. D. F. (2009). A Social Ontology for Appraising Sustainability of Construction Projects and Developments. *International Journal of Project Management*, *27*(4), 313–322. doi:10.1016/j.ijproman.2008.04.003

Eid, M. (2002). A sustainable approach to the project management odyssey. In *Proceedings of the PMI Research Conference: Frontiers of Project Management Research and Application*. Philadelphia PA: Project Management Institute.

Eid, M. (2009). *Sustainable Development & Project Management*. Cologne, Germany: Lambert Academic Publishing.

Elkington, J. (1997). *Cannibals with Forks: the Triple Bottom Line of 21st Century Business*. Oxford, UK: Capstone Publishing Ltd.

Eskerod, P., & Huemann, M. (2013). Sustainable development and project stakeholder management: What standards say. *International Journal of Managing Projects in Business*, *6*(1), 36–50. doi:10.1108/17538371311291017

Gareis, R., Heumann, M., & Martinuzzi, A. (2009). *Relating sustainable development and project management*. Paper presented at the IRNOP 2009. Berlin, Germany.

Gareis, R., Huemann, M., & Martinuzzi, A. (2011). What can project management learn from considering sustainability principles? In *Project Perspectives* (Vol. XXXIII, pp. 60–65). Amsterdam, The Netherlands: International Project Management Association.

Gareis, R., Huemann, M., & Martinuzzi, R.-A. with the assistance of Weninger, C., & Sedlacko, M. (2013). Project Management & Sustainable Development Principles. Newton Square, PA: Project Management Institute.

Gilbert, R., Stevenson, D., Girardet, H., & Stern, R. (Eds.). (1996). *Making Cities Work: The Role of Local Authorities in the Urban Environment*. London, UK: Earthscan Publications Ltd.

Goedknegt, D. (2012). Sustainability in Project Management: A case study at University of Applied Sciences Utrecht. *PM World Journal, I*(IV).

Goedknegt, D., & Silvius, A. J. G. (2012). The implementation of sustainability principles in project management. In *Proceedings of the 26th IPMA World Congress* (pp 875-882). Amsterdam, The Netherlands: International Project Management Association.

Haugan, G. (2012). *The New Triple Constraints for Sustainable Projects, Programs, and Portfolios*. Boca Raton, FL: CRC Press. doi:10.1201/b12271

Herazo, B., Lizarralde, G., & Paquin, R. (2012). Sustainable development in the building sector: A Canadian case study on the alignment of strategic and tactical management. *Project Management Journal, 43*(2), 84–100. doi:10.1002/pmj.21258

International Organization for Standardization. (2010). *ISO 26000, Guidance on Social Responsibility*. Geneva, Switzerland: International Organization for Standardization.

International Organization for Standardization. (2012). *ISO 21500:2012, Guidance on Project Management*. Geneva, Switzerland: International Organization for Standardization.

Keating, M. (1993). *The Earth Summit's Agenda for Change*. Geneva, Switzerland: Centre for our Common Future.

Keeble, J. J., Topiol, S., & Berkeley, S. (2003). Using Indicators to Measure Sustainability Performance at a Corporate and Project Level. *Journal of Business Ethics, 44*(2-3), 149–158. doi:10.1023/A:1023343614973

Keeys, L. A. (2012). Emerging Sustainable Development Strategy in Projects: A Theoretical Framework. *PM World Journal, I*(II).

Khalfan, M. M. A. (2006). Managing Sustainability within Construction Projects. *Journal of Environmental Assessment Policy and Management, 8*(1), 41–60. doi:10.1142/S1464333206002359

Klotz, L., & Horman, M. (2010). Counterfactual analysis of sustainable project delivery processes. *Journal of Construction Engineering and Management, 136*(5), 595–605. doi:10.1061/(ASCE)CO.1943-7862.0000148

Labuschagne, C., & Brent, A. C. (2005). Sustainable Project Life Cycle Management: The need to integrate life cycles in the manufacturing sector. *International Journal of Project Management, 23*(2), 159–168. doi:10.1016/j.ijproman.2004.06.003

Labuschagne, C., & Brent, A. C. (2007). Sustainability assessment criteria for projects and technologies: Judgements of industry managers. *South African Journal of Industrial Engineering, 18*(1), 19–33.

Legerman, A., Zandhuis, A., Silvius, G., Rober, R., & Stellingwerf, R. (2013). *ISO 21500 in Practice - A Management Guide*. Zaltbommel, The Netherlands: Van Haren Publishing.

Lundin, R. A., & Söderholm, A. (1995). A theory of the temporary organization. *Scandinavian Journal of Management, 11*(4), 437–455. doi:10.1016/0956-5221(95)00036-U

Maltzman, R., & Shirley, D. (2010). *Green Project Management*. Boca Raton, FL: CRC Press. doi:10.1201/EBK1439830017

Maltzman, R., & Shirley, D. (2013). Project Manager as a Pivot Point for Implementing Sustainability in an Enterprise. In A. J. G. Silvius & J. Tharp (Eds.), *Sustainability Integration for Effective Project Management* (pp. 261–278). Hershey, PA: IGI Global Publishing. doi:10.4018/978-1-4666-4177-8.ch016

Maltzman, R., Shirley, D., Mochal, T., & Krasnoff, A. (2010). *Proposed changes and reasoning for proposed changes to 5th Edition of the PMBOK® Guide*. Retrieved April 7, 2014, from http://www.green-pm.com/articles/2010-07PMIProposal.pdf

Martens, P. (2006). Sustainability: science or fiction? *Sustainability: Science, Practice, &. Policy*, *2*(1), 1–5.

McDonough, W., & Braungart, M. (2002). *Cradle To Cradle: Remaking The Way We Make Things*. New York, NY: North Point Press.

Meadows, D. H., Meadows, D. L., Randers, J., & Behrens, W. W. (1972). *The Limits to Growth*. New York, NY: Universe Books.

Office of Government Commerce. (2009). *Managing Successful Projects with PRINCE2*. Norwich.

Office of Government Commerce. (2010). Management of Risk: Guidance for Practitioners. Norwich.

Pade, C., Mallinson, B., & Sewry, D. (2008). An Elaboration of Critical Success Factors for Rural ICT Project Sustainability in Developing Countries: Exploring the Dwesa Case. *The Journal of Information Technology Case and Application*, *10*(4), 32–55. doi:10.1080/15228053.2008.10856146

Perrini, F., & Tencati, A. (2006). Sustainability and Stakeholder Management: The Need for New Corporate Performance Evaluation and Reporting Systems. *Business Strategy and the Environment*, *15*(5), 286–308. doi:10.1002/bse.538

Prieto, B. (2011). *Sustainability on Large, Complex Engineering & Construction Programs Utilizing a Program Management Approach. PM World Today, XIII*. VII.

Project Management Institute. (2010). *Code of Ethics and Professional Conduct*. Newtown Square, PA: Project Management Institute.

Project Management Institute. (2013). *A Guide to the Project Management Body of Knowledge (PMBOK Guide)* (5th ed.). Newtown Square, PA: Project Management Institute.

Robinson, J. (2004). Squaring the circle: On the very idea of sustainable development. *Ecological Economics*, *48*(4), 369–384. doi:10.1016/j.ecolecon.2003.10.017

Russell, J. (2008). Corporate social responsibility: what it means for the project manager. In *Proceedings of the 2008 PMI Europe Congress*. Project Management Institute.

Schieg, M. (2009). The model of corporate social responsibility in project management. *Business: Theory & Practice*, *10*(4), 315–321.

Shenhar, A. J., Dvir, D., Levy, O., & Maltz, A. C. (2001). Project Success: A Multidimensional Strategic Concept. *Long Range Planning*, *34*(6), 699–725. doi:10.1016/S0024-6301(01)00097-8

Silvius, A. J. G. (2013). Sustainability in Project Management Processes. In A. J. G. Silvius & J. Tharp (Eds.), *Sustainability Integration for Effective Project Management* (pp. 58–75). Hershey, PA: IGI Global Publishing. doi:10.4018/978-1-4666-4177-8.ch004

Silvius, A. J. G., & Nedeski, S. (2011). Sustainability in IS projects; A case study. *Communications of the IPMA*, *11*(4), 1–11.

Silvius, A. J. G., & Schipper, R. (2012). Sustainability in the Business Case. In *Proceedings of the 26th IPMA World Congress* (pp. 1062 – 1069). Amsterdam, The Netherlands: International Project Management Association.

Silvius, A. J. G., & Schipper, R. (2014). Sustainability in project management: A literature review and impact analysis. *Social Business*, *4*(1), 63–96. doi:10.1362/204440814X13948909253866

Silvius, A. J. G., Schipper, R., & Nedeski, S. (2013). Sustainability in Project Management: Reality Bites. *PM World Journal, II*(II).

Silvius, A. J. G., Schipper, R., Planko, J., van den Brink, J., & Köhler, A. (2012). *Sustainability in Project Management*. Farnham, UK: Gower Publishing.

Silvius, A. J. G., van den Brink, J., & Köhler, A. (2009). Views on Sustainable Project Management. In K. Kähköhnen, A. S. Kazi, & M. Rekola (Eds.), *Human Side of Projects in Modern Business*. Helsinki, Finland: IPMA Scientific Research Paper Series.

Taylor, T. (2010). *Sustainability Interventions - for Managers of Projects and Programmes*. Salford, UK: The Higher Education Academy – Centre for Education in the Built Environment.

Tharp, J. (2013). Sustainability in Project Management: Practical Applications. In A. J. G. Silvius & J. Tharp (Eds.), *Sustainability Integration for Effective Project Management* (pp. 182–193). Hershey, PA: IGI Global Publishing. doi:10.4018/978-1-4666-4177-8.ch011

Thoumy, M., & Vachon, S. (2012). Environmental projects and financial performance: Exploring the impact of project characteristics. *International Journal of Production Economics*, *140*(1), 28–34. doi:10.1016/j.ijpe.2012.01.014

Tiron-Tudor, A., & Ioana-Maria, D. (2013). Project Success by Integrating Sustainability in Project Management. In A. J. G. Silvius & J. Tharp (Eds.), *Sustainability Integration for Effective Project Management* (pp. 106–127). Hershey, PA: IGI Global Publishing.

Turner, J. R. (2010). Responsibilities for Sustainable Development in Project and Program Management. In H. Knoepfel (Ed.), *Survival and Sustainability as Challenges for Projects*. Zurich, Switzerland: International Project Management Association.

Turner, J. R., & Müller, R. (2003). On the nature of the project as a temporary organization. *International Journal of Project Management*, *21*(3), 1–8.

van den Brink, J. (2009). Duurzaam projectmanagement: verder kijken dan je project lang is (Sustainable Project Management: Looking Beyond the Project) *Projectie, 4* (In Dutch).

van den Brink, J. (2013). How Positive Psychology can Support Sustainable Project Management. In A. J. G. Silvius & J. Tharp (Eds.), *Sustainability Integration for Effective Project Management* (pp. 245–260). Hershey, PA: IGI Global Publishing. doi:10.4018/978-1-4666-4177-8.ch015

Visser, W. T. (2002). Sustainability reporting in South Africa. *Corporate Environmental Strategy*, *9*(1), 79–85. doi:10.1016/S1066-7938(01)00157-9

Winnall, J.-L. (2013). Social Sustainability to Social Benefit: Creating Positive Outcomes through a Social Risk. In A. J. G. Silvius & J. Tharp (Eds.), *Sustainability Integration for Effective Project Management* (pp. 95–105). Hershey, PA: IGI Global Publishing. doi:10.4018/978-1-4666-4177-8.ch006

World Commission on Environment and Development. (1987). *Our Common Future*. Oxford, UK: Oxford University Press.

Zoete, L. de. (2010). PMBOK of Prince 2. *Automatisering Gids*, April (in Dutch).

KEY TERMS AND DEFINITIONS

Project: A temporary organization of materials and/or resources, performing a non-routine set of processes consisting of coordinated and controlled activities, with start and end dates, in order to achieve specified project objectives.

Project Deliverable: A tangible or intangible object produced as a result of the project that is intended to be delivered to a customer, either internal or external.

Project Management: The planning, monitoring and controlling of project delivery and support processes, aimed at realizing benefits for stakeholders.

Project Risk: An uncertain event or set of events that, should it occur, will have an effect on the achievement of the objectives of the project.

Project Stakeholder: A person, group or organization that has interest or concern in the project, its resources, its deliverable or its effect.

Sustainable Development: Development that meets the needs of the present without compromising the ability of future generations to meet their own needs.

Sustainable Project Management: The planning, monitoring and controlling of project delivery and support processes, with consideration of the environmental, economic and social aspects of the life-cycle of the project's resources, processes, deliverables and effects, aimed at realizing benefits for stakeholders, and performed in a transparent, fair and ethical way that includes proactive stakeholder participation.

Chapter 15
Managing Project Sustainability: A Tool for Project Managers

Gilman C. K. Tam
Independent Researcher, Hong Kong

ABSTRACT

Managing project sustainability is becoming important in the last two decades since the Earth Summit in 1992. An increasing number of projects have built in sustainability considerations into project design and implementation. Recent research findings show that lack of sustainability knowledge for project managers is a key barrier to drive projects and programs contributing towards a sustainable society. Definitions and approaches (pillar-based and principles-based) to sustainability in project management together with project manager competence requirements are discussed. The purpose of this chapter is to devise an assessment tool for project managers incorporating the concept of pillar-based and principles-based sustainability approaches as well as the EIA-driven and objectives-led assessment methodologies. Criteria for selecting assessment scheme appropriate to various project initiatives are developed. Integrating selected assessment methodology into sustainability evaluation framework within the project life cycle forms a complete tool. This chapter contributes to devising a practical assessment tool for project managers in managing project sustainability.

INTRODUCTION

Apart from the threat of hostilities and terrorism, it seems certain that climate change and the exhaustion of natural fossil fuel resources will provide the biggest challenges in the future. We shall need effective project managers to deal with these challenges if humankind is to survive. (Lock, 2007, p. 5)

Lock raises concern about sustainability of humankind (Lock, 2007). He is well aware that project managers need to face the kind of challenges like climate change and lack of fossil fuel in the days to come. Project managers are becoming part of the solution to human survival or sustainable development – a popular term after Gro Harlem Brundtland releasing the well-known "Brundtland Report" in 1987. She puts down the definition of

DOI: 10.4018/978-1-4666-8433-1.ch015

sustainable development as "the development that meets the needs of the present without compromising the ability of future generations to meet their own needs" (Brundtland, 1987). Her basic emphases are on long-term aspects of the concept of sustainability and equity between the present and future generations. The context in which Brundtland's definition is embedded indicates that '*needs*' include a sound environment, a just society and a healthy economy (Diesendorf, 2000). It links to what people perceive for a change in behavior, attitudes, and consumption patterns, etc. towards sustainability and equity, and how society perceives and values the environment. In the eyes of Diesendorf, 'Development' covers social and economic improvement in a broad sense and which may or may not involve economic growth. The emphasis is on 'qualitative improvement in human-being' or 'unfolding of human potential' as discussed by the ecological economist, Herman Daly (Diesendorf, 2000).

The Agenda 21, which is a comprehensive blueprint of action as adopted by more than 178 governments at the United Nations in the 1992 Earth Summit in Rio de Janeiro, Brazil, called for global partnership and drove governments, business and industry for sustainable development (UNCED, 1992). While most discussions on sustainability and sustainable development focus on political or policy level issues and global concerns, a research supported by the U.S. Agency for International Development (USAID), the United Nations Environment Programme (UNEP) and the University of Minnesota addressed the equally important focus at the project level – how to conduct project for better performing sustainable development. Gregersen, Lundgren and White (1994) in their policy brief suggested changing the project approach to assure more sustainable benefit flows through project activities for the sake of improving the contribution of projects to sustainable development and avoiding unsustainability (Gregersen, Lundgren, & White, 1994).

Project exists in a relatively turbulent environment and change is the purpose of the project itself and uncertainty is inherent in the objectives of that project. A Guide to the Project Management Body of Knowledge, PMBoK (4th edition) published by the Project Management Institute (PMI) recognizes "… Projects can also have social, economic, and environmental impacts that far outlast the projects themselves" (PMI, 2008). Munier (2005, p. 21) in his book "Introduction to Sustainability: Road to a Better Future" mentions that "Sustainability as a process often involves making an analysis to determine the best course of action when several projects, plans, programs, and options are considered" (Munier, 2005). The Association for Project Management (APM) in their "APM Supports Sustainability Outlooks" (APM, 2006) recognizes that many people involved in projects and programmes have the ability and capacity to be involved and influence at personnel, corporate, government and project level. Since project management is becoming a common way of managing business (Bredillet, 2000; Turner, 2009), the awareness of project manager and his/her team members to meeting the challenges of sustainability in project delivery would have made contributions to mankind.

Sustainability is a broad and subjective concept (Lim & Yang, 2009). Project managers need to understand sustainability and its relationship to project management before they can make contributions towards a sustainable world. In the project management community, sustainability emerges as a subject in the recent academic research. For instance, Gareis, Huemann and Martinuzzi (Gareis, Huemann, & Martinuzzi, 2009) presented a paper titled "Relating sustainable development and project management" at The International Research Network on Organizing by Projects (IRNOP) in the IRNOP IX Research Conference (Berlin, Germany, 11-13, October 2009) and another paper of related topic was presented at the Project Management Institute (PMI) Research and Education Conference 2010 (Washington, D.C., USA, 11-14, July

2010) (Gareis, Huemann, & Martinuzzi, 2010); and Silvius, van den Brink and Köhler (2010) presented a paper titled "The concept of sustainability and its application to project management" at the International Project Management Association (IPMA) International Expert Seminar 2010 (Zurich, Switzerland, 18-19, February 2010) (Silvius, van den Brink, & Köhler, 2010). In 2013, Silvius and Tharp have edited a book entitled "Sustainability Integration for Effective Project Management" (Silvius & Tharp, 2013). These research activities confirm the suggestion of Lock (2007) that effective project managers are required to deal with the challenges of climate change or sustainability for the well-being of humankind.

Recent development at corporate and project levels, some authors adopt Business Excellence Model (BEM), for example the European Foundation for Quality Management (EFQM) model, to address performance excellence in organization while Keeys, Huemann and Turner (2013) propose a conceptual framework for integrating project strategy for sustainable development within the context of corporate sustainability strategy (Keeys, Huemann, & Turner, 2013). Craddock has established linkages among BEM, project sustainability and project success that he applies BEM to project environment with sustainability as criteria for success (Craddock, 2013). Gareis (2013) opines that principles of sustainable development need to be considered in the project initiation and project management processes. With different objectives and tasks in different organizations, project initiation focuses on deciding whether an investment is to be made or not. The objectives of project management process are to perform the project successfully in according to its defined objectives and manage the project complexity and dynamics. For strategic investment and organization decision, Gareis recognizes that, from sustainable development perspective, project initiation process is more important than project management process (Gareis, 2013).

From above, it shows that many authors are becoming aware of sustainability extending from corporate level to project level through corporate sustainability strategy, project strategy down to process level. To deliver projects in a sustainable way with outcomes having positive sustainable impacts on the society, sustainability assessment within the project management process is important to drive for success. Though people understand the necessity of assessing sustainability, there is no unified approach to such assessment. Furthermore, except some authors such as Silvius and Schipper (Silvius & Schipper, 2010) and Tam (Tam, 2013) in the project management community wrote on sustainability assessment, there is generally a lack of guiding principles for project managers to conduct sustainability assessment which hinders the promotion of positive and minimization of negative project impacts towards a sustainable society.

The lack of existing knowledge and common understanding among project stakeholders on sustainability issues has called for the need to build a decision-making tool in order to enhance sustainability deliverables in projects. The purpose of this chapter is to provide an assessment tool to project managers for managing project sustainability impacts whether by ways of ex-ante assessment or ex-post evaluation. It includes a proposed sustainability evaluation framework and assessment methodologies for use in the project management process. To better understand the subject, background information such as the barriers to sustainability, sustainability approaches, definitions of sustainability in project management and program management are provided. Rationale for sustainability assessment and related sustainability competence for project manager are discussed. In the next section, the systemic view of sustainability together with highlight of barriers is introduced.

THE BARRIERS TO SUSTAINABILITY

Understanding of sustainability from a system perspective helps project managers in decision making. The concept of sustainability can be viewed as a system or a particular system state where the system's inputs and outputs remain sufficiently balanced over time to avoid system collapse or disruptive change (Peattie, 2011). By analogy to students learning physics in their experiment class testing electricity relationship of voltage (V) and current (I) (Ohm's Law: $I = V/R$) in an electric circuit consisting of resistor (R). They would find that there is a linear relationship between voltage and current in a linear electric circuit up till a state where the resistor was burnt. It is because the resistor was operating at a state beyond its limit. It is no longer to sustain with increased pressure (voltage applied). In other words, a system can only be sustainable within its limit. A system can be vulnerable and be destroyed fast, for example, a giant corporation (Enron) can be collapsed within a short period of time. Maintaining system sustainability whether it is a physical or social system needs to understand its inherent architecture.

Sustainability is about integrating economic, environmental and social aspects; about integrating short term and long term aspects; and about consuming the income and not the capital (Dyllick & Hockerts, 2002). The integration of both social and natural (or physical) systems as a whole is important to understand key sustainability issues. The notion of a system incorporates a number of components that interrelate with each other. The components can be grouped together to be understood as a whole and in terms of how that whole interacts with its neighborhood environment. For a sustainable system, the relationships among its components must be sustainable and the relationship between the system and its environment must not be destabilizing (Peattie, 2011). Project manager is a key member in the team for project design, planning, executing, monitor and control. Their views and understanding of the concept of sustainability and their attitudes towards managing project would greatly impact on project success sustainably. Integrating the concept of sustainability in project management would stretch the "system boundaries" of project management (Silvius & Schipper, 2010).

My recent research through a survey on project managers explores their familiarity to the concept of sustainable development. The question of familiarity calls for integrating environmental criteria (e.g. using renewable energy) and social criteria (e.g. protecting cultural heritage) into project objectives. The result is a bit encouraging. With 101 convenience samples from project managers, there are only 4 respondents (4.0%) answer "not at all" and 21 respondents (20.8%) respond "a little". There are 76 respondents who are having either "fairly" (30.7%), "familiar" (26.7%) or "very familiar" (17.8%) knowledge towards the concept of sustainable development. By the same token, there are many project managers who are trying to build in the concept of sustainability into their project objectives.

In the same study, I have identified several major hurdles in promoting project sustainability. Not surprisingly, "lack of sustainability knowledge and expertise" were told by 75 respondents which becomes top barrier. It is followed by two barriers having 70 votes each on "lack of interest from project sponsor/investor" and "managers' mindsets". The barrier of "lack of interest from customers" having 69 responses ranked third in the study. There are other barriers such as due to "organizational culture" (63 responses), "absence of appropriate tools and processes (e.g. guidelines)" (54 responses) and "government regulatory support" (53 responses).

Some project managers in the study put forward their opinions. Some of them reflect that existence of barriers is related to mentality of project managers and sponsors, etc. For example, one responds that "to me, sustainability is the responsibility of the sponsor and customer, not the project manager nor a sustainability expert." Another mention about economic benefits: "there is a growing awareness of Sustainability but the project sponsor will only consider these issues if there is increase in ROI (Return on Investment). The only factor that mitigates the above is where the sponsor wishes to show his 'green' credentials and is not concerned with ROI. This usually happens where the project is 'iconic' and a 'statement' is being made either with government sanction or on a personal level by the sponsor/ owner."

The study shows that barriers to managing project sustainability do exist. It is necessary to strengthen knowledge of sustainability (top barrier) to project managers and sponsors. Some project managers do not find themselves involved in building a sustainable society through their contributions in project development. Others still think that project economic benefit is more significant than other benefits such as environmental or social. In the following sections, a tool for project managers is developed to help in the absence of appropriate tools and processes for managing project sustainability.

THE SUSTAINABILITY APPROACH

The Three-Pillar Approach

Following to the Brundtland Report in 1987 and the Earth Summit in 1992, many researchers are researching the concept and meaning of sustainability. It typically considers three main areas of concern, namely: environmental (planet), social (people), and economic (prosperity) (Gibb, 2004). John Elkington in his 1998 book "*Cannibals with Forks: the Triple Bottom Line of 21st Century Business*" refers these main areas of concern to as the Triple Bottom Line (TBL) (Elkington, 2004). This TBL or three-pillar approach is commonly used in analyzing problems, nevertheless, some would prefer other pillar approaches such as the two intersecting pillars (the ecological and the human) or five-pillar approach (ecological, economic, political, social and cultural) to assess sustainability (Gibson, 2006).

Considering sustainability through a three-pillar approach, it involves the promotion of:

Economic sustainability – increasing profitability through efficient use of resources (human, materials, financial), effective design and good management, planning and control; Environmental sustainability – preventing harmful and irreversible effects on the environment by efficient use of natural resources, encouraging renewable resources, protecting the soil, water, air from contaminations and others; and Social sustainability – responding to the needs of society including users, neighbours, community, workers and other project stakeholders. (Zainul Abidin & Pasquire, 2007).

The three-pillar approach is commonly used in analyzing problem which presents the advantage of its simplicity over other approaches. It is easy to conceptualize by intersecting three circles representing economic, environmental and social aspects of sustainability (Gibson, 2001). The TBL separating the concept of sustainability into three pillars tends to build up the so called "silo effect". It means that individual pillar tends to competing resource and always involving trade-off in decision making. It is difficult to promote inter-linkages and interdependencies of various pillars (Pope, Annandale, & Morrison-Saunders, 2004). This reductionist approach dividing the holistic concept of sustainability into three pillars runs the risk of having the sum of the parts being less than the whole (Pope et al., 2004).

The Principles-Based Approach

Other than pillars approach, Gibson (2001) promotes the use of principles-based approach to sustainability assessment. Sustainability criteria are generated from those principles in place rather than derived from TBL goals. He argues that the principles-based approach could handle the interlinkages and interdependencies of pillars without the necessity of competing for resource and trade-offs. Gibson (2006) takes this approach and utilizes a set of general sustainability requirements (core obligations) for sustainability-oriented decision makers. These core generic criteria include:

1. Socio-ecological system integrity;
2. Livelihood sufficiency and opportunity;
3. Intra-generational equity;
4. Inter-generational equity;
5. Resource maintenance and efficiency;
6. Socio-ecological civility and democratic governance;
7. Precaution and adaptation; and
8. Immediate and long term integration (Gibson, 2006).

These principles cover various aspects in a system for sustainability: short term development and long term equity; human and the ecology as a whole; efficient and effective use of resources; managing risk from opportunity perspective; and integrate collective ideas for decision making, etc. The specific of each item and the package as a whole for the core generic criteria must be defined in context (define "what" and "how" as part of project specification). See the Appendix for detail requirements of core generic criteria.

Selection of different sustainability approach for assessment would lead to different sustainability outcomes in the route to a sustainable world. For instance, considering a land redevelopment project, social sustainability impact assessment under the three-pillar approach would many a time consider more on current impacts to residents in terms of provision of better environment to the community and jobs creation etc. But for the principles-based approach, it has to consider inter-generational and intra-generational equity, for example, preserving part of the heritage of the community for future generations. As a consequence, a different decision would be made. Although pillar view is easy to be conceptualized, it is not necessarily reflecting a holistic view of sustainability due to inherent difficulty in promoting the between pillars sustainability contributions. Principles-based view, on the other hand, covers a wider scope in assessing sustainability contributions on strategies, policies, plans, programs and projects. However, use of such view in the real world is still subject to limitations, for instance, unavoidable trade-offs, context dependent and competence of project managers in handling such assessment activities. In the section below, the sustainability competence requirements for project managers are discussed.

PROJECT MANAGER SUSTAINABILITY COMPETENCE

Mui and Sankaran (2004) suggest that project considering sustainability (e.g. urban renewal project) requires project managers to adopt a holistic perspective and a cradle-to-grave approach in managing project. They have identified that current project management body of knowledge ignores the professional knowledge of sustainability and that no guidance on suitability of generalizing specialists (project management specialist with general sustainability knowledge) or specializing generalists (sustainability manager with general project management knowledge) taking the role of project leader (Mui & Sankaran, 2004).

Mui et al. (2004) comment that project participants should possess sustainability knowledge and the infrastructure project team leader should have experience as generalizing specialist rather than specializing generalist. Furthermore, they find that sustainability is a contemporary issue considered by many global nations as an essential task for maintaining the future prosperity of human beings. To accomplish such a task, these nations adopt a multi-disciplinary and integrated project team approach to implement the change.

In their research on an urban renewal project, Mui et al. (2004) suggest that "individuals who are generalizing specialists – who have appropriate technical and management skills, a system approach perspective, and an ability to create an open culture in teams – are the preferred choice to serve as team leaders" (p. 31).

In the same study as reported earlier on project management community, one of the questions focused on job responsibility about project sustainability activities as shown below:

Care of project sustainability (economic, environmental and social) activities is the job of sustainability manager (professional specialized in sustainability activities) and not the job of project manager.

Out of the samples, sixty (60) responses did not agree with the statement (Strongly Disagree: 15; Disagree: 45; Neutral: 20; Agree: 16; Strongly Agree: 5). In other words, most respondents (59.4%) think that project related sustainability activities should be the responsibility of project manager. When the respondents were asked about whether "Sustainability as essential knowledge area shall be included in the published guidebook of project management body of knowledge", seventy five (75) respondents responded either agree or strongly agree in a five points Likert Scale (Strongly Disagree: 1; Disagree: 3; Neutral: 22; Agree: 49; Strongly Agree: 26) which represented 74.3%. This indicates an urgent need for the inclusion of sustainability knowledge area in the project management body of knowledge to help project managers in this respect. This triangulated the suggestion of Mui et al. that the project management body of knowledge should include this essential knowledge area and should emphasize the importance of a multi-disciplinary and integrated approach (Mui & Sankaran, 2004).

Though project managers are recognized by most of the survey respondents as responsible person for project sustainability works, they are not supported by the project management body of knowledge. The lack of literature covering sustainability in the realm of project management needs to be remedied to gain competitive advantages in today's world. Raising awareness and developing sustainability mindsets within the project team are important. Establishing a culture of care to the environment, people (stakeholders); and the communities involved in would help the delivery of project. Understanding of what sustainability means at a big picture level as well as what it means at a tangible day-to-day level is part of the challenge (Griffiths, 2007).

As will be discussed below under "The Assessment Methodology" section, there is no universal sustainability assessment approach. There is also no right or wrong on decision made about choosing which sustainability approach. The sustainability requirements are subject to the context of policy, programme, plan and project. As such, to be able to assess sustainability requirements with the aim of promoting positive impacts and minimizing negative impacts, project managers are required to be able to develop competence in understanding various sustainability issues. As Lock (2007) suggests that "We shall need effective project managers to deal with these challenges if humankind is to survive". Project manager needs to identify sustainability impacts due to the project, develop mitigation plan within the project life cycle process to which project manager makes a balance or even trade-off on chosen solutions with a target to maximize overall positive sustainability effects.

Since project sustainability impact is context dependent, project managers working on nuclear power station, for instance, choose to focus on certain sustainability competence requirements that others project managers (e.g. new product development project) may choose to develop a different set of competence requirements. However, the basic needs of a sound environment, a just society and a healthy economy (Brundtland, 1987; Diesendorf, 2000) in project development are the same. These basic needs drive project managers in identifying sustainability requirements during project reviews and that project managers exercise their sustainability competence in promoting positive impacts and minimizing negative impacts overall whether adopting pillars approach or core generic criteria for assessing sustainability.

Nurturing sustainability competence as a managerial competency in professional people alongside other core competences resulting in outcomes that are financially sound, environmentally sustainable and socially responsible is important (Jaafari, 2007). It is also a capability requirement for project manager to assess sustainability impacts. Jaafari (2007) recommends teaching sustainability through project-based learning to professionals rather than discipline-based learning, as it provides a paradigm for creativity and achievement of balanced solutions through engagement in realistic assignments. The following sections would help project managers in building relevant sustainability skills for their upcoming projects.

THE SUSTAINABILITY IN PROJECT MANAGEMENT

Project management as an evolving academic discipline and professional practice was developing in response to the needs of society. For instance, early days of modern project management focused on efficiency of managing project; and then focus has been changed to effective implementation of corporate strategy and effecting organizational change in the 1990s (Baccarini, 1999). Shenhar and Dvir describe central concept of project management since 2000 as adaptation (one size does not fit all); strategic alignment (connect project management to business); and globalization (offshore projects) (Shenhar & Dvir, 2004). External environmental influences including economic, political, community, and ecological impacts started to become essential dimensions on assessing policies, programs, plans, and projects after the 1992 Earth Summit. Public opposition to construction of nuclear power station due to safety reason was one manifestation (Baccarini, 1999). Project management plays a role in sustainability.

Sustainability is not a simple concept to define and there are a large number of interpretations (Epstein, 2008; Pope et al., 2004; Robert, Daly, Hawken, & Holmberg, 1997). Early development was largely influenced by Brundtland (1987) through her report "Our Common Future" and her definition of sustainable development. She has pointed out intra-generational development and inter-generational equity; and the needs of sound environment, just society and healthy economy. According to Eid (2002, p. 206), "The goal of sustainability is the process of systematically and effectively integrating vital environmental and social concerns into economic development, financial planning, and project management". In his opinion, the integration of project management, sustainability and industry competitiveness (for example, quality, markets, equitable market conditions, etc.) would deliver a clearer business case for sustainable construction (Eid, 2002). In fact, other industry sectors, for example agribusiness and food production, chemicals, forestry, general manufacturing, infrastructure, mining, oil and gas, as well as power industry, would also have been benefited with clearer business case by adoption of the goal of sustainability.

In the last two decades since the Earth Summit, an increasing number of projects have built in sustainability considerations into project design and implementation. For instance, Mohamed Eid (2002) in his paper at the PMI Research Conference 2002 brought in an example of construction industry in the U.K. that construction companies have to face challenges to integrate the vital environmental and social considerations into their daily management. More recently, large scale projects, infrastructure projects in particular, have no alternative but to consider the impacts due to environmental and social risks as demanded by lending institutions in the early stage of their project development. Accidents happened in operating facilities may also have changed the degree of focus and requirements in project sustainability assessments, for instance the Fukushima nuclear power accident in Japan happened on March 11, 2011, has directed other nuclear power projects under development worldwide to re-consider environmental, health and safety issues making references to this catastrophic accident. These changes reflect the fact that focus and degree of significance about the contents of sustainability assessments on project may have changed with the needs of the society.

Labuschagne and Brent (2004) describe clear understanding of the various project life cycles and their interactions between life cycles and the external environment and society as prerequisite for managing project sustainability (Labuschagne & Brent, 2004). Project management with increasing emphasis on handling external environmental factors has set the tone for it being an active driver for sustainability. Typically, three-pillar approach is widely adopted in the project community. Many project managers are working towards these goals. In practice, it would be easier for project managers to assess project sustainability impacts by this approach due to ease of conceptualization. Other principles-based approach can also be selected if project managers find it appropriate to assess the same from a different perspective. Definition is needed to help them framing their activities towards sustainability in project management.

Definitions

Tam (2010a) suggests a definition of "Sustainability in Project Management" with reference to the definition of project management under the APM Body of Knowledge (APM BoK, 5th edition). The quoted portion below is taken out from the APM BoK (APM, 2006):

The promoting of positive and minimizing of negative sustainability impacts (economic; environmental; and social) within "the process by which projects are defined, planned, monitored, controlled and delivered such that the agreed benefits are realized" and contributing to a sustainable society (Tam, 2010a).

Two key components are included in this definition reflecting the attributes of sustainability in project management:

1. Promoting positive impacts and minimizing negative impacts on economic sustainability; environmental sustainability; and social sustainability within the project development process; and
2. The recognition of such project benefits realized is contributing to a sustainable society.

The sustainability requirements are subject to the context of policies, programs, plans and projects. In other words, to be able to assess sustainability requirements with the aim of promoting positive impacts and minimizing negative impacts, project managers shall be able to develop competence in understanding various sustainability issues, identifying impacts due to the project, develop mitigation plan within the project life cycle process to which project manager shall make a balance or even trade-off on chosen solutions with a target to maximize overall positive sustainability effects.

Program management unlike project management concerns more about effectiveness (do the right project) than efficiency (do the project right) (Dinsmore & Cooke-Davies, 2006). With emergent input in a turbulent environment, program manager makes use of current information (sensemaking) to identify options (ideation) for comparison (elaboration) and decision (choice) which form the learning loop. Once decision is made, project manager will at a later time take over the project(s) where sustainability in project management is being observed. In other words, for the part of sustainability in program management, program manager shall put more emphasis on the learning loop leading to a 'choice'.

To define "Sustainability in Program Management", Tam (2010b) is again making reference to the definition of program management under the APM BoK. He suggests that the emphasis on sustainability impacts and contribution to a sustainable society is the same as in the definition of "Sustainability in Project Management". The quoted portion below is taken out from the APM BoK (APM, 2006):

The promoting of positive and minimizing of negative sustainability impacts (economic; environmental; and social) within the process of "coordinated management of related projects, which may include related business-as-usual activities that together achieve a beneficial change of a strategic nature for an organization" and contributing to a sustainable society (Tam, 2010b).

Under the three-pillar approach, program manager has to assess the suggested program options in the dimension of economic sustainability, environmental sustainability, and social sustainability before making a 'choice'. Depending on context, program manager would ask a number of questions within each dimension to assess the program sustainability impacts. Assessment of the program options in the elaboration process for choice aims at promoting positive sustainability impacts of the three dimensions and minimizing negative impacts of the same. Program manager together with team members shall be able to develop competence in understanding various sustainability issues, identifying impacts due to the program options. Program manager shall be capable of making a balance or even trade-off on chosen solutions with a target to maximize overall positive sustainability effects. The below section details sustainability evaluation framework that help project managers to conduct required assessment. Detail discussion on program sustainability evaluation framework is beyond the scope of this chapter.

SUSTAINABILITY EVALUATION FRAMEWORK

To facilitate project manager in assessing sustainability impacts and devising mitigation plans during various stages of project life cycle, a project sustainability evaluation framework is developed as shown in Figure 1 (Tam, 2010a). The project sustainability evaluation framework is based on the APM Body of Knowledge (5th edition) defined project life cycle (APM, 2006) which adopts the three-pillar approach. It shows that project economic sustainability, environmental sustainability, and social sustainability are part of the project review process where it has to be reviewed during various stages of project life cycle. Project managers make reference to previous project experience including the nature of the project and its context to identify appropriate potential impacts for review. The list under various sustainability dimensions in the framework is non exhaustive, nevertheless, it can be taken as a starting point for sustainability competence development towards project manager as a generalizing specialist (defined in section before – "Project Manager Sustainability Competence") for infrastructure projects.

Alternate to the framework based on the three-pillar approach above, Figure 2 shows the same sustainability evaluation framework, however, making reference to the principles-based approach. The basic framework structure is the same but project manager needs to construct relevant sustainability assessment criteria for the project with the employed principles. Take socio-ecological system integrity (see Appendix for requirement) for building a coal fired power station as example, project manager needs to make sure that a number of requirements has been put in place for project review, for example, monitoring extinction risk of endangered species, impact of acidic gas emissions to the nearby community, and proper design of zero discharge of waste water to river, etc. To cater for project complexity, project manager requires to develop assessment requirements with his/her team members or subject specialists are invited to make contributions to such development.

Figure 1. Sustainability evaluation framework for project management: Three-Pillar Approach *(Tam, 2010a)*

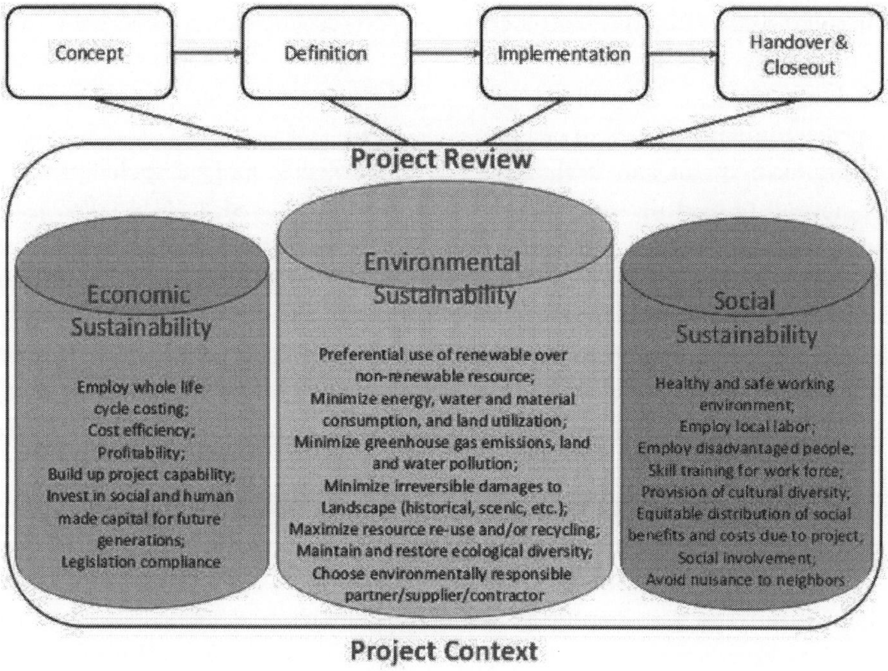

Figure 2. Sustainability evaluation framework for project management: Principles-Based Approach

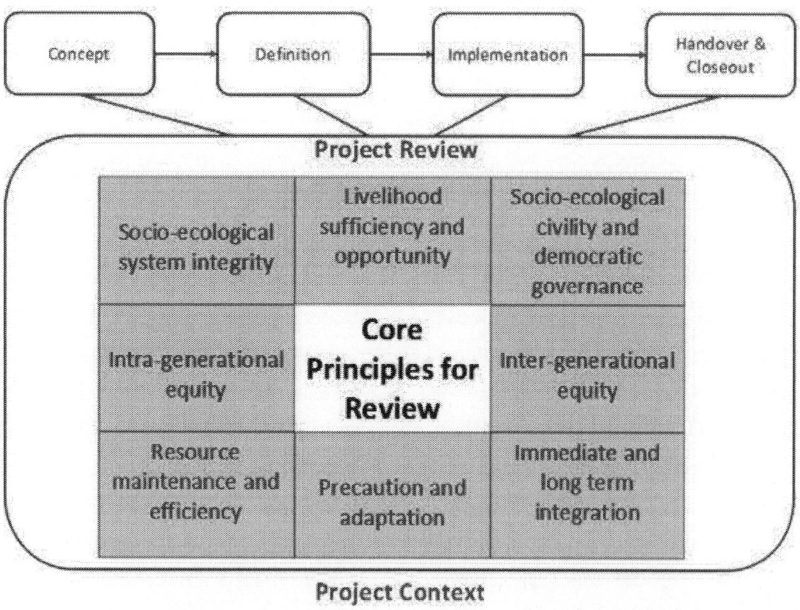

The framework described above defines sustainability evaluation processes that are performed throughout the life of a project. In the framework, project review is linked to various stages of the project life cycle. Most importantly, project manager has to accept that sustainability assessment and evaluation are part of the normal project review process. It is not an addendum to their normal project activities. The framework taking three-pillar approach and principles-based approach are of no difference in review format but of difference in the route to a sustainable society. Reasons behind have been discussed in "The Sustainability Approach" section above. Project managers have to make reference to their project setting to identify which approach has to be adopted in sustainability evaluation framework for impact assessment. For purpose of this chapter, substances of each of the sustainability dimensions are discussed in below section.

THE SUSTAINABILITY ASSESSMENT

Traditional appraisal process of project life cycle has been much concentrated on the assessment of financial and technical feasibility (Lopes & Flavell, 1998). Grundy (1998) indicates a similar effect in doing strategy implementation projects that "We hold the view that wherever possible, benefits (however soft and less tangible) should be targeted – and preferably in economic (or financial) terms. This does not mean that projects should be exactly evaluated (in financial terms) – but one would want to see potential benefits illustrated financially" (Grundy, 1998). Other considerations such as environmental impact effect of the project process or the impact of project result on the community will likely be considered for the purpose of meeting certain objectives. For example, the Equator Principles Financial Institutions (EPFIs) require proposed projects to conduct social and environmental assessment (Equator Principles). The EPFIs commit not to provide loans to projects seeking "project finance or project-related corporate loan" unless they have to comply with Equator Principles with respect to social and environmental policies and procedures (EPFI, 2013).

Project appraisal including the assessment of non-financial aspects (such as the managerial role, strategic and synergistic issues, social, political, environmental and technical links, and organizational factors) help identifying risk dimensions (Lopes & Flavell, 1998) and their relative importance to the success of project. The strong emphasis on efficiency in the traditional project appraisal process can lead to outcomes that are unacceptable from the point of view of inter-generational equity (together with intra-generational equity form the two core principles of sustainable development) (Labuschagne & Brent, 2004). Project managers for the analysis of environmental and social impacts must ensure that any future environmental liabilities and costs, as well as social impacts resulting from the implementation of the project are taken into consideration at the project decision gates (Labuschagne, Brent, & Claasen, 2005). To this end, there is a need to assess other sustainability impacts both positive and negative at the appraisal process on top of economic benefit assessment.

Sustainability needs to be treated as part of project visions. The commitment for it needs to be planted as early as possible to ensure smooth flow of process and acceptability among the project participants (Addis & Talbot, 2001; Zainul Abidin, 2005). To include environmentally sustainable practices in the design, construction and operational phases of a project and care for its social and economic aspects of project performance, Griffiths (2007) opines that presence of a sustainability management framework help project management. Griffiths (2007) finds it important to raise awareness and develop mindsets within the project team to establish a culture of care to environment, people (stakeholders) and the communities involved in (Griffiths, 2007). Clear understanding of various project life cycles, the interaction between life cycles, and the external environment and society are a prerequisite for aligning project management frameworks with the principles of sustainable development (Labuschagne & Brent, 2004). In the following sub-sections, aspects of various sustainability assessments are discussed. Understanding of sustainability assessment contents would help application of such contents to project evaluations (ex-ante and ex-post) within the selected assessment framework and methodology.

Economic Sustainability Assessment

Gregersen & Contreras (1992) in the "Economic Assessment of Forestry Project Impacts" published by the Food and Agriculture Organization of the United Nations (FAO) introduce the methodology for the assessment of likely economic impacts of potential or proposed projects (ex-ante impact assessments) and impacts after a project is implemented (ex-post impact assessments). Economic impact assessment is not a mechanistic accounting exercise. It is an attempt to assess a project or activity in a variety of ways the real value to society and to individual groups within society. The intent of such assessment is to provide background for making more informed decisions regarding the use of scarce resources available to society (Gregersen & Contreras, 1992) from the perspective of economic sustainability.

Unlike Zainul Abidin (2005) considers whole life cycle; cost efficiency; and risk assessment, etc. in measuring economic issues for construction project, Gregersen et al. in assessing forestry projects put emphasis on questions related to financial efficiency (overall cash flow); benefits/costs distribution amongst interested parties (who pays and who gains?); and economic efficiency to assess economic sustainability. The financial efficiency analysis always have to be done from a specific interested party's point of view (e.g. government, business, and individual) and economic efficiency analysis concerns with the costs and benefits to society as a whole, regardless of who pays and who gains. Both kinds of analysis concern with profitability, but economic efficiency looks at profitability from the society point of view. It is the return society as a whole can obtain with a given use of its limited resources (Gregersen et al., 1992).

Comparing the questions asked for the ex-post evaluation on project economic sustainability assessment, people focus on Financial Efficiency would ask: "Were costs and RETURNS as initially expected? (If not, why did actual costs and returns in the project differ from planned?) What is the ex-post FINANCIAL rate of return (ROR) compared with the ex-ante ROR? Are FINANCIAL benefits from the project continuing and can they be sustained?" For people with Economic Efficiency perspective, they would ask: "Were the actual costs and BENEFITS of the project in line with the planned ones? If not, why did they differ? What is the ex-post ECONOMIC rate of return in relation to the ex-ante rate provided by the project plan? Are the ECONOMIC benefits from the project sustainable over time?" As such, project managers trying to build in sustainability criteria into project objectives are recommended to adopt not only financial but also economic efficiency perspective in assessing project sustainability.

Environmental Sustainability Assessment

George (1999) suggests that the two principles of inter-generational equity and intra-generational equity are valid test for sustainable development across all people affected by the development. When the environmental impacts of the proposed project are strictly local, this means just the local community. When they are national, it must include the entire public in the country. When they are global, it must include the whole world's population. The inter-generational equity is a necessary condition for sustainability and the intra-generational equity is a necessary condition for development (George, 1999). These principles are embedded in Principle 3 of the Rio Declaration on Environment and Development of the Earth Summit for sustainable development "to equitably meet developmental and environmental needs of present and future generations" (United Nations, 1992).

To assess whether or not a proposed development is carrying sustainability, it is required to test from the perspectives of "Is it equitable for future generations" and "Is it equitable for the present generation?" George (1999) suggests a set of 18 criteria in a framework to be developed by expanding on the two equity principles. It is intended for environmental impact assessment of projects in industrial countries and the same can be amended for projects in developing countries. For a proposed development to be classified as sustainable development, it must satisfy all of the 18 criteria. The principle of intra-generational equity is considered at three levels:

Local or national impact with 4 criteria:

Criterion #1: "Have all groups or individuals affected by the project been identified, and have the impacts on them been assessed, using a full social impact assessment where appropriate?"
Criterion #2: "Will the Environmental Impact Assessment (EIA) report be published and made readily available to all members of the public?"
Criterion #3: "Will all members of the public have the opportunity to comment on the proposals, and will their views be taken into account before a decision is made?" and
Criterion #4: "If indigenous people or other minority groups are affected, have suitable provisions been made for their participation in project decisions?"

Transnational impact with 1 criterion:

Criterion #5: "Have transboundary impacts been properly assessed where appropriate, with the participation of the affected public?" and

Global impact with 6 criteria:

Criterion #13: "Have all potential global impacts been considered?"
Criterion #14 Focus on Biodiversity: "Does the assessment quantify any natural habitat that will be lost which is important for species conservation?"
Criterion #15 Focus on Biodiversity: "Is an equivalent area set aside for replacement/ regeneration?"
Criterion #16 Focus on Biodiversity: "Has a satisfactory justification been made for the habitat area lost through the project, as a proportion of the total area of this type of habitat, in such a way that the overall rate of loss will not exceed the equilibrium regeneration rate?"
Criterion #17 Focus on Greenhouse Gases: "If the project produces greenhouse gas emissions, is it shown to make an appropriate contribution to reducing emissions in accordance with the Kyoto agreement?" and
Criterion #18 on other Global Impacts: "Has a satisfactory justification been made for any other global impact, in terms of a compensating global benefit that is globally acceptable?"

Concerning inter-generational equity, to determine whether a proposed development has to be addressed either by strong sustainability (as a necessary requirement in the development) or weak sustainability (as a good enough choice in the development), two criteria are included as preliminary test (criterion #6: "Have any potentially critical ecosystem factors that may be affected been identified?" and criterion #7 "Has the risk of serious or irreversible damage arising from any such impact been satisfactorily assessed, using risk assessment techniques if appropriate?").

For a development with strong sustainability consideration, it has to observe more stringent requirement (criterion #8: "If the risk of serious or irreversible damage is significant, or if the project adds to a risk that is already significant, will the impact be fully mitigated, in kind, such that there will be zero adverse residual impact?"). If it is determined that weak sustainability consideration would be sufficient to address inter-generational equity issues within environmental sustainability, then 4 criteria have to be adopted (criterion #9: "Have any specific groups or individuals adversely affected by an impact expressed satisfaction with the compensation offered, or has any dispute been satisfactorily arbitrated?", criterion #10: "Has the natural capital that the project will convert into other forms of capital been identified?", criterion #11: "Has an appropriate socio-economic appraisal been carried out?" and criterion #12: "Does this socio-economic appraisal demonstrate that total capital will be conserved?") (George, 1999)

Social Sustainability Assessment

Assessment of social impacts for sustainability includes the processes of analyzing, monitoring and managing the intended and unintended social consequences, both positive and negative, of planned interventions (policies, programs, plans, projects) and any social change processes invoked by those interventions. The major purpose of such assessment is to bring about a more sustainable and equitable biophysical and human environment. It has a strong links with a wide range of specialist sub-fields involved in the assessment such as: aesthetic impacts (landscape analysis); archaeological and cultural heritage impacts (both tangible and non-tangible); community impacts; cultural impacts; demographic impacts; development impacts; economic and fiscal impacts; gender impacts; health and mental health impacts; impacts on indigenous rights; infrastructural impacts; institutional impacts; leisure and tourism impacts; political impacts (human rights, governance, democratization, etc.); poverty; psychological impacts; resource issues (access and ownership of resources); impacts on social and human capital; and other impacts on societies. As such, comprehensive assessment cannot normally be undertaken by a single person, but requires a team approach (Vanclay, 2003). It is convenient to conceptualize social impacts from people's way of life; their culture; their community; political systems; environment; health and wellbeing; personal and property rights; and their fears and aspirations (Vanclay, 2003) in assessing social sustainability. Lopes et al. (1998) suggest that it is better to rely on experts, in-house or external consultants, to carry out such assessment (Lopes & Flavell, 1998).

To cope with mitigating social risks, Lopes et al. (1998) have made some suggestions as below:

- At project design stage, social characteristics of the project have to be taken into account; it has to make the project compatible with local values; build up internal flexibility to allow for changes in relation to socio-cultural information; and to eliminate or modify aspects if they make the project socially unfeasible;
- Project developer has to learn about the country and the people where the project is located;
- It has to compensate fairly to parties concerned for damages and that local values and traditions have to be taken into account;
- It is important to listen to what people say. Establishment of Liaison Committees is good for the project where all social partners (external stakeholders) can meet to discuss and receive information on the project. The project team can take advantage of this committee to listen to people's proposals and views where improvement can be made early in the appraisal stage;
- The project team has to persuade people of the project's benefits by giving them priority on the benefits of the project (e.g. employment opportunity, local community investment, etc.);

- Alignment of the company's objectives with the objectives of the country (through project strategy);
- Training of managers to be aware of the outside world and deal with social problems;
- The project team and upon project completion the operation team, have to develop good links with the local communities throughout the whole life of the project (e.g. through general support to local activities, etc.);
- Seeking a good public image to the project would help resolving other social risks;
- If project appraisal determines that the project is to be at a high social risk, it is advisable to postpone it or start with a pilot project.

The above on the basis of three-pillar approach illustrates that each sustainability assessment aspect has wide range of considerations within its dimension. Up to this stage, the sustainability evaluation framework together with its ingredient for assessment has been discussed. As there are many kinds of project initiatives (from facilities upgrading to building infrastructure) and purpose of sustainability assessment, a range of assessment methodology are available for selection. Integrating selected assessment methodology into framework of choice forms a complete tool for managing project sustainability. In the section below, details of selection of relevant impact assessment methodology are discussed.

THE ASSESSMENT METHODOLOGY

There are two forms of methodology applicable to assessing sustainability impacts of policies, plans, programs and projects. They are "EIA-driven" (bottom-up from baseline) and "Objectives-led" (top-down with sustainability criteria for aspired state of society) (Pope et al., 2004). As the name implies, EIA-driven is originating from environmental impact assessment which is typically a reactive, ex-post process with a view to evaluate the acceptability of sustainability impacts and to identify potential modifications to improve the outcomes. EIA-driven sustainability assessment needs benchmarking for comparison. To this end, industrial standards, best practices and lessons learned from previous experience are taken as baselines for evaluation. It is argued that EIA-driven assessment tends to focus on reducing negative impacts against baseline conditions and minimizing mal-practices. It is not a tool to promote the concept of sustainability as a societal goal (Pope et al., 2004). This sustainability assessment methodology aims to ensure that impacts are not unacceptably negative overall. It means that the project under assessment does not lead to a less sustainable outcome.

Unlike EIA-driven assessment, objectives-led assessment aims to be a proactive, ex-ante process being included as part of development process for policies, plans, programs and projects rather than evaluating them after the facts. It assesses the contributions of proposal to aspiration objectives, rather than against baseline conditions. Objectives-led assessment does not need baselines as in EIA-driven methodology. However, it is important to have the aspired criteria developed which lead the initiative towards the goal of a sustainable society. It requires clearly defined pillar objectives or outcomes derived from principles-based approach against which the assessment can be conducted. Thus it is found to be more compatible to the concept of promoting sustainability (Pope et al., 2004).

Depending on needs, both the EIA-driven and objectives-led methodologies can be applied to assess initiatives under either the pillar-based or principles-based approach. Hence, there are four different schemes available to assess project sustainability. They are:

1. Pillar-based approach with EIA-driven assessment;

2. Pillar-based approach with objectives-led assessment;
3. Principles-based approach with objectives-led assessment; and
4. Principles-based approach with EIA-driven assessment. Figure 3 shows the four schemes with applications.

Selection of sustainability assessment approach and methodology depends on need. There is no right or wrong in choosing assessment scheme. Whether be it required to evaluate completed projects or conduct assessment on initiatives, the tool described prior could be applied. However, commercial projects and government initiatives may have different requirements in choosing approach to fit for their purposes.

Generally speaking, commercial projects doing ex-post evaluation would seek to use pillar-based EIA-driven assessment methodology. It can be understood that commercial project sponsors do not offer themselves to promote sustainability aspiration objectives. Hence, project managers are likely to compare their project performance to industry best practices. It naturally adopts industry benchmarks on economic, environmental and social sustainability performance as project TBL targets. For example, project manager would conduct sustainability performance evaluation upon completion of car manufacturing system project and that results are included in the corporate social responsibility (CSR) report.

As before mentioned, project sponsors and project managers would tend to choose pillar-based approach for purely commercial project ex-post evaluation. In the same vein, commercial project initiative, e.g. power plant project to be invested by Independent Power Producer (IPP), they would also consider pillar-based ex-ante assessment. For major development in a community, local government may not be satisfied with taking minimum TBL baseline as targets. Some aspiration states of sustainability would likely be included as objectives for the initiative. Hence, for ex-ante assessment, pillar-based objectives-led methodology can be adopted.

Unlike commercial projects normally taking pillar-based assessment approach, other programs or projects, e.g. government proposed airport development program, may choose principles-based approach for assessment. Since this assessment approach covers a wider scope than the pillar-based approach as aforementioned, it would be suitable for assessing large scale community projects

Figure 3. Selection of sustainability impacts assessment methodology

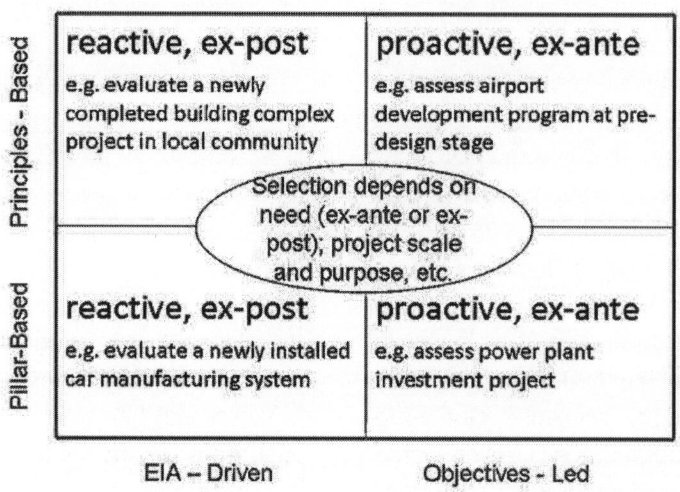

where between pillars objectives can be covered. Furthermore, states of sustainability aspiration can be proposed and that principles-based objectives-led methodology can be utilized for such project ex-ante assessment.

For those program or project taking ex-ante principles-based objectives-led assessment, results can be used as basis for ex-post evaluation upon project completion. For example, a building complex project within the airport development program has gone through ex-ante assessment utilizing principles-based objectives-led methodology. The results can be taken as basis for evaluation upon completion of project. Same principles-based approach should be observed in doing the ex-post principles-based EIA-driven assessment.

Selection Criteria

When selecting an assessment scheme for assessing or evaluating a project or initiative, the following criteria have to be observed:

1. *Does the project or initiative likely to have issue of inter-generational equity?* It is a key concern for managing project sustainability. If an initiative do have inter-generational equity issue (e.g. turning farmland into industrial park), pillar-based EIA-driven assessment methodology would not be a good choice due to between pillar issues could hardly be taken care of. Principles-based objectives-led assessment scheme with aspiration would provide a clear focus to address the inter-generational equity issue.
2. *Does it a project or initiative with obvious minor externality impact?* There are projects that have minor impacts on the external environment or community. For instance, a virtual project team building a computer model for analyzing job satisfaction of in house staff would prefer pillar-based EIA-driven assessment methodology. Other assessment schemes would not be suitable. Project managers may consider pillar-based EIA-driven scheme as basic assessment form for managing projects with minor externality impact.
3. *Does it an ex-ante assessment or ex-post evaluation?* Ex-ante assessment, which is in a sense of proactive in nature, would incorporate aspired objectives in the assessment. Hence, objectives-led assessment is adopted whether it is taken under the pillar-based or principles-based approach. On the other hand, ex-post evaluation is reactive in nature with pre-determined best practices or agreed criteria, EIA-driven assessment would match with the requirements.
4. *Does it a community project or project which is purely commercial?* Project objectives are different for those purely commercial projects and community (including government and NGO) projects. The impression that commercial organizations would preferably choose minimum requirements to satisfy laws and regulations and that pillar-based approach is chosen over the principles-based approach in managing project sustainability. Though increasing amount of national and multi-national business organizations making exceptional sustainability contributions in recent decades, most organizations are driven by profitability as prime consideration over other sustainability goals. Further research on change in organizational behavior towards managing project sustainability after the Earth Summit would be necessary for project managers to learn more about the recent development in this respect.

The four criteria discussed previously reflect the guidance on selection of assessment approaches and methodologies. They are not absolute in nature and that variations can be accepted on conditions of “fit for purpose”. For purpose of this chapter, “fit for purpose” covers not only the obvious purpose proposed by the project team but also any purpose determined at the time of assessment as a result of stakeholder consultation.

Consider the following example case: 'A multinational firm intended to mine a gold-bearing local mineral by using dangerous chemical compounds to obtain the precious metal. There was the danger of groundwater contamination due to the tailings that would result from the mining process. Local people stormed the municipality under the slogan "water is more precious than gold" and forced the local municipal council to call for a non-binding referendum on the construction of the mining project. Most of the people voted against the project though it would have created 300 direct jobs and about 1,300 indirect job opportunities. The people considered their social and health development was far more important than economic gain. The referendum has indefinitely postponed the project for development. People choose to forego the economic benefits that the project would have brought, traded those off in order to preserve the place as it is for generations to come. This is the very essence of sustainability (Munier, 2005).' It shows from this example case the firm did not successfully win the project (and the support from local people). In retrospect, the firm should have done an ex-ante assessment before launching the project. The assessment results would then be available to help the firm fine-tuning the project and lobbying the local community. Appropriate adoption of pillar-based or principles-based approach for sustainability assessment would encourage stakeholders responding to the initiative. For example, some projects do not display much between pillar issues, then pillar-based assessment could be sufficient. Otherwise, principles-based assessment would be appropriate to handle those between pillar concerns. Protection of clean water source is not only an environmental concern, for instance, it actually involves the questions of cost implication and the water quality level of acceptance from the local community. The results obtained from principles-based assessment, in this case, would generate insight that local people may have interested and the firm may lobby the local community more effectively and efficiently. Making reference to the assessment scheme selection criteria above, this gold mining project is a community involved project involving inter-generational equity issue and that an ex-ante assessment is necessary. Principles-based approach with objective-led scheme is recommended. This helps the firm assessing the needs of local people directly and efficiently. Principles like inter-generational equity; precaution and adaption, etc., applied to the initiative would directly address clean water protection issue.

CONCLUSION

Project management is an active driver towards a sustainable world. However, managing project sustainability is handicapped by the lack of knowledge and common understanding among project stakeholders on sustainability issues. My recent research confirms the view of Mui et al. (2004) that project manager with knowledge in sustainability should be responsible for taking a leading role in managing project sustainability. Nevertheless, there are barriers in this respect. A decision-making tool is manifested as necessity in order to enhance sustainability deliverables in projects. Project managers need to develop relevant sustainability competence as part of their project management skills. In this chapter, sustainability approaches (three-pillar and principles-based) together with definitions of sustainability in project management and program management are introduced. Project manager sustainability competence requirements are discussed and that sustainability evaluation framework taking pillar-based and principles-based approaches is being developed. As three-pillar approach is commonly used due to ease of conceptualization, various considerations within each of the sustainability dimensions are discussed and followed by developing assessment schemes for ex-ante and ex-post assessments. The philosophy of EIA-driven and objectives-led assessment is presented. Selection criteria are developed to help project managers in choosing appropriate sustainability impacts assessment methodology. Integrating assessment methodology into sustainability evaluation framework within project life cycle forms a complete tool. This chapter contributes to devising a practical assessment tool for project managers in managing project sustainability.

REFERENCES

Addis, B., & Talbot, R. (2001). Sustainable Construction Procurement: A Guide to Delivering Environmentally Responsible Projects. London, UK: Construction Industry Research and Information Association (CIRIA).

APM. (2006). *The APM Body of Knowledge* (5th ed.). The Association for Project Management.

Baccarini, D. (1999). *History of Project Management*. New SOuth Wales, Australia: Curtin University of Technology.

Bredillet, C. N. (2000). *Proposition of a systemic and dynamic model to design life-long learning structure: The quest of the missing link between men, team, and organizational learning*. Paper presented at the PMI Research Conference 2000: Project Management Research at the Turn of the Millennium. Paris, France.

Brundtland, G. H. (1987). *Our Common Future*. Oxford, UK: Oxford University Press.

Craddock, W. T. (2013). How business excellence models contribute to project sustainability and project success. In G. Silvius & J. Tharp (Eds.), *Sustainability Integration for Effective Project Management* (pp. 1–19). Hershey, PA: IGI Global. doi:10.4018/978-1-4666-4177-8.ch001

Diesendorf, M. (2000). Sustainability and sustainable development. In D. Dunphy, J. Benveniste, A. Griffiths, & P. Sutton (Eds.), *Sustainability: The corporate challenge of the 21st century* (pp. 19–37). Sydney, Australia: Allen & Unwin.

Dinsmore, P. C., & Cooke-Davies, T. J. (2006). *The Right Projects Done Right: From Business Strategy to Successful Project Implementation*. San Francisco, CA: John Wiley & Sons, Inc.

Dyllick, T., & Hockerts, K. (2002). Beyond the business case for corporate sustainability. *Business Strategy and the Environment*, *11*(2), 130–141. doi:10.1002/bse.323

Eid, M. (2002). *A sustainable approach to the project management odyssey. Proceedings of the PMI Research Conference: Frontiers of Project Management Research and Application*. Philadelphia PA: Project Management Institute.

Elkington, J. (2004). Enter the triple bottom line. In A. Henriques & J. Richardson (Eds.), *The triple bottom line, does it all add up? Assessing the sustainability of business and CSR* (pp. 1–16). London, UK: Earthscan Publication Ltd.

EPFI. (2013). *Equator Principles III: Equator Principles Financial Institutions*. Retrieved May 7, 2014, from http://www.equator-principles.com/resources/equator_principles_III.pdf

Epstein, M. J. (2008). *Making Sustainability Work: Best Practices in Managing and Measuring Corporate Social, Environmental, and Economic Impacts*. San Francisco, CA: Berrett-Koehler Publishers, Inc.

Gareis, R. (2013). Re-thinking project initiation and project management by considering principles of sustainable development. In G. Silvius & J. Tharp (Eds.), *Sustainability Integration for Effective Project Management* (pp. 129–143). Hershey, PA: IGI Global. doi:10.4018/978-1-4666-4177-8.ch008

Gareis, R., Huemann, M., & Martinuzzi, A. (2009). *Relating sustainable development and project management.* Paper presented at the IRNOP 2009. Berlin, Germany.

Gareis, R., Huemann, M., & Martinuzzi, A. (2010, July). *Relating sustainable development and project management: A conceptual model.* Paper presented at the 2010 PMI Research and Education Conference. Washington, DC.

George, C. (1999). Testing for sustainable development through environmental assessment. *Environmental Impact Assessment Review, 19*(2), 175–200. doi:10.1016/S0195-9255(98)00038-9

Gibb, A. (2004). Safety, health, and environment. In P. W. G. Morris & J. K. Pinto (Eds.), *The Wiley Guide to Managing Projects*. Hoboken, NJ: John Wiley & Sons, Inc. doi:10.1002/9780470172391.ch22

Gibson, R. B. (2001). *Specification of sustainability-based environmental assessment decision criteria and implications for determining "significance" in environmental assessment. University of Waterloo*. Canada: Canadian Environmental Assessment Agency.

Gibson, R. B. (2006). Sustainability assessment: Basic components of a practical approach. *Impact Assessment and Project Appraisal, 24*(3), 170–182. doi:10.3152/147154606781765147

Gregersen, H., & Contreras, A. (1992). *Economic Assessment of Forestry Project Impacts*. Rome, Italy: Food and Agriculture Organization of the United Nations.

Gregersen, H. M., Lundgren, A. L., & White, T. A. (1994). Improving project management for sustainable development: Policy Brief No.7. Madison, WI: Midwest Universities Consortium for International Activities, Inc. (MUCIA).

Griffiths, K. (2007, February). *Project sustainability management in infrastructure projects.* Paper presented at the 2nd International Conference on Sustainability Engineering and Science. Auckland, New Zealand.

Grundy, T. (1998). Strategy implementation and project management. *International Journal of Project Management, 16*(1), 43–50. doi:10.1016/S0263-7863(97)00016-1

Jaafari, A. (2007). Thinking of sustainability as a dimension of managerial competency. *PM World Today, IX*(IX).

Keeys, L. A., Huemann, M., & Turner, R. (2013). Integrating project strategy for sustainable development: A conceptual framework. In G. Silvius & J. Tharp (Eds.), *Sustainability Integration for Effective Project Management* (pp. 20–38). Hershey, PA: IGI Global. doi:10.4018/978-1-4666-4177-8.ch002

Labuschagne, C., & Brent, A. C. (2004). *Sustainable project life cycle management: Aligning project management methodologies with the principles of sustainable development.* Paper presented at the 2004 PMSA International Conference, 10-12 May 2004, Johannesburg, South Africa.

Labuschagne, C., Brent, A. C., & Claasen, S. J. (2005). Environmental and social impact considerations for sustainable project life cycle management in the process industry. *Corporate Social Responsibility and Environmental Management, 12*(1), 38–54. doi:10.1002/csr.76

Lim, S. K., & Yang, J. (2009). *A Delphi study on the critical sustainability criteria and indicators for Australian road infrastructure projects.* Paper presented at the 3rd CIB International Conference on Smart and Sustainable Built Environments, Delft University of Technology. Delft, The Netherlands.

Lock, D. (2007). *Project Management* (9th ed.). Hampshire, UK: Gower Publishing Limited.

Lopes, M. D. S., & Flavell, R. (1998). Project appraisal: A framework to assess non-financial aspects of projects during the project life cycle. *International Journal of Project Management, 16*(4), 223–233. doi:10.1016/S0263-7863(97)00055-0

Mui, D. H. F., & Sankaran, S. (2004). An effective project management-based application model for sustainable urban renewal in Hong Kong. *Project Management Journal, 35*(4), 15–34.

Munier, N. (2005). *Introduction to Sustainability: Road to a Better Future*. Dordrecht, The Netherlands: Springer.

Peattie, K. (2011). Developing and delivering social science research for sustainability. In A. Franklin & P. Blyton (Eds.), *Researching Sustainability: A Guide to Social Science Methods, Practice and Engagement*. Oxon, UK: Earthscan.

PMI. (2008). *A Guide to the Project Management Body of Knowledge (PMBOK Guide)* (4th ed.). Newtown Square, PA: Project Management Institute.

Pope, J., Annandale, D., & Morrison-Saunders, A. (2004). Conceptualising sustainability assessment. *Environmental Impact Assessment Review, 24*(6), 595–616. doi:10.1016/j.eiar.2004.03.001

Robert, K.-H., Daly, H., Hawken, P., & Holmberg, J. (1997). A compass for sustainable development. *International Journal of Sustainable Development and World Ecology, 4*(2), 79–92. doi:10.1080/13504509709469945

Shenhar, A. J., & Dvir, D. (2004). Project management evolution: Past history and future research directions. In D. P. Slevin, D. I. Cleland & J. K. Pinto (Eds.), Innovations: Project Management Research 2004 (pp. 57-64). Newton Square. PA: Project Management Institute.

Silvius, A. J. G., & Schipper, R. (2010, November). *A maturity model for integrating sustainability in projects and project management*. Paper presented at the 24th IPMA World Congress. Istanbul, Turkey.

Silvius, A. J. G., van den Brink, J., & Köhler, A. (2010, Februray). *The concept of sustainability and its application to project management*. Paper presented at the IPMA International Expert Seminar 2010 - Survival and Sustainability as Challenges for Projects. Zurich, Switzerland.

Silvius, G., & Tharp, J. (Eds.). (2013). *Sustainability Integration for Effective Project Management*. Hershey, PA: IGI Global. doi:10.4018/978-1-4666-4177-8

Tam, G. C. K. (2010a, February). *Sustainability competence requirements for project manager*. Paper presented at the IPMA International Expert Seminar 2010 - Survival and Sustainability as Challenges for Projects. Zurich, Switzerland.

Tam, G. C. K. (2010b). The program management process with sustainability considerations. *Journal of Project. Program & Portfolio Management, 1*(1), 17–27.

Tam, G. C. K. (2013). Sustainability assessment for project managers. In G. Silvius & J. Tharp (Eds.), *Sustainability Integration for Effective Project Management* (pp. 288–302). Hershey, PA: IGI Global. doi:10.4018/978-1-4666-4177-8.ch018

Turner, J. R. (Ed.). (2009). *The handbook of project-based management: Leading strategic change in organizations* (3rd ed.). New York, NY: McGraw-Hill.

UNCED. (1992). *Agenda 21, Chapter 1: Preamble. United Nations Conference on Environment & Development.*

United Nations. (1992). Rio declaration on environment and development. *Report of the United Nations Conference on Environment and Development*. Rio de Janeiro, Brazil.

Vanclay, F. (2003). SIA Principles: International principles for social impact assessment. *Impact Assessment and Project Appraisal*, *21*(1), 5–11. doi:10.3152/147154603781766491

Zainul Abidin, N. (2005). *Using Value Management to Improve the Consideration of Sustainability within Construction*. (Unpublished doctoral dissertation). Loughborough University, Loughborough, United Kingdom.

Zainul Abidin, N., & Pasquire, C. L. (2007). Revolutionize value management: A mode towards sustainability. *International Journal of Project Management*, *25*(3), 275–282. doi:10.1016/j.ijproman.2006.10.005

KEY TERMS AND DEFINITIONS

EIA-Driven Assessment: It is typically an assessment of bottom-up from baseline, reactive, ex-post process with a view to evaluate the acceptability of sustainability impacts and to identify potential modifications to improve the outcomes. EIA-driven sustainability assessment needs benchmarking for comparison. Thus industrial standards, best practices and lessons learned from previous experience are taken as baselines for evaluation.

Generalizing Specialist: Project management specialist with general sustainability knowledge.

Objectives-Led Assessment: It is a top-down assessment with sustainability criteria for aspired state of society which aims to be a proactive, ex-ante process being included as part of development process for policies, plans, programs and projects rather than evaluating them after the facts. It assesses the contributions of proposal to aspiration objectives, rather than against baseline conditions.

Pillar-Based Approach: A reductionist approach dividing the holistic concept of sustainability into normally three pillars for project analysis and improvement. The three main areas of concern are, namely: environmental (planet), social (people), and economic (prosperity).

Principles-Based Approach: It utilizes a set of general principles to construct sustainability requirements for sustainability-oriented decision and assessment. Sustainability criteria are generated from those principles. It covers a wider scope than pillar-based approach, for instance it also addresses the between pillars issue, in assessing sustainability impacts on strategies, policies, plans, programs and projects.

Specializing Generalist: Sustainability manager with general project management knowledge.

Sustainability in Program Management: The promoting of positive and minimizing of negative sustainability impacts (economic; environmental; and social) within the process of coordinated management of related projects, which may include related business-as-usual activities that together achieve a beneficial change of a strategic nature for an organization and contributing to a sustainable society.

Sustainability in Project Management: The promoting of positive and minimizing of negative sustainability impacts (economic; environmental; and social) within the process by which projects are defined, planned, monitored, controlled and delivered such that the agreed benefits are realized and contributing to a sustainable society.

APPENDIX

Table 1. Core generic criteria for sustainability assessment

	Core Generic Criteria	Requirements
1	Socio-ecological system integrity	Build human-ecological relations to establish and maintain the long-term integrity of socio-biophysical systems and protect the irreplaceable life support functions upon which human and ecological well-being depends.
2	Livelihood sufficiency and opportunity	Ensure that everyone and every community has enough for a decent life and that everyone has opportunities to seek improvements in ways that do not compromise future generations' possibilities for sufficiency and opportunity.
3	Intra-generational equity	Ensure that sufficiency and effective choices for all are pursued in ways that reduce dangerous gaps in sufficiency and opportunity (and health, security, social recognition, political influence, and so on) between the rich and the poor.
4	Inter-generational equity	Favour present options and actions that are most likely to preserve or enhance the opportunities and capabilities of future generations to live sustainably.
5	Resource maintenance and efficiency	Provide a larger base for ensuring sustainable livelihoods for all, while reducing threats to the long-term integrity of socio-ecological systems by reducing extractive damage, avoiding waste and cutting overall material and energy use per unit of benefit.
6	Socio-ecological civility and democratic governance	Build the capacity, motivation and habitual inclination of individuals, communities and other collective decision-making bodies to apply sustainability requirements through more open and better informed deliberations, greater attention to fostering reciprocal awareness and collective responsibility, and more integrated use of administrative, market, customary and personal decision-making practices.
7	Precaution and adaptation	Respect uncertainty, avoid even poorly understood risks of serious or irreversible damage to the foundations for sustainability, plan to learn, design for surprise, and manage for adaption.
8	Immediate and long term integration	Apply all principles of sustainability at once, seeking mutually supportive benefits and multiple gains.

(Gibson, 2006).

Section 4

Information and Communication Technologies for Sustaining Livelihoods

Chapter 16
The Influence of Information and Communication Technologies on Societies and their Cultures:
A Historical Perspective

Lee Allen
University of Memphis, USA

ABSTRACT

In this chapter, the various ways technologies have exerted influence upon cultures and societies since the dawn of human existence is examined. Be it man-made fire, sharpened stone tools and weapons, or cave paintings, humans are always inventing "something" to sustain or improve their lives and/or livelihoods, and generally make their existence more tolerable – and comfortable. The culture surrounding and thus influenced by technological advances differs from traditional definitive criteria of groups. A technologically-influenced society and culture is identified by its populace's ability to access and use its defining technologies. Nowadays social communication and interactions often occur with others across cultures, continents and socioeconomic systems as constantly evolving information technologies emerge as communication tools. In order to understand the role of technology's influence on our societies, we must understand the historical significance of various information and communications technologies' influence on culture and how changes in our interactions and relationships across all groups have occurred as a result.

INTRODUCTION

It is a rather incontrovertible notion that, today, computer-based technology affects every person on this planet whether they are cognizant of this fact or not. From orbiting satellites photographing every square inch of land in even the remotest parts of the world (that can then be viewed on home computers), to hand-held devices that simultaneously provide communication, informa-

DOI: 10.4018/978-1-4666-8433-1.ch016

tion, calculation, and entertainment functionality, advanced computer technologies are ubiquitous, and a fact of life in the twenty-first century. Yet as we examine the influence of modern technologies on our lives, either directly or indirectly, many conclude that what we are experiencing now is somehow a new phenomenon, that once upon a time during simpler times, we, as a society, were somehow less affected by the existing technologies prevalent during those happier days. Indeed, popular commentators and broadcasting editorialists lament that these are highly complex times that we live in, and publicly pine for less gadget-oriented days. On closer scrutiny – and with a modicum of research – these assertions are found to be false, misleading, and disingenuous, and of course pander to the baser instincts of a highly suggestible and often fearful audience.

In an historical analysis of the impact and influence of technologies on their contemporary societies, it is obvious that tidal waves of change have been induced by the introduction of seemingly insignificant (or at least taken for granted) discoveries or inventions by humans (Gallivan & Srite, 2005; Hughes, 2004; Winston, 2003; Williams & Edge, 1996; Layton, 1974; Fleck, 1958). For the sake of brevity, an exhaustive review will not be undertaken here; however key developments in human productivity and intellectual endeavors based on technological advances will be examined, and their relative societal and cultural impacts explored.

EARLY CULTURALLY INFLUENTIAL TECHNOLOGIES

The Written Word

In Plato's Phaedrus (Jowett, 2008), the Greek philosopher Socrates questioned the use of writing: "He would be a very simple person…who should leave in writing or receive in writing any art under the idea that the written word would be intelligible or certain; or who deemed that writing was at all better than knowledge and recollection of the same matters" (p. 70). Thus in the time of Socrates, the 5th century B.C.E., the technology being questioned was what certainly most of us now take for granted as a basic – even elemental – form of communication: handwriting.

The impact of the written word as a form of communication is, of course, indisputable. Whether transmitted via inscribed rock, tree bark, or papyrus, written communication of human thoughts and deeds has been a technological development that has influenced countless societies, cultures, and civilizations. To even attempt to measure the impact of this now-common form of communication on the subsequent history of the world is in itself a daunting if not futile endeavor. Yet, incredible as it may seem, at one time the development of an alphabet and writing were considered of questionable value by Socrates and many of his contemporaries who preferred that their philosophies and discourse be distributed in oration.

The effect on society and their surrounding cultures was immutable: what was once considered to be in the exclusive domain of anointed sages and their charges was now available to even among the most common – allowing that one had to learn to read, as well. This was a skill that was long only selectively shared, so as to maintain a certain distance regarding learned men versus their illiterate counterparts. But eventually even common folk were encouraged to read; mostly by those who sought to disseminate the word of God – or local authority – as they knew it.

The Printing Press

Likewise, after millennia of transcribing such valued tomes as the Bible and Beowulf by hand, toiling in ill-lit towers or dank cellars, another technological development came about to alter the history of humankind. In Mainz, Germany, in the 1440s a goldsmith and tinkerer armed with the knowledge of earlier movable-type technologies in Asia (Pan, 1998), and taking advantage of the availability of relatively low cost paper replacing expensive parchment, developed the first printing press (Meggs & Purvis, 2006).

This technology immediately revolutionized the way – and the speed – in which information could be distributed. Soon the texts of everything from the Bible to ancient Greek and Latin texts to treatises of localized interest could be disseminated – so long as the publishing entity had the remuneration required for printing such documents (Eisenstein, 2005). The recorded word and the knowledge contained within were no longer to be maintained within the exclusive domain of the most learned, nor the wealthiest. Now – in theory, anyway – any citizen on the European continent was free to learn the wisdom of the ancients, as well as the "Word of God". It was towards this latter purpose, again, that the more common folk – merchants, artisans, draftsmen, bureaucrats – were encouraged to become literate and familiarize themselves with Holy Scripture. However, interest in the classical literature of the Greek and Roman authors – Plato, Homer, Plutarch, and Tacitus among many others – was increasing exponentially as the royalty and religious leaders sought to out-do each other in terms of their patronage of great artists and other purveyors of the renascent interest in the "humanities". The general citizenry benefited as this rivalry among sponsoring patrons typically played itself out in public, where the grandiosity of the work of Michelangelo could be displayed in Rome while Donatello was showcased in Florence, and Titian in Venice. So the cultural and societal changes wrought by the technology that enabled the written word to be delivered extensively within a relatively short period of time helped create an entire era we know of as the Renaissance. It should be acknowledged that other technological improvements were also involved, such as more stable pigments and canvas along with the ability to transport raw materials, such as marble, over greater distances more efficiently. But the eventual spread of literacy among the merchant class – if not quite yet the peasantry – was caused by the new technology of its time, and helped an era to revolutionize the thinking of humankind. Indeed, by the beginning of the sixteenth century, over twenty million books had been printed by presses in 236 cities and distributed throughout Western Europe (Febvre & Martin, 1976).

Early Communication Technologies

The next technology to affect great swaths of the society surrounding it was the relatively rapid development of a series of improvements in long-distance communications. Humankind has sought to communicate over great distances since primitive and more advanced societies used, varyingly: sound (struck logs or drums); fire and smoke (signal fires and smoke signals); light (reflective surfaces, mirrors); and animal and human effort (pigeons, runners, messengers, calling posts) (Holzmann & Pehrson, 1994). Use of these has been documented in ancient Egyptian hieroglyphics, in ancient Greece by Homer (The Iliad), and the ancient Babylonians (Epic of Gilgamesh). Some of these communication systems are still in use today, as well as widely used modes that have evolved from them (semaphore flags, bicycle messengers).

However it was not until the development of the first telegraph systems in late eighteenth century France that there occurred, within the next hundred years, an explosion of technological innovation and invention in the area of distance communications. From Samuel Morse's first electro-magnetic telegraph in the 1830s to the laying of the first successful transatlantic telegraph cable in 1866, and finally to the development of the telephone in 1876, the nineteenth century was one of incredible telecommunications advances, many of which are still in place today. By the turn of the nineteenth to the twentieth century, Guglielmo Marconi's telegraphy via electromagnetic signals announced the arrival of wireless telecommunications.

So how was this rapid evolution of communications technology received by the inhabitants of societies impacted by these developments, especially when considering the overall pace of technological development over the past millennia?

A reporter, writing an article titled "The Telephone" in the November 4, 1876 edition of the New York Tribune provides us with some insight into how this now ubiquitous device was initially greeted:

"The tele-phone is a curious device that might fairly find place in the magic of Arabian Tales. Of what use is such a device?" (King, 2005, p. 4). The reporter then speculates as to its practical potential use such as allowing "officials who are far apart to talk with each other without interference of an [telegraph] operator" and "some lover might wish to pop the question directly into the ear of a lady…though miles away" (King). Fortunately the reporter redeems himself somewhat by ending with the statement that "it is not for us to guess how courtships will be carried on in the Twentieth Century" (King). If only that reporter were here to witness what has transpired since!

THE TWENTIETH CENTURY

Technology as Entertainment

As we know, the telephone connected the vast landscapes of the United States and eventually other nations in ways unimaginable in earlier times; to actually send and receive not simply a coded message, but the human voice over great distances seemed indeed something out of fairy tales, or at the very least, the then-nascent literature of science fiction. Almost simultaneously, another great development was connecting people over the American continent; it had all started with Marconi's late nineteenth century invention of wireless telegraphy, and rapidly improved upon by early radio technology pioneers Lee de Forest, Harold Arnold, and Edwin Armstrong. By 1934, the broadcasting of radio waves across the countryside was in full swing with three major national networks (two them still in business today) and over 35 million listeners: the age of commercial radio broadcasting had arrived (Balk, 2005).

For the first time, sophisticated entertainment by world-renowned artists could be received and listened to in the comfort of one's home. The days of a family member having to learn to play an instrument such as the piano, organ, guitar, or ukulele to provide home entertainment were – regrettably, for many – over (Boal-Palheiros & Hargreaves, 2001).

The advent of the telephone and radio communication technologies boom was the first instance of a technological advancement directly affecting the lives of everyone – not just the merchant class, or the military, or scientists, or only the very wealthy. For the first time, such transformative technologies were not only available to nearly all of society, they were becoming necessities. By this time society had become dependent on both the telephone and radio not only for everyday information and communications but also for law enforcement, weather-related agricultural and safety reasons, and – in the case of radio – entertainment (Lull, 1987).

Another evolution in the new technologies' effect on society in the early-to-mid twentieth century was on its increasing influence on younger and younger citizens. The major radio networks began to broadcast "family friendly" fare during what advertisers recognized as the "prime time": that time between dinner and bedtime that, thanks to the increasing availability of electric lighting in the home during the 1920s, was now pushed later than had been customary in lantern-lit rural and working class homes (Douglas, 2004). So during the early evening hours such general audience shows as Fibber McGee and Molly targeted not only the fathers and mothers relaxing after the evening meal, but also the children who listened along with them. Darker, more adult-themed shows such as The Shadow or Suspense were broadcast later, after the kids were all safely tucked in bed (Douglas, 2004).

Soon broadcasters, and their all-important advertisers, began to see that there was another potential audience emerging, and perhaps, for the first time a technology turned its attention to a much younger audience. While the film industry, in full bloom during the 1930s despite the Great Depression, had featured children as stars since the Shirley Temple and Little Rascals movies, these movies did not necessarily have young children as their primary audience in mind, despite the ages of the stars (Wojcik-Andrews, 2000). Many of Shirley Temple's and the Little Rascals films contain adult themes with children either as foils for evil adults (Shirley Temple) or as smaller versions of scheming adults (Spanky and his gang). To be sure, children certainly enjoyed such fare along with various cartoon shorts and serialized cliff-hangers shown in theaters on Saturday afternoon at half-price matinees. However, it was not until Walt Disney's feature length Snow White (1937) that the Hollywood film industry seemed to fully recognize young children as the primary audience for some of its full-length fare (Forgacs, 1992).

So as Hollywood began to explore the nascent children's market, radio broadcasters recognized that their audience was practically waiting for them, sitting by their radios. As the realities of Depression-era economics precluded extravagant expenditures for most, going to a movie was an occasional luxury allowed in a much-restricted entertainment budget. Though far more costly than a pair of movie theater tickets, people demonstrated that they were willing to purchase relatively expensive radios (often on payment plans) because of what they truly saw as a far better return on investment. While a movie created a diversion for an hour or two, a radio could provide potentially years of consistently available – and free, aside from the initial cost of the radio itself – family entertainment. Thus, "by 1935, 70 per cent of all households had at least one (radio) set, twice as many as owned telephones" and "by the end of 1939, the number of radios had more than doubled to 44 million (including 6.5 million in cars), 86 per cent of all homes were covered and listening averaged more than four-and-a-half hours per day" (Marquis, 1984, p.405). With this amount of "market penetration", radio broadcast networks and their advertising sponsors began to expand their audiences, increasingly tailoring programs to specific niche genres: dramas (Lux Radio Theater, Hollywood Radio Theater), mysteries (Escape, The Whistler), detective stories (Philip Marlowe, The Falcon), comedies (Our Miss Brooks, The Jack Benny Show), and of course, shows geared towards children's interests. Many of the children's shows were, in contrast to the half-hour to one-hour formats of the adult fare, serialized five-to-fifteen minute installments of characters popularized in the Sunday "funnies" (comic strips) such as The Adventures of Flash Gordon; perhaps to accommodate perceived shorter attention spans even then. Among the first of the successful long-running serialized radio shows dedicated specifically to children's listening was The Cinnamon Bear, a special series broadcast between Thanksgiving and Christmas which aired from 1937 and continued well into the 1950s (Boemer, 1989). The show set the precedent for children's programming for years to come: the advertisements specifically targeted children's increasing buying power which was, while still limited by the Depression, increasing and emerging as an influential force in U.S. commerce. Breakfast cereals and Cracker Jacks were among the first to add value to their products by including inexpensive toys such as decoder rings and miniature cutout dolls or tiny cars in order to increase demand by children; thereby increasing sales by pressuring parents and influencing buying decisions (Reisch, 2008; Yerxa, 2013).

From 1941 to 1945 many industries were redirected to provide materiel for the U.S. war effort. It was left mostly to the radio broadcasters to provide uplifting programming and boost morale for the soldiers abroad as well as those working back at home to support them. Because many women had joined the workforce, children were increasingly allowed more freedom and leisure time (Miller & Swanson, 1958). Aside from the less expensive Saturday matinees, radio was the key provider of children's entertainment, especially during the early evening hours, and on Sunday mornings when many radio station hosts read the comic strips for the youngest of their listeners. This was as much to temporarily fill in during the soldier-fathers' absence while fighting abroad as it was to provide temporary respite for exhausted working mothers on one of their few days off (Douglas, 2004).

The result of this enhanced programming for children was a long-lasting effect on the generation of children who were raised during the 1940s; these children became the first generation of consumers of products designed and produced specifically for them. During the 1950s, the first generation of "teenagers" emerged: automobile-worshipping, rebellious, and for the first time, regular consumers of products specifically manufactured for them: tighter fitting blue jeans, fast food that could be ordered and consumed without leaving their prized automobiles, and, of course, rock and roll music (Goldman, 1960; Miller & Nowak, 1977; Morris, 1993) . By the late 1940s the transition from big band to boogie-woogie music became facilitated as jazz and rhythm and blues artists previously unknown to the white audience began to evolve from the relative obscurity what was then known as "race records" towards the mainstream (Roy, 2004). Though the popular music sales and radio performance charts were still segregated (as they are still in large part to this day), "crossover" artists began to emerge selling to both a black audience and more accepting white teenage audience who were primarily interested in the "danceability" and relative "wildness" of the music. Thus, black performers such as Chuck Berry and Little Richard could be heard blasting from the cars and ultra-portable AM transistor receivers of teenagers throughout the United States and Western Europe, thanks to the power of radio that now transcended borders (Fatherley & McFarland, 2014). This then led to the advent of Elvis Presley who successfully blended not only rhythm and blues and rock and roll, but the predominantly heretofore rural country and western styles, helping the development of "rock-a-billy": the hybrid result of wedding rock and roll to "hillbilly" music (Escott & Hawkins, 1992; Floyd & Marsh, 1998). With Elvis, retailers now had yet another avenue for profit-making from teens: the spin-off merchandising of celebrity-related items. Everything was offered, from lunch pails to toy guitars, clocks and watches to bubblegum. Elvis Presley's image sold, and sold big – and worldwide (Guralnick, 1995). The previously disinterested consumer industries now took notice, and the continuing era of marketing specifically to teenagers had begun in full; yet another example of a technology – in this case radio – directly influencing society.

Television

However, Elvis Presley's fame and instantly recognizable image was not the product of radio technology alone. Another phenomenal, culturally influential force also began in the late 1940s: television. The effect of this truly amazing technological innovation – broadcasting live and recorded actors' performances and their voices across the airwaves directly into people's homes – was not completely realized until the early-to-mid 1950s. But because of technical improvements in both television receivers and broadcasting quality, coupled with lowering prices and increased disposable income in post-war America, when it was fully realized, a giant step in the evolution of the culture of the United States and elsewhere in the world took place.

The technology of television literally changed everything in the early 1950s (Huston et al., 1992); the culture and societies of the entire planet underwent a profound transformation due to its influence, and this time, children were not only highly involved in the spreading influence, they were essential to its widespread dissemination as a cultural influence. Beginning with early children's TV shows such as the Howdy-Doody

Hour to the Mickey Mouse Club, from Lassie to Rin Tin Tin, television broadcasters had already identified young audiences for its advertisers. Even television shows such The Adventures of Davy Crockett which was produced by Disney Studios as family-hour fare, saw an unforeseen effect demand for officially released show-related merchandise: the Davy Crockett coonskin cap, lunchbox, and toy accoutrement sales were rivaled only by those generated by those bearing Elvis Presley's image. But in the case of Davy Crockett, and later Mickey Mouse Club merchandise, these were children buying, at least via parent proxy (Forbes, 2003). The first toy ever advertised on television was the still-popular Mr. Potato Head, selling for 98 cents at the time – 1952 – and requiring a real potato, became a sought-after Christmas and birthday present as television directly influenced the society, its children, and their spending habits (Walsh, 2005; Mittell, 2003). With the booming prosperity of post-War America, such items that would not have even been remotely considered only ten years earlier were now must-haves for little boys and girls across the United States, and eventually, the rest of the world. Television was the first technological innovation that literally "grew up" with a generation, from its infancy and the quaint stereotypes it depicted of wholesome American values, to the turbulence of the early 1960s (Uslaner,1998; McAllister & Giglio, 2005). Television shows again catered geared to that same generation, now teens befuddled in the wake of the Cuban Missile Crisis, the Kennedy assassination, the Civil Rights movement, and the Vietnam War brought live to the living room each evening. But of course the next "big thing" that would again change society and culture was again brought via television; but it was not through a single popular program: it was the first U.S. performance by the Beatles on the Ed Sullivan Show in February 1964 (Inglis, 2000).

With the arrival of the Beatles, once again modern society and its culture were to become profoundly affected. Because television now reached into nearly every American home, the broadcasters almost immediately understood that something big had changed, but they were not sure what. They also realized that their primary audience for exploiting this change was the nations' youth: not the youngest this time, but those who had been raised on television as children in the 1950s, and were now approaching adulthood. Because TV networks were not yet certain in this nascent movement who would come to be known as the counterculture in the U.S., they stepped uncertainly into the waters even as radio once again became a dominant technological force in society. Music was everywhere; from radio sets, mono- and stereo phonographs, cars, and record stores, popular music led by the so-called British Invasion and now imitated on our shores, was the siren's call to a generation raised on TV but now seemingly turning its back on it (Alvey, 2004).

Networks scrambled in an attempt to cater to this audience with musical variety shows featuring everything from the resurgent folk music scene (Hootenanny) to rock and roll (Shindig) and crass, exploitative pandering to younger teens and "teeny boppers" on shows such as Where the Action Is (featuring the costumed Paul Revere and the Raiders as the house band) broadcasted nationally on weekday afternoons after school; and the incredibly vacuous Beatles Saturday morning cartoon show. The overall effect, initially, was to be largely ignored by the majority of American youth whose viewing they sought. There was no marketing schema built in to this generation of young people at this time in their lives – because of the on-going Vietnam war and the military draft that accompanied it; the civil rights demonstrations and the brutal force exerted on to stop them; the riots that ensued after such confrontations; all of these were broadcast into not only the homes but also the minds of the viewers, young and old. The result was that the younger audience no longer wanted to have anything to do with that society, and television, along with its giant corporate sponsors and manipulative advertising profiteers, were seen as part of the problem in the world: the enemy – there was no selling anything these people had to offer to American youth (Braunstein, 2002).

Of course there were notable exceptions: the Sonny and Cher Show was successful as a watered-down version of a counter-culture couple, made safe for viewers by showing only a harmless, farcical side of their make-believe lives; and there was also such silly fare as Rowan and Martin's Laugh-In which managed to introduce some fairly pointed satire via the Lily Tomlin's portrayal of a mean-spirited telephone operator. But the most notable exception was the Smothers Brothers Show: often a no-holds barred commentary on the situation in which America found itself in the late 1960s, with thinly disguised, and often confrontational, social satire. The show also featured arguably the best of the musical performers raised to near-heroic stature by the youth culture, including legendary performances by the Who and Jefferson Airplane. Inevitably, the Smothers Brothers confrontational style wore on their network and the sponsors who insisted on changes lest they quit their sponsorship of the program. The Brothers refused to budge on matters of principle, thus the network and advertisers won out in the end, and perhaps the lone candle of counter-culture representation on commercial television was extinguished, and thereby further distancing young adult viewers (Bianculli, 2009).

For young children, the New York-based Children's Television Workshop (CTW) in 1969 produced one of the most ground-breaking and influential children-oriented programs ever: Sesame Street (Fisch, Truglio & Cole, 1999; Fisch, 2004; Jenkins, 2006).

Because of its strong emphasis on learning rather than pure entertainment for children, the show is still going strong over 40 years later, and spawned other educationally-oriented shows in the 1970s such as Schoolhouse Rock and CTW's The Electric Company. Mr. Roger's Neighborhood, which first aired in 1968, moved to PBS in 1971 and provided fare for even younger viewers until 2008 (Coates, Pusser, & Goodman, 1976).

Interestingly, from the late 1960s through the mid-1970s, and until the arrival of a very different type of TV show – Saturday Night Live – most of network television's desired young audience ignored the medium completely and turned to radio, now with hipper, edgier non-formats exemplified by college and university free-form and "underground" radio programming (Wall, 2007). Record albums were played in their entirety, commercial-free, and low-key hosts, who often shared a chemically-altered state of mind with the listeners, set the decidedly laid-back tone (Keith, 1997; Walker, 2004). And many teens simply chose to retreat to their bedrooms or basements and listen to their own growing collections of vinyl records, along with cassette and 8-track tapes of their favorite artists. For various reasons older technologies dominated the youth culture during this period (Bindas & Heineman, 1994).

THE 1970s AND 1980s

The First Cell Phone

In terms of technological advances and, especially, their influence on the larger society, the period between 1970 and 1980 was relatively quiet. Certainly new ground-breaking technological breakthroughs were being made: In 1973 the first truly self-contained wireless cellular telephone was introduced by the Motorola Communications Systems Division and its lead developer, Martin Cooper (Farley, 2007). Although the development of the wireless cellular phone had begun as early as 1948, it was not until Motorola plunged ahead to enter the market with its first telephone creation, the first true innovation in telephony since the Alexander Graham Bell introduced the first telephone nearly a hundred years earlier.

That first "portable" cellular phone would hardly be recognizable as such today, as it weighed a whopping 30-ounces! Another drawback is that there were also no wireless cellular towers to provide access for the phone, save for within the confines established by the Motorola laboratories in New York City to complete a taunting phone call to telecommunications rival AT&T Bell Labs and a news reporter.

However in ten years, by 1983, the first commercial wireless cellular towers were erected in select locations (mostly large cities such as New York and Chicago) and a reduced size version of the Motorola cel phone, the Dynatac, was introduced. It had been pared down to a mere 16 ounces and was available at the initial price of $3,500! The trend towards cellular phones had begun, though, and by 1990 the U.S. had over one million cellular phone service subscribers (Farley, 2007). However when compared with the immense global impact cellular phone technology would soon have, the initial societal reaction to its introduction amounted to less of a bang than a yawn.

The Home Computer

Another very important technological development initiated during the 1970s was the start of the home computer industry. The first entry in this early arena was the Altair 8800, produced by Micro Instrumentation and Telemetry Systems (MITS) and introduced in January 1975. The Altair 8800 boasted an early Intel 8080 2MHz processor (as compared to Intel's latest i7 processor, at 3.20 GHz) and an operating system, Altair Basic, that was Microsoft's first product (Freiberger & Swaine, 2000). The pricing, as sold via specialized magazines such as Popular Electronics, was also relatively buyer-friendly: $439 for the kit, and $621 assembled (Ceruzzi, 2003).

After the relative success of the first Altair computers, other players started to invest in developing their own products. Notably, Steve Jobs and Steve Wozniak developed the Apple I computer as nothing more than a wood-mounted circuit boards array prototype in 1976 (Wozniak, 2007). But by 1977 Apple Inc. introduced the fully-formed Apple II for the relatively high introductory price of $1298, especially for a machine with computing power limited to 4 Kb of RAM and a MOS 6502 1.0 MHz processor (Carlton & Kawasaki, 1997).

The market seemed buoyant enough for several competitors to enter the fray, one of the most famous (or infamous) among them being the TRS-80 introduced in September 1977 by the Tandy Corporation, manufactured by Kyocera in Japan and sold at Radio Shack stores. Interestingly, and due most likely to its competitive pricing ($599) and ready-made retail distribution advantage, 200,000 units of the TRS-80 sold between its introduction in 1977 and 1981. While hardly significant in numbers by today's standards, the market niche for home computing was growing. IBM followed in 1981 introducing its first fully functional home computer with the PC (personal computer) label, the 5150, but again, despite its well-known brand, a buyer-inhibiting price between $1,565 and $3,000, depending on features. So it should come as no surprise that when the Commodore 64 was introduced in 1982, at the price of a mere $595, seventeen million were sold during its twelve year run, when production was ceased in 1994 (Reimer, 2005).

Personal home computers really had its only "revolution" during the 1980s with the arrival of the first Apple Macintosh. Its mark on the society and culture at the time was mostly imprinted by the airing of the "1984" television advertisement during Superbowl XVIII which depicted a lone individualist destroying the projected image of an Orwellian "Big Brother" figure (presumably standing in for the dominant IBM and thus Microsoft, empire). The Macintosh was revolutionary for its time as it was the introduction of both the Graphic User Interface (GUI) rather than the strictly text-based interface of the time, plus the innovation of the hand-controlled mouse interface, rather than total reliance on the computer keyboard to operate. These were definite innovations which forced IBM and Microsoft to scramble to develop the Windows interface which would not be ready until late 1985, and would not be considered truly competitive with Apple's GUI until the release of Windows 3.1 in 1992 (Terry,1994; Jansen,1998).

But even with such innovations, home computing had not yet reached the level of social and cultural influence it would eventually achieve in just a few years later. Again, pricing may have had a significant impact on this delay: the first Macintosh sold for $1,995 while the first GUI-interface IBM computers sold for $1,350 for monochrome screen and $1,695 for color capacity (Miller, 1987). When accounting for inflation, these were considerable amounts of money at the time, for most people.

The First 'Net

Another technological advance was begun in 1969 by the Defense Advanced Research Projects Agency (DARPA), a branch of the Pentagon. The project, which evolved throughout the 1970s, was initially developed as the DARPAnet (later shortened to ARPAnet as it evolved towards primarily civilian scientific research purposes). Beginning as a relatively small local area network connecting several universities in California (Hauben & Hauben, 1997) by the late 1980s ARPAnet was a full-fledged wide area network (WAN) connecting universities and various research institutes worldwide. This network was still a closed system of computers connected via modems and standard telephone lines. It was password protected with increasing layers of security added as would-be hackers from then-Communist Eastern European attempted to gain entry into high-level U.S. defense projects conducted at several of the connected institutions; and thus opening potential electronic backdoors into the Pentagon itself (Stoll, 1989). Thus this network that allowed computers to transmit data and thus communicate between each other across the globe, while of very keen interest to- and used by- scientists, researchers, and defense contractors, remained largely unknown to most of the general population, even by the end of the 1980s.

Occasionally Hollywood would cast a glance towards some of the doomsday potential of these connected computers spawning such fare during the 1980s as War Games (1983), which managed to incorporate elements of Arpanet, video gaming, and the Cold War as potential players in a thermonuclear doomsday scenario caused by a supercomputer run amok. For the most part this seemed more distant science fiction scenario than the near future, and did not contribute much to the national consciousness, or prevalent culture at the time.

Cable Television and MTV

Television also experienced an evolution beginning in the mid-1970s with the arrival of coaxial cable broadcasting; for the first time, the major national networks had competition in the form of local and national broadcasting cable-only broadcasters. Everything from ultra-specialized local programming to 24-hour televangelists to the then-new and paid subscription-only Home Box Office, the technology of television had evolved only slightly with the addition of cable access, but the impact cable made on society's new view of television and its subsequent cultural impact in the 1980s far outweighed the relatively minor technical innovation introduced by cable access. One of the most influential by-products introduced at the dawn of cablevision, was, aside from subscription movie and pay-per-view channels, introduced in 1981 – Music Television, far better known as MTV.

There is no doubt that MTV, which was available only via cable television technology at the time of its introduction, created a shift in our culture – as well as cultures abroad – that would last for years to come (de Mooij, 2004; Banks, 1997; Greeson & Williams, 1986). This time the targeted audience was again the teenager – that readily-identified entity that had not been of much commercial interest in terms of advertising since the 1950s. But this was a new generation – somewhat ironically the sons and daughters of those who were teenagers in the 1950s – and, as it turned out, they were the perfect audience. With innovations in sound and video technologies delivered via cable at speeds and bandwidth dwarfing what could be broadcast via traditional airwaves, the look of cable TV, and especially the expensively-produced music videos, proved to be the visual treat, or "eye candy", that brought in more and more young viewers. Hybrid cartoon and music video shows such as Beavis and Butthead helped seal the compact between ever younger viewers and MTV during the early 1990s. During recent years, mostly due to the increased availability of ever more specialized cable channels and newer technologies, MTV has lost most of its influence on youth culture, and has also jumped on the bandwagon with teen-oriented "reality shows" with varying success (Horwitz, 2006). However in other aspects, MTV has remained a cultural trendsetter on a global scale, by focusing on hip-hop and rap musical videos on pioneering shows such as Yo! MTV Raps. The influence of U.S. "hip-hop culture" has been extended via an expanding global urban audience, largely due to MTV's international programming (McLeod, 1999; Garofalo, 1994).

Video Player/Recorders

Nearly concomitant with the arrival of cable television was the revival of the video tape recorder. Professional video tape recording and playback had been available since the 1950s, and indeed, once available, many television programs were recorded on video tape rather than the more expensive 32mm film to cut costs (Jorgenson, 1998; Sugaya, 1998a). But beginning in the mid-1960s, smaller, more portable video recording units began to be manufactured by such companies as RCA and Ampex, as well as an early entry by Sony, all monochromatic using ½" tape. These smaller video recorders were occasionally found in schools and universities where they were used to capture student performances, as well as used in local independent television broadcasting stations as low cost alternatives to live programming (Sugaya, 1998b).

But as cable television began to provide more diverse content without commercial interruption, viewers increasingly felt the desire to capture some of this programming, be they movies or favored TV shows, so as to enable its viewing at a later time than when broadcast. The era of the home video recorder – and player – had arrived. Sony, JVC, and Panasonic entered the market with two competing formats: Sony Betamax and VHS. This technology was significant in many ways – not the least of because it enabled the viewer/customer to be almost in complete control of their entertainment in terms of content and timing, much unlike the previous dependence on broadcasters' scheduling of shows.

Despite initial efforts to fight the VCR in the courts, Hollywood eventually recognized the market for older movies no longer shown in theaters, and also that their revenues would be greatly diminished if all a viewer had to do was wait for his or her favorite movie to appear on HBO, tape it, then watch it until something else was recorded on top of it. The emergence of video movie rentals began: soon on nearly every corner independently-owned video rental stores appeared offering not only Hollywood blockbusters, but classic films and more obscure foreign fare (Dirks, 2010) . Eventually, national chain retailers took over the independent video rental stores, and the variety of movies dwindled to those deemed to bring in the most revenue at that location.

Video Games

Perhaps the technological innovation with the longest lasting and continuous impact on culture to emerge from the 1970s is the video game. With the first commercially available home video game units such as the Atari 2600 in 1977, video games moved from the realm of the arcade and bars to the home. This time the primary initial recipients of the technology innovation were children, especially boys between the ages of 8 and 14 (NIMF, 2010). Along with the primitive (though now nostalgia-inducing) tick-tock repetition of video Pong, to the popular Asteroids, Space Invaders, and Donkey Kong, the first huge video game hit to crossover from the arcade to the home television set was Pac-Man. Introduced in the arcade standalone version in 1980, the home version was first sold in 1982 for the Atari 2600 home video game system. By the end of 1983 Pac-Man had sold over seven million copies, but Atari over-estimated its market, leading to a glut of home video game product and a subsequent collapse of the market for such products in 1983-84 (Kent, 2001).

Along with the MTV success phenomenon, video gaming began to insinuate itself into the American cultural fabric. Hollywood jumped on the chance to exploit a darker side of video gaming in films such as Disney's Tron (1982) and The Last Starfighter (1983). However, video gaming was not as culturally significant – at first – as MTV was during the 1980s because games were mostly played in isolation, or with close friends and family in the home. The larger effect of video games would be felt later with the availability of the commercial outgrowth of the still-relatively unknown Arpanet.

A Culturally Influential – though "Lesser" – Technology

One aside in this overview of technology-as-cultural-influence: one cannot complete a review of technologies that emerged in the 1980s without noting one that subsequently created a significant sub-culture that exists to this day: the skateboard. The skateboard was first developed and introduced in the 1950s as a hybrid of surfing (another culturally significant import, from Hawaii) and roller skating, which itself saw somewhat of a renaissance during the 1980s in the arena-sized roller rinks typically situated strategically close to shopping malls. But the sport, or art, as one may see it, of skateboarding took on an entirely different cultural aspect than previously seen. Rising as a risk-taking and often law-breaking movement in Southern California (primarily in and around Venice Beach), skateboarding obtained an aura that attracted mainly boys aged 10-18 mostly due to its rough-and-tumble – and often quite dangerous – outlaw image (Brooke, 1999). The boys who participated wholeheartedly in skateboarding did so in public places that would challenge their skills, and literally risk their necks. It also became a spectator sport: once the domain of a group of friends showing off for each other, the public venues for the skateboarders became larger and more dangerous, as boys competed to see who could pull off the most acrobatically extreme stunt. At first authorities attempted to seal off areas where large groups of "'boarders" and their fans would gather, but eventually, seeing that the gatherings would simply move on to different venues, municipalities began to construct concrete parks specifically designed for skateboarding. These parks also were created with a modicum of safety in their design, so while the majority of 'boarders were content to hone their skills there, the more daring of these continued to challenge the pre-existing environment by skateboarding off stairwells, ramps, and other more dangerous venues (Borden, 2001).

The sub-culture created by the technology of the skateboard and its adherents has impacted modern society in many ways; visible not only through the continuing popularity of the loose-fitting, knee-length cargo-style shorts known as "baggies", to the slip-on canvas deck shoes favored by 'boarders (Vans), but through targeted marketing of the preferred musical styles of 'boarders (anarchic punk-rock and "thrash") which has had its own travelling outdoors music festivals since 1995, sponsored by one their corporate beneficiaries: the Vans Warped Tour. However, it is not only through directly-related products that skateboarding has influenced modern culture: the rise in interest in extreme sports that involve what many consider to be excessive risk-taking, has somehow managed to gain entrance into the Olympic Games programs. In fact, a direct off-shoot of skateboarding, with many former as well as current skateboarders competing, is now a fully-accepted sport in the Winter Olympics: snowboarding (Heino, 2000).

THE 1990s

The Internet and the Birth of the World Wide Web

By 1988 the original self-contained wide area computer network, ARPAnet and its research spinoff NSFnet, had become so large that signs of instability were beginning occur in the various pathways around the globe (Okin, 2005). In 1989 at the CERN laboratories in Geneva, Switzerland, scientists Tim Berners-Lee and Robert Cailliau conducted research that would begin to transform the concept of the network backbone that supported Arpanet and its derivatives globally (Berners-Lee, Cailliau, Groff, & Pollermann, 1992). The process was to develop an independently monitored – that is, with no geo-politically opportunistic entities involved – system for computers around the globe to connect to and communicate through. This was, of course, what would become known as the Internet and its hyper-text transfer protocol, or http (Connolly, 1999). Tim Berners-Lee saw the Internet as something greater than just a network of linked computers (Berners-Lee, 1989); by 1991 the World Wide Web (WWW) became the term that better accommodated what this new network had truly become – an interconnected web of globally connected computers (Berners-Lee, 1992).

Once again, a technological advance that would change nearly everything within the next twenty years was initially of interest primarily to researchers and academics. Research data was exchanged via online databases utilizing a communication entry-point protocol called Gopher, and various search engines, some with names taken from teenage comic book characters: Archie, Veronica, and Jughead (Collins, 1994). Of course, access to these data repositories did not exactly elicit keen interest by the general public, and thus remained a decidedly niche resource in the early 1990s. But slowly, as word of this new technology that allowed for multiple parties to communicate synchronously or asynchronously spread, interest among users grew. Because of their proximity to its academic use, faculty and students at universities and colleges were among the first to start Usenet newsgroups, user-created online venues for anything from serious scientific discussions to debates on the relative merits of the latest Star Trek spinoff show. Eventually, the capability to expand synchronous online communications from one-on-one "chats" to multiple-user "chat rooms" that allowed users to address whole groups online or to engage in more personal dialogue with selected users (Santoro, 1994). These soon grew into venues that contained "adult only" topics and other specific interest groups. Comments left on "electronic bulletin boards" could be responded to asynchronously, which led to the ubiquitous "comments" sections available on virtually any news or editorial website today. MUDs (Multi-user dungeons) and MOOs (MUD, Object Oriented) became the first online communities that counted early computer game developers and devotees among its users (Shah & Romine, 1995). Futurist Howard Rheingold, among other contemporaries, touted the building of "online communities" in a series of bestselling books (Katz, 2005). Listservs enabled users to send messages simultaneously to such groups because alongside this new avenue for communication came electronic mail – or, as we are all-too-familiar with nowadays – email. Email, which predates the Internet, was first developed in 1972 by Ray Tomlinson, but its global prevalence would not arrive until years later (Hardy, 1996).

As interest continued to grow, some researchers were attempting to move the Internet from a wholly computer text-based communications tool to a virtual environment that would include varied text fonts, graphics, photos, and colorful background schemas – as well as "links" to other such locations in the newly-created "cyberspace". They were somewhat limited by the bandwidth made available by the first generation of commercial phone modems, devices that converted data into communications capable of being transported via telephone lines to another such device. The earliest modems had the bandwidth capacity of only 300 bits per second, but improved during the 1980s to speeds of 14.4 kilobits per second (kbps). In the 1990s this soon evolved into modems capable of 28 kbps and eventually topped out at the rate of 56 kbps, the maximum transfer rate that a typical copper-wire telephone line is capable of handling (this has changed since the introduction of optical fiber lines). Users began to use modems to access electronic Bulletin Board Systems (BBS), allowing the download and upload of news, data, software, and, of course, communicating with other users.

By 1993, the National Center for Supercomputing Applications (NCSA) at the University of Illinois Urbana-Champaign had developed Mosaic, arguably the first true interface "web browser" with advanced graphics capability (Schatz & Hardin, 1994). Because of its somewhat limited distribution (again primarily via academic institutions or downloaded from NCSA), the next evolution in graphical user interface (GUI) Web browsers proved to be the real groundbreaker: in 1995, Netscape released Navigator 1.0. It was the first truly user-friendly web browser that could easily be installed on a connected computer by simply inserting a 3½" computer diskette pre-loaded with the Netscape Navigator installer program (Virnoche, 1998). Perhaps a minute later and, depending on the rate of the user's Internet connection, a new virtual world was now available to the user: a magical heretofore nonexistent world made of bits and bytes but with attributes of real-world value. One could find information from across the globe nearly instantaneously, see images uploaded in distant lands, and of course, one could shop. The dawn of the commercial use of the Internet, or World Wide Web, had arrived, bringing with it millions of curious users almost immediately. One of the first Internet-based online shopping venues was Amazon.com launched in 1995, and whose visionary entrepreneur creator, Jeff Bezos anticipated what the world opened by Netscape could lead to in terms of commercial potential. Web space then, as now, was practically free after one took into account the initial hardware and software costs of setting up computer servers, routers, and hub installations which decrease in cost over time (Anderson, 2009). And advertising could easily be accomplished by creating key words linked to the content that would lead potential customers using a web browser (Young, 1998).

From 1994 to 2000, use of the number of World Wide Web users increased from approximately 23,000,000 users in 1994 (WDVL, 2010) to 360,985,492 users as of December 31, 2000 (IWS, 2010). And while during this period the predominant demographic for users in the United States remained mostly white males between the ages of 18 to 54 years, this too was rapidly changing. By 2000, 42% of Internet users were women; 28% were black; and 13% were over the age of 65 (University of Maryland, 2010).

Everything Is Digital

The first compact disc (CD) to be produced was The Visitors by the Swedish pop group ABBA in 1982, and in the 25 year period between 1982 to 2007, over 200 billion music CDs were legitimately recorded and distributed (BBC, 2007), utterly obscuring other previously popular formats such as the vinyl record and the audio cassette in terms of sales volume (although the vinyl format still has some strong adherents and audio cassettes still enjoy sales in some parts of the third world). It also became easy and quite affordable to record, or "burn", digital files from a computer to a blank, recordable compact disc. The next obvious step soon occurred: if a CD was nothing more than a collection of digitized musical files, why not burn those onto a second CD to give to friends; or, better yet, why not simply share the digitized files to other computers by compressing and making those music files available – for free – to be downloaded via the World Wide Web? And thus, by the late 1990s, online digital music sharing caught the attention of the recording industry and many artists who then sought to put an end to it via the legal systems. The former due to revenues lost to such "piracy", and the latter more concerned about musical integrity, but also to lost potential royalties, and therefore income as well (RIAA, 2002).

Mention must also be made of the newly digitized versions of movies that became available in the 1990s: the digital video disc (DVD) made its first appearance in 1996, and video cassettes soon joined the eight-track and cassette tape in the clearance bin of history. Again because the product became recreated in the bits and bytes process of digitalization, movies also became the target of piracy that would eventually – as increased bandwidth would allow – see their digital form transferred online (Cover, 2005).

Technology in Schools

Users of the Internet were getting younger, as well. During the initial large push for computers in the classroom – mostly due to efforts by Apple Computers to target this new market in the early 1990s – many of the computers were set up as standalone machines to run software for a specific instructional goal. IBM soon followed Apple into the educational computer market via EduQuest. Most IBM EduQuest computers were sold to school districts as packages bundled with software and connected to each other via Local Area Networks (LAN) using software systems such as SchoolView, developed with GeoWorks, and ICLAS developed with Novell (Groeber, 2010). IBM EduQuest' s educational network venture was one of the first examples of widespread use of Integrated Learning Systems (ILS), connected computer systems that allowed teachers or other facilitators to monitor and record student progress using the software provided (Becker & Hativa, 1994). By comparison, and unsurprisingly, Apple advertised their educational products as intended for the students' and teachers' individual exploration and creativity, and steered mostly clear of the ILS market. Though still in widespread use today via such popular software packages as Read 180 and Scholastic Math, there has been some controversy over the overall cost-to-benefits value of Integrated Learning Systems in schools (White, 1993; Bailey, 1993).

But as popular demand for Internet access grew by the mid-1990s, so did schools also begin to realize the learning potential of having computers connected to a World Wide Web, with access to visuals from geographic areas deemed mostly unreachable but for textbook photographs and aging 16mm film reels. The demand for increased public and school access had increased so much that in 1996, the U.S. Congress authorized the creation of the Universal Service Administrative Company: Schools & Libraries Division under the auspices of the Federal Communications Commission. The E-Rate was born.

The E-Rate, funded by a small amount added to every telephone carrier's customer phone bill, held the promise of providing funds for Internet and telecommunications infrastructure to benefit public libraries as well as public and private schools who had to apply and endure rigorous (and often bureaucratic) accountability and procedural scrutiny. But the overall effect was positive: schools and libraries, and thus students, teachers, and library patrons could now access the Internet/World Wide Web for free from local areas. The Congressional Research Service reported that Internet access in public schools rose from 35% to 95% between 1994 and 1999, and access in individual classrooms rose from 3% to 63% (Stedman & Osorio-O'Dea, 2001), providing access to many residing in urban and rural areas who would have otherwise waited years for local access to the Internet. Now the technology of the Internet was available to common folk, not just those who could afford to buy computers and monthly subscription rates to companies AOL, CompuServe, or EarthLink. The widespread availability of the Internet began to affect society and culture on an almost universal level starting in the mid-1990s; the effect would be massive, and irreversible.

THE NEW MILLENIUM

The First Decade

The end of the 20th and the beginning of the 21st century was very notably defined by the fear of a potential negative impact of technologies on society, particularly on businesses and scientific endeavors ranging from research supercomputers to NASA: Y2K, also known as the millennium bug. Due to a lack of planning or lack of foresight, early computer programmers had not thought what internal computer "clocks" would do when programs using two digits representative of the year ('97, '98, '99) would encounter the turn of the century. It was feared that the resulting 00 year date would occur as an ostensibly impossible configuration for programs, as if resetting the clock. Many of the effects were unknown, thus as the year 2000 approached societies around the globe, dependent on computers and related technologies programmed years before, fretted about what would occur when the date arrived. United States governmental agencies such as the Dept. of Defense and Dept. of Justice, Federal Aviation Agency, (FAA), the Federal Emergency Management Agency (FEMA), the Government Accounting Office (GAO) all developed contingency plans in preparing for potentially catastrophic system failures; even the President had formed a Council on Year 2000 Conversion. Common folk worried if airport control towers, or even computer equipment on board airplanes, might fail to respond or stop working entirely, along with other computerized systems as traffic and train signals, electrical grids, and nuclear reactors (Yourdon & Yourdon, 1997).

The good news was that as the date changed to January 1, 2000, not much happened, at least in most countries. The scramble to reprogram and prepare for the worst mostly paid off, and while some populations suffered various temporary setbacks, most notably Japan; so despite a few relatively minor glitches, everyone survived mostly unscathed by the millennium bug (BBC News, Jan.1, 2000).

The Age of the Internet

With the first truly global technological scare behind us, the world was ready to charge into the new century with rapidly-changing technologies, exceeding even the speed as defined by Moore's Law. First published in the April 1965 issue of Electronics magazine, Intel co-founder Gordon Moore's prediction stated that the price of each unit of computer processing power would drop by 50% price every two years. In the first decade of the 21st century, the Internet challenged even that prediction which had held true for nearly four decades. According to Chris Anderson (2009), editor-in-chief of Wired magazine:

"What the Internet does is combine [processors, bandwidth, and storage]... compounding the price declines with a triple play of technology... As a result the net annual deflation rate of the online world is 50 percent, which is to say that whatever it costs YouTube to stream a video today will cost half as much in a year." (p. 13)

Because of the combination of increasing computing power, storage space, and Internet speed with diminishing costs, and despite the so-called "dot-com bust" of 2001, where several large Internet-dependent companies failed within a short time period as the NASDAQ index plummeted (Galbraith & Hale, 2004), the 2000s saw the incredible growth of online everything: retail commerce, entertainment, travel arrangements, banking, and even education. Since 2000, new technologies have influenced every aspect of Western society, and have now permeated most Eastern societies, notably Japan, South Korea, India, and of course, China. China has become the leading exporter, by far, of electronics, telecommunications, and computer-based technologies, followed by Asian countries Malaysia and Thailand (WTO, 2009). And India has gained the reputation as the leading provider of business process (information technology) outsourcing (Friedman, 2005), as anyone who has used telephone technical support has undoubtedly noticed.

The new power of the Internet is not restricted to commercial use; indeed, as during its Arpanet infancy when it was used almost exclusively for research by universities and scientific communities, the Web has allowed access to heretofore hidden data and resources literally at the touch of our fingertips. Libraries around the world allow access to vast stores of knowledge that once would have required travel to distant lands and authorization via a bureaucratic chain-of-command, and gigantic databases house important information dating back years. These online-accessible archives occasionally require the intermediary services of a professional whose expertise lies in knowing precisely how and where to look in seeking information. Thus the role of the librarian in our society has undergone a dramatic shift: from a person knowledgeable of the contents to be found within the confines of a particular library, to a specialist in information science with the knowledge and expertise to research the contents of libraries and information repositories across the globe (Cassell & Hiremath, 2006).

Video Games Revisited

It is worth noting that unlike the first home video game wave that hit the youth and young adult market in the late 1970s and early 1980s, the possibility of playing video games with partners or foes from across the globe changed the dynamics of electronic games entirely. Added to the aforementioned rapidly evolving speed, power, and capacity paired with declining costs, video games sales soared in the 2000s. Smaller and more versatile game controllers, such as the Sony PlayStation, a unit capable of playing Blu-ray videos and downloading online videos and music, or the Nintendo Wii which has altered the stereotypical couch-potato image of the video gamer have, quite literally, changed the game. Online gamers participating in massively multiplayer online game (MMOG) virtual reality-style games such as World of Warcraft, Final Fantasy, and Second Life (more of a virtual world than merely a game) now number in the hundreds of millions worldwide (comScore, 2007). Handheld devices have also evolved from the now-quaint first Nintendo GameBoy to the sophisticated Nintendo DSi with Internet browsing capability and built-in cameras.

Some of the unforeseen consequences of the widespread availability of inexpensive computer and Internet technologies are evidenced in children in South Korea who have developed addictions to the Internet, and video games in particular, so severe that deprogramming camps have been created to help stop behaviors that have led to serious health issues (Block, 2008). Other countries, including the United States, have also identified Internet addiction as a societal ill (Byun et al., 2008).

Digital Mobility

Of course for adults (and, increasingly, children) who prefer to have a single, portable multifunction unit with them, cellular telephones no longer simply make phone calls; wireless mobile phones are also capable of taking digital photos; downloading and playing music; mobile file storage; identifying location or getting directions via Global Positioning Systems (GPS); Internet browsing; and text-messaging and email. And those are features the simpler models! Other types of devices, such as the Blackberry, Apple iPhone, Google Android and Nexus One, and Microsoft's Phone 7 are more aptly labeled mobile computing devices, since the capabilities seem more akin to home computer systems, rather than mere mobile telephones. The ubiquity of mobile phone use throughout the world has actually led to a decline in traditional landline telephony, and in regions of the world once thought too perilous or unstable to build an extensive telephone infrastructure; relatively easy and inexpensive cellular phone towers are solely providing telecommunications for these areas (Friedman, 2005).

The increasing global community of mobile phone users has extended into the demographic of children; it is not unheard of to find five- or six-year-old children using telephones to stay in touch with friends and family members, and even text-messaging each other. And increasingly, educators across the world have discovered the power of hand-held mobile devices and phones to incorporate teaching and learning, particularly in more remote areas of the world. Mobile learning, or M-Learning, is now in widespread use in countries such as China, Pakistan, India, Japan, and parts of sub-Saharan Africa. The devices are used to transmit lessons and tests, and also by students to enhance projects by using the camera functions common to cellular phones nowadays (Motlik, 2008).

Virtual Lives

One of the increasingly noted trends in how technology is affecting our society is the rise of the virtual persona; Andy Warhol was certainly prescient in his vision that "in the future everyone will be famous for fifteen minutes", but he underestimated the duration of the "fame" aspect, however that might be interpreted. With the advent of so-called social media, or Web 2.0, tools, common people find themselves constantly updating their "audiences", real or imagined, with the latest information on their whereabouts, goings-on, and other tidbits from their everyday existence. My Space, Facebook, YouTube, Twitter, and blogs (Web logs) broadcast every minute detail that a person or group wishes to tell someone, or everyone – plus allows others to weigh in on such details, with occasionally tragic results (Luo, 2009; Groholt, Ekeberg, & Haldorsen, 2006; Kidd et al., 2006). The increased reliance on such online venues to create a virtual existence apart from reality has attracted the naive, the mentally unstable, and of course, the criminally-intentioned, to wander the digital crowd in search of thrills or victims. Recent FBI statistics provide a terrifying view of just how often the Internet is used for other, less-than-wholesome motives (Wolak, Finkelhor, & Mitchell, 2004). However others will argue that the Internet is no more or less dangerous to children than any other type of social interaction, and that education, rules and adult supervision are required just as in the "real" world (Wolak, Finkelhor, Mitchell, & Ybarra, 2008).

Another dark side to the widespread accessibility of the Web is its use to perpetrate fraudulent and even criminal intentions; many of us have received the email pleas or entreaties to send funds thus granting us access to even larger funds. It is also known to law enforcement agencies that racist fringe groups as well as overtly terroristic entities such as Al Qaeda routinely recruit new converts to their cause by the use of Websites featuring long propagandistic messages and videos glorifying violence in the name of their fight (Gruen, 2006; Weimann, 2006).

And there is no doubt that the political parties and associated causes, with their ardent computer-equipped supporters, have changed the way information – as well as disinformation – is disseminated today. There certainly is no end in sight for such use of the power of the Web, and recent examples include the President of the United States now broadcasting messages to constituents via YouTube streaming video.

Technologies Today

As we have entered the second decade of the new millennium, a consistent trend is clearly visible within the constant barrage of new technologies, and can be identified as a synergistic confluence – where multiple technologies converge to create new functional interdependencies, as witnessed by the increasing reliance on the mobile phone/computing device. It has been announced that test markets are in effect to determine the desirability of a pocket-sized mobile device's capability of receiving and viewing live high definition (HD) television (Shin, 2006; Kumar, 2007). This is an excellent example of how all of the recent trends towards the synergistic confluence of previously disparate technologies seem to have one trait in common: the ultimate goal of the product is entertainment. This is also evidenced in the booming "home theater experience" market, as stores compete in selling audio and visual components that will work together with a computer interface and the Internet to bring not just rented video cassettes or DVDs, but the digitized products streamed via the Web into our living rooms, bedrooms, or any other location where a device capable of receiving a broadband signal is found (Kidd et al., 1999). Television (network and cable), movies, radio, music, and surfing the Web: all together in one assemblage of devices connected to one another. Adult, children, and teenage programming, along with specialized Spanish-language, sports, music, comedy, religious, and political channels now offer a smorgasbord of entertainment, information, and the resulting hybrid of the two, "infotainment" for nearly every possible demographic, including children. Specifically marketing to children has achieved what targeted marketing has sought and accomplished in other areas: creating a specialized niche demographic that all media (television, radio, film, Internet, music) can now reach unrestrictedly (Bhattacharyya & Kohli, 2007). The influence of technology and its retail beneficiaries has now fully extended to every demographic available – and may result in unintended consequences, such as the perception of the prolongation of childhood and expansion of adolescence and increasing juvenility (Cross, 2014).

CONCLUSION

The new century's defining technologies and its ubiquitous influence on our societies and cultures is defined by no single vehicle, medium, or device; it is defined by the infinite variety of choices that surround us, and the multiple possibilities – as well as the potential dangers – such choices offer (McCray, 2014). As we have seen, previous societies and cultures have benefitted and advanced because of the introduction of a "disruptive innovation" (Bower & Christensen, 1995); it will be up to us, as the human beings responsible for the development and use of new technologies, to see that our new-found tools and resources provide positive outcomes for our future, as well as the future of our children.

REFERENCES

Alvey, M. (2004). 'Too many kids and old ladies': Quality demographics and 1960s US television. *Screen*, *45*(1), 40–62. doi:10.1093/screen/45.1.40

Anderson, C. (2009). *Free: The future of a radical price*. New York: Hyperion.

Bailey, G. D. (1993). Wanted: A road map for understanding integrated learning systems. In G. D. Bailey (Ed.), *Computer-Based Integrated Learning Systems* (pp. 3–9). Englewood Cliffs, NJ: Educational Technology Publications.

Balk, A. (2005). *The rise of radio, from Marconi through the golden age*. Jefferson, NC: McFarland.

Banks, J. (1997). MTV and the globalization of popular culture. *International Communication Gazette, 59*(1), 43–60. doi:10.1177/0016549297059001004

Becker, H. J., & Hativa, N. (1994). History, theory, and research concerning integrated learning systems. *International Journal of Educational Research, 21*(1), 5–12. doi:10.1016/0883-0355(94)90019-1

Berners-Lee, T. (1989). *Information management: A proposal*. CERN Report. Retrieved April 14, 2010, from http://cds.cern.ch/record/369245/files/dd-89-001.pdf

Berners-Lee, T. (1992). The world-wide web. *Computer Networks and ISDN Systems, 25*(4–5), 454–459. doi:10.1016/0169-7552(92)90039-S

Berners-Lee, T., Cailliau, R., Groff, J.-F., & Pollermann, B. (1992). World-Wide Web: The Information Universe. *Internet Research, 2*(1), 52–58. doi:10.1108/eb047254

Bhattacharyya, R., & Kohli, S. (2007). Target Marketing to Children – The Ethical Aspect. In *Proceedings of the International Marketing Conference on Marketing &* Society (pp. 69-74). IIMK Publishing. Retrieved April 14, 2010, from http://dspace.iimk.ac.in/bitstream/2259/387/1/69-74.pdf

Bianculli, D. (2009). *Dangerously funny: The uncensored story of "The Smothers Brothers Comedy Hour"*. Beaverton, OR: Touchstone.

Bindas, K. J., & Heineman, K. J. (1994). Image is everything? Television and the counterculture message in the 1960s. *Journal of Popular Film and Television, 22*(1), 22–37. doi:10.1080/01956051.1994.9943663

Block, J. J. (2008). Issues for DSM-V: Internet Addiction. *The American Journal of Psychiatry, 165*(3), 306–307. doi:10.1176/appi.ajp.2007.07101556 PMID:18316427

Boal-Palheiros, G. M., & Hargreaves, D. J. (2001). Listening to music at home and at school. *British Journal of Music Education, 18*(2), 103–118. doi:10.1017/S0265051701000213

Boemer, M. L. (1989). *The children's hour: radio programs for children 1929-1956*. Lanham, MD: Scarecrow Press.

Borden, I. (2001). *Skateboarding, space and the city: Architecture and the body*. Oxford, UK: Berg.

Bower, J. L., & Christensen, C. M. (1995). Disruptive technologies: Catching the wave. *Harvard Business Review, 73*(1), 43–53.

Braunstein, P. (2002). Forever Young: Insurgent youth and the Sixties culture of rejuvenation. In P. Braunstein & M. W. Doyle (Eds.), *Imagine Nation: The American Counterculture of the 1960s and 1970s* (pp. 243–273). New York, NY: Routledge.

Brooke, M. (1999). The concrete wave: The history of skateboarding. Toronto, Canada: Warwick.

Byun, S., Ruffini, C., Mills, J. E., Douglas, A. C., Niang, M., Stepchenkova, S., & Blanton, M. et al. (2008). Internet Addiction: Metasynthesis of 1996–2006 quantitative Research. *Cyberpsychology & Behavior, 12*(2), 203–207. doi:10.1089/cpb.2008.0102 PMID:19072075

Carlton, J., & Kawasaki, G. (1997). *Apple: The inside story of intrigue, egomania, and business blunders*. New York: Random House.

Cassell, K. A., & Hiremath, U. (2006). *Reference and information services in the 21st century: An introduction*. New York, NY: Neal-Schuman.

Ceruzzi, P. E. (2003). *A history of modern computing*. Cambridge, MA: MIT Press.

Coates, B., Pusser, H. E., & Goodman, I. (1976). The influence of "Sesame Street" and "Mister Rogers' Neighborhood" on children's social behavior in the preschool. *Child Development*, *47*(1), 138–144. doi:10.2307/1128292

Collins, M. (1994). Internet information management tools. *Communication Education*, *43*(2), 112–119. doi:10.1080/03634529409378968

Compact disc hits 25th birthday. (2007). Retrieved April 14, 2010, from BBC News website: http://news.bbc.co.uk/2/hi/6950845.stm?lsm

comScore. (2007). *Worldwide online gaming community reaches 217 million people*. Retrieved April 17, 2010, from comScore website: http://www.comscore.com/Press_Events/Press_Releases/2007/07/Worldwide_Online_Gaming_Grows

Connolly, D. (1999). *CERN httpd*. Retrieved April 10, 2010, from http://www.w3.org/Daemon/

Cover, R. (2005). DVD time: temporality, audience engagement and the new TV culture of digital video. *Media International Australia: Incorporating Culture & Policy*, (117), 137.

Cross, G. (2014). *Jaded Children, Callow Adults*. Retrieved April 11, 2014, from The Chronicle of Higher Education website: http://chronicle.com/article/Jaded-Children-Callow-Adults/145117

de Mooij, M. K. (2004). *Consumer behavior and culture: consequences for global marketing and advertising*. Thousand Oaks, CA: Sage.

Dirks, T. (2010). The history of film. *Film History, 1970s*. http://www.filmsite.org/70sintro.html Retrieved April 5, 2010

Douglas, S. J. (2004). *Listening in: Radio and the American imagination*. Minneapolis: University of Minnesota Press.

Eisenstein, E. L. (2005). The printing revolution in early modern Europe (2nd, rev. ed.). Cambridge, UK: University Press.

Escott, C., & Hawkins, M. (1992). *Good rockin' tonight: Sun Records and the birth of rock'n'roll*. New York: St. Martin's Griffin.

Farley, T. (2007). The Cell-Phone Revolution. *American Heritage*, *22*(3), 8–19.

Fatherley, R. W., & MacFarland, D. T. (2014). *The birth of top 40 radio: The Storz stations' revolution of the 1950s and 1960s*. Jefferson, NC: MacFarland & Co.

Febvre, L., & Martin, H. (1976). *The coming of the book: the impact of printing 1450-1800*. London: New Left Books.

Fisch, S. M. (2004). *Children's learning from educational television: Sesame Street and beyond*. New York: Routledge.

Fisch, S. M., Truglio, R. T., & Cole, C. F. (1999). The impact of Sesame Street on preschool children: A review and synthesis of 30 years' research. *Media Psychology*, *1*(2), 165–190. doi:10.1207/s1532785xmep0102_5

Fleck, A. (1958). Technology and its social consequences. In C. Singer, E.J. Holmyard, A.R. Hall & T.I. Williams (Eds.) A History of Technology. Volume V: The Late Nineteenth Century, c. 1850 to c. 1900 (pp. 814-841). Oxford, UK: Clarendon.

Floyd, J., & Marsh, D. (1998). Sun Records: An oral history. New York: Avon.

Forbes, B. D. (2003). Mickey Mouse as icon: Taking popular culture seriously. *Word & World*, *23*(3), 242–252.

Forgacs, D. (1992). Disney animation and the business of childhood. *Screen*, *33*(4), 361–374. doi:10.1093/screen/33.4.361

Freiberger, P., & Swaine, M. (2000). *Fire in the valley: The making of the personal computer*. New York, NY: McGraw-Hill.

Friedman, T. L. (2005). *The World is Flat: A Brief History of the Twenty-First Century*. New York: Farrar, Straus and Giroux.

Galbraith, J. K., & Hale, T. (2004). *Income distribution and the information technology bubble. University of Texas Inequality Project Working Paper 27, January 14, 2004*. Retrieved April 11, 2010, from University of Texas website: http://utip.gov.utexas.edu/papers/utip_27.pdf

Gallivan, M., & Srite, M. (2005). Information technology and culture: Identifying fragmentary and holistic perspectives of culture. *Information and Organization*, *15*(4), 295–338. doi:10.1016/j.infoandorg.2005.02.005

Garofalo, R. (1994). Culture versus Commerce: The Marketing of Black Popular Music. *Public Culture*, *7*(1), 275–288. doi:10.1215/08992363-7-1-275

Goldman, E. (1960). *The crucial decade and after: America from 1945 to 1960*. New York: Vintage Books.

Greeson, L. E., & Williams, R. A. (1986). Social Implications of Music Videos for Youth: An Analysis of the Content and Effects of MTV. *Youth & Society*, *18*(2), 177–189. doi:10.1177/0044118X86018002005

Groeber, M. (2010). *IBM EduQuest*. Retrieved April 10, 2010, from http://www.mgroeber.de/nathan/devices/eduquest.html

Groholt, B., Ekeberg, O., & Haldorsen, T. (2006). Adolescent suicide attempters: What predicts future suicidal acts? *Suicide & Life-Threatening Behavior*, *36*(6), 638–650. doi:10.1521/suli.2006.36.6.638 PMID:17250468

Gruen, M. (2006). Innovative recruitment and indoctrination tactics by extremists: Video games, hip-hop, and the world wide web. In James Forest (Ed.) The making of a terrorist: Recruitment, training, and root causes; Vol. 1: Recruitment. 4-17. Westport, CT: Praeger.

Guralnick, P. (1995). *Last train to Memphis: The rise of Elvis Presley*. New York: Little, Brown and Co.

Hardy, I. R. (1996). The Evolution of ARPANET Email. Thesis, Department of History, University of California, Berkeley, CA.

Hauben, M., & Hauben, R. (1997). *Netizens: On the history and impact of Usenet and the Internet*. Hoboken, NJ: Wiley-IEEE.

Heino, R. (2000). New sports: What is so punk about snowboarding? *Journal of Sport and Social Issues*, *24*(2), 176–191. doi:10.1177/0193723500242005

Holzmann, G. J., & Pehrson, P. (1994). *The early history of data networks*. Hoboken, NJ: Wiley-IEEE.

Horwitz, J. (2006). *Does MTV really matter anymore*? Retrieved March 29, 2010, from: http://www.ilounge.com/index.php/backstage/comments/does-mtv-really-matter-any-more

Hughes, T. P. (2004). *Human-built world: How to think about technology and culture*. Chicago, IL: The University of Chicago.

Huston, A. C., Donnerstein, E., Fairchild, H., Feshbach, N. D., Katz, P. A., Murray, J. P., & Zuckerman, D. et al. (1992). *Big world, small screen: The role of television in American society*. Lincoln, NE: University of Nebraska Press.

Inglis, I. (2000). The Beatles are coming! Conjecture and conviction in the myth of Kennedy, America, and the Beatles. *Popular Music and Society*, *24*(2), 93–108. doi:10.1080/03007760008591769

Internet World Stats. (2010). *Internet Usage Statistics: The Internet Big Picture-World Internet Users and Population Stats*. Retrieved April 10, 2010, from http://www.wdvl.com/Internet/History/

Jansen, B. J. (1998). The graphical user interface. *ACM SIGCHI Bulletin*, *30*(2), 22–26. doi:10.1145/279044.279051

Jenkins, H. (2006). *Convergence culture: Where old and new media collide*. New York, NY: NYU press.

Jorgenson, F. (1998). Early fixed-head video recorders. In E. D. Daniel, C. D. Mee, & M. H. Clark (Eds.), *Magnetic Recording: The First 100 Years* (pp. 137–152). Hoboken, NJ: Wiley-IEEE.

Katz, M. (2005). Internet gurus: Prominent Internet professionals. In *Proceedings of the III Congrés Internacional Comunicació i Realitat, Barcelona* (pp.157-169). Retrieved April 10, 2010, from http://cicr.blanquerna.url.edu/2005/Abstracts/PDFsComunicacions/vol1/03/Katz_Merav.pdf

Keith, M. C. (1997). *Voices in the purple haze: Underground radio and the Sixties*. Santa Barbara, CA: Praeger.

Kent, S. (2001). *The ultimate history of video games: From Pong to Pokémon - the story behind the craze that touched our lives and changed the world*. New York: Three Rivers.

Kidd, C. D., Orr, R., Abowd, G. D., Atkeson, C. G., Essa, I. A., MacIntyre, B., & Newstetter, W. et al. (1999). The aware home: A living laboratory for ubiquitous computing research. In N. Streitz, J. Siegel, V. Hartkopf, & S. Konomi (Eds.), *Cooperative buildings. Integrating information, organizations, and architecture* (pp. 191–198). Berlin: Springer. doi:10.1007/10705432_17

Kidd, S., Henrich, C. C., Brookmeyer, K. A., Davidson, L., King, R. A., & Shahar, A. (2006). The social context of adolescent suicide attempts: Interactive effects of parent, peer, and school social relations. *Suicide & Life-Threatening Behavior*, *36*(4), 386–395. doi:10.1521/suli.2006.36.4.386 PMID:16978093

King, D. C. (2005). *World wars and the modern age*. Hoboken, NJ: John Wiley & Sons.

Kumar, A. (2007). *Mobile TV: DVB-H, DMB, 3G systems and rich media applications*. Burlington, MA: Elsevier. doi:10.1016/B978-0-240-80946-5.50005-7

Layton, E. T. (1974). Technology as knowledge. *Technology and Culture*, *15*(1), 31–41. doi:10.2307/3102759

Lull, J. (1987). *Popular music and communication*. Thousand Oaks, CA: Sage.

Luo, J. S. (2009). The Facebook phenomenon: Boundaries and controversies. *Primary Psychiatry*, *16*(11), 19–21.

Marquis, A. G. (1984). Written on the wind: The impact of radio during the 1930s. *Journal of Contemporary History*, *19*(3), 385–415. doi:10.1177/002200948401900302

McAllister, M. P., & Giglio, J. M. (2005). The commodity flow of U.S. children's television. *Critical Studies in Media Communication*, *22*(1), 26–44. doi:10.1080/0739318042000331835

McCray, W. P. (2014). *The technologists' siren song*. Retrieved April 11, 2014, from The Chronicle of Higher Education website: http://chronicle.com/article/The-Technologists-Siren-Song/145107

McLeod, K. (1999). Authenticity within hip-hop and other cultures threatened with assimilation. *Journal of Communication*, *49*(4), 134–150. doi:10.1111/j.1460-2466.1999.tb02821.x

Meggs, P. B., & Purvis, A. W. (2006). *Meggs' history of graphic design* (4th ed.). Hoboken, NJ: Wiley & Sons.

Miller, D. R., & Swanson, G. E. (1958). *The changing American parent*. New York: Wiley.

Miller, D. T., & Nowak, M. (1977). *The fifties*. New York, NY: Doubleday.

Miller, M. (1987). Short looks: IBM PS/ Model 25. *InfoWorld*, *9*(33), 44.

Mittell, J. (2003). The great Saturday morning exile: Scheduling cartoons on television's periphery in the 1960s. In C. A. Stabile & M. Harrison (Eds.), *Prime time animation: Television animation and American culture* (pp. 33–54). New York: Routledge.

Morris, G. (1993). Beyond the beach: Social and formal aspects of AIP's beach party movies. *Journal of Popular Film and Television*, *21*(1), 30–48. doi:10.1080/01956051.1993.9943970

Motlik, S. (2008). Technical evaluation report 63: Mobile learning in developing nations. *International Review of Research in Open and Distance Learning*, *9*(2), 1–7.

National Institute on Media and the Family. (2010). Retrieved April 5, 2010, from http://www.mediafamily.org/activitiesandquizzes/decactivity.shtml

Okin, J. R. (2005). *The Internet revolution: The not-for-dummies guide to the history, technology, and use of the Internet*. Winter Harbor, ME: Ironbound.

Pan, J. (1997). On the origin of printing in the light of new archaeological discoveries. *Chinese Science Bulletin*, *42*(12), 976–981. doi:10.1007/BF02882611

Plato. (2008). *Phaedrus*. (B. Jowett, Trans.). Forgotten Books.

Reimer, J. (2005). *Total share: 30 years of personal computer market share figures*. Retrieved March 30, 2010, from the Ars Technica website: http://arstechnica.com/old/content/2005/12/total-share.ars

Reisch, L. (2008). The nature and culture of consumption in consumption societies. In Reisch (Ed.), Rethinking consumer behavior for the well-being of all: Reflections on individual consumer responsibility (pp. 15-21). Strasbourg, Austria: Council of Europe Publishing.

RIAA. (2002). *Recent study illustrates Internet piracy's impact on music market*. Retrieved April 16, 2010, from the RIAA.org website: http://www.riaa.org/PR_STORY.CFM?ID=491

Roy, W. G. (2004). "Race records" and "hillbilly music": Institutional origins of racial categories in the American commercial recording industry. *Poetics*, *32*(3–4), 265–279. doi:10.1016/j.poetic.2004.06.001

Santoro, G. M. (1994). The internet: An overview. *Communication Education*, *43*(2), 73–86. doi:10.1080/03634529409378965

Schatz, B. R., & Hardin, J. B. (1994). NCSA Mosaic and the World Wide Web: Global hypermedia protocols for the Internet. *Science*, *265*(5174), 895–901. doi:10.1126/science.265.5174.895 PMID:17782140

Shah, R., & Romine, J. (1995). *Playing MUDs on the Internet*. New York: Wiley & Sons.

Shin, D. H. (2006). Prospectus of mobile TV: Another bubble or killer application? *Telematics and Informatics*, *23*(4), 253–270. doi:10.1016/j.tele.2005.08.001

Stedman, J. B., & Osorio-O'Dea, P. (2001). *E-Rate for schools: Background on telecommunications discounts through the Universal Service Fund (98-604 EPW).* Congressional Research Service. Retrieved April 10, 2010, from Policy Archive website: http://www.policyarchive.org/handle/10207/bitstreams/655.pdf

Stoll, C. (1989). *The cuckoo's egg: Tracking a spy through the maze of computer espionage.* New York: Doubleday.

Sugaya, H. (1998). Helical-scan recorders for broadcasting. In E. D. Daniel, C. D. Mee, & M. H. Clark (Eds.), *Magnetic Recording: The First 100 Years* (pp. 170–181). Hoboken, NJ: Wiley-IEEE.

Sugaya, H. (1998). Consumer video recorders. In E. D. Daniel, C. D. Mee, & M. H. Clark (Eds.), *Magnetic Recording: The First 100 Years* (pp. 182–200). Hoboken, NJ: Wiley-IEEE.

Terry, N. P. (1994). GUI Wars: The Windows Litigation and the Continuing Decline of Look and Feel. *Arkansas Law Review*, *47*, 93–155.

University of Maryland College Park. (2000). *Estimated Internet usage by basic general social survey demographics.* Retrieved April 10, 2010, from http://www.webuse.umd.edu/tutorial/SDA-GSS_Tutorial.pdf

Uslaner, E. M. (1998). Social capital, television, and the "mean world": Trust, optimism, and civic participation. *Political Psychology*, *19*(3), 441–467. doi:10.1111/0162-895X.00113

Virnoche, M. E. (1998). The Seamless web and communications equity: The shaping of a community network. *Science, Technology & Human Values*, *23*(2), 199–220. doi:10.1177/016224399802300203

Walker, J. (2004). *Rebels on the air: An alternative history of radio in America.* New York: NYU Press.

Wall, T. (2007). Finding an alternative: Music programming in US college radio. *Radio Journal: International Studies in Broadcast & Audio Media*, *5*(1), 35–54.

Walsh, T. (2005). *Timeless toys: Classic toys and the playmakers who made them.* Riverside, NJ: Andrews McMeel.

Web Developer's Virtual Library. (2010). *History of the Internet and the World Wide Web.* Retrieved April 10, 2010, from Web Developer's Virtual Library.com website: http://www.wdvl.com/Internet/History

Weimann, G. (2006). Terrorist dot com: Using the internet for terrorist recruitment and mobilization. In J. Forest (Ed.), The making of a terrorist: Recruitment, training, and root causes, Vol. 1: Recruitment (pp. 53-65). Westport, CT: Praeger.

White, M. (1993). Are ILSs good education? In G. D. Bailey (Ed.), *Computer-Based Integrated Learning Systems* (pp. 115–119). Englewood Cliffs, NJ: Educational Technology Publications.

Williams, R., & Edge, D. (1996). The social shaping of technology. *Research Policy*, *25*(6), 856–899. doi:10.1016/0048-7333(96)00885-2

Winston, M. (2003). Children of invention. In M. Winston & R. Edelbach (Eds.), *Society, Ethics, and Technology* (2nd ed.). Belmont, CA: Thomson/Wadsworth.

Wojcik-Andrews, I. (2000). *Children's films: History, ideology, pedagogy, theory.* New York: Garland.

Wolak, J., Finkelhor, D., & Mitchell, K. (2004). Internet-initiated sex crimes against minors: Implications for prevention based on findings from a national study. *The Journal of Adolescent Health*, *35*(5), 424–433. doi:10.1016/j.jadohealth.2004.05.006 PMID:15488437

Wolak, J., Finkelhor, D., Mitchell, K. J., & Ybarra, M. L. (2008). Online "predators" and their victims: Myths, realities, and implications for prevention and treatment. *The American Psychologist*, *63*(2), 111–128. doi:10.1037/0003-066X.63.2.111 PMID:18284279

World Trade Organization. (2009). *Statistics International trade statistics 2009 - Merchandise trade by product*. Retrieved April 12, 2010, from WTO.org website: http://www.wto.org/english/res_e/statis_e/its2009_e/its09_merch_trade_product_e.htm

Wozniak, S. (2007). iWoz: Computer geek to cult icon: How I invented the personal computer, co-founded Apple, and had fun doing it. New York: W.W. Norton & Co.

Y2K bug fails to bite. (No Date). Retrieved April 11, 2010, from BBC News website: http://news.bbc.co.uk/2/hi/science/nature/585013.stm

Yerxa, D. A. (2013). The Invention of the American Meal: An Interview with Abigail Carroll. *Historically Speaking*, *14*(5), 26–28. doi:10.1353/hsp.2013.0055

Young, J. S. (1998). *Forbes greatest technology stories: Inspiring tales of the entrepreneurs*. New York: John Wiley & Sons.

Yourdon, E., & Yourdon, J. (1997). *Time bomb 2000: What the year 2000 computer crisis means to you!* Upper Saddle River, NJ: Prentice Hall.

KEY TERMS AND DEFINITIONS

Communications: Oral, written, electronic, and technologically-enhanced interactions between human beings.

Computers: Electronic equipment and devices that allow the rapid processing, calculation, and visual representation of information.

Culture: The customs and key indicators of socially accepted norms of a society.

Internet: A network of inter-related access points allowing the rapid transmission of information and entertainment.

Mobile Technologies: Hand-held and portable devices used in communications by transmitting voice and/or visual information.

Radio: Transmission and reception of audio information and entertainment.

Societies: Groupings of human beings by mutual consent and agreed-upon standards and rules.

Technology: Human inventions designed to sustain or improve lives and/or livelihoods to make existence more tolerable and/or comfortable.

Video: Transmission and reception of visual information and entertainment.

World Wide Web: The aggregate of all interconnected equipment and devices via Internet access points.

Chapter 17
ICTs in Schools and Their Relationship with Indigenous Communities of Patagonia

Flavio Leandro Caldas
Provincial College of Technical Education (EPET) No. 12, Argentina

Leandro Norberto Giglioli
Provincial College of Technical Education (EPET) No. 12, Argentina

ABSTRACT

UNESCO indicates that one of the biggest problems we face in the early twenty-first century is the abolition of differences between individuals and cultures. Intercultural education is therefore paramount. With their potential for allowing members of different countries and cultures to meet and interact, ICTs (Information and Communication Technologies) offer an interesting array of tools for tackling this matter. Argentina acknowledges the right of indigenous people to access bilingual and intercultural education, and seeks to improve teachers' skills to achieve a better quality of education that allows equal opportunities. However, the reality is that schools in the Patagonian province of Neuquén are still far from achieving this target. This article presents data on the use of ICTs in Patagonian schools, based on the opinion of students from both aboriginal and urban backgrounds. It also analyzes the relationship between students' performance and the use of technological tools.

INTRODUCTION

Since the reform of the Argentinean Constitution in 1994, the government has always acknowledged the ethnic and cultural pre-existence of aboriginal people. This implies the recognition of the multicultural and multiethnic nature of our country, at the same time demanding its respect and appraisal. Argentina addressed this issue at the 169th convention of the International Labor Organization (ILO) on Indigenous and Tribal People which was implemented from 2001 onwards, in this way promoting the "respect and appraisal of cultural diversity and constitutionally acknowledging the rights of the indigenous population".

From that reform onwards the right of these aboriginal people to a bilingual and intercultural education was also granted. This right has not been

DOI: 10.4018/978-1-4666-8433-1.ch017

fully implemented yet, although partial improvements have been made towards this national goal.

Taking the new National Education Law of 2006 as a starting point, the need to provide schooling for all Argentineans, disregarding their race, creed, location, age, etc., has been stated, aiming for an education system that grants opportunities to all its participants in order to obtain a quality education (Hernández & Calcagno, 2003). We understand that the educational system cannot waste this opportunity to amend its mistakes and inequalities, or at least, to attempt that change.

The new didactic and technological tools, above all those known as ICTs (Information and Communication Technologies), have become an integral part of everyday life, but have had little effect on the aboriginal students of the Neuquén province. Some students feel comfortable with the arrival of these tools because they see advertisements on the Internet, on television, at the cinema, or hear them on the radio (Bautista, 2004; Mominó, Sigalés & Meneses, 2008), whereas others may feel a certain sense of rejection. Outside of school, for these youths ICTs represent something close to amusement, while for adults they mean the possibility of further integration into the labor market. For both groups, ICTs represent the attractive possibility of communicating and feeling part of a group.

The reality is that new technologies are spreading worldwide due to globalization and openly becoming the transmitters of a neoliberal consumerist model around the planet by means of the so-called Information Society (Murillo García, 2010; Ferrer, 2010;Ferrán et al., 2010). By undertaking a comparison between the appearance of print and public schooling, we can infer that we are on the brink of a great change in the traditional educational model, in which all the education providers are daily participants and should have full responsibility in the aforementioned change.

The National Education Law is clear in its meaning, and in Chapter 1, Article 11, it promotes two essential topics for education in the Patagonian region: "To develop the required competencies for the use of the new languages triggered by the information and communication technologies. To ensure respect for these indigenous peoples' language and cultural identity, promoting the value of multiculturalism in the students' education".

Figure 1. "Conectar Igualdad" portal

The Government itself is aware of the deficiencies in the furthering of these goals, according to the DiNIECE report (2005) related to "the educational policies to prevent academic failure". This report "contemplates the need to continue working on the digital literacy and the management of computer resources", which were never completely implemented in the Patagonia region and which are still an unresolved matter for the integration of ICTs into curriculum practices, although some steps were taken four years ago, with the arrival of the National State program "Conectar Igualdad" (2010).

From the abovementioned issue springs the present article, which contains information generated from data collected in one secondary school in San Martín de los Andes in the year 2014, emphasizing the role played by students from rural areas, and who belong to or are descended from Mapuche communities.

All Latin American countries, to a greater or lesser extent, boast a rich and diverse cultural patrimony. In them the western Iberian culture (Spanish and Portuguese) remains and coexists with the aboriginal cultures of pre-Columbian origin and, in some cases, even with African cultural heritage (Antinao, 1998; Binstock et al., 2008; Del Álamo, 2003). Nevertheless, this cultural diversity is not acknowledged as valuable, nor is itproperly reflected in the educational system, which is predominantly shaped by Western culture. In the case of Neuquén and the aforementioned Mapuche community, these tendencies remain, despite the fact that schools have a high percentage of students descending from the original aboriginal population.

The objective of this research is to get a sense of the situation of the students in intercultural schools of Neuquén in connection with the use of ICTs, and their relation to their performance, attempting to formulate some methodological proposals to teach curriculum content by means of the inclusion of new technologies in the classroom.

So as to organize the research, the following topics have been considered within the current educational context, analyzing the factors that influence the academic performance of those students belonging to rural schools in Neuquén:

1. The intercultural nature of schools as a central issue for the future of schooling. Any school that is located in a region where there are two or more cultures co-existing must consider intercultural education as the only possible way to optimize the teaching-learning process. There must exist a well-developed base in order to promote tolerance and respect for diversity, and taking the analysis of national and regional curriculum is a starting point.
2. The expectations students have of the use of ICTs. The responsible and effective use of the ICTs inside and outside the classroom could improve not only the academic performance of the students, but also could increase collaborative work amongst students.
3. The use of ICTs in the classroom. Focusing on the expectations that the students have regarding their academic performance, we aim to analyze
4. The acceptance of ICTs as a tool for teaching and learning. We understand that ICTs play a major role not only in the educational process, but also in the creation of a skilled workforce and the inclusion of members of aboriginal communities in the sustainable development of their socioeconomic system.

Despite these studies and suggestions, traditional lectures are still a constant and are taught in a similar way to that of the mid-twentieth century. They are classes in which subjects are formally presented, conceived as a group of facts, proceedings and known solutions which are to be found in the textbook; in which students are thought to understand when they can follow a rote process to obtain the right answer; and in which the job of the teacher, interpreted as that of the holder of truth, consists in showing each process step by step, without taking into account the financial, social or cultural differences of the students.

PROBLEM IDENTIFICATION

The original topic of this research arises from a problem found in the educational framework of certain rural communities in the Patagonia region. The results published in Caldas and Garcia-Valcárcel (2013) were of particular interest, since they showed the lack of public policies providing for the introduction of ICTs in primary and secondary schools in Argentina. This publication has discussed the implementation of the at that time new governmental program "Conectar Igualdad" (PCI). Using this work as a starting point, we wish to investigate how the program was implemented in the Patagonia region, and how it affected the students and teachers of secondary schools in the area. Our study will focus on the students from Mapuche communities and the impact this program had on their socioeconomic situation. In order to do this, we surveyed students from the secondary school Escuela Provincial de Educación Técnica 12 (E.P.E.T. 12), located in the Patagonian town of San Martín de los Andes, in the Neuquén province, and used that sample as a small representation of the current situation.

Our study will center its attention on the Mapuche community and the PCI, trying to answer the following major questions:

- Has the PCI improved the quality of academic performance and social interaction in the student overall population?
- Has any change been observed in the experiences of students of Mapuche origin?
- Is there a substantive policy concerning the execution of the PCI, so that it can be implemented to its full extent; that is, has the deployed equipment been complemented with courses or any other type of professional training for the use of the offered technologies?
- Has the program been reevaluated in order to assess the extent of its success?

ICTs IN THE ARGENTINEAN EDUCATIONAL SYSTEM

Until now, the equipment and connectivity processes in Argentinean schools have been the result of several intermittent initiatives from the public sector (National Ministry of Education, state governments or city councils), from non-governmental organizations, or from the private sector. Within this context, the ways in which this equipment and connectivity has been integrated in schools have also varied: from donations and contributions of computers deprived of any pedagogic content and/or prior awareness for their beneficial use in the classroom, to programs driven by intensive training for teachers and oriented towards the development of science and technology projects.

This variety of initiatives, their multiple sources of funding, and their intermittence, have rendered it difficult to keep an up-to-date record of schools' are progress in technological infrastructure in the different jurisdictions of the country. Moving beyond the importance of having a precise account of the state of the equipment and connectivity in the nation's schools, which could be included in the annual lists of the National Office of Information and Education Quality Assessment (Dirección Nacional de Información y Evaluación de Calidad Educativa, DiNIECE), it is imperative to trace a national map that provides this kind of information in order to diagnose the situation of the use of ICTs in the Argentinean education system as soon as possible. Then it would be possible to assess in what measure and in what way the integration of the ICTs in schools has impacted the educational quality of each school.

The state of the availability and technological resources in Patagonian schools proves to be unbalanced if we compare the different Patagonian regions. The supplying of computer equipment has not necessarily meant access to connectivity; mainly because the first initiatives in this respect came before affordable and available broadband connections. In these cases, connectivity has always been considered a second stage in the integration process of ICTs in schools. On the other hand, the "List of teaching institutions and their annexes" does not offer any detail about the characteristics or the distribution of the equipment that the schools own. This kind of information, which is essential to make a diagnosis on the state of the computer apparatus in a school, has not yet been published.

ICTs in Rural Schools Settled in Aboriginal Communities

According to this situation, which increases in those rural schools situated in aboriginal communities, deciding ICTs policies with just criteria implies prioritizing those deprived suburban or rural areas, which are more disconnected and more unprotected in terms of education.

Regarding the state of ICTs in rural schools, it is possible to allege direct and indirect evidence of the need to overcome some deficiencies. Though there was a rise in the availability of ICTs in rural areas, mere equipment is not enough to promote change (DiNIECE, 2005). Moreover, these advances are still insufficient and unequal in comparison with urban schools. Another deficit is that there is little evidence for those successful actions that many schools perform in relation to ICTs, which are necessary inputs for the construction of more efficient policies.

One of the most vulnerable sectors when it comes to the right to a quality education and the chances to access information is the indigenous children and adolescents who inhabit rural areas. The education aimed at these indigenous people adopts its own particular characteristics different in relation to the non-indigenous population. Nevertheless, it is possible and necessary to establish relationships between ICTs and indigenous edu-

Figure 2. Members of aboriginal communities receiving the PCI netbook

cation that reduces not only the digital gaps, but also those related to culture, identity and social immigration.

Some benefits are also generated when an education policy pertinent to ICTs that takes into account the quality and impact on the childhood and adolescent indigenous population is implemented. ICTs are tools that make possible a wide range of opportunities and favorable results. In order for this to happen, conditions which later need to be enhanced must be generated, for a profitable use of ICTs in rural indigenous communities can greatly change the precarious education dynamics that currently characterize many of these institutions. A school situated in an aboriginal community becomes the cultural and economic center of that region, and if that particular school is in tune with the ICTs it can also benefit both the families and development of the local community. (Magadan, 2008, p.118)

ICTs could also add value to the regions' intercultural and bilingual education on various levels. It would be possible to work in conjunction with the "Confederación de Organizaciones Mapuche" (COM) so as to, after a thorough analysis confirmed by consensus, allow the elaboration of a feasible action plan.

The curriculum is a fundamental issue in the inclusion of intercultural education in schools located within indigenous communities. The Board of Education is currently working on creating a consensus proposal from the COM, the government and the teachers' union who have formed an Intercultural Education headquarters, its chief being the Mapuche teacher Graciela Aquito.

The ICTs and their Inclusion in Secondary Schools with Mapuche Students

The Patagonian secondary education system achieved an important change in the past few years, since the implementation of the statewide program "Conectar Igualdad" in the region. More than 50000 netbooks were delivered to schools, and Internet access points were installed in almost every high school in the province. Such actions require public policies that allow the adoption of the technological tools and the design of a new educational paradigm. Now the teachers are no longer the experts in the use of the ICTs, but instead this role has been handed on to the students.

Figure 3. E.P.E.T. 12, in San Martín de los Andes, Neuquén

This inversion of roles requires the teachers to mediate and have a higher degree of tolerance than before in order to accept this new fact; that is, that the teacher no longer owns all information, and is no longer in a position of absolute power as once was the case.

Additionally, in Neuquén's rural region there is a large amount of students that originate from indigenous Mapuche communities, and they are always ready to reclaim their ancestral rights. The Mapuche population stands out above other Argentinean indigenous populations because of their energy and the amount of press the media is always ready to give them. It is because this attitude that they want to truly own and control the tools that the ICTs provide.

Furthermore, the labor market continuously demands employees with knowledge in the use of ICTs and their applications; and due to this demand, young Mapuches are now considered for jobs that their parents and grandparents would never have imagined they could aspire to.

THE NEUQUÉN PROVINCE: EDUCATION AND SOCIOECONOMIC PROCESSES

Over the past years, the ICTs have been imposing new socioeconomic scenarios on every country of Latin America. This has surprised the entire continent, delaying the equal distribution of quality education to all the students of the region. To this inequality we have to add the challenge of promoting and integrating new forms of technological education without widening the economical gap between the social classes that received a deficient education and those that, meanwhile, were able to access an elite-level education. To include the ICTs to improve equality and quality of education is challenge that must be confronted.

The province of Neuquén is remarkable for the large aboriginal population that lives within its limits and because of the financial relevance of tourism to the area. These two groups –the Mapuches and the tourists– form a socioeconomic symbiosis, in which the Mapuche community has proposed new touristic destinations for the economic development of the community. This cooperation requires the use of ICTs for the broadcasting and sales of these touristic goods. The growth of touristic market in the area has influenced the regional economies, and the indigenous communities have diversified their offering using the Web in order to include this economic opportunity in their commercial portfolio. Many tourists feel attracted by the prospect of meeting these aboriginal communities from Patagonia, and they are glad to have the opportunity to stay one night inside a cabin located on Mapuche land, managed by people of this community.

The ski resort situated in Mount Batea Mahuida and the cabins in Lolen are just some of the new Mapuche entrepreneurship that give an idea of the economic development of this aboriginal population due to their efficient use of ICTs.

From a sociological point of view, schools among Mapuche communities represent an advance in (urban) society within a totally different setting. In an interview with rural teacher Luis Martínez, he clearly stated that "...the school is conceived for us (the urban community) and then it has been transferred to rural areas, and, on top of that, into a Mapuche community...we have exchanged fortresses for schools... Introducing a Mapuche boy into a classroom is very hard because he is in the country all day long, and to *confine* him within a classroom for a couple of hours seems a penance to him."

The following items characterize the education in Neuquén, allowing us to approximately understand its state:

1. Only half of the population reaches the primary school level. Furthermore, only half of the people that start primary schools complete this level; that is, a quarter of the total population concludes the most basic level of education.

2. Only 44% of the population achieves a secondary level of education.
3. Literacy has increased in the 90s (from a 92.3% in 1980 to a 94.7% in 1991). Despite these optimistic numbers, in most rural areas, and hence in the Mapuche communities within the province, important inequalities appear with respect to urban areas. (C.P.E, 2010).

The structural problems of the education system, namely attrition and academic failure, could be solved by endorsing the broadening of the education offer, both quantitatively and qualitatively, and would not be left only to the good will of the teachers of Neuquén as seems to be the intention of the political spheres.

The Presence of the Mapuche Community on the Web

If we were to do a web search, we would notice the vast amount of websites that make reference to the Mapuche Nation, in historical, descriptive, informative, and other terms. We will also be able to observe a variety of webpages that promote the Mapuche culture and their reclaims. From this viewpoint, the Mapuche community has used the Internet as a tool so as to allow the access and participation in the Web of other communities. In that way, the general population forms particular views regarding the Mapuches; views that can be positive, negative, or of reaffirmation of the Mapuches' identity. The following should be treated as a sample of the reach of the Mapuche population on the Web:

- http://www.avkinpivkemapu.com.ar/
- http://liwenmapu.wordpress.com/
- http://paismapuche.org/
- http://www.mapuche-nation.org/
- https://www.facebook.com/pages/Confederaci%C3%B3n-Mapuche-de-Neuqu%C3%A9n/444250588989024

RESEARCH METHODOLOGY

Based on the results of a previous publication of Caldas and Garcia-Valcárcel (2013), we determined to focus on the opinion of high-school students on the use of ICTs, paying particular attention to those students of Mapuche origin. Since the abovementioned article was published much has changed in the Argentinean education system; specifically, the governmental PCI. The arrival of these netbooks was an important occurrence; hence it will be our frame of reference when talking about ICTs in secondary schools' classrooms and in this article from now on.

Research was carried out in the technical high-school E.P.E.T. 12, in the town of San Martín de los Andes, since this school has a considerable number of students of Mapuche background. This school was considered to be representative of the current educational situation regarding ICTs, with a total student body of approximately 650 students.

In order to perform this study, a qualitative survey was conducted with 107 students from the chosen secondary school, 19 of which belong to the Mapuche community. The survey gathered personal and academic data, with questions that went from the students' opinion regarding the relationship between academic performance and the use of their netbooks; to how they thought this new piece of hardware improved their social skills. This survey was complemented by a series of interviews of key faculty members.

Because some of the information we required is in documents of a confidential nature, we obtained authorization from the principal of the institution in order to access them.Once the surveying process finished, we processed the qualitative data and so as to obtain variables. This allowed us to interpret the data, and establish any dependence relationship between key variables with the aid of the statistical software package SPSS©. Finally, we were able to present these statistical results in a coherent manner in the attempt to draw several conclusions. It is worth mentioning that Fisher's exact test was used alongside Pearson's chi-squared test in order to examine the data, since the sample of students from Mapuche background was sometimes too small for regular Pearson's chi-squared test. As you will observe, we have pointed out that the frequencies are sometimes smaller than the minimum required for Pearson's test to be reliable, and therefore used Fisher's test, as it is an acceptable measure to take into account when working with small samples.

THE STUDENTS' OPINION: ANALYSIS AND INTERPRETATION OF DATA

Personal and Social Features of the Students

This study covers students from 2nd to 4th grade (7th to 12th grade in the U.S.), with ages ranging from 12 to 18 years. As mentioned in the previous study, this discrepancy in age may be due to several factors, since some students:

- Had to retake a year in primary school.
- Had to retake a year in secondary school.
- Dropped-out in favor of working.
- Started when they were older than the average.

We chose students that were currently in these grades because they have been in possession of these netbooks for over two years by now, and therefore had more experience with the equipment than students that just started the first level of secondary school.

It is worth to observe that classrooms are heterogeneous with respect to the background of the students. Students from Mapuche background represent approximately 18% of our sample, the rest being students coming from various urban schools.

Owning a Technology vs. Knowing How to Use It

With the implementation of the governmental PCI, every high school student now has acquired a netbook; therefore it has become pointless in a way to analyze how many of these students possess one. However, owning a piece of equipment does not mean owning the knowledge on how to use it. To make complete use of something one requires, it could be argued, is to not only own that element or tool, but to also own the knowledge in order to use it properly. To further emphasize this point, we may highlight some the results of the survey, showing that 18% of the sample did not particularly enjoy using computers in general; even though most of them (82%) had one or more at home. The PCI guarantees only the delivery of the equipment, but does not yet complement this investment with training so that the students can effectively use this resource. Therefore, much of this investment is gone to waste, not granting to the students as many benefits as it could.

Moreover, the lack of training could degenerate through improper use of this equipment, consequently bringing adverse effects to the users, who are the students in this case. The survey shows these effects, with 50% of the students viewing their performance diminish with the coming of the netbooks also mentioning that in fact they use it only for their leisure, playing videogames while they should be finish coursework. Still, one should point out that these students represent a small minority of the total sample.

Expectations and Attitude towards the ICTs

The attitude that every person who is involved with the educational system has towards any given element, contributes to the students' academic performance; that is, the outlook of faculty, students, parents, and all other educational staff (Tartwijk, 2008; García-Valcarcel, 2008; Ferrer,

Figure 4. Perception of performance change due to the use of ICTs

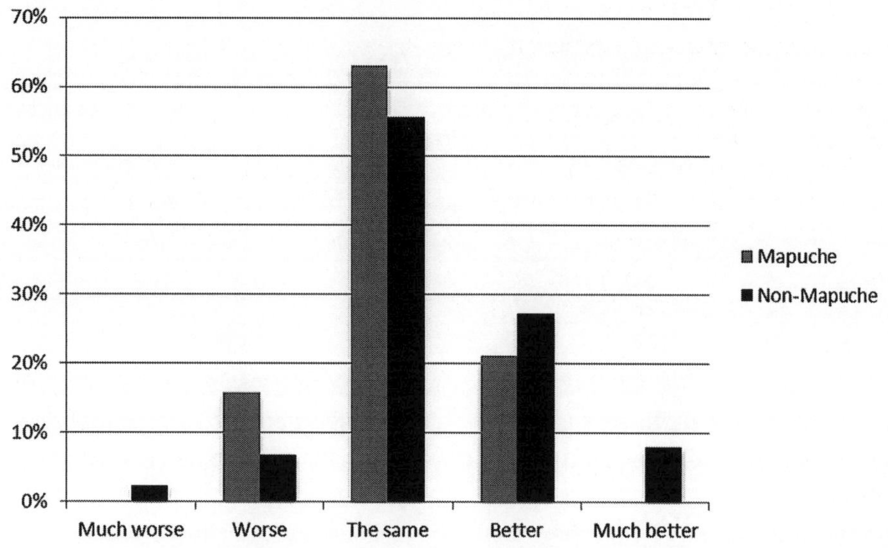

2010). By attitude we mean the mental state that conditions an individual to perceive and react in a certain way to the environment that surrounds him or her.

In contrast to what we could state from the study of primary level students in Caldas and Garcia-Valcárcel (2013), many teenagers in secondary school do not seem to perceive any effect of the use of ICTs on their academic progress. In fact, only 32% of them think that the introduction of the netbooks in their repertoire has improved their academic performance. More than half of the students of the sample (57%) believe there has been no significant change since this program took effect, with only 10% asserting the use of ICTs such as the netbook has lowered their academic level.

Moreover, the one may observe from Figure 4 that the perception students from Mapuche origin have about the role of ICTs in their performance differ significantly from the opinion of the rest of their peers.

One may infer a variety of causes for this phenomenon; for example, students from Mapuche origin might have not been exposed to such technologies as early in their lives as students from other backgrounds. Moreover, this gap might widen when we observe that there is no standardized training method or policy so that these students are not as intimidated as they might feel. According to Petit (2006), the use of ICTs in the school is highly significant in relation to the attitudes that can be generated with their implementation, both in the students and in their families. Hence, when we observe that only 41% of the total student sample shares their netbook with their relatives, we are observing a particular attitude towards these technologies.

Therefore, the attitude of Mapuche students towards the new available technologies is not improving, but could eventually worsen if nothing is done at an institutional level in order to correct this situation.

Academic Performance and ICTs: The Effectiveness of the PCI

We could argue that academic performance is mainly the sum of two factors: academic learning, and academic progress. In the Argentinean educational system, and most educational systems around the world, learning is evaluated by examinations or tests designed to assess how much

Table 1. Perception of academic performance vs. use of netbooks inside the classroom (Pearson's chi-squared and Fisher's exact tests)

	Value	df	Asymptotic *p* (Two-Tailed)	Exact *p* (Two-Tailed)	Exact *p* (One-Tailed)
Pearson's chi-squared	17.422[a]	8	0.026	0.029	
Likelihood ratio	18.798	8	0.016	0.019	
Fisher's exact test	17.152			0.011	
Linear correlation	7.624	1	0.006	0.005	0.003
Number of valid cases	107				

[a]66.7% of the expected frequencies have values less than 5. The minimum expected frequency is 0.22.

of the content offered by the professors is being assimilated by the students. Consequently, academic progress is the measured change between examinations; and this period of time between exams is usually well defined by the State and its organisms. In this sense, the educational system in Argentina follows the utopian structure that is portrayed in Comenius (1907).

As we can appreciate from Table 1, there exists a dependent relationship between the perception students have of the ICTs affecting (for better or worse) their academic performance and in what degree the same students use their netbooks inside the classroom. In Figure 4 we observe the opinion of the majority of students in the sample, regardless of their background; these latest results from Table 1 are pointing out a possible solution to this issue, as simple as allowing and encouraging students to use their netbooks inside the classroom for academic activities.

The ICTs in the Schools

The use of computers and other such technologies in primary school is neither established nor regulated within the Neuquén province (Caldas, 2010). This lack of policy was present in the secondary level until recently, and hence one can still observe great disparities between students depending on their school of origin. Students from urban primary schools usually have parents with a certain economic level, a level that parents of students attending rural schools can rarely attain. So far, the PCI is being tested in two rural schools in Patagonia, and the project of their inclusion has just started for primary school.

The path from primary to secondary school is characterized by a development of the teenager that is soon to become an adolescent, if he or she is not one already. This development includes a need to become part of a group, to integrate with their peers, particularly at the beginning of their adolescence. At this stage is when one can appreciate the increased use of ICTs; and it is at this point where they should be taught how to use them efficient and responsibly.

This integration occurs inside and outside the classroom alike, and therefore the use of the netbooks in the classroom for academic purposes should be encouraged. However, this behavior is not as widely observed amongst the students that come from Mapuche communities, as it is shown in the Table 2.

The table shows that the variances are not the same, as stated by the value of *p* for Levene's test, which is obviously greater than 5%. The two-tailed *p*-value shows the significance of the dependence of the two variables considered, indicating that the two groups greatly differ between each other in terms of netbook usage inside the classroom.

Students in general agree that the use of the netbooks inside the classroom is minimal. Nonetheless, there is a clear difference between the two groups that have contributed in this study;

Figure 5. How much are the ICTs used inside the classroom?

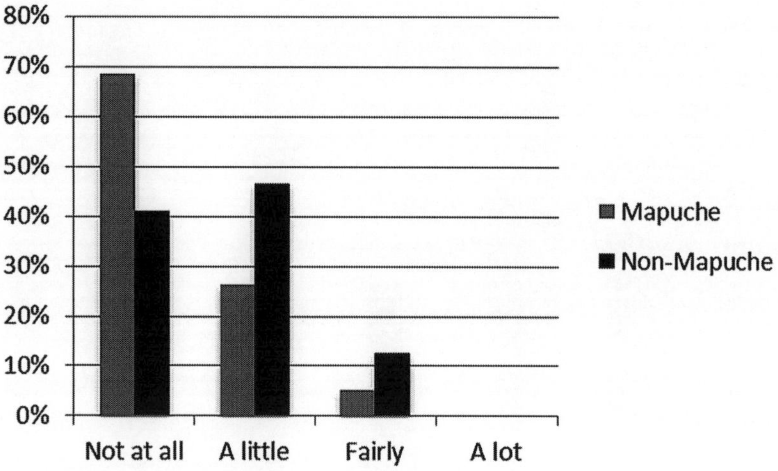

students from Mapuche communities do not make the most of the resource offered to them, as it one may appreciate from Figure 5. This may create a situation of disadvantage that could possibly ends up creating tensions and widening the gap between the two groups, instead of making it one. As a society, this is one of the reasons we should intently consider the training of these students on the use of the ICTs, as social inequalities can subsequently develop into economic inequalities.

Fisher's independence test for the relationship between group projects and Mapuche results in a $p = 0.033$, fairly below under the 5% boundary. This is another indicator that points to the differences between the two groups, as it is presented in Figure 6. Group projects are essential for any style of education, particularly if one is trying to achieve a multicultural viewpoint. Furthermore, the sample was taken from a technical school, where group projects are a center factor in the students' education.

Professors and Teaching with the ICTs

We could now refer to both netbooks and other ICTs alike when we say that professors are usually skeptical towards the use of these new technologies, seeing them more like an imposition on them rather than a tool to improve their teaching. We show Figure 7 as a clear way to present the viewpoints of many professors.

Table 2. Usage of netbooks inside the classroom vs. students' background (t-test)

	Levene's Test to Assess Equality of Variances		t-Test for Median Equality				
	F	*p* for Levene	t	df	*p* (Two-Tailed)	Median Difference	Error on the Median Difference
Equal variance has been assumed	0.967	0.328	2.068	105	0.041	0.347	0.198
Equal variance has not been assumed			2.244	28.918	0.033	0.347	0.167

Figure 6. Use of ICTs in collaborative work

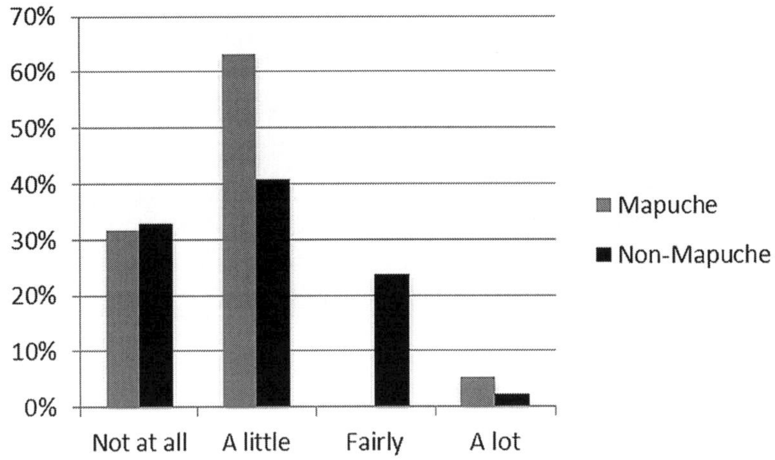

Figure 7. Professors teaching with their netbooks

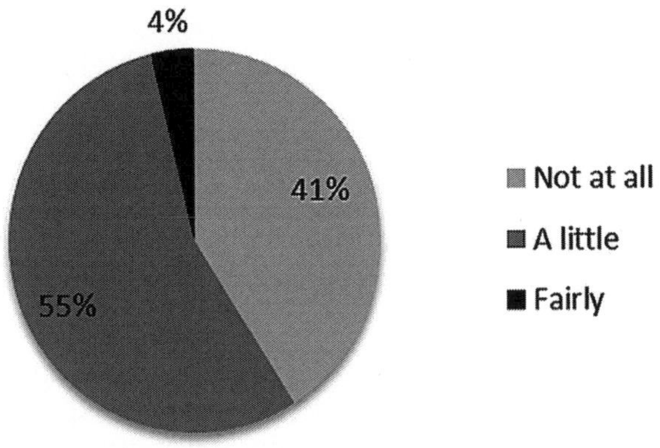

The fact that professors do not use the equipment offered to them in order to teach is perfectly plausible and acceptable; although they are not setting the best example for their students in terms of using the technologies now available in an efficient way to complete their work. But some professors do not welcome the use of netbooks inside the classroom, and there have been cases where they prohibit the use of such tools, claiming that they are only used to distract their students. For example, one surveyed student said "We cannot use it [the netbook] in the classroom. I used it at home, and it has helped me with my homework."

If the students are using this resource to engage in entertainment activities, such as videogames, the solution should not be the ban of netbooks inside the classroom, but instead they should be taught the correct and responsible use of this tool. This way, students will cease to view the ICTs as an end to entertain themselves, but a means to a greater end, which is their better insertion into the socioeconomic reality.

From the statistical analysis that we performed for this study we can state that there exists a dependent relationship between perceived academic performance and how much the students use the netbooks to complete homework. The dependence was shown by both Pearson's chi-squared and Fisher's exact tests, with significance (0.022 and 0.008, respectively) well below the probabilistic cut-off. That means that, if taught how to use the netbooks responsibly and efficiently, the students might change their attitude towards the use of the netbooks, and have a more gratifying academic experience.

Strengths and Weaknesses of the PCI

As a result of the student survey and the interviewed faculty members, we have the PCI to have the following characteristics:

Strengths:

- The fact that the PCI is a nationwide program. Amongst the interviewed teachers it is stressed the importance of social and educational policies reaching the whole nation.
- The possibility for the students to bring their netbooks back home, generating a domino effect, since the students' families will be able to use this technology and assimilate many of the concepts offered by the ICTs.
- Incorporation of new profiles in the information technology functions inside of the schools with a more comprehensive and wider view of the homework. The figure of the "Network Manager" is highlighted.
- Better offers and more opportunities for teacher training. It is worth to mention that these offers are usually free of charge and can be completed online.

Weaknesses:

- The delay in the delivery of the equipment and the lack of network connectivity of some educational establishments, emphasized by the amount of complaints presented by several teachers.
- The lack of basic training for students, for them to know how to handle and manage the new equipment when it is just delivered.
- Sometimes the universality and equality of the program is lost, as some students belong to other groups that do not accept the use of netbooks.

CONCLUSION AND RECOMMENDATIONS

The state of deferment in the exercise of the rights to education on behalf of the indigenous population in Argentina is changing. While these populations present a manifest heterogeneity with regard to the social and economic state in which they find themselves, several of them share a situation that can undoubtedly be considered complex.

Research evidence suggests, however, that this situation is the consequence of complex historical processes. The arrival of the PCI to the Patagonian high-schools could be one way to struggle against this deferment, offering possibilities to those environments where these communities are placed. On the other hand, the bonds between the schools and these communities do not always generate positive synergies and are marked by the way in which schools approach working with aboriginal populations, and by how the community itself welcomes and integrates principals and teachers.

Comprehensive and overarching policies are necessary to guarantee the access and continued school attendance of children and adolescents in the system; that is, initiatives that understand not only those aspects linked to education, but also to health and protection. From an educational point of view, the PCI has deployed new equipment and has improved the infrastructure of schools that serve these communities.

Another element to pay attention to is the instruction teachers receive in order to see to the demands of this multicultural population. How should they approach working in communities that preserve their native language, as well as the definition and scope of an intercultural education, are unresolved issues. Specific practices in bilingual literacy result in tensions between the education ministry committees, the characteristics of the schools themselves (essentially the human resources available) and the relationship with the community.

In addition, the current right of the indigenous population to receive an education is not only linked to the full participation of their native language in the teaching process, but also to the maintained recognition of their indigenous cultures, promoting the development of rich and varied traditions. The reach of the concept of interculturalism and its implementation is also problematic. There exists a great heterogeneity in the ways to deal with the literacy process and in the use of cultural contents characteristic of these populations in the school curriculum. In other words, principals and teachers have a relatively wide degree of discretionary powers when it comes to defining and teaching intercultural education in the specific contexts in which they work. In that way, different notions and practices that express divergent interpretations of the right to an intercultural education are recorded. Some teachers relate the concept with the acknowledgment and transitory use of the native language in the process of transmission of the Spanish language. Others do it with an explicit acknowledgement of "respect" for the indigenous culture, which implies an acceptance of the way they behave, though not the significant incorporation of specific cultural contents. Finally, some make an effort to incorporate into the curriculum elements and aspects of the indigenous culture in a more integrated way. Taking this situation into consideration, we assert the need not only to define specific policies regarding bilingualism and interculturalism, but also to exercise a regular control of these same policies.

It is extremely necessary to improve the academic conditions under which adolescents from indigenous populations enter secondary schools, as well as the instruction of teachers and managers in cooperative work, interculturalism and ICT insertion. These policies aim essentially to contribute to overcoming feelings of inferiority and dropouts among these youths; only then will we be able to seriously speak about equal opportunities.

According to the teachers and the principal of the technical school E.P.E.T. 12, the program "Conectar Igualdad" is perceived as a policy that improves public education by:

1. Generating equal opportunities amongst the whole student body.
2. Decreasing the digital literacy gap between different communities.
3. Articulation between the PCI and other previous ICTs experiences in schools, as the PROMSE and the PROMEDU programs.
4. Awarding greater reach, universality, and swiftness in the implementation of integration policies for the aboriginal communities of Neuquén.

Proposed Recommendations

We hope that this research generates proposals to be analyzed by the proper authorities, so that the introduction of the ICTs in the schooling system becomes paramount. Furthermore, we feel the following recommendations to be necessary conditions to be met if these technologies are to improve the Patagonian educational system:

- Means of evaluating and monitoring the rate and direction of the change produced by the PCI in students and faculty must be generated. They should take into account indicators referring to the students' academic performance: dropout index, ratio of students that retake a grade, students' and teachers' skills at using ICTs, collaborative work and peer integration. We realize that the compilation of such an extensive amount of data is a challenge for any one individual; but this could easily be accomplished by the state in the next national census.
- Educational spaces for debate, reflection, and critical thinking, about the emergent pedagogic model should be created.

- It is important to extend ICTs training to both students and their families in order to increase the effectiveness of this program.
- We recommend holding conferences which promote awareness for both the student body and the faculty, so that social networks are used in a responsible and respectful manner.

REFERENCES

Alsina, M. R. (1997). Elementos para una comunicación intercultural. *CIDOB d'Afers Internacionals, 36,* 11-21. Retrieved February 6, 2010, from http://www.raco.cat/index.php/Revista CIDOB/article/viewFile/28020/27854

Antinao, N. (1998). *La Cultura Mapuche.* Neuquén, Argentina: Universidad Nacional del Comahue.

Area, M. (2008). Innovación pedagógica con TIC y el desarrollo de las competencias informacionales y digitales, *Investigación en la escuela, 64,* 5-18.

Ballester, A. (2002). *El aprendizaje significativo en la práctica: Cómo hacer el aprendizaje significativo en el aula.* Retrieved from http://www.aprendizajesignificativo.es/mats/El_aprendizaje_significativo_en_la_practica.pdf

Bautista, A. (Ed.). (2004). *Las nuevas tecnologías de la enseñanza.* Madrid, Spain: Ediciones Akal.

Binstock, G., Cerrutti, M., & Duro, E. (2008). *Acceso y permanencia educativa de niños y adolescentes en comunidades Kolla, Mapuche, Mbya Guaraní y Wichien la Argentina.* Buenos Aires, Argentina: Government of Argentina.

Bonder, G. (2008). Juventud, género TIC: Imaginarios en la construcción de la sociedad de la información en América Latina. In *Proceedings of the ARBOR Ciencia, Pensamiento y Cultura CLXXXIV 733,* (pp. 917-934). Retrieved February 16, 2010, from http://arbor.revistas.csic.es/index.php/ arbor/article/view/234/235

Brynin, M. (2006). Gender, technology and jobs. *The British Journal of Sociology, 57*(3), 437–453. doi:10.1111/j.1468-4446.2006.00119.x PMID:16939595

Burbules, N. (2001). *Educación: riesgos y promesas de lasnuevastecnologías de la información.* Barcelona, Spain: Granica.

Cabero, J. (2004). Reflexiones sobre las tecnologías como instrumentos culturales. In Martínez, F., & Castaño, C. (2008). La segunda brecha digital y las mujeres. *Telos.* Retrieved November 20, 2009, fromhttp://www.campusred.net/TELOS/articuloAutorInvitado.asp?idarticulo=2&rev=75

Caldas, F. (2010).*La inserción de las TICs en las escuelas rurales Patagónicas desde una perspectiva intercultural* (Unpublished doctoral dissertation). University of Salamanca, Spain.

Caldas, F., & Garcia-Valcárcel, A. (2013). The Role of ICTs in Rural Schools of Patagonia. *Multiculturalism in Technology-Based Education, 1*(4), 38–58.

Castaño, C., Martín, J., & Vázquez, S. (2009). *E-inclusion and social welfare in Spain: a gender perspective.* Bremen, Germany: GICT. Retrieved November 5, 2010, from http://www.informatik.unibremen.de/soteg/gict2009/proceedings/GICT2009_Castano.pdf

Cebrián de la Serna, M. (Ed.). (2009). *Las Tecnologías de la información y comunicación para el desarrolloeducativo de los pueblos indígenas*. Andalucía, Spain: GTEA.

Comenius, J. A. (1907). *The Great Didactic* (Didactica Magna). Retrieved May 15, 2014, from https://ia600406.us.archive.org/32/items/cu31924031053709/cu31924031053709.pdf

Consejo Provincial de Educación. (2010). *Consejo Provincial de Educación: Información estadística de la deserción y repitencia en la provincia del Neuquén*. Neuquén, Argentina: Author.

Crook, C. (1998). *Ordenadores y aprendizaje colaborativo*. Madrid, Spain: Morata.

Del Álamo, O. (2003). Esperanza tecnológica: Internet para los pueblos indígenas de América Latina. *Instituciones y Desarrollo*, *14*(15), 43–79.

Díaz, R. (2001). *Trabajo docente y diferencia cultural: lecturas antropológicas para una Identidad desafiada*. Madrid, Spain: Abya Yala, Miño y Dávila.

DiNIECE. (2005). *Políticas sociales y acceso a educación, salud y programas de alivio a la pobreza*. Retrieved February 22, 2011, from http://www.civil-society.oas.org/Spanish/Decentralization_2-politicas_sociales.doc

E-igualdad. (2007). *Sociedad de la Información y Género: unanálisis de laspolíticaspúblicas. Estado de situación, iniciativas y propuestas*. Retrieved November 15, 2010, from http://www.e-igualdad.net/fichero.aspx?id=199&titulo=Estudiode Políticascompleto

Ferrer, F., Armengol, C., Belvis, E., Massot, M., & Pàmies, J. (2010). *Evaluación del Programa Pizarra Digital en Aragón*. Barcelona, Spain: Universidad Autónoma de Barcelona.

García-Valcárcel, A. (2008). *Investigación y Tecnologías de la información y Comunicación al servicio de la Innovación Educativa*. Salamanca, Spain: Universidad de Salamanca.

García-Valcárcel, A., & Tejedor, F. J. (2009). Evaluación de medios didácticos y proyectos TIC. In J. De Pablos (Ed.), *Tecnología Educativa: La formación del profesorado en la era de Internet* (pp. 271–302). Málaga, Spain: Aljibe.

Government of Argentina. (2010). *Conectar Igualdad*. Retrieved May 12, 2014, from http://www.conectarigualdad.gob.ar

Hernández, I., & Calcagno, S. (2003). *Los pueblos indígenas y la Sociedad de la Información en América Latina y el Caribe*. Santiago de Chile, Chile: CEPAL.

International Labor Organization. (1997). 169th Convention: Indigenous and tribal people. Retrieved April 30, 2010, from http://www.ilo.org/indigenous/Resources/Publications/lang--en/docName-- WCMS_100897/index.htm

Lewis, R. (1998). Trabajo y aprendizaje en Comunidades distribuidas. In C. Vizcarro & J. León (Eds.), *Nuevas Tecnologías para el aprendizaje* (pp. 191–220). Madrid, Spain: Pirámide.

Magadan, C. (2008). *Las TIC en las escuelas rurales argentinas: Las TIC del aula a la agenda política*. Buenos Aires, Argentina: UNICEF Argentina.

Mominó, J., Sigalés, C., & Meneses, J. (2008). *La escuela en la sociedad red: internet en la Educación Primaria y Secundaria*. Barcelona, Spain: Ariel.

Murillo García, J. L. (2010). Programas Escuela 2.0 y Pizarra Digital: Un paradigma de mercantilización del sistema educativo a través de las TICs. *REIFOP*, *13*(2), 65–78.

Petit, C. (2006). *La generación Tecno cultural.* Buenos Aires, Argentina: Government of Argentina.

Quintero, A., & Hernández, A. (2005). El profesor ante el reto de integrarlas TIC en los procesos de enseñanza. *Revista Enseñanza, 23*, 305–321.

Slavsky, L. (2006). Tecnologías de la información y la comunicación para jóvenes mapuches. *Novedades de Antropología, 15*(54), 12–13.

Tejedor, F. J., & García-Valcárcel, A. (2005). Condicionantes (actitudes, conocimientos, usos, intereses, necesidades formativas) a tener en cuenta en la formación del profesorado no universitario en TIC. Revista Enseñanza, 23, 115-142. Retrieved December 31, 2010, from http://e-spacio.uned.es/fez/eserv.php?pid=bibliuned:20225&dsID=condicionantes__tener.pdf

Tello, E. (2007). Las tecnologías de la información y comunicaciones (TIC) y la brecha digital: Su impacto en la sociedad de México. RUSC, 4(2), 1-8. Retrieved September 15, 2010, from http://www.uoc.edu/rusc/4/2/dt/esp/tello.pdf

KEY TERMS AND DEFINITIONS

ICTs: Information and Communication Technologies, such as radio, television, cellphones, software, hardware, internet connection, etc.

Indigenous: Aboriginal or native to a given region.

Intercultural: Characteristic of the interaction between two or more cultures.

Mapuche: Ethnic group indigenous to the Patagonia region spanning southern Argentina and Chile.

Neuquen: Argentinean province, located in the Patagonian region.

Patagonia: Geographical region located in the south of Argentina, characterized by an arid and cold climate.

PCI: Programa Conectar Igualdad (Connecting Equality Program). Argentinean federal government initiative aimed at reducing educational inequality through the distribution of ICTs in school systems throughout Argentina.

Chapter 18
How Can ICTs Contribute towards a More Sustainable Future?

Albena Antonova
Sofia University, Bulgaria

ABSTRACT

Since antiquity technological innovations endanger environmental balance and there is major need to keep this balance in check. Any new technology generates more business activity, leading to increased resource extraction and waste and directly affecting natural ecosystems. Thus technological progress and economic growth are based on unsustainable practices. In the last few decades, information and communication technologies (ICT) accelerated globalized business activity by making the world smaller, more connected and smarter. ICT gradually transformed all aspects of human life including work, learning, and leisure; it has a global impact on business processes and practices, communication, logistics and transportation, finance, and commerce among other aspects. This resulted in wealth accumulation, resource depletion and social divide which have led to problems, directly and indirectly, such as scarcity of natural resources, global warming, climate change, population growth, and increasing youth unemployment. This chapter outlines some of the challenges of the new technologies and ICT practices. It proposes a practice-oriented framework for adoption of more sustainable ICT strategy in companies.

INTRODUCTION

Historically, human progress and development of technologies have created a negative impact on environmental stability and integrity of ecosystems. For 10 millennia, technological innovations have fundamentally transformed the human life. Innovations gradually leaded to resource extinction, environmental exploitation and represent a global trend for the future. In the beginning of 21st century, people could not even imagine the world without technologies. However in order to continue to benefit from technologies people have to make substantial changes in their current business practices and general perceptions. Financial and economic global crises, combined with frequent natural disasters make planning of business operations unpredictable with markets

DOI: 10.4018/978-1-4666-8433-1.ch018

being unstable and investments riskier. In the same time, global economic activity has tripled in size since 1980, and is predicted to quintuple in the next 50 years.

The concepts of sustainable development were defined 30 years ago. However, only recently businesses and social communities have opened the discussion for a truly sustainable future. Do we still have time to reverse the global trends? Some of the most urgent problem areas for businesses nowadays are: scarcity of natural resources and their rising prices; fuels; minerals; fresh water; energy; environmental factors (ecosystems integrity, waste management and global warming effects, increased number of natural cataclysms); and social factors (cost of living, increased world population, aging society, mobility and migrations). More generally, politicians, researchers, and companies still miss the holistic approach for coping with increased sustainability challenges. The high complexity of the term "sustainability" makes possible for myriad different interpretations. Moreover, different contexts of applying sustainable concepts and tools lead to overall misunderstanding and perplexity.

Globalization and fast emergence of new technologies resulted in accelerated production and consumption models that provoked irreversible economic, social, and environment changes. New technology-based innovations formed the backbone of the recent economic growth, fueling the market competition and catalyzing social and environmental footprints around the globe. Information technologies transformed the logic of business operations and accelerated the globalization processes. Nowadays information technologies are practically involved in every aspect of human activity including business, education, communication, and entertainment. More specifically, IT plays and increasingly important role in innovations and R&D processes; cost-effectiveness and efficiency; customer services; and finally they have general impact on business competitiveness. Information technologies represent a unique expanding economy sector having large influence on overall economic activity.

Widely spread across businesses all over the world, usually ICT can have very detrimental influence on organizational environmental footprint (Jenkin, Webster, & McShane, 2011). Information technologies have short product life spans (e.g., laptops, 3–4 years; networks, 5–7 years); their manufacturing and disposal have resulted in toxic hotspots; and a large portion of organizations' electricity costs (and concomitant greenhouse gas emissions) is due to IT energy use (e.g., office buildings, 26%; data centers, 95%) (Jenkin, Webster, & McShane, 2011). In contrast to other technologies, information technologies, and especially information systems, have a large potential to reverse the negative impact. As discovered by Gartner (2007), ICTs are responsible for about 2% of global carbon emissions. The main contributing sectors within the ICT industry include the energy requirements of PCs and monitors (40%), data centres, which contribute a further 23%, and fixed and mobile telecommunications that contribute 24% of the total emissions. However, the majority of researches cited by Molla et al. (2008) believe in the potential of technologies to create sustainable business and society. It is estimated that 'Green' IT/IS can have positive impact on the environment with the potential to reduce global emissions by 15% (The Climate Group, 2008). Even dominating corporate reports in the field of green IT/IS speculate that IT has a potential to create new competitive opportunities, to reduce carbon emissions, and to improve overall business efficiency (Molla et al., 2008).

The objective of the chapter is to identify the current trends of ICT and to propose a concise holistic framework for companies to enhance their development and implementation of green IT technologies. Moreover, there is a discussion of several practical aspects and examples. It starts with a short overview of recently emerged concepts of green, sustainable and clean technologies, focusing on green IT. Some related concepts are then discussed as well as sustainable development, sustainable and eco-innovations, sustainable manufacturing.

The second part proposes a holistic model for ICT development and implementation in companies. There it highlights the possible role of ICT to enhance companies and business organizations to approach sustainability in a practical and affordable manner. As information technologies play increasingly important roles in any aspect of the business, education and social development, IT can have major influence on sustainable development in micro-aspects. This chapter also discusses different approaches for implementation of information technologies in business settings for improving sustainable development and elaborates on a general framework for sustainable business. Finally there is a general overview of how information technologies can lead to number of sustainable transformations in business, educational and manufacturing processes, and business practices.

BACKGROUND

The background part of the chapter outlines the basic trends and terms that are emerging in research and professional/business literature in the last years. Sustainable development, sustainable manufacturing and sustainable and eco-innovations is presented as general and fundamental concepts that are influencing development of ICT sector. After that some more attention is put on different technologies aspects – green and clean. Finally detailed analysis is made on Green IT and the number of its modifications – green information systems, green networks and green computing.

Sustainable Development

Sustainable development is a well-used oxymoron as the concepts of growth endanger sustainability. The issue of sustainability is extraordinary in both magnitude and complexity and as such is one of the greatest challenges faced by modern society (Ramani et al., 2010). In 1986 sustainable development was defined as a political concept in the Brundtland Report as "...development that meets the needs of the present without compromising the ability of future generations to meet their own needs" (UN, 1987). Sustainability goes beyond the ecological aspects and scarcity of natural resources, as it also includes social and economic stability (Harmakoorpi, 2009). At the 2005 World Summit it was assumed the "three pillars" of sustainability (environment, social, and economic), built on the concepts of the triple bottom line (TBL), developed by John Elkington (1994). The triple bottom line attempts to incorporate financial, environmental, and social capital into a comprehensive framework that can help companies analyze their current processes, innovate, and identify new sources of revenue and cost reduction. According to the research of Arena et al. (2009), along with economical, ecological and social development, technological development should be considered as well. In summary, sustainable development stands for (Filho, 2000):

- Systematic, long-term use of natural resources;
- The modality of development that enables countries to progress, economically and socially, without destroying their environmental resources;
- The type of development which is socially just, ethically acceptable, morally fair and economically sound; and
- The type of development where environmental indicators are as important as economic indicators.

According to Seliger, Kim, Kernbaum, & Zettl (2008), sustainability is a directive to enhance human living standards while improving the availability of natural resources and ecosystems for future generations. Although important and politically accepted, the concepts of sustainability often miss practical implementation in companies and social communities. Some of the key problem issues with sustainability can be summarized as:

- Too theoretical,
- Too broad,
- Too recently recognized,
- No personnel to deal with,
- It demands substantial resources,
- It lacks scientific base, and
- Too much of a fashion-word (i.e. fad) (Jucker, 2002).

In general, people are generally not aware of sustainability ideas and principles. Although there is widespread popularity of the term "sustainability" in political and social documents, several studies in UK and Germany revealed that people cannot cite any meaningful description of the sustainability (Jucker, 2002). Due to the broad and complex scope of sustainability, people are rather concerned for environment issues and wildlife protection, putting the focus away from economical and social development. Thus to progress with sustainable development, people need to consider practical issues and case studies, best practices and good examples. This will enable them to go into specifics and understand sustainability as something relevant to them, valuable and achievable.

Sustainable Manufacturing

Manufacturing industries are largely promoted to become a driving force for the creation of a sustainable society (OECD, 2009). It is recognized that manufacturing companies can design and implement integrated sustainable practices and develop products and services that contribute to better environmental performance. Moreover, many other challenges to traditional manufacturing companies exists (Anityasari, 2008) and these include increased risk for overproduction, due to fast evolving customer requirements; constant need to frequent up-to-date knowledge; expansion of business scope from design and manufacturing to provision of complex services; and end-solutions approach. Hence, manufacturing should adapt to increased expectations.

Sustainable manufacturing is a business practice of the industrial sector, which expands all the company's processes and decisions into the broader social and natural environments in which the company operates in and affects with its actions. This is executed with the explicit objective of reducing or eliminating any negative impact, while pursuing the desired level of technological and economic performance (Leahu-Aluas, 2010). The US Department of Commerce defines sustainable manufacturing as "...the creation of manufactured products that use processes that minimize negative environmental impacts, conserve energy and natural resources, are safe for employees, communities, and consumers and are economically sound..." (Leahu-Aluas, 2010).

Following the detailed literature review of Arena et al. (2009) about the state-of-the-art in sustainable manufacturing, there have been outlined different factors and sub-factors for sustainable manufacturing. The authors identified several sub-dimensions of sustainable manufacturing grouped around 4 dimensions:

1. **Ecological:** Resources – materials, energy, water; depletion and pollution – emissions, biodiversity and waste; human behaviour and activities: products and services, compliance, transport,
2. **Economical:** Economic performance, indirect economic impact, market presence,
3. **Social:** Work practices and work conditions, diversity and equal opportunities, relations with the community, social policy compliance, consumer health and safety and human rights, and
4. **Technological:** Increasing the productivity of natural resources, shift from overconsumption to biological models, moving from ownership to solution-based business models, reinvesting in natural capital.

The life cycle analysis (LCA) addresses all phases of the product life cycle, including the design phase, raw material production phase, manufacturing phase, distribution phase, usage phase, and end of life phase. LCA aims to maximize total product performances during the product lifetime. The life-cycle approach advocates for the attainment of total product performance, not only from an economics perspective but also from social and environmental perspectives.

Eco-Innovation and Sustainable Innovations

Some of the concepts of sustainability discussed above include idea of eco-innovation. The definition of eco-innovation, provided by Reid & Miedzinski (2008), states that "eco-innovation is the creation of novel and competitively priced goods, processes, systems, services and procedures designed to satisfy human needs and provide better quality of life for everyone, with a whole-life-cycle minimal use of natural resources (materials including energy and surface area) per unit output, and a minimal release of toxic substances." However, eco-innovation and sustainable innovations are not synonyms.

Harmaakorpi (2009) claims that sustainable innovation is an umbrella term and stands for: ecologically sustainable development; participatory innovation (including customers, employees, users and the general public); continuous innovation (the ability to continuously regenerate and break boundaries); global innovation (innovation in global cooperation using knowledge distributed everywhere); innovative management (or management encouraging innovation in organizations and society). The authors Maxwell, Sheate, & van der Vorst (2003) highlight that sustainable innovation is innovation aiming to generate benefits that are collective in terms of the environment, society and economy while reflecting a new out-of-the-box approach that very often challenges traditional systems.

Thus many scholars understand sustainable innovations as a form of disruptive innovations that are continuously changing and threatening existing economic and social models. This explains why it is extremely difficult for companies and politicians to accept, and work for, this fundamental change, and why they often prefer to substitute the term with eco-efficiency, dematerialization and ecology-friendly production (Charter, 2004). Arvidsson & Mannervik (2009) also discuss the need for revolutionary change in the innovation system, emphasizing that the old dominant conceptual model for innovations is outdated and has to be replaced by a new one.

Clean/Green Technologies

Hart (1997) decomposes sustainable development into clean technologies (i.e., environmentally sustainable technologies) and sustainable vision (i.e., plan for moving towards sustainable development) as part of the sustainability portfolio. "Clean technology" stays for the concept that both efficiency and productivity can be increased by using new processes, products and services, while at the same time reducing greenhouse gas emissions and protecting natural resources (DCTI, 2013) Thus Clean technologies are competitive with, if not superior to, their conventional counterparts. Many also offer significant additional benefits, notably their ability to improve the lives of those in both developed and developing countries. The Deutches CleanTech Institute, together with KPMG and institute developed a complex framework (DCTI, 2013) including: environmentally friendly energy and energy storage; solid waste management, sustainable water management, sustainable mobility, resource efficiency, energy efficiency.

"Green" has become a popular term for describing things that are good for the environment, generally healthful and economically sensible (Prothero & Fitchett, 2000). Green in the modern business language is the color of environment, future-orientation, ethical and responsible business. In the professional literature, terms like green IT, green IS, green networks and green computing emerged, often used as synonyms.

Green IT

One of the widely accepted definitions proposed by Watson et al. (2008) is based on the differences between green IT and green IS. In general, information technologies transmit process or store information. Therefore, green IT should focus on energy efficiency and equipment utilization. That is why Molla et al. (2008) considers green IT mainly as data center efficiency and narrowly defined green IT as technologies and tools to reduce power, cooling and real estate costs, associated with data centers operations (Molla et al., 2008).

Among popular definitions is that of Watson et al. (2008): 'Green IT' addresses energy consumption and waste associated with the use of hardware and software, tends to have a direct and positive impact. Examples include improving the energy efficiency of hardware and data centers, consolidating servers using virtualization software, and reducing waste associated with obsolete equipment (Watson, Boudreau, Chen, & Huber, 2008).

From practitioners' points of view, a global survey conducted in 2009 highlight that to companies Green IT means lowering electric and cooling costs and promoting sustainable energy practices (Accenture, 2009).

After providing an overview of green IT definitions in literature, Molla et al. (2008) proposes holistic conceptualization of green IT from 4 perspectives: sourcing perspective (purchase green technologies); operation perspective (energy efficiency); service perspective (overall services for sustainability as measuring and analytical tools for greenhouse gas); and an IT life management perspective (waste and life-cycle management).

From a supply chain perspective green supply chain refers to integrating environmental thinking into the product design, sourcing, manufacturing, warehousing, distributing and end of life product management aspects of a supply chain. Thus, from a strategic perspective, green strategy articulates a business' intention to cultivate good environmental stewardship while at the same time pursuing economic goals (Olson, 2008).

Green IS

Green information systems represent an integrated and cooperating set of software using information technologies to support individual, group, organizational or societal goals. Therefore, green IS refers to the development and use of information systems to support or enable environmental sustainability initiatives and, thus, tends to have an indirect and positive impact. Examples include: collaborative group software and telepresence systems to enable remote meetings and reduce the negative environmental impacts associated with travel; environmental information systems to track and monitor environmental variables such as waste, emissions, toxicity, water consumption, and carbon footprints; and supply chain systems to optimize product routing and transportation, thus reducing the amount of energy consumed moving products (Watson, Boudreau, Chen, & Huber, 2008).

Some other relevant definitions include green computing, defined by Talebi and Way (2009) as "a discipline that studies, develops and promotes techniques for improving energy efficiency and reducing waste in the full life cycle of computing equipment from initial manufacture, through delivery, use, maintenance, recycling and disposal in an economically realistic way" (Talebi & Way 2009). Chilamkurti, Zeadally, & Mentiplay (2009) describe Green Networking as covering all aspects of the network (personal computers, peripherals, switches, routers, and communication media). Energy efficiencies of all network components must be optimized to have a significant impact on the overall energy consumption by these components. Consequently, these efficiencies gained by having a Green Network will reduce CO_2 emissions and thus will help mitigate global warming. The Life Cycle Assessment (LCA) of the components must be considered. LCA is the valuation of the environmental impacts on a product from cradle to grave.

KEY ASPECTS OF GREEN IT/IS

Green IT

Some of the common criteria for defining what green products include: energy use, greenhouse gas production, raw material source, emissions (air, water), waste production, water usage, land use, end of life, toxicity, use and exposure. Any of these metrics is complex to measure and to estimate along the end-product value chain. Many of the authors and definitions above point out that green IT is mainly focused on energy efficiency and equipment utilization. Green IT substantially addresses issues related to reduced energy consumption and waste management. Moreover, one of the major concerns is the rise of datacenters (Dunn, 2010). There are estimates that in 2020 they will be 5 times more datacenters than there was 2002. Another important aspect is related to electronic waste, including obsolete computer and television equipment, mobile phones, old cables and additional IT equipment. As the number of users of ICT devices constantly increase and the lifespan of these products is between 1-3 years, e-waste is constantly accumulating and it generates serious problems in the environment.

Therefore, according to (Watson, Boudreau, Chen, & Huber, 2008) Green IT can refer to:

- Designing energy efficient chips and disk drives;
- Replacing personal computers with energy efficient thin clients;
- Use of virtualization software to run multiple operating systems on one server;
- Reducing the energy consumption of data centers;
- Using renewable energy sources to power data centers;
- Reducing electronic waste from obsolete computing equipment;
- Promoting telecommuting and remote computer administration to reduce transportation emissions.

Some recent technologies supporting Green IT include cloud computing, data centers, virtualization, social networks and Web 2.0, mobile computing and storage trends, nanotechnology and cooling systems, remote control systems, and energy management systems. The emphasis on services and cloud computing provide many promising technologies such as SaaS (software as a service), PaaS (Platform as a service), and IaaS (infrastructure as a service). In this case users don't need to purchase software licenses and up-dates or to install new programs on their computers, but can access the Internet and use the application services on-line (for example Google docs).

The list above can be largely improved as Green IT is perceived only as a final good or product, and rarely as part of larger ecosystem. The use of IT technologies is incremental as it depends on software development and software efficiency. People don't need ICT equipment per se; they require complex services involving multiple applications and supporting equipment. End-users, managers, system administrators and clients will purchase and use IT equipment only as a consequence of the services it will obtain. Therefore, Green IT should be analyzed from the service science perspective (Antonova, 2012), covering value co-creation processes with end-users. Taking into account this perspective, there should be highlight on the role of software development, quality assurance models, and studies of human-computer interaction and usability tests. Therefore Green IT should not put the focus on how to create new, better and energy-efficient equipment, but how to increase user satisfaction and utility from running quality and efficient software applications while saving time and efforts and improving quality of human-computer interaction. Many social practices can aid to improve ICT use. For example, limiting the use of Cc (i.e. Carbon copy) function on e-mails can significantly reduce the time for e-mail processing.

Green IS

Many researchers highlight the difference between green *in* IT and green *with* IT. Green IS generally refers to the design and implementation of information systems that contribute to sustainable business processes. Green IS, for example, helps an organization to (Watson, Boudreau, Chen, & Huber, 2008):

- Reduce transportation costs with a fleet management system and dynamic routing of vehicles to avoid traffic congestion and minimize energy consumption;
- Support team work and meetings when employees are distributed throughout the world, and thus reduce the impact of air travel. IS can move remote working beyond telecommuting to include systems that support collaboration, group document management, cooperative knowledge management, and so forth;
- Track environmental information (such as toxicity, energy used, water used, etc.) about the creation of products, their components, and the fulfillment of services;
- Monitor a firm's operational emissions and waste products to manage them more effectively; and
- Provides information to consumers so they can make green choices more conveniently and effectively.

Application of green information systems can lead to a substantial improvement in company performance and efficiency. Green IS has a greater potential than green IT because it tackles a much larger problem. It can make entire systems more sustainable compared to reducing the energy required to operate information technologies.

With development of new high-technology products and services, and the emerging complex business models, the end-users can improve the overall use of products and services without the need to possess them. The key concepts of service science and value creation can enhance many green IS practices while leading to successful business models and practices. Green IS can substantially decrease the popularity of product possession models and promote service in use models. Moreover they can largely increase self-services and therefore optimize business expenditures, client satisfaction, and need.

HOW TO TRANSFORM GREEN IT/IS TO SUSTAINABLE IT/IS: INTEGRATIVE FRAMEWORK

In order to facilitate the adoption of Green IS/IT, different authors proposed several models for adoption and measurement of Green IT/IS. For example Philipson (2010) proposed a green IT framework – RMIT model, called Green IT framework. Here 4 IT concepts are covered (equipment lifecycle, end-user computing, enterprise and data centers, IT as low-carbon enabler) in 5 perspectives – attitude, police, practice, technology, metrics. Based on these sections, Philipson (2010) approaches a quantified methodology to survey respondents and identify a Green IT readiness index, allowing public authority to obtain data in order to compare different industries and different periods. However, the model proposed is focused mainly on the green IT perspective.

After analysing some of the key terms covered by Green IT/IS, it is critical to understand how companies can interpret and adopt sustainable IT/IS framework. From a practical standpoint, the model is based on the considerations that:

1. Sustainable IS/IT should cover all 3 aspects of sustainability – environment, economy and society, moreover, it should support both green IT/IS and green with IT/IS approaches;
2. Sustainable IS/IT should be produced by sustainable manufacturing practice and should facilitate sustainable manufacturing processes;
3. Sustainable IS/IT is a complex ecosystem of interactions, aiming to reduce resource use and improve overall efficiency, including many technological and business practices;
4. Sustainable IS/IT leads to short term and long-term business benefits and involve large pull of interconnections in company;

A sustainable IS/IT model should cover all substantial business processes of the IS/IT lifecycle. Therefore it includes management, social and technological aspects, which highlight the role of participants in the complex eco-system:

- Conception (R&D, eco-innovations), supply of raw materials (country of origin, quality, price, eco-aspects – suppliers screening);
- Delivery of raw materials (stock piles, delivery policy, SCM);
- Production (energy consumption, pollution, quality standards, production processes, employees (work conditions, office/production energy consumption, equipment) environment (environment screening);
- Delivery of final products (stock, delivery policy, SCM), trade agreements, service;
- Marketing &after sale policy (promote durability, promote buy-back policy, repairing, guarantees, long-term service);
- Business models (provide products/services people want and need – accent on conception phase and user-co-creation; open innovation processes, attention on resource use, holistic vision of the company role in the economy; testing and evaluation, living labs;
- Main results - increase efficiency, increase services and not in products.

In consideration of these stated considerations, the model of sustainable IT/IS is proposed below with the aim to improve visibility of the key sustainability issues. The model combines TBL with increased efficiency and cost/resources optimization. More importantly, it cover LCA analysis and cradle-to-cradle approach, and facilitates companies through implementation of an IS/IT strategy and to easily identify how they use and deploy IT in their business. It aims to provide a general understanding of inter-relationship between various complementary terms within the Sustainability field. Finally the framework proposes a comprehensive and multidimensional challenge in defining the road ahead and the options for sustainable future development.

The reference model (Figure 1) includes 3 main reference fields – operate in environmental integrity, strive for financial profitability, and promote social equity. Companies should discover how IT/IS on one hand responds to these conditions and on the other hand leads to these in the context of their corporate use. The environmental management includes waste minimization, energy management and water conservation. Therefore companies should adopt practices and specialized systems to assess its energy efficiency and greenhouse gas effects. Time is another crucial resource and therefore companies need to consider that sustainable technologies are time-efficient and save/budget time for development, use and exploitation. Quality is a substantial part of any technology solution. The quality of IT/IS equipment is a prerequisite for use and intention to use the IT systems by users. At the same time IT/IS can support various quality assurance processes including assessments of value and quality obtained from end-users. Lean manufacturing approaches allow companies to focus on leading processes and features, concentrating on resources optimization and smarter technologies. For example new emerging practices as additive manufacturing (3D printing) can replace other much more energy-consuming technologies. Materials and inventory management requires careful policy for materials purchase, based on the principle of material substitution. Inventory management can be facilitated and improved by specific tracking and logistic systems. Corporate social responsibility (CSR) becomes a popular business practice as capability to comply with the mounting demands of different environmental groups and government regulations and practice socially oriented moral management is a major concern and an issue that might affect competitiveness. Open innovations and living labs can improve interactions between the company with end-users and third parties. Last, adoption of innovative business models and social practices will lead to substantial changes. Green purchasing programs and eco-innovations designate the continuous process of improvement, involving marketing and promotion factors across the supply chain. Life cycle analysis is the crucial element in any technology or product in the company as it shows its ecological footprint from the cradle till the final disposal.

DISCUSSION

Bleischwitz, Giljum, Kuhndt, & Schmidt-Bleek (2009) identified three main industrial areas that employ the majority of the earth resources and impacts ecology, economy and sustainable development in a global scale. The three industries are housing, mobility and food production, together with their overall supply chain and subsectors. Careful optimization of ICT use in these sectors could largely influence the production process and use of natural resources, chemicals and energy, change of consumer choice and customer habits,

Figure 1. Sustainable IS/IT reference model

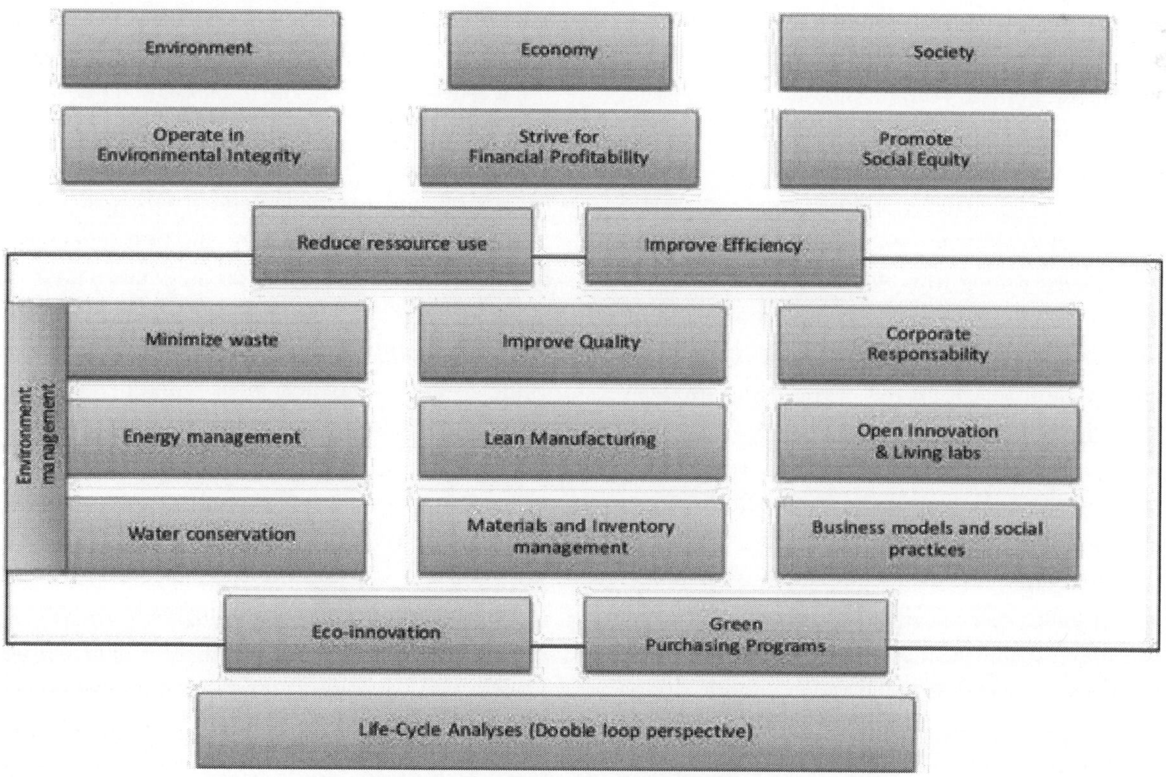

and can generally decrease waste and optimize the economic structure. Thus focusing a company's sustainable IS/IT practices and optimization of the information use in these specific sectors can lead to substantial improvement both in economy and ecology. Moreover, Bleischwitz et al. (2009) believe that companies will be the main drivers of eco-innovations and sustainable progress, propagating production and delivery of eco-innovative products and technologies and educating customers and citizens for sustainable use practices.

While ICTs continue to transform commercial, business and social practices on the global landscape, we can expect that new technologies will continue to emerge. Soon it is expected that new coming ubiquitous and pervasive technologies (such as augmented reality, additive manufacturing—3D printing, Internet of things, future internet and robotics) will bring many new challenges for sustainable development. These new IT/IS applications will substantially change the way products and services are designed, produced and consumed. Undoubtedly this will have larger impacts on the earth's ecosystems, employment, social divide and sustainable development as a whole. Robots and additive manufacturing systems can significantly reduce the need for a low-skill labour force. Moreover, today robots can replace the highly qualified work of surgeons, while smart toilet systems can become personal bio labs, transforming fundamentally the healthcare system. At the same time the youth unemployment is increasing globally, while public social systems and pension funds are put at risk from the very large aging population.

Historically technologies and new discoveries have been continuously transforming the business and have led to social unrest since the first industrial revolution. Thus "dehumanizing" business by applying more technology solutions should not mean that working places and jobs have to disappear, or that the social and economic divide should increase. New technologies lead to new level of development. The global economy realizes an expanding wealth accumulation according to the recent reports (Credit Swiss, 2013), reaching new levels of productivity and efficiency. New emerging technologies open many new opportunities. It can be expected there to be the emergence of a new sensor-enabled digital world, where the objects have "senses" to collect and process information, accumulated through hearing, seeing, communicating, reacting, deciding, memorizing and storing. This can lead on the one hand to minimizing resource usage and waste ("cost" oriented approach) and on the other hand, it can provide improved services, based on synergy of value networks for customers (becoming "profit-centers").

However, the fast implementation of technologies in different social contexts can threaten many professions, industries and economic sectors, so the society needs to set up new understanding about the "risk price" for technology adoption. Sustainable development should become priority to companies, the public and the entire society. Instead of continuing short-term production, companies have to reconsider how to improve the quality and durability of products and services in order to limit the waste of resources during its whole life-cycle and improving recycling and ecological balance. Thus in order to change the concepts of resource extraction and use, companies will need additional support to redefine production processes, business models and value-creation mechanisms. Therefore, companies should move from simple end-products to complex service sales, designing value co-creation experiences with clients while concentrating on revenue perspectives.

CONCLUSION

Since innovations and technologies have general impact on environment, and lead to substantial growth and exploitation of economic resources, sustainability is a key concern when designing and developing new products and services. ICTs should be considered in every sector - from employing electricity and energy resources, to responsible for substantial waste accumulation. On the other hand, ICT can improve many existing production and business practices that can lead to more sustainable business and technologies.

This chapter proposes a new model for understanding sustainable technologies, that can enhance companies to understand how sustainable their ICT strategies are and which aspects are covered. While discussing different concepts of ICT, the focus on green, eco or clean are just labels toward a more general paradigm shift. ICT has too often been considered a "driver for the business", and as such has been viewed in the silo of the specific project for which it is needed. By viewing ICT strategically across the entire organization and even fundamental social infrastructure, ICT can become the "engine of the business" (Accenture, 2009).

REFERENCES

Accenture. (2009). *Green Technology – Driving economic and environmental benefits from ICT.*

Anityasari, M. (2008). Inserting the Concepts of Sustainable Manufacturing into Industrial, Engineering Curriculum –A Framework of Thoughts. In *Proceedings of the 9th Asia Pacific Industrial Engineering & Management Systems (APIEMS) Conference* (pp. 517-526). Bali, Indonesia.

Antonova, A. (2012). Service science, value creation and sustainable development. In N. Delener (Ed.), *Service Science Research, Strategy, and Innovation: Dynamic Knowledge Management Methods* (pp. 157–196). Hershey, PA: IGI Global. doi:10.4018/978-1-4666-0077-5.ch010

Arena, M., Duque, N., Terzi, S.. Bengo, I., Azzone, G., & Garetti, M. (2009). A state-of-the-art of industrial sustainability, definitions, tools and metrics. *Int. J. Product Lifecycle Management, 4*(1/2/3), 207-251.

Arvidsson, N., & Mannervik, U. (2009). *The Innovation Platform: Enabling balance between growth and renewal.* Sweden: VINNOVA.

Barnatt, C. (N.d.). *Explaining the future.* Retrieved October, 2012, from www.explainingthefuture.com

Bleischwitz, R., Giljum, S., Kuhndt, M., & Schmidt-Bleek, F. (2009). *Eco-innovation- Putting the EU on the path to a resource and energy efficient economy.* Brussels, Belgium: European Parliament.

Charter, M. (2004). Sustainable Innovations. In *Proceedings of the Business Council for Sustainable Development of Taiwan (BCSD-Taiwan).* Washington, DC: World Business Council for Sustainable Development.

Chilamkurti, N., Zeadally, S., & Mentiplay, F. (2009). Green networking for major components of ICT systems. *EURASIP Journal on Wireless Communications and Networking*, (35), 1–7.

Credit Swiss Research Institute. (2013). *Global Wealth Report 2013.* Retrieved October, 2013, from http://thenextrecession.files.wordpress.com/2013/10/global-wealth-report.pdf

DCTI. 2013 Definition for CleanTech and CleanTech Framework, http://www.dcti.de/en/cleantech/definition.html

Dunn, H. (2010). Jamaica. In The Association for Progressive Communications (APC) & Humanist Institute for Cooperation with Developing Countries (Hivos) (Eds.), *Global Information Society Watch 2010: Focus on ICTs and Environmental Sustainability* (pp. 148-151). Melville, South Africa: APC. Retrieved from http://www.giswatch.org/hopetondunn%40gmail.com

Elkington, J. (1994). Towards the Sustainable Corporation: Win-Win-Win Business Strategies for Sustainable Development. *California Management Review*, *36*(2), 90–100. doi:10.2307/41165746

Filho, W. (2000). Dealing with misconseptions on the concept of sustainability. *International Journal of Sustainability in Higher Education*, *1*(1), 9–19. doi:10.1108/1467630010307066

Harmaakorpi, V. (2009). Sustainable innovation: What is it? Estonia, Latvia, Lithuania. Poland: Baltic Rim Economies.

Hart, S. (1997). Beyond Greening: Strategies for a sustainable world. *Harvard Business Review*, *1997*(January-February), Retrieved from https://hbr.org/1997/01/beyond-greening-strategies-for-a-sustainable-world/ar/1

Jenkin, T. A., Webster, J., & McShein, L. (2011). An agenda for 'Green' information technology and systems research. *Information and Organization*, *21*(1), 17–40. doi:10.1016/j.infoandorg.2010.09.003

Jucker, R. (2002). Sustainability? Never heard of it! *International Journal of Sustainability in Higher Education*, *3*(1), 8–18. doi:10.1108/14676370210414146

Leahu-Aluas, S. (2010). *Sustainable Manufacturing: An Overview for Manufacturing Engineers*. Resource.

Maxwell, D., Sheate, W., & van der Vorst, R. (2003). Sustainable Innovation in Product and Service Development. In *Proceedings of the Towards Sustainable Product Design 8 Conference*. Surrey, UK: Centre for Sustainable Design.

Molla, A., Cooper, V., Corbitt, B., Deng, H., Peszynski, K., Pittayachawan, S., & Teoh, S. (2008). E-readiness to G-readiness: developing a green information technology readiness framework. In *Proceedings of the 19th Australasian Conference on Information Systems*. Sydney, Australia: Australasian Conferences on Information Systems (ACIS).

OECD. (2009). *Sustainable Manufacturing and Eco-Innovation, Synthesis report*. Retrieved October, 2011, from http://www.oecd.org/dataoecd/15/58/43423689.pdf Document.

Olson, E. (2008). Creating an enterprise-level Greener strategy. *The Journal of Business Strategy*, *29*(2), 22–30. doi:10.1108/02756660810858125

Philipson, G. (2010). A green ICT framework: Understanding and measuring green ICT. *Connection research, 2010*.

Prothero, A., & Fitchett, J. A. (2000). Greening Capitalism: Opportunities for a Green Commodity. *Journal of Macromarketing*, *20*(1), 46–55. doi:10.1177/0276146700201005

Ramani, K., Ramanujan, D., Bernstein, K., Zhao, F., Sutherland, J., Handwerker, C., & Thurston, H. et al. (2010). Integrated Sustainable Life Cycle Design: A Review. *Journal of Mechanical Design*, *132*(9), 091004. doi:10.1115/1.4002308

Reid, A., & Miedzinski, M. (2008). *SYSTEMATIC Innovation Panel on eco-innovation*. Final report for sectoral innovation watch. Retrieved from www.europe-innova.org

Seliger, G., Kim, H.-J., Kernbaum, S., & Zettl, M. (2008). Approaches to sustainable manufacturing. *International Journal of Sustainable Manufacturing*, *1*(1/2), 58–77. doi:10.1504/IJSM.2008.019227

Talebi, M., & Way, T. (2009). Methods, metrics and motivation for a green computer science program. In *Proceedings of the 40th ACM (Association of Computing Machinery) Technical Symposium*. New York, NY: ACM. doi:10.1145/1508865.1508995

The Climate Group. (2008). *SMART 2020: Enabling the low carbon economy in the information age*. Report by the Climate Group on behalf of the Global e-Sustainability Initiative (GeSI), The Climate Group, London. Retrieved from http://www.smart2020.org/

UN (United Nations). (1987). *Our Common Future, Report of the World commission on environment and development*. Retrieved January, 2009, from http://www.un-documents.net/wced-ocf.htm

Watson, R. T., Boudreau, M. C., Chen, A., & Huber, M. H. (2008). Green IS: Building sustainable business practices. In R. T. Watson (Ed.), *Information Systems*. Athens, GA: Global Text Project.

WWF (World Wildlife Fund). (2009). *From Green IT to greening with IT*. White paper. Washington, DC: WWF.

KEY TERMS AND DEFINITIONS

Eco-Innovations: Innovations in products, services and processes that lead to more environment-friendly practices – including limiting and re-use of raw materials – decreasing waste and product disposal.

Green IS: Design and implementation of information systems that contribute for sustainable future in long-term, including technologies and business models that limit the resource use, increase energy efficiency and contribute for reconstitution of business and social practices.

Green IT: Cradle-to-cradle approach for information technologies, including design, implementation, deployment, use, recycling and disposal of IT devices (digital devices; computer-enhanced devices).

Sustainable Development: Development based on economic, social and technological progress, using limited consumption of natural resources, having minimal impact to the environment; Sustainable development should lead to the increase of humankind knowledge in order to cope on socially just and responsible for the future generations' way with environment limitations, resource use, overcoming natural and human-provoked crisis and cataclysms.

Sustainable Innovations: Innovations in products, services and processes that lead to more sustainable for the planet practices and long-term benefits. These innovations should cover the three pillars of sustainability – to be environmentally friendly, to be economically sound, to be socially just.

Ubiquitous and Pervasive Technologies: Digitally-enabled products and technologies that will enhance data and information collection, processing and delivery and Internet connectivity, increasing products usability and capacity for service delivery.

Compilation of References

79/409/EEC. (1979). *Council Directive 79/409/EEC of 2 April 1979 on the conservation of wild birds*. (Vol. 79/409/EEC): Official Journal L 103, 25/04/1979.

92/43/EEC. (1992). *Council Directive 92/43/EEC of 21 May 1992 on the conservation of natural habitats and of wild fauna and flora*. (Vol. 92/43/EEC): Official Journal of E.U., L 206, 22.7.1992.

Aas, C., Ladkin, A., & Fletcher, J. (2004). Stake-holder Collaboration and Heritage Management. *Annals of Tourism Research*, *32*(1), 28–48. doi:10.1016/j.annals.2004.04.005

Abdeen, M. O. (2008). Green energies and environment. *Renewable & Sustainable Energy Reviews*, *12*(7), 1789–1821. doi:10.1016/j.rser.2006.05.009

Abdeen, M. O. (2009). Principle of low energy building design: Heating, ventilation and air conditioning. *Cooling India: India's Premier Magazine on the Cooling Industry*, *5*(4), 26–46.

Abdeen, M. O. (2012). Clean and green energy technologies: Sustainable development and environment. *Sky J. Agric. Res.*, *1*(2), 28–50.

Accenture. (2009). *Green Technology – Driving economic and environmental benefits from ICT.*

Achman, R. (2013). Stakeholders' Perspectives on Sustainability in Project Management. In A. J. G. Silvius & J. Tharp (Eds.), *Sustainability Integration for Effective Project Management* (pp. 321–336). Hershey, PA: IGI Global Publishing. doi:10.4018/978-1-4666-4177-8.ch020

Adams, W. M. (2006). *The future of sustainability: Rethinking environment and development in the twenty-first century*. IUCN. Retrieved May 1, 2011, from http://cmsdata.iucn.org/downloads/ iucn_future_of_sustanability.pdf

Addis, B., & Talbot, R. (2001). Sustainable Construction Procurement: A Guide to Delivering Environmentally Responsible Projects. London, UK: Construction Industry Research and Information Association (CIRIA).

Adey, P. (2010). *Mobility*. Abingdon, UK: Routledge.

AFD. (2012). *4th Focus Area: Supporting municipalities in their sustainable development*. Retrieved March 24, 2014, from http://www.afd.fr/lang/en/home/pays/mediterranee-et-moyen-orient/geo/turquie/tr-axes-strategiques-strategie-Turquie-strateji-turkiye/axe-4-accompagner-les-municipalites-dans-leur-developppement-urbain-durable

Ağdağ, O. N. (2009). Comparison of old and new municipal solid waste management systems in Denizli, Turkey. *Waste Management (New York, N.Y.)*, *29*(1), 456–464. doi:10.1016/j.wasman.2008.01.012 PMID:18346887

Agnew, J. A., & Duncan, J. S. (Eds.). (1989). *The power of place: bringing together geographical and sociological imaginations*. Boston, MA: Unwin Hyman.

Aguilar, M. (2009). *Examining Destination Marketing from the Lens of Sustainability*. Unpublished master's thesis. Arizona State University, Phoenix, AZ.

Ahern, D. K. (2007). Challenges and Opportunities of eHealth Research. *American Journal of Preventive Medicine*, *32*(5), 75–82. doi:10.1016/j.amepre.2007.01.016 PMID:17466822

Ahern, J., Cilliers, S., & Niemelä, J. (2014). The concept of ecosystem services in adaptive urban planning and design: A framework for supporting innovation. *Landscape and Urban Planning*, *125*(0), 254–259.

Akadiri, P. O., Olomolaiye, P. O., & Chinyio, E. A. (2013). Multi-criteria evaluation model for the selection of sustainable materials for building projects. *Automation in Construction*, *30*(2), 113–125. doi:10.1016/j.autcon.2012.10.004

Alberti, M. (2008). *Advances in Urban Ecology. Integrating Humans and Ecological Processes in Urban Ecosystems*. New York, NY: Springer.

Aldred, R. (2012). Incompetent or too competent? Negotiating everyday cycling identities in a motor dominated society. *Mobilities*, *8*(2), 252–271. doi:10.1080/17450101.2012.696342

Allen, A. (2003). Environmental planning and management of the peri-urban interface: Perspectives on an emerging field. *Environment and Urbanization*, *15*(1), 135–147.

Al-Saleh, Y. M., & Taleb, H. N. (2010). The integration of sustainability within value management practices: A study of experienced value managers in the GCC countries. *Project Management Journal*, *41*(2), 50–59. doi:10.1002/pmj.20147

Alsina, M. R. (1997). Elementos para una comunicación intercultural. *CIDOB d'Afers Internacionals, 36,* 11-21. Retrieved February 6, 2010, from http://www.raco.cat/index.php/RevistaCIDOB/article/viewFile/28020/27854

Alternatif Enerji Web Sitesi. (2013). *Turkey's First Green Public Building in Küçükçekmece*. Retrieved March 24, 2014, from http://www.alternatifenerji.com/turkeys-first-green-public-building-at-kucukcekmece.html

Alvey, M. (2004). 'Too many kids and old ladies': Quality demographics and 1960s US television. *Screen*, *45*(1), 40–62. doi:10.1093/screen/45.1.40

AlWaer, H., Sibley, M., & Lewis, J. (2008). Different Stakeholder Perceptions of Sustainability Assessment. *Architectural Science Review*, *51*(1), 48–59. doi:10.3763/asre.2008.5107

Amati, M. (2008). *Urban Green Belts in the Twenty-first Century*. Sydney, Australia: Ashgate.

Amnesty International. (2010). *Kenya: Risking Rape to Reach a Toilet: Women's Experiences in the Slums of Nairobi, Kenya*. (AFR 32/006/2010).

Anderson, C. (2009). *Free: The future of a radical price*. New York: Hyperion.

Andriantiatsaholiniaina, L., Kouikoglou, V. S., & Phillis, Y. A. (2004). Evaluating strategies for sustainable development: Fuzzy logic reasoning and sensitivity analysis. *Ecological Economics*, *48*(2), 149–172. doi:10.1016/j.ecolecon.2003.08.009

Anityasari, M. (2008). Inserting the Concepts of Sustainable Manufacturing into Industrial, Engineering Curriculum –A Framework of Thoughts. In *Proceedings of the 9th Asia Pacific Industrial Engineering & Management Systems (APIEMS) Conference* (pp. 517-526). Bali, Indonesia.

Annual Survey of Health Information Exchange. (2009). eHealth initiative, Migrating Toward Meaningful Use: *The State of Health Information Exchange.* A Report based on the Results of the eHealth Initiative's 2009.

Anonymous, . (2011). *The Board's Sustainability Book*. London, UK: Arthur D. Little.

Antinao, N. (1998). *La Cultura Mapuche*. Neuquén, Argentina: Universidad Nacional del Comahue.

Antonova, A. (2012). Service science, value creation and sustainable development. In N. Delener (Ed.), *Service Science Research, Strategy, and Innovation: Dynamic Knowledge Management Methods* (pp. 157–196). Hershey, PA: IGI Global. doi:10.4018/978-1-4666-0077-5.ch010

APM. (2006). *The APM Body of Knowledge* (5th ed.). The Association for Project Management.

Area, M. (2008). Innovación pedagógica con TIC y el desarrollo de las competencias informacionales y digitales, *Investigación en la escuela, 64*, 5-18.

Arena, M., Duque, N., Terzi, S.. Bengo, I., Azzone, G., & Garetti, M. (2009). A state-of-the-art of industrial sustainability, definitions, tools and metrics. *Int. J. Product Lifecycle Management*, *4*(1/2/3), 207-251.

Armsworth, P. R., Dally, G. C., Karelva, P., & Sanchirico, J. N. (2006). Land market feedbacks can undermine biodiversity conservation. *The National Academy of Sciences of the SUA*, *103*(14), 5403–5408.

Arts, B. (2006). Non-state Actors in Global Governance: New Arrangements Beyond the State. In M. Koenig-Archibugi & M. Zürn (Eds.), *New Modes of Governance in the Global System: Exploring Publicness, Delegation and Inclusiveness* (pp. 177–200). Basingstoke, London: Palgrave Macmillan.

Arvidsson, N., & Mannervik, U. (2009). *The Innovation Platform: Enabling balance between growth and renewal*. Sweden: VINNOVA.

Ashford, N., & Hall, R. (2011). The Importance of Regulation-Induced Innovation for Sustainable Development. *Sustainability*, *3*(1), 270–292. doi:10.3390/su3010270

ASHRAE. (2003). Energy efficient design of new building except new low-rise residential buildings. BSRIASHRAE proposed standards 90-2P-1993. Atlanta, GA: American Society of Heating, Refrigerating, and Air Conditioning Engineers Inc.

ASHRAE. (2005). Commercial/Institutional Ground Source Heat Pump Engineering Manual. Atlanta, GA: American Society of heating, Refrigeration and Air-conditioning Engineers, Inc.

Aslund, A. (2008). *Russian energy and the European Union: Perspectives of Gazprom*. Peter G. Peterson Institute for International Economics. Retrieved May 9, 2014, at http://www.iie.com/publications/papers/aslund0508.pdf

Association for Project Management. (2006). *APM supports sustainability outlooks*.

Atvur, S. (2009). Yerel Gündem 21 ve Çevre: Anltalya Kent Konseyi Örneği. *Sosyal Bilimler Dergisi*, *33*(2), 231–241.

Australian National University. (2014) National Centre for Geographic & Resource Analysis in Primary Health Care (GRAPHC) on-line mapping and related geospatial analysis systems: A GRAPHC Project. Retrieved May, 2014, from http://aphcri.anu.edu.au/projects/anu/national-centre-geographic-resource-analysis-primary-health-care-graphc-line-mapping

Ausubel, J. H., Meyer, P. S., & Wernick, I. K. (2001). Death and the human environment: The United States in the 20th century. *Technology in Society*, *23*(2), 131–146. doi:10.1016/S0160-791X(01)00005-7

Avery, L. M., Anchang, K. Y., Tumsweige, V., Strachan, N., & Goude, P. J. (2014, November). Potential for Pathogen reduction in anaerobic digestion and biogas generation in Sub-Saharan Africa. *Biomass and Bioenergy*, *70*, 112–124. doi:10.1016/j.biombioe.2014.01.053

Baccarini, D. (1999). *History of Project Management*. New SOuth Wales, Australia: Curtin University of Technology.

Badiru, A. B. (2010). The many languages of sustainability. *Industrial Engineer*, *42*(11), 30–34.

Baev, P. (2008). *The East-West maneuvering in Russia's energy policy: Could oil and gas exports to China endanger Europe's energy security?* Working paper. International Peace Research Institute, Oslo (PRIO). Retrieved May 8, 2014, at http://www.fni.no/russcasp/Russia-China-energy-Baev.pdf

Baev, P. (2009). *Russian energy policy and military power: Putin's quest for greatness*. London: Routledge.

Baharuddin, H. G., & Simula, M. (1996). Timber certification in transition. Study on the development in the formulation and implementation of certification schemes for all internationally traded timber and timber products. Yokohama, Japan: International Tropical Timber Organization (ITTO).

Bahloul, H. & Özcan, Ü. (2006). *Municipal Partnership in Turkey: Situation Analysis*. Report Supported by UNDP.

Bailey, G. D. (1993). Wanted: A road map for understanding integrated learning systems. In G. D. Bailey (Ed.), *Computer-Based Integrated Learning Systems* (pp. 3–9). Englewood Cliffs, NJ: Educational Technology Publications.

Baker Institute. (2013). *Shale Gas and U.S. National Security*. Baker Institute. Retrieved May 7, 2014, from http://bakerinstitute.org/center-for-energy-studies/shale-gas-and-us-national-security/

Bakker, K. (2003). Archipelagos and networks: Urbanization and water privatization in the south. *The Geographical Journal*, *169*(4), 328–341. doi:10.1111/j.0016-7398.2003.00097.x

Balk, A. (2005). *The rise of radio, from Marconi through the golden age*. Jefferson, NC: McFarland.

Ballester, A. (2002). *El aprendizaje significativo en la práctica: Cómo hacer el aprendizaje significativo en el aula*. Retrieved from http://www.aprendizajesignificativo.es/mats/El_aprendizaje_significativo_en_la_practica.pdf

Banar, M., Cokaygil, Z., & Ozkan, A. (2009). Life cycle assessment of solid waste management options for Eskisehir, Turkey. *Waste Management (New York, NY)*, *29*(1), 54–62. doi:10.1016/j.wasman.2007.12.006 PMID:18280731

Banister, D., Watson, S., & Wood, C. (1997). Sustainable cities: Transport, energy, and urban form. *Environment and Planning. B, Planning & Design*, *24*(1), 125–143. doi:10.1068/b240125

Banks, J. (1997). MTV and the globalization of popular culture. *International Communication Gazette*, *59*(1), 43–60. doi:10.1177/0016549297059001004

Barabaro, S., Coppolino, S., Leone, C., & Sinagra, E. (1978). Global solar radiation in Italy. *Solar Energy*, *20*(5), 431–438. doi:10.1016/0038-092X(78)90163-9

Barbone, S., Groot, J., Horam, R., Liuni, S., & Imerti, V. (2011). *Project Management for European Sustainable Development*. Foundation for European Sustainable Tourism.

Barcelona Energy Agency (BEA). (2009). *Barcelona Solar Thermal Ordinance (OST)*. Retrieved December 11, 2009, from http://www.barcelonaenergia.cat/eng/operations/ost.htm

Barnatt, C. (N.d.). *Explaining the future*. Retrieved October, 2012, from www.explainingthefuture.com

Barnes, T. G., & Adams, L. (1999). *A guide to Urban Habitat Conservation Planning*. Lexington, KY: University of Kentucky. Retrieved from College of Agriculture; http://www.ca.uky.edu/agc/pubs/for/for74/for74.htm

Barroso, J. M. (2014). *Letter from President Barroso to President Putin*. Retrieved April 22, 2014, from http://europa.eu/rapid/press-release_STATEMENT-14-132_en.htm

Baruah, D. (1995). Utilisation pattern of human and fuel energy in the plantation. *Journal of Agriculture and Soil Science*, *8*(2), 189–192.

Baum, S., Kendall, E., Muenchberger, H., Gudes, O., & Yigitcanlar, T. (2010). Geographical information systems: An effective planning and decision-making platform for community health coalitions in Australia. *Health Information Management Journal*, *39*(3), 28–33. PMID:21905331

Baur, C. (2008). An analysis of factors underlying e-health disparities. *Cambridge Quarterly of Healthcare Ethics*, *17*(4), 417–428. doi:10.1017/S0963180108080547 PMID:18724881

Bautista, A. (Ed.). (2004). *Las nuevas tecnologías de la enseñanza*. Madrid, Spain: Ediciones Akal.

Beardsley, K., Thorne, J. H., Roth, N. E., & Gao, S. (2009). Assessing the influence of rapid urban growth and regional policies on biological resources. *Landscape and Urban Planning*, *93*(3-4), 172–183.

Beccali, M., Cellura, M., & Mistretta, M. (2003). Decision-making in energy planning. Application of the Electre method at regional level for the diffusion of renewable energy technology. *Renewable Energy*, *28*(13), 2063–2087. doi:10.1016/S0960-1481(03)00102-2

Becker, H. J., & Hativa, N. (1994). History, theory, and research concerning integrated learning systems. *International Journal of Educational Research*, *21*(1), 5–12. doi:10.1016/0883-0355(94)90019-1

Beissinger, S. R., & Westphal, M. I. (1998). On the use of demographic models of population viability in endangered species management. *The Journal of Wildlife Management*, *62*(3), 821–841.

Bendewald, M., & Zhai, Z. J. (2013). Using carrying capacity as a base line for building sustainability assessment. *Habitat International*, *37*(1), 22–32. doi:10.1016/j.habitatint.2011.12.021

Bergmans, F. (2006). Integrating People, Planet and Profit. In J. Jonker & M. de Witte (Eds.), *Management Models for Corporate Social Responsibility* (pp. 117–125). Berlin, Germany: Springer. doi:10.1007/3-540-33247-2_14

Bernard, P., Charafeddine, R., Frohlich, K. L., Daniel, M., Kestens, Y., & Potvin, L. (2007). Health inequalities and place: A theoretical conception of neighbourhood. *Social Science & Medicine, 65*(9), 1839–1852. doi:10.1016/j.socscimed.2007.05.037 PMID:17614174

Berners-Lee, T. (1989). *Information management: A proposal*. CERN Report. Retrieved April 14, 2010, from http://cds.cern.ch/record/369245/files/dd-89-001.pdf

Berners-Lee, T. (1992). The world-wide web. *Computer Networks and ISDN Systems, 25*(4–5), 454–459. doi:10.1016/0169-7552(92)90039-S

Bernstein, J. (2005). Sustainable Development Governance Challenges in the New Millennium. In M. Berglund (Ed.), *International Environmental Law-making and Diplomacy Review 2004* (pp. 31–50). Joensuu: University of Joensuu, Department of Law.

Betsill, M. M., & Bulkeley, H. (2004). Transnational networks and global environmental governance: The cities for climate protection program. *International Studies Quarterly, 48*(2), 471–493. doi:10.1111/j.0020-8833.2004.00310.x

Beyer, K. M. M., & Rushton, G. (2009). Mapping cancer for community engagement. *Preventing Chronic Disease, 6*(1), 1–8. PMID:19080009

Bhattacharyya, R., & Kohli, S. (2007). Target Marketing to Children – The Ethical Aspect. In *Proceedings of the International Marketing Conference on Marketing* & Society (pp. 69-74). IIMK Publishing. Retrieved April 14, 2010, from http://dspace.iimk.ac.in/bitstream/2259/387/1/69-74.pdf

Bianculli, D. (2009). *Dangerously funny: The uncensored story of "The Smothers Brothers Comedy Hour"*. Beaverton, OR: Touchstone.

Bindas, K. J., & Heineman, K. J. (1994). Image is everything? Television and the counterculture message in the 1960s. *Journal of Popular Film and Television, 22*(1), 22–37. doi:10.1080/01956051.1994.9943663

Binstock, G., Cerrutti, M., & Duro, E. (2008). *Acceso y permanencia educativa de niños y adolescentes en comunidades Kolla, Mapuche, Mbya Guaraní y Wichien la Argentina*. Buenos Aires, Argentina: Government of Argentina.

Bleischwitz, R., Giljum, S., Kuhndt, M., & Schmidt-Bleek, F. (2009). *Eco-innovation- Putting the EU on the path to a resource and energy efficient economy*. Brussels, Belgium: European Parliament.

Block, J. J. (2008). Issues for DSM-V: Internet Addiction. *The American Journal of Psychiatry, 165*(3), 306–307. doi:10.1176/appi.ajp.2007.07101556 PMID:18316427

Boal-Palheiros, G. M., & Hargreaves, D. J. (2001). Listening to music at home and at school. *British Journal of Music Education, 18*(2), 103–118. doi:10.1017/S0265051701000213

Boemer, M. L. (1989). *The children's hour: radio programs for children 1929-1956*. Lanham, MD: Scarecrow Press.

Boentje, J. P., & Blinnikov, M. S. (2007). Post-Soviet forest fragmentation and loss in the Green Belt around Moscow, Russia (1991–2001): A remote sensing perspective. *Landscape and Urban Planning, 82*(4), 208–221.

Bolinger, M., & Wiser, R. (2009). Wind power price trends in the United States: Struggling to remain competitive in the face of strong growth. *Energy Policy, 37*(3), 1061–1071. doi:10.1016/j.enpol.2008.10.053

Bonder, G. (2008). Juventud, género TIC: Imaginarios en la construcción de la sociedad de la información en América Latina. In *Proceedings of the ARBOR Ciencia, Pensamiento y Cultura CLXXXIV 733*, (pp. 917-934). Retrieved February 16, 2010, from http://arbor.revistas.csic.es/index.php/ arbor/article/view/234/235

Borden, I. (2001). *Skateboarding, space and the city: Architecture and the body*. Oxford, UK: Berg.

Boschi-Pinto, C., Lanata, C. F., Mendoza, W., & Habte, D. (2006). Diarrheal Diseases. In D. T. Jamison, R. G. Feachem, M. W. Makgoba, E. R. Bos, F. K. Baingana, K. J. Hofman, & K. O. Rogo (Eds.), *Disease and mortality in Sub-Saharan Africa*. Washington, DC: World Bank.

Bos, E., My, T., Vu, E., & Bulatao, R. (1994). *World population projection: 1994-95*. Baltimore, MD & London, UK: World Bank by the John Hopkins University Press.

Bostancı, S. H. (2012). Eco-Municipalities and Municipal Applications for Sustainability. In Ö. Yalçıner-Ercoşkun (Ed.), *Green and Ecological Technologies for Urban Planning: Creating Smart Cities* (pp. 310–328). Hershey, PA: IGI Global. doi:10.4018/978-1-61350-453-6.ch017

Boulos, M. N. K., & Al-S horbaji, N. M. (2014). On the Internet of Things, smart cities and the WHO Healthy Cities. *International Journal of Health Geographics*, *12*(10), 1–6.

Bower, J. L., & Christensen, C. M. (1995). Disruptive technologies: Catching the wave. *Harvard Business Review*, *73*(1), 43–53.

Boyd, S., & Butler, R. (1997). Sustainable Tourism Development in Protected Areas. *International Journal of Heritage Studies*, *10*(3), 309–319.

Brandoni, C., & Polonara, F. (2012). The role of municipal energy planning in the regional energy-planning process. *Energy*, *48*(1), 323–338. doi:10.1016/j.energy.2012.06.061

Braunstein, P. (2002). Forever Young: Insurgent youth and the Sixties culture of rejuvenation. In P. Braunstein & M. W. Doyle (Eds.), *Imagine Nation: The American Counterculture of the 1960s and 1970s* (pp. 243–273). New York, NY: Routledge.

Bredillet, C. N. (2000). *Proposition of a systemic and dynamic model to design life-long learning structure: The quest of the missing link between men, team, and organizational learning*. Paper presented at the PMI Research Conference 2000: Project Management Research at the Turn of the Millennium. Paris, France.

Breen, R. (2004). The Comparative Study of Social Mobility. In R. Breen (Ed.), *Social Mobility in Europe* (pp. 37–75). Oxford, UK: Oxford University Press. doi:10.1093/0199258457.003.0003

Bregalia, L. (2005). Keeping World Heritage in the Family: A Geneology of Maya Labour at Chichen Itza. *International Journal of Heritage Studies*, *8*(3), 247–265.

Brent, A. C., & Labuschagne, C. (2006). Social indicators for sustainable project and technology life cycle management in the process industry. *International Journal of Life Cycle Assessment*, *11*(1), 3–15. doi:10.1065/lca2006.01.233

Brent, A. C., & Petrick, W. (2007). Environmental Impact Assessment (EIA) during project execution phases: Towards a stage-gate project management model for the raw materials processing industry of the energy sector. *Impact Assessment and Project Appraisal*, *25*(2), 111–122. doi:10.3152/146155107X205832

Breuste, J. H. (2010). Allotment Gardens as Part of Urban Green Infrastructure: Actual Trends and Perspectives. In N. Müller, P. Werner, & J. G. Kelcey (Eds.), *Central Europe. Urban Biodiversity and Design*. Oxford, UK: Wiley-Blackwell.

Breuste, J., Niemelä, J., & Snep, R. P. H. (2008). Applying landscape ecological principles in urban environments. *Landscape Ecology*, *23*(10), 1139–1142.

Brooke, M. (1999). The concrete wave: The history of skateboarding. Toronto, Canada: Warwick.

Browne, R., & Knodel, M. (2008). *Sustainability in Hanover*. Hanover: PRS Policy Brief 0708-08.

Brown, G., Montag, J., & Lyon, K. (2012). Public Participation GIS: A Method for Identifying Ecosystem Services. *Society & Natural Resources: An International Journal*, *25*(7), 633–651. doi:10.1080/08941920.2011.621511

Brown, J., Cairncross, S., & Ensink, J. H. J. (2013). Water, sanitation, hygiene and enteric infections in children. *Archives of Disease in Childhood*, *98*(8), 629–634. doi:10.1136/archdischild-2011-301528 PMID:23761692

Brown, L. (2009). *Plan B 4.0: Mobilizing to Save Civilization*. Washington, DC: Earth Policy Institute.

Brown, M. A., & Sovacool, B. K. (2007). Developing an energy sustainability index to evaluate energy policy. *Interdisciplinary Science Reviews*, *32*(4), 335–349. doi:10.1179/030801807X211793

Brugmann, J. (1996). Planning for sustainability at the local government level. *Environmental Impact Assessment Review*, *16*(4), 363–379. doi:10.1016/S0195-9255(97)81658-7

Bruner, A. G., Gullison, R. E., Rice, R. E., & da Fonseca, G. A. B. (2001). Effectiveness of parks in protecting tropical biodiversity. *Science*, *291*(5501), 125–128.

Brynin, M. (2006). Gender, technology and jobs. *The British Journal of Sociology*, *57*(3), 437–453. doi:10.1111/j.1468-4446.2006.00119.x PMID:16939595

BSR/GlobeScan. (2012). *2012 BSR/GlobeScan State of Sustainable Business Poll*. Retrieved January 8, 2013, from http://www.globescan.com/commentary-and-analysis/press-releases/press-releases-2012/244-new-poll-of-business-leaders-highlights-sustainability-priorities-for-global-companies.html

Buchholz, T. S., Volk, T. A., & Luzadis, V. A. (2007). A participatory systems approach to modeling social, economic, and ecological components of bioenergy. *Energy Policy*, *35*(12), 6084–6094. doi:10.1016/j.enpol.2007.08.020

Burbules, N. (2001). *Educación: riesgos y promesas de lasnuevastecnologías de la información*. Barcelona, Spain: Granica.

Burstrom, B., Macassa, G., Oberg, L., Bernhardt, E., & Smedman, L. (2005). Equitable child health interventions: The impact of improved water and sanitation on inequalities in child mortality in Stockholm, 1878 to 1925. *American Journal of Public Health*, *95*(2), 208–216. doi:10.2105/AJPH.2003.034900 PMID:15671452

Burström, F. (1999). Materials accounting and environmental management in municipalities. *Journal of Environmental Assessment Policy and Management*, *1*(3), 297–327. doi:10.1142/S1464333299000247

Burström, F. (2000). *Environment and Municipalities: Towards a Theory on Municipal Environmental Management*. Stockholm, Sweden: KTH/Högskoletryckeriet.

Busche, S., Doris, E., Braccio, R., Lippert, D., Finch, P., O'Toole, D., & Fetter, J. (2010). *Clean Energy Policy Analysis: Impact Analysis of Potential Clean Energy Policy Options for the Hawaii Clean Energy Initiative*. Technical Report. NREL/TP-742-47891.

Butera, F. (2008). Towards the Renewable Built Environment. In P. Droege (Ed.), *Urban Energy Transition: From Fossil Fuels to Renewable Power* (pp. 329–364). Oxford, UK: Elsevier. doi:10.1016/B978-0-08-045341-5.00014-1

Byrne, J., Wang, Y.-D., Kim, J.-D., Lee, H., & Kim, J.-W. (2004). *Energy Revolution: 21 Century Energy and Environmental Strategy*. Maeil Business Newpaper.

Byun, S., Ruffini, C., Mills, J. E., Douglas, A. C., Niang, M., Stepchenkova, S., & Blanton, M. et al. (2008). Internet Addiction: Metasynthesis of 1996–2006 quantitative Research. *Cyberpsychology & Behavior*, *12*(2), 203–207. doi:10.1089/cpb.2008.0102 PMID:19072075

Cabero, J. (2004). Reflexiones sobre las tecnologías como instrumentos culturales. In Martínez, F., & Castaño, C. (2008). La segunda brecha digital y las mujeres. *Telos*. Retrieved November 20, 2009, fromhttp://www.campusred.net/TELOS/articuloAutorInvitado.asp?idarticulo=2&rev=75

Cadman, T. (2011). *Quality and Legitimacy of Global Governance: Case Lessons from Forestry*. Basingstoke: Palgrave Macmillan. doi:10.1057/9780230306462

Cadman, T. (2013). Applying an Empirical Evaluation to the Governance Legitimacy of Carbon Offset Mechanisms on the Basis of Stakeholder Perceptions. In T. Cadman (Ed.), *Climate Change and Global Policy Regimes: Towards Institutional Legitimacy* (pp. 79–95). Basingstoke: Palgrave Macmillan. doi:10.1057/9781137006127.0012

Cadman, T. (Ed.). (2013b). *Climate Change and Global Policy Regimes: Towards Institutional Legitimacy*. Basingstoke: Palgrave Macmillan. doi:10.1057/9781137006127

Cadman, T., & Marseni, T. (2011). The Governance of Climate Change: Evaluating the Governance Quality and Legitimacy of the United Nations' REDD-plus Programme. *International Journal of Climate Change: Impacts and Responses*, *2*(3), 103–124.

CAEEDAC. (2000). *A descriptive analysis of energy consumption in agriculture and food sector in Canada*. Final Report, February 2000.

Cairncross, S., & Feachem, R. G. (1983). *Environmental health engineering in the tropics: an introductory text*. West Sussex, England: Wiley.

Cai, Y., Huang, G., Lin, Q., Nie, X., & Tan, Q. (2009). An optimization-model-based interactive decision support system for regional energy management systems planning under uncertainty. *Expert Systems with Applications*, *36*(2, Part 2), 3470–3482. doi:10.1016/j.eswa.2008.02.036

Caldas, F., & Garcia-Valcárcel, A. (2013). The Role of ICTs in Rural Schools of Patagonia. *Multiculturalism in Technology-Based Education*, *1*(4), 38–58.

Campbell, H. E., & Corley, E. A. (2012). *Urban Environmental Policy Analysis*. Armonk, NY: M.E. Sharpe.

Canadian Business for Social Responsibility. (2010). *CSR Governance Guidelines*. Toronto, Canada: Canadian Business for Social Responsibility.

Cantrell, J., & Wepfer, W. (1984). Shallow Ponds for Dissipation of Building Heat: A case Study. *ASHRAE Transactions*, *90*(1), 239–246.

Carbone, M. (2005). Sustainable Tourism in Developing Countries: Poverty Alleviation, Participatory Planning, and Ethical Issues. *European Journal of Development Research*, *17*(3), 559–565. doi:10.1080/09578810500209841

Carley, S. (2009). Distributed generation: An empirical analysis of primary motivators. *Energy Policy*, *37*(5), 1648–1659. doi:10.1016/j.enpol.2009.01.003

Carlton, J., & Kawasaki, G. (1997). *Apple: The inside story of intrigue, egomania, and business blunders*. New York: Random House.

Carson, R. (1962). *Silent Spring*. Boston, MA: Houghton Mifflin.

Carstensen, T. A., & Ebert, A. (2012). Cycling cultures in Northern Europe: from "golden age" to "renaissance". In J. Parkin (Ed.), *Cycling and sustainability* (pp. 23–58). UK: Emerald Group Publishing Limited. doi:10.1108/S2044-9941(2012)0000001004

Casault, K. (2011). Publication of Social Responsibility News and its Impacts on Mining Sector Investors' Behavior.*Proceedings of the 2011 Northeast Decision Sciences Institute Conference* (pp. 201-206). Houston, TX: Decision Sciences Institute.

Cashore, B., Auld, G., & Newsom, D. (2004). *Governing Through Markets: Forest Certification and the Emergence of Non-State Authority*. New Haven, London: Yale University Press.

Caslake, L. F., Connolly, D. J., Menon, V., Duncanson, C. M., Rojas, R., & Tavakoli, J. (2004). Disinfection of Contaminated Water by Using Solar Irradiation. *Applied and Environmental Microbiology*, *70*(2), 1145–1151. doi:10.1128/AEM.70.2.1145-1150.2004 PMID:14766599

Cassell, K. A., & Hiremath, U. (2006). *Reference and information services in the 21st century: An introduction*. New York, NY: Neal-Schuman.

Castaño, C., Martín, J., & Vázquez, S. (2009). *E-inclusion and social welfare in Spain: a gender perspective*. Bremen, Germany: GICT. Retrieved November 5, 2010, from http://www.informatik.unibremen.de/soteg/gict2009/proceedings/GICT2009_Castano.pdf

Cebrián de la Serna, M. (Ed.). (2009). *Las Tecnologías de la información y comunicación para el desarrolloeducativo de los pueblos indígenas*. Andalucía, Spain: GTEA.

Cellini, R. (2011). Is UNESCO Recognition Effective in Fostering Tourism? A Comment on Yang, Lin and Han. *Tourism Management*, *32*(2), 452–454. doi:10.1016/j.tourman.2010.01.018

Centers for Disease Control and Prevention. (1999). Achievements in Public Health, 1990-1999: Changes in the Public Health System.[MMWR]. *Morbidity and Mortality Weekly Report*, *48*(50), 849–859. PMID:10563522

Central Intelligence Agency. (2009). *The World Factbook 2009*. Washington, DC: Central Intelligence Agency. Retrieved August 6, 2012, from https://www.cia.gov/library/publications/download/download-2009/index.html

Central Northern Adelaide Health Service. (2008). *Central Northern Adelaide Health Service Social Health Atlas 2008*. Retrieved November 24, 2008, from http://www.publichealth.gov.au/interactive_mapping/sa_sha_cnahs_2005/atlas.html

Ceruzzi, P. E. (2003). *A history of modern computing*. Cambridge, MA: MIT Press.

Cesari, C. (2010). World Heritage and Mosaic Universalism: A View from Palestine. *Journal of Social Archaeology*, *10*(3), 299–324. doi:10.1177/1469605310378336

Chadwick, E. (1843). *Report on the sanitary condition of the labouring population of Great Britain. A supplementary report on the results of a spiecal inquiry into the practice of interment in towns*. London, UK: H. M. Stationery.

Chambers, E. (2009). From Authenticity to Significance: Tourism on the Frontier of Culture and Place. *Futures*, *41*(6), 353–359. doi:10.1016/j.futures.2008.11.003

Chang, H. W., & Chang, H. L. (2003). A strategic study of bicycle tourism in Taiwan. *Journal of the Eastern Asia Society for Transportation Studies*, *5*, 1675–1685.

Charter, M. (2004). Sustainable Innovations. In *Proceedings of the Business Council for Sustainable Development of Taiwan (BCSD-Taiwan)*. Washington, DC: World Business Council for Sustainable Development.

Chavan, M. (2005). An appraisal of environment management systems. *Management of Environmental Quality*, *16*(5), 444–463. doi:10.1108/14777830510614321

Checkley, W., Buckley, G., Gilman, R. H., Assis, A. M. O., Guerrant, R. L., Morris, S. S., & Black, R. E. et al.The Childhood Malnitrition and Infection Network. (2008). Multi-country analysis of the effects of diarrhoea on childhood stunting. *International Journal of Epidemiology*, *37*(4), 816–830. doi:10.1093/ije/dyn099 PMID:18567626

Chhabra, D. (2009). Proposing a Sustainable Marketing Framework for Heritage Tourism. *Journal of Sustainable Tourism*, *17*(3), 313–320. doi:10.1080/09669580802495758

Chhabra, D. (2010). *Sustainable Marketing of Cultural and Heritage Tourism*. London: Routledge.

Chhabra, D. (2012). Authenticity of the objectively authentic. *Annals of Tourism Research*, *39*(1), 499–502. doi:10.1016/j.annals.2011.09.005

Chiesura, A. (2004). The role of urban parks for the sustainable city. *Landscape and Urban Planning*, *68*(4), 129–138.

Chilamkurti, N., Zeadally, S., & Mentiplay, F. (2009). Green networking for major components of ICT systems. *EURASIP Journal on Wireless Communications and Networking*, (35), 1–7.

Choi, H., & Sirakaya, E. (2006). Sustainability Indicators for Managing Community Tourism. *Tourism Management*, *27*(6), 1274–1289. doi:10.1016/j.tourman.2005.05.018

Choi, S., Lehto, X., & Morrison, A. (2007). Destination image representation on the web: Content analysis of Macau travel related websites. *Tourism Management*, *28*(1), 118–129. doi:10.1016/j.tourman.2006.03.002

Christensen, T. H., Godskesen, M., Gram-Hassen, K., Quitzau, M., & Ropke, I. (2007). Greening the Danes? Experience with consumption and environment policies. *Journal of Consumer Policy*, *30*(2), 91–116. doi:10.1007/s10603-007-9029-2

CIA. (2014). World Factbook. Retrieved April 28, 2014, from https://www.cia.gov/library/publications/the-world-factbook/geos/rs.html

CIFOR. (Centre for International Forestry research) (2010). *Simply REDD: CIFOR's Guide to Forests, Climate Change and REDD*. Bogor: CIFOR. Retrieved October 1, 2010, from www.cifor.cgiar.org/publications/pdf_files/.../MediaGuide_REDD.pdf

Clapp, J. (2005). Global Environmental Governance for Corporate Responsibility and Accountability. *Global Environmental Politics*, *5*(3), 23–34. doi:10.1162/1526380054794916

Coates, B., Pusser, H. E., & Goodman, I. (1976). The influence of "Sesame Street" and "Mister Rogers' Neighborhood" on children's social behavior in the preschool. *Child Development*, *47*(1), 138–144. doi:10.2307/1128292

Coenen, F. (2001). Probing the Essence of LA21 as a Value-Added Approach to Sustainable Development and Local Democracy. In W. M. Lafferty (Ed.), *Sustainable Communities in Europe* (pp. 153–179). London, UK: Earthscan.

Coetzee, W., Nierkel, M., & Saayman, M. (2006). Applying Economic Guidelines for Responsible Tourism in a World Heritage Site. *Koedoe*, *50*(1), 54–60.

Cogălniceanu, D. (1999). *Managementul capitalului natural*. Bucureşti: Ars Docendi.

Cogeneration and On-site Power Production (COSPP). (2005). *Stationary fuel cells*. Retrieved January 7, 2010, from http://www.cospp.com/display_article/272983/122/ARTCL/none/TECHS/1/Stationary-fuel-cells/

Cohen, A. (2007). *Europe's strategic dependence on Russian energy.* Retrieved December 5, 2010, from http://www.heritage.org/research/reports/2007/11/europes-strategic-dependence-on-russian-energy

Cohen, A. (2012). *Doctrine of the Energy Security for the Russian Federation.* Retrieved May 7, 2014, from http://sei.irk.ru/promo/doktrina-energeticheskoy-bezopasnosti-rossii/ - in Russian.

Cohen, B. (2006). Urbanization in developing countries: Current trends, future projections, and key challenges for sustainability. *Technology in Society*, *28*(1), 63–80. doi:10.1016/j.techsoc.2005.10.005

Cohen, E. (2007). Authenticity in Tourism Studies. *Tourism Recreation Research*, *32*(2), 75–82. doi:10.1080/02508281.2007.11081279

Coker, R., & Martin, R. (2006). Introduction: The importance of law for public health policy and practice. *Public Health, 120. Supplement*, *1*(0), 2–7.

Collins, M. (1994). Internet information management tools. *Communication Education*, *43*(2), 112–119. doi:10.1080/03634529409378968

Comenius, J. A. (1907). *The Great Didactic* (Didactica Magna). Retrieved May 15, 2014, from https://ia600406.us.archive.org/32/items/cu31924031053709/cu31924031053709.pdf

Commission of the European Communities (CEC). (1997). *Towards a Urban Agenda in the European Union. COM (1997) 197.* Bruxell.

Commission of the European Communities (CEC). (1998). *Sustainable Urban Development in the European Union: a Framework for Action. COM (1998).* Bruxell.

Commission of the European Communities (CEC). (1999). *Green Paper on the Urban Environment. COM (1999) 218.* Bruxell.

Commission of the European Communities (CEC). (2001). *A Sustainable Strategy for a Better World: a European Strategy for Sustainable Development. COM (2001) 264.* Bruxell.

Commission of the European Communities (CEC). (2001). *European transport policy for 2010: Time to decide. COM (2001) 370.* Bruxell.

Commission of the European Communities (CEC). (2004). *Towards a Thematic Strategy on the Urban Environment. COM (2004) 60 final.* Bruxell.

Commission of the European Communities (CEC). (2007). *Towards a new culture for urban mobility.* Green Paper. Retrieved from http://www.eur-lex.europa.ue

Commission of the European Communities (CEC). (2011). *Roadmap to a Single European Transport Area: Towards a competitive and resource efficient transport system.* White Paper. COM/2011/0144 final, Bruxell.

Compact disc hits 25th birthday. (2007). Retrieved April 14, 2010, from BBC News website: http://news.bbc.co.uk/2/hi/6950845.stm?lsm

comScore. (2007). *Worldwide online gaming community reaches 217 million people.* Retrieved April 17, 2010, from comScore website: http://www.comscore.com/Press_Events/Press_Releases/2007/07/Worldwide_Online_Gaming_Grows

Connolly, D. (1999). *CERN httpd.* Retrieved April 10, 2010, from http://www.w3.org/Daemon/

Connolly, J., & Prothero, A. (2003). Sustainable Consumption: Consumption, Consumers and the Commodity Discourse. *Consumption Markets & Culture*, *6*(4), 275–291. doi:10.1080/1025386032000168311

Consejo Provincial de Educación. (2010). *Consejo Provincial de Educación: Información estadística de la deserción y repitencia en la provincia del Neuquén.* Neuquén, Argentina: Author.

Conway, M. D., Rizzuto, C. D., & Weiss, L. M. (2008). *A better way to speed the adoption of vaccines.* Retrieved November 20, 2008, from http://www.mckinseyquarterly.com/home.aspx

Conway, F. (2014). Local and Public Heritage at a World Heritage Site. *Annals of Tourism Research*, *44*(30), 143–155. doi:10.1016/j.annals.2013.09.007

Cooper, P., & Vargas, C. (2004). *Implementing Sustainable Development: From Global Policy to Local Action.* Lanham, MD: Rowman & Littlefield Publishers, Inc.

Cooper, R. S., Kennelly, J. F., & Orduñez-Garcia, P. (2006). Health in Cuba. *International Journal of Epidemiology*, *35*(4), 817–824. doi:10.1093/ije/dyl175 PMID:16931525

Cormio, C., Dicorato, M., Minoia, A., & Trovato, M. (2003). A regional energy planning methodology including renewable energy sources and environmental constraints. *Renewable & Sustainable Energy Reviews*, *7*(2), 99–130. doi:10.1016/S1364-0321(03)00004-2

Corrales, L. F., Izurieta, R., & Moe, C. L. (2006). Association between intestinal parasitic infections and type of sanitation system in rural El Salvador. *Tropical Medicine & International Health*, *11*(12), 1821–1831. doi:10.1111/j.1365-3156.2006.01737.x PMID:17176347

Costanza, R., d'Arge, R., de Groot, R., Farber, S., Grasso, M., Hannon, B., & van den Belt, M. et al. (1997, May). The value of the world's ecosystem services and natural capital. *Nature*, *387*, 253–260.

Cover, R. (2005). DVD time: temporality, audience engagement and the new TV culture of digital video. *Media International Australia: Incorporating Culture & Policy*, (117), 137.

Craddock, W. T. (2013). How Business Excellence Models Contribute to Project Sustainability and Project Success. In A. J. G. Silvius & J. Tharp (Eds.), *Sustainability Integration for Effective Project Management* (pp. 1–19). Hershey, PA: IGI Global Publishing. doi:10.4018/978-1-4666-4177-8.ch001

Crawford, L. (2007). Global Body of Project Management Knowledge and Standards. In P. W. G. Morris & J. K. Pinto (Eds.), *The Wiley Guide to Managing Projects*. Hoboken, NJ: John Wiley and Sons, Inc. doi:10.1002/9780470172391.ch46

Credit Swiss Research Institute. (2013). *Global Wealth Report 2013*. Retrieved October, 2013, from http://thenextrecession.files.wordpress.com/2013/10/global-wealth-report.pdf

Cresswell, T. (2006). The Right to Mobility: The Production of Mobility in the Courtroom. *Antipode*, *38*(4), 735–754. doi:10.1111/j.1467-8330.2006.00474.x

Croll, P. R., & Croll, J. (2007). Investigating risk exposure in e-health systems. *International Journal of Medical Informatics*, *76*(5-6), 460–465. doi:10.1016/j.ijmedinf.2006.09.013 PMID:17126069

Crook, C. (1998). *Ordenadores y aprendizaje colaborativo*. Madrid, Spain: Morata.

Cross, G. (2014). *Jaded Children, Callow Adults*. Retrieved April 11, 2014, from The Chronicle of Higher Education website: http://chronicle.com/article/Jaded-Children-Callow-Adults/145117

Cumming, O. (2009). The sanitation imperative: A strategic response to a development crisis. *Desalination*, *248*(1-3), 8–13. doi:10.1016/j.desal.2008.05.031

Curry, E. (2010). Water Scarcity and the Recognition of the Human Right to Safe Freshwater. *Northwestern Journal of International Human Rights*, *9*(1), 103–121.

Curtis, V., & Cairncross, S. (2003). Effect of washing hands with soap on diarrhoea risk in the community: A systematic review. *The Lancet Infectious Diseases*, *3*(5), 275–281. doi:10.1016/S1473-3099(03)00606-6 PMID:12726975

Curtis, V., Kanki, B., Mertens, T., Traore, E., Diallo, I., Tall, F., & Cousens, S. (1995). Potties, pits and pipes: Explaining hygiene behaviour in Burkina Faso. *Social Science & Medicine*, *41*(3), 383–393. doi:10.1016/0277-9536(94)00341-P PMID:7481932

D'Apote, S. L. (1998). IEA biomass energy analysis and projections. In *Proceedings of Biomass Energy Conference: Data, Analysis and Trends*. Paris, France.

Database of State Incentives for Renewables and Efficiency (DSIRE). (2014) *DSIRE RPS Data Spreadsheet*. Retrieved June 11, 2014, from http://www.dsireusa.org/rpsdata/index.cfm

Daub, C., & Ergenzinger, R. (2005). Enabling sustainable management through a new multi-disciplinary concept of customer satisfaction. *European Journal of Marketing*, *39*(9/10), 998–1217. doi:10.1108/03090560510610680

David, J. M. (2000). Developing hydrogen and fuel cell products. *Energy World*, *303*(0), 16–17.

Davies, D., Gray, S., Gardner, G., & Harland, G. (2001). *A quantitative study of the attitudes of individuals towards cycling*. TRL Report 481, Crowthorne. Retrieved December 13, 2013, from http://www.trl.co.uk/online_store/reports_publications/trl_reports/cat_traffic_and_transport_planning/report_a_quantitative_study_of_the_attitudes_of_individuals_to_cycling.htm

DCTI. 2013 Definition for CleanTech and CleanTech Framework, http://www.dcti.de/en/cleantech/definition.html

de Mooij, M. K. (2004). *Consumer behavior and culture: consequences for global marketing and advertising*. Thousand Oaks, CA: Sage.

De Vos, P., De Ceukelaire, W., Malaise, G., Pérez, D., Lefèvre, P., & Van Der Stuyft, P. (2009). Health through People's Empowerment: A Rights-Based Approach to Participation. *Health and Human Rights*, *11*(1), 23–35. doi:10.2307/40285215 PMID:20845848

Del Álamo, O. (2003). Esperanza tecnológica: Internet para los pueblos indígenas de América Latina. *Instituciones y Desarrollo*, *14*(15), 43–79.

Department of Business, Economic Development and Tourism, State of Hawaii (DBEDT). (2014). *Hawaii Energy Facts and Figures*. Retrieved June 12, 2014, from http://energy.hawaii.gov/wp-content/uploads/2011/08/HI-Energy-FactsFigures_May2014.pdf

Deshmukh, S. S., & Deshmukh, M. K. (2009). A new approach to micro-level energy planning--A case of northern parts of Rajasthan, India. *Renewable & Sustainable Energy Reviews*, *13*(3), 634–642. doi:10.1016/j.rser.2007.11.015

Díaz, R. (2001). *Trabajo docente y diferencia cultural: lecturas antropológicas para una Identidad desafiada*. Madrid, Spain: Abya Yala, Miño y Dávila.

Diesendorf, M. (2000). Sustainability and sustainable development. In D. Dunphy, J. Benveniste, A. Griffiths, & P. Sutton (Eds.), *Sustainability: The corporate challenge of the 21st century* (pp. 19–37). Sydney, Australia: Allen & Unwin.

Dill, J. (2009). Bicycling for Transportation and Health: The Role of Infrastructure. *Journal of Public Health Policy*, *30*(S1), 95–110. doi:10.1057/jphp.2008.56 PMID:19190585

DiMaggio, P. J., Hargittai, E., Neuman, R., & Robinson, J. (2001). Social implications of the Internet. *Annual Review of Sociology*, *27*(1), 307–336. doi:10.1146/annurev.soc.27.1.307

Ding, G. K. C. (2008). Sustainable construction—The role of environmental assessment tools. *Journal of Environmental Management*, *86*(3), 451–464. doi:10.1016/j.jenvman.2006.12.025 PMID:17289255

DiNIECE. (2005). *Políticas sociales y acceso a educación, salud y programas de alivio a la pobreza*. Retrieved February 22, 2011, from http://www.civil-society.oas.org/Spanish/Decentralization_2-politicas_sociales.doc

Dinsmore, P. C., & Cooke-Davies, T. J. (2006). *The Right Projects Done Right: From Business Strategy to Successful Project Implementation*. San Francisco, CA: John Wiley & Sons, Inc.

Dirks, T. (2010). The history of film. *Film History*, *1970s*, •••. http://www.filmsite.org/70sintro.html Retrieved April 5, 2010

Dolan, P. (2002). The Sustainability of 'Sustainable Consumption'. *Journal of Macromarketing*, *22*(2), 170–181. doi:10.1177/0276146702238220

Domac, J., Segon, V., Przulj, I., & Rajic, K. (2011). Regional energy planning methodology, drivers and implementation--Karlovac County case study. *Biomass and Bioenergy*, *35*(11), 4504–4510. doi:10.1016/j.biombioe.2011.07.018

Dorian, J. P., Franssen, H. T., & Simbeck, D. R. (2006). Global challenges in energy. *Energy Policy*, *34*(15), 1984–1991. doi:10.1016/j.enpol.2005.03.010

Douglas, S. J. (2004). *Listening in: Radio and the American imagination*. Minneapolis: University of Minnesota Press.

Drain, P. K., & Barry, M. (2010). Fifty Years of U.S. Embargo: Cuba's Health Outcomes and Lessons. *Science*, *328*(5978), 572–573. doi:10.1126/science.1189680 PMID:20430999

Dresang, L. T., Brebrick, L., Murray, D., Shallue, A., & Sullivan-Vedder, L. (2005). Family Medicine in Cuba: Community-Oriented Primary Care and Complementary and Alternative Medicine. *The Journal of the American Board of Family Practice*, *18*(4), 297–303. doi:10.3122/jabfm.18.4.297 PMID:15994475

Drost, A. (1992). Developing Sustainable Tour- ism for WHS. *Annals of Tourism Research*, *23*(2), 479–492. doi:10.1016/0160-7383(96)83345-7

D'Sa, A. (2005). Integrated resource planning (IRP) and power sector reform in developing countries. *Energy Policy, 33*(10), 1271–1285. doi:10.1016/j.enpol.2003.12.003

Duchin, F. (1995). *Global scenarios about lifestyle and technology, the sustainable future of the global system.* Tokyo: United Nations University.

Duffie, J. A., & Beckman, W. A. (1980). *Solar Engineering of Thermal Processes*. New York, NY: J. Wiley and Sons.

Duhl, L. J. (1996). An ecohistory of health: The role of 'healthy cities'. *American Journal of Health Promotion, 10*(4), 258–261. doi:10.4278/0890-1171-10.4.258 PMID:10159706

Duhl, L. J., & Sanchez, A. K. (1999). *Healthy cities and the city planning process. A Background Documentation on Links Between Health And Urban Planning*. Copenhagen, Denmark: WHO, Regional Office for Europe.

Dumbaugh, E., & Li, W. (2010). Designing for the Safety of Pedestrians, Cyclists, and Motorists in Urban Environments. *Journal of the American Planning Association, 77*(1), 69–88. doi:10.1080/01944363.2011.536101

Dunn, H. (2010). Jamaica. In The Association for Progressive Communications (APC) & Humanist Institute for Cooperation with Developing Countries (Hivos) (Eds.), *Global Information Society Watch 2010: Focus on ICTs and Environmental Sustainability* (pp. 148-151). Melville, South Africa: APC. Retrieved from http://www.giswatch.org/hopetondunn%40gmail.com

Dur, F., Yigitcanlar, T., & Bunker, J. (2009, March). *A decision support system for sustainable urban development: the integrated land use and transportation indexing model.* Paper presented at the Postgraduate Infrastructure Conference. Brisbane, Australia: Queensland University of Technology.

Dutt, B. (1982). Comparative efficiency of energy use in rice production. *Energy, 6*(0), 25.

Duvigneaud, P. (1974). *La synthèse écologique*. Paris, France: Doin.

Dyllick, T., & Hockerts, K. (2002). Beyond the business case for corporate sustainability. *Business Strategy and the Environment, 11*(2), 130–141. doi:10.1002/bse.323

Dzwairo, B., Hoko, Z., Love, D., & Guzha, E. (2006). Assessment of the impacts of pit latrines on groundwater quality in rural areas: A case study from Marondera district, Zimbabwe. *Physics and Chemistry of the Earth Parts A/B/C, 31*(15–16), 779–788. doi:10.1016/j.pce.2006.08.031

Earth Charter Initiative. (2000). *The Earth Charter.* Retrieved May 6, 2006, from http://www.earthcharterinaction.org/

Ecosystem, U. Legambiente. (2011). *XV Report about environmental quality of Italian provinces.* Retrieved from http:/www.legambiente.eu

Edum-Fotwe, F. T., & Price, A. D. F. (2009). A Social Ontology for Appraising Sustainability of Construction Projects and Developments. *International Journal of Project Management, 27*(4), 313–322. doi:10.1016/j.ijproman.2008.04.003

Edwards, P., & Tsuorus, A. D. (2006). *A Healthy City is an Active City: A Physical Activity Planning Guide.* World Health Organization.

Eid, M. (2002). A sustainable approach to the project management odyssey. In *Proceedings of the PMI Research Conference: Frontiers of Project Management Research and Application.* Philadelphia PA: Project Management Institute.

Eid, M. (2009). *Sustainable Development & Project Management.* Cologne, Germany: Lambert Academic Publishing.

E-igualdad. (2007). *Sociedad de la Información y Género: unanálisis de laspolíticaspúblicas. Estado de situación, iniciativas y propuestas.* Retrieved November 15, 2010, from http://www.e-igualdad.net/fichero.aspx?id=199&titulo=Estudiode Políticascompleto

Eisenstein, E. L. (2005). The printing revolution in early modern Europe (2nd, rev. ed.). Cambridge, UK: University Press.

Elkington, J. (1994). Towards the Sustainable Corporation: Win-Win-Win Business Strategies for Sustainable Development. *California Management Review, 36*(2), 90–100. doi:10.2307/41165746

Elkington, J. (1998). *Cannibals with Forks: the Triple Bottom Line of 21st Century Business*. Gabriola Island, British Columbia: New Society Publishers.

Elkington, J. (2004). Enter the triple bottom line. In A. Henriques & J. Richardson (Eds.), *The triple bottom line, does it all add up? Assessing the sustainability of business and CSR* (pp. 1–16). London, UK: Earthscan Publication Ltd.

Emrealp, S. (2005). *Yerel Gündem 21 Uygulamalarına Yönelik Kolaylaştırıcı Bilgiler El Kitabı. Türkiye- İstanbul: IULA-EMME (UCLG-MEWA)*. Yayını.

Energy Charter Secretariat. (2010). *Energy Charter*. Retrieved December 5, 2013, from http://www.encharter.org/

Energy Information Administration (EIA). (2009). *Capacity of Distributed Generators by Technology Type*. Retrieved January 7, 2010, from http://www.eia.doe.gov/cneaf/electricity/epa/epat2p7b.html

Energy Information Administration. (2013). *Russia Country Report*. Retrieved April 28, 2014, from http://www.eia.gov/countries/cab.cfm?fips=rs

Energy Information Administration. (2014). *Energy Intensity*. U.S. Energy Information Administration. Retrieved April 13, 2014, from http://www.eia.gov/cfapps/ipdbproject/iedindex3.cfm?tid=92&pid=47&aid=2&cid=CG1,&syid=2007&eyid=2011&unit=BTUPUSDM

Energy Information Administration. (of the U.S. Department of Energy). (2013). *International Energy Outlook 2013*. Retrieved April 7, 2014, from http://www.eia.gov/forecasts/ieo/pdf/0484(2013).pdf

EPFI. (2013). *Equator Principles III: Equator Principles Financial Institutions*. Retrieved May 7, 2014, from http://www.equator-principles.com/resources/equator_principles_III.pdf

Epstein, M. J. (2008). *Making Sustainability Work: Best Practices in Managing and Measuring Corporate Social, Environmental, and Economic Impacts*. San Francisco, CA: Berrett-Koehler Publishers, Inc.

Escott, C., & Hawkins, M. (1992). *Good rockin' tonight: Sun Records and the birth of rock'n'roll*. New York: St. Martin's Griffin.

Eskerod, P., & Huemann, M. (2013). Sustainable development and project stakeholder management: What standards say. *International Journal of Managing Projects in Business*, *6*(1), 36–50. doi:10.1108/17538371311291017

Espinosa, A., Harnden, R., & Walker, J. (2008). A complexity approach to sustainability - Stafford Beer revisited. *European Journal of Operational Research*, *187*(2), 636–651. doi:10.1016/j.ejor.2007.03.023

Esty, D. C., Levy, M., Srebotnjak, T., & de Sherbinin, A. (2005). *Environmental Sustainability Index: Benchmarking national environmental stewardship*. New Haven, CT: Yale Center for Environmental Law & Policy.

Esty, D., & Winston, A. (2006). *Green to Gold: How Smart Companies Use Environmental Strategy to Innovate, Create Value, and Build Competitive Advantage*. New Haven, CT: Yale University Press.

Eurobarometer. (2011). *Future of transport. Analytical report. Flash EB Series #312*. Retrieved December 12, 2013, from http://ec.europa.eu/public_opinion/flash/fl_312_en.pdf

European Commission. (2006). *EU-Russia Energy Dialog: Eight progress report*. Retrieved April 15, 2014, from http://ec.europa.eu/energy/russia/joint_progress/doc/progress8_en.pdf

European Commission. (2009). *Natura 2000 barometer - December 2008*. Natura 2000. European Commission DG ENV Nature Newletter, 8-9.

European Commission. (2010). *Europe in figures - Eurostat yearbook 2010*. Luxembourg: Publications Office of the European Union.

European Commission. (2013b). *Renewable Energy Progress Report*. Retrieved April 16, 2014, at http://eur-lex.europa.eu/legal-content/EN/TXT/PDF/?uri=CELEX:52013DC0175&from=EN

European Commission. (2014). *Guidelines on State aid for environmental protection and energy 2014-2020*. Retrieved May 11, 2014 at http://ec.europa.eu/competition/sectors/energy/eeag_en.pdf

European Commission. (2014a). *European Commission*/Trade/Russia. Retrieved April 22, 2014, from http://trade.ec.europa.eu/doclib/docs/2006/september/tradoc_111720.pdf

European Cyclists' Federation (ECF). (2013). *Calculating the economic benefits of cycling in EU-27*. Retrieved February 10, 2014, from www.ecf.com

European Environment Agency (EEA). (2006). *Urban sprawl in Europe. "The ignored challenge" Report*. Copenhagen. Retrieved June 12, 2012, from www.eea.europa.eu/publications/eea_report_2006_10

European Environment Agency (EEA). (2010). *The European environment state and outlook 2010. Urban environment*. Copenhagen, Denmark: Publications Office of the European Union. Retrieved March 10, 2011, from www.europa.eu

European Photovoltaic Industry Association (EPIA). (2014) *2013: Record-year for solar photovoltaics, accelerating market globalisation*. Retrieved June 11, 2014, from http://www.epia.org/fileadmin/user_upload/Press_Releases/Global_Market_Outlook_2014_Press_Release.pdf

European Union. (2014a). *European Union/External Service/Russia*. Retrieved April 22, 2014, from http://eeas.europa.eu/russia/index_en.htm

European Union. (2014b). *European Union/Trade in Goods with Russia*. Retrieved April 27, 2014, from http://trade.ec.europa.eu/doclib/docs/2006/september/tradoc_113440.pdf

European Wind Energy Association (EWEA). (2009a). *Global Statistics-US, China & Spain Lead World Wind Power Market in 2007*. Retrieved 7 January, 2010, from http://www.ewea.org/index.php?id=1487

European Wind Energy Association (EWEA). (2009b). *Legal framework for wind energy*. Retrieved November 24, 2009, from http://www.ewea.org/index.php?id=197

EWEA. (2003). *Wind force 12*. Brussels: EWEA.

Falkner, R. (2003). Private Environmental Governance and International Relations: Exploring the Links. *Global Environmental Politics*, *3*(2), 72–87. doi:10.1162/152638003322068227

Farley, T. (2007). The Cell-Phone Revolution. *American Heritage*, *22*(3), 8–19.

Farrell, B., & Ward, L. T. (2005). Seven Steps towards Sustainability: Tourism in the Context of New Knowledge. *Journal of Sustainable Tourism*, *13*(2), 109–122. doi:10.1080/09669580508668481

Fatherley, R. W., & MacFarland, D. T. (2014). *The birth of top 40 radio: The Storz stations' revolution of the 1950s and 1960s*. Jefferson, NC: MacFarland & Co.

Fatusi, A. O., & Hindin, M. J. (2010). Adolescents and youth in developing countries: Health and development issues in context. *Journal of Adolescence*, *33*(4), 499–508. doi:10.1016/j.adolescence.2010.05.019 PMID:20598362

Febvre, L., & Martin, H. (1976). *The coming of the book: the impact of printing 1450-1800*. London: New Left Books.

Feinstein, C. D., Orans, R., & Chapel, S. W. (1997). The Distributed Utility: A New Electric Utility Planning and Pricing Paradigm. *Annual Review of Energy and the Environment*, *22*(1), 155–185. doi:10.1146/annurev.energy.22.1.155

Fernando, R. (2012). Sustainable globalization and implications for strategic corporate and national sustainability. *Corporate Governance*, *12*(4), 579–589. doi:10.1108/14720701211267883

Ferrer, F., Armengol, C., Belvis, E., Massot, M., & Pàmies, J. (2010). *Evaluación del Programa Pizarra Digital en Aragón*. Barcelona, Spain: Universidad Autónoma de Barcelona.

Fidler, C. (2010). Increasing the Sustinability of a Resource Development: Aboriginal Engagement and Negotiated Agreements. *Environment, Development and Sustainability*, *12*(2), 233–244. doi:10.1007/s10668-009-9191-6

Filho, W. (2000). Dealing with misconseptions on the concept of sustainability. *International Journal of Sustainability in Higher Education*, *1*(1), 9–19. doi:10.1108/1467630010307066

Fisch, S. M. (2004). *Children's learning from educational television: Sesame Street and beyond*. New York: Routledge.

Fisch, S. M., Truglio, R. T., & Cole, C. F. (1999). The impact of Sesame Street on preschool children: A review and synthesis of 30 years' research. *Media Psychology*, *1*(2), 165–190. doi:10.1207/s1532785xmep0102_5

Fitzpatrick, P., Fonseca, A., & McAllister, M. L. (2011). From the Whitehourse Mining Initiative Towards Sustinable Mining: Lessons Learned. *Journal of Cleaner Production, 19*(4), 376–384. doi:10.1016/j.jclepro.2010.10.013

Flachsland, C., Marschinski, R., & Edenhofer, O. (2009). To link or not to link: Benefits and disadvantages of linking cap-and-trade systems. *Climate Policy, 9*(4), 358–372. doi:10.3763/cpol.2009.0626

Fleck, A. (1958). Technology and its social consequences. In C. Singer, E.J. Holmyard, A.R. Hall & T.I. Williams (Eds.) A History of Technology. Volume V: The Late Nineteenth Century, c. 1850 to c. 1900 (pp. 814-841). Oxford, UK: Clarendon.

Floyd, J., & Marsh, D. (1998). Sun Records: An oral history. New York: Avon.

Flynn, B. C. (1996). Healthy cities: Toward worldwide health promotion. *Annual Review of Public Health, 17*(1), 299–309. doi:10.1146/annurev.pu.17.050196.001503 PMID:8724229

Forbes, B. D. (2003). Mickey Mouse as icon: Taking popular culture seriously. *Word & World, 23*(3), 242–252.

Forest, M., Konijnendijk, C. C., & Randrup, T. B. (Eds.). (1999). *COST action E12 research and development in urbanforestry in Europe*. Luxembourg: Office for Official Publications of the European Communities.

Forgacs, D. (1992). Disney animation and the business of childhood. *Screen, 33*(4), 361–374. doi:10.1093/screen/33.4.361

Freiberger, P., & Swaine, M. (2000). *Fire in the valley: The making of the personal computer*. New York, NY: McGraw-Hill.

Friedman, T. L. (2005). *The World is Flat: A Brief History of the Twenty-First Century*. New York: Farrar, Straus and Giroux.

Frumkin, H. (2009). Healthy Communities, Green Communities. In S. Piedmont-Palladino & T. Mennel (Eds.), *Green Community* (pp. 118–125). APA Planners Press.

Fuller, R. A., Irvine, K. N., Devine-Wright, P., Warren, P. H., & Gaston, K. J. (2007). Psychological benefits of greenspace increase with biodiversity. *Biology Letters, 3*(4), 390–394.

Fullerton, L., McGettigan, K., & Stephens, S. (2010). Integrating Management and Marketing Strategies at Heritage Sites. *International Journal of Culture, Tourism, and Hospitality Research, 4*(2), 108–117. doi:10.1108/17506181011045181

Fyall, A., & Rakic, T. (2006). The Future Market for WHS. In A. Leask & A. Fyall (Eds.), *Managing World Heritage Sites*. New York: Butterworth Heinemann.

Galbraith, J. K., & Hale, T. (2004). *Income distribution and the information technology bubble. University of Texas Inequality Project Working Paper 27, January 14, 2004*. Retrieved April 11, 2010, from University of Texas website: http://utip.gov.utexas.edu/papers/utip_27.pdf

Galla, A. (Ed.). (2012). *World Heritage: Benefits Beyond Borders*. Cambridge, UK: Cambridge University Press. doi:10.1017/CBO9781139567657

Gallivan, M., & Srite, M. (2005). Information technology and culture: Identifying fragmentary and holistic perspectives of culture. *Information and Organization, 15*(4), 295–338. doi:10.1016/j.infoandorg.2005.02.005

Gant, R., Robinson, G., & Faza, S. (2011). Land-use change in the 'edgelands': Policies and pressures in London's rural–urban fringe. *Land Use Policy, 28*(1), 266–279.

García-Valcárcel, A. (2008). *Investigación y Tecnologías de la información y Comunicación al servicio de la Innovación Educativa*. Salamanca, Spain: Universidad de Salamanca.

García-Valcárcel, A., & Tejedor, F. J. (2009). Evaluación de medios didácticos y proyectos TIC. In J. De Pablos (Ed.), *Tecnología Educativa: La formación del profesorado en la era de Internet* (pp. 271–302). Málaga, Spain: Aljibe.

Gareis, R., Huemann, M., & Martinuzzi, A. (2009). *Relating sustainable development and project management.* Paper presented at the IRNOP 2009. Berlin, Germany.

Gareis, R., Huemann, M., & Martinuzzi, R.-A. with the assistance of Weninger, C., & Sedlacko, M. (2013). Project Management & Sustainable Development Principles. Newton Square, PA: Project Management Institute.

Gareis, R. (2013). Re-thinking project initiation and project management by considering principles of sustainable development. In G. Silvius & J. Tharp (Eds.), *Sustainability Integration for Effective Project Management* (pp. 129–143). Hershey, PA: IGI Global. doi:10.4018/978-1-4666-4177-8.ch008

Gareis, R., Huemann, M., & Martinuzzi, A. (2011). What can project management learn from considering sustainability principles? In *Project Perspectives* (Vol. XXXIII, pp. 60–65). Amsterdam, The Netherlands: International Project Management Association.

Garofalo, R. (1994). Culture versus Commerce: The Marketing of Black Popular Music. *Public Culture*, *7*(1), 275–288. doi:10.1215/08992363-7-1-275

Garrard, J., Rose, G., & Lo, S. (2008). Promoting transportation cycling for women: The role of bicycle Infrastructure. *Preventive Medicine*, *46*(1), 55–59. doi:10.1016/j.ypmed.2007.07.010 PMID:17698185

Gatersleben, B., & Haddad, H. (2010). Who is the typical bicyclist? *Transportation Research Part F: Traffic Psychology and Behaviour*, *13*(1), 41–48. doi:10.1016/j.trf.2009.10.003

Gatersleben, B., & Uzzell, D. (2002). Sustainable transport and quality of life. In W. R. Black & P. Nijkamp (Eds.), *Social Change and Sustainable Transport* (pp. 135–140). Bloomington, IN: Indiana University Press.

Geerlings, H., Shiftan, Y., & Stead, D. (2012). The Complex Challenge of Transitions Towards sustainable Mobility: An introduction. In Geerlings, Shiftan, & Stead (Eds.), Transition towards Sustainable Mobility, (pp.1-9). Ashgate.

Gemeinsame Landesplanung Berlin und Brandenburg. (2001). *Regionalparks in Brandenburg und Berlin*. Potsdam: Ministerium für Landwirtschaft. Umweltschutz und Raumordnung des Landes Brandenburg/Senatsverwaltung für Stadtentwicklung des Landes Berlin.

George, C. (1999). Testing for sustainable development through environmental assessment. *Environmental Impact Assessment Review*, *19*(2), 175–200. doi:10.1016/S0195-9255(98)00038-9

Georgi, J. N., & Dimitriou, D. (2010). The contribution of urban green spaces to the improvement of environment in cities: Case study of Chania, Greece. *Building and Environment*, *45*(6), 1401–1414.

Geothermal Energy Association (GEA). (2009). *Geothermal 101: Basics of Geothermal Energy Production and Use*. Washington, D.C.: Geothermal Energy Association.

Geothermal Energy Association (GEA). (2013). *2013 Geothermal Power: International Market Overview*. Retrieved June 11, 2014, from http://geo-energy.org/events/2013%20International%20Report%20Final.pdf

Gerald, S. (2012). Why we disagree about climate change: A different viewpoint. *Energy & Environment*, *23*(8), 76–95.

Gibb, A. (2004). Safety, health, and environment. In P. W. G. Morris & J. K. Pinto (Eds.), *The Wiley Guide to Managing Projects*. Hoboken, NJ: John Wiley & Sons, Inc. doi:10.1002/9780470172391.ch22

Gibson, R. B. (2001). *Specification of sustainability-based environmental assessment decision criteria and implications for determining "significance" in environmental assessment. University of Waterloo*. Canada: Canadian Environmental Assessment Agency.

Gibson, R. B. (2006). Sustainability assessment: Basic components of a practical approach. *Impact Assessment and Project Appraisal*, *24*(3), 170–182. doi:10.3152/147154606781765147

Gilbert, R., Stevenson, D., Girardet, H., & Stern, R. (Eds.). (1996). *Making Cities Work: The Role of Local Authorities in the Urban Environment*. London, UK: Earthscan Publications Ltd.

Gill, N., Waitt, G., & Head, L. (2009). Local engagements with urban bushland: Moving beyond bounded practice for urban biodiversity management. *Landscape and Urban Planning*, *93*(3-4), 184–193.

Givoni, B. (1998). *Climate consideration in building and urban design*. New York, NY: Van Nostrand Reinhold.

Glaas, E., & Juhola, S. (2013). New levels of climate adaptation policy: Analysing the institutional interplay in the Baltic Sea Region. *Sustainability*, *1*(0), 56–122.

Global Wind Enery Council (GWEC). (2014). *Global Wind Report Annual Market Update 2013*. Retrieved June 11, 2014, from http://www.gwec.net/wp-content/uploads/2014/04/GWEC-Global-Wind-Report_9-April-2014.pdf

Godzimirski, J. (2009). *Russian Energy Strategy 2030*. Norwegian Institute of international Affairs. Retrieved May 5, 2014, from http://www.fni.no/russcasp/Godzimirski_2009_03_25_Russian_energy_sector_2030.pdf

Goedknegt, D. (2012). Sustainability in Project Management: A case study at University of Applied Sciences Utrecht. *PM World Journal, I*(IV).

Goedknegt, D., & Silvius, A. J. G. (2012). The implementation of sustainability principles in project management. In *Proceedings of the 26th IPMA World Congress* (pp 875-882). Amsterdam, The Netherlands: International Project Management Association.

Goldman, E. (1960). *The crucial decade and after: America from 1945 to 1960*. New York: Vintage Books.

Goldthau, A. (2008a). Russia's energy weapon. *EU Energy Policy Blog February 17*. Retrieved May 1, 2014, from http://www.energypolicyblog.com/?p=118

Goldthau, A. (2008b). *Resurgent Russia? Rethinking Energy Inc.: Five Myths about the "Energy Superpower."* Hoover Institution. Retrieved May 1, 2014, from http://www.hoover.org/publications/policyreview/14931716.html

Gordon, A., Simondson, D., White, M., Moilanen, A., & Bekessy, S. (2009). Integrating conservation planning and landuse planning in urban landscapes. *Landscape and Urban Planning*, *91*(4), 183–194.

Gorham, R. (2002). Car dependence as a social problem: A critical essay on the existing literature and future needs. In W. R. Black & P. Nijkam (Eds.), *Social Change and Sustainable Transport* (pp. 107–116). Bloomington, IN: Indiana University Press.

Görkem, O., & Öztürk, Y. (2014). Gastronomic Reflections of Cittaslow Movement on Local Cuisine: The Case Study of Seferihisar (İzmir, Turkey). *Turizam*, *18*(1), 11–21.

Gotting-Frosinki, J., & Grigoleit, B. (Eds.). (2000). *Regionalparks in Brandenburg and Berlin – Strategies for Sustainable Development in the Metropolitan Area*. Berlin, Germany: Saladruck.

Götz, R. (2008). *Managing European-Russian energy independence*. Retrieved September 28, 2013, from http://www.swp-berlin.org/fileadmin/contents/products/arbeitspapiere/Oslo_Dec_13__ks.pdf

Government of Argentina. (2010). *Conectar Igualdad*. Retrieved May 12, 2014, from http://www.conectar-igualdad.gob.ar

Government, A. C. T. (2014). Drinking fountains with refill stations locations. Retrieved May 7, 2014, from http://www.timetotalk.act.gov.au/consultations/?engagement=drinking-fountains-with-refill-stations-locations

Grahn, P. (1994). Green structures—the importance for health of nature areas and parks. *European Regional Planning*, *56*, 89–112.

Greeson, L. E., & Williams, R. A. (1986). Social Implications of Music Videos for Youth: An Analysis of the Content and Effects of MTV. *Youth & Society*, *18*(2), 177–189. doi:10.1177/0044118X86018002005

Gregersen, H. M., Lundgren, A. L., & White, T. A. (1994). Improving project management for sustainable development: Policy Brief No.7. Madison, WI: Midwest Universities Consortium for International Activities, Inc. (MUCIA).

Gregersen, H., & Contreras, A. (1992). *Economic Assessment of Forestry Project Impacts*. Rome, Italy: Food and Agriculture Organization of the United Nations.

Griffiths, K. (2007, February). *Project sustainability management in infrastructure projects*. Paper presented at the 2nd International Conference on Sustainability Engineering and Science. Auckland, New Zealand.

Grigoroudis, E., Kouikoglou, V. S., & Phillis, Y. A. (2012). Approaches for measuring sustainability. In P. Olla (Ed.), *Global sustainable development and renewable energy systems* (pp. 101–130). Hersey, PA: IGI Global. doi:10.4018/978-1-4666-1625-7.ch006

Grigoroudis, E., Kouikoglou, V. S., & Phillis, Y. A. (2013a). A fuzzy paradigm for the sustainability evaluation of energy systems. In F. Cavallaro (Ed.), *Assessment and simulation tools for sustainable energy systems: Methodology and applications* (pp. 205–224). New York, NY: Springer. doi:10.1007/978-1-4471-5143-2_10

Grigoroudis, E., Kouikoglou, V. S., & Phillis, Y. A. (2013b). SAFE 2013: Sustainability of countries updated. *Ecological Indicators*, *38*, 61–66. doi:10.1016/j.ecolind.2013.10.022

Grimason, A. M., Davison, K., Tembo, K. C., Jabu, G. C., & Jackson, M. H. (2000). Problems associated with the use of pit latrines in Blantyre, Republic of Malawi. *The Journal of the Royal Society for the Promotion of Health*, *120*(3), 175–182. doi:10.1177/146642400012000307 PMID:11077806

Groeber, M. (2010). *IBM EduQuest*. Retrieved April 10, 2010, from http://www.mgroeber.de/nathan/devices/eduquest.html

Groholt, B., Ekeberg, O., & Haldorsen, T. (2006). Adolescent suicide attempters: What predicts future suicidal acts? *Suicide & Life-Threatening Behavior*, *36*(6), 638–650. doi:10.1521/suli.2006.36.6.638 PMID:17250468

Gromov, A. (2009). *Energy Strategy of Russia for the year 2030: Approaches, priorities and reference points*. Retrieved May 5, 2014, from http://www.energystrategy.ru/ab_ins/source/Gromov_MGIMO-23.10.09.ppt

Gromov, A. (2009). *Russian energy strategy for the period up to 2030: the Way to the innovative energy development*. Retrieved May 5, 2014, from http://www.iea.org/work/2008/neet_russia/Gromov.pdf

Gruen, M. (2006). Innovative recruitment and indoctrination tactics by extremists: Video games, hip-hop, and the world wide web. In James Forest (Ed.) The making of a terrorist: Recruitment, training, and root causes; Vol. 1: Recruitment. 4-17. Westport, CT: Praeger.

Grundy, T. (1998). Strategy implementation and project management. *International Journal of Project Management*, *16*(1), 43–50. doi:10.1016/S0263-7863(97)00016-1

Gudes, O., Yigitcanlar, T., & Pathak, V. (2009, March). *A community health support system for the planning of healthy cities*. Paper presented at the Postgraduate Infrastructure Conference. Brisbane, Australia: Queensland University of Technology.

Gudes, O., Kendall, E., Yigitcanlar, T., Han, J., & Pathak, V. (2012). Developing a competitive city through healthy decision-making City Competitiveness and Improving Urban Subsystems: Technologies and Applications. In M. Bulu (Ed.), *City Competitiveness and Improving Urban Subsystems: Technologies and Applications* (pp. 107–121). Hershey, PA: IGI Global. doi:10.4018/978-1-61350-174-0.ch006

Gudes, O., Kendall, E., Yigitcanlar, T., Pathak, V., & Baum, S. (2010). Rethinking health planning: A framework for organising information to underpin collaborative health planning. *Health Information Management Journal*, *39*(2), 18–29. PMID:20577020

Guerin, H. (2000). Marketing: Complement or Compromise. In N. Buttimer, C. Rynee, & H. Guerin (Eds.), *The Heritage of Ireland*. Cork, Ireland: The Collins Press.

Guerrant, R. L., Hughes, J. M., Lima, N. L., & Crane, J. (1991). Diarrhea in Developed and Developing Countries: Magnitude, Special Settings, and Etiologies. *Reviews of Infectious Diseases*, *12*(Supplement 1), S41–S50. doi:10.1093/clinids/12.Supplement_1.S41 PMID:2406855

Guralnick, P. (1995). *Last train to Memphis: The rise of Elvis Presley*. New York: Little, Brown and Co.

Gwatkin, D. R. (2003). How well do health programmes reach the poor? *Lancet*, *361*(9357), 540–541. doi:10.1016/S0140-6736(03)12558-5 PMID:12598134

Haddow, K. H. (2013). Consultation, the Way Forward. *Journal of Energy & Natural Resources Law*, *31*(1), 81–91.

Hadfield, A. (2008). EU–Russia Energy Relations: Aggregation and Aggravation. *Journal of Contemporary European Studies*, *16*(2), 231–248. doi:10.1080/14782800802309953

Hall, O., & Scrase, J. (1998). Will biomass be the environmentally friendly fuel of the future? *Biomass and Bioenergy*, *15*(4-5), 357–367. doi:10.1016/S0961-9534(98)00030-0

Hall, R. (2013). Diamond Mining in Canada's Northwest Territories: A Colonial Continuity. *Antipode*, *45*(2), 376–393. doi:10.1111/j.1467-8330.2012.01012.x

Hamel, G. (2000). *Leading the Revolution*. Boston, MA: Harvard Business School Press.

Hamel, G., & Breen, B. (2007). *The Future of Management*. Boston, MA: Harvard Business School Press.

Han, J. H., & Lee, S. H. (2013). Planning ubiquitous cities for social inclusion. *International Journal of Knowledge-Based Development*, *4*(2), 157–172. doi:10.1504/IJKBD.2013.054092

Han, J. H., Sunderland, N., Kendall, E., Gudes, O., & Henniker, G. (2010). The need for an equitable approach to e-health: Spatial variation in internet accessibility, chronic disease and disadvantage. *Health Information Management Journal*, *39*(2), 30–36. PMID:20577021

Hanley, J. G. (2007). Public Health, London's Levels and the Politics of Taxation, 1840-1860. *Social History of Medicine*, *20*(1), 21–38. doi:10.1093/shm/hkl084

Hansen, U., & Schrader, U. (1997). A Modern Model of Consumption for a Sustainable Society. *Journal of Consumer Policy*, *20*(4), 443–468. doi:10.1023/A:1006842517219

Hanson, S. (Ed.). (1995). *The Geography of Urban Transportation*. New York: Guilford Press.

Hardy, I. R. (1996). The Evolution of ARPANET Email. Thesis, Department of History, University of California, Berkeley, CA.

Harmaakorpi, V. (2009). Sustainable innovation: What is it? Estonia, Latvia, Lithuania. Poland: Baltic Rim Economies.

Harris, J., & Nelson, J. (1993). Monitoring Tourism from a Whole Economy Perspective: A Case from Indonesia. In J. Nelson, R. Butler, & G. Wall (Eds.), *Tourism and Sustainable Development: Monitoring, Planning and Managing* (pp. 179–196). Waterloo, Canada: Department of Geography Publications Series, University of Waterloo.

Hart, S. (1997). Beyond Greening: Strategies for a sustainable world. *Harvard Business Review*, *1997*(January-February), Retrieved from https://hbr.org/1997/01/beyond-greening-strategies-for-a-sustainable-world/ar/1

Hartz, A. (2006). Der Regionalpark Saar – Zwischenbilanz, Projekte, Masterplan. In Ministerium für Umwelt des Saarlandes (MfU), Akademie für Raumforschung und Landesplanung (ARL), & LAG-Hessen/Rheinland-Pfalz/Saarland (Eds.), Kooperation als Erfolgsfaktor für Regionen im Wandel (pp. 42-45). Saarbrücken.

Hassan, S. (2000). Determinants of Marketing Competitiveness in an Environmentally Sustainable Tourism Industry. *Journal of Travel Research*, *38*(3), 239–245. doi:10.1177/004728750003800305

Hasse, J. E., & Lathrop, R. G. (2003). Land resource impact indicators of urban sprawl. *Applied Geography (Sevenoaks, England)*, *23*(2-3), 159–175.

Hauben, M., & Hauben, R. (1997). *Netizens: On the history and impact of Usenet and the Internet*. Hoboken, NJ: Wiley-IEEE.

Haufler, V. (2001). *A Public Role for the Private Sector: Industry Self-regulation*. Washington, DC: Carnegie Endowment for International Peace.

Haugan, G. (2012). *The New Triple Constraints for Sustainable Projects, Programs, and Portfolios*. Boca Raton, FL: CRC Press. doi:10.1201/b12271

Hawaii Clean Energy Initiative (HCEI). (2009). *How can Oahu reach 70% clean energy?: Hawaii Powered*. Hawaii Clean Energy Initiative, and Booz Allen Hamilton.

Hawken, P. (2007). *Blessed Unrest: How the Largest Movement in the World Came into Being and Why No One Saw It Coming*. New York, NY: Viking/Penguin Group.

Haywood, M. (1990). Revisiting and Implementing the Marketing Concept as It Applies to Tourism. *Tourism Management*, *11*(3), 195–206. doi:10.1016/0261-5177(90)90042-8

Healthy Cities Illawarra. (2010). *Working with the community for a healthier, safer, greener and more caring Illawarra. Wollongong: Illawarra city council.* Retrieved October 10, 2010, from http://www.healthycitiesill.org.au/contactus.htm

Hede, A. (2007). World Heritage listing and the Evolving Issues Related to Tourism and Heritage: Cases from Australia and New Zealand. *Journal of Heritage Tourism*, *2*(3), 133–144. doi:10.2167/jht055.0

Heino, R. (2000). New sports: What is so punk about snowboarding? *Journal of Sport and Social Issues*, *24*(2), 176–191. doi:10.1177/0193723500242005

Held, D., McGrew, A. G., Goldblatt, D., & Perraton, J. (1999). *Global Transformations: Politics, Economics and Culture*. London: Polity Press.

Helm, D. (2007). *The Russian dimension and Europe's external energy policy*. University of Oxford. Retrieved May 12, 2014, at http://www.dieterhelm.co.uk/node/655

Herazo, B., Lizarralde, G., & Paquin, R. (2012). Sustainable development in the building sector: A Canadian case study on the alignment of strategic and tactical management. *Project Management Journal*, *43*(2), 84–100. doi:10.1002/pmj.21258

Herguner, B. (2012). Local Administrative Reforms in Turkey and the Philippines with regard to Agenda21: Profiling Contexts, Parallelisms, and Contrasts. *International Journal of Business and Social Science*, *3*(19), 107–116.

Hernández, I., & Calcagno, S. (2003). *Los pueblos indígenas y la Sociedad de la Información en América Latina y el Caribe*. Santiago de Chile, Chile: CEPAL.

Heuermann, K., & Chhabra, D. (2014). The Darker Side of Dark Tourism: An Authenticity Perspective. *Tourism Analysis*, *19*(2), 213–225. doi:10.3727/108354214X13963557455766

Hirt, S., & Kovachev, A. (2006). The changing spatial structure of post-socialist Sofia. In S. Tsenkova & Z. Nedović-Budić (Eds.), *The Urban Mosaic of Post-Socialist Europe, Contributions to Economics, Part II* (pp. 113–130). Heidelberg, Germany & New York, NY: Physica-Verlag.

Hochschild, A. R. (1997). *The Time Bind. When Works Becomes Home and Home Becomes Work*. New York: Metropolitan Books.

Holland, L., & Boon Foo, Y. (2003). Differences in environmental reporting practices in the UK and the US: The legal and regulatory context. *The British Accounting Review*, *35*(1), 1–18. doi:10.1016/S0890-8389(02)00127-0

Holltzman, Y. (2013). A strategy of innovation through the development of a portfolio of innovation capabilities. *Journal of Management Development*, *33*(1), 24–31. doi:10.1108/JMD-11-2013-0138

Holtz, G., Brugnach, M., & Pahl-Wostl, C. (2008). Specifying 'regime': A framework for defining and describing regimes in transition research. *Technological Forecasting and Social Change*, *75*(5), 623–643. doi:10.1016/j.techfore.2007.02.010

Holzmann, G. J., & Pehrson, P. (1994). *The early history of data networks*. Hoboken, NJ: Wiley-IEEE.

Hopwood, B., Mellor, M., & O'Brien, G. (2005). Sustainable Development: Mapping Different Approaches. *Sustainable Development*, *13*(1), 38–52. doi:10.1002/sd.244

Horwitz, J. (2006). *Does MTV really matter anymore*? Retrieved March 29, 2010, from: http://www.ilounge.com/index.php/backstage/comments/does-mtv-really-matter-any-more

Hughes, T. P. (2004). *Human-built world: How to think about technology and culture*. Chicago, IL: The University of Chicago.

Humphreys, D. (2006). *Logjam: Deforestation and the Crisis of Global Governance*. London: Earthscan.

Huston, A. C., Donnerstein, E., Fairchild, H., Feshbach, N. D., Katz, P. A., Murray, J. P., & Zuckerman, D. et al. (1992). *Big world, small screen: The role of television in American society*. Lincoln, NE: University of Nebraska Press.

IAEA. (2005). *Energy indicators for sustainable development: Guidelines and methodologies*. Vienna: International Atomic Energy Agency.

IAEA. (2005). *Energy indicators for sustainable development: Guidelines and methodologies*. Vienna: International Atomic Energy Agency. Retrieved July 27, 2014, from http://www-pub.iaea.org/MTCD/ publications/PDF/Pub1222_web.pdf

Iannucci, J. (1994). *The Distributed Utility: Is This the Future?* Paper presented at the 5th National Conference on Integrated Resource Planning. Washington, D.C.

Ianoş, I. (2004). *Dinamica urbană. Aplicaţii la oraşul şi sistemul urban românesc*. Bucureşti: Tehnică.

Ianoş, I., Pumain, D., & Racine, J. B. (Eds.). (2000). *Integrated Urban Systems and Sustainability of Urban Life*. Bucureşti, Romania: Editura Tehnică.

Iatridis, D. S. (1990). Cuba's Health Care Policy: Prevention and Active Community Participation. *Social Work*, *35*(1), 29–35. PMID:2315760

IEA. (2002). *World energy outlook: Energy and poverty*. Paris: International Energy Agency. Retrieved July 31, 2012, from http://www.iea.org//textbase/nppdf/free/2000/weo2002.pdf

IEA. (2007). *Key energy statistics 2007*. Paris: International Energy Agency.

IEA. (2011c). *Energy statistics of Non-OECD countries*. Paris: International Energy Agency.

IEA. (2011d). *Energy statistics of OECD countries*. Paris: International Energy Agency.

IHA. (2003). *World Atlas & Industry Guide*. United Kingdom: The International Journal Hydropower & Dams.

Imura, H. (2010). Eco-Cities: Re-Examining Concepts and Approaches. In L. L. Fook & C. Gang (Eds.), *Towards a Liveable and Sustainable Urban Environment: Eco-Cities in East Asia*. Singapore: World Scientific. doi:10.1142/9789814287777_0002

Inglis, I. (2000). The Beatles are coming! Conjecture and conviction in the myth of Kennedy, America, and the Beatles. *Popular Music and Society*, *24*(2), 93–108. doi:10.1080/03007760008591769

Ingram, J. C., & Wilkie, D. (2008). Governance of the Global Carbon Market: Does Scale Matter? WCS Working Paper Series. In K. Redford & C. Grippo (Eds.), *WCS Working Paper 36, Protected Areas, Governance and Scale*. Bronx, NY: Wildlife Conservation Society.

Institute of Economic Strategy. (2014). Retrieved May 7, 2014, from http://www.energystrategy.ru/ - in Russian.

Institute of Energy Systems. (2014) Retrieved May 7, 2014, from http://sei.irk.ru/index.php - in Russian.

Intergraph. (2006). P.A.T.Z.-Zona Aglomeratiei Urbane si Zona Metropolitana ale Municipiului Bucuresti.

International Council on Mining and Metals. (2003). *10 Principles*. London, UK: International Council on Mining and Metals. Retrieved August 6, 2012, from http://liveassets.iucn.getunik.net/downloads/minicmmstat.pdf

International Energy Agency (IEA). (2008). *Energy Technology Perspectives: Scenarios & Strategies to 2050*. Paris, France: International Energy Agency.

International Energy Agency Implementing Agreement on Ocean Energy Systems (IEA-OES). (2007). Annual Report 2007. Retrieved June 13, 2014 from http://www.oreg.ca/docs/IEA_docs/IEA_Annual_Report_2007.pdf

International Institute for Sustainable Development (IISD) Reporting Services. (N.D.). *GEF STAP Considers REDD, Forest Conservation and Sustainable Forest Management*. Retrieved October 1, 2010, from http://climate-l.org/news/gef-stap-considers-redd-forest-conservation-and-sustainable-forest-management/

International Labor Organization. (1997). 169th Convention: Indigenous and tribal people. Retrieved April 30, 2010, from http://www.ilo.org/indigenous/Resources/Publications/lang--en/docName-- WCMS_100897/index.htm

International Organization for Standardization. (2010). *ISO 26000, Guidance on Social Responsibility*. Geneva, Switzerland: International Organization for Standardization.

International Organization for Standardization. (2012). *ISO 21500:2012, Guidance on Project Management*. Geneva, Switzerland: International Organization for Standardization.

Internet World Stats. (2010). *Internet Usage Statistics: The Internet Big Picture-World Internet Users and Population Stats*. Retrieved April 10, 2010, from http://www.wdvl.com/Internet/History/

Iojă, I. C., Pătroescu, M., Vânău, G., & Iojă, A. (2007). Noise pollution in Bucharest urban parks. Paper presented at the SECOTOX Conference and the International Conference on Environemental Management, Engineering, Planning and Economics (CEMEPE), Salonic.

Iojă, I. C., Pătroescu, M., Rozylowicz, L., Popescu, D. V., Vergheleţ, M., Zotta, M. I., & Felciuc, M. (2010). The efficacy of Romania's protected areas network in conserving biodiversity. *Biological Conservation*, *143*(11), 2468–2476.

Iržikevičius, R. (2014). *Europe discusses an Energy Union*. Retrieved on May 10, 2014, from http://www.lithuaniatribune.com/67212/europe-discusses-an-energy-union-201467212/

Isfort, ANAV-ASSTRA. (2013). *10° Rapporto sulla mobilità in Italia*. Retrieved from www.isfort.it

Isfort. (2014). *La domanda di mobilità degli italiani*. Retrieved from www.isfort.it

Ispra, Istituto Superiore per la Protezione e la Ricerca Ambientale. (2013). *Qualità dell'ambiente urbano. VII rapporto*. Retrieved from www.isprambiente.it

Israel, B. A., Schulz, A. J., Parker, E., & Becker, A. B. (2001). Community-based participatory research: Policy recommendations for promoting a partnership approach in health research. *Education for Health*, *14*(2), 182–197. doi:10.1080/13576280110051055 PMID:14742017

Istat, Istituto Nazionale di Statistica. (2014). *Focus Mobilità urbana*. Retrieved from www.istat.it

Italia, A. (2007). *Urban ecosystem Europe. An integrated assessment on the sustainability of 32 European cities*. Retrieved March 10, 2012, from www.ambienteitalia.it

IUCN. (1994). *Guidelines for Protected Area Management Categories*. Gland, Switzerland: IUCN.

Jaafari, A. (2007). Thinking of sustainability as a dimension of managerial competency. *PM World Today*, *IX*(IX).

Jacobs, A. B. (1980). *Making City Planning Work*. Chicago, IL: American Planning Association.

Jaffe, J., & Stavins, R. N. (2007). *Linking Tradable Permit Systems for Greenhouse Gas Emissions: Opportunities, Implications, and Challenges. Report prepared for the International Emissions Trading Association*. IETA.

Jamerozy, U. (2007). Marketing of Tourism: A Paradigm Shift towards Sustainability. *International Journal of Culture. Tourism and Hospitality Research*, *1*(2), 117–130.

James, P., Tzoulas, K., Adams, M. D., Barber, A., Box, J., Breuste, J., & Ward Thompsons, C. et al. (2009). Towards an integrated understanding of green space in the European built environment. *Urban Forestry & Urban Greening*, *8*(2), 65–75.

Jansen, B. J. (1998). The graphical user interface. *ACM SIGCHI Bulletin*, *30*(2), 22–26. doi:10.1145/279044.279051

Jeju Special Self-Governing Province. (2009). *Jeju's Mid- and Long-Term Roadmap of New and Renewable Energy Planning*.

Jenkins, H. (2006). *Convergence culture: Where old and new media collide*. New York, NY: NYU press.

Jenkins, H., & Yakovleva, N. (2006). Corporate Social Responsibility in the Mining Industry: Exploring Trends in Social and Environmental Disclosure. *Journal of Cleaner Production*, *14*(3-4), 271–284. doi:10.1016/j.jclepro.2004.10.004

Jenkin, T. A., Webster, J., & McShein, L. (2011). An agenda for 'Green' information technology and systems research. *Information and Organization*, *21*(1), 17–40. doi:10.1016/j.infoandorg.2010.09.003

Jiang, Y. H., & Guo, X. C. (2009). Urban traffic development strategies based on the concept of green transportation. *Journal of Hefei University of Technology*, *7*, 1086–1090.

Jim, C., & Chen, W. (2009). Ecosystem services and valuation of urban forests in China. *Cities (London, England)*, *26*(4), 187–196.

Johnson, J. (2002). A conceptual model for enhancing community competitiveness in the new economy. *Urban Affairs Review*, *37*(6), 763–779. doi:10.1177/107874037006001

Jon, A. P. (1979). The Impact of Sanitary Reform upon American Urban Planning, 1840-1890. *Journal of Social History*, *13*(1), 83–103. doi:10.1353/jsh/13.1.83 PMID:11632375

Jones, P. G., Beebe, S. E., Tohme, J., & Galwey, N. W. (1997). The use of geographical information systems in biodiversity exploration and conservation. *Biodiversity and Conservation*, *6*(7), 947–958.

Jones, P., Hillier, D., Comfort, D., & Eastwood, I. (2005). Sustainable Retailing and Consumerism. *Management Research News*, *28*(1), 34–33. doi:10.1108/01409170510784760

Jordan, A., Wurzel, R., & Zito, A. (2005). The Rise of 'New' Policy Instruments in Comparative Perspectives: Has Governance Eclipsed Government? *Political Studies*, *53*(3), 441–469. doi:10.1111/j.1467-9248.2005.00540.x

Jorgenson, F. (1998). Early fixed-head video recorders. In E. D. Daniel, C. D. Mee, & M. H. Clark (Eds.), *Magnetic Recording: The First 100 Years* (pp. 137–152). Hoboken, NJ: Wiley-IEEE.

Joyce, P., Green, R., & Winch, G. (2006). A new construct for visualizing and designing e-fulfilment systems for quality healthcare delivery. *The TQM Magazine*, *18*(6), 638–651. doi:10.1108/09544780610707129

Jucker, R. (2002). Sustainability? Never heard of it! *International Journal of Sustainability in Higher Education*, *3*(1), 8–18. doi:10.1108/14676370210414146

Junginger, M., & Faaij, A. (2005). *IEA Bioenergy task 40-Country report for the Netherlands*. Paris, France: International Energy Agency.

Kadıköy Municipality. (2013). *Kadıköy Municipality Actions Against Climate Change and Energy Efficiency Operations*.

Kammerud, R., Ceballos, E., Curtis, B., Place, W., & Anderson, B. (1984). Ventilation cooling of residential buildings. *ASHRAE Trans Part 1B*, *90*(1), 226–252.

Kanellos, T., & Valos, M. (2010). *Green Marketing and the Green Consumer: Integrating Environmental Marketing into the Firm's Overall Business Strategy*. Faculty of Business and Law, Deakin University.

Kanudia, A., & Loulou, R. (1999). Advanced bottom-up modelling for national and regional energy planning in response to climate change. *International Journal of Environment and Pollution*, *12*(2/3), 191–216. doi:10.1504/IJEP.1999.002292

Kapp, R. W. Jr. (2014). Clean Water Act (CWA), US. In P. Wexler (Ed.), *Encyclopedia of Toxicology* (3rd ed., pp. 979–981). Oxford: Academic Press. doi:10.1016/B978-0-12-386454-3.00830-7

Katsikas, S., Lopez, J., & Pernul, G. (2008). The challenge for security and privacy services in distributed health settings. *Studies in Health Technology and Informatics*, *134*, 113–125. PMID:18376039

Katz, M. (2005). Internet gurus: Prominent Internet professionals. In *Proceedings of the III Congrés Internacional Comunicació i Realitat, Barcelona* (pp.157-169). Retrieved April 10, 2010, from http://cicr.blanquerna.url.edu/2005/Abstracts/ PDFsComunicacions/vol1/03/Katz_Merav.pdf

Kaufmann, V., Bergman, M. M., & Joice, D. (2004). Motility: Mobility as capital. *International Journal of Urban and Regional Research*, *28*(4), 745–756. doi:10.1111/j.0309-1317.2004.00549.x

Kavanaugh, S., & Rafferty, K. (1997). Ground source heat pumps. Design of Geothermal Systems for Commercial and Institutional Buildings. Atlanta, GA: American Society of heating, Refrigeration and Air-conditioning Engineers, Inc.

Keating, M. (1993). *The Earth Summit's Agenda for Change*. Geneva, Switzerland: Centre for our Common Future.

Keeble, J. J., Topiol, S., & Berkeley, S. (2003). Using Indicators to Measure Sustainability Performance at a Corporate and Project Level. *Journal of Business Ethics*, *44*(2-3), 149–158. doi:10.1023/A:1023343614973

Keeys, L. A. (2012). Emerging Sustainable Development Strategy in Projects: A Theoretical Framework. *PM World Journal, I*(II).

Keeys, L. A., Huemann, M., & Turner, R. (2013). Integrating project strategy for sustainable development: A conceptual framework. In G. Silvius & J. Tharp (Eds.), *Sustainability Integration for Effective Project Management* (pp. 20–38). Hershey, PA: IGI Global. doi:10.4018/978-1-4666-4177-8.ch002

Keith, M. C. (1997). *Voices in the purple haze: Underground radio and the Sixties*. Santa Barbara, CA: Praeger.

Keles, R. (1997). *The common heritage of mankind and the new concepts of responsibility*. Retrieved March 12, 2010, from http://biopolitics.gr/biowp/b-i-o-e-library/sociology/

Kellerman, A. (2012). *Daily Spatial Mobilities. Physical and virtual*. Surrey, UK: Ashgate Publishing Group.

Kelley, I. (2008). *Energy in America*. University of Vermont Press, University Press of New England.

Kemp, D., Bond, C., Franks, D., & Cote, C. (2010). Mining, Water and Human Rights: Making the Connection. *Journal of Cleaner Production*, *18*(15), 1553–1562. doi:10.1016/j.jclepro.2010.06.008

Kent, S. (2001). *The ultimate history of video games: From Pong to Pokémon - the story behind the craze that touched our lives and changed the world*. New York: Three Rivers.

Kenworthy, J., & Laube, F. (1996). Automobile dependence in cities. An international comparison of urban transport and land use patterns with implication for sustainability. *Environmental Impact Assessment Review*, *16*(4-6), 279–308. doi:10.1016/S0195-9255(96)00023-6

Khalfan, A., Roaf, V., Grimes, H., Langford, M., Fairstein, C., Russell, A., & Kiefer, T. (2007). *Manual on the Right to Water and Sanitation*. OHRE, AAAS, SDC and UN-HABITAT.

Khalfan, M. M. A. (2006). Managing Sustainability within Construction Projects. *Journal of Environmental Assessment Policy and Management*, *8*(1), 41–60. doi:10.1142/S1464333206002359

Khan, J. (2004). *Local politics of renewable energy: project planning, siting conflicts and citizen participation*. Lund, Sweden: Lund University.

Kidd, C. D., Orr, R., Abowd, G. D., Atkeson, C. G., Essa, I. A., MacIntyre, B., & Newstetter, W. et al. (1999). The aware home: A living laboratory for ubiquitous computing research. In N. Streitz, J. Siegel, V. Hartkopf, & S. Konomi (Eds.), *Cooperative buildings. Integrating information, organizations, and architecture* (pp. 191–198). Berlin: Springer. doi:10.1007/10705432_17

Kidd, S., Henrich, C. C., Brookmeyer, K. A., Davidson, L., King, R. A., & Shahar, A. (2006). The social context of adolescent suicide attempts: Interactive effects of parent, peer, and school social relations. *Suicide & Life-Threatening Behavior*, *36*(4), 386–395. doi:10.1521/suli.2006.36.4.386 PMID:16978093

Kilbourne, W. (1998). Green Marketing, a Theoretical Perspective. *Journal of Marketing Management*, *14*(6), 641–655.

Kilbourne, W., McDonagh, P., & Prothero, A. (1997). Sustainable Consumption and Quality of Life: A Macromarketing Challenge to the Dominant Social Paradigm. *Journal of Macromarketing*, *17*(2), 4–24. doi:10.1177/027614679701700103

King, D. C. (2005). *World wars and the modern age*. Hoboken, NJ: John Wiley & Sons.

Kipfer, S., & Keil, R. (2002). Toronto Inc? Planning the competitive city in the new Toronto. *Antipode a radical journal of Geography*, *34*(2), 227–264.

Kiron, D., Kruschwitz, N., Reeves, M., & Goh, E. (2013, Winter). The Benefits of Sustainability-Driven Innovation. *MIT Sloan Management Review*, *54*(2), 69–73.

Kirsch, S. (2010). Sustainable Mining. *Dialectical Anthropology*, *34*(1), 87–93. doi:10.1007/s10624-009-9113-x

Kivenzor, G. (2007). Brand Equity Aberrations: Heritage Brand Perception Effects in Russian Markets. *Academy of Marketing Science Review*, *10*, 1–20.

Klotz, L., & Horman, M. (2010). Counterfactual analysis of sustainable project delivery processes. *Journal of Construction Engineering and Management*, *136*(5), 595–605. doi:10.1061/(ASCE)CO.1943-7862.0000148

Kluge, E. H. (2007). Secure e-health: Managing risks to patient health data. *International Journal of Medical Informatics*, *76*(5-6), 402–406. doi:10.1016/j.ijmedinf.2006.09.003 PMID:17084665

Knappett, P. S. K., Escamilla, V., Layton, A., Mckay, L. D., Emch, M., Williams, D. E., & Van Geen, A. et al. (2011). Impact of population and latrines on fecal contamination of ponds in rural Bangladesh. *The Science of the Total Environment*, *409*(17), 3174–3182. doi:10.1016/j.scitotenv.2011.04.043 PMID:21632095

Koch, F. (2006). Housing markets and urban regimes – The case of Warsaw. In F. Eckardt & I. Elander (Eds.), *Urban Governance. Future Urban Research in Europe*. Berlin, Germany: Berliner Wissenschaftsverlag.

Kollman, K., & Prakash, A. (2002). EMS-based Environmental Regimes as Club Goods: Examining Variations in Firm-level Adoption of ISO 14001 and EMAS in U.K., U.S. and Germany. *Policy Sciences*, *35*(1), 43–67. doi:10.1023/A:1016071810725

Konga, F., Yin, H., Nakagoshi, N., & Zong, Y. (2010). Urban green space network development for biodiversity conservation: Identification based on graph theory and gravity modelling. *Landscape and Urban Planning*, *95*(1-2), 16–27.

Konteh, F. H. (2009). Urban sanitation and health in the developing world: Reminiscing the nineteenth century industrial nations. *Health & Place*, *15*(1), 69–78. doi:10.1016/j.healthplace.2008.02.003 PMID:18359263

Kouikoglou, V. S., & Phillis, Y. A. (2009). On the monotonicity of hierarchical sum-product fuzzy systems. *Fuzzy Sets and Systems*, *160*(24), 3530–3538. doi:10.1016/j.fss.2009.02.001

Kouloumpis, V. D., Kouikoglou, V. S., & Phillis, Y. A. (2008). Sustainability assessment of nations and related decision making using fuzzy logic. *IEEE Systems Journal*, *2*(2), 224–236. doi:10.1109/JSYST.2008.925256

Kramer, D., & Doran, P. (2008). Protected area establishment and the endogenous effect of residential. Paper presented at the the annual meeting of the International Congress for Conservation Biology, Convention Center. Chattanooga, TN.

Kramer, D., & Doran, P. (2010). Land conversion at the protected area's edge. *Conservation Letters*, *3*(5), 349–358.

Krizek, K. J. (2012). Cycling, urban form and cities: what do we know and how should we respond? In J. Parkin (Ed.), *Cycling and sustainability* (pp. 23–58). UK: Emerald Group Publishing Limited. doi:10.1108/S2044-9941(2012)0000001007

Krizek, K. J., & Stonebraker, E. W. (2011). Assessing options to enhance bicycle and transit integration. *Journal of Transportation Research Board*, *2217*(-1), 162–167. doi:10.3141/2217-20

Kühn, M. (1999). Kulturlandschaften zwischen Schutz und Nutzung. Modellhafte Planungsansätze einer nachhaltigen Freiraum- und Landschaftsentwicklung. REGIO Beiträge des IRS, 14.

Kumar, A. (2007). *Mobile TV: DVB-H, DMB, 3G systems and rich media applications*. Burlington, MA: Elsevier. doi:10.1016/B978-0-240-80946-5.50005-7

Kuntz, D. (1994). The Politics of Suffering: The Impact of the U.S. Embargo on the Health of the Cuban People. Report to the American Public Health Association of a Fact-Finding Trip to Cuba, June 6-11, 1993. *Journal of Public Health Policy*, *15*(1), 86–107. doi:10.2307/3342609 PMID:8027364

Labuschagne, C., & Brent, A. C. (2005). Sustainable Project Life Cycle Management: The need to integrate life cycles in the manufacturing sector. *International Journal of Project Management*, *23*(2), 159–168. doi:10.1016/j.ijproman.2004.06.003

Labuschagne, C., & Brent, A. C. (2007). Sustainability assessment criteria for projects and technologies: Judgements of industry managers. *South African Journal of Industrial Engineering*, *18*(1), 19–33.

Labuschagne, C., Brent, A. C., & Claasen, S. J. (2005). Environmental and social impact considerations for sustainable project life cycle management in the process industry. *Corporate Social Responsibility and Environmental Management*, *12*(1), 38–54. doi:10.1002/csr.76

Lam, H. L., Varbanov, P. S., & Klemes, J. J. (2011). Regional renewable energy and resource planning. *Applied Energy*, *88*(2), 545–550. doi:10.1016/j.apenergy.2010.05.019

Lammerts van Beuren, E. M., & Blom, E. M. (1997). *Hierarchical Framework For The Formulation Of Sustainable Forest Management Standards*. Leiden: The Tropenbos Foundation.

Lamont, M. J. (2009). Reinventing the wheel: A definitional discussion of bicycle tourism. *Journal of Sport & Tourism*, *14*(1), 5–23. doi:10.1080/14775080902847363

Laurence, D. (2011). Establishing a Sustainable Mining Operation: An Overview. *Journal of Cleaner Production*, *19*(2-3), 278–284. doi:10.1016/j.jclepro.2010.08.019

Lawton, P., Meczynski, M., & Barber, A. (2013). Policies towards Place Attraction and Policies for Place Retention. In S. Musterd & Z. Kovacs (Eds.), *Place-making and policies for competitive cities* (pp. 105–148). Chichester, West Sussex, United Kingdom: Wiley Blackwell. doi:10.1002/9781118554579.ch8

Layton, E. T. (1974). Technology as knowledge. *Technology and Culture*, *15*(1), 31–41. doi:10.2307/3102759

Le Cog, C. (2009). Russian gas suply and common energy policy. *Baltic Rim Economies. Bimonthly Review, Expert Article 330.*

Leahu-Aluas, S. (2010). *Sustainable Manufacturing: An Overview for Manufacturing Engineers*. Resource.

Lederer, M. (2011). From CDM to REDD+—What do we know for setting up effective and legitimate carbon governance? *Ecological Economics*, *70*(11), 1900–1907. doi:10.1016/j.ecolecon.2011.02.003

Legerman, A., Zandhuis, A., Silvius, G., Rober, R., & Stellingwerf, R. (2013). *ISO 21500 in Practice - A Management Guide*. Zaltbommel, The Netherlands: Van Haren Publishing.

Letema, S., Van Vliet, B., & Van Lier, J. B. (2014). Sanitation policy and spatial planning in urban East Africa: Diverging sanitation spaces and actor arrangements in Kampala and Kisumu. *Cities (London, England)*, *36*, 1–9. doi:10.1016/j.cities.2013.08.003

Lewis, R. (1998). Trabajo y aprendizaje en Comunidades distribuidas. In C. Vizcarro & J. León (Eds.), *Nuevas Tecnologías para el aprendizaje* (pp. 191–220). Madrid, Spain: Pirámide.

Liberatore, A. (1997). The Integration of Sustainable Developemnt Objectives into EU Policy-Making: Barriers and Prospects. In S. Baker, M. Kousis, D. Richardson, & S. Young (Ed.), The Politics of Sustainable Development: Theory, Policy and Practice Within the European Union. Routledge.

Li, J., & Colombier, M. (2009). Managing carbon emissions in China through building energy efficiency. *Journal of Environmental Management*, *90*(8), 2436–2447. doi:10.1016/j.jenvman.2008.12.015 PMID:19344996

Li, L., & Revesz, P. (2004). Interpolation methods for spatio-temporal geographic data. *Computers, Environment and Urban Systems*, *28*(3), 201–227.

Lim, S. K., & Yang, J. (2009). *A Delphi study on the critical sustainability criteria and indicators for Australian road infrastructure projects.* Paper presented at the 3rd CIB International Conference on Smart and Sustainable Built Environments, Delft University of Technology. Delft, The Netherlands.

Lin, K., & Chang, T. C. (2013). Everyday crises: Marginal society livelihood vulnerability and adaptability to hazards. *Progress in Development Studies*, *13*(1), 45–78. doi:10.1177/146499341201300101

Lipschutz, R., & Mayer, J. (1996). *Global Civil Society and Global Environmental Governance: The Politics of Nature from Place to Planet*. New York: State University of New York Press.

Liuhto, K. (2010). *Energy in Russia's foreign policy: Electronic Publications of Pan-European Institute*. Retrieved April 24, 2014, from http://www.utu.fi/fi/yksikot/tse/yksikot/PEI/raportit-ja-tietopaketit/Documents/Liuhto_final_netti.pdf

Li, X. (2005). Diversification and localization of energy systems for sustainable development and energy security. *Energy Policy*, *33*(17), 2237–2243. doi:10.1016/j.enpol.2004.05.002

Lock, D. (2007). *Project Management* (9th ed.). Hampshire, UK: Gower Publishing Limited.

Lockwood, C. (2006). Building the green way. *Harvard Business Review*, *84*(6), 129–137. PMID:16770900

Lopes, M. D. S., & Flavell, R. (1998). Project appraisal: A framework to assess non-financial aspects of projects during the project life cycle. *International Journal of Project Management*, *16*(4), 223–233. doi:10.1016/S0263-7863(97)00055-0

Lovins, A. (1977). *Soft Energy Paths: Toward a Durable Peace.* San Francisco: Friends of the Earth International.

Luh, J., Baum, R., & Bartram, J. (2013). Equity in water and sanitation: Developing an index to measure progressive realization of the human right. *International Journal of Hygiene and Environmental Health*, *216*(6), 662–671. doi:10.1016/j.ijheh.2012.12.007 PMID:23333082

Lull, J. (1987). *Popular music and communication.* Thousand Oaks, CA: Sage.

Lumsdon, L. (2000). Transport and tourism: Cycle tourism - a model for sustainable development? *Journal of Sustainable Tourism*, *8*(5), 361–377. doi:10.1080/09669580008667373

Lundin, R. A., & Söderholm, A. (1995). A theory of the temporary organization. *Scandinavian Journal of Management*, *11*(4), 437–455. doi:10.1016/0956-5221(95)00036-U

Luo, J. S. (2009). The Facebook phenomenon: Boundaries and controversies. *Primary Psychiatry*, *16*(11), 19–21.

Lyon, S. (2007). Balancing Values of Outstanding Universality with Conservation and Management at the Three United Kingdom Cultural WHS. *Journal of Heritage Tourism*, *2*(1), 53–63. doi:10.2167/jht028.0

Maeng, D., & Nedovic-Budic, Z. (2010). Relationship between ICT and urban form in knowledge-based development: Empirical analysis of Washington, DC metro region. *International Journal of Knowledge-Based Development*, *1*(1-2), 97–117. doi:10.1504/IJKBD.2010.032588

Magadan, C. (2008). *Las TIC en las escuelas rurales argentinas: Las TIC del aula a la agenda política*. Buenos Aires, Argentina: UNICEF Argentina.

Mäkinen, H. (2010). The future of natural gas as the European Union's energy source – risks and possibilities. *Electronic Publications of Pan-European Institute.* 9/2010. Retrieved May 5, 2014, from http://www.utu.fi/fi/yksikot/tse/yksikot/PEI/raportit-ja-tietopaketit/Documents/Mäkinen_final.pdf

Maltzman, R., Shirley, D., Mochal, T., & Krasnoff, A. (2010). *Proposed changes and reasoning for proposed changes to 5th Edition of the PMBOK® Guide*. Retrieved April 7, 2014, from http://www.green-pm.com/articles/2010-07PMIProposal.pdf

Maltzman, R., & Shirley, D. (2010). *Green Project Management*. Boca Raton, FL: CRC Press. doi:10.1201/EBK1439830017

Maltzman, R., & Shirley, D. (2013). Project Manager as a Pivot Point for Implementing Sustainability in an Enterprise. In A. J. G. Silvius & J. Tharp (Eds.), *Sustainability Integration for Effective Project Management* (pp. 261–278). Hershey, PA: IGI Global Publishing. doi:10.4018/978-1-4666-4177-8.ch016

Mancisidor, I. M. A., Uraga, P. D. B., Mancisidor, I. M. A., & López, P. R. A. (2009). European Union's renewable energy sources and energy efficiency policy review: The Spanish perspective. *Renewable & Sustainable Energy Reviews*, *13*(1), 100–114. doi:10.1016/j.rser.2007.07.003

Manning, T. (1999). Indicators of tourism sustainability. *Tourism Management*, *20*(1), 179–181.

Maragkogianni, M., Papaefthimiou, S., & Zopounidis, C. (2013). Emissions Trading Schemes in the Transportation sector. In Vasile, Turek, & Subic (Eds.), Sustainable Technologies, Policies, and Constraints in the Green Economy (pp. 269-289). Hershey, PA: IGI Global. doi:10.4018/978-1-4666-4098-6.ch015

Maraseni, T. N. (2013). Evaluating the clean development mechanism. In T. Cadman (Ed.), *Quality and Legitimacy of Global Governance: Case Lessons from Forestry* (pp. 96–110). Basingstoke: Palgrave Macmillan.

Margules, C. R., & Pressey, R. L. (2000). Systematic conservation planning. *Nature*, *405*(6783), 243–253.

Marletto, G. (2011). Structure, Agency and change in the car regime. A review of literature. *European Transport*, *47*, 71–88.

Márquez, M. (2009). Health-workforce development in the Cuban health system. *Lancet*, *374*(9701), 1574–1575. doi:10.1016/S0140-6736(09)61919-X PMID:19897113

Marquis, A. G. (1984). Written on the wind: The impact of radio during the 1930s. *Journal of Contemporary History*, *19*(3), 385–415. doi:10.1177/002200948401900302

Marsh, J. (1993). The Potential Organization and Components of a Tourism Sustainability Index. In J. Nelson, R. Butler, & G. Wall (Eds.), *Tourism and Sustainable Development: Monitoring, Planning and Managing* (pp. 234–238). Waterloo, Canada: Department of Geography Publications Series, University of Waterloo.

Martens, P. (2006). Sustainability: science or fiction? *Sustainability: Science, Practice, &. Policy*, *2*(1), 1–5.

Marull, J., Pino, J., Mallarach, J. M., & Cordobilla, M. J. (2007). A Land Suitability Index for Strategic Environmental Assessment in metropolitan areas. *Landscape and Urban Planning*, *81*(3), 200–212.

Maxwell, D., Sheate, W., & van der Vorst, R. (2003). Sustainable Innovation in Product and Service Development. In *Proceedings of the Towards Sustainable Product Design 8 Conference*. Surrey, UK: Centre for Sustainable Design.

May, P. (2005). Regulation and Compliance Motivations: Examining Different Approaches. *Public Administration Review, 34*(65/1), 31-44.

McAllister, M. P., & Giglio, J. M. (2005). The commodity flow of U.S. children's television. *Critical Studies in Media Communication, 22*(1), 26–44. doi:10.1080/0739318042000331835

McCray, W. P. (2014). *The technologists' siren song*. Retrieved April 11, 2014, from The Chronicle of Higher Education website: http://chronicle.com/article/The-Technologists-Siren-Song/145107

McDonald, S., & Oates, C. J. (2006). Sustainability: Consumer perceptions and marketing strategies. *Business Strategy and the Environment, 15*(3), 157–170. doi:10.1002/bse.524

McDonough, W., & Braungart, M. (2002). *Cradle To Cradle: Remaking The Way We Make Things*. New York, NY: North Point Press.

McDowall, W., & Eames, M. (2006). Forecasts, scenarios, visions, backcasts and roadmaps to the hydrogen economy: A review of the hydrogen futures literature. *Energy Policy, 34*(11), 1236–1250. doi:10.1016/j.enpol.2005.12.006

McGuigan, J., Conroy, G., & Elmore, M. (1998). Solar disinfection of drinking water contained in transparent plastic bottles: Characterizing the bacterial inactivation process. *Journal of Applied Microbiology, 84*(6), 1138–1148. doi:10.1046/j.1365-2672.1998.00455.x PMID:9717300

McKercher, B., Ho, P., & du Cros, H. (2004). Attributes of Popular Culture Attractions in Hong Kong. *Annals of Tourism Research, 31*(2), 393–407. doi:10.1016/j.annals.2003.12.008

McLeod, K. (1999). Authenticity within hip-hop and other cultures threatened with assimilation. *Journal of Communication, 49*(4), 134–150. doi:10.1111/j.1460-2466.1999.tb02821.x

McLeod, M. (2010). "We Cubans Are Obligated Like Cats to Have a Clean Face": Malaria, Quarantine, and Race in Neocolonial Cuba, 1898-1940. *The Americas, 67*(1), 57–81. doi:10.1353/tam.0.0272

Meadows, D. H., Meadows, D. L., Randers, J., & Behrens, W. W. (1972). *The Limits to Growth*. New York, NY: Universe Books.

Meckel, R. A. (1998). *Save the babies: American public health reform and the prevention of infant mortality, 1850-1929*. University of Michigan Press.

Meggs, P. B., & Purvis, A. W. (2006). *Meggs' history of graphic design* (4th ed.). Hoboken, NJ: Wiley & Sons.

Mehling, M. (2009). *Global Carbon Market Institutions: An Assessment of Governance Challenges and Functions in the Carbon Market*. Climate Strategies.

Mercier, M. E., & Boone, C. G. (2002). Infant mortality in Ottawa, Canada, 1901: Assessing cultural, economic and environmental factors. *Journal of Historical Geography, 28*(4), 486–507. doi:10.1006/jhge.2002.0442

Merriman, P. (2009). Auto mobility and the Geographies of the Car. *Geography Compass, 3*(5), 586–599. doi:10.1111/j.1749-8198.2009.00219.x

Metin, E., Eröztürk, A., & Neyim, C. (2003). Solid waste management practices and review of recovery and recycling operations in Turkey. *Waste Management (New York, N.Y.), 23*(5), 425–432. doi:10.1016/S0956-053X(03)00070-9 PMID:12893015

Meyer, P. E., & Winebrake, J. J. (2009). Modeling technology diffusion of complementary goods: The case of hydrogen vehicles and refueling infrastructure. *Technovation, 29*(2), 77–91. doi:10.1016/j.technovation.2008.05.004

Michigan State University. (2014). *globalEDGE Energy*. Retrieved April 25, 2014 from http://globaledge.msu.edu/industries/energy

Miller, D. R., & Swanson, G. E. (1958). *The changing American parent*. New York: Wiley.

Miller, D. T., & Nowak, M. (1977). *The fifties*. New York, NY: Doubleday.

Miller, G. (2001). The Development of indicators for sustainable tourism: Results of a Delphi survey of tourism researchers. *Tourism Management*, *22*(4), 351–362. doi:10.1016/S0261-5177(00)00067-4

Miller, M. (1987). Short looks: IBM PS/ Model 25. *InfoWorld*, *9*(33), 44.

Miller, P., & Hirschhorn, N. (1995). The Effect of a National Control of Diarrheal Diseases Program on Mortality: The Case of Egypt. *Social Science & Medicine*, *40*(10), S1–S30. doi:10.1016/0277-9536(95)00001-N PMID:7638641

Mill, R., & Morrison, A. (2006). *The Tourism System* (pp. 143–147). Dubuque, IA: Kendall Hunt Publishing Company.

Milov, V., Coburn, L., & Danchenko, I. (2006). Russia's energy policy: 1992-2005. *Eurasian Geography and Economics*, *47*(3), 285–313. doi:10.2747/1538-7216.47.3.285

Mines and Communities. (2001). *London Declaration*. Retrieved August 6, 2012, from http:www.minesandcommunities.org/article.php?a=8470

Mining Association of Canada. (2004). *Towards Sustainable Mining Guiding Principles*. Ottawa, Ontario: Mining Association of Canada.

Mining Association of Canada. (2007). *Biodiversity Conservation Management Framework*. Ottawa, Ontario: Mining Association of Canada.

Mining Association of Canada. (2008). *Aboriginal and Community Outreach Framework*. Ottawa, Ontario: Mining Association of Canada.

Mining Association of Canada. (2009). *Energy and GHG Emissions Management Guidance Document*. Ottawa, Ontario: Mining Association of Canada.

Mining Association of Canada. (2011). *Tailings Management Protocol*. Ottawa, Ontario: Mining Association of Canada.

Mining Association of Canada. (2011b). *A Guide to the Audit and Assessment of Tailings Facilities Management*. Ottawa, Ontario: Mining Association of Canada.

Mining Association of Canada. (2011c). *Developing an Operation, Maintenance, and Surveillance Manual for Tailings and Water Management Facilities*. Ottawa, Ontario: Mining Association of Canada.

Mining Association of Canada. (2011d). *A Guide to the Management of Tailings Facilities*. Ottawa, Ontario: Mining Association of Canada.

Mining Association of Canada. (2011e). *Safety and Health Framework*. Ottawa, Ontario: Mining Association of Canada.

Mining Association of Canada. (2013b). *Biodiversity Conservation Management Protocol*. Ottawa, Ontario: Mining Association of Canada.

Mining Association of Canada. (2013c). *Energy and GHG Emissions Management Protocol*. Ottawa, Ontario: Mining Association of Canada.

Mining Association of Canada. (2013e). *Crisis Management Planning Reference Guide*. Ottawa, Ontario: Mining Association of Canada.

Mining Association of Canada. (2014b). *Research Findings: Public Opinion Tracking Study*. Complied by Abacus Data.

Mining Watch Canada. (2011). *About Us*. Retrieved December 10, 2011, from http://www.miningwatch.ca/about-us-1

Ministry of Economy, Trade and Industry (METI). (2009). *Japan Hydrogen and Fuel Cell Demonstration Project (JHFC) project was launched for the Future of the Earth*. Retrieved October 22, 2009, from http://www.jhfc.jp/e/jhfc/index.html

Ministry of Energy and Mineral Resources-Indonesia & National Council on Climate Change-Indonesia (MEMR & NCCC-Indonesia). (n.d.). *Geothermal in Indonesia Low Carbon Development: Profile, Status and Role of Market Mechanism*. Retrieved June 12, 2014, from http://www.thepmr.org/system/files/documents/Geothermal+in+Indonesia+Low+Carbon+Development+R2.pdf

Ministry of Environment (MOE). (2014). Seminar on promotional policies for electric vehicles. March 20-21, Jeju International Convention Center.

Ministry of Knowledge and Economy (MKE). (2008). *New & Renewable Energy White Paper 2008*. Gwacheon: Korean Ministry of Knowledge and Economy.

Ministry of Trade, Industry and Energy (MOTIE) & Korea Energy Economics Institute (KEEI). (2013) 2013 Year Book of Regional Energy Statistics. Korea: Korea Energy Economics Institute.

Minkler, M. (2000). Using Participatory Action Research to build Healthy Communities. *Public Health Reports*, *115*(2-3), 191–197. doi:10.1093/phr/115.2.191 PMID:10968753

Minkler, M., & Wallerstein, N. (2003). Introduction to community based participatory research. In M. Minkler & N. Wallerstein (Eds.), *Community Based Participatory Research for Health* (pp. 3–26). San Francisco, CA: Jossey-Bass.

Mitchell, D. (2008). *A Note on Rising Food Prices*. Washington, DC: The World Bank. doi:10.1596/1813-9450-4682

Mittell, J. (2003). The great Saturday morning exile: Scheduling cartoons on television's periphery in the 1960s. In C. A. Stabile & M. Harrison (Eds.), *Prime time animation: Television animation and American culture* (pp. 33–54). New York: Routledge.

Mkandawire, T. (2008). Quality of groundwater from shallow wells of selected villages in Blantyre District, Malawi. *Physics and Chemistry of the Earth Parts A/B/C*, *33*(8–13), 807–811. doi:10.1016/j.pce.2008.06.023

Molla, A., Cooper, V., Corbitt, B., Deng, H., Peszynski, K., Pittayachawan, S., & Teoh, S. (2008). E-readiness to G-readiness: developing a green information technology readiness framework. In *Proceedings of the 19th Australasian Conference on Information Systems*. Sydney, Australia: Australasian Conferences on Information Systems (ACIS).

Mominó, J., Sigalés, C., & Meneses, J. (2008). *La escuela en la sociedad red: internet en la Educación Primaria y Secundaria*. Barcelona, Spain: Ariel.

Montis, A. D. (2014). Strategic environmental assessment of energy planning tools. A study of Italian regions and provinces. *Environmental Impact Assessment Review*, *46*, 32–42. doi:10.1016/j.eiar.2014.01.006

Mooney, G., & Fohtung, N. G. (2008). Issues in the measurement of social determinants of health. *Health Information Management Journal*, *37*(3), 26–30. PMID:18941263

Moore, E., Cooley, H., Christian-Smith, J., & Donnelly, K. (2014). Sustainable Water Jobs. In E. Moore, H. Cooley, J. Christian-Smith, & K. Donnelly (Eds.), *The World's Water* (Vol. 8, pp. 35–61). Island Press/Center for Resource Economics. doi:10.5822/978-1-61091-483-3_3

Morgan, G., Apt, J., & Lave, L. (2005). The US, Electric Power Sector and Climate Change Mitigation. The Pew Center on Global Climate Change, Arlington, VA (June 2005).

Morris, G. (1993). Beyond the beach: Social and formal aspects of AIP's beach party movies. *Journal of Popular Film and Television*, *21*(1), 30–48. doi:10.1080/01956051.1993.9943970

Morrow, K. (2012). Rio+20, the green economy and reorienting sustainable development. *Environmental Law Review*, *14*(4), 15–23.

Moszynski, P. (2006). Worldwide water crisis is a "silent emergency," UN agency says. *BMJ (Clinical Research Ed.)*, *333*(7576), 986–986. doi:10.1136/bmj.333.7576.986-a PMID:17095767

Motlik, S. (2008). Technical evaluation report 63: Mobile learning in developing nations. *International Review of Research in Open and Distance Learning*, *9*(2), 1–7.

Moutinho, J. (2006). From Technological Determinism to Regional Development: Lessons Learned from the Portuguese Digital Cities Program (1998-2006). In P. Cunningham & M. Cunningham (Eds.), *Exploiting the Knowledge Economy: Issues, Applications, Case Studies*. Amsterdam, The Netherlands: IOS Press.

Mudd, G. (2007). Global trends in Gold Mining: Towards Quantifying Environmental and Resource Sustainability? *Resources Policy*, *32*(1-2), 42–56. doi:10.1016/j.resourpol.2007.05.002

Mui, D. H. F., & Sankaran, S. (2004). An effective project management-based application model for sustainable urban renewal in Hong Kong. *Project Management Journal*, *35*(4), 15–34.

Munasinghe, M. (2004). Sustainable development: Basic concepts and application to energy. In C. Cleveland (Ed.), *Encyclopedia of Energy* (pp. 789–808). New York, NY: Elsevier Academic Press. doi:10.1016/B0-12-176480-X/00441-1

Munier, N. (2005). *Introduction to Sustainability: Road to a Better Future*. Dordrecht, The Netherlands: Springer.

Murillo García, J. L. (2010). Programas Escuela 2.0 y Pizarra Digital: Un paradigma de mercantilización del sistema educativo a través de las TICs. *REIFOP*, *13*(2), 65–78.

Musterd, S., & Kovacs, Z. (Eds.). (2013). *Place-making and policies for competitive cities*. Chichester, West Sussex, United Kingdom: Wiley Blackwell. doi:10.1002/9781118554579

Musterd, S., & Murie, A. (Eds.). (2010). *Making competitive cities*. Oxford: Wiley-Blackwell.

Najam, A., Runnalls, D., & Halle, M. (2007). *Environment and Globalization: Five Propositions*. Winnipeg, Canada: International Institute of Sustainable Development.

National Institute on Media and the Family. (2010). Retrieved April 5, 2010, from http://www.mediafamily.org/activitiesandquizzes/decactivity.shtml

National Renewable Energy Laboratory (NREL). (2008). *20% Wind Energy by 2030*. US Department of Energy.

Nelson, J., & Payne, R. (1993). An Introduction to Tourism and Sustainable Development with Special Reference to Monitoring. In J. Nelson, R. Butler, & G. Wall (Eds.), *Tourism and Sustainable Development: Monitoring, Planning and Managing* (pp. 3–19). Waterloo, Canada: Department of Geography Publications Series, University of Waterloo.

Newman, P. W. G., & Kenworthy, J. R. (1999). *Sustainability and Cities. Overcoming Automobile Dependence*. Washington, DC: Island Press.

Newman, P., & Thornley, A. (1996). *Urban planning in Europe: international competition, national systems, and planning projects*. London: Routledge.

Nidumolu, R., Prahalad, C. K., & Rangaswami, M. R. (2009). Why Sustainability Is Now the Key Driver of Innovation. *Harvard Business Review*, (September): 2009.

Nieuwenhuis, P., Wells, P., & Vergragt, P. J. (2004). Introduction to the Special Issue on Technological Change and Regulation in the Car Industry. *Greener Management International*, *47*, 5–11. doi:10.9774/GLEAF.3062.2004.au.00003

Nijkamp, P. (2008). XXQ factors for sustainable urban development: A systems economics view. *Roumanian Journal of Regional Science*, *2*(1), 1–34.

Nijkamp, P., & Volwahsen, A. (1990). New directions in integrated regional energy planning. *Energy Policy*, *18*(8), 764–773. doi:10.1016/0301-4215(90)90029-4

Nilüfer Municipality. (2014). *Useful Information*. Retrieved May 2, 2014, from http://www.nilufercity.eu/index.php?s=i&id=12

Njeru, J. (2013). 'Donor-driven' neoliberal reform processes and urban environmental change in Kenya: The case of Karura Forest in Nairobi. *Progress in Development Studies*, *13*(1), 17–25. doi:10.1177/146499341201300105

Northridge, M. E., Sclar, E. D., & Biswas, P. (2003). Sorting out the connections between the built environment and health: A conceptual framework for navigating pathways and planning healthy cities. *Journal of Urban Health*, *80*(4), 556–568. doi:10.1093/jurban/jtg064 PMID:14709705

Novick, L. F., Morrow, C. B., & Mays, G. P. (2008). *Public health administration: Principles for population-based management* (2nd ed.). Burlington, MA: Jones and Bartlett Pub.

Nuryunti, W. (1996). Heritage and Postmodern Tourism. *Annals of Tourism Research*, *23*(2), 249–260. doi:10.1016/0160-7383(95)00062-3

Nyenje, P. M., Foppen, J. W., Kulabako, R., Muwanga, A., & Uhlenbrook, S. (2013). Nutrient pollution in shallow aquifers underlying pit latrines and domestic solid waste dumps in urban slums. *Journal of Environmental Management*, *122*(0), 15–24. doi:10.1016/j.jenvman.2013.02.040 PMID:23542227

O'Sullivan, M., & Watling, D. (2011). Visions for a walking and cycling focused urban transport system. *Journal of Transport Geography*, *19*(6), 1580–1589. doi:10.1016/j.jtrangeo.2011.03.011

Odeku, K. O., Maveneka, A., & Konanani, R. H. (2013). Consequences of Country's Withdrawal from Climate Change Agreements: Implications for Carbon Emissions Reduction. *Journal of Human Ecology (Delhi, India)*, *41*(1), 17–24.

Odum, E. P. (1971). Fundamental of ecology (Third Edition). Philadelphia, London, & Toronto: W. B. Saunders.

OECD. (2004). *Implementing sustainable urban travel policies: moving ahead. National policies to promote cycling*. Paris, France: OECD.

OECD. (2005). *OECD Factbook 2005*. Paris: OECD Publications.

OECD. (2009). *Annual Report 2009*. Paris, France: OECD.

OECD. (2009). *Sustainable Manufacturing and Eco-Innovation, Synthesis report*. Retrieved October, 2011, from http://www.oecd.org/dataoecd/15/58/43423689.pdf Document.

OECD/IEA. (2004). *Renewables for power generation: status and prospect*. UK: OECD.

Office of Government Commerce. (2009). *Managing Successful Projects with PRINCE2*. Norwich.

Office of Government Commerce. (2010). Management of Risk: Guidance for Practitioners. Norwich.

Ogle, M. (1993). Domestic Reform and American Household Plumbing, 1840-1870. *Winterthur Portfolio*, *28*(1), 33–58. doi:10.1086/496603

Okin, J. R. (2005). *The Internet revolution: The not-for-dummies guide to the history, technology, and use of the Internet*. Winter Harbor, ME: Ironbound.

Okkan, P. (1993). Reducing CO_2 emissions-How do heat pumps compete with other options? *IEA Heat Pump Centre Newsletter*, *11*(3), 24–26.

Oktay, S. Ö., & Çetin, N. İ. (2013). *Proposal of A Local-Specific Environmental Assessment Method for Yedikule Neighbourhood, İstanbul*. Dublin, Ireland: AESOP-ACSP Joint Congress.

Olewiler, N. (2006). Sustainability for urban areas: The role of natural capital indicators. *Cities (London, England)*, *23*(3), 184–195.

Olivier, J. G. J., Janssens-Maenhout, G., & Peters, J. A. H. W. (2012). *Trends in global CO_2 emissions. 2012 Report. The Hague: PBL Netherlands Environmental Assessment Agency*. Ispra: Joint Research Centre.

Olson, E. (2008). Creating an enterprise-level Greener strategy. *The Journal of Business Strategy*, *29*(2), 22–30. doi:10.1108/02756660810858125

Onda, K., Crocker, J., Kayser, G. L., & Bartram, J. (2014). Country clustering applied to the water and sanitation sector: A new tool with potential applications in research and policy. *International Journal of Hygiene and Environmental Health*, *217*(2-3), 379–385. doi:10.1016/j.ijheh.2013.07.017 PMID:24054545

Osborn, F. J. (1969). *Green Belt Cities*. London: Evelyn, Adams & Mackay.

Pacione, M. (2005). *Urban Geography. A global perspective*. Abingdon, UK: Routledge.

Packard, V. (1960). The Waste Makers. Penguin, Harmondsworth. In Robins, N. (1999). Making sustainability bite: Transforming global consumption patterns. *The Journal of Sustainable Product Design*, *10*, 7–15.

Pade, C., Mallinson, B., & Sewry, D. (2008). An Elaboration of Critical Success Factors for Rural ICT Project Sustainability in Developing Countries: Exploring the Dwesa Case. *The Journal of Information Technology Case and Application*, *10*(4), 32–55. doi:10.1080/15228053.2008.10856146

Page, S. J. (2009). *Transport and Tourism: Global perspectives*. Harlow, UK: Prentice Hall.

Pan, J. (1997). On the origin of printing in the light of new archaeological discoveries. *Chinese Science Bulletin*, *42*(12), 976–981. doi:10.1007/BF02882611

Parker, C., Mitchell, A., Trivedi, M., & Mardas, N. (2009). *The little REDD+ book*. Oxford: Global Canopy Programme.

Parkin, J., & Koorey, G. (2012). Nework planning and infrastructure design. In J. Parkin (Ed.), *Cycling and sustainability* (pp. 131–160). UK: Emerald Group Publishing Limited. doi:10.1108/S2044-9941(2012)0000001008

Parto, S. (1999). Aiming Low. In R. B. Gibson (Ed.), *Voluntary Initiatives: The New Politics of Corporate Greening* (pp. 182–198). Peterborough, Canada: Broadview Press.

Pătroescu, M., & Iojă, C. (2004). The role of the parks in Bucharest city ecosystem. Paper presented at the Lucrarile simpozionului Dimitrie Cantemir 25.

Pătroescu, M., Niţă, M. R., Iojă, I. C., & Vânău, G. (2009). New residential areas in Bucharest Metropolitan Area - location, type and characteristics. Paper presented at the 14th International Conference on Urban Planning, Regional Development and Information Society REAL CORP 2009. Barcelona, Spain.

Pătroescu, M., Dragomirescu, Ş., Iojă, I. C., & Niţă, M. R. (2008). Regional activities parks – partenership opportunities in environmental protection. *Present Environment and Sustainable Development, 1*(1), 71–81.

Pătroescu, M., Iojă, C., Necşuliu, R., & Brăilescu, C. (2004). The quality of oxygenating surfaces. The green areas of Bucharest. A case studies. *Revue Roumaine de Geographie, 47-48*, 205–216.

Pattberg, P. H. (2005). The Forest Stewardship Council: Risk and Potential of Private Forest Governance. *Journal of Environment & Development, 14*(3), 356–374. doi:10.1177/1070496505280062

Patuelli, R., Mussoni, M., & Candela, G. (2013). *The Effects of World Heritage Sites on Domestic Tourism: A Spatial Interaction Model for Italy.* The Rimini Centre for Economic Analysis. Retrieved April 20, 2014, from http://link.springer.com/article/10.1007/s10109-013-0184-5#page-1

Pearce, T. D., Ford, J. D., Prno, J., Duerden, F., Pittman, J., Beaumier, M., & Smit, B. et al. (2010). Climate Change and Mining in Canada. *Mitigation and Adaptation Strategies for Global Change, 16*(3), 347–368. doi:10.1007/s11027-010-9269-3

Peattie, K. (2011). Developing and delivering social science research for sustainability. In A. Franklin & P. Blyton (Eds.), *Researching Sustainability: A Guide to Social Science Methods, Practice and Engagement.* Oxon, UK: Earthscan.

Peattie, K., & Charter, M. (1994). Green marketing. *The Marketing Book, 5*, 726–755.

Pedersen, A. O., Nyhuus, S., Blindheim, T., & Werlgeland Krog, O. M. (2004). Implementation of a GIS-based management tool for conservation of biodiversity within the municipality of Oslo, Norway. *Landscape and Urban Planning, 68*(4), 429–438.

PEFC. (2005). *Certification and Accreditation Procedures.* Annex 6, version 11 April 2005.

Perdan, S., & Azapagic, A. (2011). Carbon trading: Current schemes and future developments. *Energy Policy, 39*(10), 6040–6054. doi:10.1016/j.enpol.2011.07.003

Perdue, W. C., Stone, L. A., & Gostin, L. O. (2003). The built environment and its relationship to the public's health: The legal framework. *American Journal of Public Health, 93*(9), 1390–1394. doi:10.2105/AJPH.93.9.1390 PMID:12948949

Perlmutt, D. (2001). Bank of America executive to retire after 23 years. *Charlotte Observer.* Retrieved January 31, 2001, from http://www.charlotte.com/mld/charlotte/archives/

Pernille, M. (2004). Danish lessons on district heating. *Energy Resource Sustainable Management and Environmental, March/April*, 16-17.

Perovic, J., & Orttung, R. (2007). Russia's energy policy: Should Europe worry? *Russian Analytical Digest, 18*(7). Retrieved September 27, 2013, from www.russlandanalysen.de

Perovic, J., Orttung, R., & Wenger, A. (Eds.). (2009). *Russian energy power and foreign relationships: Implications for conflict and cooperation.* Oxon, UK: Routledge.

Perrini, F., & Tencati, A. (2006). Sustainability and Stakeholder Management: The Need for New Corporate Performance Evaluation and Reporting Systems. *Business Strategy and the Environment, 15*(5), 286–308. doi:10.1002/bse.538

Petit, C. (2006). *La generación Tecno cultural.* Buenos Aires, Argentina: Government of Argentina.

Philadelphia Water Department. (2002). *Philadelphia Water Department Baxter Water Treatment Plant.* Source Water Assessment Report. (ME350056), 221.

Philipson, G. (2010). A green ICT framework: Understanding and measuring green ICT. *Connection research, 2010.*

Phillis, Y. A., & Andriantiatsaholiniaina, L. (2001). Sustainability: An ill-defined concept and its assessment using fuzzy logic. *Ecological Economics*, *37*(3), 435–456. doi:10.1016/S0921-8009(00)00290-1

Phillis, Y. A., & Davis, B. J. (2009). Assessment of corporate sustainability via fuzzy logic. *Journal of Intelligent & Robotic Systems*, *55*(1), 3–20. doi:10.1007/s10846-008-9289-3

Phillis, Y. A., Grigoroudis, E., & Kouikoglou, V. S. (2011). Sustainability ranking and improvement of countries. *Ecological Economics*, *70*(3), 542–553. doi:10.1016/j.ecolecon.2010.09.037

Phillis, Y. A., Kouikoglou, V. S., & Andriantiatsaholiniaina, L. (2003). Sustainable development: A definition and assessment. *Environmental Engineering and Management Journal*, 2(4), 345–355.

Phillis, Y. A., Kouikoglou, V. S., & Zhu, X. (2010). Fuzzy assessment of material recyclability and its applications. *Journal of Intelligent & Robotic Systems*, *55*(1), 21–38. doi:10.1007/s10846-008-9290-x

Pickett, S. T. A., Cadenasso, M. L., Grove, J. M., Nilon, C. H., Pouyat, R. V., Zipperer, W. C., & Costanza, R. (2001). Urban ecological systems: Linking terrestrial ecological, physical, and socioeconomic components of metropolitan areas. *Annual Review of Ecology Evolution and Systematics*, *32*, 127–157.

Pickford, J. (1980). UN Water and Sanitation Decade. *Habitat International*, *5*(3/4), 459–467. doi:10.1016/0197-3975(80)90032-6

Pignatelli, S., & Musumeci, S. (2003). Comparison of Three Oral Rehydration Strategies in the Treatment of Acute Diarrhea in a Tropical Country. *Current Therapeutic Research*, *64*(3), 189–202. doi:10.1016/S0011-393X(03)00021-3 PMID:24944365

Pink, S. (2007). Sensing Cittàslow: Slow living and the constitution of the sensory city. *The Senses and Society*, *2*(1), 59–77. doi:10.2752/174589207779997027

Pink, S. (2008). Sense and sustainability: The case of the Slow City movement. *Local Environment*, *13*(2), 95–106. doi:10.1080/13549830701581895

Placet, M., Anderson, R., & Fowler, K. M. (2005). Strategies for Sustainability. *Research Technology Management*, *48*(5), 32–41.

Plato. (2008). *Phaedrus*. (B. Jowett, Trans.). Forgotten Books.

Polat, E. (2012). An Approach for Land-Use Sustainability Assessment Using Decision Support Systems, AHP and GIS. In Ö. Yalçıner-Ercoşkun (Ed.), *Green and Ecological Technologies for Urban Planning: Creating Smart Cities* (pp. 310–329). Hershey, PA: IGI Global.

Pomering, A., Noble, G., & Johnson, L. (2011). Conceptualizing a Contemporary Marketing Mix for Sustainable Tourism. *Journal of Sustainable Tourism*, *19*(8), 953–969. doi:10.1080/09669582.2011.584625

Pont, S. J., Grijalva, C. G., Griffin, M. R., Scott, T. A., & Cooper, W. O. (2009). National Rates of Diarrhea-Associated Ambulatory Visits in Children. *The Journal of Pediatrics*, *155*(1), 55–61. doi:10.1016/j.jpeds.2009.01.075 PMID:19394047

Pope, J., Annandale, D., & Morrison-Saunders, A. (2004). Conceptualising sustainability assessment. *Environmental Impact Assessment Review*, *24*(6), 595–616. doi:10.1016/j.eiar.2004.03.001

Porter, M. (1985). *Competitive Advantage: Creating and Sustaining Superior Performance*. New York, NY: Free Press.

Porter, M. E. (1995). The Competitive Advantage of the Inner City. *Harvard Business Review*, *74*, 61–78.

Potoski, M., & Prakash, A. (2005). Green Clubs and Voluntary Governance: ISO 14001 and Firms' Regulatory Compliance. *American Journal of Political Science*, *49*(2), 235–248. doi:10.1111/j.0092-5853.2005.00120.x

Prahalad, C. (2005). *The Fortune at the Bottom of the Pyramid: Eradicating Poverty Through Profits*. Upper Saddle River, NJ: Wharton School Publishing.

Prahalad, C. K., & Krishnan, M. (2007). *The new age of innovation: Driving Co-created Value Through Global Networks*. New York, NY: McGraw-Hill.

Prieto, B. (2011). *Sustainability on Large, Complex Engineering & Construction Programs Utilizing a Program Management Approach. PM World Today, XIII*. VII.

Primack, R. B., Pătroescu, M., Rozylowicz, L., & Iojă, I. C. (2008). *Fundamentele conservării diversităţii biologice*. Bucureşti: AGIR.

Probe International. (2013). *Shale Oil*. Retrieved May 7, 2014, from http://probeinternational.org/library/wp-content/uploads/2013/02/pwc-shale-oil1.pdf

Project Management Institute. (2010). *Code of Ethics and Professional Conduct*. Newtown Square, PA: Project Management Institute.

Project Management Institute. (2013). *A Guide to the Project Management Body of Knowledge (PMBOK Guide)* (5th ed.). Newtown Square, PA: Project Management Institute.

Pronello, C., & Camusso, C. (2011). Travellers' profiles definition using statistical multivariate analysis of attitudinal variables. *Journal of Transport Geography*, *19*(6), 1294–1308. doi:10.1016/j.jtrangeo.2011.06.009

Prothero, A., & Fitchett, J. A. (2000). Greening Capitalism: Opportunities for a Green Commodity. *Journal of Macromarketing*, *20*(1), 46–55. doi:10.1177/0276146700201005

Pruss, A., & Mariotti, S. P. (2000). Preventing trachoma through environmental sanitation: A review of the evidence base. *Bulletin of the World Health Organization*, *78*(2), 258–266. PMID:10743299

Pucher, J., & Buehler, R. (2008). Making cycling irresistible: Lessons from the Netherlands, Denmark and Germany. *Transport Reviews*, *28*(4), 495–528. doi:10.1080/01441640701806612

Pucher, J., & Buehler, R. (2009). Integrating Bicycle and Public Transport in North America. *Journal of Public Transportation*, *12*(3), 79–104. doi:10.5038/2375-0901.12.3.5

Pullin, A. S., Baldi, A., Can, O. E., Dieterich, M., Kati, V., Livoreil, B., & Sousa-Pinto, I. et al. (2009). Conservation Focus on Europe: Major Conservation Policy Issues That Need to Be Informed by Conservation Science. *Conservation Biology*, *23*(4), 818–824.

Pumain, D., & Saint-Julien, T. (1997). *L'analyse spatiale. 1. Localisation dans l'espace*. Paris: Arman Colin.

Quaid, A. (2002). The Sustainability inventory: A tool to assist US Municipalities advance towards sustainability. *Local Environment*, *7*(4), 447–452. doi:10.1080/1354983022000027545

Quintero, A., & Hernández, A. (2005). El profesor ante el reto de integrarlas TIC en los procesos de enseñanza. *Revista Enseñanza*, *23*, 305–321.

Raines, S. S. (2003). Perceptions of Legitimacy and Efficacy in International Environmental Management Standards: The Impact of the Participation Gap. *Global Environmental Politics*, *3*(3), 47–78. doi:10.1162/152638003322469277

Rainey, D. L. (2006). *Sustainable Business Development: Inventing the Future through Strategy, Innovation and Leadership*. Cambridge, UK: Cambridge University Press. doi:10.1017/CBO9780511617607

Rainey, D. L. (2010). *Enterprise-wide Strategic Management: Achieving Sustainable Success through Leadership, Strategies and Value Creation*. Cambridge, UK: Cambridge University Press.

Rainey, D. L., & Araujo, R. (2014). *The Pursuit of Sustainability: Creating Business Value through Strategic Leadership, Holistic Perspectives, and Exceptional Performance*. Charlotte, NC: Information Age Publishing.

Rakic, T., & Leask, A. (2006, June). *World Heritage List: historical development, current status and future scenarios*. Paper presented at the Cutting Edge Research in Tourism Conference-New Directions Challenges and Applications Conference. Surrey, UK.

Rakic, T., & Chambers, D. (2007). World Heritage: Exploring the Tension between the Universal and the National. *Journal of Heritage Tourism*, *2*(3), 145–155. doi:10.2167/jht056.0

Ramachandra, T. (2009). RIEP: Regional integrated energy plan. *Renewable & Sustainable Energy Reviews*, *13*(2), 285–317. doi:10.1016/j.rser.2007.10.004

Ramani, K., Ramanujan, D., Bernstein, K., Zhao, F., Sutherland, J., Handwerker, C., & Thurston, H. et al. (2010). Integrated Sustainable Life Cycle Design: A Review. *Journal of Mechanical Design*, *132*(9), 091004. doi:10.1115/1.4002308

Raphael, A. T. (2012). Energy and Climate Change: Critical reflection on the African Continent; Is There an Ideal REDD+ Program? An Analysis. *Journal Sustainable Development in Africa*, *14*(6), 25–36.

Rautenstrauch, L. (1995). Funktionsverteilung zwischen Stadt und Umland. *Das Bauzentrum*, *3/1995*, 15–26.

Rawlinson, R. (1853). *On the drainage of towns*. Paper presented at the Minutes of the Proceedings Ambulatory VisiOn the Drainage of Towns.

Rees, W. E. (1999). The built environment and the ecosphere: A global perspective. *Building Research and Information*, *27*(4), 206–220. doi:10.1080/096132199369336

Regidor, E., Pascual, C., Martínez, D., Calle, M. E., Ortega, P., & Astasio, P. (2011). The role of political and welfare state characteristics in infant mortality: A comparative study in wealthy countries since the late 19th century. *International Journal of Epidemiology*, *40*(5), 1187–1195. doi:10.1093/ije/dyr092 PMID:21737401

Reid, A., & Miedzinski, M. (2008). *SYSTEMATIC Innovation Panel on eco-innovation*. Final report for sectoral innovation watch. Retrieved from www.europe-innova.org

Reimer, J. (2005). *Total share: 30 years of personal computer market share figures*. Retrieved March 30, 2010, from the Ars Technica website: http://arstechnica.com/old/content/2005/12/total-share.ars

Reisch, L. (2008). The nature and culture of consumption in consumption societies. In Reisch (Ed.), Rethinking consumer behavior for the well-being of all: Reflections on individual consumer responsibility (pp. 15-21). Strasbourg, Austria: Council of Europe Publishing.

RIAA. (2002). *Recent study illustrates Internet piracy's impact on music market*. Retrieved April 16, 2010, from the RIAA.org website: http://www.riaa.org/PR_STORY.CFM?ID=491

Ridley, J., & Jones, L. (2002). *User and Public Involvement in Health Services: A Literature Review*. Edinburgh, Scotland: Partners in Change, SHS Trust.

Robert, K.-H., Daly, H., Hawken, P., & Holmberg, J. (1997). A compass for sustainable development. *International Journal of Sustainable Development and World Ecology*, *4*(2), 79–92. doi:10.1080/13504509709469945

Robins, N. (1999). Making sustainability bite: Transforming global consumption patterns. *The Journal of Sustainable Product Design*, *10*, 7–15. http://www.poptel.org.uk/iied/smg/pubs/susbite.html Retrieved July 2, 2007

Robinson, J. (2004). Squaring the circle: On the very idea of sustainable development. *Ecological Economics*, *48*(4), 369–384. doi:10.1016/j.ecolecon.2003.10.017

Roettger, G. (2007). *Over a barrel: Where Russian energy policy leaves Europe with regards to its energy security*. (Unpublished Master's thesis). Naval Postgraduate School, Monterey, CA.

Romanova, T. (2008). The Russian perspective on the energy dialogue. *Journal of Contemporary European Studies*, *16*(2), 219–230. doi:10.1080/14782800802309938

Romeijn, P. (1999) *Green Gold: on Variations in Truth in Plantation Forestry*. Heelsum: Treemail.

Roriz, L. (2001). *Determining the potential energy and environmental effects reduction of air conditioning systems*. Commission of the European Communities DG TREN.

Rosenau, J. (2003). *Distant Proximities: Dynamics Beyond Globalization*. Princeton, Oxford: Princeton University Press.

Rosenberg, C. E. (1987). *The cholera years, the United States in 1832, 1849, and 1866*. Chicago, USA: University of Chicago Press. doi:10.7208/chicago/9780226726762.001.0001

Rowe, G., & Frewer, L. J. (2009). Public Participation Methods: A framework for evaluation. *Science, Technology & Human Values*, *25*(1), 3–29. doi:10.1177/016224390002500101

Roy, W. G. (2004). "Race records" and "hillbilly music": Institutional origins of racial categories in the American commercial recording industry. *Poetics*, *32*(3–4), 265–279. doi:10.1016/j.poetic.2004.06.001

Rudnitsky, J., & Mazneva, E. (2014). *Gazprom Sees Growth in Europe as Net Falls Below Estimates*. Blumberg/Business Week, April 29, 2014. Retrieved May 2, 2014, from http://www.businessweek.com/news/2014-04-29/gazprom-2013-net-falls-to-1-dot-14-trillion-rubles-below-estimates

Rufat, S., & Suditu, B. (2008). Bucarest, faire la ville entre héritages et mimétisme. *L'Espace Geographique*, *4*(37), 327–337.

Ruggie, J. G. (2003). Taking Embedded Liberalism Global: The Corporate Connection. In D. Held & M. Koenig-Archibugi (Eds.), *Taming Globalisation: Frontiers of Governance* (pp. 93–129). Cambridge: Polity Press.

Russell, J. (2008). Corporate social responsibility: what it means for the project manager. In *Proceedings of the 2008 PMI Europe Congress*. Project Management Institute.

Russian American Business. (2009). *Energy Strategy 2030*. Retrieved March 5, 2014, from *http://*russianamericanbusiness.org/we*b_CURRENT/articles/545/1/* Energy-strategy-2030

Russian Government. (2013). *Federal Law No. 250*. Retrieved April 25, 2014, from http://www.minfin.ru/common/upload/library/2013/12/main/FZ349-FZ_ot_021213.pdf

Sadiki, F. A. (2012). *Sustainable Tourism Marketing Strategies at UNESCO World Heritage Sites (UNLV Theses/Dissertations/Professional Papers/Capstones; Paper 1477)*. Las Vegas, NV: University of Las Vegas University Libraries.

Saipradist, A., & Staiff, R. (2007). Crossing the Cultural Divide: Western Tourists and Interpretation at Ayutthaya World Heritage Site, Thailand. *Journal of Heritage Tourism*, *2*(3), 211–224. doi:10.2167/jht061.0

Salet, W. (2007). New metropolitan spaces and metropolitan strategies in the face of modernisation, *Metropoles, 2*, 1-26. Retrieved August, 2012, from http://metropoles.revues.org/262

Salon, D., Sperling, D., Meier, A., Murphy, S., Gorham, R., & Barrett, J. (2010). City carbon budgets: A proposal to align incentives for climate-friendly communities. *Energy Policy*, *38*(4), 2032–2041. doi:10.1016/j.enpol.2009.12.005

San Diego Association of Governments. (2009). *Regional Energy Strategy*. Retrieved November 29, 2010, from http://www.sandag.org/uploads/publicationid/publicationid_1476_10631.pdf

Santiso, R. (1997). Effects of chronic parasitosis on women's health. *International Journal of Gynaecology and Obstetrics: the Official Organ of the International Federation of Gynaecology and Obstetrics*, *58*(1), 129–136. doi:10.1016/S0020-7292(97)02865-8 PMID:9253675

Santoro, G. M. (1994). The internet: An overview. *Communication Education*, *43*(2), 73–86. doi:10.1080/03634529409378965

Sarıyer Municipality. (2012). *Two green investments in the future of Sarıyer*. Retrieved March 22, 2014, from http://en.sariyer.bel.tr/news/654/two-green-investments-in-the-future-of-sariyer.aspx

Sauter, R., & Bauknecht, D. (2009). Distributed Generation: Transforming the Electricity Network. In I. Scrase & G. MacKerron (Eds.), *Energy for The Future: A New Agenda* (pp. 147–164). New York, NY: Palgrave MacMillan.

Schäffler, A., & Swilling, M. (2013). Valuing green infrastructure in an urban environment under pressure — The Johannesburg case. *Ecological Economics*, *86*(0), 246–257.

Schatz, B. R., & Hardin, J. B. (1994). NCSA Mosaic and the World Wide Web: Global hypermedia protocols for the Internet. *Science*, *265*(5174), 895–901. doi:10.1126/science.265.5174.895 PMID:17782140

Schieg, M. (2009). The model of corporate social responsibility in project management. *Business: Theory & Practice*, *10*(4), 315–321.

Schmidlin, T., Huerlimann, E., Silue, K. D., Yapi, R. B., Houngbedji, C., Kouadio, B. A., & Raso, G. et al. (2013). Effects of Hygiene and Defecation Behavior on Helminths and Intestinal Protozoa Infections in Taabo, Cote d'Ivoire. *PLoS ONE*, *8*(6). PMID:23840358

Scholte, J. A. (2000). *Globalization: The Critical Introduction*. New York, NY: Palgrave.

Scholte, J. A. (2004). Civil Society and Democratically Accountable Global Governance. *Government and Opposition*, *39*(2), 211–233. doi:10.1111/j.1477-7053.2004.00121.x

Schultz, S. K., & Mcshane, C. (1978). To engineer the metropolis: Sewers, sanitation, and city planning in late-nineteenth-century America. *The Journal of American History*, *65*(2), 389–411. doi:10.2307/1894086 PMID:11614685

Schulz, A., & Northridge, M. E. (2004). Social determinants of health: Implications for environmental health promotion. *Health Education & Behavior*, *31*(4), 455–471. doi:10.1177/1090198104265598 PMID:15296629

Seliger, G., Kim, H.-J., Kernbaum, S., & Zettl, M. (2008). Approaches to sustainable manufacturing. *International Journal of Sustainable Manufacturing*, *1*(1/2), 58–77. doi:10.1504/IJSM.2008.019227

Selwyn, T. (1996). Introduction. In T. Selwyn (Ed.), *The Tourist Image: Myths and Myth Making in Tourism* (pp. 1–33). Chichester, UK: John Wiley and Sons, Ltd.

Sener, I., Eluru, N., & Bhat, C. R. (2009). Who Are Bicyclists? Why and How Much Are They Bicycling? *Transportation Research Record*, *2134*(1), 63–72. doi:10.3141/2134-08

Senge, P. (2008). *The Necessary Revolution: How Individuals and Organizations Are Working Together to Create A Sustainable World*. New York, NY: Doubleday Publishing Group.

Seres, S. (2008). *Analysis of technology transfer in CDM projects*. Bonn: UNFCCC Secretariat.

Shah, R., & Romine, J. (1995). *Playing MUDs on the Internet*. New York: Wiley & Sons.

Shaviv, E. (1989). The influence of the thermal mass on the thermal performance of buildings in summer and winter. In T. C. Steemers & W. Palz (Eds.), *Science and Technology at the service of architecture* (pp. 470–472). Dordrecht: Kluwer Academic Publishers.

Sheer, H. (2004). *The Solar Economy: Renewable Energy for a Sustainable Global Future*. London, UK: Earthscan.

Sheller, M., & Urry, J. (2000). The City and the Car. *International Journal of Urban and Regional Research*, *24*(4), 737–757. doi:10.1111/1468-2427.00276

Shenhar, A. J., & Dvir, D. (2004). Project management evolution: Past history and future research directions. In D. P. Slevin, D. I. Cleland & J. K. Pinto (Eds.), Innovations: Project Management Research 2004 (pp. 57-64). Newton Square. PA: Project Management Institute.

Shenhar, A. J., Dvir, D., Levy, O., & Maltz, A. C. (2001). Project Success: A Multidimensional Strategic Concept. *Long Range Planning*, *34*(6), 699–725. doi:10.1016/S0024-6301(01)00097-8

Shim, J. P., Warkentin, M., Courtney, J. F., Power, D. J., Sharda, R., & Carlsson, C. (2002). Past, present, and future of decision support technology. *Decision Support Systems*, *33*(2), 111–126. doi:10.1016/S0167-9236(01)00139-7

Shin, D. H. (2006). Prospectus of mobile TV: Another bubble or killer application? *Telematics and Informatics*, *23*(4), 253–270. doi:10.1016/j.tele.2005.08.001

Shore, W. B. (2006). Land-use, transportation and sustainability. *Technology in Society*, *28*(1-2), 27–43. doi:10.1016/j.techsoc.2005.10.014

Sieverts, T. (1999). *Zwischenstadt*. Braunschweig, Wiesbaden: Zwischen Ort und Welt, Raum und Zeit, Stadt und Land.

Silvius, A. J. G., & Schipper, R. (2010, November). *A maturity model for integrating sustainability in projects and project management*. Paper presented at the 24th IPMA World Congress. Istanbul, Turkey.

Silvius, A. J. G., Schipper, R., & Nedeski, S. (2013). Sustainability in Project Management: Reality Bites. *PM World Journal*, *II*(II).

Silvius, A. J. G., van den Brink, J., & Köhler, A. (2010, Februray). *The concept of sustainability and its application to project management*. Paper presented at the IPMA International Expert Seminar 2010 - Survival and Sustainability as Challenges for Projects. Zurich, Switzerland.

Silvius, A. J. G., & Schipper, R. (2012). Sustainability in the Business Case. In *Proceedings of the 26th IPMA World Congress* (pp. 1062 – 1069). Amsterdam, The Netherlands: International Project Management Association.

Silvius, A. J. G., van den Brink, J., & Köhler, A. (2009). Views on Sustainable Project Management. In K. Kähköhnen, A. S. Kazi, & M. Rekola (Eds.), *Human Side of Projects in Modern Business*. Helsinki, Finland: IPMA Scientific Research Paper Series.

Simonsen, P. S., & Jørgensen, B. (1998). Cycle tourism. An economic and environmental sustainable form of tourism? In C. Simonsen, S. Jørgensen, L. Robbins (Eds.), *Cycling tourism*. Unit of Tourism Research at Research Centre of Bornholm. Retrieved from www.crt.dk/media/Cycling_tourism.pdf

Singh, J. (2000). *On farm energy use pattern in different cropping systems in Haryana, India*. Unpublished master's thesis, International Institute of Management-University of Flensburg, Germany.

Sirakaya, E., Jamal, T., & Choi, H. (2001). In Search of Sustainable Tourism Indicators. In D. Weaver (Ed.), *Encyclopedia of Ecotourism* (pp. 411–432). Oxford, UK: Oxford University Press.

Sitarz, D. (1992). *Agenda 21: The Earth Summit Strategy to save our planet*. Boulder, CO: Earth Press.

Sivkov, S. I. (1964). On the computation of the possible and relative duration of sunshine. *Trans. Main Geophys Obs*, *160*(0), 21–39.

Sivkov, S. I. (1964). To the methods of computing possible radiation in Italy. *Trans. Main Geophys Obs*, *160*(0), 1–20.

Skjærseth, J. B., Stokke, O. S., & Wettestad, J. (2006). Soft Law, Hard Law, and Effective Implementation. *Global Environmental Politics*, *6*(3), 104–120. doi:10.1162/glep.2006.6.3.104

Slavsky, L. (2006). Tecnologías de la información y la comunicación para jóvenes mapuches. *Novedades de Antropología*, *15*(54), 12–13.

Smith, M. G. (2012). *Enhancing Water Conservation Strategies in NYC: Saving Water to Save Energy*. (Unpublished master's thesis). School of Architecture, Pratt Institute, New York, NY.

Smith, W. P., & Zollner, P. A. (2005). Sustainable management of wildlife habitat and risk of extinction. *Biological Conservation*, *125*(3), 287–295.

Socco, C. (2010). *Il Piano Urbano di Mobilità Sostenibile. Annessi*. Osservatorio Città Sostenibili, Department Territorio Politecnico and University of Turin.

Soerensen, H. C., & Weinstein, A. (2006). *Ocean Energy: Position paper for IPCC*. Retrieved June 13, 2014, from http://www.eu-oea.com/euoea/files/ccLibraryFiles/Filename/000000000400/Ocean_Energy_IPCC_final.pdf

SolarCentury. (2009). *The Merton Rule*. Retrieved December 11, 2009, from http://www.solarcentury.co.uk/Knowledge-Base/The-Merton-Rule

Solomon, B., & Banerjee, A. (2006). A global survey of hydrogen energy research, development and policy. *Energy Policy*, *34*(7), 781–792. doi:10.1016/j.enpol.2004.08.007

Sovacool, B. K., & Brown, M. A. (2010). Competing dimensions of energy security: An international perspective. *Annual Review of Environment and Resources*, *35*(1), 77–108. doi:10.1146/annurev-environ-042509-143035

Sovacool, B. K., & Mukherjee, I. (2011). Conceptualizing and measuring energy security: A synthesized approach. *Energy*, *36*(8), 5343–5355. doi:10.1016/j.energy.2011.06.043

Sovacool, B. K., & Watts, C. (2009). Going Completely Renewable: Is it Possible (Let Alone Desirable)? *The Electricity Journal*, *22*(4), 95–111. doi:10.1016/j.tej.2009.03.011

Spiegel, J. M., & Yassi, A. (2004). Lessons from the Margins of Globalization: Appreciating the Cuban Health Paradox. *Journal of Public Health Policy*, *25*(1), 85–110. doi:10.1057/palgrave.jphp.3190007 PMID:15134135

Stavins, R. N. (2001). *Experience with Market-Based Environmental Policy Instruments*. Discussion Paper 01-58. Washington, DC: Resources for the Future.

Stedman, J. B., & Osorio-O'Dea, P. (2001). *E-Rate for schools: Background on telecommunications discounts through the Universal Service Fund (98-604 EPW)*. Congressional Research Service. Retrieved April 10, 2010, from Policy Archive website: http://www.policyarchive.org/handle/10207/bitstreams/655.pdf

Steele, J. (1997). *Sustainable architecture: principles, paradigms, and case studies*. New York, NY: McGraw-Hill Inc.

Steg, L., & Gifford, R. (2005). Sustainable transportation and quality of life. *Journal of Transport Geography*, *13*(1), 59–69. doi:10.1016/j.jtrangeo.2004.11.003

Stepek, G., Buttle, D. J., Duce, I. R., & Behnke, J. M. (2006). Human gastrointestinal nematode infections: Are new control methods required? *International Journal of Experimental Pathology*, *87*(5), 325–341. doi:10.1111/j.1365-2613.2006.00495.x PMID:16965561

Sterman, J. D. (2006). Learning from evidence in a complex world. *American Journal of Public Health*, *96*(3), 505–514. doi:10.2105/AJPH.2005.066043 PMID:16449579

Stern, E., Gudes, O., & Svoray, T. (2009). Web-Based Traditional Public Participation Comprehensive Planning: A Comparative Study. *Environment & Planning B*, *36*(6), 1067–1085. doi:10.1068/b34113

Stern, N. (2006). *Stern Review: The economics of climate change*. London: HM Treasury.

Stoll, C. (1989). *The cuckoo's egg: Tracking a spy through the maze of computer espionage*. New York: Doubleday.

Strauss, J. (2013). Does housing drive state-level job growth? Building permits and consumer expectations forecast a state's economic activity. *Journal of Urban Economics*, *73*(1), 77–93. doi:10.1016/j.jue.2012.07.005

Strohbach, M. W., Haase, D., & Kabisch, N. (2009). Birds and the city: Urban biodiversity, land use, and socioeconomics. *Ecology and Society*, *14*(2), 31.

Subramanian, P. M. (2000). Plastics recycling and waste management in the U.S. *Resources, Conservation and Recycling*, *28*(3), 253–263. doi:10.1016/S0921-3449(99)00049-X

Sugaya, H. (1998). Consumer video recorders. In E. D. Daniel, C. D. Mee, & M. H. Clark (Eds.), *Magnetic Recording: The First 100 Years* (pp. 182–200). Hoboken, NJ: Wiley-IEEE.

Sugaya, H. (1998). Helical-scan recorders for broadcasting. In E. D. Daniel, C. D. Mee, & M. H. Clark (Eds.), *Magnetic Recording: The First 100 Years* (pp. 170–181). Hoboken, NJ: Wiley-IEEE.

Suthar, S., Bishnoi, P., Singh, S., Mutiyar, P. K., Nema, A. K., & Patil, N. S. (2009). Nitrate contamination in groundwater of some rural areas of Rajasthan, India. *Journal of Hazardous Materials*, *171*(1–3), 189–199. doi:10.1016/j.jhazmat.2009.05.111 PMID:19545944

Sykora, L., & Ourednícekin, M. (2007). Sprawling post-communist metropolis: Commercial and residential suburbanization in Prague and Brno, the Czech Republic. In E. Razin, M. Dijst, & C. Vázquez (Eds.), *Employment Deconcentration in European Metropolitan Areas* (pp. 209–233). Dordrecht: Springer.

Szekely, F., & Strebel, H. (2013). Incremental, radical and game-changing: Strategic innovation for sustainability. *Corporate Governance*, *13*(5), 467–481. doi:10.1108/CG-06-2013-0084

Talebi, M., & Way, T. (2009). Methods, metrics and motivation for a green computer science program. In *Proceedings of the 40th ACM (Association of Computing Machinery) Technical Symposium*. New York, NY: ACM. doi:10.1145/1508865.1508995

Talu, N. (2007). *Sürdürülebilir kalkınma durum değerlendirme raporu, Sürdürülebilir Kalkınmanın Sektörel Politikalara Entegrasyonu Projesi*. Retrieved March 27, 2010, from http://www.bayindirlik.gov.tr/turkce/kentlesme/skdurumdegerlendirmeraporu.pdf

Tam, G. C. K. (2010a, February). *Sustainability competence requirements for project manager*. Paper presented at the IPMA International Expert Seminar 2010 - Survival and Sustainability as Challenges for Projects. Zurich, Switzerland.

Tam, G. C. K. (2010b). The program management process with sustainability considerations. *Journal of Project. Program & Portfolio Management*, *1*(1), 17–27.

Tam, G. C. K. (2013). Sustainability assessment for project managers. In G. Silvius & J. Tharp (Eds.), *Sustainability Integration for Effective Project Management* (pp. 288–302). Hershey, PA: IGI Global. doi:10.4018/978-1-4666-4177-8.ch018

Tang, B., Wong, S., & Lee, A. K. (2007). Green belt in a compact city: A zone for conservation or transition? *Landscape and Urban Planning*, *79*(3-4), 358–373.

Tarr, J. A. (1979). The Separate vs. Combined Sewer Problem: A Case Study in Urban Technology Design Choice. *Journal of Urban History*, *5*(3), 308–339. PMID:11614824

Tarr, J. A., McCurley, J. III, McMichael, F. C., & Yosie, T. (1984). Water and Wastes: A Retrospective Assessment of Wastewater Technology in the United States, 1800-1932. *Technology and Culture*, *25*(2), 226–263. doi:10.2307/3104713 PMID:11611516

Task Force on Climate Change Prime Minister's Office. (2008). *Comprehensive Plan on Combating Climate Change*. Seoul: Task Force on Climate Change Prime Minister's Office.

Tate, J. E., Burton, A. H., Boschi-Pinto, C., Steele, A. D., Duque, J., & Parashar, U. D. (2012). 2008 estimate of worldwide rotavirus-associated mortality in children younger than 5 years before the introduction of universal rotavirus vaccination programmes: A systematic review and meta-analysis. *The Lancet Infectious Diseases*, *12*(2), 136–141. doi:10.1016/S1473-3099(11)70253-5 PMID:22030330

Taylor, J. (2001). Authenticity and Sincerity in Tourism. *Annals of Tourism Research*, *28*(1), 7–26.

Taylor, M. S., Ha, M., Frank, J., & Whiter, N. (1990). The Risk Approach in Diarrheal Disease Intervention in Grenada. *Social Science & Medicine*, *30*(10), 1089–1095. doi:10.1016/0277-9536(90)90295-4 PMID:2363059

Taylor, T. (2010). *Sustainability Interventions - for Managers of Projects and Programmes*. Salford, UK: The Higher Education Academy – Centre for Education in the Built Environment.

Tejedor, F. J., & García-Valcárcel, A. (2005). Condicionantes (actitudes, conocimientos, usos, intereses, necesidades formativas) a tener en cuenta en la formación del profesorado no universitario en TIC. Revista Enseñanza, 23, 115-142. Retrieved December 31, 2010, from http://e-spacio.uned.es/fez/eserv.php?pid=bibliuned:20225&dsID=condicionantes__tener.pdf

Tello, E. (2007). Las tecnologías de la información y comunicaciones (TIC) y la brecha digital: Su impacto en la sociedad de México. RUSC, 4(2), 1-8. Retrieved September 15, 2010, from http://www.uoc.edu/rusc/4/2/dt/esp/tello.pdf

Tepecik, A., & Anderson, E. (2006). *Sustainable Development within the Region: Strategies and the Complex Social System- What Turkey and the U.S.A. Can Learn from Skåne, Sweden*. Retrieved May 3, 2014, from http://www.bth.se/tks/esp.nsf/

Terrados, J., Almonacid, G., & Hontoria, L. (2007). Regional energy planning through SWOT analysis and strategic planning tools: Impact on renewables development. *Renewable & Sustainable Energy Reviews*, *11*(6), 1275–1287. doi:10.1016/j.rser.2005.08.003

Terris, M. (1989). The Health Status of Cuba: Recommendations for Epidemiologic Investigation and Public Health Policy. *Journal of Public Health Policy*, *10*(1), 78–87. doi:10.2307/3342945 PMID:2715341

Terry, N. P. (1994). GUI Wars: The Windows Litigation and the Continuing Decline of Look and Feel. *Arkansas Law Review*, *47*, 93–155.

Thakur, C., & Mistra, B. (1993). Energy requirements and energy gaps for production of major crops in India. *Agricultural Situation of India*, *48*(10), 665–689.

Tharp, J. (2013). Sustainability in Project Management: Practical Applications. In A. J. G. Silvius & J. Tharp (Eds.), *Sustainability Integration for Effective Project Management* (pp. 182–193). Hershey, PA: IGI Global Publishing. doi:10.4018/978-1-4666-4177-8.ch011

The California Energy Commission. (2007). *2007 Integrated Energy Policy Report*. Retrieved May 10, 2010, from http://www.energy.ca.gov/2007_energypolicy/

The Climate Group. (2008). *SMART 2020: Enabling the low carbon economy in the information age*. Report by the Climate Group on behalf of the Global e-Sustainability Initiative (GeSI), The Climate Group, London. Retrieved from http://www.smart2020.org/

The Economist Intelligence Unit Limited. (2003). *Russian Renewables Business Brief: Power Economics*. Retrieved October 3, 2009, from the Business Source Complete database.

The Economist Intelligence Unit Limited. (2013). *Russia Energy Report*. The Economist Intelligence Unit Limited. Retrieved May 2, 2014, from the Business Source Complete database.

The Economist. (2014). *Output/Prices/Jobs*. Retrieved May 4, 2014, from http://www.economist.com/news/economic-and-financial-indicators/21601526-output-prices-and-jobs

The World Commission of Environment and Development. (1987). *Our Common Future*. Oxford, UK: Oxford University Press.

Thoumy, M., & Vachon, S. (2012). Environmental projects and financial performance: Exploring the impact of project characteristics. *International Journal of Production Economics*, *140*(1), 28–34. doi:10.1016/j.ijpe.2012.01.014

Thrift, N. (2004). Driving in the city. *Theory, Culture & Society*, *21*(4-5), 41–59. doi:10.1177/0263276404046060

Tibor, T., & Feldman, I. (1996). *ISO 14000: A Guide to the New Environmental Management Standards*. Chicago: Irwin Professional Publishing.

Timothy, D. J. (2011). *Cultural heritage and tourism: An introduction*. Bristol, UK: Channel View Publications.

Timothy, D., & Boyd, S. (2006). Heritage Tourism in the 21st Century: Valued Traditions and New Perspectives. *Journal of Heritage Tourism*, *1*(1), 1–16.

Tinuade, O., John, O., Saheed, O., Oyeku, O., Fidelis, N., & Olabisi, D. (2006). Parasitic etiology of childhood diarrhea. *Indian Journal of Pediatrics*, *73*(12), 1081–1084. doi:10.1007/BF02763049 PMID:17202634

Tiron-Tudor, A., & Ioana-Maria, D. (2013). Project Success by Integrating Sustainability in Project Management. In A. J. G. Silvius & J. Tharp (Eds.), *Sustainability Integration for Effective Project Management* (pp. 106–127). Hershey, PA: IGI Global Publishing.

Tomes, N. (1998). *The gospel of germs: men, women, and the microbe in American life*. Cambridge, MA: Harvard University Press.

Toprak, Z., & Palabıyık, H. (2000). Participation and civil society: The experiences of Izmir local agenda 21 (1995–2000). *Turkish Public Administration Annual*, *24-26*(1).

Tratalos, J., Fuller, R. A., Warren, P. H., Davies, R. G., & Gaston, K. J. (2007). Urban form, biodiversity potential and ecosystem services. *Landscape and Urban Planning*, *83*(4), 308–317.

Travisi, C., & Camagni, R. (2005). *Sustainability of Urban Sprawl: Environmental-Economic. Indicators for the Analysis of Mobility Impact in Italy*. The Fondazione Eni Enrico Mattei. Retrieved from http://www.feem.it/Feem/Pub/Publications/WPapers/default.htm

Tsioliaridou, E., Bakos, G., & Stadler, M. (2006). A new energy planning methodology for the penetration of renewable energy technologies in electricity sector: Application for the island of Crete. *Energy Policy*, *34*(18), 3757–3764. doi:10.1016/j.enpol.2005.08.021

Tsoutsos, T., Drandaki, M., Frantzeskaki, N., Iosifidis, E., & Kiosses, I. (2009). Sustainable energy planning by using multi-criteria analysis application in the island of Crete. *Energy Policy*, *37*(5), 1587–1600. doi:10.1016/j.enpol.2008.12.011

Tukahirwa, J. T., Mol, A. P. J., & Oosterveer, P. (2013). Comparing urban sanitation and solid waste management in East African metropolises: The role of civil society organisations. *Cities (London, England)*, *30*(0), 204–211. doi:10.1016/j.cities.2012.03.007

Tukker, A., Cohen, M. J., de Zoysa, U., Hertwich, E., Hofstetter, P., Inaba, A., & Stø, S. et al. (2006). The Oslo Declaration on Sustainable Consumption. *Journal of Industrial Ecology*, *10*(1-2), 9–14. doi:10.1162/108819806775545303

Turban, E. (1993). *Decision support and expert systems: management support systems*. Upper Saddle River, New Jersey, USA: Prentice Hall PTR.

Turner, J. R. (2010). Responsibilities for Sustainable Development in Project and Program Management. In H. Knoepfel (Ed.), *Survival and Sustainability as Challenges for Projects*. Zurich, Switzerland: International Project Management Association.

Turner, J. R. (Ed.). (2009). *The handbook of project-based management: Leading strategic change in organizations* (3rd ed.). New York, NY: McGraw-Hill.

Turner, J. R., & Müller, R. (2003). On the nature of the project as a temporary organization. *International Journal of Project Management*, *21*(3), 1–8.

TWAS. (2008). *Sustainable energy for developing countries*. Trieste: The Academy of Sciences for the Developing World.

Uiterkamp, A. J. M. S., & Vlek, C. (2007). Practice and Outcomes of Multidisciplinary Research for Environmental Sustainability. *The Journal of Social Issues*, *63*(1), 175–197. doi:10.1111/j.1540-4560.2007.00502.x

UN (United Nations). (1987). *Our Common Future, Report of the World commission on environment and development*. Retrieved January, 2009, from http://www.un-documents.net/wced-ocf.htm

UN Committee on Economic, Social and Cultural Rights (CESCR). (2003). *General Comment No. 15: The Right to Water* (Arts. 11 and 12 of the Covenant). 20 January 2003, E/C.12/2002/11, Retrieved from http://www.refworld.org/docid/4538838d11.html

UN General Assembly. (1966). *International Covenant on Economic, Social and Cultural Rights*. 16 December 1966, United Nations, Treaty Series, vol. 993, p. 3, Retrieved from http://www.refworld.org/docid/3ae6b36c0.html

UN General Assembly. (2010). *Resolution 15/9, Human rights and access to safe drinking water and sanitation*. A/HRC/RES/15/9 (6 October 2010), Retrieved from http://daccess-dds-ny.un.org/doc/UNDOC/GEN/G10/166/33/PDF/G1016633.pdf?OpenElement

UNCED. (1992). *Agenda 21, Chapter 1: Preamble.United Nations Conference on Environment & Development*.

UNDESA. (2007). *Energy indicators for sustainable development: Country studies on Brazil, Cuba, Lithuania, Mexico, Russian Federation, Slovakia and Thailand*. New York: United Nations. Retrieved July 31, 2012, from http://www.un.org/esa/sustdev/publications/energy_indicators/chapter2.pdf

UNEP. (1987). *Our common future: The world commission on environment and development*. Oxford: Oxford University Press.

UNESCO. (2002). *Operational Guidelines for the Implementation of the World Heritage Convention*. Paris, France: UNESCO.

UNFCCC. (2011). Addendum. Part Two: Action taken by the Conference of the Parties at its sixteenth session. In *Proceedings of the Conference of the Parties on Its Sixteenth Session*. Retrieved from http://unfccc.int/resource/docs/2010/cop16/eng/07a01.pdf

United Nation Children's Fund & World Health Organization. (2013). *Progress on Drinking Water and Sanitation 2013 Update*. Retrieved March 20, 2014 from http://apps.who.int/iris/bitstream/10665/81245/1/9789241505390_eng.pdf

United Nation. (2014). *International Decade for Action 'Water for Life' 2005-2015*. Retrieved March 20, 2014, from http://www.un.org/waterforlifedecade/sanitation.shtml

United Nations (UN). (2003). World urbanisation project: the 2002 revision. New York, NY: The United Nations Population Division.

United Nations Development Programme (UNDP). (2000). *World energy assessment: energy and the challenge of sustainability.* Retrieved January 20, 2010, from http://www.energyandenvironment.undp.org/undp/indexAction.cfm?module=Library&action=GetFile&DocumentAttachmentID=1020

United Nations Development Project. (2013). *National human development report in the Russian Federation.* Retrieved May 15, 2014, from http://hdr.undp.org/en/countries/profiles/RUS

United Nations Development Project. (2013). *Oil and gas in Russia: MarketLine industry profile*. Retrieved April 29, 2014, from the Business Source Complete database (Reference code: 0153-2116 (September)).

United Nations Framework Convention on Climate Change (UNFCCC). (2009). *The draft of the Copenhagen Climate Change Treaty* (pp. 3–181).

United Nations, Department of Economic and Social Affairs, Population Division. (2014). *World Urbanization Prospects: The 2014 Revision, Highlights* (ST/ESA/SER.A/352). Retrieved January 30, 2015, from www.esa.un.org

United Nations, Economic Commission for Europe. (2008). *Working Together for Sustainable and Healthy Transport: Guidance on Supportive Institutional Conditions for Policy Integration of Transport, Health and Environment.* Retrieved June 10, 2012, from www.unece.org

United Nations. (1992). Rio declaration on environment and development. *Report of the United Nations Conference on Environment and Development*. Rio de Janeiro, Brazil.

United States Geological Service. (2011). *2009 Minerals Yearbook: Canada*. Washington, DC: United States Department of the Interior, United States Geological Survey.

University of Maryland College Park. (2000). *Estimated Internet usage by basic general social survey demographics*. Retrieved April 10, 2010, from http://www.webuse.umd.edu/tutorial/SDA-GSS_Tutorial.pdf

UN-REDD. (2010). *The UN-REDD Programme*. Retrieved March 23, 2010, from http://www.un-redd.org/UNREDDProgramme/tabid/583/language/en-US/Default.aspx

Urbanczyk, R. (2010). *PRESTO Cycling Policy Guide. Promotion of Cycling*. Retrieved June 22, 2012, from www.presto-cycling.eu

Urry, J. (2004). The "System" of Auto mobility. *Theory, Culture & Society*, *21*(4-5), 25–29. doi:10.1177/0263276404046059

Urry, J. (2006). Inhabiting the car. *The Sociological Review*, *54*(S1), 7–31. doi:10.1111/j.1467-954X.2006.00635.x

Urry, J. (Ed.). (2007). *Mobilites*. Cambridge, UK: Polity Press.

Uslaner, E. M. (1998). Social capital, television, and the "mean world": Trust, optimism, and civic participation. *Political Psychology*, *19*(3), 441–467. doi:10.1111/0162-895X.00113

Vajjhala, S. P. (2005, July). Integrating GIS and participatory mapping in community development planning. In *25th Annual ESRI International Users Conference*. San Diego, CA.

Valdés, N. P. (1971). Health and Revolution in Cuba. *Science and Society*, *35*(3), 311–335.

Valentin, E. K. (2001). SWOT analysis from a resource-based view. *Journal of Marketing*, *9*(2), 54–68.

Valkila, N., & Saari, A. (2012). Perceptions Held by Finnish Energy Sector Experts Regarding Public Attitudes to Energy Issues. *J. Sustainable. Dev.*, *5*(11), 23–45.

van Agtmael, A. (2007). *The Emerging Markets Century: How a New Breed of World-Class Companies is Overtaking the World*. New York, NY: Free Press.

van den Brink, J. (2009). Duurzaam projectmanagement: verder kijken dan je project lang is (Sustainable Project Management: Looking Beyond the Project) *Projectie, 4* (In Dutch).

van den Brink, J. (2013). How Positive Psychology can Support Sustainable Project Management. In A. J. G. Silvius & J. Tharp (Eds.), *Sustainability Integration for Effective Project Management* (pp. 245–260). Hershey, PA: IGI Global Publishing. doi:10.4018/978-1-4666-4177-8.ch015

Van der Helm, R. (2009). The vision phenomenon: Towards a theoretical underpinning of visions of the future and the process of envisioning. *Futures*, *41*(2), 96–104. doi:10.1016/j.futures.2008.07.036

Van Leeuwen, E. S., Vreeker, R., & Rodenburq, C. A. (2006). A framework for quality of life assessment of urban green areas in Europe: An application to District Park Reudnitz Leipzig. *International Journal of Environmental Technology and Management*, *6*(1-2), 111–122.

Vanclay, F. (2003). SIA Principles: International principles for social impact assessment. *Impact Assessment and Project Appraisal*, *21*(1), 5–11. doi:10.3152/147154603781766491

Vargas-Parra, M. V., Villalba, G., & Gabarrell, X. (2013). Applying exergy analysis to rainwater harvesting systems to assess resource efficiency. *Resources, Conservation and Recycling*, *72*(0), 50–59. doi:10.1016/j.resconrec.2012.12.008

Vine, E. (2008). Strategies and policies for improving energy efficiency programs: Closing the loop between evaluation and implementation. *Energy Policy*, *36*(10), 3872–3881. doi:10.1016/j.enpol.2008.06.038

Virnoche, M. E. (1998). The Seamless web and communications equity: The shaping of a community network. *Science, Technology & Human Values*, *23*(2), 199–220. doi:10.1177/016224399802300203

Vision, S. (2010). *Spatially Enabling Government – 'Healthtracks' wins 2010 WA Spatial Excellence*. Retrieved November 30, 2010, from http://www.spatialvision.com.au/index.php/latest-news-spatially-enabling-government.html

Visser, W. T. (2002). Sustainability reporting in South Africa. *Corporate Environmental Strategy*, *9*(1), 79–85. doi:10.1016/S1066-7938(01)00157-9

Voinov, A., & Smith, C. (1994). *Dimensions of sustainability*. Paper presented at the 1st International Symposium of Ecosystem Health & Medicine. Ottawa, Canada. Retrieved May 1, 2011, from http://www.uvm.edu/~gundiee/AV/PUBS/DS/Sust_Dim.html

Waddock, S. (2008). Building a New Institutional Infrastructure for Corporate Responsibility. *The Academy of Management Perspectives*, *22*(3), 87–108. doi:10.5465/AMP.2008.34587997

Wager, J. (1995). Developing a strategy for the Angkor world heritage site. *Tourism Management*, *16*(7), 515–523. doi:10.1016/0261-5177(95)00069-Z

Walker, C. L. F., Rudan, I., Liu, L., Nair, H., Theodoratou, E., Bhutta, Z. A., & Black, R. E. et al. (2013). Global burden of childhood pneumonia and diarrhoea. *Lancet*, *381*(9875), 1405–1416. doi:10.1016/S0140-6736(13)60222-6 PMID:23582727

Walker, J. (2004). *Rebels on the air: An alternative history of radio in America*. New York: NYU Press.

Walle, A. H. (1998). *Cultural tourism: a strategic focus*. Boulder, CO: Westview Press, Inc.

Wall, T. (2007). Finding an alternative: Music programming in US college radio. *Radio Journal: International Studies in Broadcast & Audio Media*, *5*(1), 35–54.

Walsh, T. (2005). *Timeless toys: Classic toys and the playmakers who made them*. Riverside, NJ: Andrews McMeel.

Wang, Y., Byrne, J., Boo, K., Yun, S., & Soh, Y. (1996). *A spatially-integrated energy planning model for Korea's sustainable development*. Seoul: Korean Ministry of Commerce, Industry and Energy.

Ward, J. W., & Warren, C. (2007). *Silent victories: the history and practice of public health in twentieth-century America*. Oxford, UK: Oxford University Press.

Warren, M. (2002). What Can Democratic Participation Mean Today? *Political Theory*, *30*(5), 677–701. doi:10.1177/0090591702030005003

Warschauer, M. (2003). *Technology and Social Inclusion: Rethinking the Digital Divide*. Cambridge, MA: MIT Press.

Wateraid. (2014). *Risking rape to reach a toilet in India's slums*. Retrieved December 12, 2014, from http://www.wateraid.org/news/news/risking-rape-to-reach-a-toilet-in-india-slums

Watson, R. T., Boudreau, M. C., Chen, A., & Huber, M. H. (2008). Green IS: Building sustainable business practices. In R. T. Watson (Ed.), *Information Systems*. Athens, GA: Global Text Project.

WCED. (1987). *Our common future*. Oxford, UK: Oxford University Press.

Weaver, M. (2012). Canadian Mining and Corporate Social Responsibility: Advancing Corporate Interest and Community Engagement. *Global Conference on Business and Finance Proceedings*, *7*(2), 582-592.

Web Developer's Virtual Library. (2010). *History of the Internet and the World Wide Web*. Retrieved April 10, 2010, from Web Developer's Virtual Library.com website: http://www.wdvl.com/Internet/History

Webb, K. (2012). Multi-level Corporate Responsibility and the Mining Sector: Learning from the Canadian Experience in Latin America. In V. K. Aggarwal (Ed.), *Business and Politics* (pp. 1–43). Boston, MA: De Gruyter. doi:10.1515/bap-2012-0022

Webster, D., & Muller, L. (2000). *Urban Competitiveness Assessment in Developing Country Urban Regions: The Road Forward.* Paper presented at the Urban Group, INFUD, World Bank. Washington, DC: World Bank.

WEC. (2013). *World energy scenarios: Composing energy futures to 2050*. London: World Energy Council. Retrieved July 25, 2014, from http://www.worldenergy.org/wp-content/uploads/2013/09/World-Energy-Scenarios_Composing-energy-futures-to-2050_Full-report.pdf

WEC. (2013). *World energy trilemma: Time to get real – The case for sustainable energy investment*. London: World Energy Council. Retrieved July 25, 2014, from http://www.worldenergy.org/wp-content/uploads/2013/09/2013-Time-to-get-real-the-case-for-sustainable-energy-investment.pdf

WEF. (2013). *The Global Energy Architecture Performance Index Report 2014*. New York: World Economic Forum and Accenture. Retrieved July 25, 2014, from http://www3.weforum.org/docs/ WEF_EN_NEA_Report_2014.pdf

Weidmann, K., Hennings, N., Schmidt, S., & Wuestefeld, T. (2011). The Importance of Brand Heritage as a Key Performance Driver in Marketing Management. *Journal of Brand Management*, *19*(3), 182–194. doi:10.1057/bm.2011.36

Weimann, G. (2006). Terrorist dot com: Using the internet for terrorist recruitment and mobilization. In J. Forest (Ed.), The making of a terrorist: Recruitment, training, and root causes, Vol. 1: Recruitment (pp. 53-65). Westport, CT: Praeger.

Wen, L. M., & Rissel, C. (2008). Inverse associations between cycling to work, public transport, and overweight and obesity: Findings from a population based study in Australia. *Preventive Medicine*, *46*(1), 29–32. doi:10.1016/j.ypmed.2007.08.009 PMID:17904210

White, M. (1993). Are ILSs good education? In G. D. Bailey (Ed.), *Computer-Based Integrated Learning Systems* (pp. 115–119). Englewood Cliffs, NJ: Educational Technology Publications.

Whitmore, A. (2006). The Emperor's New Clothes: Sustainable Mining? *Journal of Cleaner Production*, *14*(3-4), 309–314. doi:10.1016/j.jclepro.2004.10.005

WHO [World Health Organisation]. (1999). Health: creating healthy cities in the 21st century. In D. Satterthwaite (Ed.), *The Earthscan Reader in Sustainable Cities* (pp. 137-172). London, UK: Earthscan.

WHO [World Health Organisation]. (2008). Framework and Standards for Country Health Information Systems. *Health Metrics Network*. Retrieved March 12, 2009, from http://www.who.int/healthmetrics/documents/framework/en/

Wickramasinghe, N. S., Fadlalla, A. M. A., Geisler, E., & Schaffer, J. L. (2005). A Framework For Assessing E-Health Preparedness. *International Journal of Electronic Healthcare*, *1*(3), 316–334. doi:10.1504/IJEH.2005.006478 PMID:18048213

Wikle, T. A., & Finchum, A. (2003). The emerging GIS degree landscape. *Computers, Environment and Urban Systems*, *27*(2), 107–122.

Willard, B. (2005). *The Next Sustainability Wave: Building Boardroom Buy-*. Gabriola Island, BC: New Society Publishers.

Williams, N., McDonnell, M., & Seager, E. (2005). Factors influencing the loss of an endangered ecosystem in an urbanising landscape: A case study of native grasslands from Melbourne, Australia. *Landscape and Urban Planning*, *71*(1), 35–49.

Williams, R., & Edge, D. (1996). The social shaping of technology. *Research Policy*, *25*(6), 856–899. doi:10.1016/0048-7333(96)00885-2

Winnall, J.-L. (2013). Social Sustainability to Social Benefit: Creating Positive Outcomes through a Social Risk. In A. J. G. Silvius & J. Tharp (Eds.), *Sustainability Integration for Effective Project Management* (pp. 95–105). Hershey, PA: IGI Global Publishing. doi:10.4018/978-1-4666-4177-8.ch006

Winston, M. (2003). Children of invention. In M. Winston & R. Edelbach (Eds.), *Society, Ethics, and Technology* (2nd ed.). Belmont, CA: Thomson/Wadsworth.

Winter, T. (2007). Rethinking tourism in Asia. *Annals of Tourism Research*, *34*(1), 27–44. doi:10.1016/j.annals.2006.06.004

Wittemyer, G., Elsen, P., Bean, W. T., Burton, A. C., & Brashare, J. S. (2008). Accelerated human population growth at protected area edges. *Science*, *321*(5885), 123–126.

Woehrel, S. (2009). *Russian energy policy towards neighboring countries*. Congressional Research Service Report for Congress (May 20). Retrieved April 27, 2013, from http://www.fas.org/sgp/crs/row/RL34261.pdf

Wojcik-Andrews, I. (2000). *Children's films: History, ideology, pedagogy, theory*. New York: Garland.

Wolak, J., Finkelhor, D., & Mitchell, K. (2004). Internet-initiated sex crimes against minors: Implications for prevention based on findings from a national study. *The Journal of Adolescent Health*, *35*(5), 424–433. doi:10.1016/j.jadohealth.2004.05.006 PMID:15488437

Wolak, J., Finkelhor, D., Mitchell, K. J., & Ybarra, M. L. (2008). Online "predators" and their victims: Myths, realities, and implications for prevention and treatment. *The American Psychologist*, *63*(2), 111–128. doi:10.1037/0003-066X.63.2.111 PMID:18284279

Wolf, J. H. (2001). *Don't Kill Your Baby: Public Health and the Decline of Breastfeeding in the 19th and 20th Centuries*. Columbus, Ohio: Ohio State University Press.

Wolf, J. H. (2007). Saving Babies and Mothers: Pioneering Efforts to Decrease Infant and Maternal Mortality. In J. W. Ward & C. Warren (Eds.), *Silent victories: the history and practice of public health in twentieth-century America* (p. 484). Oxford, UK: Oxford University Press.

Wong, J. K. F., & Wylie, A. (2010). Community- and Hospital-based Teaching in the Medical Currirulum: Examples from Cuba and the UK. *International Journal of Canadian Studies*, *2*(3/4), 343–350.

World Energy Outlook. (2012). *International Energy Agency*. Retrieved April 28, 2014, from http://www.worldenergyoutlook.org/publications/weo-2012/

World Energy Outlook. (2013). *Renewable Energy Outlook*. International Energy Agency. Retrieved April 16, 2014, at http://www.worldenergyoutlook.org/media/weowebsite/2013/WEO2013_Ch06_Renewables.pdf

World Health Organization, & Unicef, United Nation Children's Fund. (2013). *Progress on Sanitation and Drinking Water*. 2013 Update. 40.

World Health Organization, & Unicef, United Nations Children's Fund. (2009). *Diarrhoea: Why children are still dying and what can be done*. 68.

World Health Organization, United Nations, United Nations Children's Fund, & The World Bank. (2013). Levels and Trends in Child Mortality. *Report*, *2013*, 34.

World Health Organization. (2013a). *Children: Reducing Mortality. WHO Factsheet* (Fact Sheet Number 178), 4.

World Health Organization. (2013b). *Diarrhoeal Disease. WHO Factsheet* (330). 4.

World Resources Institute. (2006). *EarthTrends: Environmental information*. Washington, D.C.: World Resources Institute. Retrieved July 31, 2012 from http://earthtrends.wri.org

World Trade Organization. (2009). *Statistics International trade statistics 2009 - Merchandise trade by product*. Retrieved April 12, 2010, from WTO.org website: http://www.wto.org/english/res_e/statis_e/its2009_e/its09_merch_trade_product_e.htm

World Wild Fund for Nature (WWF). (2012). *Igniting the Ring of Fire, A Vision for Developing Indonesia's Geothermal Power*. Retrieved June 13, 2014, from http://awsassets.wwf.or.id/downloads/geothermal_report.pdf

Wozniak, S. (2007). iWoz: Computer geek to cult icon: How I invented the personal computer, co-founded Apple, and had fun doing it. New York: W.W. Norton & Co.

Wu, J., & Boggess, W. (1999). The optimal allocation of conservation funds. *Journal of Environmental Economics and Management*, *38*(3), 302–332. doi:10.1006/jeem.1999.1091

WWF (World Wildlife Fund). (2009). *From Green IT to greening with IT.* White paper. Washington, DC: WWF.

Y2K bug fails to bite. (No Date). Retrieved April 11, 2010, from BBC News website: http://news.bbc.co.uk/2/hi/science/nature/585013.stm

Yalçıner – Erçoşkun, Ö. (2012). A Paradigm Shift towards Urban Resilience. In Ö. Yalçıner-Ercoşkun (Ed.), Green and Ecological Technologies for Urban Planning: Creating Smart Cities (pp. 1-17). Hershey, PA: IGI Global.

Yalcintas, M., & Kaya, A. (2009). Conservation vs. renewable energy: Cases studies from Hawaii. *Energy Policy*, *37*(8), 3268–3273. doi:10.1016/j.enpol.2009.04.029

Yaldiz, O., Ozturk, H., & Zeren, Y. (1993). *Energy usage in production of field crops in Turkey*. Paper presented at 5th International Congress on Mechanisation and Energy Use in Agriculture. Kusadasi, Turkey.

Yang, F., Zeng, G., Du, C., Tang, L., Zhoua, J., & Li, Z. (2008). Spatial analyzing system for urban land-use management based on GIS and multi-criteria assessment modeling. *Progress in Natural Science*, *18*(10), 1279–1284.

Yeager, B. A. C., Huttly, S. R. A., Bartolini, R., Rojas, M., & Lanata, C. F. (1999). Defecation practices of young children in a Peruvian shanty town. *Social Science & Medicine*, *49*(4), 531–541. doi:10.1016/S0277-9536(99)00119-7 PMID:10414812

Yergin, D. (2008). *Oil at the "break point."* Special Report. Testimony before the US Congress Joint Economic Committee in Washington, DC, June 25, 2008. Retrieved October 16, 2009, from http://www2.cera.com/news/DYergin_June2008_Testimony.pdf

Yerxa, D. A. (2013). The Invention of the American Meal: An Interview with Abigail Carroll. *Historically Speaking*, *14*(5), 26–28. doi:10.1353/hsp.2013.0055

Yilmaz, P., Hakan Hocaoglu, M., & Konukman, A. E. S. (2008). A pre-feasibility case study on integrated resource planning including renewables. *Energy Policy*, *36*(3), 1223–1232. doi:10.1016/j.enpol.2007.12.007

Yli-Pelkonen, V., & Kohl, J. (2005). The role of local ecological knowledge in sustainable urban planning: perspectives from Finland. *Sustainability: Science, Practice, & Policy*, *1*(1), 3–14.

Yli-Pelkonen, V., & Niemelä, J. (2005). Linking ecological and social systems in cities: Urban planning in Finland as a case. *Biodiversity and Conservation*, *14*(8), 1947–1967.

Yongsi, H. B. (2007). Diarrheal diseases in the history of public health. *Archives of Medical Research*, *38*(2), 159–163. doi:10.1016/j.arcmed.2006.11.001 PMID:17227723

Young, J. S. (1998). *Forbes greatest technology stories: Inspiring tales of the entrepreneurs*. New York: John Wiley & Sons.

Yourdon, E., & Yourdon, J. (1997). *Time bomb 2000: What the year 2000 computer crisis means to you!* Upper Saddle River, NJ: Prentice Hall.

Yu, S. M., Tu, Y., & Luo, C. (2011). *Green Retrofitting Costs and Benefits: A New Research Agenda*. IRES Working Paper Series, 22.

Yue, C., & Wang, S. (2006). GIS-based evaluation of multifarious local renewable energy sources: A case study of the Chigu area of southwestern Taiwan. *Energy Policy*, *34*(6), 730–742. doi:10.1016/j.enpol.2004.07.003

Zainul Abidin, N. (2005). *Using Value Management to Improve the Consideration of Sustainability within Construction*. (Unpublished doctoral dissertation). Loughborough University, Loughborough, United Kingdom.

Zainul Abidin, N., & Pasquire, C. L. (2007). Revolutionize value management: A mode towards sustainability. *International Journal of Project Management*, *25*(3), 275–282. doi:10.1016/j.ijproman.2006.10.005

Zawahri, N., Sowers, J., & Weinthal, E. (2011). The Politics of Assessment: Water and Sanitation MDGs in the Middle East. *Development and Change*, *42*(5), 1153–1177. doi:10.1111/j.1467-7660.2011.01730.x PMID:22175085

Zhuplev, A. (2013). Russian Energy Sector: Megatrends, Drivers and Strategic Implications. Paper presented at the Academy of International Business Meeting, Moscow, Russia.

Zhuplev, A., & Shein, V. (2004). Administrative Culture in a Borderless World: Russia. In J. Jabbra & O. Dwivendi (Eds.), Administrative Culture in the Borderless World. Willowdale, Ontario, Canada: de Sitter Publications.

Zhuplev, A. (2008). Economic internationalization of Russia: Roots, trends, and scenarios. *International Political Science Review*, *29*(1), 99–119. doi:10.1177/0192512107083449

Zito, P., & Salvo, G. (2011). Toward an urban transport sustainability index: An European comparison. *European Transport Research Review*, *3*(4), 179–195. doi:10.1007/s12544-011-0059-0

Zoete, L. de. (2010). PMBOK of Prince 2. *Automatisering Gids*, April (in Dutch).

About the Contributors

Ken D. Thomas is the Honors Lecturer in Biosystems Engineering of both the Honors College and Department of Biosystems Engineering at Auburn University. He received both his B.Sc. Chemical & Process Engineering and MSc Environmental Engineering from the University of the West Indies, St. Augustine and Ph.D. Civil Engineering (Environmental & Water Resources Engineering [EWRE]) from the University of South Florida (USF). His current research interests are in sustainability science, sustainable development and sustainable development engineering, especially in a West Indian context, and engineering education.

***

Lee E. Allen, Ed.D. (University of Memphis) is an Associate Professor and Program Coordinator for the School Library Information Specialist program in the Department of Instruction and Curriculum Leadership for which he currently serves as Interim Chair. Dr. Allen has served as technology consultant on numerous federal and state grants, and is the Principal Investigator for the Institute of Library & Museum Services' Laura Bush 21st Century Librarian grant in partnership with urban and rural school districts in Tennessee. He is currently the online course development director for the West Tennessee Regional STEM Innovation Collaboratory grant. Dr. Allen's research focuses on the integration of information technologies in the development and use of knowledge and skills in the classroom, libraries, and everyday learning opportunities and environments.

Albena Antonova is a lecturer at Sofia University, Faculty of Economics and Business Administration in the field of IST implementation in business and economy. She works on a number of research projects, related to technology implementation, serious games, knowledge management and others. Her main research interests include knowledge management, emerging technologies, serious games, business and management education, service science, e-learning and TEL models and methods, e-Business, technology entrepreneurship, open innovations and innovations management and living labs. Currently she has more than 30 publications in the field.

Seda H. Bostancı received her B.Sc., M.Sc. degrees from Mimar Sinan Fine Arts University (MSGSÜ), Urban and Regional Planning Department (B.Sc.), in 2000, and Urban Design (M.Sc.) in 2002 respectively. Then she received a Ph.D. from Istanbul Technical University, Urban and Regional Planning Department in 2008. From 2004 to 2010, she worked as an urban planner in Sarıyer Municipality Planning Department and joined the design process of 1/1000 scale Master Plan processes of Kilyos, Demirciköy and Rumelifeneri. Since 2010 she has been working as a Local Governments Program coordinator at Okan

University. In 2012 she became Assistant Professor in the same department. Her research interests are urban design, urban aesthetics, mathematical methods in urban design, eco-municipalities and urbanization. Her main articles are: Bostancı, S.H., & Ocakçı, M. (2011). Innovative Approach to Aesthetic Evaluation Based on Entropy, *European Planning Studies, 19*(4); Bostancı, S.H. (2011). Eco-Municipalities and Municipal Applications for Sustainability, chapter in Green and Ecological Technologies for Urban Planning: Creating Smart Cities, In O. Yalciner Ercoskun (Ed.), IGI Global, pp. 310-328.

Tim Cadman is a Research Fellow with the Institute for Ethics, Governance and Law at Griffith University, Queensland, Australia, and an Adjunct Lecturer with the Australian Centre for Sustainable Business and Development at the University of Southern Queensland. He specialises in the governance of sustainable development, including forest management, climate change, and finance. His first monograph, *Quality and legitimacy of global governance: case lessons from forestry* was published in 2011, followed by an edited collection *Climate change and global policy regimes: towards institutional legitimacy* in 2013. His active research includes developing quality of governance standards for REDD+ and forest management in Nepal and Papua New Guinea, and tracking the integrity systems associated with the UN climate change regime. He established the Forest Stewardship Council in Australia in 2002 and also assists multi-stakeholders in environmental conflict mediation and negotiation.

Flavio Leandro Caldas earned his doctorate in Educational Technology from the University of Salamanca in 2011. His research focuses on the relationship between educational technology and native peoples of the Americas, and has taken him to Spain, Peru, Argentina and Chile. His work has been featured in a variety of Argentinean publications. Dr. Caldas also holds a degree in Cultural Management, Tourism and Patrimony from the Ortega y Gasset Foundation and a civil engineering degree from the UTN de la Plata. From 2004 to 2007, he served as Subsecretary of Culture of the city of San Martin de Los Andes.

Wei-Ming Chen received her Ph.D. degree from University of Delaware, USA in 2014 and her dissertation is entitled as *Mapping Alternative Energy Paths for Taiwan to Reach a Sustainable Future: an Application of the LEAP Model.* She has great interest in climate change and sustainable energy policy research, focusing on policies for East Asian countries, especially Taiwan, South Korea, and Japan. She is now a postdoctoral fellow at National Taiwan University of Science and Technology and is implementing a national energy project of inter-governmental communication. The purpose of this project is design a communication mechanism and procedure for bridging various governmental agencies, in order to facilitate the development of renewable energy and low-carbon technologies in Taiwan. She expects that she will contribute new knowledge into the field of energy and environmental policy, both in Asia and in the world.

Deepak Chhabra is an Associate Professor and a Senior Sustainability Scientist at Arizona State University, Phoenix (Arizona, United States). Her research interests include economic impact, sustainable marketing and ethical consumption of tourism products. She works on a variety of research projects focused on topics such as marketing and economic impact of heritage and nature-based tourism. Currently she has approximately 45 refereed publications in the field. She has also recently authored a book titled 'Strategic Marketing in Hospitality and Tourism: Building a Smart Online Agenda.'

Cristiana Maria Ciocănea is a Research Assistant at the Centre for Environmental Research and Impact Studies within the University of Bucharest and a Teaching Assistant Collaborator at Faculty of Geography, University of Bucharest. She holds a Ph.D. in Geography since 2013 with the paper Structural and functional changes of urban landscape determined by consumption patterns of society - case study 3rd District of Bucharest and a B.Sc. degree in Psychology since 2008. She has collaboratively published more than 10 articles in national and international journals and participated at numerous conferences regarding urban and rural ecology, urban sprawl, urban landscape, urban and regional planning and biodiversity conservation. Since 2009 she has been an active member in research teams with national and international contracts regarding urban landscape dynamics, urban environmental quality, land use conflicts, consumption patterns of society, perception of urban landscape, public perception of conservation activities and importance of protected areas.

Sarah Jane Edwards is the Senior Urban Planner for the Australian Capital Territory Government's Education and Training Directorate and is a Ph.D. Candidate at the University of Western Australia, having transferred her Ph.D. Candidature from the University of Tokyo in 2014. Sarah Jane's research expertise is in the interaction between health and planning, economic development and planning as well as Japanese planning policy. She was awarded the prestigious Australian Postgraduate Award Scholarship in 2014 and the Japanese Government Postgraduate Scholarship also known at the MEXT Scholarship in 2006. Between 2012 and 2014, Sarah Jane was a Professional Adjunct with Dr. Rachel Davey at the Centre for Research & Action in Public Health at the University of Canberra. Sarah Jane also has extensive public policy experience and has worked for the Commonwealth Departments of Immigration and Health. She is fluent in Japanese and while at the University of Tokyo with the International Development and Regional Planning Research Unit, she completed research on urban regeneration in regional Japan, regional China and the Ueno business district in central Tokyo. Sarah Jane is currently based in Perth focusing on research.

Leandro Norberto Giglioli graduated from Middlebury College in 2013 with a B.A. in Mathematics. His involvement in this project stems from a lifelong passion for technology coupled with coupled with years spent immersed in education. This is his first academic foray into the social sciences, his previous research having centered on measure theory and functional analysis.

Monica Gray, Ph.D., M.P.H., C.P.H. is an Assistant Professor of Civil and Environmental Engineering at The Lincoln University. She simultaneously received her Ph.D. in Civil and Environmental Engineering (Water Resources concentration) and Masters of Public Health (Environmental & Occupational Health concentration) from the University of South Florida, Tampa. She also received a Masters in Biological Engineering from the University of Georgia, Athens and B.S. in Agricultural Engineering from the University of the West Indies, Trinidad. Prior to arriving at The Lincoln University, Dr. Gray managed the global curriculum portfolio for over a hundred and twenty programs in sixteen countries at Arcadia University and work as an Environmental Engineer and Environmental Health Program Director at the Philadelphia Housing Authority and Organica Biotechnology. Her research interest is in the area of systems approaches for sustainable environmental management and community health with particular focus on water resources and sanitation systems. This includes water and wastewater treatment, reuse and management. Her current research project is the identification and modelling of Pharmaceutical and Personal Care Products (PPCPs) in community water.

Evangelos Grigoroudis is an Associate Professor of management of quality processes in the School of Production Engineering and Management of the Technical University of Crete, Greece (2002-). He received his Ph.D. degree in 1999 from the same institution. He has received distinctions from the Hellenic Operational Research Society, the Academy of Business and Administrative Sciences, the World Automation Congress, the Foundation of Ioannis and Vasileia Karayianni, the Technical University of Crete, and the State Scholarships Foundation of Greece. He acts as reviewer for more than 50 scientific journals, and he is associate editor of several journals including *Operational Research: An International Journal* and *International Journal of Decision Support Systems*. He is author/editor of 10 books on the measurement of service quality, the business strategy and management, and the multicriteria decision aid approaches, as well as of a significant number of research reports and papers in scientific journals and conference proceedings. His research interests include service quality measurement processes, customer and employee satisfaction, performance evaluation, business excellence, operational research (evaluation methodologies and techniques), multicriteria decision analysis, data analysis (qualitative data analysis methods), and marketing (market and customer satisfaction surveys).

Ori Gudes, Ph.D. led the Epidoros project (formerly known as HDSS) within the Logan-Beaudesert Health Coalition (LBHC). This project combined complex and diverse datasets along with a decision support strategy, to increase the effectiveness of participatory planning and decision -making in Logan-Beaudesert. This project was awarded the Queensland Spatial Excellence Award under the research and innovation category (2011) by the SSSI and SIBA. Dr. Gudes was responsible for managing and leading the research and development activities in this project. In his previous research work (M.A. thesis) he developed a web-based GIS Public Participation tool for a neighbourhood in Tel-Aviv, Israel. This study examined a real-world case of neighbourhood revitalization. Dr. Gudes' thesis won the 3rd Place in the Annual Thesis contest of the Israeli Planning Association for 2007. Dr. Gudes' Ph.D. thesis has been nominated for the QUT outstanding award for 2012, and passed with only minor revisions. Currently, Dr. Gudes holds a research fellow position at the department of spatial sciences, Curtin University, Perth, WA, Australia. His area of research is focused on: GeoHealth, GIS and Health, Health planning, urban planning, and spatial analysis.

Jong Chul Huh received his M.S. and Ph.D. degrees from Inha University in 1982 and 1992, respectively. He has been with the Department of Mechanical System Engineering, Jeju National University since 1984, and is now a professor. He serves as an editor of the Journal of the Korean Solar Energy Society. His research areas are wind resource, clean energy development and wind turbine design.

Margee Hume is the Head of the Strategy, Human Resource Management and marketing discipline at Central Queensland University. Professor Margee Hume specialises in service experience mapping, innovation, and IT service management. Her focus is on sustainable work communities' research. Her research primarily focuses in the non-profit sector and health sector management.

Michelle Edith Jarvie-Eggart has a Ph.D. in environmental engineering and a Graduate Certificate in Sustainability from Michigan Technological University. She is also a registered professional engineer in the states of Oregon and Michigan, with work experience in the water/wastewater and mining industries. She currently works for the consulting firm Barr Engineering, where assists clients in mining and other heavy industries with sustainability and environmental compliance. She is also an adjunct Assistant Professor for the University of Maryland University College's master's program in environmental management.

Vassilis S. Kouikoglou received the diploma in electrical engineering from the National Technical University of Athens, Athens, Greece, in 1985 and the Ph.D. degree in production engineering and management from the Technical University of Crete, Chania, Greece, in 1989. Since 1991, he has been with the Department of Production Engineering and Management, Technical University of Crete, Crete, Greece, where he is a professor and has served as chairman. His research interests are in modeling and optimization of production networks and environmental systems. He is an Editor of *the Journal of Intelligent and Robotic Systems*.

Federico Lopez-Casero is a policy researcher working for the Forest Conservation, Livelihoods and Rights Project at the Institute for Global Environmental Strategies (IGES). IGES is a research institute based in Japan that conducts strategic policy research to support sustainable development in the Asia-Pacific region. The focus of Federico's present work is on exploring policy options to prevent trade in illegal timber, primarily through procurement policies and border control.

Tek Maraseni, Ph.D. has over 20 years work experience in carbon and forest related areas in different countries including Nepal, Thailand and Australia. Whilst working with the Ministry of Forests and Soil Conservation in Nepal (1991-2003), he worked closely with several forests stakeholders and delivered trainings on several NRM issues. In 2002/2003, he worked at the Asian Institute of Technology (Thailand) on a Capacity Development for CDM project implemented by the UNEP. Currently, he is the Deputy Director with the Australian Centre for Sustainable Catchments, Australia, and also a Senior International Scientist with the Chinese Academy of Sciences, Lanzhou, China. He has produced over 90 publications including two books in the last seven years. His published work has been recognized by several national and international fellowships/grants/awards. During this time he has supervised nine Ph.D. students, marked Ph.D. theses and reviewed journal articles in ten international journals.

Helen Muga, Ph.D. is an Assistant Professor in civil engineering at the University of Mount Union, Alliance, Ohio. She worked as a postdoctoral researcher in the Civil & Environmental Engineering department at the University of South Florida, Tampa, Florida. She received a Ph.D. in Environmental Engineering from Michigan Technological University, Michigan, USA, a Masters degree in Environmental Engineering from Michigan Technological University, Michigan, USA, a Masters degree in Chemical Engineering from Curtin University of Technology, Australia, and a Bachelors degree in Chemistry from the University of Papua New Guinea. Her research interests include water and wastewater engineering, sustainability, life cycle engineering, green engineering, diffusion and adoption of green technology, and international development work.

Mihaita Iulian Niculae is a research assistant at the Centre for Environmental Research and Impact Studies at the University of Bucharest. Mihaiti studies landscape ecology, the dynamics of the countryside and conservation planning and has taken courses in environmental economics and management at the Luigi Bocconi Comercial University, Milan. Mihaiti's work was presented in national and international scientific conferences and by publishing a several number of articles in international databases indexed journals. Since 2006, Mihaiti has been an active participant in research projects related to biodiversity conservation and integrated waste management.

Mihai Răzvan Niţă, Ph.D. is a researcher at the Centre for Environmental Research and Impact Studies and Lecturer at the Faculty of Geography, University of Bucharest in Geography since 2011. Dr. Niţă's main research topics include green infrastructures, environmental conflicts and environmental impact assessments.

Abdeen Mustafa Omer (B.Sc., M.Sc., Ph.D.) is an Associate Researcher at Energy Research Institute (ERI), UK. He obtained both his Ph.D. degree in the Built Environment and Master of Philosophy degree in Renewable Energy Technologies from the University of Nottingham, UK. He is a qualified Mechanical Engineer with a proven track record within the water industry and renewable energy technologies. He graduated from University of El Menoufia, Egypt with B.Sc. in Mechanical Engineering. His previous experience involved being a member of the research team at the National Council for Research/Energy Research Institute in Sudan and working director of research and development for National Water Equipment Manufacturing Co. Ltd., Sudan. He has been listed in the WHO'S WHO in the World 2005, 2006, 2007 and 2010. He has published over 200 papers in peer-reviewed journals, 50 review articles, 5 books and 50 chapters in books.

Diana Andreea Onose is an assistant researcher at the Centre for Environmental Research and Impact Studies, University of Bucharest and a has Ph.D. with the thesis Modeling interdependencies between structural components, urban functions and environmental quality in Bucharest from the perspective of sustainable land planning. In 2010 she graduated with masters in Environmental Sciences – Integrated Environmental Assessment with the paper Efficiency in applying the fractal method in the assessment of equipotential ecological areas in an urban ecosystem. Case study: Bucharest Sector 1. She benefited from an ERASMUS scholarship in Environmental Sciences at the Polytechnic University of Valencia, Spain (2007) and a Ph.D. research stage at the University of Barcelona (2012). The research activity is mainly focused in urban and rural ecology, impact assessment and geographical information systems. She is an active member on research teams that study urban and rural ecology.

Youn Cheol Park, Ph.D. is currently a Visiting Scholar at the University of Illinos Urbana-Champaign and a Professor of Mechanical Engineering at Jeju National University (JNU), Jeju, Korea. Prior to his Visiting appointment he was the Director for the Center for Clean Energy Development at JNU. Dr. Park holds a Ph.D. (1997), M.S. (1992), and B.E. (1990) in Mechanical Engineering, all from Korea University.

Virendra Pathak has a Ph.D. in the area of Geo-informatics from the Indian Institute of Technology, Kanpur, India. He has a diverse academic background with M.E. in Remote Sensing and Photogrametry, and B.E. in Civil Engineering. He has twenty years of experience in academia in India, Australia, and Canada. Dr. Pathak is currently associated with the Institute of Engineering & Technology, U.P. Technical University, Lucknow, India. He is involved in teaching Geo-informatics related subjects. His research interests are in the area of applications of geospatial technologies for urban development including higher education policy and management. He has been into academic administration and presently coordinating a World Bank assisted technical education quality improvement program.

Maria Pătroescu is a professor at the Faculty of Geography and director of the Centre for Environmental Research and Impact Studies, University of Bucharest. She holds a Ph.D. in Geography since 1982 with Subcarpathians between Buzau and Ramnicu-Sarat: ecological potential and biological exploitation. Since 1997 she has been the Ph.D. coordinator. Her didactic and research activity are focused on several representative areas: biodiversity conservation, environmental geography, human ecology and biogeography. She attended several training sessions at prestigious universities inclusive of: Lomonosov University, Moscow, Ecole Normale Superieure, Fontenay/Saint-Cloud, University Paris I, Phanteone-Sorbonne, Liverpool Hope College, Tokyo Metropolitan University, Geophile Research Center, Lyon. She is the honorary president of Carpatho-Danubian's Center of Geoecology, an NGO in Romania, which does extensive work in education for environmental protection and conservation. Over her career, she has coordinated 90 national and 8 international projects won by competition. Since 2004 she has been the chairman of the Scientific Board of Iron Gates Natural Park.

Yannis A. Phillis received his diploma in electrical and mechanical engineering from the National Technical University of Athens, Greece, in 1973 and the M.S., Engineer Degree, and Ph.D. degrees from the University of California, Los Angeles, in control systems in 1978, 1979, and 1980, respectively. From 1980 to 1986, he was with Boston University, Boston, MA. Since 1986, he has been with the Department of Production Engineering and Management, Technical University of Crete (TUC), Chania, Greece where he is professor and director of the CAM Laboratory. He was Rector of TUC for 12 years. In 1992 and between 2005 and 2007 he was visiting professor at UCLA's Chemical Engineering Department. In 2008 he was Onassis Foundation Senior Visiting Fellow in the US. His research interests are in stochastic control, discrete-event systems, and applications in manufacturing networks and environmental systems. Dr. Phillis is Book Editor of the Journal of Intelligent and Robotic Systems, Advisory Board Member for the IEEE Systems Journal, Associate Editor for the International Journal of Engineering Management, Member of the Editorial Advisory Board for the Environmental Engineering and Management Journal, and was on the Editorial Board of the Encyclopedia of Life Support Systems, and past Editor of the IEEE Robotics and Automation Magazine. He is the recipient of numerous honors including a "Lifetime Achievement Award," at the World Automation Conference 2010, Kobe, Japan.

Donatella Privitera is an economic geography Associate Professor at University of Catania, Italy, with a M.S. Degree in Agri-Business from the Catholic University of Milan. Prior to becoming a full-time academic, she has had experience working in a multinational company (Kraft General Food, Italy) in marketing. She has taught the economy of landscape and marketing of agricultural products for the Faculty of Agriculture at University Mediterranea of Reggio Calabria, Italy. She is currently teaching economic geography with a specialty in tourism and regional development. She is a member of the Italian Geographic Society (SGI), Society Italian of Agricultural Economists (SIDEA) and European Association of Agricultural Economists (EAAE). She has presented papers at several conferences, and published in international books in association with her research interests in the following areas: transport geography; sustainable cities; information and communication technologies with rural development; green economy; regional planning and its implications for tourism. She has participated in the EU project HERODOT-INTERREG IIIB and she is participating in cooperative national research projects. She is a nominated expert for Calabria and Sicily to manage projects involving university-industry knowledge transfer.

David L. Rainey, Ph.D. is an internationally-known author, educator, and business consultant. He is a leading authority on sustainable development, strategic leadership, strategic management, strategic innovation, product development, and energy management. He is a strategist and pragmatist developing innovative solutions to the challenges in today's turbulent business environment. Dr. Rainey has over thirty-five years of experience and leadership in industry and academia. He is a professor of management in the Lally School of Management and Technology at Rensselaer Polytechnic Institute. Dr. Rainey is a visiting professor at the Technical University of Munich and an associate of the Center for the Study of Corporate Sustainability in Buenos Aires, Argentina. Dr. Rainey is the author of *Product Innovation: Leading Change through Integrated Product Development* (2005), *Sustainable Business Development: Inventing the Future through Strategy, Innovation and Leadership* (2006) and *Enterprise-wide Strategic Management: Achieving Sustainable Success through Leadership, Strategies and Value Creation* (2010). The books are published by Cambridge University Press. His two new books published by Information Age Publishing include: *Visionary Strategic Leadership: Sustaining Success through Strategic Direction, Corporate Management, and High-level Programs* (2014) and *The Pursuit of Sustainable Leadership: Becoming a Successful Strategic Leader through Principles, Perspectives, and Professional Development* (2013). His next two books are: *Full-spectrum Strategic Leadership: Being on the Cutting Edge through Innovative Solutions, Integrated Systems and Enduring Relationships* and *The Pursuit of Sustainability: Creating Business Value through Strategic Leadership, Holistic Perspectives and Exceptional Performance.* Dr. Rainey earned a B.S. in Mechanical Engineering, a M.B.A., and Master of Science degrees in Engineering Science and Business Management. He earned a Ph.D. from Rensselaer Polytechnic Institute.

Dmitry A. Shtykhno is a Professor of the Comparative Economics Department at the Comparative Economics Department of the Plekhanov Russian University of Economics (PRUE), Moscow, Russia. In 1999 he obtained the Ph.D. degree. From 2001 to 2006 he worked a Program Director at the CHN University Qatar. Since 2006, at PRUE, he has worked as Deputy Dean of the Graduate School, Dean of the School of Business, Head of the International Office, and currently is Director of the Strategy Development Center. He has published several papers in the fields of management and international business. His research interests include international business, comparative and cross cultural management, and entrepreneurship in developing economies.

Gilbert Silvius, Ph.D. (1963) is professor of project and programme management at LOI University of Applied Sciences and principal consultant at Van Aetsveld change and project management. He is an internationally experienced consultant/trainer in project management and member of the international enable2change network of project management experts. As a practitioner, Gilbert has over 20 years hands-on experience in organizational change and IT projects. Gilbert is considered one of the leading experts in the field of sustainability in project management, with over a dozen papers and several books published on the topic. He was awarded the 2013 Sustainability Award of the international Green Project Management organization. Gilbert holds a Ph.D. in information sciences from Utrecht University and masters' degrees in economics and business administration.

Gilman C. K. Tam is an independent researcher and is currently taking on the asset management role for a multinational independent power producer. He has gained extensive practical experience in power plant project development, construction, commissioning, and maintenance both in Hong Kong and China. Gilman is a member of The Institution of Engineering and Technology (IET) in the UK; member of The American Society of Heating, Refrigerating and Air-Conditioning Engineers (ASHRAE); and member of Project Management Institute (PMI) in the US. He is a Project Management Professional (PMP). Gilman holds M.Sc. degree with distinction in Energy from the Heriot-Watt University in the UK and M.B.A. degree from the Newport University in the US. Gilman is working on project management research at the doctoral level with a focus on sustainability in project management. His major research interest includes the development of practical sustainability tools for project managers.

Gabriel Ovidiu Vânău is a geographer whose research interests focus on the land use and environmental planning, urban-rural interaction and linkages, protected areas governance in relation to economic development. Vânău holds a doctorate in geography from the University of Bucharest. His doctoral thesis examined the fringe of Bucharest as an urban-rural interface. He works as a research assistant at the Centre for Environmental Research and Impact Studies and as a teaching assistant at the Faculty of Geography, both within the University of Bucharest. He is strongly committed to integrating education and outreach into research projects, particularly by exposing his students to the excitement of scientific research.

Young-Doo Wang is Professor and Associate Director of the Center for Energy and Environmental Policy (CEEP) at the University of Delaware. He is also Director of the Energy and Environmental Policy Graduate Program (ENEP), which is administered by CEEP. He is co-director of the Joint Institute for a Sustainable Energy and Environmental Future (JISEEF), an innovative research and policy advocacy organization headquartered in Korea with the mission of promoting peaceful and sustainable policy options for Northeast Asia. Dr. Wang currently serves as a member of the External Research and Technical Advisory Board (ERTAB) to review Nevada's NSF EPSCoR Research Infrastructure Improvement Grant. His work has been funded by the World Bank, the W. Alton Jones Foundation, the Blue Moon Fund, the National Science Foundation, the U.S. Department of Energy, the U.S. Environmental Protection Agency, the National Renewable Energy Laboratory, the Korea Energy Economics Institute, the Korea Electricity Power Corporation, among others. Dr. Wang's recent books include: *Green Energy Economies* (2014) published by Transaction Publishers; *Energy Revolution: 21st Century Energy and Environmental Strategy* (2004) published by the Maeil Business Newspaper (a prestigious publisher in Korea); and *Water Conservation-Oriented Rates: Strategies to extend Supply, Promote Equity, and Meet Minimum Flow Levels* (2005) published by the American Water Works Association. He has published over 150 research articles in the areas of energy, environment, and sustainable development.

Tan Yigitcanlar is an Associate Professor at the School of Civil Engineering and Built Environment, Queensland University of Technology and an Executive Director at the World Capital Institute, Brisbane, Australia. He has been responsible for research, teaching, training and capacity building programs in the fields of urban and regional planning, development and management in esteemed Australian, Finnish, Japanese and Turkish universities. The main foci of his research are advocating and promoting knowledge-based urban development and sustainable urban, infrastructure and transport development in city-regions. He is an Associate Editor of the *International Journal of Knowledge Based Development* and *International Journal of Environmental Science and Technology*, and carries the Chairman role of the annual *Knowledge Cities World Summits*. He has published extensively in the field and his publications include two authored books—*Knowledge and the City*, *Sustainable Urban Water Environment*—and six edited books—*Knowledge-Based Urban Development*, *Creative Urban Regions*, *Knowledge-Based Development for Cities and Societies*, *Sustainable Urban and Regional Infrastructure Development*, *Rethinking Sustainable Development*, and *Building Prosperous Knowledge Cites.*

Anatoly Zhuplev, a Fulbright Scholar, has been a management professor at the College of Business Administration at Loyola Marymount University since 1990. Prior to joining the faculty, Zhuplev taught at Northeastern University and the Moscow Management Institute. He also worked for several non-profit organizations in Russia. He is the recipient of numerous academic awards during his 15-year tenure in Russian education; he has also received the Award for Outstanding Contribution to the Loyola Marymount University MBA Program. Zhuplev is a member of the International Management Development Association, on the Editorial Board of the *Journal of East-West Business* and a member of the Editorial Review Board for the *Journal of Transnational Management.*

Index

A

B

C

D

E

F

G

H

I

J

L

M

N

O

P

Q

R

S

T

U

9 781466 68

Printed by BoD™in Norderstedt, Germany